ALFRED LORD TENNYSON

A MEMOIR

BY HIS SON

I have lived my life, and that which I have done
May He within Himself make pure!

New York
THE MACMILLAN COMPANY
LONDON: MACMILLAN & CO., LTD.
1911

Set up and electrotyped.   Published September, 1897.   Reprinted
October, November twice, 1897; January, March, August, September,
1898; June, 1899.
New edition in one volume September, 1905 ; February, 1911.

Norwood Press
J. S. Cushing & Co. — Berwick & Smith Co.
Norwood, Mass., U.S.A.

THESE VOLUMES ARE DEDICATED

BY PERMISSION

TO THE QUEEN

An Unpublished Version of "To the Queen," 1851.

THE NOBLEST MEN METHINKS ARE BRED
 OF OURS THE SAXO-NORMAN RACE;
  AND IN THE WORLD THE NOBLEST PLACE,
MADAM, IS YOURS, OUR QUEEN AND HEAD.

YOUR NAME IS BLOWN ON EVERY WIND,
 YOUR FLAG THRO' AUSTRAL ICE IS BORNE,
  AND GLIMMERS TO THE NORTHERN MORN,
AND FLOATS IN EITHER GOLDEN IND

I GIVE THIS FAULTY BOOK TO YOU,
 FOR, THO' THE FAULTS BE THICK AS DUST
  IN VACANT CHAMBERS, I CAN TRUST
YOUR WOMAN'S NATURE KIND AND TRUE.

CONTENTS.
VOL. I.

CONTENTS.

CONTENTS.
VOL. II.

PREFACE.

Unpublished Sonnet

(*Written originally as a preface to "Becket"*).

Old ghosts whose day was done ere mine began,
If earth be seen from your conjectured heaven,
Ye know that History is half-dream — ay even
The man's life in the letters of the man.
There lies the letter, but it is not he
As he retires into himself and is:
Sender and sent-to go to make up this,
Their offspring of this union. And on me
Frown not, old ghosts, if I be one of those
Who make you utter things you did not say,
And mould you all awry and mar your worth;
For whatsoever knows us truly, knows
That none can truly write his single day,
And none can write it for him upon earth.

" History is half-dream — ay even
The man's life in the letters of the man";

but besides the letters of my father and of his friends
there are his poems, and in these we must look for the
innermost sanctuary of his being. For my own part, I
feel strongly that no biographer could so truly give him
as he gives himself in his own works; but this may be
because, having lived my life with him, I see him in every
word which he has written; and it is difficult for me so

far to detach myself from the home circle as to pourtray him for others. There is also the impossibility of fathoming a great man's mind; his deeper thoughts are hardly ever revealed. He himself disliked the notion of a long, formal biography, for

> "None can truly write his single day,
> And none can write it for him upon earth."

However he wished that, if I deemed it better, the incidents of his life should be given as shortly as might be without comment, but that my notes should be final and full enough to preclude the chance of further and unauthentic biographies.

For those who cared to know about his literary history he wrote "Merlin and the Gleam." From his boyhood he had felt the magic of Merlin — that spirit of poetry — which bade him know his power and follow throughout his work a pure and high ideal, with a simple and single devotedness and a desire to ennoble the life of the world, and which helped him through doubts and difficulties to "endure as seeing Him who is invisible."

> Great the Master,
> And sweet the Magic,
> When over the valley,
> In early summers,
> Over the mountain,
> On human faces,
> And all around me,
> Moving to melody,
> Floated the Gleam.

In his youth he sang of the brook flowing through his upland valley, of the "ridgéd wolds" that rose above his home, of the mountain-glen and snowy summits of his early dreams, and of the beings, heroes and fairies, with which his imaginary world was peopled. Then was heard the "croak of the raven," the harsh voice of those who were unsympathetic —

> The light retreated,
> The landskip darken'd,
> The melody deaden'd,
> The Master whisper'd
> "Follow the Gleam."

Still the inward voice told him not to be faint-hearted but to follow his ideal. And by the delight in his own romantic fancy, and by the harmonies of nature, "the warble of water," and "cataract music of falling torrents," the inspiration of the poet was renewed. His Eclogues and English Idylls followed, when he sang the songs of country life and the joys and griefs of country folk, which he knew through and through.

> Innocent maidens,
> Garrulous children,
> Homestead and harvest,
> Reaper and gleaner,
> And rough-ruddy faces
> Of lowly labour.

By degrees, having learnt somewhat of the real philosophy of life and of humanity from his own experience, he rose to a melody "stronger and statelier." He celebrated the glory of "human love and of human heroism" and of human thought, and began what he had already devised, his Epic of king Arthur, "typifying above all things the life of man," wherein he had intended to represent some of the great religions of the world. He had purposed that this was to be the chief work of his manhood. Yet the death of his friend, Arthur Hallam, and the consequent darkening of the whole world for him made him almost fail in this purpose; nor any longer for a while did he rejoice in the splendour of his spiritual visions, nor in the Gleam that had "waned to a wintry glimmer."

> Clouds and darkness
> Closed upon Camelot;
> Arthur had vanish'd
> I knew not whither,
> The king who loved me,
> And cannot die.

Here my father united the two Arthurs, the Arthur of the Idylls and the Arthur "the man he held as half divine." He himself had fought with death, and had come out victorious to find "a stronger faith his own," and a hope for himself, for all those in sorrow and for universal humankind, that never forsook him through the future years.

> And broader and brighter
> The Gleam flying onward,
> Wed to the melody,
> Sang thro' the world.
>
> * * * * *
>
> I saw, whenever
> In passing it glanced upon
> Hamlet or city,
> That under the Crosses
> The dead man's garden,
> The mortal hillock,
> Would break into blossom;
> And so to the land's
> Last limit I came.

Up to the end he faced death with the same earnest and unfailing courage that he had always shown, but with an added sense of the awe and the mystery of the Infinite.

> I can no longer,
> But die rejoicing,
> For thro' the Magic
> Of Him the Mighty,
> Who taught me in childhood,
> There on the border
> Of boundless Ocean,
> And all but in Heaven
> Hovers the Gleam.

That is the reading of the poet's riddle as he gave it to me. He thought that " Merlin and the Gleam " would probably be enough of biography for those friends who urged him to write about himself. However, this has not been their verdict, and I have tried to do what he said that I might do, and have endeavoured to give briefly something of what people naturally wish to know, something about his birth, homes, school, college, friendships, travels, and the leading events of his life, enough to present the sort of insight into his history and pursuits which one wants, if one desires to make a companion of a man. The picture of his early days has been mainly sketched from what he and my mother have told me. My difficulty in arranging the later chapters has been how to choose, and how to throw aside, from the mass of material[1]. I have quoted from many manuscripts never

[1] My thanks are due to Professor Henry Sidgwick and Professor Palgrave, who have helped me to make my selection from upwards of 40,000 letters.

meant for the public eye, many of which I have burnt according to his instructions. Among those that I have collected here, the most interesting to me are my father's unpublished poems, letters, — and notes on his own life and work left me for publication after his death, Arthur Hallam's letters, Edward Fitzgerald's private MS notes [1] (some of which he gave me, and some of which have been lent to me by Mr Aldis Wright), and the journal of our home life. This last is a simple record of daily something-nothings.

If there appear, in the Reminiscences kindly contributed by his different friends, to be any discrepancies, let it be remembered that the many-sided man has sympathy with many and various minds, and that the poet may be like the magnetic needle, which, though it can be moved from without, yet in itself remains true to the magnetic pole.

According to my father's wish, throughout the memoir my hand will be as seldom seen as may be, and this accounts for the occasionally fragmentary character of my work. The anecdotes and sayings here related have been mostly taken down as soon as spoken, and are hence, I trust, not marred or mended by memory, which, judging from some anecdotes of him recently published, is wont to be a register not wholly accurate. "Fingunt simul creduntque."

Such reviews as I have quoted are chiefly those which have met with my father's approbation as explanatory commentaries. For my own part, I have generally refrained from attempting to pronounce judgment either on his poems or on his personal qualities and characteristics; although more than any living man I

[1] Generally signed E. F. G. throughout this work.

have had reason to appreciate his splendid truth and
trustfulness, his varied creative imagination, and love of
beauty, his rich humour, his strength of purpose, the
largeness of his nature, and the wide range of his genius.
If I may venture to speak of his special influence over
the world, my conviction is, that its main and enduring
factors are his power of expression, the perfection of his
workmanship, his strong common sense, the high purport
of his life and work, his humility, and his open-hearted
and helpful sympathy —

"Fortezza, ed umilitade, e largo core."

CHRONOLOGY OF THE BOOKS OF POEMS.

1827.—POEMS BY TWO BROTHERS. London: Printed for W. Simpkin and R. Marshall, Stationers'-Hall-Court; and J. and J. Jackson. Louth: 1827. Published in two sizes.

1829.—TIMBUCTOO. A Poem which obtained the Chancellor's Medal at the Cambridge Commencement, 1829. By A. Tennyson, of Trinity College. 8vo.

1830.—POEMS, CHIEFLY LYRICAL. By Alfred Tennyson. London: Effingham Wilson, Royal Exchange, Cornhill, 1830. 12mo.

1832.—POEMS, BY ALFRED TENNYSON. London: Edward Moxon, 64 New Bond Street (dated 1833). 12mo.

1833.—THE LOVER'S TALE, privately printed in London.

1842.—POEMS, BY ALFRED TENNYSON. London: Edward Moxon, Dover Street, 1842. 2 vols., 12mo.

1843.—THE SAME. Second edition. London: 1843. 2 vols., 12mo.

1845.—THE SAME. Third edition. London: 1845. 2 vols., 12mo.

1846.—THE SAME. Fourth edition. London: 1846. 2 vols., 12mo.

1847.—THE PRINCESS. A Medley. By Alfred Tennyson. London: Edward Moxon, Dover Street, 1847. 12mo.

1848.—THE SAME. Second edition. London: 1848 (with addition of dedication to Henry Lushington).

1848.—POEMS, BY ALFRED TENNYSON. Fifth edition. London: Edward Moxon, Dover Street, 1848. 12mo.

1850.—IN MEMORIAM. London: Edward Moxon, Dover Street, 1850. 12mo. (Appointed Poet-laureate Nov. 19.)

1850.—THE PRINCESS. Third edition (altered, with songs added). London : Edward Moxon, Dover Street, 1850. 12mo.

1850.—POEMS, BY ALFRED TENNYSON. Sixth edition. London : 1850. 12mo. (*After reading a Life and Letters* included.)

1851.—POEMS, BY ALFRED TENNYSON. Seventh edition. London : 1851. 12mo. (*Come not when I am dead, Edwin Morris, The Eagle,* and the dedication *To the Queen* included.)

1851.—THE PRINCESS. Fourth edition., London : 1851. 12mo. *This edition first has the passages describing the Prince's weird seizures.*

1851.—IN MEMORIAM. Fourth edition. London : 1851. 12mo. (*O Sorrow, wilt thou live with me ?* added.)

1852.—ODE ON THE DEATH OF THE DUKE OF WELLINGTON. By Alfred Tennyson, Poet-laureate. London : Edward Moxon, Dover Street, 1852. 8vo.

1853.—POEMS, BY ALFRED TENNYSON. Eighth edition. London : 1853. 12mo. (With an alteration in the *Dream of Fair Women*, and lines *To E. L.* added.)

1853.—THE PRINCESS. Fifth edition (the final text). London : 1853. 12mo.

1854.—CHARGE OF THE LIGHT BRIGADE, published in the *Examiner*, Dec. 9th, 1854, then printed for the soldiers before Sebastopol, August, 1855.

1855.—MAUD, AND OTHER POEMS. By Alfred Tennyson, D.C.L., Poet-laureate. London : Edward Moxon, 1855. 12mo.

1857.—POEMS BY ALFRED TENNYSON. Illustrations by D. G. Rossetti, J. E. Millais, and others. Edward Moxon. Royal 8vo.

1859.—IDYLLS OF THE KING. By Alfred Tennyson, D.C.L., Poet-laureate. London : Edward Moxon & Co., Dover Street, 1859. 12mo.

1861.—THE SAILOR BOY. London : Emily Faithfull & Co., Victoria Press.

1862.—IDYLLS OF THE KING. A new edition. London : 1862. 12mo. (with Dedication to the Prince Consort).

1862.—ODE : MAY THE FIRST, 1862, FOR THE OPENING OF THE INTERNATIONAL EXHIBITION. London : Edward Moxon & Co. (published also in *Fraser*, June, 1862).

1863.—WELCOME TO ALEXANDRA. 4 pages. London : Edward Moxon & Co.

1864.—ENOCH ARDEN, ETC. By Alfred Tennyson, D.C.L., Poet-laureate. London: Edward Moxon & Co., Dover Street, 1864. 12mo.

1865.—SELECTIONS from the works of Alfred Tennyson, D.C.L., Poet-laureate. London: Edward Moxon & Co., Dover Street, 1865. 16mo.
This was published in Moxon's Miniature Poets, and contains six new poems, viz.: ' The Captain,' 'On a Mourner,' 'Home They Brought Him Slain with Spears,' and three 'Sonnets to a Coquette.'

1867.— THE VICTIM. } Printed by Sir Ivor Guest (Lord Wimborne), THE WINDOW. } set to music by Sir Arthur Sullivan.

1869.—THE HOLY GRAIL, AND OTHER POEMS. By Alfred Tennyson, D.C.L., Poet-laureate. London: Strahan & Co., Publishers, 56 Ludgate Hill, 1869. 12mo.

1870.—THE WINDOW, OR THE SONG OF THE WRENS. With music by Arthur Sullivan. London: Strahan, 1871 (Dec. 1870).

1871.—MINIATURE EDITION OF COMPLETE WORKS. London: Strahan & Co.

1871.—THE LAST TOURNAMENT. *Contemporary Review*, December.

1872.—GARETH AND LYNETTE, ETC. By Alfred Tennyson, D.C.L., Poet-laureate. London: Strahan & Co., 56 Ludgate Hill, 1872. 12mo.

1872.—THE LIBRARY EDITION OF THE COMPLETE WORKS. In seven volumes. London: Strahan & Co., 1872. Large 8vo. (The Idylls of the King in sequence with Epilogue to the Queen.)

1874.—A WELCOME TO THE DUCHESS OF EDINBURGH. H. S. King & Co.

1874.—THE CABINET EDITION (H. S. King & Co.) contained: *In the Garden at Swainston, The Voice and the Peak, England and America.*

1875.—QUEEN MARY. A Drama, by Alfred Tennyson. London: Henry S. King & Co., 1875. 12mo.

1876.—QUEEN MARY, produced at the Lyceum Theatre.

1876.—HAROLD. A Drama, by Alfred Tennyson. London: Henry S. King & Co. (dated 1877). 12mo.

1879.—THE LOVER'S TALE. By Alfred Tennyson. London: C. Kegan Paul & Co., 1 Paternoster Square, 1879. 12mo.

1879.—THE FALCON, produced at the St. James' Theatre.

1880.—COLLECTED SONNETS. By Charles Tennyson Turner with memorial lines by Alfred Tennyson. Edited (with a short preface) by Hallam Tennyson. London: C. Kegan Paul. 12mo.

1880.—BALLADS AND OTHER POEMS. By Alfred Tennyson. London: C. Kegan Paul & Co., 1 Paternoster Square, 1880. 12mo.

1881.—THE CUP, produced at the Lyceum Theatre.

1882.—THE PROMISE OF MAY, produced at the Globe Theatre.

1884.—THE CUP AND THE FALCON. By Alfred Lord Tennyson, Poet-laureate. London: Macmillan & Co., 1884. 12mo.

1884.—A NEW SINGLE-VOLUME EDITION OF WORKS. Revised by the Author with corrections. Macmillan & Co.

1884.—BECKET. By Alfred Lord Tennyson, Poet-laureate. London: Macmillan & Co., 1884. Crown 8vo.

1885.—TIRESIAS, AND OTHER POEMS (including *Once more the Heavenly Power*, published in *The Youth's Companion*, Boston, U.S.A., 1884). By Alfred Lord Tennyson, D.C.L., Poet-laureate. London: Macmillan & Co., 1885. 12mo.

1886.—A NEW LIBRARY EDITION OF COMPLETE WORKS. In ten volumes (revised, with additions by the author). London: Macmillan & Co. (Also a new single-volume Edition, with slight alterations. Macmillan & Co.)

1886.—LOCKSLEY HALL SIXTY YEARS AFTER, ETC. By Alfred Lord Tennyson, D.C.L., Poet-laureate. London and New York: Macmillan & Co., 1886. 12mo.

1887.—CARMEN SAECULARE. An ode in honour of the Jubilee of Queen Victoria. *Macmillan's Magazine*, April.

1889.—DEMETER AND OTHER POEMS. Macmillan & Co., London and New York. 12mo. (20,000 copies sold in first week.)

1889.—A NEW AND REVISED SINGLE-VOLUME EDITION OF WORKS (with many additions). Macmillan & Co.

1892.—THE FORESTERS, ROBIN HOOD AND MAID MARIAN. London and New York: Macmillan & Co. 12mo. Produced at Daly's Theatre in New York, March 17.

1892.—THE SILENT VOICES. Order of Service in Westminster Abbey, Oct. 12th. Printed for copyright purposes. London and New York: Macmillan & Co.

1892.—Oct. 28th. THE DEATH OF ŒNONE, AKBAR'S DREAM AND OTHER POEMS. London and New York: Macmillan & Co. 12mo. Also large paper Edition with five steel portraits.

1893.—BECKET, AS ARRANGED FOR THE STAGE BY HENRY IRVING (revised by Alfred Lord Tennyson).   Macmillan & Co.

1894.—THE COMPLETE SINGLE-VOLUME EDITION OF THE WORKS, with last alterations, etc.   London : Macmillan & Co.

In Rowe's *Coming of Arthur,* and *Passing of Arthur;* G.C. Macaulay's *Gareth and Lynette,* and *Marriage of Geraint,* and *Geraint and Enid;* Ainger's *Tennyson for the Young;* Rowe's *Aylmer's Field;* Rowe's *Selections from Tennyson;* Palgrave's Golden Treasury Selection of *Lyrical Poems;* Dawson's *Princess;* Rolfe's *Enoch Arden, and Selections,* whenever there was any doubtful point in the notes, I referred it to my father : so that in the later editions of these annotated volumes the commentaries may be considered tolerably accurate.

POEMS PUBLISHED IN THE " NINETEENTH CENTURY."

My father contributed the following poems to the *Nineteenth Century :* in 1877, " Prefatory Sonnet " (March), and " Montenegro " (May), and "To Victor Hugo " (June), and " Achilles over the Trench " (August) ; and in March, 1878, he contributed " The Revenge " ; in April, 1879, " The Defence of Lucknow, with a Dedicatory Poem to Princess Alice " ; in May, 1880, " De Profundis " ; in November, 1881, " Despair " ; in September, 1882, " To Virgil " ; in March, 1883, " Frater ave atque vale " ; in February, 1892, " On the death of the Duke of Clarence and Avondale."

George Pitt of Strathfieldsaye = Lady Jane Pitt[1]

Jane = Christopher Hildeyard
Dorothy = George Clayton of Grimsby

Ralph Tennyson, of Barton and of Wrawby, 1672-1735 = Dorothy Chapman

Michael Tennyson, of Preston, York, Stainton = Elizabeth Clayton and Lincoln, 1721-1796

1775
George Tennyson, M.P., of Bayons Manor, 1750-1835 = Mary Turner, of Caistor, 1753-1825

Mary = John Bourne of Dalby

Elizabeth = Matthew Russell, M.P. of Brancepeth Castle

6th Aug., 1805
Rev. George Clayton Tennyson, M.A., LL.D., of Somersby, 1778-1831 = Elizabeth Fytche, of Louth, 1781-1865

The Right Hon. Charles Tennyson d'Eyncourt, M.P. of Bayons Manor, 1784-1861

George, May, 1806-1806, born at Tealby
Frederick, June, 1807- = Maria Giuliotti
Charles, July, 1808-1879 = Louisa Sellwood

13th June, 1850
ALFRED, Aug. 6th, 1809-1892 = EMILY SARAH SELLWOOD, 1813-1896, daughter of Henry Sellwood, Esq., of Berks.
Somersby

= Alan Ker, Judge of High Court of Jamaica
= Capt. Jesse, R.N.

Mary, Sept., 1810-1884
Emilia, Oct., 1811-1889
Engaged to A. H. Hallam, d. 1833
Edward, Jan., 1813-1890, born at Somersby = 1st Harriet West, 2nd Louisa Maynard
Arthur, May, 1814-
Septimus, Sept., 1815-1866
Matilda, Sept., 1816-
Cecilia, Oct., 1817- = Prof. Edmund Law Lushington, D.C.L., of Park House, Maidstone
Horatio, Sept., 1819- = 1st Charlotte d. of Dudley Cary Elwes, 2nd Catharine West

1884
Hallam Tennyson = Audrey Boyle
1852-

1878
Lionel Tennyson = Eleanor Locker
1854-1886

Charles Bruce Locker
1879-

Michael Sellwood
1883-

Alfred Browning Stanley
1878-

Harold Courtenay
1896-

Lionel Hallam
1889-

Alfred Aubrey
1891-

1 Daughter of John Earl Rivers and Catherine daughter of William Lord Morley.

CHAPTER I.

BOYHOOD.

1809–1827.

The Tennysons may probably in their origin have been Danes, and they appear to have first settled north of the Humber, in Holderness. The earliest notice of the family that can be found is that in 1343 one John Tenison charged certain persons with forcibly taking away his goods and chattels at Paulfleet to the amount of £40. In 1528 John Tennyson of Ryall directs that his body should be buried in the kirk-garthe of All Hallows at Skekelinge. To Margaret his wife he devises one ox-yard of land and half a close called Stockett Croft during her widowhood. Bequests are also made to his several children. One of them named William, who was possibly a Mayor, afterwards leaves to John, his son, his "best mace, and to Paul Church, twenty pence." He desires to be buried in the same kirk-garthe of All Hallows. From these Tennysons, through a Lancelot Tennyson of Preston, and Ralph Tennyson, who raised a troop of horse to support William III., descends Michael of Lincoln, my father's great-grandfather. Michael was remembered by my grandfather, the Rev. Dr George Clayton Tennyson, as taking him into his bed and talking to him about the stars.

Half-way between Horncastle and Spilsby, in a land

of quiet villages, large fields, gray hillsides and noble tall towered churches, on the lower slope of a Lincolnshire wold, the pastoral hamlet of Somersby nestles, embosomed in trees.

Here, on the 6th of August, 1809, was born, in his father's rectory, Alfred Tennyson. He was the fourth of twelve children, eight sons and four daughters, most of them more or less true poets, and of whom all except two have lived to 70 and upward. Dr Tennyson baptized the boy two days after he was born, following the Prayer-book instruction that people "defer not the Baptism of their children longer than the first or second Sunday next after their birth."

"Here's a leg for a babe of a week!" says doctor; and
    he would be bound,
There was not his like that year in twenty parishes
    round [1],

was said of him; nevertheless during his infancy three times after convulsions he was thought to be dead.

In 1892 I visited the old home, and when I returned, told my father that the trees had grown up obscuring the view from the Rectory, and that the house itself looked very desolate. All he answered was, "Poor little place!" He always spoke of it with an affectionate remembrance; of the woodbine that climbed into the bay window of his nursery; of the Gothic vaulted dining-room with stained glass windows, making, as my uncle Charles Turner used to say, "butterfly souls" on the walls; of the beautiful stone chimney-piece carved by his father; of the pleasant little drawing-room lined with book-shelves, and furnished with yellow curtains, sofas and chairs, and looking out on the lawn. This lawn was overshadowed on one side by wych-elms, and on the other by larch and sycamore trees.

[1] See "The Grandmother."

Here, my father said, he made his early song "A spirit haunts the year's last hours." Beyond the path, bounding the green sward to the south, ran in the old days a deep border of lilies and roses, backed by hollyhocks and sunflowers. Beyond that was

> A garden bower'd close
> With plaited alleys of the trailing rose,
> Long alleys falling down to twilight grots,
> Or opening upon level plots
> Of crowned lilies, standing near
> Purple-spiked lavender —

sloping in a gradual descent to the parson's field, at the foot of which flows, by "lawn and lea," the swift, steep-banked brook, where are "brambley wildernesses," and "sweet forget-me-nots," and in which the "long mosses sway." The charm and beauty of this brook,

>   That loves
> To purl o'er matted cress and ribbed sand,
> Or dimple in the dark of rushy coves,
> And swerves to left and right thro' meadowy curves
> That feed the mothers of the flock[1],

haunted him through life.

Near Somersby the stream joins another from Holywell, and their confluence may be referred to in the lines:

> By that old bridge, which, half in ruins then,
> Still makes a hoary eyebrow for the gleam
> Beyond it, where the waters marry.

"Flow down, cold rivulet, to the sea" was the poem more especially dedicated to the Somersby stream, and not, as some have supposed, "The Brook," which is designed to be a brook of the imagination.

The orchard on the right of the lawn forms a sunny

---

[1] "Ode to Memory," which he considered one of the best among his very early and peculiarly concentrated Nature-poems.

little spot that awoke in his mind pleasant memories. "How often," he said, "have I risen in the early dawn to see the golden globes lying in the dewy grass among those apple trees." He delighted too to recall the rare richness of the bowery lanes: the ancient Norman cross standing in the churchyard, close to the door of the quaint little church: the wooded hollow of Holywell: the cold springs flowing from under the sandstone rocks: the flowers, the mosses, and the ferns. When there I looked in vain for the words "Byron is dead," which he had carved on a rock when he was fourteen, on hearing of Byron's death (April 19th, 1824), "a day when the whole world seemed to be darkened for me."

Like other children, the Tennysons had their imaginative games; they were knights and jousted in mock tournaments, or they were "champions and warriors, defending a field, or a stone-heap, or again they would set up opposing camps with a king in the midst of each. The king was a willow-wand stuck into the ground, with an outer circle of immortals, to defend him, of firmer, stiffer sticks. Then each party would come with stones, hurling at each other's king and trying to overthrow him[1]." Stories are told too about their boyish pranks in the old red-bricked house with embattled parapet (Baumber's Farm), said to have been built by Vanbrugh, which adjoins the Rectory garden, and is erroneously called by some " The Moated Grange." " At all events, whatever may have happened," my father writes, " The Moated Grange is an imaginary house in the fen; I never so much as dreamed of Baumber's farm[2] as the abode of Mariana, and the character of Baumber was so ludicrously unlike the Northern Farmer, that

---

[1] Taken from the account which my father gave Mrs Thackeray Ritchie.

[2] The localities of my father's subject-poems are wholly imaginary, although he has done for general Mid-Lincolnshire scenery what Virgil did for Mantua.

it really makes me wonder how any one can have the
face to invent such stories." I think that their childhood, despite the home circumstances which will be
presently noticed, could not have been in the main unhappy. Their imaginative natures gave them many
sources of amusement. One of these lasted a long
time: the writing of tales in letter form, to be put
under the vegetable dishes at dinner, and read aloud
when it was over. I have heard from my uncles
and aunts that my father's tales were very various in
theme, some of them humorous and some savagely
dramatic; and that they looked to him as their most
thrilling story-teller. Among historical events the doings
of Wellington and Napoleon were the themes of story
and verse. Yet Somersby was so far out of the world
that the elder children say they did not hear of the
battle of Waterloo at the time. They had however an
early memory that " the coach drove through Somersby,
the horses decorated with flowers and ribbons, and
this might have been in honour of Wellington's great
victory."

My aunt Cecilia (Mrs Lushington) narrates how in
the winter evenings by the firelight little Alfred would
take her on his knee, with Arthur and Matilda leaning
against him on either side, the baby Horatio between
his legs; and how he would fascinate this group of young
hero-worshippers, who listened open-eared and open-
mouthed to legends of knights and heroes among
untravelled forests rescuing distressed damsels, or on
gigantic mountains fighting with dragons, or to his tales
about Indians, or demons, or witches. The brothers
and sisters would sometimes act one of the old English
plays; and the elder members of the family thought
that my father, from his dramatic rendering of his parts
and his musical voice, would turn out an actor.

When he was seven years old he was asked, " Will

you go to sea or to school?" He said, "To school," thinking that school was a kind of paradise; so he was taken to the house of his grandmother at Louth. His mother had been born in that town, being daughter of the vicar, the Rev. Stephen Fytche[1]; and he was sent to the Grammar School there, then under the Rev. J. Waite, a tempestuous, flogging master of the old stamp. He remembered to his dying day sitting on the stone steps of the school on a cold winter's morning, and crying bitterly after a big lad had brutally cuffed him on the head because he was a new boy. I still have the books which he used there, his *Ovid*, *Delectus*, *Analecta Græca Minora*, and the old *Eton Latin Grammar*, originally put together by Erasmus, Lilly and Colet.

Among the incidents in his school life he would recall that of walking in a procession of boys, decked with ribbons, at the proclamation of the Coronation of George IV., and how the, old women said that " The boys made the prettiest part of the show." Later in school life, he one day stood on a wall and made a political speech to his school-fellows, but was promptly ordered down by an usher, who asked him whether he wished to be the parish beadle.

Two facts that his grandmother told him at this time impressed him. One was that she had become blind from cataract, and then had a dream that she saw; and, that, although couching for cataract was not common in those days, owing to this dream she had gone to

---

[1] George Clayton Tennyson of Tealby, clerk, and Elizabeth Fytche of Louth, spinster, were married in Louth Church by license on the 6th August 1805 by Wolley Jolland, Vicar, in the presence of John Fytche and Charles Tennyson. The Fytches were a county family of old descent. The first name on the Fytche pedigree is John Fitch of Fitch Castle in the North, who died in the 25th year of Edward I. His descendant Thomas Fitch was knighted by Charles II. 1679, served the office of High Sheriff in Kent, and was created baronet, Sept. 7th, 1688.

London, and had been operated on successfully. The second was that she remembered having seen a young widow[1], dressed in white, on her way to be strangled (her body afterwards to be burnt) for poisoning her husband.

A few years ago the present master of Louth School gave a holiday in my father's honour. The compliment gratified him; yet he said, " How I did hate that school ! The only good I ever got from it was the memory of the words, 'sonus desilientis aquae,' and of an old wall covered with wild weeds opposite the school windows. I wrote an English poem there, for one of the Jacksons; the only line I recollect is ' While bleeding heroes lie along the shore[2].' "

In 1820 he left Louth and came home to work under his father.

When twelve years old he wrote the following literary epistle (the earliest of those now remaining) to his aunt Marianne Fytche.

SOMERSBY.

My dear Aunt Marianne,

When I was at Louth you used to tell me that you should be obliged to me if I would write to you and give you my remarks on works and authors. I shall now fulfil the promise which I made at that time. Going into the library this morning, I picked up "Sampson Agonistes," on which (as I think it is a play you like)

1 "Women who were found guilty of murdering their husbands, or of the other offences comprised under the terms high or petit treason, were publicly burnt, by a law which was not abolished till 1790. A stake ten or eleven feet high was planted in the ground. An iron ring was fastened near the top, and from it the culprit was hung while the faggots were kindled under her feet. The law enjoined that she should be burnt alive, but in practice the sentence was usually mitigated, and she was strangled before the fire touched her body."

Lecky's *England in the Eighteenth Century*, Vol. I. p. 506.

2 See Professor J. W. Hales' account of Louth School in the *Gentleman's Magazine*, Dec. 1892. See Appendix, p. 497.

I shall send you my remarks. The first scene is the
lamentation of Sampson, which possesses much pathos
and sublimity. This passage,

> Restless thoughts, that like a deadly swarm
> Of hornets arm'd, no sooner found alone,
> But rush upon me thronging, and present
> Times past, what once I was, and what am now,

puts me in mind of that in Dante, which Lord Byron
has prefixed to his " Corsair," " Nessun maggior dolore,
Che ricordarsi del tempo felice, Nella miseria." His
complaint of his blindness is particularly beautiful,

> O loss of sight, of thee I most complain!
> Blind among enemies! O worse than chains,
> Dungeon or beggary, or decrepit age!
> Light, the prime work of God, to me is extinct,
> And all her various objects of delight
> Annulled, which might in part my grief have eased,
> Inferior to the vilest now become
> Of man or worm; the vilest here excel me:
> They creep, yet see; I, dark in light, exposed
> To daily fraud, contempt, abuse, and wrong,
>   *   *   *   *   *   *   *   *
> Scarce half I seem to live, dead more than half.
> O dark, dark, dark, amid the blaze of noon,
> Irrecoverably dark, total eclipse
> Without all hope of day!
> O first created beam, and thou great Word,
> "Let there be light!" and light was over all.—

I think this is beautiful, particularly

> O dark, dark, dark, amid the blaze of noon.

After a long lamentation of Sampson, the Chorus
enters, saying these words :

> This, this is he. Softly awhile;
> Let us not break in upon him:
> O change beyond report, thought, or belief!
> See how he lies at random, carelessly *diffused.*

If you look into Bp. Newton's notes, you will find that
he informs you that " This beautiful application of the

word 'diffused' is borrowed from the Latin." It has the same meaning as " temere " in one of the Odes of Horace, Book the second,

> Sic temere, et rosâ
> Canos odorati capillos,

of which this is a free translation, " Why lie we not at random, under the shade of the plantain (sub platano), having our hoary head perfumed with rose water?" To an English reader the metre of the Chorus may seem unusual, but the difficulty will vanish, when I inform him that it is taken from the Greek. In line 133 there is this expression, " Chalybean tempered steel." The Chalybes were a nation among the ancients very famous for the making of steel, hence the expression " Chalybean," or peculiar to the Chalybes: in line 147 "the Gates of Azzar"; this probably, as Bp. Newton observes, was to avoid too great an alliteration, which the "Gates of Gaza" would have caused, though (in my opinion) it would have rendered it more beautiful: and (though I do not affirm it as a fact) perhaps Milton gave it that name for the sake of novelty, as all the world knows he was a great pedant. I have not, at present, time to write any more. perhaps I may continue my remarks in another letter to you: but (as I am very volatile and fickle) you must not depend upon me, for I think you do not know any one who is so fickle as

Your affectionate nephew,

A. TENNYSON.

P.S. Frederick informed me that grandmamma was quite growing dissipated, going out to parties every night. The Russels and grandmamma are to be at Dalby on Tuesday the 23rd, and I also hope to be taken by papa and mamma who are invited. Frederick made mamma promise to write him an account of the visit, but if I go, I shall take the trouble from mamma.

His second earliest letter is a piece of nonsense with which he favoured his sisters' governess.

La Mancha.

My dear Dulcinea,

Pursuant to your request and the honour of Knight-errantry, and in conformity to my bump of conscientiousness (which has grown so enormous since my visit to you that I can scarce put on my helmet), I now intend, as far as lies in my power, to fulfil that promise which the lustre of your charms extorted from me. Know then, most adorable mistress of my heart, that the manuscripts which your angelic goodness and perfection were pleased to commend are not with me. If however my memory, assisted by the peerless radiance of your divine favour, avail me aught, I will endeavour to illume the darkness of my imagination with the recollection of your glorious excellence, till I produce a species of artificial memory unequalled by the *Memoria Technica* of Mr Gray. Who would not remember when thus requested? It would cause a dead idiot to start afresh to life and intellect. Accept then, soul of my soul, these effusions, in which no Ossianic, Miltonic, Byronic, Milmanic, Moorish, Crabbic, Coleridgic etc. fire is contained.

The first is a review of death:

Why should we weep for those who die? etc.

The second is a comparison:

> Je fais naître la lumière
> Du sein de l'obscurité.   (Rousseau.)

How gaily sinks the gorgeous sun, etc.
And now farewell, my incomparable Dulcinea. In the truest spirit of knight-errantry,

Yours ever, Don Quixote.

As to his earliest attempts at poetry, he wrote the following note for me in 1890:

"According to the best of my recollection, when I was about eight years old, I covered two sides of a slate with Thomsonian blank verse in praise of flowers for my brother Charles, who was a year older than I was, Thomson then being the only poet I knew. Before I could read, I was in the habit on a stormy day of spreading my arms to the wind, and crying out 'I hear a voice that's speaking in the wind,' and the words 'far, far away' had always a strange charm for me. About ten or eleven Pope's *Homer's Iliad* became a favourite of mine and I wrote hundreds and hundreds of lines in the regular Popeian metre, nay even could improvise them, so could my two elder brothers, for my father was a poet and could write regular metre very skilfully."

[I give one example:

Can I forget thee? In the festive hall,
Where wit and beauty reign and minstrelsy,
My heart still fondly shall recur to thee,
Thine image still recall.

Can I forget thee? In the gloomy hour,
When wave on wave tempestuous passions roll,
Thou, loved ideal, still shalt soothe my soul,
And health and peace restore.

Farewell, my choicest blessings round thee wait,
And kindred angels guard thine angel form,
Guide and protect thee in life's rudest storm,
And every blast of fate[1]!]

[1] These lines are copied from my grandfather's scrapbook, a book which with others in his library he bound in leather with his own hands. His sister Mrs Matthew Russell also dabbled in poetry, and Dr Tennyson writes to her about some of her compositions in 1825: "You do wrong to confess you are long in making verses, for no one would conceive it from the peculiar ease of the metre. You are not however singular: Gray hammer'd at his verses with great difficulty, and yet they have immortalized his name. Æschylus, the great Greek tragedian, with great difficulty once composed three verses in three days: a poetaster came to Æschylus, and boasted that he had composed three thousand in the same time. 'Your three thousand verses,' said Æschylus, 'will last only for three days, whereas my three verses will last for ever.' Your soliloquy is very beautiful, and so beautiful that I have transcribed it amongst my choice selections."

The note continues — " My father once said to me, ' Don't write so rhythmically, break your lines occasionally for the sake of variety.'

' Artist first, then Poet,' some writer said of me. I should answer, ' Poeta nascitur non fit '; indeed, ' Poeta nascitur et fit.' I suppose I was nearer thirty than twenty before I was anything of an artist.

At about twelve and onward I wrote an epic of six thousand lines à la Walter Scott, — full of battles, dealing too with sea and mountain scenery, — with Scott's regularity of octo-syllables and his occasional varieties. Though the performance was very likely worth nothing I never felt myself more truly inspired. I wrote as much as seventy lines at one time, and used to go shouting them about the fields in the dark. All these early efforts have been destroyed, only my brother-in-law Edmund Lushington begged for a page or two of the Scott poem. Somewhat later (at fourteen) I wrote a Drama in blank verse, which I have still, and other things. It seems to me, I wrote them all in perfect metre."

These poems made my grandfather say with pardonable pride, " If Alfred die, one of our greatest poets will have gone ": and at another time, " I should not wonder if Alfred were to revive the greatness of his relative, William Pitt [1]."

His grandmother, the sister of the Reverend Samuel Turner, would assert: " Alfred's poetry all comes from me." My father remembered her reading to him, when a boy, " The Prisoner of Chillon " very tenderly. Sam Turner, on the contrary, smashed the bottom out of his glass of rum and water on the dinner table, as he inveighed against " this new-fangled Byron."

When at his grandfather's desire my father wrote a poem on his grandmother's death, the old gentleman gave

[1] See p. xxii.

him half a guinea with these words, " Here is half a guinea
for you, the first you have ever earned by poetry, and take
my word for it, the last." He himself was not a great
hand at versification. Two lines of his are extant, describing the crest of the Boynes, a goat drinking out of a
stream. His younger son had previously made these lines,

> On yonder bank a goat is stood,
> He seems to sip the silver flood,

which were corrected by the old gentleman as follows,

> On yonder bank a goat I spy,
> To sip the flood he seems to try.

Owing to a caprice of my great-grandfather's,
my grandfather, who was the elder son, was disinherited in favour of his only brother, Charles (Tennyson
d'Eyncourt [1]), and so deprived of a position for which he
would seem to have been well fitted. A neighbouring
squire, being told by my great-grandfather of his intention, remonstrated, " George, if you do this you'll
certainly be damned, you will indeed "; but, in spite of
the remonstrance and the risk, the estate was left away
from the elder son.

As compensation for being disinherited, my grandfather was appointed not only Rector of Somersby and
Wood Enderby, but also Incumbent of Benniworth and
Vicar of Great Grimsby, for those were the days of
pluralists. Not that he could have been a grasping man,
for on one occasion a wealthy land-owner (whose heir
was a remote relation and a poor farm-labourer) announced his intention of leaving all his property to
Dr Tennyson. But this my grandfather felt was unjust,
and accordingly took the first opportunity of offending

---

[1] Charles took the name of d'Eyncourt because, according to Burke and
other heralds, the Tennysons represent the two branches of the old Norman
family of d'Eyncourt.

his would-be benefactor in order that he might change
his mind. The ruse was successful, as the sequel
proved, for the estate devolved upon the rightful
heir.

Undoubtedly the disinheritance of my grandfather
created a feeling of injustice in his mind which descended
to his sons, though my father used to reflect in later
years how little this early trial personally affected them
and the d'Eyncourt sons; the cousins were always good
friends.

My grandfather had no real calling for the ministry
of the Church, yet he faithfully strove to do his duty.
He was a man of great ability, and considerably in
advance of his age in his theological tenets, although
in his sermons he could not escape the academic style
of his time; for example: "The benevolent genius of
Christianity affords the strongest presumption of its verity.
The Almighty, so infinitely benevolent, can only wish to
ensure the happiness of His creatures in the truths which
He communicates, in the laws which He imposes, and
in the doctrines which He promulgates. This indeed is
so self-evident that it might be laid down as a rule that
if any religion have not a benevolent tendency, this very
circumstance is a sufficient refutation of its proceeding
from God. What is revealed to us by Christianity but
the Redemption of the whole human race by the merits
of a crucified Saviour, and the glorious assurance of a
future state of existence?"

The Lincolnshire folk among whom he lived were
in the early part of this century apt to be uncouth
and mannerless. A type of rough independence was
my grandfather's coachman, who, blamed for not keeping the harness clean, rushed into the drawing-room,
flung the whole harness on the floor and roared out:
"Clean it yourself then." It was perhaps the same
man, who at the time of the Reform Bill said, "I

suppose, Master Awlfred, your aunt Mrs Bourne will be going up to London before they begin *to kill the quality*."

(This aunt was a rigid Calvinist, who would weep for hours because God was so infinitely good. " Has He not damned," she cried, "most of my friends? But *me, me* He has picked out for eternal salvation, *me* who am no better than my neighbours." One day she said to her nephew, " Alfred, Alfred, when I look at you, I think of the words of Holy Scripture — 'Depart from me, ye cursed, into everlasting fire.'")

Again the Somersby cook was a decided character, and " Master Awlfred " heard her in some rage against her master and mistress exclaim: " If you raäked out Hell with a smaäll-tooth coämb you weän't find their likes," a phrase which long lingered in his memory.

Yet notwithstanding their roughness the poor were fond of the "stern Doctor," as they called him, and would "do anything for him." Here perhaps I should mention that the sense of his father's unkindness and injustice preyed upon his nerves and his health, and caused him at times to be terribly despondent. More than once Alfred, scared by his father's fits of despondency, went out through the black night, and threw himself on a grave in the churchyard, praying to be beneath the sod himself [1].

---

[1] In one of his books I have found this unfinished prayer, composed by him, and written in his boyish hand; it begins thus :

" O Lord God Almighty, high above all height, Omniscient and Omnipresent, Whose lifetime is eternity, wilt Thou condescend to behold from the throne of Thy inexpressible Majesty the work of Thine own Hands kneeling before thee? Thou art the God of Heaven and of Earth. Thou hast created the immeasurable sea. Thou hast laid the foundations of the world that it should not be moved for ever. Thou givest and Thou takest life, Thou destroyest and Thou renewest. Blessed be Thy name for ever and ever."

The prayer continues with an appeal for pity to Christ — " Who did leave the right hand of the Father to endure the agonies of the crown of thorns," and " of the Cross."

No doubt the children profited by the dominating force of their father's intellect. A Hebrew and Syriac scholar, he perfected himself in Greek, in order that he might teach his sons. All that they learnt of languages, of the fine arts, of mathematics, and natural science, until they went to Cambridge, was learnt from him. My father said that he himself received a good but not a regular classical education. At any rate he became an accurate scholar, the author "thoroughly drummed" into him being Horace; whom he disliked in proportion. He would lament, " They use *me* as a lesson-book at schools, and they will call me 'that horrible Tennyson.' It was not till many years after boyhood that I could like Horace. Byron expressed what I felt, ' Then farewell Horace whom I hated so.' Indeed I was so over-dosed with Horace that I hardly do him justice even now that I am old."

The boys had one great advantage, the run of their father's excellent library. Amongst the authors most read by them were Shakespeare, Milton, Burke, Goldsmith, Rabelais, Sir William Jones, Addison, Swift, Defoe, Cervantes, Bunyan and Buffon.

Dr Tennyson's social powers were famous throughout the country side. The tradition lingered long among old barristers that, as young men, when they came to Spilsby on circuit, they were always anxious to persuade Dr Tennyson to dine with them because of his geniality and brilliant conversation.

To this sketch of my grandfather, my uncle Arthur adds a few words.

A scene comes before me of Frederick, Charles and Alfred having a regular scrimmage with lesson-books, and of my father suddenly coming round the corner. I didn't wait to see what happened, but bolted; our father's tall form appearing was generally at such moments the signal for a regular " scatter," but, although very severe, he had great tenderness of heart. I can well recollect him by my bedside, almost weeping, when I had a bad paroxysm of croup. Alfred had the same tenderness in spite of his somewhat gruff manner: he was notable among his brothers for strength and independence of character. His was a very gentle nature and I never remember quarrelling with him. He was very kind to us who were younger than he was, and I remember his tremendous excitement when he got hold of Bewick for the first time: how he paced up and down the lawn for hours studying him, and how he kept rushing in to us in the schoolroom to show us some of the marvellous wood-cuts, and to let us have a share in this new pleasure of his. Indeed he was always a great reader; and if he went alone he would take his book with him on his walk. One day in the winter, the snow being deep, he did not hear the Louth mail coming up behind. Suddenly "Ho! ho!" from the coachman roused him. He looked up, and found a horse's nose and eyes over his shoulder, as if reading his book. Like my father, Alfred had a great head, so that when I put on his hat it came down over my face. He too like my father [1] had a powerful frame, a splendid physique, and we used to have gymnastics over the large beam in his attic den, which was in the gable looking westward. Alfred and I often took long rambles together, and on one particular afternoon, when we were in the home fields talking of our respective futures, he said most emphatically, "Well, Arthur, I mean to be famous." (From his earliest years he felt that he was a poet, and earnestly trained himself to be worthy of his vocation.) For our less active amusements we carved in wood and moulded with clay, and one of my earliest recollections of Alfred is watching him form with clay a Gothic archway in the bole of an old tree.

In the poem of "Isabel" my father more or less described his mother, who was a "remarkable and saintly woman." "One of the most innocent and tender-hearted ladies I ever saw," wrote Edward Fitzgerald.

---

[1] He stood six feet two, and was strong and energetic. Tim Green, the Somersby rat-catcher, a great ally of the young Tennysons, said, "I remember the oud Doctor. What a clip he used to goä betweeän them chooörches o' Somersby an' Enderby!"

She devoted herself entirely to her husband and her children.

> The world hath not another
> (Tho' all her fairest forms are types of thee,
> And thou of God in thy great charity)
> Of such a finish'd chasten'd purity.

She had been among the beauties of the county. When she was almost eighty, a daughter, under cover of her deafness, ventured to mention the number of offers of marriage which had been made to her mother, naming twenty-four. Suddenly, to the amusement of all present, the old lady said emphatically, and quite simply, as for truth's sake, " No, my dear, twenty-five." She had a great sense of humour, which made her room a paradise for the children. They inherited her love of animals [1] and her pity "for all wounded wings." And my father was even then a keen observer of the habits of birds and beasts and ants and bees; was " wise in winged things, and knew the ways of Nature," of which he had the true poet's love. In later life this led to an earnest study of science.

As a boy he would reel off hundreds of lines such as these:

> When winds are east and violets blow,
> And slowly stalks the parson crow.

And

> The quick-wing'd gnat doth make a boat
> Of his old husk wherewith to float
> To a new life! all low things range
> To higher! but I cannot change.

[1] The boys of a neighbouring village used to bring their dogs to my grandmother's windows and beat them in order to be bribed to leave off, or to induce her to buy them.

To the aggravation of the neighbouring gamekeepers he would spring all their traps, and more than one of them threatened that, if they caught " that there young gentleman who was for ever springing the gins," they would duck him in the pond.

He liked to tell of an owl and a monkey of famous memory. Sitting at night by the open window in his own particular little attic (now used as a store-room for apples and lumber), he heard the cry of a young owl and answered it. The owl came nestling up to him, fed out of his hand, and finally took up its permanent abode with the family. Sometimes it would perch on my grandmother's head, and was so constantly with her that her pet monkey was made jealous. The monkey was a droll fellow: he would imitate the housemaid scrubbing the floor, and his prime luxury was to singe the hair of his back at a candle. One luckless day he was sitting in a corner of the sill outside the attic window, the owl in the opposite corner. The monkey glared at the owl; the owl watched the monkey with solemn round eyes, — the monkey, advancing and retiring, and gibbering like a little Frenchman all the while. The little Frenchman at last plucked up courage, rushed at his solemn opponent, took him by the leg, and hurled him to the ground. " One of the most comical scenes," my father said, " that I have ever witnessed." The owl was eventually drowned in the well; dying, it is supposed, a Narcissus death of vanity.

" Like Wordsworth on the mountains," said Fitzgerald, " Alfred too, when a lad abroad on the wold, sometimes of a night with the shepherd, watched not only the flock on the greensward, but also

the fleecy star that bears
Andromeda far off Atlantic seas ":

2—2

Two of Alfred's earliest lines were:

The rays of many a rolling central star,
Aye flashing earthwards, have not reach'd us yet.

There is a story current in the family that Frederick,
when an Eton school-boy, was shy of going to a neighbouring dinner-party to which he had been invited.
" Fred," said his younger brother, " think of Herschel's
great star-patches, and you will soon get over all that."
Of the few families in the neighbourhood the Tennysons were most intimate with the Rawnsleys. Mr
Rawnsley, who was Rector of Halton, was appointed by
Dr Tennyson one of the guardians of his children. For
his son Drummond my father had a strong friendship
which lasted through life, having been first attracted
to him by a certain unworldliness of nature.
In the summer-time Dr and Mrs Tennyson took
their holiday by the seaside, mostly at Mablethorpe.
From his boyhood my father had a passion for the sea,
and especially for the North Sea in wild weather—

The hollow ocean-ridges roaring into cataracts:

and for the glorious sunsets over the flats —

The wide-wing'd sunset of the misty marsh.

The cottage [1] to which the family resorted was close
under the sea bank, " the long low line of tussocked dunes."
" I used to stand on this sand-built ridge," my father
said, " and think that it was the spine-bone of the world."
From the top of this, the immense sweep of marsh inland [1]
and the whole weird strangeness of the place greatly

[1] Or even a lowly cottage whence we see
    Stretch'd wide and wild the waste enormous marsh,
    Where from the frequent bridge,
    Like emblems of infinity,
    The trenchéd waters run from sky to sky.

                                    "Ode to Memory."

moved him. On the other side of the bank at
low tide there is an immeasurable waste of sand and
clay. "Nottingham and Lincoln foälk moästly coom
'ere," one of the Mablethorpe fishermen grumbled, "a
vast sight of 'em, soom taime (time), but they saäys it
is a mighty dool plaäce with a deäl o' sand, becos there
isn't naw band nor pier like: but howsoomever, the wind
blaws the poor things a bit, an' they weshes their bodies
i' the waäves." At night on the shore, when the tide
is full, the sound is amazing. All around there is a
low murmur of seething foam,

> Like armies whispering where great echoes be.

"Nowhere," wrote Drummond Rawnsley, "are the
waves in a storm higher than in the North Sea": nowhere have the breakers a more thunderous roar than
on this Lincolnshire coast: and sometimes at half-tide
the clap of the wave falling on the flat shore can be
heard for miles, and is accurately described in "The
Last Tournament":

> As the crest of some slow-arching wave,
> Heard in dead night along that table-shore,
> Drops flat, and after the great waters break
> Whitening for half a league, and thin themselves,
> Far over sands marbled with moon and cloud,
> From less and less to nothing.

Fitzgerald writes: "I used to say Alfred never
should have left old Lincolnshire, where there were not
only such good seas, but also such fine Hill and Dale
among 'The Wolds,' which he was brought up in, as
people in general scarce thought on."

In 1827 my uncle Frederick went from Eton, where
he was captain of the school, to Trinity College, Cambridge: and in March of this year *Poems by Two Brothers*

was published by Jackson of Louth. When these poems were written, my uncle Charles was between sixteen and eighteen, and my father between fifteen and seventeen.

The brothers were promised the liberal sum of £20, having however to take more than half of this in books out of Jackson's shop. According to the fashion of the day, quotations from various authors were freely interspersed throughout the little volume, and the motto at the beginning was " Haec nos novimus esse nihil." Their preface states, " We have passed the Rubicon and we leave the rest to fate, though its edict may create a fruitless regret that we ever emerged 'from the shade' and courted notoriety."

As an outburst of youthful poetic enthusiasm, the book is not wanting in interest and a certain charm, although full of the boyish imitation of other poets. Unlike Swift, who exclaimed on re-reading his early work, " What a genius I had when I wrote that!" my father could hardly tolerate what he called his " early rot." But latterly he said, " Some of it is better than I thought it was!" In consequence of the unearthing of this MS by Messrs Jackson it fell to me to publish the second edition, sixty years after the publication of the first, and to endeavour to initial the poems. Yet I cannot be sure of the authorship of each, even though the original manuscript has been in my hands, for the poems are not always copied out by their respective authors. But the initials which I gave received the sanction and authority of my uncle Frederick, as far as his memory served him. He himself was the author of four of the poems, that had generally been attributed to Charles.

The only contemporary criticism is in the *Literary Chronicle* (May 1827):

This little volume exhibits a pleasing union of kindred tastes, and contains several little pieces of considerable merit.

My uncle Charles would say that, on the afternoon of publication, my father and he hired a carriage with some of the money earned; and driving away fourteen miles, over the wolds and the marsh, to Mablethorpe, their favourite waste sea-shore, "shared their triumph with the winds and waves."

UNPUBLISHED POEMS OF BOYHOOD.

(Fragments written at 14 or 15 years of age.)

I showed the following early fragments to the late Master of Ballioi and by his advice I publish them. He said, "They are most original, and it is wonderful how the whelp could have known such things." They were omitted from the *Poems by Two Brothers*, being thought too much out of the common for the public taste.

(*A scene, written at* 14.)

ACT I, SC. I (IN SPAIN).

DRAMATIS PERSONÆ.

CARLOS (a spirited stripling with a spice of suspicion and a preponderance of pride).
MICHAEL (his old attendant).

Moonlight.

Carl. Hear you the sound of wheels?
Mich.   No, faith, not I.
Carl. Methinks they tarry somewhat. What's the
        clock?
Mich. Half way toward midnight.
Carl.   Why, they should be here.
Mich. 'Tis a clear night, they will be here anon.
Carl. Hist! what was that?

Mich.   The night gale in those trees.
Carl.   How beautifully looks the moonbeam through
The knotted boughs of this long avenue
Of thick dark oaks, that arch their arms above,
Coeval with the battlemented towers
Of my old ancestors !
I never look upon them but I glow
With an enthusiastic love of them.
Methinks an oak-tree never should be planted
But near the dwelling of some noble race ;
For it were almost mockery to hang it
O'er the thatch'd cottage, or the snug brick box
Of some sleek citizen.
Ye proud aristocrats whose lordly shadows,
Chequer'd with moonlight's variation,
Richly and darkly girdle these gray walls, —
I and my son's sons and our offspring, all
Shall perish, and their monuments, with forms
Of the unfading marble carved upon them,
Which speak of us to other centuries,
Shall perish also, but ye still shall flourish
In your high pomp of shade, and make beneath
Ambrosial gloom. Thou dost remember, Michael,
How, when a boy, I joy'd to place me on
The hollow-stemm'd and well-nigh leafless oak
Which towers above the lake that ripples out
In the clear moonshine.
Mich.   You were wont to call it
Your throne.
Carl.   I was so, Michael.
Mich.   You'd sit there
From dawn till sunset looking far away
On the blue mountains, and most joyful when
The wanton wind came singing lustily
Among the moss-grown branches, and threw back
Your floating hair.

Carl.   Ha! Ha! Why even then
My Spanish blood ran proudly in my veins.

Mich. Ay, Ay, I warrant you, and when I came
And would have call'd you down to break your
    fast,
You would look down and knit your baby brows
Into your father's frown, and beckon me
Away.

Carl.   Ha! Ha! 'twas laughable, and yet
It show'd the seeds of innate dignity
That were within me; did it not, good Michael?

Mich. And when your age had somewhat riper grown,
And I was wont to dandle you upon
My knee, and ask you whether you would be
A great man in your time,
You'd weave your waxen fingers in these locks
(They are gray now) and tell me you were great
Already in your birth.

Carl.   Ha! by St James
Mine was no vulgar mind in infancy,
Ev'n then the force of nature and high birth
Had writ nobility upon my brow.
Hark! they are coming.

Extract from a Play also written at 14

(according to an entry made by my grandfather at the beginning
of the MS).

THE DEVIL (speaks)

(*going to the timepiece*).

Half after midnight! these mute moralizers,
Pointing to the unheeded lapse of hours,
Become a tacit eloquent reproach

Unto the dissipation of this Earth.
There is a clock in Pandemonium,
Hard by the burning throne of my great grandsire,
The slow vibrations of whose pendulum,
With click-clack alternation to and fro,
Sound " Ever, Never " thro' the courts of Hell,
Piercing the wrung ears of the damn'd that writhe
Upon their beds of flame, and whensoe'er
There may be short cessation of their wails,
Through all that boundless depth of fires is heard
The shrill and solemn warning " Ever, Never ":
Then bitterly I trow they turn and toss
And shriek and shout to drown the thrilling noise.
Half after midnight !   (*Looking again at the timepiece.*)
                    Wherefore stand I here?
Methinks my tongue runs twenty knots an hour:
I must unto mine office.
                              (*Exit abruptly.*)

After reading the *Bride of Lammermoor* he wrote
the following:

THE BRIDAL.*

The lamps were bright and gay
    On the merry bridal-day,
When the merry bridegroom
    Bore the bride away!
A merry, merry bridal,
    A merry bridal-day!
And the chapel's vaulted gloom
    Was misted with perfume.
" Now, tell me, mother, pray,
    Why the bride is white as clay,
Although the merry bridegroom
    Bears the bride away,

On a merry, merry bridal,
  A merry bridal-day?
And why her black eyes burn
  With a light so wild and stern?"
"They revel as they may,"
  That skinny witch did say,
"For — now the merry bridegroom
  Hath borne the bride away —
Her thoughts have found their wings
  In the dreaming of past things:
And though girt in glad array,
  Yet her own deep soul says nay:
For tho' the merry bridegroom
  Hath borne the bride away,
A dark form glances quick
  Thro' her worn brain, hot and sick."
And so she said her say —
  This was her roundelay —
That tho' the merry bridegroom
  Might lead the bride away,
Dim grief did wait upon her,
  In glory and in honour.

    *   *   *   *   *

In the hall, at close of day, .
  Did the people dance and play,
For now the merry bridegroom
  Hath borne the bride away.
He from the dance hath gone
  But the revel still goes on.
Then a scream of wild dismay
  Thro' the deep hall forced its way,
Altho' the merry bridegroom
  Hath borne the bride away;
And, staring as in trance,
  They were shaken from the dance. —

Then they found him where he lay
Whom the wedded wife did slay,
Tho' he a merry bridegroom
Had borne the bride away,
And they saw *her* standing by,
With a laughing crazed eye,
On the bitter, bitter bridal,
The bitter bridal-day.

THE COACH OF DEATH.*

(A fragment.)

Far off in the dun, dark occident,
    Behind the burning Sun:
Where his gilding ray is never sent,
    And his hot steeds never run:

There lies a land of chilling storms,
    A region void of light,
A land of thin faces and shadowy forms,
    Of vapours, and mist, and night.

There never green thing will gaily spring
    In that unwholesome air,
But the rickety blast runs shrilly and fast
    Thro' the bony branches there.

When the shadow of night's eternal wings
    Envelopes the gloomy whole,
And the mutter of deep-mouth'd thunderings
    Shakes all the starless pole,

Thick sobs and short shrill screams arise
    Along the sunless waste,
And the things of past days with their horrible eyes
    Look out from the cloudy vast.

And the earth is dry, tho' the pall of the sky
    Leave never an inch of blue;
And the moaning wind before it drives
    Thick wreaths of cloudy dew.

Whoever walks that bitter ground
    His limbs beneath him fail;
His heart throbs thick, his brain reels sick:
    His brow is clammy and pale.

But some have hearts that in them burn
    With power and promise high,
To draw strange comfort from the earth,
    Strange beauties from the sky.

———————

Dark was the night, and loud the roar
    Of wind and mingled shower,
When there stood a dark coach at an old Inn door
    At the solemn midnight hour.

That Inn was built at the birth of Time:
    The walls of lava rose,
Cemented with the burning slime
    Which from Asphaltus flows.

No sound of joy, no revelling tones
    Of carouse were heard within:
But the rusty sign of a skull and cross-bones
    Swung creaking before the Inn.

No taper's light look'd out on the night,
    But ever and anon
Strange fiery eyes glared fiercely thro'
    The windows of shaven bone.

And the host came forth, and stood alone
    And still in the dark doorway:
There was not a tinge on each high cheek bone,
    But his face was a yellow gray.

The skin hung lax on his long thin hands;
  No jolly host was he;
For his shanks were shrunken to willow wands
  And his name was Atrophy!

Dimly the travellers look'd thro' the glooms,
  Worn and wan was their gaze, I trow,
As the shrivell'd forms of the shadowy grooms
  Yoked the skeleton horses to.

They lifted their eyes to the dead, pale skies,
  And above the barkless trees
They saw the green verge of the pleasant earth,
  And heard the roar of her seas.

They see the light of their blest firesides,
  They hear each household voice:
The whisper'd love of the fair young wives;
  And the laugh of their rose-lipp'd boys.

The summer plains with their shining leaves,
  The summer hills they see;
The dark vine leaves round the rustling eaves,
  And the forests, fair and free.

There came a gaunt man from the dark Inn door,
  A dreadnought coat had he:
His bones crack'd loud, as he stept thro' the crowd,
  And his boots creak'd heavily.

Before his eyes so grim and calm
  The tingling blood grew chill,
As each put a farthing into his palm,
  To drive them where he will.

His sockets were eyeless, but in them slept
  A red infernal glow;
As the cockroach crept, and the white fly leapt
  About his hairless brow.

They mounted slow in their long black cloaks,
   The tears bedimm'd their sight:
The grim old coachee strode to the box,
   And the guard gasp'd out "All's right."

The leaders bounded, the guard's horn sounded:
   Far away thro' the night ran the lengthen'd tones:
As the quick wheels brush'd, and threw up the dust
   Of dead men's pulverised bones.

Whose blood in its liveliest course would not pause
   At the strife of the shadowy wheels,
The chattering of the fleshless jaws,
   And the beat of the horny heels?

Deep dells of snow sunk on each side below
   The highway, broad and flat,
As the coach ran on, and the sallow lights shone
   Dimly and blurly with simmering fat.

Vast wastes of starless glooms were spread
   Around in the chilling air,
And heads without bodies and shapes without heads
   Went leaping here and there.

O Coachee, Coachee, what lights approach
   With heavenly melodies?
Oh! those are the lights of the Paradise coach,
   That so gaily meet their eyes!

With pleasant hymns they soothe the air
   Of death, with songs of pride:
With sackbut, and with dulcimer,
   With psaltery they ride.

These fear not the mists of unwholesome damps
   That through that region rove,
For all wreath'd with green bays were the gorgeous
     lamps,
   And a bright archangel drove.

They pass'd (an inner spirit fed
    Their ever-burning fires,)
With a solemn burst of thrilling light,
    And a sound of stringéd lyres.

With a silver sound the wheels went round,
    The wheels of burning flame;
Of beryl, and of amethyst
    Was the spiritual frame.

Their steeds were strong exceedingly:
    And rich was their attire:
Before them flow'd a fiery stream;
    They broke the ground with hoofs of fire.

They glitter'd with a stedfast light,
    The happy spirits within;
As stars they shone, in raiment white,
    And free from taint of sin.

CHAPTER II.*

CAMBRIDGE.

1828–1830.

I past beside the reverend walls
  In which of old I wore the gown;
  I roved at random thro' the town,
And saw the tumult of the halls;

And heard once more in College fanes
  The storm their high-built organs make,
  And thunder-music, rolling, shake
The prophets blazon'd on the panes:

And caught once more the distant shout,
  The measured pulse of racing oars
  Among the willows; paced the shores
And many a bridge, and all about

The same gray flats again, and felt
  The same, but not the same; and last
  Up that long walk of limes I past
To see the rooms in which *he* dwelt.

Another name was on the door:
  I linger'd; all within was noise
  Of songs, and clapping hands, and boys
That crash'd the glass, and beat the floor;

Where once we held debate, a band
  Of youthful friends, on mind and art,
  And labour, and the changing mart,
And all the framework of the land.

On February 20th, 1828, my father and my uncle Charles matriculated at Trinity College, Cambridge, where their elder brother Frederick was already a distinguished scholar, and had won the University medal for the best Greek ode on the Pyramids.

Of their entrance into Cambridge, — my father told me that they had left the coach and were walking down Trumpington Street in the dusk of the evening, when a proctor addressed him, "What are you doing without your cap and gown, sir, at this time of night?" To which, not being aware of the dignity of the personage who addressed him, he promptly retorted, " I should like to know what business it can be of yours, sir."

They first occupied rooms at No. 12 Rose Crescent, moving afterwards to Trumpington Street, No. 57 Corpus Buildings. Although they knew but few men when beginning their University career, and were shy and reserved, they soon joined themselves to a set of friends who were all more or less remarkable. At first my father writes to his aunt, Mrs Russell: "I am sitting owl-like and solitary in my rooms (nothing between me and the stars but a stratum of tiles). The hoof of the steed, the roll of the wheel, the shouts of drunken Gown and drunken Town come up from below with a sea-like murmur. I wish to Heaven I had Prince Hussain's fairy carpet to transport me along the deeps of air to your coterie. Nay, I would even take up with his brother Aboul-something's glass for the mere pleasure of a peep. What a pity it is that the golden days of Faerie are over! What a misery not to be able to consolidate our gossamer dreams into reality! When, my dearest Aunt, may I hope to see you again? I know not how it is, but I feel isolated here in the midst of society. The country is so disgustingly level, the revelry of the place so monotonous, the studies of the University so uninteresting, so much matter of fact. None but dry-headed, calculating, angular little gentlemen can take much delight in them.

I have been seeking ' Falkland' for a long time without success. Those beautiful extracts from it, which you showed me at Tealby, haunt me incessantly; but wishes, I think, like telescopes reversed, seem to set their objects at a greater distance."

"I can tell you nothing of his college days," writes Edward Fitzgerald to a friend, "for I did not know him till they were over, tho' I had seen him two or three times before: I remember him well, a sort of Hyperion."

With his poetic nature, and warmth of heart, he soon made his way. Fanny Kemble, who used to visit her brother John, said of him when at College, "Alfred Tennyson was our hero, the great hero of our day." Another friend describes him as "Six feet high, broad-chested, strong-limbed, his face Shakespearian, with deep eyelids, his forehead ample, crowned with dark wavy hair, his head finely poised, his hand the admiration of sculptors, long fingers with square tips, soft as a child's but of great size and strength. What struck one most about him was the union of strength with refinement." On seeing him first come into the Hall at Trinity, Thompson [1] said at once, "That man must be a poet." Arthur Hallam "looked up to him as to a great poet and an elder brother [2]."

Hallam said to Trench in 1832: "Alfred's mind is what it always was, or rather, brighter, and more vigorous. I regret, with you, that you have never had the oppor-tunity of knowing more of him. His nervous tempera-ment and habits of solitude give an appearance of affectation to his manner, which is no interpreter of the man, and wears off on further knowledge. Perhaps you would never become very intimate, for certainly your bents of mind are not the same, and at some points they intersect; yet I think you would hardly fail to see much for love, as well as for admiration." Blakesley described Alfred as "Truly one of the mighty of the earth."

The friends among whom he lived were Spedding (author of the Life of Bacon), Milnes (afterwards Lord Houghton), Trench (afterwards Archbishop of Dublin),

---

[1] Afterwards Master of Trinity.
[2] A. H. Hallam was born on February 1st, 1811.

Alford (afterwards Dean of Canterbury), Brookfield, Blakesley (afterwards Dean of Lincoln), Thompson, Stephen Spring Rice, Merivale (afterwards Dean of Ely), J. M. Kemble, Heath (Senior Wrangler 1832), Charles Buller, R. Monteith, Tennant, and above all Hallam. Some summers ago my father and I went to see Hallam's rooms, at No. 3, G, New Court, in which with these friends he had spent so many happy hours. Of this band of men Lord Houghton spoke in 1866 at the opening of the New Cambridge Union: " I am inclined to believe that the members of that generation were, for the wealth of their promise, a rare body of men such as this University has seldom contained." They were a genial, high-spirited, poetical [1] set, full of speculation and of enthusiasm for the great literature of the past, and for the modern schools of thought, and despised rhetoric and sentimentalism. Fitzgerald comments thus in one of his unpublished MS notes:

The German School, with Coleridge, Julius Hare, etc. to expound, came to reform all our notions. I remember that Livy and Jeremy Taylor were the greatest poets next to Shakespeare. I am not sure if you were not startled at hearing that Eutropius was the greatest lyric poet except Pindar. You hadn't known he was a poet at all. I remember A. T. quoting Hallam (the great historian) as pronouncing Shakespeare "the greatest man." I thought such dicta rather peremptory for a philosopher. " Well," said A. T., " the man one would wish perhaps to show as a sample of mankind to those in another planet." He used sometimes to quote Milton as the sublimest of all poets, and his two similes, one about the " gunpowder ore," and the other about " the fleet," as the grandest of all similes. He thought that " ' Lycidas ' was a touchstone of poetic taste." Of Dryden, " I don't know how it is, but Dryden always seems greater than he shows himself to be."

[1] The modern poets in the ascendant among them were Wordsworth, Coleridge, Shelley, Keats; but Byron's " comet blaze " was evidently on the wane.

His friends noted that my father had from the first a deep insight into character, and would often turn upon them with a sudden terse criticism when they thought him far away in the clouds [1].

Fitzgerald remembered that of someone suddenly pronouncing a dogma he said, " That's the swift decision of one who sees only half the truth ";

And of a very different character, somewhat apologetic, " There's a want of central dignity in him."

A few of his Cambridge contemporaries have been drawn in verse by him [2].

The then well-known Cambridge orator S— was partly described in the poem, " A Character." He was " a very plausible, parliament-like, self-satisfied speaker at the Union Debating Society."

Another verse-portrait my father quoted to me, which he remembered with pleasure that Hallam had praised:

[1] "We were looking one day at the portrait of an elderly politician in his bland, family aspect: A. T. (with his eye-glass), ‘ It looks rather like a retired panther.’ So true !" MS Note, E. F. G.

[2] Of Brookfield he wrote in 1875 for Lord Lyttelton's preface to " Sermons, by the late Rev. William Henry Brookfield ":

> Old Brooks, who loved so well to mouth my rhymes,
> How oft we two have heard St Mary's chimes !
> How oft the Cantab supper, host and guest,
> Would echo helpless laughter to your jest !
> How oft with him we paced that walk of limes,
> Him, the lost light of those dawn-golden times.

(It was of him that the late Dr Thompson wrote : — " He was far the most amusing man I ever met, or shall meet. At my age it is not likely that I shall ever again see a whole party lying on the floor for purposes of unrestrained laughter, while one of their number is pouring forth, with a perfectly grave face, a succession of imaginary dialogues between characters, real and fictitious, one exceeding another in humour and drollery.")

Of Kemble my father said in a sonnet published in 1830 :

> My hope and heart is with thee — thou wilt be
> A latter Luther and a soldier priest.

(*Unpublished.*)

Thy soul is like a landskip, friend,
   Steeple, and stream, and forest lawn,
   Most delicately overdrawn
With the first twilight of the even,
   Clear-edged, and showing every bend
   Of each dark hill against the Heaven,
Nor wanting many a sombre mound,
   Stately and mild, and all between
   Valleys full of solemn sound,
   And hoary holts on uplands green,
And somewhat loftier antient heights
Touch'd with Heaven's latest lights.

Of Blakesley he said, " He ought to be Lord Chancellor, for he is a subtle and powerful reasoner, and an honest man." Blakesley, he observed another time, was honestly indignant at gaining the Chancellor's Medal, which, he asserted, " ought to have gone to young Kennedy."

Later, of James Spedding he remarked, " He was the Pope among us young men — the wisest man I know."

Of Hallam himself, " He would have been known, if he had lived, as a great man but not as a great poet; he was as near perfection as mortal man could be[1]."

Whewell, who was his tutor, he called " the lion-like man," and had for him a great respect. It is reported that Whewell, recognizing his genius, tolerated in him certain informalities which he would not have overlooked in other men. Thus, " Mr Tennyson, what's the compound interest of a penny put out at the Christian era up to the present time? " was Whewell's good-natured call to

[1] " And over those ethereal eyes
The bar of Michael Angelo.

These lines I wrote from what Arthur Hallam said after reading of the prominent ridge of bone over the eyes of Michael Angelo: ' Alfred, look over my eyes ; surely I have the bar of Michael Angelo ! ' " A. T.

attention in the Lecture Room while my father was reading Virgil under the desk.

Once, when Whewell had made himself unpopular, a tumult arose among the undergraduates, who lined the street from the Senate House to Trinity Gate and hooted him, shouting "Billy Whistle!" (Whewell's nickname). As he passed between them, Hallam, Spring Rice, and my father, raised a cheer for him. He saw my father and bade him come instantly to his rooms. Whewell began, "I was sorry to see, Mr Tennyson, that you were at the head of that very disorderly mob outside the Senate House." "But," answered my father, "my friends and I were not heading the mob, we were cheering you!" Whereat Whewell said nothing, but smiled grimly to himself with evident pleasure, inviting him to breakfast next morning.

Another Cambridge story about Whewell, but perhaps of later date, my father would tell somewhat in this way. At 12 o'clock one night, horns and trumpets and bugles and drums began to play from all the windows round Trinity New Court, and a man, who had been expelled that day, strummed on a piano which had been set in the middle of the lawn; and there was the fiend's own row. Presently Whewell, who lived in Nevile's Court, next to the New Court, was heard thundering at his door which had been tied with a rope; '$τρὶς μὲν ὀρέξατ' ἰὼν$' and at the third charge he broke through, rushed out, found all the windows closed, lights extinguished, dead silence everywhere, only the expelled man standing immovable by the piano under a cold round moon. Whewell strode to the piano, the expelled man ran for his life round and round the colonnades of Nevile's Court; thrice he ran round, Whewell pursuing. At last Whewell caught him. "Do you know who I am, sir?" said Whewell, panting. "Yes," was the answer, "Old Whistle, who made that mistake in his *Dynamics*." Thereupon Whewell, seeing that he was the man who had been expelled, took him by the scruff of the neck, carried him to the great gate, and shot him out like bad rubbish.

As a young man my father's friends have often described him to me as having Johnsonian common sense and a rare power of expression, very genial, full of enjoyment, full of sensitiveness and full of humour, though with the passionate heart of a poet, and sometimes feeling the melancholy of life. He passed through "moods of misery unutterable," but he eventually shook them off. He remembered how, when in London almost for the first time, one of these moods came over him, as he realized that "in a few years all its inhabitants would be lying horizontal, stark and stiff in their coffins."

Despite such passages of gloom he worked on at his poems, wrote Latin and Greek odes[1], read his classics

---

[1] Before he had left Somersby for Cambridge, he had written in Greek hexameters an Homeric book on the Seven against Thebes, and an Ovidian poem about the death of a young girl who had died for love of the Apollo Belvedere.

In his note-book, mixed up with translations of Aristophanes, and of Greek philosophers, and with astronomical diagrams, I find this fragment, mainly of value as showing at what an early date physical science began to penetrate his verse :

The Moon.   (Unpublished fragment.)

*   *   *   *   *   *

Deep glens I found, and sunless gulfs,
   Set round with many a toppling spire,
And monstrous rocks from craggy snouts
   Disploding globes of roaring fire.

Large as a human eye the sun
   Drew down the West his feeble lights;
And then a night, all moons, confused
   The shadows from the icy heights.

["A night, all moons," means that when seen from the airless moon all the principal stars and planets would be very large and bright in the black heavens, and strike the eye there as the moon strikes the eye here.]

and history and natural science [1]. He also took a lively interest in politics. He was among the young supporters of the Anti-slavery Convention, and advocated the Measure for abolishing subscription to the Thirty-nine Articles, while admiring as statesmen Canning, Peel, and the Duke of Wellington. England was in a state of ferment with the hope or dread of the Reform Bill. Farms were fired, ricks were burnt, and "sanguine Lazarus felt a vacant hand Fill" with the rich man's purse. In the poem addressed to Mary Boyle my father tells how he helped to "hand the bucket from the well," and to quench a conflagration in a homestead near Cambridge.

At one of these farm fires he heard a countryman saying, "Now we shall get our taters cheaper." "You fools," said my father, although he largely sympathized with the labourers in their demands, "you are all going the way to make taters dearer." Some undergraduates with over-zeal began to pull down the farmer's house in order to help him to preserve the materials from fire. The poor man held them back, comically but naturally remonstrating, "Leave me, sirs, I pray you, the little property that the fire has spared!"

My father's note-book contains these unpublished lines:

> I, loving Freedom for herself,
>   And much of that which is her form,
> Wed to no faction in the state,
>   A voice before the storm,
> I mourn in spirit when I think
>   The year, that comes, may come with shame,
> Lured by the cuckoo-voice that loves
>   To babble its own name.

That "deep chord which Hampden smote" pulsed

---

[1] " I kept a tame snake in my rooms. I liked to watch his wonderful sinuosities on the carpet." A. T.

through the life of the young men of the day. These riots of the poorer classes filled my father with an earnest desire to do something to help those who lived in misery among the "warrens of the poor." Indeed from first to last he always preached the onward progress of liberty, while steadily opposed to revolutionary license —

> Freedom free to slay herself, and dying while they shout her name.

Asked what politics he held: "I am of the same politics as Shakespeare [1], Bacon, and every sane man."

Carlyle's account of Sterling best describes, as far as I can gather, the typical intellectual undergraduate of my father's set: who hated the narrow and ignorant Toryism to be found in country districts: who loathed parties and sects: who reverenced the great traditions and the great men of past ages, and eagerly sympathized with the misfortunes and disabilities of his fellow-men.

He tells how Sterling, famous already for the brilliance of his talk, had at Cambridge "a wide and rather genial circle of comrades." They had among them a society called the "Apostles": of which my father was an early member. "On stated evenings," Carlyle goes on, "was much logic, and other spiritual fencing, and ingenuous collision — probably of a really superior quality in that kind; for not a few of the then disputants have since proved themselves men of parts, and attained distinction in the intellectual walks of life."

It is of the "Apostles" that Sterling writes to Trench: "Pray let me see you as soon as you reach London, and

---

[1] " Some critics," he said to me more than once, "object to Shakespeare's *aristocratic* view of his clowns, because he makes them talk such poor stuff, but they forget that his clowns occasionally speak as real truths as Hamlet, and that sometimes they utter very profound sayings. That is the glory of Shakespeare, he can give you the incongruity of things."

in the mean time commend me to the brethren, who, I trust, are waxing daily in religion and radicalism."

Arthur Hallam, in a letter to Gladstone, says of Frederick Maurice: "The effects which he has produced on the minds of many at Cambridge by the single creation of that society of 'Apostles' (for the spirit though not the form was created by him) is far greater than I can dare to calculate, and will be felt, both directly and indirectly, in the age that is upon us."

There were regular meetings of the society as distinguished from the almost daily gatherings in one or another man's rooms, at all of which much coffee was drunk, much tobacco smoked. The Apostle who proposed the subject for discussion, generally stood before the mantelpiece, and said his say. Douglas Heath writes that the image he has carried away of my father is of one "sitting in front of the fire, smoking and meditating, and now and then mingling in the conversation." With one short phrase he was wont to sum up the issue of the arguments. Heath continues: "I cannot satisfy myself as to the time when I became an Apostle, or when I made acquaintance with A. T. My belief is that he had already become an honorary member extraordinary. In the usual course a member had to read essays in regular succession, or give a dinner in default during a certain period, after which he became honorary. But A. T. was, I suppose, bored by this, and the society was content to receive him, his poetry and wisdom unfettered." "Ghosts" was the subject of an essay written by my father for the Society, but he was too shy to deliver it. The preface alone has survived [1].

These friends not only debated on politics but read their Hobbes, Locke, Berkeley, Butler, Hume, Bentham, Descartes and Kant, and discussed such questions as the Origin of Evil, the Derivation of Moral Senti-

[1] For the prologue of "Ghosts" see Appendix, p. 497.

ments, Prayer and the Personality of God[1]. Among
the Cambridge papers I find a remarkable sentence on
" Prayer" by Arthur Hallam.

With respect to prayer, you ask how am I to distinguish the
operations of God in me from motions in my own heart? Why
should you distinguish them or how do you know there is any
distinction? Is God less God because He acts by general laws
when He deals with the common elements of nature?...That
fatal mistake which has embarrassed the philosophy of mind
with infinite confusion, the mistake of setting value on a thing's
origin rather than on its character, of assuming that *composite*
must be less excellent than simple, has not been slow to extend
its deleterious influence over the field of practical religion.

My father seems to have propounded in some college
discussion the theory, that the " development of the
human body might possibly be traced from the radiated,
vermicular, molluscous and vertebrate organisms." The
question of surprise put to him on this proposition was
" Do you mean that the human brain is at first like a
madrepore's, then like a worm's, etc.? but this cannot be
for they have no brain[2]."

At this time, with one or two of his more literary
friends, he took great interest in the work which Hallam
had undertaken, a translation from the *Vita Nuova* of

[1] Three questions discussed by the Society were: (1) Have Shelley's
poems an immoral tendency? Tennyson votes " No." (2) Is an intelligible
First Cause deducible from the phenomena of the Universe? Tennyson
votes " No." (3) Is there any rule of moral action beyond general
expediency? Tennyson votes " Aye."

I have a note to my father from Tennant saying: " Last Saturday we
had an Apostolic dinner when we had the honour, among other things, of
drinking your health. Edmund Lushington and I went away tolerably
early; but most of them stayed till past two. John Heath volunteered a
song; Kemble got into a passion about nothing but quickly jumped out
again; Blakesley was afraid the Proctor might come in; and Thompson
poured large quantities of salt upon Douglas Heath's head because he talked
nonsense."

[2] Letter from A. H. Hallam. Most of his philosophical and religious
letters to my father have been lost.

Dante, with notes and prefaces. For this task Hallam, who in 1827 had been in Italy with his parents and had drunk deep of the older Italian literature, says that he was perfecting himself in German and Spanish, and was proposing to plunge into the Florentine historians and the medieval Schoolmen. He writes to my father: " I expect to glean a good deal of knowledge from you concerning metres which may be serviceable, as well for my philosophy in the notes as for my actual handiwork in the text. I purpose to discuss considerably about poetry in general, and about the ethical character of Dante's poetry."

My father said of his friend: " Arthur Hallam could take in the most abstruse ideas with the utmost rapidity and insight, and had a marvellous power of work and thought, and a wide range of knowledge. On one occasion, I remember, he mastered a difficult book of Descartes at a single sitting."

On June 6th, 1829, the announcement was made that my father had won the prize medal for his poem in blank verse on "Timbuctoo [1]." To win the prize in anything

---

[1] From Somersby, after his father's death (1831 probably), he wrote to the printer Metcalfe, who had asked permission to include " Timbuctoo " in a collection of Cambridge Prize Poems:

SOMERSBY.

SIR, As you intend to reprint the Cambridge Prize Poems, it would seem odd to leave mine out, tho' for my own part I had much rather you had not thought of it. Prize Poems (without any exception even in favour of Mr. Milman's "Belvedere") are not properly speaking "Poems" at all, and ought to be forgotten as soon as recited. I could have wished that poor " Timbuctoo " might have been suffered to slide quietly off, with all its errors, into forgetfulness: however as I do not expect to turn you from your purpose of republishing the p^e p^s, I suppose mine must be printed along with them: only for "cones of Pyramids," which is nonsense (p. 10), I will thank you to substitute "peaks of Pyramids."

I am, Sir, yours truly,

ALFRED TENNYSON.

(As the poem is now published this is the sole correction. My father would say, "'The Lover's Tale' and 'Timbuctoo' are in no way imitative of

but rhymed heroics was an innovation. My grandfather had desired him to compete, so unwillingly he patched up an old poem on " The Battle of Armageddon," and came out prizeman over Milnes, Hallam and others.

Charles Wordsworth (afterwards Bishop of St Andrews) writes to his brother Christopher Wordsworth, Sept. 4th, 1829 (see *Annals of my Early Life*, C. Wordsworth, 1890):

What do you think of Tennyson's Prize poem ("Timbuctoo")? If such an exercise had been sent up at Oxford, the author would have had a better chance of being rusticated, with the view of his passing a few months at a Lunatic Asylum, than of obtaining the prize. It is certainly a wonderful production ; and if it had come out with Lord Byron's name, it would have been thought as fine as anything he ever wrote.

Arthur Hallam writes, Sept. 14th, 1829, to W. E. Gladstone :

I am glad you liked my queer piece about Timbuctoo. I wrote it in a sovereign vein of poetic scorn for anybody's opinion, who did not value Plato and Milton just as much as I did. The natural consequence was that ten people out of twelve laughed or opened large eyes ; and the other two set about praising highly, what was plainly addressed to them, not to people in general. So my vanity would fain persuade me, that, like some of my betters, I " fit audience found, tho' few." My friend Tennyson's poem, which got the prize, will be thought by the ten sober persons afore-mentioned twice as absurd as mine ; and to say the truth, by striking out his prose argument, the Examiners have done all in their power to verify the concluding words, " All was night." The splendid imaginative power that pervades it will be seen through all hindrances. I consider Tennyson as promising fair to be the greatest poet of our generation, perhaps of our century.

any poet, and, as far as I know, nothing of mine after the date of ' Timbuctoo' was imitative. As for being original, nothing can be said which has not been said in some form or another before.")

I asked Dean Merivale, last survivor, except Douglas Heath, of that Cambridge set, to give me his recollections.   He answered:

> Believe me that I have not written a letter for several months, but you will, I am sure, allow me to make this exception to your very kind note.   I only wish I could give you any accurate recollection of your honoured father which would be worthy of your acceptance on such an occasion. You have seen, no doubt, the many contemporary diaries of those who rejoice to set down their reminiscences of so great and so loveable a member of their set....May I be excused for recording a recollection of which I was proud — that of being allowed or enjoined by the Vice-Chancellor to declaim his " Timbuctoo[1] " in the Senate House in the summer of 1829, which he declined to do from the modesty which too often beset him ?

The Dean also enclosed the following letter, written, my father said, " under a horror of publicity " which made him " feel as Cowper did."

July 29th, 1829.

MY DEAR MERIVALE,

Will you write and tell me whether you can read my poem at Commencement or not, since I must come up to Cambridge if you cannot ?   I hope you found my letter sufficiently clear relatively to corrections.   The Vice-Chancellor observed to me, " We cannot do these things quite so well by proxy as with the person himself, to whom several of my objections might have been stated and answered immediately."   I hope you have somewhat recovered from the shock of your grandmother's sudden death.   I consider it as rather remarkable that on the morning when we were at Hampstead I seemed to myself to have some presentiment of it, and could not shake the idea from my mind, though I could not give utterance to

---

[1] Matthew Arnold told G. L. Craik that when, as a youth, he first read " Timbuctoo " he prophesied the greatness of Tennyson.

it; you remember my asking you whether either of your grandmothers was dead, and telling you that both mine were.

Believe me, dear Merivale,
          Yours most truly, A. TENNYSON.

In 1829 my uncle Charles won a Bell Scholarship by the beauty of his translations. One sentence survived in my father's memory:

"And the ruddy grape shall droop from the desert thorn."

The brothers Charles and Alfred would humorously describe how *Much Ado about Nothing* was played by their friends in March, 1830. Kemble as Dogberry, Hallam as Verges, Milnes as Beatrice. When Beatrice sat down, her weight was such that she crashed through the couch, and sank on the floor, nothing to be seen but a heap of petticoats, much to the discomfiture of the players and the immeasurable laughter of the spectators. The incident used to remind my father by contrast of Kemble's observation to someone who was playing the part of Falstaff, " Pooh, you should see my sister: she does Falstaff better than any man living." My father, I may add, was famous in some parts of Shakespeare, especially in Malvolio.

In certain College rooms he was often asked to declaim the many ballads which he knew by heart, " Clerke Saunders," " Helen of Kirkconnel," " May Margaret," and others: and also his own poems "The Hesperides," " The Lover's Tale" (written 1827), " The Coach of Death "; and he would improvise verses by the score full of lyrical passion. I quote again from Edward Fitzgerald: "'Oriana' Tennyson used to repeat in a way not to be forgotten at Cambridge tables."

For his exercise he either rowed, or fenced, or took

long walks, and would go any distance to see "a bubbling
brook."   " Somehow," he would say, " water is the
element I love best of all the four."

His first volume, *Poems, chiefly Lyrical*, was published in 1830 by Effingham Wilson, also the publisher
of Robert Browning's *Paracelsus*. Favourable reviews
appeared by Sir John Bowring in the *Westminster*, by
Leigh Hunt in the *Tatler*, and by Arthur Hallam in
the *Englishman's Magazine*.

The *Westminster* article (January 1831) contained
this prophetic notice of " The Poet ":

> If our estimate of Mr Tennyson be correct, he too is a poet;
> and many years hence may he read his juvenile description of
> that character with the proud consciousness that it has become
> the description and history of his own work.

Arthur Hallam's enthusiasm was worthy of his true
and unselfish friendship, and helped my father through
the years of darkness and disparagement that were soon
to come.

> There is a strange earnestness in his worship of beauty
> which throws a charm over his impassioned song, more easily
> felt than described, and not to be escaped by those who have
> once felt it....The features of original genius are clearly and
> strongly marked. The author imitates no one; we recognize
> the spirit of his age, but not the individual form of this or that
> writer. His thoughts bear no more resemblance to Byron or
> Scott, Shelley or Coleridge, than to Homer or Calderon, Firdusi
> or Calidasa. We have remarked five distinctive excellencies
> of his own manner. First, his luxuriance of imagination, and
> at the same time his control over it. Secondly, his power of
> embodying himself in ideal characters, or rather moods of
> character, with such accuracy of adjustment that the circum-
> stances of the narrative seem to have a natural correspondence
> with the predominant feeling and, as it were, to be evolved from
> it by assimilative force. Thirdly, his vivid, picturesque delinea-
> tion of objects, and the peculiar skill with which he holds all of
> them *fused*, to borrow a metaphor from science, in a medium of

strong emotion. Fourthly, the variety of his lyrical measures and the exquisite modulation of harmonious words and cadences to the swell and fall of the feelings expressed. Fifthly, the elevated habits of thought, implied in these compositions, and importing a mellow soberness of tone, more impressive to our minds than if the author had drawn up a set of opinions in verse, and sought to instruct the understanding rather than to communicate the love of beauty to the heart.

Coleridge[1], indeed, for whose prose my father never much cared, but to whose poetry, especially " Kubla Khan," " The Ancient Mariner," and "Christabel," he was devoted, was more reserved in his praise about the first two ventures:

I have not read through all Mr Tennyson's poems, which have been sent to me; but I think there are some things of a good deal of beauty in what I have seen. The misfortune is, that he has begun to write verses without very well understanding what metre is[2].

" The first ' Mariana ' and the ' Arabian Nights ' were the two poems that marked the volume (1830) as something to be thought about." " The affectation " (in

[1] Arthur Hallam visited Coleridge at Highgate and wrote about him in his poem of " Timbuctoo ":

> "Methought I saw a face whose every line
> Wore the pale cast of thought, a good old man,
> Most eloquent, who spake of things divine.
> Around him youths were gather'd, who did scan
> His countenance so grand and mild, and drank
> The sweet sad tears of wisdom."

[2] Concerning this criticism my father said in 1890: " Coleridge did not know much about my poems, for he confounded Charles and me. From what I have heard he may have read *Glen-river* in ' above the loud Glenriver,' and *tendril-twine* in the line ' mantled with flowering tendriltwine ' dactylically; because I had an absurd antipathy to hyphens, and put two words together as one word. If that was the case, he might well have wished that I had more sense of metre. But so I, an old man, who get a poem or poems every day, might cast a casual glance at a book, and seeing something which I could not scan or understand, might possibly decide against the book without further consideration."

the volume), E. F. G. adds, "was not of *the man*; but of the time and society he lived in, and from which he had not yet emerged to his proper and distinct altitude. Two years afterwards he took his ground with 'The Miller's Daughter,' 'Palace of Art,' 'Dream of Fair Women,' etc."

On the appearance of the poems Hallam wrote the following letter to my grandmother:

My dear Madam,

As I have at last the pleasure of sending to Alfred his long-expected book, I take this opportunity of begging that you will accept from me a copy of some poems which I originally intended to have published in the same volume. To this joint publication, as a sort of seal of our friendship, I had long looked forward with a delight which I believe was no way selfish. But there are reasons which have obliged me to change my intention, and withdraw my own share of the work from the Press. One of these was the growing conviction of the exceeding crudeness of style which characterized all my earlier attempts....I have little reason to apprehend your wasting much time over that book, when I send you along with it such a treasure in your son's poetry. He is a true and thorough poet, if ever there was one; and tho' I fear his book is far too good to be popular, yet I have full faith that he has thrown out sparks that will kindle somewhere, and will vivify young generous hearts in the days that are coming to a clearer perception of what is beautiful and good.

Believe me yours very sincerely,

A. H. Hallam.

During the summer my father joined Arthur Hallam, and both started off for the Pyrenees, with money for the insurgent allies of Torrijos, — a noble, accomplished, truthful man, worthy to be a leader. He it was who had raised the standard of revolt against the Inquisition and the tyranny of Ferdinand, King of Spain. Alfred and

Arthur held a secret meeting with the heads of the conspiracy on the Spanish border, and were not heard of by their friends for some weeks [1].

John Frere and James Spedding wrote to my uncle Charles inquiring about them, and about my grandfather who was also abroad, and he answers:

To John Frere.

SOMERSBY, *July 27th*, 1830.

From Hallam I heard just now: he complains rather of the heat, and says Alfred is delighted with his journey, though regretting the impermanence of his impressions in the hurry of travel. My father has returned from his tour and I am much surprised to see him so well after the neck-break adventures he has encountered. On one occasion, proceeding along in a small carriage over the mountains, he was hurled down a precipice and stunned, but saved himself from certain death by convulsively grasping a pine that grew out of a ledge: while the driver, carriage and horse were dashed to atoms thousands of feet below him. Again, at the Carnival in Rome, a man was stilettoed in his arms, drawing first suspicion and then violence on his person: the excess of which he prevented by exclaiming that he was an Englishman and had not done the deed. Again, he was suddenly seized with giddiness on the verge of a precipice, and only preserved by the presence of mind of a person near him. At another (time) he was near being buried alive.

To James Spedding.

I expect the travellers home every day; I heard twice from Hallam, who mentioned the middle of September as the most probable period of their return, but a dozen counter-resolutions may come athwart their homeward intention even yet for what I know. Hallam's last letter was dated from Cauteretz, Dép[t]. des Hautes Pyrénées, but from what he there intimated of return about this time, it would be foolish in you to hazard your good things in an epistle directed thither. The said Hallam or one of

[1] No further information upon this business has been preserved.

his fellow-travellers, it should seem, wrote a letter to Tennant with full intention, I guess, of its getting further than Perpignan; but Tennant a short time back informed me that he had received a communication from les Administrateurs de la Poste, advertising him of a letter which had taken up its abode at Perpignan on account of its not being paid to the coast. What news it contained "no one dreameth," or whether it was written previous or subsequent to my last receipts from the Continent. Kemble is said to be at Gibraltar. Trench either on the way thither or arrived, and Hallam expressed some apprehensions on the score of their safety, but I hope with you there is not much fear in the present posture of things. Thank you for sending Southey my sonnets, thank you for cheering my heart with the worthy man's good opinion, and thank you for your letter and address.

Before going further it may be as well to pick up the threads of the story of this Spanish insurrection. Torrijos the leader had hoped to restore such a measure of freedom as the Cortes had secured for Spain, in the Constitution which had been framed after the Peninsular War. This was the Constitution to which Ferdinand had sworn when he returned from his long captivity in Bayonne, but which he speedily renounced, dissolving the Cortes and restoring the Inquisition. In 1820, revolution having followed revolution, the Cortes met again, under protection of part of the army, and the Inquisition was abolished. This state of things did not last. In 1823 Ferdinand was, by help of the Duc d'Angoulême, proclaimed absolute King. Again despotism prevailed. Many Liberals fled to England. Of these Carlyle gives a pathetic description as they were seen, chiefly about Euston Square and the new Church of St Pancras — "stately tragic figures, in proud threadbare cloaks," who had acknowledged General Torrijos as their chief. A fiery sympathy had been kindled in the hearts of many of the "Apostles" by this romantic band : some of whom had, after seven years' banishment, "got shipping as private passengers in one craft or the other ; and, by degrees or at once, arrived all at Gibraltar;— Boyd (Sterling's cousin), one or two young democrats of Regent Street, the fifty picked Spaniards, and Torrijos[1]."

Among the Pyrenean revolutionists met by Arthur Hallam and my father the chief man was one Señor Ojeda, who informed them that he desired "couper la gorge à tous les curés," then clapping his hand on his heart murmured "mais vous connaissez mon cœur"— "and a pretty black one it is," thought my father.

After the travellers had returned, a report reached Somersby that John Kemble, who had joined the insurgents in the South, had been caught and was to be tried for his life. Away my father posted for miles in the early dawn to try and find someone of authority at Lincoln or elsewhere, who knew the Consul at Cadiz and would help him to save his friend. The report turned out to be untrue and Kemble came back safe and sound.

But on the last night of November, 1831, Torrijos and his gallant companions left Gibraltar in two small vessels; the British Governor, on occasion of the fresh rising of General Mina against Spanish despotism, having intimated that Gibraltar must not shelter rebels against Spain.

They set sail for Malaga, were chased by Spanish guardships, and ran ashore at Fuengirola near Malaga. They barricaded themselves in a farm-house, were surrounded by vastly superior forces and compelled to surrender.

All the fifty-six (Boyd among them) perished by military execution on the Esplanade of Malaga[2].

My father returned from the expedition in improved health. From this time forward the lonely Pyrenean

[1] Carlyle's *John Sterling*, p. 64 (ed. 1871).
[2] Carlyle's *John Sterling*, p. 77.

peaks, the mountains with "their streaks of virgin snow," like the Maladetta, mountain "lawns and meadow-ledges midway down," and the "long brook falling thro' the clov'n ravine," were a continual source of inspiration; he had written part of "Œnone" in the valley of Cauteretz. His sojourn there was also commemorated one and thirty years afterwards in "All along the Valley."

He came home impressed with the "lightheartedness" of the French; but, infinitely preferring the freer air of England," he writes: "Someone says that nothing strikes a traveller more on returning from the Continent than the look of an English country town. Houses not so big, nor such rows of them as abroad, but each man's house little or big distinct from one another, his own castle, built according to his own means and fancy, and so indicating the Englishman's free individual humour. I am struck on returning from France with the look of good sense in the London people[1]."

UNPUBLISHED POEM, 1828.

By a Brook.

Townsmen, or of the hamlet, young or old,
Whithersoever you may wander now,
Where'er you roam from, would you waste an hour,
Or sleep thro' one brief dream upon the grass,
Pause here. The murmurs of the rivulet,
Rippling by cressy isles or bars of sand,
Are pleasant from the early Spring to when,
Full fields of barley shifting tearful lights
On growing spears, by fits the lady ash
With twinkling finger sweeps her yellow keys.

---

[1] Quoted from MS by E. F. G. (date of letter uncertain).

UNPUBLISHED POEMS, WRITTEN (1828–1831) AT CAMBRIDGE.*

Anacaona.

[My father liked this poem but did not publish it, because the natural history and the rhymes did not satisfy him. He evidently chose words which sounded well, and gave a tropical air to the whole, and he did not then care, as in his later poems, for absolute accuracy.]

I

A dark Indian maiden,
　Warbling in the bloom'd liana,
Stepping lightly flower-laden,
　By the crimson-eyed anana,
Wantoning in orange groves
　Naked, and dark-limb'd, and gay,
Bathing in the slumbrous coves,
In the cocoa-shadow'd coves,
　Of sunbright Xaraguay,
Who was so happy as Anacaona,
　The beauty of Espagnola,
　The golden flower of Hayti?

2

All her loving childhood
　Breezes from the palm and canna
Fann'd this queen of the green wildwood,
　Lady of the green Savannah:
All day long with laughing eyes,
　Dancing by a palmy bay,
In the wooded paradise,
The cedar-wooded paradise
　Of still Xaraguay:
None were so happy as Anacaona,
　The beauty of Espagnola,
　The golden flower of Hayti!

3

In the purple island,
  Crown'd with garlands of cinchona,
Lady over wood and highland,
  The Indian queen, Anacaona,
Dancing on the blossomy plain
  To a woodland melody:
Playing with the scarlet crane[1],
The dragon-fly and scarlet crane,
  Beneath the papao tree!
Happy, happy was Anacaona,
  The beauty of Espagnola,
  The golden flower of Hayti!

4

The white man's white sail, bringing
  To happy Hayti the new-comer,
Over the dark sea-marge springing,
  Floated in the silent summer:
Then she brought the guava fruit,
  With her maidens to the bay;
She gave them the yuccaroot,
Maizebread and the yuccaroot,
  Of sweet Xaraguay:
Happy, happy Anacaona,
  The beauty of Espagnola,
  The golden flower of Hayti!

5

Naked, without fear, moving
  To her Areyto's mellow ditty,
Waving a palm branch, wondering, loving,
  Carolling " Happy, happy Hayti!"
She gave the white men welcome all,
  With her damsels by the bay;

[1] Perhaps the scarlet ibis, *guava rubra*, not now known to visit Hayti.

For they were fair-faced and tall,
They were more fair-faced and tall,
   Than the men of Xaraguay,
And they smiled on Anacaona,
   The beauty of Espagnola,
   The golden flower of Hayti!

6

'Following her wild carol
   She led them down the pleasant places,
For they were kingly in apparel,
   Loftily stepping with fair faces.
But never more upon the shore
   Dancing at the break of day,
In the deep wood no more, —
By the deep sea no more, —
   No more in Xaraguay
Wander'd happy Anacaona,
   The beauty of Espagnola,
   The golden flower of Hayti!

The Lark.

Full light aloft doth the laverock spring
   From under the deep, sweet corn,
And chants in the golden wakening
   Athwart the bloomy morn.
What aileth thee, O bird divine,
   That thou singest with main and with might?
Is thy mad brain drunk with the merry, red wine,
   At the very break of light?
It is not good to drink strong wine
   Ere the day be well-nigh done;
But thou hast drunk of the merry, sweet wine,
   At the rising of the sun.

Some verses of " Sir Launcelot and Queen Guinevere " were handed about at Cambridge among my
father's contemporaries.   The following unpublished
lines were among them, and kept by Edward Fitzgerald:

> Life of the Life within my blood,
>   Light of the Light within mine eyes,
> The May begins to breathe and bud,
>   And softly blow the balmy skies;
> Bathe with me in the fiery flood,
>   And mingle kisses, tears, and sighs,
> Life of the Life within my blood,
>   Light of the Light within mine eyes.

Life.

Why suffer human life so soon eclipse?
For I could burst into a psalm of praise,
Seeing the heart so wondrous in her ways,
E'en scorn looks beautiful on human lips!
Would I could pile fresh life on life, and dull
The sharp desire of knowledge still with knowing!
Art, Science, Nature, everything is full,
As my own soul is full, to overflowing —
Millions of forms, and hues, and shades, that give
The difference of all things to the sense,
And all the likeness in the difference.
I thank thee, God, that thou hast made me live:
I reck not for the sorrow or the strife:
One only joy I know, the joy of life.

To Poesy.

O God, make this age great that we may be
   As giants in Thy praise! and raise up Mind,
Whose trumpet-tongued, aerial melody
   May blow alarum loud to every wind,
   And startle the dull ears of human kind!
Methinks I see the world's renewed youth
   A long day's dawn, when Poesy shall bind
Falsehood beneath the altar of great Truth:
The clouds are sunder'd toward the morning-rise;
   Slumber not now, gird up thy loins for fight,
And get thee forth to conquer. I, even I,
Am large in hope that these expectant eyes
Shall drink the fulness of thy victory,
   Tho' thou art all unconscious of thy Might.

To —.

Thou may'st remember what I said
When thine own spirit was at strife
With thine own spirit. " From the tomb
And charnel-place of purpose dead,
Thro' spiritual dark we come
Into the light of spiritual life."
God walk'd the waters of thy soul,
And still'd them. When from change to change,
Led silently by power divine,
Thy thought did scale a purer range
Of prospect up to self-control,
My joy was only less than thine.

The Hesperides.*

[Published and suppressed by my father, and republished by me here
(with accents written by him) in consequence of a talk that I had with
him, in which he regretted that he had done away with it from among
his " Juvenilia."]

> Hesperus and his daughters three
> That sing about the golden tree. *Comus.*

The North wind fall'n, in the new-starréd night
Zidonian Hanno, wandering beyond
The hoary promontory of Soloë,
Past Thymiaterion in calméd bays
Between the southern and the western Horn,
Heard neither warbling of the nightingale,
Nor melody of the Libyan Lotus-flute
Blown seaward from the shore; but from a slope
That ran bloom-bright into the Atlantic blue,
Beneath a highland leaning down a weight
Of cliffs, and zoned below with cedar-shade,
Came voices like the voices in a dream
Continuous; till he reach'd the outer sea: —

SONG OF THE THREE SISTERS.

I

The Golden Apple, the Golden Apple, the hallow'd
    fruit,
Guard it well, guard it warily,
Singing airily,
Standing about the charméd root.
Round about all is mute,
As the snowfield on the mountain-peaks,
As the sandfield at the mountain-foot.
Crocodiles in briny creeks
Sleep and stir not: all is mute.

If ye sing not, if ye make false measure,
We shall lose eternal pleasure,
Worth eternal want of rest.
Laugh not loudly: watch the treasure
Of the wisdom of the West.
In a corner wisdom whispers. Five and three
(Let it not be preach'd abroad) make an awful mystery:
For the blossom unto threefold music bloweth;
Evermore it is born anew,
And the sap to threefold music floweth,
From the root,
Drawn in the dark,
Up to the fruit,
Creeping under the fragrant bark,
Líquid góld, hóneyswéet thró and thró..

(slow movement)

Keen-eyed Sisters, singing airily,
Looking warily
Every way,
Guard the apple night and day,
Lest one from the East come and take it away.

II

Father Hesper, Father Hesper, Watch, watch, ever
    and aye,
Looking under silver hair with a silver eye.
Father, twinkle not thy stedfast sight:
Kingdoms lapse, and climates change, and races die;
Honour comes with mystery;
Hoarded wisdom brings delight.
Number, tell them over, and number
How many the mystic fruit-tree holds,
Lest the red-comb'd dragon slumber
Roll'd together in purple folds.

Look to him, father, lest he wink, and the golden
  apple be stol'n away,
For his ancient heart is drunk with overwatchings
  night and day
Round about the hallow'd fruit-tree curl'd —
Sing awáy, sing aloúd evermóre in the wínd without
  stóp,   (*Anapæst*)
Lest his sealéd eyelid drop,
For he is older than the world.
If *hé* waken, *wé* waken,
Rapidly levelling eager eyes.
If *hé* sleep, *wé* sleep,
Dropping the eyelid over our eyes.
If the golden apple be taken
The world will be overwise.
Five links, a golden chain are we,
Hesper, the Dragon, and Sisters three
Bound about the golden tree.

III

Father Hesper, Father Hesper, Watch, watch, night
  and day,
Lest the old wound of the world be healéd,
The glory unsealéd,
The golden apple stol'n away,
And the ancient secret revealéd.
Look from West to East along:
Father, old Himala weakens, Caucasus is bold and strong.
Wandering waters unto wandering waters call;
Let them clash together, foam and fall.
Out of watchings, out of wiles,
Comes the bliss of secret smiles.
All things are not told to all,

Half-round the mantling night is drawn.
Purplefringéd with even and dawn
Hesper hateth Phosphor, evening hateth morn.

IV

Every flower and every fruit the redolent breath
  Of the warm seawind ripeneth,
    Arching the billow in his sleep:
  But the land-wind wandereth,
    Broken by the highland steep,
    Two streams upon the violet deep.
For the Western Sun, and the Western Star,
And the low west-wind, breathing afar,
    The end of day and beginning of night,
    Keep the apple Holy and Bright;
Holy and Bright, round and full, bright and blest,
    Mellow'd in a land of rest:
    Watch it warily night and day;
    All good things are in the West.
Till mid-noon the cool East light
Is shut out by the round of the tall hill brow,
  But, when the full-faced Sunset yellowly
  Stays on the flowerful arch of the bough,
  The luscious fruitage clustereth mellowly,
    Golden-kernell'd, Golden-cored,
  Sunset-ripen'd above on the tree.
  The world is wasted with fire and sword,
  But the Apple of gold hangs over the Sea!
  Five links — a Golden chain are we —
  Hesper, the Dragon, and Sisters three,
            Daughters three,
            Round about,
            All round about
  The gnarl'd bole of the charméd tree.

The Golden Apple, The Golden Apple, The hallow'd
fruit,
> Guard it well,
> Guard it warily,
> Watch it warily,
> Singing airily,
Standing about the charméd root.

Lasting Sorrow.

(Republished from *Friendship's Offering*—an album published by
Smith and Elder 1832.)

Me my own Fate to lasting sorrow doometh:
Thy woes are birds of passage, transitory:
Thy spirit, circled with a living glory,
In summer still a summer joy resumeth.
Alone my hopeless melancholy gloometh,
Like a lone cypress, thro' the twilight hoary,
From an old garden where no flower bloometh,
One cypress on an inland promontory;
But yet my lonely spirit follows thine,
As round the rolling earth night follows day;
But yet thy lights on my horizon shine
Into my night, when thou art far away;
I am so dark, alas! and thou so bright,
When we two meet there's never perfect light.

Another sonnet, "There are three things which fill
my heart with sighs," he contributed (1832) to the
Yorkshire Literary Annual.

CHAPTER III.

CAMBRIDGE, SOMERSBY AND ARTHUR HALLAM.

1830–31.

To Alfred Tennyson (at Somersby) (unpublished).

Those Gothic windows are before me now,
  Which long have shone dim-lighted in my mind;
That slope of softest green, the brook below,
Old musty stalls, and tedded hay behind —
All have I seen; and simple tho' they be,
  A mighty awe steals with them on my heart,
For they have grown and lasted as a part
Of thy dear self, up-building thine and thee:
From yon tall fir, weathering the April rain,
  Came influence rare, that deepen'd into song,
Beauty lurk'd for thee in the long gray fields,
  By tufted knolls, and, Alfred, made thee strong !
Hence are the weapons which thy spirit wields,
Musical thoughts of unexampled strain.   A. H. H.

As Sterling had been deeply moved " by the opinions and feelings which pervaded the age," and had instituted a crusade against the cold selfishness of the time; so the narrowness and dryness of the ordinary course of study at Cambridge, the lethargy there, and absence of any teaching that grappled with the ideas of the age and stimulated and guided thought on the subjects of deepest human interest, had stirred my father to wrath[1]. He cried aloud for some " soldier-priest, no sabbath-drawler of old saws," to set the world right. But however

[1] Macaulay had written of the Cambridge of his day: "We see men of four and five-and-twenty, loaded with academical honours and rewards—scholarships, fellowships, whole cabinets of medals, whole shelves of prize-books, enter into life with their education still to begin; unacquainted with the first principles of the laws under which they live,

66

gloomy his own view and that of his contemporaries was then as to the present, my father clearly saw the " Day-beam, New-risen o'er awaken'd Albion." Indeed now, as always, he was one of those " on the look-out for every new idea, and for every old idea with a new application, which may tend to meet the growing requirements of society "; one of those who are " like men standing on a watch-tower, to whom others apply and say, not 'What of the night?' but 'What of the morning and of the coming day[1]?'"

At the request of Aubrey de Vere, he consented that the following denunciatory lines, written in his undergraduate days, should be published among my notes.

Lines on Cambridge of 1830.

Therefore your Halls, your ancient Colleges,
Your portals statued with old kings and queens,
Your gardens, myriad-volumed libraries,
Wax-lighted chapels, and rich carven screens,
Your doctors, and your proctors, and your deans,
Shall not avail you, when the Day-beam sports
New-risen o'er awaken'd Albion. No!
Nor yet your solemn organ-pipes that blow
Melodious thunders thro' your vacant courts
At noon and eve, because your manner sorts
Not with this age wherefrom ye stand apart,
Because the lips of little children preach
Against you, you that do profess to teach
And teach us nothing, feeding not the heart.

In after years a great change came over Cambridge,

unacquainted with the very rudiments of moral and political science." And when Whewell in 1838 was elected to the chair of Moral Philosophy, he began his introductory address by elaborately justifying the innovation of delivering public lectures on the subject committed to his charge.

[1] Speech of the Duke of Argyll in the House of Lords, Aug. 13th, 1894.

and he was sorry that he had spoken so bitterly, for he always looked back with affection to those " dawn-golden times " passed with his friends at Trinity.   He honoured the University for the way it had adapted itself to modern requirements; and he especially approved of the University Extension movement, for spreading higher education throughout local centres in Great Britain. Every vacation after his marriage University men visited him, so that he kept level with such movements.

What impressed him most, when he went to Cambridge in 1872, was the change in the relations between don and undergraduate.   While he was keeping his terms (1828–1831) there was "a great gulf fixed" between the teacher and the taught[1], but in 1872 he found a constant personal intercourse and interchange of ideas between them.   And, as the "living word" is to each man more than the mere lecture-room exposition, this change, he thought, could not fail to have the best influence on the enlargement of the views, sympathies and aspirations of the generations to come.

A letter from Blakesley indicates an intellectual attitude somewhat similar to my father's in relation to the prevailing habits of thought in Cambridge and in society at large.

DEAR TENNYSON,

BLACKHEATH, 1830.

The present race of monstrous opinions and feelings which pervade the age require the arm of a strong Iconoclast. A volume of poetry written in a proper spirit, a spirit like that which a vigorous mind indues by the study of Wordsworth and Shelley, would be, at the present juncture, the greatest benefit the world could receive.   And more benefit would accrue from it than from all the exertions of the Jeremy Benthamites and Millians, if they were to continue for ever and a day.   I have seen Sterling two or three times since I have been in these parts, and had some conversation with him.

[1] He said to Dr Butler, " There was a want of love in Cambridge then."

Sterling, and all of his class, who have been hawked at by the mousing owls of Cambridge, suffer from the narrow-mindedness of criticism. He saw the abuses of the present system of things, which is upheld by the strong hand of power and custom, and he attacked them accordingly. For this conduct he was dubbed a radical. He soon saw that the reforms proposed by that party were totally inadequate to the end which they proposed : that if carried to their fullest effect they would only remove the symptoms and not the cause of evil; that this cause was the selfish spirit which pervades the whole frame of society at present, and that to counterbalance the effects the cause of them must be removed. This end, he at first probably thought with Shelley, might be effected by lopping off those institutions in which that selfish spirit exhibits itself, without any more effort. He afterwards saw, with Wordsworth, that this was not the true method; but that we must implant another principle with which selfishness cannot co-exist, and trust that this plant as it grows up will absorb the nourishment of the weed, in which case those wickednesses and miseries, which are only the forms in which the latter developes itself, will of their own accord die away, as soon as their principle of vegetation is withered and dried up.

Hallam has gone back to Cambridge. He was not well while he was in London; moreover, he was submitting himself to the influences of the outer world more than (I think) a man of his genius ought to do.

I shall be in Cambridge, God willing (which, considering the depth of the snow is not quite clear), to-morrow evening. I hope soon to see you there.

Believe me your affectionate friend,

J. W. BLAKESLEY.

On October 4th, 1830, Arthur Hallam wrote from Forest House, Leyton, Essex:

I am sorry, dear Alfred, that I have left your note so long unanswered; but I don't doubt you have found already that to return to one's native land is to throw oneself into the jaws of all kinds of importunate people, from creditors upwards or downwards, who leave one no time for pleasant things. Yet this excuse lies arrantly, I discover upon second thoughts. I am living here in a very pleasant place, an old country mansion, in the depths of the Forest, with cedars in the garden, the seed of which is vouched to have been brought from Lebanon, and a billiard-table within doors, by dint of which I demolish time pretty well. I have been studious too, partly after my fashion, and partly after my father's; i.e. I read six books of Herodotus with him, and I take occasional plunges into David Hartley, and Buhle's *Philosophie Moderne* for my own gratification. I cannot find that my adventures have produced quite the favourable impression on my father's mind that his letter gave me to expect. I don't mean that he blames me at all; but his old notions about the University begin to revive, and he does not seem quite to comprehend, that after helping to revolutionize kingdoms, one is still less inclined than before to trouble one's head about scholarships, degree and such gear. Sometimes I sigh to be again in the ferment of minds, and stir of events which is now the portion of other countries. I wish I could be useful; but to be a fly on that great wheel would be something. Spanish affairs, you will have seen by the papers, go on slowly: not therefore, I trust, less surely; but I wish something was done. Sterling has had little direct news for a while,. and Perina never wrote to me. Sterling has been unwell, and is going to be married. I am glad he does not go out of the Apostolic family, for his lady is to be Susan Barton, of whom you may often have heard Blakesley rave. I had a letter from Spedding the other day, full of pleasant scoffs. I found one on my return from Leighton, dated two months ago, and extolling your book above sun, moon and stars: I have written to him, but as he has not answered, he has probably quitted Upfield Lodge. I cannot make out that you have been reviewed anywhere, but I have seen no magazines, and a letter from Garden, also of very old date, gives hope of *Blackwood*. Effingham of course I shun, as I would "whipping to death, pressing and hanging." Moxon very civilly sent me two copies of Lamb's Album verses, one for you; the book is weak as water. What think you of Belgium? The opinion of everybody here seems against them; yet I cannot well conceive their present resolution, and increasing unanimity, unless the grounds of their aversion to the Dutch were stronger than it is the fashion to represent them. At all events, now blood has

flowed in torrents, all union is rendered impracticable. The
chances of a general war in Europe are great; the iniquitous
prudence of the Allied Wolves, who struck the Lion down, has
guaranteed the possession of Belgium to the Dutch crown, and
should the insurgents, as is very likely, declare they never can
submit to the government of a Thing who has made war upon
them, the inevitable consequence will be that the Prussians
will interfere to preserve the sanctity of the guarantee, and
the French to maintain the principle, that the allegiance of a
people depends on its consent, not on the autocratic transfer of
another power. 'Twas a very pretty little revolution in Saxony,
and a respectable one at Brunswick.   I am surprised you have
not heard of Frederick; have you not written to the Hôtel de
Lille? You really ought, for he may be in distress, and Temple-
ton has very likely left Paris. I beg your pardon for this stupid
note, and rest in expectation of your promised letter, which I
hope will explain your intentions for the future, and the details
of things as they are at Somersby.   Remember me most kindly
to your mother and sisters, and tell Charles to write.

Affectionately yours, A. H. H.

It may be as well to say here that all the letters from
my father to Arthur Hallam were destroyed by his
father after Arthur's death: a great loss, as these particular letters probably revealed his inner self more
truly than anything outside his poems.

In February 1831 my father left Cambridge, for
my grandfather was somewhat ailing and wished that
he should return to help his mother.

On the night of leaving he gave a supper in his
rooms, Corpus Buildings, and after supper he and his
friends all danced a quadrille. As he drove away in the
coach his last sight in Trumpington Street was "Thompson's handsome face under the light of a street lamp."

After he had gone down, the Cambridge friends forwarded him his *Alfieri*, which one of them had borrowed
from him and for which he had been making constant demands, and they also told him of the poet Wordsworth's

visit to Trinity. They told how Spedding gave him coffee in his rooms; how Wordsworth was in good talking mood but furiously alarmist, nothing but revolutions, reigns of terror; how he had said he wished that Coleridge had not written the second part of " Christabel " because this required the tale to be finished, and asserted that the conclusion of Part I., " It was a lovely sight to see," was too much laboured : how he defended " Passive Obedience " by quoting Scripture. Upon the whole, although he " said nothing very profound or original," yet the young men enjoyed his talk till one o'clock in the morning; he also was pleased with his hearers.

My father's comment on such criticism about a poet whom he loved was : " How can you expect a great man to say anything 'very profound' when he *knows* it is expected of him ? "

On a Wednesday of this March, shortly after 11 o'clock in the morning, my grandfather was found leaning back in his study chair, having passed away peacefully —

Once thro' mine own doors Death did pass,
One went, who never hath return'd.
He will not smile — not speak to me
Once more.

After Arthur Hallam's death these lines were written in " In Memoriam," referring to the double loss of his father and of his friend :

As down the garden-walks I move,
Two spirits of a diverse love
Contend for loving masterdom.

My father told me that within a week after his father's death he slept in the dead man's bed, earnestly desiring

¹ Wordsworth, according to Milnes, heard Hallam deliver his Declamation in Trinity College Chapel. " It was splendid," he writes, " to see the poet Wordsworth's face kindle as Hallam proceeded with it."

to see his ghost, but no ghost came. "You see," he said, "ghosts do not generally come to imaginative people." In a letter to his friend John Frere, my uncle Charles describes what happened:

SOMERSBY, *March 23rd,* 1831.

*   *   *   *   *   *

John, a melancholy change has taken place in our house since I saw you last. My poor father, all his life *a man of sorrow and acquainted with grief,* has gone to " that bourne from whence no traveller returns." After an illness of about a month's continuance, he died last Wednesday at eleven o'clock in the day. He suffered little, and after death his countenance, which was strikingly lofty and peaceful, was I trust an image of the condition of his soul, which on earth was daily racked by bitter fancies, and tossed about by strong troubles. We are not certain whether we shall be permitted to remain much longer in this place. We must abide the pleasure of Robinson, the next Incumbent, &c. &c.

If...I pay him a rent by which he will be a gainer, I think we are likely to be less under obligations to him than he to us. But as my father's revenues are now sequestrated we are left entirely at the will of my grandfather, who may have a house of his own to put us into.

Charles Tennyson (d'Eyncourt)[1], Dr Tennyson's brother, also writes to the co-trustee of my grandfather's property, Mr Rawnsley of Halton:

This morning's post brought me the afflicting news from Somersby. You will guess my feelings, for you know that I valued my dear brother for his thousand admirable qualities of

---

[1] The Right Hon. Charles Tennyson d'Eyncourt represented in Parliament successively Grimsby, Bletchingley, Stamford, and Lambeth. On his death in 1861, he was succeeded by his son George Hildeyard T. d'Eyncourt, who died in 1871. The Tennyson estates then passed to his brother, Admiral Edwin Tennyson d'Eyncourt, C.B., who had served with distinction in China, and in the Gulf of Finland during the Crimean War. Under an arrangement made with the Admiral, Edmund d'Eyncourt, son of Louis T. d'Eyncourt (long known as Senior Metropolitan Magistrate), now holds the property.

heart, which would have contributed to his own happiness and that of those around him if he had not given way to failings arising out of a nervous temperament. I knew him to be excellent in intention, to be naturally full of worth and goodness, and I respected and loved him. I believe he also depended on my fraternal feelings towards him, and I will, as far as I can, endeavour to justify his good opinion of me. I transmit to you his will and a codicil....I was unable to get down to Somersby, my official business requiring my presence in town. I would however have broken through all, if I could have been of use or comfort to my poor brother's widow.

From Arthur Hallam to Emily Tennyson.

1831.

I cannot help thinking that if the name of Tennyson should pass from that little region, which all your life long has been to you home, that blessed little region, "bosomed in a kindlier air, Than the outer realm of care And dole," the very fields and lanes will feel a sorrow, as if part of their appointed being had been reft from them. Yet, after all, a consecration has come upon them from the dwellers at Somersby, which, I think, is not of the things that fail. Many years perhaps, or shall I say many ages, after we all have been laid in dust, young lovers of the beautiful and the true may seek in faithful pilgrimage the spot where Alfred's mind was moulded in silent sympathy with the everlasting forms of nature. Legends will perhaps be attached to the places that are near it. Some Mariana, it will be said, lived wretched and alone in a dreary house on the top of the opposite hill. Some Isabel may with more truth be sought nearer yet. The belfry, in which the white owl sat "warming his five wits," will be shown, for six-pence, to such travellers as have lost their own. Critic after critic will track the wanderings of the brook, or mark the groupings of elm and poplar, in order to verify the "Ode to Memory" in its minutest particulars. I send down, along with this note, some numbers of the *Tatler*, containing a review of Alfred and Charles by Leigh Hunt. You will be amused with the odd style of his observations, and the frank familiarity with which he calls them by their Christian names, just as if he had supped with them a hundred times. His general remarks are nonsensical enough, but being a poet he has a keen eye for true beauty, and the judgments of his taste are worth having. Charles will be proud of this review because it is the first notice which the Press (our new despot, the Kehama, under whom the world now groans, already nearly almighty and omnipresent, but, alas! as far as ever from all-wise) has deigned to take of his "humble plot of ground." But he has had better suffrages: voices have come to him from the Lakes, and the old man of Highgate has rejoiced over him[1]. I am looking forward with eagerness to seeing Charles; would that Alfred were with him! but that will not be, and perhaps ought not to be; "the days are awa" that we have seen.

The upshot of the various transactions as to Somersby was, that the new Incumbent was willing that the Tennysons should live on at the Rectory, where they remained till 1837.

Arthur Hallam had been attached to my aunt Emily since 1829. After the first year, when Mr Hallam thought it desirable that the lovers should be separated for a time, he stayed at Somersby as often as he could spare leisure from his work; and whenever he came, he cheered all with his "bright, angelic spirit and his gentle, chivalrous manner[2]."

"I am," wrote Hallam to Trench, "now at Somersby, not only as the friend of Alfred Tennyson, but as the lover of his sister. An attachment on my part of nearly two years' standing and a mutual engagement of one year are, I fervently hope, only the commencement of a

---

[1] S. T. Coleridge.

[2] Witch-elms that counterchange the floor
    Of this flat lawn with dusk and bright;
    And thou, with all thy breadth and height
    Of foliage, towering sycamore;

    How often, hither wandering down,
    My Arthur found your shadows fair,
    And shook to all the liberal air
    The dust and din and steam of town.

union which circumstances may not impair, and the grave itself may not conclude."

My aunt Emily had eyes "with depths on depths," and "a profile like that on a coin," "testa Romana," as an old Italian said of her. All the Tennyson sons and daughters except Frederick had the colouring of Italy or the south of France with dark eyes and hair. This foreign colouring may possibly have been derived from a Huguenot ancestor, a relation of Madame de Maintenon. On the Continent my father was never taken for an Englishman, and even in Ireland in 1848, when he was at Valentia, an Irishman rose up from among the fern and heather, and said, "From France, your honour?" thinking, as he confessed, that he was a Frenchman come to head a revolution.

While Hallam was at Somersby, after the morning's work the Tennysons and he would generally go for long walks together beyond the "bounding hill." Not only was my father fond of walking, but of "putting the stone" and other athletic feats. Mrs Lloyd of Louth writes: "In proof of his strong muscular power, when showing us a little pet pony on the lawn at Somersby one day he surprised us by taking it up and carrying it." Brook-field remarked: "It is not fair, Alfred, that you should be Hercules as well as Apollo." Fitzgerald notes: "Alfred could hurl the crowbar further than any of the neighbouring clowns, whose humours, as well as those of their betters, knight, squire, landlord and lieutenant, he took quiet note of, like Chaucer himself." Yet as he wandered over the wold, or by the brook, he often seemed to be in dreamland, so that one who often saw him then called him "a mysterious being, seemingly lifted high above other mortals, and having a power of intercourse with the spirit-world not granted to others."

In the evening he lived much in his attic den, but now and then came down and listened to the singing and playing of his sisters. He had a love for the simple style of Mozart, and for our own national airs and ballads, and played himself a little on the flute, but only "cared for complicated music as suggesting echoes of winds and waves." The sisters were all very musical, my aunt Mary playing the harp and accompanying the brothers and sisters who sang. Fitzgerald speaks of music in College days, and says:

A. T. was not thought to have an ear for music; I remember little of his execution in the line except humming over "the weary pund o' tow," which was more because of the weary moral, I think, than for any music's sake. Carlyle once said, "The man must have music dormant in him, revealing itself in *verse.*" I remember A. T.'s speaking of Haydn's "Chaos," which he had heard at some Oratorio. He said, "The violins *spoke* of *light.*" Carlyle, who was apt to look on poetry as a waste of talents which ought to be employed in other heroic work, took at once to A. T.: among other signs of the man, remarking his voice, "like the sound of a pinewood," he said.

In past years many friends of Somersby days have told me of the exceeding consideration and love which my father showed his mother, and how much they were struck by the young man's tender and deferential manner towards her, and how he might often be found in her room reading aloud, with his flexible voice, Shakespeare, Milton, Chaucer, Spenser and Campbell's patriotic ballads. When Arthur Hallam was with them, Dante, Petrarch, Tasso and Ariosto were the favourite poets: and it was he who taught my aunt Emily Italian, and made her a proficient scholar.

Arthur Hallam to Emily Tennyson.

Lady, I bid thee to a sunny dome,
  Ringing with echoes of Italian song;
  Henceforth to thee these magic halls belong,
And all the pleasant place is like a home:
Hark! on the right, with full piano tone,
  Old Dante's voice encircles all the air:
  Hark yet again! like flute tones mingling rare
Comes the keen sweetness of Petrarca's moan.

Pass thou the lintel freely; without fear
  Feast on the music.   I do better know thee
  Than to suspect this pleasure thou dost owe me
Will wrong thy gentle spirit, or make less dear
  That element whence thou must draw thy life,
  An English maiden and an English wife.

CHAPTER IV.

ARTHUR HALLAM.

1831–1833.

Thy leaf has perish'd in the green,
And, while we breathe beneath the sun,
The world which credits what is done
Is cold to all that might have been.

So here shall silence guard thy fame;
But somewhere, out of human view,
Whate'er thy hands are set to do
Is wrought with tumult of acclaim.

In the spring of 1831 my father was much distressed about the condition of his eyes and feared that he was going to lose his sight, "a sad thing to barter the universal light even for the power of ' Tiresias and Phineus, prophets old.'" He took to a milk diet for some months, which apparently "did good." At all events his eyesight was strong enough to allow him to study *Don Quixote* in the original. He also records that one night he "saw the moonlight reflected in a nightingale's eye, as she was singing in the hedgerow [1]." He adds that her voice vibrated with such passion that he wrote of

The leaves
That tremble round the nightingale

[1] Owing to his extreme short-sight he could see objects at a short distance better than anyone: and at a long distance with his eye-glass or

in "The Gardener's Daughter." Hallam told him at this
time that " The nightingale with long and low preamble,"
in the sonnet which I give, was "worth an estate in
Golconda."

> Check every outflash, every ruder sally
> Of thought and speech, speak low, and give up wholly
> Thy spirit to mild-minded Melancholy:
> This is the place. Thro' yonder poplar alley,
> Below, the blue green river windeth slowly,
> But in the middle of the sombre valley,
> The crisped waters whisper musically,
> And all the haunted place is dark and holy.
> The nightingale, with long and low preamble,
> Warbled from yonder knoll of solemn larches,
> And in and out the woodbine's flowery arches
> The summer midges wove their wanton gambol,
> And all the white-stemm'd pinewood slept above,
> When in this valley first I told my love.

My father contributed " Anacreontics," " No More [1],"
and " A Fragment," to a literary annual *The Gem*; and
Moxon, who had some sparks of poetry in him, and had
come into possession of the *Englishman's Magazine*,
wished to start with a "flash number," and asked
Hallam to persuade my father to forward him a poem
which would appear along with contributions from
Wordsworth, Southey, and Charles Lamb. Hallam
urged him (July 15th, 1831) to send " The Sisters,"

spectacles he could see as far as any long-sighted person. At this time he
went to see Brodie for his eyes, and began to talk so learnedly about them,
that Brodie raised his hand saying: "Wait; remember I *never* see medical
students without a fee." His hearing was extraordinarily keen, and this he
held to be a compensation for his short-sight: he "could hear the shriek
of a bat," which he said was the test of a fine ear.

[1] " No More" is written out in Arthur Hallam's handwriting in a
common-place book belonging to Archdeacon Allen, and is dated by Arthur
Hallam 1826. Although my father considered the poem crude, it is remarkable for a boy of seventeen.

or "Rosalind," or the "Southern Mariana," and begged him not to disdain a mode of publication which Schiller and Goethe chose for their best compositions. He pointed out that the fugitive pieces might form part of a volume hereafter.

Hallam was at Hastings "listening all day to the song of the larks on the cliffs," and reading *Destiny* and *Inheritance*. He had no answer from Alfred, or any of his brothers, so wrote again:

HASTINGS, *July* 26*th*, 1831.

I have been expecting for some days an answer to my letter about Moxon; but I shall not delay any longer my reply to your last, and before this is sent off yours may come. I, whose imagination is to yours as Pisgah to Canaan, the point of distant prospect to the place of actual possession, am not without some knowledge and experience of your passion for the past. To this community of feeling between us, I probably owe your inestimable friendship, and those blessed hopes which you have been the indirect occasion of awakening. But what with you is universal and all-powerful, absorbing your whole existence, communicating to you that energy which is so glorious, in me is checked and counteracted by many other impulses, tending to deaden the influence of the senses which were already less vivacious by nature. When I say the senses, I mean those employed in the processes of imagination, viz. sight and hearing. You say pathetically, "Alas for me! I have more of the Beautiful than the Good!" Remember to your comfort that God has given you to see the difference. Many a poet has gone on blindly in his artist pride. I am very glad you have been reading Erskine [of Linlathen]. No books have done me so much good as his, and I always thought you would like them if they came in your way. His doctrine may not be the truth, but it may contain it still, and this is my own view of the case. You perhaps will be angry when I tell you that I sent your sonnet about the "Sombre Valley" to Moxon[1], who is charmed with it, and has printed it off. I confess this is a breach of trust on my part, but I hope for your forgiveness...

A. H. H.

[1] Published in the *Englishman's Magazine* for August.

The two friends, after a tour taken by Hallam in Devon, Cornwall and Yorkshire, met at Sheffield to talk over literary plans for the future. Hallam wrote that he was " in the humbler station of critic," while " Alfred is brimful of subjects and artist thoughts." The " Apostles " and their little band of Cambridge friends expressed themselves warmly as to Hallam's article on the *Poems, chiefly Lyrical.* After his holiday Hallam returned to his reading of law, and enjoyed " the old fellow Blackstone," culling for Alfred poetic words like " foréstal." " The Dream of Fair Women," Hallam was of opinion, should be published soon, for it would establish the poet at once in general reputation. The friends interchanged thoughts on the political state of the world and on Ireland especially, which is " the most volcanic point." They had grave arguments about the Church, and were exercised about the St Simonians, whose opinions on many points " resembled those of Shelley, although they were much more practical." Miss Austen's novels were read and notes compared. My father preferred *Emma* and *Persuasion*, and Hallam wrote, " *Emma* is my first love, and I intend to be constant. The edge of this constancy will soon be tried, for I am promised the reading of *Pride and Prejudice.*"

My father meets Fanny Kemble, whom he holds " supreme in Juliet," and she speaks of him as having " the grandest head of any man whom she has clapt eyes on." Adelaide Kemble copies out " The Sisters," " raving about it at intervals in the most Siddonian tone," and Fanny has set the ballad to music; " she inclines however to think it too painful, and to wish such things should not be written." Her " enthusiasm is high " over some of the manuscript poems in the forthcoming 1832 volume, especially " The Lady of Shalott."

Her own play, *Francis I.*, runs for several nights
(March 1832). "It is a remarkable production for
seventeen; the language is very pure, free, elegant
English and strictly dramatic. There is none of that
verbiage which is called mere poetry in it. She must
have nourished her childhood with the strong wine of
our old drama": so writes Hallam, who was more
conversant with that old drama than any of his
Cambridge contemporaries.

The Hunchback is then given, and Hallam writes
that "The scene in the second Act, where Fanny
Kemble plays fine lady, was excellent, but the tragic
parts yet finer: for instance where Clifford comes in
as Secretary, and afterwards where she expostulates with
Master Walter. Her 'Clifford, why don't you speak to
me?' and 'Clifford, is it you?' and her 'Do it,' with
all the accompanying speech, I shall never forget."

Hallam and my father in their rambles through
London, and in their smokes in Hallam's den at the top
of the house in the "long unlovely street," touched on all
imaginable topics. Hallam was busy writing essays on
modern authors; and these and my father's 1832 volume
were frequent subjects of discussion. The unsettled
condition of the country and the misery of the poorer
class weighed upon them. It seemed difficult to young
men, starting in life, to know how to remedy these
evils, but they determined not to lose hold of the Real
in seeking the Ideal. Hallam writes: "Where the ideas
of time and sorrow are not, and sway not the soul with
power, there is no true knowledge in Poetry or Philosophy."

On my father's return to Somersby, the correspondence recommenced. Hallam desires the publication of
"The Lover's Tale," for there are "magnificent passages
in that poem. The present casket, faulty as it is, is yet the
only one in which the precious gems contained therein

can be preserved." The author thinks it too diffuse and will not publish. Hallam answers that, since his is "the only printed copy of the 'Lover's Tale,' he shall make a fortune by lending it out at five shillings a head." One day he reads "Œnone" to his father, who "seems to like Juno's speech, but is called away in the middle of Venus'," so the friends do not obtain the great man's criticism.

Meanwhile the colloquial critic of *Blackwood*, "Christopher North," had delivered his judgment on *Poems, chiefly Lyrical* in a comically aggressive though not wholly unfriendly article[1].

The following two letters were written by Arthur Hallam about this review, and the poems which were to appear in the volume of 1832:

[Undated.]

Professor Wilson has thought fit to have a laugh at you and your critics, amongst whom so humble a thing as myself, has not, as you will perceive, escaped. I suppose one ought to feel very savage at being attacked, but somehow I feel much more amused. He means well I take it, and as he has extracted nearly your whole book, and has in his soberer mood spoken in terms as high as I could have used myself of some of your best poems, I think the review will assist rather than hinder the march of your reputation. They little know the while that you despise the false parts of your volume quite as vehemently as your censors can, and with purer zeal, because with better knowledge.

April 10*th*, 1832.

I don't know that you ought to publish this spring, but I shall never be easy or secure about your MSS until I see them fairly out of your control. The Ballad of "The Sisters" was very popular at Cambridge. Indeed it is very perfect. Monteith showed his ignorance by wishing the murdering lady

---

[1] For example in the criticism of the song entitled "The Owl," he says, "Alfred is as an owl: all that he wants is to be shot, stuffed and stuck into a glass case, to be made immortal in a museum." (*Blackwood's Mag.* Vol. XXXI.)

to have been originally the rival of the seduced lady, which idea was of course scouted by the wiser listeners, that is, all the rest, as substituting a commonplace melodramatic interest for the very poetic interest arising from your conception of the character.   All were anxious for the " Palace of Art," etc., and fierce with me for not bringing more.   Venables is a great man (at Cambridge), also Dobson.   New customs, new topics, new slang phrases have come into vogue since *my* day, which yet was but yesterday.   I don't think I could reside again at Cambridge with any pleasure.   I should feel like a melancholy Pterodactyl winging his lonely flight among the linnets, eagles and flying fishes of our degenerate post-Adamic world.   I have seen Gaskell, who is in the ninth heaven of happiness, going to be married the end of May.   I have taken to my law again, and a little to my other studies.   The [first Reform] Bill is now in the second reading, and will pass by a very small majority.   The cholera is certainly abating; the preliminary symptoms have been very widely prevalent; disorders which are cured without difficulty in our rank of life turn to malignant cholera in the poor.   Casimir Périer has had it but is recovering.   The heroes of July are cutting the throats of physicians and wine merchants as you will see by the papers.

The report about Macaulay in Tennant's letter has no great foundation : at least he has not seen your book.   I think Mac has some poetic taste, and would appreciate you.

Yours affectionately,

A. H. H.

Spedding wrote from Cambridge to Thompson (May 4th, 1832):

Only think of an "Apostolic" dinner next Friday, 11th inst. ; present, Hallam, Trench, Kemble, Arthur Buller, Martineau, Pickering, Donne I hope, etc. etc.   Only think of Heath's essay on Niebuhr the day after !   Only think of the " Palace of Art," of which you may see part of a stanza, horribly misquoted, at what should have been the beginning of this sheet !   Only think of all these things, and others which your own fruitful imagination will readily suggest !   By the way, are you not tired by this time of the monotony and manufacture of your infernal county ? or if you are still wandering on the sea-shore, does not your soul feel very much like

> A still salt pool, lock'd in with bars of sand
> Left on the shore, that hears all night
> The plunging seas draw backward from the land
> Their moon-led waters white?

Do you not begin to sigh for apostolic conversation, and your dear lodgings, and River-Gods of " Mighty Michael Angelo," and the massed chestnut boughs that promise soon to put out their leaves?

Charles Merivale also wrote to Thompson that " A daily divan continued to sit throughout the term," and that the " ' Palace of Art ' was read successively to each man as he came up from the vacation." He continues :

Though the least eminent of the Tennysonian Rhapsodists, I have converted by my readings both my brother and your friend (or enemy?) Richardson to faith in the " Lotos-eaters." They rather scoff at the former (the " Palace of Art "), and ask whether " The abysmal depths of personality " means the *Times* newspaper ?

Spedding wrote again to Thompson, June 21st, 1832 :

We talk out of the " Palace of Art," and the " Legend of Fair Women." The great Alfred is here (in London), i.e. in Southampton Row, smoking all the day, and we went from this house on a pilgrimage to see him, to wit, two Heaths, my brother and myself, and meeting Allen on the way we took him along with us, and when we arrived at the place appointed we found A. T. (Alfred Tennyson), and A. H. H. (Arthur Hallam), and J. M. K. (Kemble), and we made a goodly company, and did as we do at Cambridge, and but that you were not among us, we should have been happy.

And on July 18th, 1832, Spedding writes :

I say, a new volume by A. T. is in preparation, and will, I suppose, be out in Autumn. In the meantime I have no copy of the " Palace of Art," but shall be happy to repeat it to you when you come ; no copy of the " Legend of Fair Women," but can repeat about a dozen stanzas which are of the finest; no copy of the conclusion of " Œnone," but one in pencil which none but myself can read.

This July my father and Hallam went for a tour on the Rhine.

Arthur Hallam to Emily Tennyson.

NONNENWERTH, *July* 16*th*, 1832.

I expect, as far as I can calculate (but a traveller's calculations are always liable to be deranged by unforeseen chances), to be in England by the end of this month, and then I shall go straight to Somersby. I had better tell you something of what Alfred and I have been doing. My last letter, I think, was from Rotterdam.

We resumed our steam-boat last Wednesday morning, and came on slowly up the Rhine; the banks of which are more uniformly ugly and flat as far as Cologne than any country I ever saw of so great an extent. Really, until yesterday, we had seen nothing in the way of scenery that deserved going a mile to see. Cologne is the paradise of painted glass: the splendour of the windows in the churches would have greatly delighted you. The Cathedral is unfinished, and if completed on the original plan, would be the most stupendous and magnificent in the world. The part completed is very beautiful Gothic. Alfred was in great raptures, only complaining he had so little time to study the place. There is a gallery of pictures quite after my own heart, rich, glorious old German pictures, which Alfred accuses me of preferring to Titian and Raffaelle. In the Cathedral we saw the tomb and relics of the three kings, Gaspar, Melchior, and Balthazar, the patrons of Cologne and very miraculous persons in their day, according to sundry legends. The tomb is nearly all of pure massy gold, studded with rich precious stones.

From Cologne we came on to Bonn, which really bears a sort of family-likeness to Cambridge. Here the Rhine begins to be beautiful; and yesterday we took a luxurious climb up the Drachenfels, looked around at the mild vine-spread hillocks, and "river-sundered champaign clothed with corn," ate cherries under the old castle-wall at the top of the crag, then descended to a village below, and were carried over in a boat to the place from which I am writing. And what is that? Ten years ago it was a large convent of Benedictine nuns; now it is a large and comfortable hotel, still retaining the form of the Convent, the Cloisters, cell-like rooms, etc. It stands on an island in the middle of the river; you will understand the size of the isle, when I tell you it is rather larger, according to Alfred, than that of the Lady of Shalott, and the stream is rather more rapid than our old acquaintance that ran down to Camelot. The prospect from the window and gardens is most beautiful, the mountains, as they are called, Drachenfels being one, on one bank of the river, and Rolandseck towering up on the other, with the hills about Bingen glooming in the distance.

After their return Arthur Hallam writes to Alfred:

1832.

My dear Alfred,

Thanks for your batch of MSS. The lines to J. S. are perfect. James [Spedding], I am sure, will be most grateful. The "Old Year" is excellent. The "Little Room" is mighty pleasant[1].

Remember the maxim of the Persian sage: "εἰ διάζεις, ἀπέχου." Your epigram to North is good, but I have scruples whether you should publish it. Perhaps he may like the lines and you the better for them; but "μερμηρίζω." I think the "Lover's Tale" will be liked, as far as I can remember its old shape. Moxon is in ecstasies with the "May Queen"; he says the volume must make a great sensation. He and your friends are anxious that it should be out before the storm of politics is abroad. The French Fleet has got the start of you, and I fear Antwerp may be taken before your last revise is ready; but still you may be beforehand with the elections, which is more

---

[1] (*Note by my father.*)

As soon as this poem was published, I altered the second line to "All books and pictures ranged aright"; yet "Dear room, the apple of my sight" (which was much abused) is not so bad as

"Do go, dear rain, do go away."

A. T.

important. There has been some delay this week, owing to want of types, but the (printer's) devils are full of promise to set up immediately. Moxon has sent me the revises of " The Palace," with the notes; they are, I believe, correct, yet I would know whether you altered " pouring glorious scorn" into " frowning," etc. In the course of next week I shall send you two compositions of my own, the one very trifling, an article of three pages only, in the *Foreign Quarterly*, the other, a pamphlet Moxon has just published for me on Rossetti's *Disquisizioni sullo spirito Antipapale* [1]. I hope you will like it; yet I have not forgotten that the last time I sent you a publication of mine you did not even deign to read it. When should I have done the like by one of yours? Perhaps you may retort with justice, that this question is like the American's remark in Mrs Trollope, to an Englishman, who had never read Bryant's poems, " How illiberal you English are! just let me ask you, what you would say to one of us that had never read Milton or Shakespeare, or any of *your* great authors! " Fare thee well, old trump, poems are good things but flesh and blood is better. I only crave a few words.

Ever yours affectionately, A. H. H.

After staying at Kitlands.

DORKING, *October* 10*th*, 1832.

MY DEAR ALFRED,

I must snatch a few minutes from the overwhelming mass of law business which is now on my hands, just to talk with you about the first-proof. I had it sent down to me while I was staying at Heath's. The weather was miserably rainy, so, after breakfast, we adjourned to an arbour in the garden, and while Thompson, who was also staying there, furnished cheroots, I furnished proof-sheets. After mature examination, we came, in full conclave, to some decisions, of which you shall have the benefit. We think the type very pretty, but are rather sorry the book will not bind up with its predecessor. We admire the Buonaparte sonnet but we strongly urge the substitution of

---

[1] Among other papers Hallam wrote then were the brief though remarkable memoirs of Petrarch, Burke, and Voltaire, for the *Gallery of Portraits* published by the Society for the Diffusion of Useful Knowledge.

"dreamer" for "madman." The stanzas "All good things" seem
to us perfect. The "Lady" (of Shalott) reads charmingly in print:
the more I read it, the more I like it. You were, indeed, happily
inspired when the idea of that poem first rose in your imagination.
We had a long battle with Mr Heath, a famous lawyer, but no
man of letters, about the last stanza in the proof. We flatter
ourselves we floored him; to be sure we were three to one, but he
fought well. The principal point of attack was "cloud-white"; he
said it was absurd to explain a fixed colour as pearl by the most
variable hue in the world, that of a cloud. We recovered ourselves
with all the grace of practised combatants, and talked learnedly
about the context of feeling, and the conformity of the lady's
dress to her magical character, till at last our opponent left us
in possession of the field, declaring still between his teeth, that,
for his part, he thought poetry ought to be sense. In one place
a whole line was omitted. Douglas Heath read, "sudden
laughters of the Tay" (Jay); without ever suspecting the
misprint. I hear Tennant has written to dissuade you from
publishing "Kriemhild," "Tarpeia" (in the "Fair Women").
Don't be humbugged, they are very good; you may put a
note or two if you will, yet Milton did not to "Paradise Lost."
Rogers the poet has been staying here, and speaks of you with
admiration. Have you written to Moxon? He is anxious to
have the rest of the MSS.

Ever your most affectionate ARTHUR.

My father wrote to Mr Moxon, in consequence of
this letter from Arthur Hallam:

20 *Nov.* 1832.

DEAR SIR,

After mature consideration, I have come to
a resolution of not publishing the last poem in my little
volume, entitled, "Lover's Tale": it is too full of faults
and tho' I think it might conduce towards making me
popular, yet, to my eye, it spoils the completeness of the
book, and is better away; of course whatever expenses
may have been incurred in printing the above must
devolve on me solely.

The vol. can end with that piece titled to J. S.

We, who live in this corner of the world, only get our letters twice or thrice a week: which has caused considerable delay: but on receipt of this you may begin to dress the volume for its introduction into the world, as soon as you choose.

Believe me, Sir, yours very truly,

ALFRED TENNYSON.

P.S. The title-page may be simply

POEMS

BY ALFRED TENNYSON

(don't let the printer squire me).

Be so good as to send me five copies.

Among the poems in this volume were " The Lady of Shalott " (so-called from an Italian novelette, " Donna di Scalotta "), " Mariana in the South," " The Miller's Daughter," " Œnone," " The Palace of Art," " The Lotos-Eaters," " The Dream of Fair Women," " The May Queen," and " To James Spedding " on the death of his brother Edward. After its publication Arthur Hallam wrote to my father, referring to a review of the book in the *Quarterly* (No. XLVII. 1833):

[*Undated.*]

Your book continues to sell tolerably and Moxon says the *Quarterly* has done good. Rogers defends you publicly as the most promising genius of the time. Sir Robert Inglis told my father he had heard from unquestionable authority that Alfred Tennyson was an assumed name like Barry Cornwall. I endeavoured to shake his scepticism, I fear without effect. I hear to-day that a question is put up at the Cambridge Union, " Tennyson or Milton, which the greater poet?"

*   *   *   *   *

My father met Milman one day who denies altogether having written the infamous article [in the *Quarterly*]. He says he has made a rule never to cut up any living poet. Once he made an exception in the case of a foreigner, and to his horror when at Florence he found himself invited to meet him at breakfast. Rogers thinks the first volume decidedly superior to the second....I don't quite comprehend this.

From Arthur Hallam.

[*Undated.*]

Ὦ μοι, Διογενὲς Πατρόκλεις, οἷον ἔειπες;

You are very impertinent about my talent of letter-writing; I never said I composed my letters, now at least; formerly I did in some sort, when Plancus was consul, and Gaskell my correspondent and hero of romance. Am I not thereby entitled to say of myself, as Mrs Langley said of her daughters, "Whatever accomplishment I may possess in that way, it is entirely self-taught"?

That labour, if labour it was, was one of love. It had nothing of the file. I composed a letter as I composed a poem. Heart and mind went into it, and why? — because I couldn't help it. I was full of thoughts so new to me that I was afraid of losing them, and took every way to treasure them : so dear they were too that I could not rest till those I loved were familiar with them.

I have been reading Mrs Jameson's *Characteristics*, and I am so bewildered with similes about groves and violets, and streams of music, and incense and attar of roses, that I hardly know what I write. Bating these little flummeries of style, it is a good book, showing much appreciation of Shakespeare and the human heart *ἐν διὰ δυοῖν.*

I went again to Effingham Wilson's shop to-day; he was bland and submissive, promising to send me the account as soon as he should have time to make it out. I am confident the £11 [1] will be found a mistake. A rumour is current that Mrs Arkwright has set "Oriana" to music! All the world loves her music, and "Oriana" has a fair chance of becoming as stale as the "Captive Knight." The country is in jeopardy hourly increasing. Yesterday I saw (perhaps) the last king of England go down to open the first assembly of delegates from a sovereign people. It is an unmanageable house. O'Connell

---

[1] The sum my father received for the 1830 volume.

raves. Government menaces. Your uncle [C. Tennyson d'Eyn-court] seems to be manœuvring to be chief of the Penultimate Radicals, the Girondists, one might call them from their position, were they not alike destitute of genius and patriotism. But there can be no doubt that, if the Mountain continues unshaken, it must increase, and that more faint-hearted crew to which your uncle belongs will adhere to it. O'Connell's speech is said to have been very effective. He and Sheil on one side; Macaulay and Stanley on the other, there will be some fine spectacles of intellectual combat.

Ever yours affectionately, A. H. H.

My father did not view the political situation so gloomily as did Arthur Hallam. It was the "dead waste and middle of the night" when the news of the passing of the Reform Bill for England and Wales had reached Somersby. This "Firm Bill," as the Lincolnshire people called it, had stirred all hearts; and my father and some of his brothers and sisters at once sallied out into the darkness, and began to ring the church bells madly. The new parson, horrified at hearing his bells rung and not merely rung but furiously clashed without his leave, came rushing into his church, and in the pitch blackness laid hold of the first thing which he could clap hand to, and this happened to be my aunt Cecilia's little dog — which forthwith tried to bite. The Tennysons then disclosed themselves amid much laughter; and the parson, who I suppose was a Tory of the old school, was with difficulty pacified. More than once my father thought of turning this scene into verse as an interesting picture of the times. The advice as to sensitiveness[1] which Hallam

[1] Jowett writes to me: "Your father was very sensitive and had an honest hatred of being gossiped about. He called the malignant critics and chatterers 'mosquitoes.' He never felt any pleasure at praise (except from his friends), but he felt a great pain at the injustice of censure. It never occurred to him that a new poet in the days of his youth was sure to provoke dangerous hostilities in the 'genus irritabile vatum,' and in the old-fashioned public."

gave my father at this time was wise; since the
Quarterly review could not but disturb the equanimity
of a mind peculiarly liable to be annoyed by captious
and unintelligent criticism[1]. Hallam urged him to find
amusement in those hair-splitting critics, " who are the
bane of great art," and to assure himself that even these
reviews would bring him into notice. His friends were
of opinion that even the sneering savage *Quarterly*
attack would be innocuous, for the *Review* was known in
London to be the organ of a party, both in politics and
literature. They cheered him by telling him that his
very creative originality and unlikeness to any poet, his
uncommon power over varied metres and rare harmonies
of sound and sense, needed the creation of a taste for
his work before he could be appreciated. " To raise the
many," Hallam wrote, " to his own real point of view,
the artist must employ his energies, and create energy
in others: to descend to their position is less noble, but
practicable with ease." However the estimation in which
the *Quarterly* was then held throughout the country was
given by an old Lincolnshire squire, who assured my
father that " The *Quarterly* was the next book to God's
Bible."

My father's attitude towards his critics is illustrated
in the following letter[2], written by him to " Christopher
North " in reference to a pamphlet by Mr Lake, which

---

[1] More than once the writer in the *Quarterly* wilfully misinterprets the
lines and poems. For instance, in " The Miller's Daughter" my father
describes the mill-pool, and says:

> A water-rat from off the bank
> Plunged in the stream.

This is explained by the reviewer as the poet "likening the first intrusion of
love into the virgin bosom of the miller's daughter to the plunging of a
water-rat."

[2] This letter was found in a rag-store in Dundee in September 1895 and
forwarded to me by C. M. Falconer.

he thought " Christopher North " might be disposed to notice.

SOMERSBY, SPILSBY, LINCOLNSHIRE.

SIR,

Tho' I *am* " the star of little Britain," I assure you I do not rise or set there very cordially. I prefer vegetating in a very quiet garden where I neither see nor hear anything of the great world of literature — not lighting even upon *Maga* once a year. Nevertheless, in the lack of better things, a composition, mistermed a Satyre, entitled *Criticism and Taste*, and particularly remarkable for the want of either, was forwarded to me, a day or two ago, by the author — with a note; he thinks I ought to promote the circulation of his book for the good of my own, does he? so then I am to be pioneered — perhaps patronized, by Mr John Lake. Now, Sir, hew me piecemeal, cut me up any way you will, exhaust all your world of fun and fancy upon me, but do not suspect me — tho' I may have done, written, said foolish things, not excepting a silly squib to Christopher North — do not dream that I can, now or ever, own any one grain of sympathy with the ravings of this unhappy coxcomb. I would rather request you, if you do not object to meet me on such dirty ground, to shake hands over the puddle he has made.

Five months after it had been printed I saw the critique[1] from which Mr L. has drawn his inspiration. I considered it at the time as somewhat too skittish and petulant, tho' it was redeemed to me by a tone of boisterous and picturesque humour such as I love. My gall might have risen a little — that it could never have contained much bitterness the weakness of my epigram ought, I think, to prove; for I trust that you will give me credit for being able to write a better.

[1] The *Blackwood* article by Wilson.

I could wish that some of the poems there broken
on your critical wheel were deeper than ever plummet
sounded. Written as they were before I had attained
my nineteenth year they could not but contain as many
faults as words. I never wish to see them or hear of
them again — much less to find them dragged forward
once more on your boards, if you should condescend to
divide Mr L. from his one idea by replying to him.
Perhaps you should not use him too harshly — tho' his
arrogance deserves reproof; a consideration of the real
imbecility of his nature ought to blunt the weapon.

Someone (I think M. in his cups) told a friend of
mine that you were the author of an article on me in
the *Quarterly*. I do not believe it; for I could not
recognise one spark of genius or a single touch of true
humour or good feeling. Moreover the man misprints
me, which is worse than lying — but now that we have
shaken hands (for I trust, we have) I find that you owe
me an explanation. Somewhere or other you state
" Alfred is a gentleman " — to which I answer with Con-
rade and Borachio, " Yea, sir, we hope ": you say afterwards, that I have forgotten what was due to myself in
that character, because having previously sent you " a
copy with a grateful superscription " I had publicly disclaimed much relish for your approbation. Now upon
mine honour as a gentleman, I did never send or cause
to be sent any such presentation-copy, or write, indite,
or cause to be written or indited any superscription,
grateful or ungrateful, to any Editor of any Review or
Magazine whatsoever.

Apologising for having thus far incroached on your
valuable time......[1]

The next decade wrought a marvellous abatement
of my father's real fault, which was undoubtedly " the

[1] The signature of this letter has been cut off.

tendency, arising from the fulness of a mind which had not yet learned to master its resources freely, to over-crowd his composition with imagery...to which may be added an over-indulgence in the luxuries of the senses, a profusion of splendours, harmonies, perfumes, gorgeous apparel, luscious meats and drinks and 'creature comforts' which rather pall upon the sense, and make the glories of the outward world a little too obscure and overshadow the world within[1]."

"Alfred continued writing," as Spedding says, "like a crocodile, sideways and onward": and defines one aspect of the poet's work in this sort of way:

(What Thor, armed with his hammer, said to the Bard before dinner.)

Wherever evil customs thicken,
Break thro' with the hammer of iron rhyme,
Till priest-craft and king-craft sicken,
But pap-meat-pamper not the time
With the flock of the thunder-stricken.
If the world caterwaul, lay harder upon her
Till she clapperclaw no longer,
Bang thy stithy stronger and stronger,
Thy rhyme-hammer *shall* have honour.

Yet a poet cannot live his true life without sympathy, and he fancied that England was an unsympathetic atmosphere, and half resolved to live abroad in Jersey, in the south of France, or in Italy. He was so far persuaded that the English people would never care for his poetry, that, had it not been for the intervention of his friends, he declared it not unlikely that after the death of Hallam he would not have continued to write.

[1] Spedding's *Reviews and Discussions*.

Spedding wrote[1], as to this second volume: " The reception (of the poems), though far from triumphant, was not inauspicious; for while they gained him many admirers, they were treated, even by those critics whose admiration, like their charity, begins and ends at home, as sufficiently notable to be worth some not unelaborate ridicule. The admiration and the ridicule served alike to bring them into notice...The superiority of his second collection of poems lay not so much in the superior workmanship (it contained perhaps fewer that were equally perfect in their kind) as in the general aim and character. If some of the blossom was gone, it was amply repaid by the more certain promise of fruit. Not only was the aim generally larger, the subjects and interest more substantial, and the endeavour more sustained, but the original and distinctive character of the man appeared more plainly. His genius was manifestly shaping a peculiar course for itself, and finding out its proper business; the moral soul was beginning more and more to assume its due predominance, not in the way of formal preaching (the proper vehicle of which is prose), but in the shape and colour which his creations unconsciously took, and the feelings which they were made insensibly to suggest."

To his aunt, Mrs Russell, my father wrote the two following letters:

SOMERSBY.

DEAREST AUNT,

What think you of the state of affairs in Europe? Burking and cholera have ceased to create much alarm. They are our least evils, but reform and

[1] In 1842.

St Simonism are, and will continue to be, subjects of the highest interest.   The future is so dark in the prospect that I am ready to cry out with the poet:

> The empty thrones call out for kings,
> But kings are cheap as summer-dust.
> The good old time hath taken wings,
> And with it taken faith and trust,
> And solid hope of better things.

Reform (not the measure, but the instigating spirit of reform, which is likely to subsist among the people long after the measure has past into a law) will bring on the confiscation of Church property, and maybe the downfall of the Church altogether: but the existence of the sect of the St Simonists[1] is at once a proof of the immense mass of evil that is extant in the nineteenth century, and a focus which gathers all its rays.   This sect is rapidly spreading in France, Germany and Italy, and they have missionaries in London.   But I hope and trust that there are hearts as true and pure as steel in old England, that will never brook the sight of Baal in the sanctuary, and St Simon in the Church of Christ.   I should delight in having a line from you or Emma.

Believe me,

Ever yours most affectionately,

A. T.

---

[1] See an interesting account of Saint-Simon and his followers in Lecky's *Democracy and Liberty*, Vol. II. pp. 207–215.

SOMERSBY, *March* 10*th*, 1833.

MY DEAREST AUNT,

I am much grieved to find that your kind-hearted letter to me has been lying so many days unanswered. I was at Mablethorpe, a bathing-place on our bleak, flat Lincolnshire coast, when it arrived at Somersby, and as there is no species of post between the latter and the former place, I have only just now received it together with some others. I have sent Emma's[1] picture to 15 Portland Place. I recollect when I first saw it, thinking that it did not do her justice: it wanted her life and vivacity. I would have forwarded this portrait to you long ago, and likewise visited you by the proxy of a letter, but to me as to Dante, "La diritta via era smarrita," for I knew not where you were. What astrologer can point out the place of any star that moves perpetually under a cloud?

You have been singing too in your solitude, and I should like much to hear some of your melodies, but a malicious fatality always seems to thwart me: the ghost of some ex-amateur, jealous of your notes, thrusts himself between me and any possible piano you may sit down to. My grandfather had lately a very severe fit of the gout, — Mr B.[2] stayed two nights in the house, — but our last accounts are that he is pretty well recovered and rides out, I believe, as usual.

Mary remembers having once met you at Tealby: I wish you knew her better — she is a girl of great feeling

---

[1] Her daughter, Lady Boyne.

[2] Mr B——, the county doctor, would miss out his "h's," and say: "Mr Tennyson, I work 'ard and get up so early that I 'eat my own grate." He was in the habit of riding about at night with a gig-lamp fastened to each foot, for fear of being run over.

and very warm in her attachments to her female friends, and true feeling is all that is really valuable on the windy side of the grave. For myself, I drag on somewhat heavily thro' the ruts of life, sometimes moping to myself like an owl in an ivy-bush, or that *one* sparrow which the Hebrew mentioneth as sitting on the housetop (a passage which used always to make me uncomfortable), and sometimes smoking a pipe with a neighbouring parson and cursing O'Connell for as double-dyed a rascal as ever was dipped in the Styx of political villainy[1]. Last year, however, Hallam and myself steamed up the Rhine as far as Bingen; we had the pleasure of being moored by a muddy island, full of stagnant dykes, in the river Maas, where we performed quarantine for a week, and saw by night the boats, from the cholera vessels stationed in the river, creeping round to the burial-place of the island with a corpse and a lantern. We at last got so enraged that we pulled down the Dutch colours and reversed them, which put the ancient skipper into such indignation that he swore he would hang us at the yard-arm.

We returned by Aix-la-Chapelle and Brussels. My mother, who, as you know, is one of the most angelick natures on God's earth, always doing good as it were by a sort of intuition, continues in tolerable health, though somewhat harassed with the cares incident to so large a family. She sends the essence of all love to you and yours, and begs me to state how happy it would make her to see you at Somersby: indeed this is a wish in which we all cordially join, tho' for my own part I have very faint hopes that you will gratify it. Many thanks for your present and letter.

Love to Emma and compliments to Gustavus[2]. I

---

[1] He softened this opinion when he came to know more about O'Connell.
[2] The baby son is the present Lord Boyne.

hope for his own peace of mind that he will have as little of the Tennyson about him as possible.

Believe me,

My dearest Aunt,

Ever your most affectionate nephew,

A. T.

During these years the Tennysons seem to have taken turns in going to London. We hear of my uncle Charles seeing his Cambridge friends in town. "Brookfield is melancholy and not fancy-free." "John Kemble is buried in Gothic manuscripts, and will only talk of Runes and Eddas, and of the brave knight Siegfried." Arthur Hallam is "as kind as ever," and Charles rides with him "through the beautiful Norwood country." In March of this year we are told that Arthur Hallam, Alfred and Mary enjoyed their sight-seeing in London together. They visited the Elgin Marbles, the Tower and the Zoological Gardens. They looked through microscopes at "moths' wings, gnats' heads, and at all the lions and tigers which lie perdus in a drop of spring water." My father would say, on looking through the microscope, "Strange that these wonders should draw some men to God and repel others. No more reason in one than in the other."

In July Arthur Hallam wrote to my father who was in Scotland :

July 31st, 1833.

I feel to-night what I own has been too uncommon with me of late, a strong desire to write to you. I do own I feel the want of you at some times more than at others ; a sort of yearning for dear old Alfred comes upon me, and that without

any particularly apparent reason. I missed you much at
Somersby — not for want of additional excitement, I was very
happy. I had never been at Somersby before without you.
However I hope you are not unpleasantly employed in the land
of cakes and broiled fish. I hear that you were charmed with
the amiability of the Gardens; I also hear in town that the old
Monteiths have been here instead of there. I trust you finished
the "Gardener's Daughter," and enriched her with a few additional beauties drawn from the ancient countenance of Monteith's
aunt. Have you encountered any Highland girl with "a shower
for her dower"? I should like much to hear your adventures,
but I daresay it will be difficult to persuade you to write to Vienna,
whither I am going on Saturday with tolerable speed. At all
events if you have any traveller's tale to tell, do not tell it often
enough to get tired of it before we meet. I am going perhaps
as far as Buda. I shall present your poetic respects to the
Danube and to certain parts of Tyrol. In the parcel which
accompanies this you will find a volume of poems by Hartley
Coleridge, much of which I think you will agree with me is
exquisitely beautiful. Probably Charles and Septimus will like
the sonnets more than you will. I desire and peremptorily
issue my orders that Emily may not be debarred from full, fair
and free reading of that book by any of her brothers.

A. H. H.

My father went with Tennant to London to say
farewell to his friend, before he set out abroad. There
was a supper at my father's lodgings, and Tennant writes
to Septimus Tennyson:

Moxon and Leigh Hunt were there, and we did not separate
till half-past four o'clock : Alfred repeated glorious fragments of
the "Gardener's Daughter," which seemed to produce proper effect
upon Leigh Hunt. Yesterday we went in a troop to see Rogers'
(the poet's) gallery of paintings : superb Titian, very beautiful
Raphael Madonna, and in fact all art gems [1]. There is a fresco

---

[1] The Titian, presumably *Noli me tangere,* and the (so-called) Giotto, a
fragment with two Apostles' heads, as well as the Madonna, which had
belonged to the Orleans collection, are now in the National Gallery.

by Giotto. In the library we found Charles' volume but *not* Alfred's. There were many proofs of the engravings that will appear in his (Rogers') forthcoming volume.

Hallam sent as a parting present to Emily Tennyson the *Pensées de Pascal*, and *Silvio Pellico*. In August he started with his father for the " Tyrol, and Salzburg." " Never have mountains seemed to him so sublime." He admired " the independence and self-respect of the Tyrolese." Vienna he compared to Paris, but found the city " more uniformly handsome." He visited the Treasure Chamber, where he saw " the largest diamond in the world." The Prater was dismal, " insipid, worse even than the Corso at Milan or the Cascine at Florence." But he revelled in the picture gallery and wrote about it as follows:

Sept. 6th, 1833.

The gallery is grand and I longed for you: two rooms full of Venetian pictures only; such Giorgiones, Palmas, Bordones, Paul Veroneses! and oh Alfred such Titians! by Heaven, that man could paint! I wish you could see his Danaë. Do you just write as perfect a Danaë! Also there are two fine rooms of Rubens, but I know you are an exclusive, and care little for Rubens, in which you are wrong: although no doubt Titian's imagination and style are more analogous to your own than those of Rubens or of any other school.

A. H. H.

That is the last letter from Arthur Hallam. With his letters I find these MS lines:

I do but mock me with the questionings.
Dark, dark, irrecoverably dark
Is the soul's eye; yet how it strives and battles
Through the impenetrable gloom to fix
That master light, the secret truth of things,
Which is the body of the Infinite God.

A. H. H.

He died at Vienna on Sept. 15th, 1833. When Mr Hallam returned from his daily walk, he saw Arthur asleep as he supposed upon the couch; a blood-vessel near the brain had suddenly burst: it was not sleep but death.

On October 1st a letter from Arthur Hallam's uncle, Henry Elton, at Clifton, brought the sorrowful news to my father:

At the desire of a most afflicted family, I write to you because they are unequal from the grief into which they have fallen to do it themselves. Your friend, sir, and my much-loved nephew, Arthur Hallam, is no more. It has pleased God to remove him from this, his first scene of existence, to that better world for which he was created. He died at Vienna, on his return from Buda, by apoplexy, and I believe his remains come by sea from Trieste. Mr Hallam arrived this morning in 3 Princes Buildings. May that Being in whose hands are all the destinies of man, and who has promised to comfort all that mourn, pour the balm of consolation on all the families, who are bowed down by this unexpected dispensation! I have just seen Mr Hallam, who begs I will tell you that he will write himself as soon as his heart will let him. Poor Arthur had a slight attack of ague, which he had often had, ordered his fire to be lighted, and talked with as much cheerfulness as usual. He suddenly became insensible, and his spirit departed without pain. On examination it was the general opinion that he could not have lived long. This was also Dr Holland's opinion. The account I have endeavoured to give you is merely what I have been able to gather, but the family of course are in too great distress to enter into details.

(*Extract of letter from John M. Kemble to Fanny Kemble[1].*)

It is with feelings of inexpressible pain that I announce to you the death of poor Arthur Hallam, who expired suddenly from an attack of apoplexy at Vienna, on the 15th of last

[1] Given me by Miss Cobbe.

month.   Though this was always feared by us as likely to occur,
the shock has been a bitter one to bear : and most of all so to
the Tennysons, whose sister Emily he was to have married.   I
have not yet had the courage to write to Alfred.   This is a loss
which will most assuredly be felt by this age, for if ever man
was born for great things he was.   Never was a more powerful
intellect joined to a purer and holier heart; and the whole
illuminated with the richest imagination, with the most sparkling
yet the kindest wit.   One cannot lament for him that he is gone
to a far better life, but we weep over his coffin and wonder that
we cannot be consoled : the Roman epitaph on two young
children *Sibimet ipsis dolorem abstulerunt, suis reliquere* (from
themselves they took away pain, to their friends they left it !) is
alway present to my mind, and somehow the miserable feeling
of loneliness comes over one even though one knows that the
dead are happier than the living.   His poor father was with him
only ; they had been travelling together in Hungary and were
on their return to England ; but there had been nothing whatever to announce the fatal termination of their journey ; indeed
bating fatigue Arthur had been unusually well.

On December 30th Henry Hallam wrote to my
father as follows :

It may remove some anxiety from the minds of yourself and
others to know that the mortal part of our dearest Arthur will
be interred at Clevedon on Friday.   I leave town to-morrow.
My first thought was not to write to you till all was over : but
you may have been apprehensive for the safety of the vessel.   I
did not expect her arrival so soon.   Use your own discretion
about telling your sister.   Mrs H. is very anxious to hear about
her ; if not too painful to her, Miss Tennyson will have the
kindness to write.   Do your utmost, my dear young friend, to
support her and yourself.   Give as little way to grief as you
may.   But I feel that my own rather increases with time ; yet
I find also that both occupation and conversation are very
serviceable.   I fear the solitary life you both lead in the country
is sadly unpropitious.   We are now all well, though my boy [1] is
not as vigorous as he should be.   God bless you all.

Affectionately yours, H. H.

[1] Harry Hallam.

In the letters from Arthur Hallam's friends there was a rare unanimity of opinion about his worth. Milnes, writing to his father, says that he had a "very deep respect" for Hallam, and that Thirlwall, in after years the great Bishop, for whom Hallam and my father had a profound affection, was "actually captivated by him." When at Cambridge with Hallam he had written: "He is the only man here of my own standing before whom I bow in conscious inferiority in everything." Alford writes: "Hallam was a man of wonderful mind and knowledge on all subjects, hardly credible at his age.... I long ago set him down for the most wonderful person I ever knew. He was of the most tender, affectionate disposition."

So "those whose eyes must long be dim with tears," Henry Hallam says, "brought him home to rest among his kindred and in his own country": and the burial took place on Jan. 3rd, 1834, in the lonely church which overlooks the Bristol Channel.

On the evening of one of these sad[1] winter days my father had already noted down in his scrap-book some fragmentary lines, which proved to be the germ of " In Memoriam":

> Where is the voice I loved? ah where
> Is that dear hand that I would press?
> Lo! the broad heavens cold and bare,
> The stars that know not my distress!
>
> * * * * *
>
> The vapour labours up the sky,
> Uncertain forms are darkly moved!
> Larger than human passes by
> The shadow of the man I loved,
> And clasps his hands, as one that prays!

[1] Francis Garden had written to Trench, Nov. 26th, 1833: "When in London, I saw a letter from poor Alfred Tennyson. Both himself and his family seemed plunged in the deepest affliction."

Later, Henry Hallam writes to my father:

It is my intention to print, for private friends only, a few of those pieces which have already appeared, with some poems and perhaps prose papers that I have in my possession.   Several of those printed in 1830, and a certain number that are in manuscript, will be included.   It will be necessary to prefix a short memoir.   I must rely on his contemporaries and most intimate friends to furnish me with part of my materials; and I should wish to have anything that may be thought most worthy of being mentioned, communicated to me by letter.   Perhaps you would do something.   I should desire to have the character of his mind, his favourite studies and pursuits, his habits and views delineated.   I shall not apply to too many persons; but it has been suggested to me that Spedding will be better able to assist me than any one else.   I do not know whether this is the case, nor do I know Mr S.'s direction.   It is somewhere in Cumberland. I shall be most happy if you can give me a better account than the last we have had of your sister; we all unite in kindest love to all.

Most truly yours, HENRY HALLAM [1].

To this volume of collected poems and essays, published some time after, Henry Hallam prefixed an introduction, in which he said " Arthur seemed to tread the earth as a spirit from a better world."   Arthur's old Eton friend Gladstone wrote: " When much time has elapsed, when most bereavements will be forgotten, he will still be remembered, and his place, I fear, will be felt to be still vacant, singularly as his mind was calculated by its native tendencies to work powerfully and for good, in an age full of import to the nature and destinies of man."

In consequence of her sudden and terrible grief my aunt Emily was ill for many months, and very slowly recovered.   "We were waiting for her," writes one of her friends, " in the drawing-room the first day since her

[1] See Appendix, p. 498, for Letters about Arthur Hallam.

loss that she had been able to meet anyone, and she came at last, dressed in deep mourning, a shadow of her former self, but with one white rose in her black hair as her Arthur loved to see her."

"The Two Voices" or "Thoughts of a Suicide" was begun under the cloud of this overwhelming sorrow, which, as my father told me, for a while blotted out all joy from his life, and made him long for death, in spite of his feeling that he was in some measure a help and comfort to his sister. But such a first friendship and such a loss helped to reveal himself to himself, while he enshrined his sorrow in his song. Tennant writes: "Alfred although much broken in spirits is yet able to divert his thoughts from gloomy brooding, and keep his mind in activity."

In the earliest manuscript of "The Two Voices" a fine verse is found which was omitted in the published edition as too dismal (after "under earth").

> From when his baby pulses beat
> To when his hands in their last heat
> Pick at the death-mote in the sheet.

Then in the same manuscript-book come the first written sections of "In Memoriam," in the following order:

> Fair ship that from the Italian shore.
> > (*written on a stray sheet*)

> With trembling fingers did we weave.
> When Lazarus left his charnel-cave.
> This truth came borne with bier and pall.
> It draweth near the birth of Christ.

And between "With trembling fingers" and "When Lazarus left his charnel-cave" he has written the first draft of his "Morte d'Arthur."

UNPUBLISHED POEMS OF THIS PERIOD.

The Statesman.*

They wrought a work which Time reveres,
  A pure example to the lands,
  Further and further reaching hands
For ever into coming years;

They worshipt Freedom for her sake;
  We faint unless the wanton ear
  Be tickled with the loud " hear, hear,"
To which the slight-built hustings shake;

For where is he, the citizen,
  Deep-hearted, moderate, firm, who sees
  His path before him? not with these,
Shadows of statesmen, clever men!

Uncertain of ourselves we chase
  The clap of hands; we jar like boys:
  And in the hurry and the noise
Great spirits grow akin to base.

A sound of words that change to blows!
  A sound of blows on armed breasts!
  And individual interests
Becoming bands of armed foes!

A noise of hands that disarrange
  The social engine! fears that waste
  The strength of men, lest overhaste
Should fire the many wheels of change!

* Copyright, 1897, by The Macmillan Company.

Ill fares a people passion-wrought,
    A land of many days that cleaves
    In two great halves, when each one leaves
The middle road of sober thought!

Not he that breaks the dams, but he
    That thro' the channels of the state
    Convoys the people's wish, is great;
His name is pure, his fame is free:

He cares, if ancient usage fade,
    To shape, to settle, to repair,
·   With seasonable changes fair,
And innovation grade by grade:

Or, if the sense of most require
    A precedent of larger scope,
    Not deals in threats, but works with hope,
And lights at length on his desire:

Knowing those laws are just alone
    That contemplate a mighty plan,
    The frame, the mind, the soul of man,
Like one that cultivates his own

He, seeing far an end sublime,
    Contends, despising party-rage,
    To hold the Spirit of the Age
Against the Spirit of the Time.

1833.

Youth.*

I

Youth, lapsing thro' fair solitudes,
　　Pour'd by long glades and meadowy mounds,
Crown'd with soft shade her deepening floods
　　That wash'd her shores with blissful sounds:

Her silver eddies in their play
　　Drove into lines and studs of light
The image of the sun by day,
　　The image of the moon by night.

The months, ere they began to rise,
　　Sent thro' my blood a prophet voice
Before the first white butterflies,
　　And where the secret streams rejoice.

I heard Spring laugh in hidden rills,
　　Summer thro' all her sleepy leaves
Murmur'd: a voice ran round the hills
　　When corny Lammas bound the sheaves:

A voice, when night had crept on high,
　　To snowy crofts and winding scars,
Rang like a trumpet clear and dry,
　　And shook the frosty winter stars.

When I was somewhat older grown
　　These voices did not cease to cry,
Only they took a sweeter tone,
　　But did not sound so joyfully:

Lower and deeper evermore
　　They grew, and they began at last
To speak of what had gone before,
　　And how all things become the past.

Life, to this wind, turn'd all her vanes,
   Moan'd in her chimneys and her eaves;
I grieved as woods in dripping rains
   Sigh over all their fallen leaves;

Beside my door at morning stood
   The tearful spirit of the time;
He moan'd, " I wander from my good!"
   He chanted some old doleful rhyme.

So lived I without aim or choice,
   Still humming snatches of old song,
Till suddenly a sharper voice
   Cried in the future " Come along."

When to this sound my face I turn'd,
   Intent to follow on the track,
Again the low sweet voices mourn'd
   In distant fields, " Come back, come back."

Confused, and ceasing from my quest,
   I loiter'd in the middle way,
So pausing 'twixt the East and West,
   I found the Present where I stay.

Now idly in my natal bowers,
   Unvext by doubts I cannot solve,
I sit among the scentless flowers
   And see and hear the world revolve:

Yet well I know that nothing stays,
   And I must traverse yonder plain:
Sooner or later from the haze
   The second voice will peal again.

II

A rumour of a mystery,
    A noise of winds that meet and blend,
An energy, an agony,
    A labour working to an end.

Now shall I rest or shall I rise?
    It is the early morning, Hark!
A voice like many voices cries,
    Comes hither throbbing thro' the dark;

Now one faint line of light doth glow,
    I follow to the morning sun,
Behind yon hill the trumpets blow,
    And there is something greatly done:

The voice cries "Come." Upon the brink
    A solitary fortress burns,
And shadows strike and shadows sink,
    And Heaven is dark and bright by turns.

"Come" and I come, the wind is strong:
    Hush! there floats upward from the gulf
A murmur of heroic song,
    A howling of the mountain wolf;

A tempest strikes the craggy walls,
    Faint shouts are heard across the glen,
A moan of many waterfalls,
    And in the pauses groans of men.

"Come" and I come, no more I sleep:
    The thunder cannot make thee dumb;
"Come" and I come, the vale is deep,
    My heart is dark, but yet I come.

Up hither have I found my way,
  The latest thunder-peal hath peal'd,
Down from the summit sweeps the day
  And rushes o'er a boundless field.

Out bursts a rainbow in the sky —
  Away with shadows! On they move!
Beneath those double arches lie
  Fair with green fields the realms of Love.

The whole land glitters after rain,
  Thro' wooded isles the river shines,
The casements sparkle on the plain,
  The towers gleam among the vines;

" Come " and I come, and all comes back
  Which in that early voice was sweet,
Yet am I dizzy in the track,
  A light wind wafts me from my feet.

Warm beats my blood, my spirit thirsts;
  Fast by me flash the cloudy streaks,
And from the golden vapour bursts
  A mountain bright with triple peaks:

With all his groves he bows, he nods,
  The clouds unswathe them from the height,
And there sit figures as of Gods
  Ray'd round with beams of living light.

8—2

CHAPTER V.*

THE 1832 VOLUME (DATED 1833).

SOLITUDE AND WORK (1833–1835).

Mighty the voices of earth, which are dull'd by the voices that say:
"All of us drift into darkness, wherein we shall all pass away!"
Better to pass then at once than seeing the darkness to stay,
But for a mightier Voice which was born of the Dawn of the Day.

It becomes no man to nurse despair,
But in the teeth of clench'd antagonisms
To follow up the worthiest.

Before following further the thread of the life, I must set down here certain notes upon the 1832 volume by my father and by Edward Fitzgerald, omitted from the last chapter, in order not to interrupt the sequence of Arthur Hallam's letters.

Fitzgerald writes on "The Lady of Shalott":

Well I remember this poem, read to me, before I knew the author, at Cambridge one night in 1832 or 3, and its images passing across my head, as across the magic mirror, while half asleep on the mail coach to London "in the creeping dawn" that followed.[1]

The key to this tale of magic "symbolism" is of deep human significance, and is to be found in the lines:

[1] MS Note, E. F. G.

> Or when the moon was overhead,
> Came two young lovers lately wed;
> "I am half sick of shadows," said
> The Lady of Shalott.

Canon Ainger in his *Tennyson for the Young* quotes the following interpretation, given him by my father:

The new-born love for something, for some one in the wide world from which she has been so long secluded, takes her out of the region of shadows into that of realities.

The idea of "Mariana in the South" came to my father as he was travelling between Narbonne and Perpignan[1], and foreign critics have found out and have appreciated this representation of southern France.

The first original manuscript verse of "The Miller's Daughter," which he altered both before and after publication, seemed to Fitzgerald too good to be lost:

> I met in all the close green ways,
> While walking with my rod and line,
> The miller with his mealy face,
> And long'd to take his hand in mine.
> He look'd so jolly and so good —
> While fishing in the milldam-water,
> I laugh'd to see him as he stood,
> And dreamt not of the miller's daughter.

"This poem," Fitzgerald writes, "as may be seen, is much altered and enlarged from the first edition of 1832; in some respects, I think, not for the better; losing somewhat of the easy character of 'talk across the walnuts and the wine.'" It shows the poet's especial love of setting his human beings in a landscape which is strictly in harmony with the subject of the poem. "The mill was no particular mill," my father writes; "if

[1] See letter from Arthur Hallam on "Mariana in the South" in Appendix, p. 500.

I thought at all of any mill it was that of Trumpington near Cambridge."

From the volume of 1832 he omitted several stanzas of "The Palace of Art" because he thought that the poem was too full. "The artist is known by his self-limitation" was a favourite adage of his. He allowed me however to print some of them in my notes, otherwise I should have hesitated to quote without his leave lines that he had excised. He "gave the people of his best," and he usually wished that his best should remain without variorum readings, "the chips of the workshop," as he called them. The love of bibliomaniacs for first editions filled him with horror, for the first editions are obviously in many cases the worst editions; and once he said to me:

> "Why do they treasure the rubbish I shot from
>   my full-finish'd cantos?
>
> νήπιοι οὐδὲ ἴσασιν ὅσῳ πλέον ἥμισυ παντός."

For himself many passages in Wordsworth and other poets had been entirely spoilt by the modern habit of giving every various reading along with the text. Besides, in his case, very often what is published as the latest edition has been the original version in his first manuscript, so that there is no possibility of really tracing the history of what may seem to be a new word or a new passage. "For instance," he said, "in 'Maud' a line in the first edition was 'I will bury myself in *my books*, and the Devil may pipe to his own,' which was afterwards altered to 'I will bury myself *in myself*, etc.': this was highly commended by the critics as an improvement on the *original* reading—but it was actually in the first MS draft of the poem."

In 1890 he wrote the following notes: "Trench said to me, when we were at Trinity together, 'Tennyson, we cannot live in art.'" "'The Palace of Art' is the embodiment of my own belief that the Godlike life is with man and for man, that

Beauty, Good and Knowledge are three sisters...
That never can be sunder'd without tears.
And he that shuts out Love, in turn shall be
Shut out from Love, and on her threshold lie,
Howling in outer darkness."

"When I first conceived the plan of the poem, I intended to have introduced both sculptures and paintings into it, but I only finished two sculptures.

One was the Tishbite whom the raven fed,
    As when he stood on Carmel-steeps
With one arm stretch'd out bare, and mock'd and said,
    'Come, cry aloud, he sleeps.'

Tall, eager, lean and strong, his cloak wind-borne
    Behind, his forehead heavenly bright
From the clear marble pouring glorious scorn,
    Lit as with inner light.

One was Olympias; the floating snake
    Roll'd round her ankles, round her waist
Knotted, and folded once about her neck,
    Her perfect lips to taste,

Down from the shoulder moved: she seeming blithe
    Declined her head: on every side
The dragon's curves melted, and mingled with
    The woman's youthful pride
Of rounded limbs —

After the old verse xxvi was

'From shape to shape at first within the womb
    The brain is moulded,' she began,
'And thro' all phases of all thought I come
    Unto the perfect man.

All nature widens upward. Evermore
  The simpler essence lower lies,
More complex is more perfect, owning more
  Discourse, more widely wise.'

In the centre of the four quadrangles of the palace
is a tower.

Hither, when all the deep unsounded skies
  Shudder'd with silent stars, she clomb,
And as with optic glasses her keen eyes
  Pierced thro' the mystic dome,

Regions of lucid matter taking forms,
  Brushes of fire, hazy gleams,
Clusters and beds of worlds, and bee-like swarms
  Of suns, and starry streams.

She saw the snowy poles and Moons of Mars,
  That mystic field of drifted light
In mid Orion, and the married stars.

The 'Moons of Mars' is the only modern reading
here, all the rest are more than half a century old."

After perusing the "marvellously compressed word-
pictures of this poem," Fitzgerald appends a personal
note to "sat smiling babe in arm."

I remember A. T.[1] admiring the abstracted look of a Murillo
Madonna at Dulwich ; the eyes of which are on you, but seem
"looking at something beyond, beyond the Actual into Abstraction."   This has been noticed of some great men ; it is the trance
of the Seer : I do not remember seeing it in A. T. himself ;
great as he was from top to toe, and his eyes dark, powerful
and serene [2].

He was still afraid of blindness, which his brother Frederick
said might accompany the perception of the inward Sublime as
in Homer and Milton.   The names of Dante and Michael Angelo

[1] Fitzgerald generally calls my father A. T.

[2] Fitzgerald afterwards altered his mind and wrote : "I have seen it in
his (A. T.'s).   Some American spoke of the same in Wordsworth.   I suppose
it may be the same with all *poets*."

in (the original form of) this poem remind me that once looking
with A. T. at two busts of Dante and Goethe in a shop window
in Regent Street, I said, "What is there wanting in Goethe
which the other has?" "The Divine[1]!"

After visiting Italy some twenty years after this poem was
written, he told me he had been prepared for Raffaelle but not for
Michael Angelo: whose picture at Florence of a Madonna dragging a "ton of a child" over one shoulder almost revolted him at
first, but drew him toward itself afterwards, and "would not out
of memory." I forget if he saw the Dresden Raffaelle[2], but he
would speak of the *Child* in it as "perhaps finer than the whole
composition, in so far as one's eyes are more concentrated on the
subject. The child seems to me the furthest reach of human
art. His attitude is a man's: his countenance a Jupiter's —
perhaps too much so." But when A. T. had a babe of his own,
he saw it was not "too much so." "I am afraid of him: babies
have an expression of grandeur which children lose, a look of
awe and wonder. I used to think the old painters overdid the
expression and dignity of their infant Christs, but I see they
didn't. This morning * * * lay half-an-hour worshipping the
bed-post on which the sunlight flickered (pure nature worship)[3].
'If,' as old Hallam said, 'one could have the history of a babe's
mind!'"

The "Dream of Fair Women" began in the first
edition of 1832 with some stanzas about a man sailing
in a balloon, but my father did not like the "balloon
stanzas" so they were cut out. As Edward Fitzgerald
said to him, "They make a perfect poem by themselves
without affecting the 'dream.'"

As when a man that sails in a balloon,
    Down-looking sees the solid shining ground
Stream from beneath him in the broad blue noon,
    Tilth, hamlet, mead and mound:

[1] To me, he said, "The Divine *intensity*," and possibly the same to
Fitzgerald. H. T.
[2] He went to Dresden on purpose to see this great picture.
[3] "Afterwards he took to fetish-worship — the worship of a gilded doll sent
him by Lear." A. T.

And takes his flags and waves them to the mob,
  That shout below, all faces turn'd to where
Glows rubylike the far-up crimson globe,
  Fill'd with a finer air:

So, lifted high, the poet at his will
  Lets the great world flit from him, seeing all,
Higher thro' secret splendours mounting still,
  Self-poised, nor fears to fall,

Hearing apart the echoes of his fame.
  While I spoke thus, the seedsman, Memory,
Sow'd my deep-furrow'd thought with many a name
  Whose glory will not die.

From the letters of that time I gather that there was
a strong current of depreciation of my father in certain
literary quarters. However he kept up his courage,
profited by friendly and unfriendly criticism, and in silence, obscurity, and solitude, perfected his art. " First
the workman is known for his work, afterwards the
work for the workman ": but it is " only the concise
and perfect work," he thought, " which will last[1]. "
That the volume of 1832 was partially successful
(three hundred copies having been sold) is obvious from
the fact that Moxon was eager to publish more by him.
Later an appreciative article by John Stuart Mill in the
London Review (July 1835) was a great encouragement.
Friendly critics, like G. S. Venables, wrote that his poems
had too much concentrated power and thought, were
too imaginative and too largely imbued with the " innermost magic," easily to excite popular interest, or to be
read at once by those whom he specially wished to
influence. Kemble had said, " In Alfred's mind the
materials of the greatest works are heaped in an abundance which is almost confusion." Notwithstanding all

[1] A. T.

hostile criticism, he had impressed himself deeply on a
limited number of minds.   He now began to base his
poetry more on the " broad and common interests of the
time and of universal humanity," although no doubt it
was harder to idealize such themes than those that
appealed mostly to the imagination.   The great Catholic
painters could express what was at the same time ideal
and real in the minds of the people : but the modern
artist has hardly ever found similar objects of high
imagination and intense popular feeling for his art to
work upon.   If, wrote Venables, in a contemporary
letter to my father, an artist could only now find out
where these objects are, he would be *the* artist of
modern times.   Venables affirmed they were not to be
sought in any transient fashions of thought, but in the
" convergent tendencies of many opinions" on religion,
art and nature, — of which tendencies he and others
believed, he said, that my father, with his commanding
intellect, and conspicuous moral courage, ought to be the
artistic exponent and unifier.   My father pondered all
that had been said and — after a period of utter prostra-
tion from grief, and many dark fits of blank despondency
— his passionate love of truth, of nature, and of humanity, drove him to work again, with a deeper and a fuller
insight into the requirements of the age.

His resolve
Upbore him and firm faith —
And beating up thro' all the bitter world,
Like fountains of sweet water in the sea,
Kept him a living soul[1].

Two pathetic lines of his written at this time are left :

O leave not thou thy son forlorn ;
Teach me, great Nature : make me live.

" Perpetual idleness," he would say, " must be one of

[1] "Enoch Arden."

the punishments of Hell." Hundreds of lines were, as he expressed it, " blown up the chimney with his pipe-smoke, or were written down and thrown into the fire, as not being then perfect enough." " The Brook " in later years was actually rescued from the waste-paper heap.

He lived for the most part at Somersby, and I give a list of his week's work; which he drew up.

Monday.	History, German.
Tuesday.	Chemistry, German.
Wednesday.	Botany, German.
Thursday.	Electricity, German.
Friday.	Animal Physiology, German.
Saturday.	Mechanics.
Sunday.	Theology.
Next Week.	Italian in the afternoon.
Third Week.	Greek. *Evenings.* Poetry.

UNPUBLISHED POEM OF THIS PERIOD.

The Mother's Ghost.

Not a whisper stirs the gloom,
    It will be the dawning soon,
We may glide from room to room,
    In the glimmer of the moon :
Every heart is lain to rest,
    All the house is fast in sleep,
Were I not a spirit blest,
    Sisters, I could almost weep !

In that cradle sleeps my child,
    She whose birth brought on my bliss:
On her forehead undefiled
    I will print an airy kiss:

See, she dreameth happy dreams,
Her hands are folded quietly,
Like to one of us she seems,
One of us my child will be.

Now and then, when he could save up a little hoard, he went to London or to visit his friends in their homes. From the occasional letters to and from them (1832–35) we can see something of what his life was and the impression which his work was then making.

Brookfield writes from Sheffield:

You and Rob Montgomery are our only brewers now! À propos to the latter, Jingling James, his namesake, dined with us last week. And now for a smack of Boswell. *Brookfield*. Glass of wine after your fish? *Montgomery*. Thank you, sir! *B*. Which vegetable, sir? *M*. A potato, if you please! *B*. Another, sir! *M*. That will do, I thank you. *B*. Talking of potatoes, sir, have you read Alfred Tennyson? *M*. Only in the reviews yet, but there are two brothers, aren't there? *B*. Both "rather pretty," but Alfred alone has been extracted at any length in the reviews. *M*. He has very wealthy and luxurious thought and great beauty of expression, and is *a poet*. But there is plenty of room for improvement, and I would have it so. Your trim correct *young* writers seldom turn out well. A young poet should have a great deal which he can afford to throw away as he gets older. Tennyson *can* afford this. But I can say little of one of whom I have seen so little.

I sent him copies of both you and Charles yesterday, and met him in the street this morning. He said he was going out of town, but we would talk about you when he came back and read you. "I read," said he, "twelve of the sonnets last night, which if I had not liked them better than other sonnets I could not have done. There are great outbreaks of poetry in them." Omitting my own interjectional queries, etc., which leave to Jemmy's remarks an over-pompous connectedness which they had not *vivâ voce*, I give you his words as nearly as I remember. They are not important, but we generally wish to know what

is said of us, whether trivial or not. At autopsychography I am
not good, if I had any idiopsychology to autopsychographize. I
am just about as happy as a fish, neither excited by mirth, nor
depressed by sadness. The Clerk's[1] letter awoke me rather this
morning; if he be yet with you tell him it had been good service
to have done so two months earlier. Writing from Somersby
where there is so much to prevent one from thinking of any
place else was certainly a meritorious exertion, and it has brought
my pardon. My love to the wretch, and let him know he shall
expiate his neglect by silence on my part, until I know whether
his address be your house. Which information do thou give
me in a day or two; and tell me all about Frederick and
Charles. From the former I never could worm a letter yet, but
unless you can coax so much of him without, I shall perhaps
make one more effort shortly. My kindest regards to all your
family.

Ever, dearest Alfred, yours,

W. H. BROOKFIELD.

P.S. I wish very much you would make a sonnet for me as
Hallam once did. I could not value it more, and should not
less, than his. It may be that I could not make a more boring
request. But I will incur nine chances of vexing you and
thereby myself for the sake of the tenth of getting what I want.

At this time Tennant shot an arrow: "May your
success in rhyming vary inversely as the number of
letters you write!" and Spedding sent to Somersby his
Union speech on Liberty, which had gained renown in
the University. The poem "You ask me, why, tho' ill at
ease" was not, as is often stated, "an edition of this
speech versified." My father said to me that he and
Spedding freely interchanged their political views, and
that therefore it was not unlikely that there should be a
similarity of thought and language. He did not think

---

[1] Charles Turner.

that he had ever read the speech when he wrote the poem.

He wrote to Spedding, begging him to "commend" a book shortly to be published by an old Louth tutor of his, Mr Dale:

SOMERSBY,
February 9th (1833[1]?).

MY DEAR JAMES,

I seize upon a halfsheet, the blank half of a printed prospectus of a translation of the "Osman Sultan's campaigns in Western Asia, from Bayezyd Ildirim to the death of Murad the Fourth (1389–1640), from the German of Joseph Von Hammer, by Thomas Aquila Dale[2]," indeed mine ancient tutor and paidagogue in times of yore. Which work commend everywhere, for, I think, he is likely to do it well, and the book will contain a map of the countries from Sinope to Tiflis, and from Odana to Bagdad. Which map will be three feet and a half by two and a half, and you will grant that our literature is marvellously deficient in works of Oriental History. And as I said before the man is mine ancient and trusty paidagogue, and moreover a good man, and one that is publishing at a loss, and one that has *not* two cloaks, wherefore it is reasonable that you should commend his book. For your letter I thank you heartily: my thanks have lost half their natural vigour and beauty; however you must recollect that half your epistle was to someone else, indeed you confessed as much in your P. S. Are we not quits then, or in the language of Mrs Jennings, "Does not one shoulder of mutton drive out another?" You should not have written to me without telling me somewhat that was interesting to myself

---

[1] The letters of this time are often undated.
[2] Published by William Straker, West Strand, 1835.

(always the first consideration!) or that bore some reference to you and yours (always the second!), or lastly, without giving me some news of the great world, for know you not I live so far apart from the bustle of life that news becomes interesting to me? I assure you that we have a spare bed and the bed is not so spare either, but a bed both plump and pulpy, and fit for "your domeship[1]," whenever you can come and see us. I express myself very clumsily, but being overawed by the memory of your calm personal dignity and dome, and melted likewise with the recollection of the many intellectual evenings we have spent together in olden days, while we sat smoking (for you know, James, you were ever fond of a pipe), — Speak for me, aposiopesis, or rather do not, for thou art an unhappy figure and born dumb and of no earthly use but to cut the throat of a clause! ———

Write to me now and then, lest I perish. Where is Tennant? I have not yet answered him: how shall I direct to him? You inquire after Charles. We see little of him: I believe his spirits are pretty good. Is Brooks at Cambridge? To him I owe a letter, and I mean to pay my debt.

Ever thine, A. T.

From Hon. Stephen Spring Rice.

CAMBRIDGE, *November 27th*, 1833.

DEAR ALFRED,

When I received your note some days back I was at first inclined to think it a pity that so much good abuse should be thrown away. Such a happy facility of assertion combined with such apparent sincerity in the expression deserved a better

---

[1] "Domeship" refers to Spedding's head.

fate than being uselessly employed on one so steeled to abuse as myself. O king! I hope that you will be sufficiently occupied till the 28th with the "Morte d'Arthur." I send Keightley's *Fairy Legends* and the other books, which it shall be my care to despatch to you to-morrow; Kemble (Anglo-Saxon *Lecturer* to the University) sends you to fill up your leisure hours a folio Saxo-Grammaticus.......to be jammed into the bowl of your pipe. Matters are going on here much as usual. I have just written by Peacock's desire to Blakesley to tell him to come here and be a lecturer, a summons which there is no doubt he will obey. Sterling is here still, and is to be at the yearly dinner [1] which takes place among "mankind," and which will come to pass on Monday next. Spedding, Alford, Donne, the two Farishes and Pickering are expected; so much for eating. I have read *Wilhelm Meister* for the first time, with which I find as many faults and beauties as every one does. What think you of that γλυκύπικρον performance? there is another question to burthen your soul with unanswered. If your health is proposed I shall oppose it on the ground of your having been an unworthy member of the Society!! I hope that you will not be able to decipher this scrawl, and so write to ask what it is about. I shall send the books to-morrow; you ought to know when to send for them.

Thine ever,

S. E. SPRING RICE.

From J. M. Kemble.

CAMBRIDGE, *November*, 1833.

DEAREST ALFRED,

I write you a line or two by this parcel to tell you what I know is no news to you, that I love you heartily and wish you were with us. There is little stirring here save that we all look with interest for news from you; I wish you could come and dine with the Apostles on Monday next: I am not sure

---

[1] The "Apostles'" dinner.

that Donne and Trench will not be with us. We are all pretty well, etc., looking out for more sprigs of the garden (or the gardener's daughter, for I suppose she was not so imperfect a woman as not to be mother as well as maid and married)? Is there no gardener's granddaughter? "Simeon Stylites" is said by the prophane, that is the mathematicians Spring Rice and Heath, to be not "the watcher on the pillar to the end," but to the nth; and I think this is an improvement; the more so as it shows your universality off, and marks that you have a touch of mathematics in you: O Alfred! could you only have made the height of the pillar a geometrical progression! Give my affectionate remembrances to Charles and Fred. Write to me, or what is better yet, come to me.

Ever your most affectionate friend,

J. M. KEMBLE.

To J. M. Kemble.

1833.

MY DEAR JOHN,

I hope this will find you at Cambridge. J. Heath wrote to me that the books should have been returned by the 21st and I received his note on the 21st. I know not what the fine is, and as to applying for any information even on Cambridge subjects to Cambridge men I hold it vanity. They are so smoke-sotted. Shamefully careless was it to have let these books lie for three weeks in Spring Rice's room. Shameful not to have sent the second volume of Keightley, and hateful the purloining of my album, which I *will* have found. If the thief be not Douglas himself, it is that luxurious, eye-glass-wearing, unconscienced fellow S. Rice, whom — fill up the chasm as you choose: if the book be returned, let it be with a blessing. Seriously speaking I am disgusted. I am heartily glad

you have got *Beowulf* out.   Some thoughts, vague ones,
I have, of coming up to Cambridge and attending your
lectures next term, always provided they be gratis.   Good
bye, dear old Jack.

Thine ever,

A. TENNYSON.

Be so good as to send me the " Morte d'Arthur "
again.

P.S.   Perhaps you would use your paternal authority
with the undergraduate whom you may suspect of being
the thief.   Douglas himself ought not to pass unreproved.
What a careless set you are!

From R. M. Milnes.

After an "Apostles' " dinner.

CAMBRIDGE, (*not dated*).

To ALFRED,
        I feel I am getting cross, and as I wish to express in
simple sincerity my hope that you will not long defer your
promist visit to me, as soon as I return to Yorkshire, which will
be in about a fortnight, I shall rock myself on the belief that
you will bring or send me something comfortable.

Yours affectionately,

RICHARD M. MILNES.

P.S.   I suppose nobody writes to you because you never
write to nobody.   John Heath and many others were full to the
brim of enquiries after you, and if you had heard the cheer that
followed the health of A. T., the Poet of the Apostles, at our
dinner, if you had !

9—2

Milnes wrote to him later about his *Memorials of a tour in Greece* which he was about to publish, and received the following answer:

December 3rd, 1833.

MY DEAR MILNES,

A letter from you was like a message from the land of shadows. It is so long since I have looked upon and conversed with you, that I will not deny but that you had withdrawn a little into the twilight. Yet you do me a wrong in supposing that I have forgotten you. I shall not easily forget you, for you have that about you which one remembers with pleasure. I am rejoiced to hear that you intend to present us with your Grecian impressions. Your gay and airy mind must have caught as many colours from the landskip you moved through as a flying soap-bubble — a comparison truly somewhat irreverent, yet I meant it not as such; though I care not if you take it in an evil sense, for is it not owed to you for your three years' silence to me whom you professed to love and care for? And in the second place, for your expression, "clearing one's mind of Greek thoughts and Greek feelings to make way for something better." It is a sad thing to have a dirty mind full of Greek thoughts and feelings. What an Augean it must have been before the Greek thoughts got there! To be done with this idle banter, I hope that in your book you have given us much glowing description and little mysticism. I know that you can describe richly and vividly. Give orders to Moxon, and he will take care that the volume is conveyed to me.

Believe me, dear Richard,

Ever thine, A. T.

Spedding writes to Thompson (1834) about William Wordsworth and Alfred Tennyson:

Wordsworth's eyes are better, but not well, nor ever likely to be. Reading inflames them and so does composing. I believe it was a series of Highland sonnets that brought on the last attack, so much worse than he had before. He read me several, that I had not seen nor heard before, many of them admirably good: also a long, romantic wizard and fairy poem, of the time of Merlin and king Arthur, very pretty but not of the first order[1]: but I should not have expected anything so good from him which was so much out of his beat. He has not advanced much in his knowledge of Alfred; but he is very modest in his refusal to praise, attributing his want of admiration to a deficiency in himself, whether from the stiffness of old age which cannot accommodate itself to a new style of beauty, or that the compass of his sympathies has been narrowed by flowing too long and strongly in one direction (N.B. He is not answerable for the English that I am writing). But he doubts not that Alfred's style has its own beauty, though he wants the faculty to enter fully into it, alleging as a parallel case the choruses in "Samson Agonistes," the measure of which he has never been able to enjoy, which comes to perhaps as high a compliment as a negative compliment can. He spoke so wisely and graciously that I had half a mind to try him with a poem or two, but that would have been more perhaps than he meant: and indeed it is always so pleasant to hear a distinguished man unaffectedly disclaiming the office of censor, that I think it fair to take him at his word. I have given a copy of Alfred's second volume to Hartley Coleridge, who, I trust, will make more of it. He had only seen it for a few minutes, and was greatly behind the age, though he admitted that A. T. was undoubtedly a man of genius, and was going to say something sharp about the *Quarterly* in a review of "The Doctor," which he was or is writing for *Blackwood*. I also sent him yesterday a copy of Charles Tennyson, accompanied with one of my most gentlemanly letters.

In June 1834 there was great distress at Somersby among the Tennysons, because the landlord threatened

---

[1] "The Egyptian Maid, or, The Romance of the Water Lily."

to cut down Enderby Wood and the Fairy Wood in Holywell, where, under the trees, the finest and earliest snowdrops blow. A hope was uttered that the fairies might haunt the desecrators. The Fairy Wood was left unscathed; and my father completed his poem, the "Sleeping Beauty"; and warmed to his work because there had been a favourable review of him lately published in far-off Calcutta.

In July he visited his friend Heath at Kitlands near Dorking, and thence journeyed with him to Worthing. When they arrived at the little seaside town on a beautiful still night, the sea was calm and golden, and there was a Cuyp-like picture of boys bathing in the glowing sunset, and of gray fishing-boats moored out in the distance. Heath tried to persuade my father to go to Brighton, for he said "The town is worth going to see, and moreover the coast is very fine, an infinitely finer place than Worthing." But my father refused, and in-sisted on returning to his work. He took Kitlands again by the way and had "lonely walks in dark valleys," and by the side of the streams which rise in Leith Hill. In his note-book on one page there is a map of Kitlands and of the surrounding country: on another there is an unpublished fragment on mine host of an ancient hostelry!

Mine Host. (*Unpublished.*)

Yon huddled cloud his motion shifts,
　　Where, by the tavern in the dale,
The thirsty horseman, nodding, lifts
　　The creaming horn of corny ale!

This tavern is their chief resort,
　　For he, whose cellar is his pride,
Gives stouter ale and riper port
　　Than any in the country-side.

Mine host is fat, and gray, and wise,
  He strokes his beard before he speaks;
And when he laughs, his little eyes
  Are swallow'd in his pamper'd cheeks.

He brims his beaker to the top,
  With jokes you never heard before,
And sometimes with a twinkling drop,
  " To those who will not taste it more!"

The following letter reached him at Kitlands from his sister Emily:

Somersby Rectory, July 12th, 1834.

My dearest Alfred,

    I certainly intend to go to Moulsey[1]. Would to God I could begin the journey immediately but it is not in my power. You will be sorry to hear that I have been considerably worse in health since your departure......And once or twice indeed I thought that the chilly hand of death was upon me : however I still exist, tho' reduced again to a great state of weakness. If possible I will journey southward soon. You know, Alfred, the great desire I have to become acquainted with the Hallam family, particularly with Ellen ; she will perhaps be the friend to remove in some degree the horrible feeling of desolation which is ever at my heart. I can no longer continue in this deepening grave of tears...depend upon it I will do all in my power to go to Moulsey. What is life to me! if I die (which the Tennysons never do) the effort shall be made. The deep unaffected kindness of the Hallams made us all weep...How long do you think of remaining at Kitlands? It would be pleasant to come while you are there. This however will scarcely be the case considering my journey will commence in about three weeks' time, if by any means I can conjure up resolution....Remember us all to "our Mr Heath " and his brother, and cannot you intimate to the sister how sorry we were not to have been able to avail ourselves, that is Mary and myself, of her kind invitation ? Take

---

[1] The Hallams' house at the time.

care of thyself that thou mayest return with new health and spirits is the ardent wish of

Thy very affectionate sister, EMILY TENNYSON.

His mother wrote him a letter at the same time:

What kind hearts the Hallams have! I hope poor Emily will be able to go to Moulsey. The pony got out of the stables and she went with one of the servants to catch it (as Harrison had gone to Horncastle), which made her very ill for some hours, but she is now as well as usual. I wish I could have induced her to begin her journey immediately, but she fancies she has something still to do before she can set out. The great lassitude she feels makes her fear she is unequal for such an exertion. I should have liked her so much to be introduced to the Hallams by you; she also considers this as very desirable. Charles is busy at present with his flock whom he is catechising, but I hope he will be able to travel with her in three weeks' time. I have found the books which Mr Heath mentions. Shall I send them by Mr Spedding? I have not heard whether or no he is at Tealby. I hope we shall see him.........Should you hear of anything likely to suit Arthur let me know. Remember me to all your friends.

His sister Mary adds a line entreating him

to lend an attentive ear to any music that may be sung, whether by way of chants, hymns, or songs, and to ascertain if Miss Heath will give the name of one or two that most affect his musical organs.

She goes on:

We were rather surprised to hear that the quaint creature Fred has set off to quaff companionless a " beaker full of the warm South," but I suppose a hot sun, south wind and cloudless sky (which constitute a humming day) and all of which are my aversion are all the world to him. And now I must bid thee adieu, hoping to see thee return as blithe as blithe can be. Remember me kindly to all at Kitlands.

When my father returned to Somersby, he had not only Emily to comfort, but also his friend Tennant, who consulted him about a great sorrow which had befallen him and craved for sympathy.

From R. J. Tennant (after a visit to Somersby).

LONDON UNIVERSITY, *August 4th,* 1834.

MY DEAR ALFRED,

I cannot delay writing to you, and cannot express my earnest gratitude for your friendship....The sight of Somersby, and *your* kindness have overcome the hard-hearted stubbornness that shut up all my feelings. Forgotten friendships have been revived, and correspondences been renewed that had long since dropped, and home feelings aroused that had slept a long sleep. ...Your very kind letter serves me every day instead of a companion ; the only way in which it is in my power to show gratitude for the repeated and continued kindness I receive from you, is by following your counsel as far as I am able, and keeping my own mind in peace.

*   *   *   *   *   *

Ever your affectionate R. J. TENNANT.

What strikes me much in this early life of my father is not only his wide power of sympathy, but also his practical good sense, shown especially in the management of home and of family. For example, now that he knew Tennant wanted an interest in life, and was a good scholar, and that his brother Horatio never looked at a book (his time at Louth School being over), it occurred to him that Horatio might be placed at Blackheath under the care of Tennant, then a master in Blackheath School. The proposition was put before Tennant, with a plain statement, that, although Horatio had more than average power, he had grown rusty and his acquirements were less than they ought to be at his age.

If he went from the lonely haunts of Somersby to
Blackheath, it was hoped that it might be " of advantage
to him, for he would see men and he never seemed to
care much about boys; but his observations upon the
men he had seen had been very just and penetrating."
So off to Blackheath by my father's decision Horatio
accordingly went.

The elder brother Frederick was just then in the
midst of music at Milan. He wrote a few lines urging
my father to publish in the spring. But he would not and
could not; his health since Hallam's death had been
"variable, and his spirits indifferent." The chief change
my father had from the monotony of Somersby life was
to drive over to Charles at Tealby, "for Lincolnshire,
a beautiful village." Their grandfather George Tennyson,
who was beginning to show signs of his approaching end,
had left the Tennyson estate of Bayons Manor and
migrated to a small house on a sandy moor, because
his son Charles Tennyson d'Eyncourt pressed to be installed in the squiredom. "One would have supposed that
such a thing," said Frederick, "would have been sufficient
to shake the last sands out of his glass." However he
lived on his moor comfortably and peaceably: and there
died in 1835.

As for his private occupations, my father was
still reading his Racine, Molière, and Victor Hugo
among other foreign literature; and had also dipped into
Maurice's work *Eustace Conway*, which appears to have
been in great disfavour, and into *Arthur Coningsby* by
John Sterling, "a dreary book"; " 'Tis a pretty piece of
work, would 'twere done!" wrote one of the friends. In
October 1834, he told Tennant he was busy copying out
his " Morte d'Arthur "; then he posted Spedding some
of the new poems for his opinion and Spedding replied as
follows:

MIRE HOUSE, KESWICK, *September* 19*th*, 1834.

MY DEAR ALFRED,

Such as it is, this letter will I expect come to you in an independent character, by the good aid of Philip van Artevelde (Henry Taylor), to whom I have a decent excuse for writing. I received by Douglas and John Heath divers of your compositions, albeit too few for my appetite: to wit, " Sir Galahad," which enjoys my unlimited admiration. The virgin knight is as beautiful a spirit as Don Quixote in a more beautiful kind, if that could be. Also " Nature, so far as in her lies," one of those pieces which nobody except yourself can write, and I think the most exquisite of an exquisite race. Of the rest I cannot find words to express what and how great is the glory. I have also the alterations of " Oh that 'twere possible," improvements I must admit, tho' I own I did not think that could have been: "Along this glimmering corridor" I had seen before, tho' not as it stands now : and

> Fair is her cottage in its place,
>   Where yon broad water sweetly, slowly glides.
> It *sees itself* from thatch to base
>   *Dream* in the sliding tides — [1]

It is perfectly true; how on earth did you find it out? Last and greatest (tho' not most perfect in its kind) I have received "The Thoughts of a Suicide [2]"; the design is so grand, and the moral, if there is one, so important that I trust you will not spare any elaboration of execution. At all events let me have the rest of it and I will tell you at large what I think ; also as many more as you can supply; remembering that double letters or parcels will not distress my circumstances. Since I saw you, I have been cultivating my body to the entire exclusion of my soul, which some say is the better part. I have rolled great stones down mountains, but stirred no hidden principle of thought or deed. I have not done anything good; nor said any good thing. I have written no prose and small verse. Perhaps I was too ambitious, for I endeavoured at nothing lower than Milton's high-learned manner. I sent the small effort to

---

[1] " Requiescat."   [2] " The Two Voices."

Tennant, but that is no reason I should not send it to you, who will laugh at it less and understand it more. After all it is but a fragment of a simile!

> Liker that far significant coach that bears
> The windy artist from his central tower
> Whither the stars come clustering to suggest
> The universal secret, she far off
> Swims on Macadam, etc. etc.

The "far significant coach" is the Cambridge Telegraph, exquisitely described by its property of conveying Professor Airy from the Observatory.

I have not forgotten my promise to write to Charles, but alas how many things are sincerely promised which are nevertheless not faithfully performed.

Ever thine, JAMES SPEDDING.

To James Spedding.

1834.

MY DEAR JAMES,

It may be you have waited some time for a reply, but you haven't waited, so say no more. I have been out or you should have heard from me before this, so, I pray you, make not any little lapse of time that may possibly have slided away into the unrecoverable between the writing of your letter and the receipt of mine precedent for further delay in answering this, for your letters do my moral and intellectual man much good. I am going to town with Emily to-morrow and I expect a token from you on my return. You ask me what I have been doing: I have written several things since I saw you, some emulative of the "$\dot{\eta}\delta\dot{v}$ $\kappa a\dot{\iota}$ $\beta\rho a\chi\dot{v}$ $\kappa a\dot{\iota}$ $\mu\epsilon\gamma a\lambda o\pi\rho\epsilon\pi\dot{\epsilon}s$[1]" of Alcaeus, others of the "$\dot{\epsilon}\kappa\lambda o\gamma\dot{\eta}$ $\tau\hat{\omega}\nu$ $\dot{o}\nu o\mu\dot{a}\tau\omega\nu$ $\kappa a\dot{\iota}$ $\tau\hat{\eta}s$ $\sigma\upsilon\nu\theta\dot{\epsilon}\sigma\epsilon\omega s$ $\dot{a}\kappa\rho\dot{\iota}\beta\epsilon\iota a$" of Simonides, one or two epical, but you can scarcely expect me to write

[1] Dion. Hal. v. 421.

them out for you: for I can scarcely bring myself to write
them out for myself, and do you think I love you better
than myself? I had thought your Paley had taught
you better. By a quaint coincidence I received your
letter, directed (I suppose) by Philip van Artevelde,
with Philip himself (not the man but the book), and I
wish to tell you that I think him a noble fellow; I close
with him in most that he says of modern poetry, tho'
it may be that he does not take sufficiently into consideration the peculiar strength evolved by such writers
as Byron and Shelley, who, however mistaken they
may be, did yet give the world another heart and new
pulses, and so are we kept going. Blessed be those
that grease the wheels of the old world, insomuch as
to move on is better than to stand still. But " Philip is
a famous man" and makes me 'shamed of my own faults.
À propos of faults I have corrected much of my last
volume, and if you will send me your copy I would insert
my corrections. Heaven knows what Douglas brought
you: as for some stanzas about a " Corridor[1]," I know
not whether there be such a poem; if there be it is very
evident you have it not rightly.

I think on second thoughts tho' much against my
will I will write thee out a poem, partly because Charles
likes it, partly to give a local habitation on this paper
and in your brain-piece to what else flies loosely thro'
the wind of my own memory like a Sibyl's leaf. Voilà!
be merciful.

(Here is copied out)

Love thou thy land with love far brought
etc.

It is said one cannot make a silken purse out of
a sow's ear, yet have you made a Miltonian out of the
Telegraph. "Cynthius aurem vellit ": your far significant

[1] See page 146, " The Little Maid."

coach drew the purse of my mouth like a sow's ear, it was not the wrong sow's ear to lay hold on, for I grinned. Kemble would have said "screamed" but I never scream, I leave that to your vivid men. I dare say you are right about the stanza in "Sir Galahad," who was intended for something of a male counterpart to St Agnes. I cannot write the "Suicide[1]" for you, 'tis too long, nor "Morte d'Arthur," which I myself think the best thing I have managed lately, for 'tis likewise too long; nor can I write any more at present, for it is much too late.

> Angels guard thee, dear Jimmy,
>   Ever thine, A. T.

P.S.   *Fragment on British Freedom.*

> Grave mother of majestic works,
>   From her isle-altar gazing down,
> Who, God-like, grasps the triple forks,
>   And, King-like, wears the crown:
>
> Her open eyes desire the truth,
>   The wisdom of a thousand years
> Is in them.   May perpetual youth
>   Keep dry their light from tears!

1835.

From J. M. Heath (the first mention of "In Memoriam").

My dear Alfred,

I sent Julia, on hearing her fears, a copy of your two companions to "Fair Ship[2]," which have been a great delight to her, and she seems to have communicated them to some others. "The Xmas[2]" is indeed most beautiful, most touching, and the

---

[1] "Two Voices."

[2] The sections of "In Memoriam" which were first written; see page 109.

latter portions of the "Fair Ship" speak to *our* hearts indeed. That last verse, is it not the expression of each voiceless thought? But the enjoyment of these will sink deeper yet. I seem sometimes as if I could not take in more than *one* thought at a time, I mean such thoughts as the mind loves to dwell on, and feed upon as it were, etc. etc. etc. I am doubtful how far I am justified in having sent you this, but I could not resist. There are many more people that take an interest in you than you are aware of. Your letter was balm to me, send me more such. I hope we shall see you in the summer.

Your very affectionate friend,

J. M. HEATH.

P.S. Thompson cometh, Spedding then, and if you ask what doeth the Spedding, why marry it is this. He bade me say in answer to all such enquiries that he, the said Spedding, was now waiting till he should grow wiser.

To James Spedding.

SOMERSBY RECTORY,
Feb. 15*th*, 1835. *Midnight.*

MY DEAR JAMES,

I shall never more have such respect for the lymphatic temperament. A promise has been broken by you, a promise generated betwixt two cigars at Gliddon's, corroborated in Holborn, and repeated in the archway of the Ball and Crown. I did write to you and you have thought me " worthy of sacred silence," but let that pass. I have heard much of your wisdom from Thompson and others, and I confess that, despite of your transgression, I have an inclination to come and see you, and if possible to bring you back with me here. Can I hear that men are wise and not look them in the face? I will come to you as Sheba came to Solomon.

> She travell'd far from Indian streams,
>   And he a royal welcome made
>   In ample chambers overlaid
> With Lebanonian cedar-beams.

I forget where I read this, and I do not know whether I shall have a royal welcome; wherefore be no more lymphatic but answer me, for I have sold my medal [1], and made money, and would visit you, and if you answer me not I shall —.

Very affectionately thine

As thou usest me, A. TENNYSON.

To James Spedding.

[*Undated.*]

MY DEAR JAMES,

I am sorry to disappoint myself (and perhaps in some slight measure you also) by postponing my visit. I am going to be from home for some time but not anywhere in your direction. The birds must sing and the furze bloom for you and Fitzgerald alone, "par nobile fratrum." I sincerely hope you have not put off any one else in the expectation of seeing me: tho' I did not state as much in my note, it was only when I first proposed it that I could have come to you. Fortune will perhaps bring me whiter days.

I know not whether you are aware that Charles has become an independent gentleman, living in a big house among chalky wolds at Caistor. His and my great uncle, Sam Turner, to whom he was heir, died some little time ago and left him property, but he complains

---

[1] This, the Chancellor's Medal for "Timbuctoo," was given back to him by his cousin Lewis Fytche in 1885.

that it is at present unavailable, talks of debts to be paid etc. etc.

John Heath writes me word that Mill is going to review me in a new Magazine, to be called the *London Review*, and favourably; but it is the last thing I wish for, and I would that you or some other who may be friends of Mill would hint as much to him. *I do not wish to be dragged forward again in any shape before the reading public at present*, particularly on the score of my old poems, most of which I have so corrected (particularly " Œnone ") as to make them much less imperfect, which you who are a wise man would own if you had the corrections. I may very possibly send you these some time.

I am in much haste and obliged to conclude, but absent or present,

Believe me

Ever your true friend and admirer, A. T.

UNPUBLISHED POEMS OF THIS PERIOD (ABOUT 1834).

Whispers.

'Tis not alone the warbling woods,
   The starr'd abysses of the sky,
The silent hills, the stormy floods,
   The green that fills the eye —
These only do not move the breast;
   Like some wise artist, Nature gives,
   Thro' all her works, to each that lives
A hint of somewhat unexprest.
Whate'er I see, where'er I move,
   These whispers rise, and fall away,
Something of pain — of bliss — of Love,
   But what, were hard to say.

The Little Maid.

Along this glimmering gallery
A child she loved to play;
This chamber she was born in! See,
The cradle where she lay!

That little garden was her pride,
With yellow groundsel grown!
Those holly-thickets only hide
Her grave — a simple stone!

CHAPTER VI.

VISITS TO THE LAKES AND ELSEWHERE.
THE "MORTE D'ARTHUR."
1836–37.

To a friend, Mrs Neville, who had lately lost her husband (written between 1830 and 1840, unpublished).

Woman of noble form and noble mind!
Whithersoever thro' the wilderness
Thou bearest from the threshold of thy friends
The sacred sorrows of as pure a heart
As e'er beat time to Nature, take with thee
Our warmest wishes, silent Guardians
But true till Death; and let them go in hope,
Like birds of passage, to return with thee
Some happy Summer morning, when the winds
Are fallen or changed; and, water'd by thy tears,
The two fair lilies growing at thy side
Have slowly prosper'd into stately flowers.

The only Tennyson who, in spite of their grand-father's wish "to make all the brothers parsons[1],"

---

[1] Alluded to in a letter from Frederick Tennyson to John Frere, April 18th, 1832. "After this long sit however I ought certainly to have some interesting passages to tongue. The foremost that presents itself is a crotchet

became a clergyman, was my uncle Charles. He had been ordained in 1835, and appointed to the curacy of Tealby, the village adjoining Bayons Manor. On May 24th, 1836, he married Louisa Sellwood, my mother's youngest sister.

My mother as a bridesmaid was taken into church by my father. They had rarely been in each other's company since their first meeting in 1830, when the Sellwoods had driven over one spring day from Horncastle, to call at Somersby Rectory. Arthur Hallam was then staying with the Tennysons; and asked Emily Sellwood to walk with him in the Fairy Wood. At a turn of the path they came upon my father, who, at sight of the slender, beautiful girl of seventeen in her simple gray dress, moving "like a light across those woodland ways," suddenly said to her: "Are you a Dryad or an Oread wandering here?" Now, as a bridesmaid, she seemed to him even lovelier:

"O happy bridesmaid, make a happy bride!"
And all at once a pleasant truth I learn'd,
For, while the tender service made thee weep,
I loved thee for the tear thou couldst not hide,
And prest thy hand, and knew the press return'd.

My uncle Arthur says: "It was then I first saw your mother, and she read to me Milton's 'Comus,' which I had not known before and which I have loved ever since."

My uncle Charles and his bride left for their honeymoon on the Rhine, a tour which was alluded to in "In Memoriam," section XCVIII.:

of my grandfather's, that we are all to take orders, myself especially, which puts me into a demisemijoram and causes me to lose time. In order to fill up this note I must add that I expect to be ordained in June, without much reason, for hitherto I have made no kind of preparation, and a pretty parson I shall make I'm thinking…"

You leave us: you will see the Rhine,
　And those fair hills I sail'd below,
　When I was there with him; and go
By summer belts of wheat and vine

To where he breathed his latest breath,
　That City.

To *that* city my father would never go, and he gave
me a most emphatic " no " when I once proposed a tour
there with him.

Under the will of Sam Turner of Caistor, my uncle
assumed the name of Turner, settling with his wife at
the vicarage of Grasby near Caistor.

The painful parting from Somersby took place in
1837. The patron, Mr Burton, and the Incumbent had
allowed the Tennysons to continue in the Rectory thus
long. My grandmother had understood that her father-in-
law would leave her the estate of Usselby, not far from the
old home; but this was not to be. Not that my grandmother was destitute; she had her jointure; and my
uncle Frederick had been left a property at Grimsby,
and all his brothers and sisters had their small " portions."
Under these circumstances the family decided that it was
best for them to leave the county and live nearer London.
My uncle Frederick was in Corfu, and remained there as
long as his cousin George d'Eyncourt, who was secretary
to Lord Nugent[1], kept his appointment. Afterwards he
went to Italy and lived near Florence on the Fiesole
Road, in a villa planned by Michael Angelo. There, so
report ran, " in a large hall, Frederick Tennyson (who
was a great lover of music) used to sit in the midst of
his forty fiddlers." Thus, his two elder brothers being
away, on my father devolved the care of the family and

---

[1] High Commissioner of the Ionian Islands.

of choosing a new home. The task was by no means easy. The mother "ruled by right of love," but knew nothing of the world. First of all a career had to be found for Horatio, the youngest brother, who wanted to be a soldier. The mother would not hear of this, and he was sent off to try his fortune in Tasmania. High Beech in Epping Forest was the home eventually selected; and there the Tennysons lived till 1840, when they went to Tunbridge Wells. Thence they moved in 1841 to Boxley near Maidstone.

Mrs Procter (Barry Cornwall's wife) once said to me:

I have known three great poets, Wordsworth, Browning and your father, and when they chose they could be more prosaic and practical than anybody on earth.

My father certainly proved his practical turn at this time in furnishing High Beech, for they say that he "did not even forget the kitchen utensils: and that throughout the furniture was pretty and inexpensive." The house and park were pleasant enough. There was a pond in the park on which in winter my father might be seen skating, sailing about on the ice in his long blue cloak.

He liked the nearness of London, whither he resorted to see his friends Spedding, Fitzgerald, Heath, Kemble, Tennant and others: but he writes that he could not often stay in town even for a night, his mother being in such a nervous state that he did not like to leave her. "The light of London flaring like a dreary dawn" was an especial admiration of his, during the evening journeys between London and High Beech. When he could leave home he would often visit in Lincolnshire, and stay both at his brother's vicarage and at the Sellwoods' in Horncastle. My mother and he were then quasi-engaged but were not able to marry owing to want of funds. They were not married until 1850, when his poems brought him a competency.

The study at High Beech, where he worked at his 1842 volume, was not the top attic, according to his usual preference, but a large room over the dining-room, with a bay window, red curtains, and a Clytie on a pedestal in the corner.

The "faithful Fitz[1]" writes that as early as 1835, when he met my father in the Lake Country, at the Speddings' (Mirehouse, by Bassenthwaite Lake), he saw what was to be part of this 1842 volume, the " Morte d'Arthur," " The Day-Dream," " The Lord of Burleigh," " Dora," and " The Gardener's Daughter." They were read out of a MS "in a little red book to him and Spedding of a night, ' when all the house was mute.' " Fitzgerald continues :

Spedding's father and mother were both alive ; and his father, who was of a practical turn, and had seen enough of poets in Shelley and Coleridge (perhaps in Wordsworth also), whom he remembered about the Lakes, rather resented our making so serious a business of verse-making, though he was so wise and charitable as to tolerate everything and everybody, except poetry and poets. He was jealous of his son James applying his great talents, which might have been turned to public and practical use, to such nonsense.

My father read them a great deal of Wordsworth, "the dear old fellow," as he called him. " The Yews of Borrowdale," " The Simplon Pass," the sonnet beginning " Two Voices," " The Solitary Reaper," " Peele Castle," the " Ode on Intimations of Immortality," " The Fountain," were among his favourites. Fitzgerald notes again :

I remember A. T. saying he remembered the time when he could see nothing in " Michael" which he now read us in admiration ; though he thought Wordsworth often clumsy

---

[1] Edward Fitzgerald.

and diffuse. There was no end of "This Thorn" in the piece that bears the name: "such hammering to set a scene for so small a drama."

My father also read Keats and Milton: saying that "Lycidas" was "a test of any reader's poetic instinct," and that "Keats, with his high spiritual vision, would have been, if he had lived, the greatest of us all (tho' his blank verse was poor), and that there is something magic and of the innermost soul of poetry in almost everything which he wrote." Then, perhaps in his weaker moments, he used to think Shakespeare greater in his sonnets than in his plays. "But he soon returned to the thought which is indeed the thought of all the world. He would have seemed to me to be reverting for a moment to the great sorrow of his own mind; and in that peculiar phase of mind he found the sonnets a deeper expression of the never-to-be-forgotten love which he felt, more than any of the many moods of many minds which appear among Shakespeare's dramas [1]."

The three friends went to Ambleside together, but Spedding was obliged to leave Fitzgerald and my father there, and go home on business. Fitzgerald says:

Alfred Tennyson staid with me at Ambleside. I will say no more than that the more I see of him, the more cause I have to think him great. His little humours and grumpinesses were so droll that I was always laughing. I must, however, say further, that I felt what Charles Lamb describes, a sense of depression at times from the overshadowing of a so much more lofty intellect than my own.

He adds a note about a row on Windermere with my father:

Resting on our oars one calm day on Windermere, whither we had gone for a week from dear Spedding's (Mirehouse), at the

---

[1] Jowett.

end of May 1835, resting on our oars, and looking into the lake quite unruffled and clear, Alfred quoted from the lines he had lately read us from the MS of "Morte d'Arthur" about the lonely lady of the lake and Excalibur —

> Nine years she wrought it, sitting in the deeps
> Upon the hidden bases of the hills.

" Not bad that, Fitz, is it[1] ? "

This kind of remark he would make when reading his own or others' poetry when he came to lines that he particularly admired, from no vanity but from a pure feeling of artistic pleasure. "The Lord of Burleigh" was also read from MS and Fitz writes: " I remember the author doubting if it were not too familiar, with its

> ' Let us see these handsome houses,'

etc. for public taste. ' But a sister,' A. T. said, ' had liked it '; we never got it out of our heads from the first hearing; and now is there a greater favourite where English is spoken ? " My father and Fitzgerald then had a contest as to who could invent the weakest Wordsworthian line imaginable. Although Fitzgerald claimed this line, my father declared that he had composed it —

A Mr Wilkinson, a clergyman.

While my father was in the Lake Country he fell in with Hartley Coleridge, who discussed Pindar with him, calling Pindar " The Newmarket poet." " Hartley was wonderfully eloquent," my father said, " and I suspect resembled his father in that respect. I liked Hartley, ' Massa ' Hartley. I remember that on one occasion Hartley was asked to dine with the family of a stiff Presbyterian clergyman, residing in the Lake district. The party sat a long time in the drawing-room waiting for dinner. Nobody talked. At last Hartley could

[1] E. F. G., MS Note.

stand it no longer, he jumped up from the sofa, kissed
the clergyman's daughter, and bolted out of the house.
He was very eccentric, a sun-faced little man. He once
went a walking tour with some friends. They suddenly
missed him, and could not find him anywhere, and did
not see him again for six weeks, when he emerged from
some inn. He was a loveable little fellow."

Sonnet to Alfred Tennyson, after meeting him for the first time.

Long have I known thee as thou art in song,
And long enjoyed the perfume that exhales
From thy pure soul, and odour sweet entails
And permanence on thoughts that float along
The stream of life, to join the passive throng
Of shades and echoes that are Memory's being;
Hearing, we hear not, and we see not, seeing,
If Passion, Fancy, Faith, move not among
The never-present moments of reflection.
Long have I viewed thee in the crystal sphere
Of verse, that like the Beryl makes appear
Visions of hope, begot of recollection.
Knowing thee now, a real earth-treading man,
Not less I love thee and no more I can.

HARTLEY COLERIDGE.

Of this visit Spedding wrote to Thompson:

Alfred left us about a week since, homeward bound, but
meaning to touch at Brookfield's on his way. The weather has
been much finer since he went; certainly, while he was here, our
northern sun did not display himself to advantage. Nevertheless
I think he took in more pleasure and inspiration than any one
would have supposed who did not know his almost personal
dislike of the present, whatever it may be. Hartley Coleridge is
mightily taken with him; and after the fourth bottom of gin,
deliberately thanked Heaven (under me, I believe, or me under
Heaven, I forget which) for having brought them acquainted.

Said Hartley was busy with an article on " Macbeth," to appear (the vegetable spirits permitting) in the next *Blackwood*. He confessed to a creed touching Destiny which was new to me; denying Free-Will (if I understood him right) in toto; but at the same time maintaining that man is solely and entirely answerable for whatever evil he does, not merely that he is to suffer for it but that he is *answerable* for it, which I do not. I could not get Alfred to Rydal Mount, he would and would not [1] (sulky one), although Wordsworth was hospitably minded towards him; and would have been more so, had the state of his household permitted, which I am sorry to say is full of sickness. ...Alfred despises the Citation and Exam. of W. Shakespeare [2].

From Edward Fitzgerald.
(*After the visit at the Speddings', Mirehouse.*)

LONDON, *July 2nd*, 1835.

DEAR TENNYSON,

I suppose you have heard of the death of James Spedding's sister-in-law : for my part I only came to know of it a day or two ago : having till then lived out of communication with any one who was likely to know of such things. After leaving you at Ambleside, I stayed a fortnight at Manchester, and then went to Warwick, where I lived a king for a month. Warwickshire is a noble shire : and the Spring being so late, I had the benefit of it through most of the month of June. I sometimes wished for you, for I think you would have liked it well....... I have heard you sometimes say that you are bound by the want of such and such a sum, and I vow to the Lord that I could not have a greater pleasure than transferring it to you on such occasions ; I should not dare to say such a thing to a small man : but you are not a small man assuredly : and even if you do not make use of my offer, you will not be offended but put it to the right account. It is very difficult to persuade people in this world that one can part with a banknote without a pang. It is one of the most simple things I have ever done to talk thus to you, I believe : but here is an end; and be charitable to me.

---

[1] He said that he did not wish to " obtrude himself on the great man at Rydal."

[2] This refers to Landor's Essay so named.

Edgeworth [1] is......a wonderful man, but I shall be very serious
with him lest he should wean you from indulging in quaint and
wonderful imaginations, and screw you up too tightly to moral
purpose.   If this sentence is unintelligible to you, I will console
you with one that is as clear as daylight.   Your muse has
penetrated into France : there has been a review of your poems
in a paper called the *Voleur*, in which you are called — guess
what! — " Jeune Enthousiaste de l'école gracieuse de *Thomas
Moore*" — this I think will make you laugh and is worth postage.
Now I have told you all that I have in my head : it is fortunate
that the sheet of paper is just spacious enough for my out-
pourings.   The " Morte d'Arthur " has been much in my mouth :
audibly : round Warwick.

> I am yours very truly, E. FITZGERALD.

P. S.   When I was at Manchester, I bought a small *Dante*
for myself : and, liking it well, the same for you : for I had never
seen the edition before, and I dare say you have not.   It is
small but very clearly printed : with little explanations at the
foot of each page, very welcome to me : the proper price was ten
shillings but I only gave three.

Leigh Hunt writes :

> 4 UPPER CHEYNE ROAD, CHELSEA.   1835.

The *Prince Arthur* [2] which I should have brought with me,
I will send to-morrow or next day by a messenger ; and the rest
shall reach you as quickly as may be.   Meanwhile may I
venture to hope that my two non-appearances will not hinder me
from having another invitation some day, or yourself from
coming to see me ?   Carlyle expresses the pleasure he should
have in meeting you here some evening....... Shall I hope to
see you at Carlyle's lecture on Monday ?

---

[1] Nephew of Maria Edgeworth, the " Little Frank " of the *Parent's
Assistant*.

[2] This copy of Malory I have still in my possession, a small book for the
pocket, published 1816, by Walker and Edwards, and much used by my
father.

From R. M. Milnes.

Your brief was infallibly pleasant. I shall wait for you in December. If you like, we will have " Freezetown" (Fryston) all to ourselves and you may smoke while I play the organ. Now be a good boy and do as you're told. Lord Northampton is getting up a charity book of poetry for the destitute family of a man of letters, born in the dead letter office, and he earnestly prays you to contribute not your mite but your might to it. I have half promised you will give him something pretty consider- able, for the fault of the book will be that the contributions are not as great in dimension as in name. He has got original things of Wordsworth, Southey, Miss Bailey, R. M. M. etc. I will love you more and more therefore if you will send some jewels directed to the Marquis of Northampton, Castle Ashby, Northampton, as soon as convenient. Your "St Agnes[1]" looks funny between Lord Londonderry and Lord W. Lennox, God her aid! I like Brookfield's sonnet eminently.......

Yours affectionately, R. M. MILNES.

P. S. You know your contribution will be at your disposal to do what you like with when the book is sold, i.e. in a year or so.

To R. M. Milnes[2].

December, 1836.

DEAR RICHARD,

As I live eight miles from my post-town and only correspond therewith about once a week, you must not wonder if this reaches you somewhat late. Your former brief I received, though some six days behind time, and stamped with the postmarks of every little market-town in the country, but I did not think it demanded an immediate answer, hence my silence.

[1] "St Agnes," published in the *Keepsake* (1837), pp. 247–48, edited by Lady Emmeline Stuart Wortley.
[2] Quoted in Wemyss Reid's *Life of Lord Houghton*.

That you had promised the Marquis I would write for him something exceeding the average length of " Annual compositions "; that you had promised him I would write at all : I took this for one of those elegant fictions with which you amuse your aunts of evenings, before you get into the small hours when dreams are true. Three summers back, provoked by the incivility of editors, I swore an oath that I would never again have to do with their vapid books, and I brake it in the sweet face of Heaven when I wrote for Lady What's-her-name Wortley. But then her sister wrote to Brookfield and said she (Lady W.) was beautiful, so I could not help it. But whether the Marquis be beautiful or not, I don't much mind; if he be, let him give God thanks and make no boast. To write for people with prefixes to their names is to milk he-goats; there is neither honour nor profit. Up to this moment I have not even seen *The Keepsake* : not that I care to see it, for the want of civility decided me not to break mine oath again for man nor woman, and how should such a modest man as I see my small name in collocation with the great ones of Southey, Wordsworth, R. M. M., etc., and not feel myself a barndoor fowl among peacocks? Goodbye.

Believe me always thine,

A. T.

Milnes was angry at the refusal, and my father answered him banteringly again:

Jan. 10th, 1837 [1].

Why what in the name of all the powers, my dear Richard, makes you run me down in this fashion? Now is my nose out of joint, now is my tail not only curled

[1] Quoted in Wemyss Reid's *Life of Lord Houghton*.

so tight as to lift me off my hind legs like Alfred Crow-
quill's poodle, but fairly between them.   Many sticks
are broken about me.   I am the ass in Homer.   I am
blown.   What has so jaundiced your good-natured eyes
as to make them mistake harmless banter for *insolent
irony*: harsh terms applicable only to —— who big as
he is, sits to all posterity astride upon the nipple of
literary dandyism, and " takes her milk for gall " ?   " Insolent irony " and " piscatory vanity," as if you had
been writing to St Anthony, who converted the soft
souls of salmon ; but may St Anthony's fire consume
all misapprehension, the spleen-born mother of five-
fold more evil on our turnip-spheroid than is malice
aforethought.

Had I been writing to a nervous, morbidly-irritable
man, down in the world, stark-spoiled with the staggers
of a mis-managed imagination and quite opprest by
fortune and by the reviews, it is possible that I might
have halted to find expressions more suitable to his
case ; but that you, who seem at least to take the world
as it comes, to doff it, and let it pass, that you, a man
every way prosperous and talented, should have taken
pet at my unhappy badinage made me lay down my
pipe and stare at the fire for ten minutes, till the stranger
fluttered up the chimney !   You wish that I had never
written that passage.   So do I, since it seems to have given
such offence.   Perhaps you likewise found a stumbling-
block in the expression " vapid books," as the angry
inversion of four commas seems so intimate.   But are
not *Annuals* vapid ?   Or could I *possibly* mean that what
you or Trench or De Vere chose to write therein must
be vapid ?   I thought you knew me better than even
to insinuate these things.   Had I spoken the same
things to you laughingly in my chair, and with my own
emphasis, you would have seen what they really meant,
but coming to read them peradventure in a fit of indi-

gestion, or with a slight matutinal headache after your
Apostolic symposium you subject them to such misinterpretation as, if I had not sworn to be true friend
to you till my latest death-ruckle, would have gone far
to make me indignant.   But least said soonest mended ;
which comes with peculiar grace from me after all this
verbiage.   You judge me rightly in supposing that I
would not be backward in doing a really charitable deed.
I will either bring or send you something for your
Annual.   It is very problematical whether I shall be
able to come and see you as I proposed, so do not
return earlier from your tour on my account ; and if I
come, I should only be able to stop a few days, for, as
I and all my people are going to leave this place very
shortly never to return, I have much upon my hands.
But whether I see you or no,

Believe me always thine affectionately,

A. TENNYSON.

I have spoken with Charles.   He has promised to
contribute to your *Annual*[1].   Frederick will, I daresay,
follow his example.   See now whether I am not doing
my best for you, and whether you had any occasion to
threaten me with that black "Anacaona[2]" and her cocoa-
shod coves of niggers.   I cannot have her strolling about
the land in this way.   It is neither good for her reputation nor mine.   When is Lord Northampton's book
to be published, and how long may I wait before I send
anything by way of contribution ?

"O that 'twere possible," afterwards the foundation
of "Maud," was sent to Lord Northampton.   Fitzgerald
also notes that in this year my father wrote a poem on

[1] *The Tribute.*   [2] p. 56.

the Queen's accession, " of which the burden was ' Here's
a health to the Queen of the Isles.' " One stanza I have
heard my father repeat :

(Unpublished.)

That the voice of a satisfied people may keep
A sound in her ears like the sound of the deep,
Like the sound of the deep when the winds are asleep ;
Here's a health to the Queen of the Isles.

A fragment of a poem about Mablethorpe he wrote
then, and gave in 1850 to the *Manchester Athenæum
Album :*

Mablethorpe.

Here often when a child I lay reclined :
   I took delight in this fair strand and free ;
Here stood the infant Ilion of the mind,
   And here the Grecian ships all seem'd to be.
And here again I come, and only find
   The drain-cut level of the marshy lea,
Gray sand-banks, and pale sunsets, dreary wind,
   Dim shores, dense rains, and heavy-clouded sea.

The following sonnet was also preserved, which he
wrote at the end of 1837 or the beginning of 1838.

Sonnet.   (Unpublished.)

To thee with whom my true affections dwell,
That I was harsh to thee, let no one know ;
It were, O Heaven, a stranger tale to tell
Than if the vine had borne the bitter sloe.
Tho' I was harsh, my nature is not so :
A momentary cloud upon me fell :
My coldness was mistimed like summer-snow,
Cold words I spoke, yet loved thee warm and well.
Was I so harsh ?   Ah dear, it could not be.
Seem'd I so cold ? what madness moved my blood

To make me thus belie my constant heart
That watch't with love thine earliest infancy,
Slow-ripening to the grace of womanhood,
Thro' every change that made thee what thou art?

It was in the latter part of 1837 or the beginning of 1838 that he appears to have first become known in America. Professor Rolfe, who has kindly interested himself in the matter, writes to me that R. W. Emerson somehow made acquaintance with the 1830 and 1832 volumes about that time and delighted in lending them to his friends.

Emerson suggested a reprint of the volumes, and Longfellow, brother of the poet, showed Prof. Rolfe a letter from Messrs C. C. Little & Co. of Boston addressed to the poet and dated April 27th, 1838, stating that they intended to publish the reprint; but for some reason this plan was not carried out.

During some months of 1837 my father was deeply immersed in Pringle's *Travels*, and Lyell's *Geology*: and from Pringle he got the image of the hungry lion used in his simile in " Locksley Hall ":

Slowly comes a hungry people, as a lion creeping nigher,
Glares at one that nods and winks behind a slowly-dying fire.

He received the following letter from Leigh Hunt, dated July 31st:

My dear Sir

Many thanks for your kind letter. It delights me to think you should find anything to like in my verses, especially " Paganini." I always fancy that if ever I write anything worthy of the name of poetry, it is when I write about music. Your communication alas! came too late for the book in question; but the editor shall know of it, and will doubtless be gratified that you have written.   I wish to send you a copy of the first number of the new series of a magazine (the *Monthly Repository*) of which I myself have become editor; but have not the face to put you to the expense of receiving it at such a distance.   Will you drop me a *word* to say whether I can forward it to any intermediate place of communication, and will you at the same time look into your desk and see if you can oblige me *with a few verses and your name to them*, for my new adventure?   You will see in some verses of mine, in the number I speak of, that I have taken a liberty with said name, in speaking of a fair and no unworthy imitator of yours, a Miss Barrett[1], who really has sparks of the "faculty divine," but what I say, as you will easily believe, has all due respect and admiration at the bottom of it; as indeed every one knows who knows anything about you, or about what I say of you.   Therefore do not hesitate to send me a Sibylline leaf if you can, and be sure I ask it for your honour and glory as well as my own advantage.   I want my magazine to be such a magazine as was never seen before, every article worth something, though *I* say it that shouldn't, and I believe you know my gallant wish to be a sort of Robin Hood of an editor, with not a man in my company that does not beat his leader.   A sonnet — a fragment — anything will be welcome, most especially if you put your name to it; and therefore for the sake of poetry and my love of it, again I say, *oblige me if you can;* and also send instantly because time begins to press.

Ever truly yours, LEIGH HUNT.

P. S.   The magazine shall come away the instant I hear from you where to send it.

In the following extract from an unpublished letter of Leigh Hunt's to S. C. Hall an interesting criticism is given of my father and his brothers Frederick and Charles:

I do not know the birth, parentage and education of Tennyson.   I am pretty sure however that he is not long come from

[1] Afterwards Mrs Barrett Browning.

Trinity College, Cambridge, and I believe him to be nephew of Tennyson d'Eyncourt, the member for Lambeth, and son of a clergyman (the last however I know still more dimly than the rest). He has a brother (Charles) whom you ought to know, if you do not know him already.

I will send you his vol. of Sonnets to-morrow, together with the only vol. which I have at home (I find) of Alfred's. If it is not the one you want, I will see who has got the other. Charles is not equal to Alfred, but still partakes of the genuine faculty. He has a graceful luxury but combining less of the spiritual with it, which, I suppose, is the reason why he has become clergyman! I was fearful of what he would come to by certain migivings in his poetry and a want of the active poetic faith.

There is also another brother, perhaps less inspired than Charles and who has only put forth a sonnet or so in public, Frederick, but still partaking of the right vein; and I think I have heard there are two of the sisters poetical! Here is a nest of nightingales for you! ***

The materials of the noblest poetry are abundant in him (Alfred), and we trust will not find any too weak corner in the sensitiveness of his nature to oppress him with their very exuberance.

Mr Gladstone, as is well-known, was Arthur Hallam's school friend, and on this account my father had a romantic desire to see him; and so called upon him about this time. I wrote to Mr Gladstone for some details of their early intercourse and he kindly replied:

10 Downing Street, Whitehall, *October*, 1892.

My dear Hallam,

I am afraid that I shall have to adjourn any attempt to record my intercourse with your father until after my resignation of my present office, and even then I fear it might have to compete with the demands of my unfinished work.

I do not think that at any time during the last forty years I have ever found myself able when in office to give continuous thoughts on any subject outside public affairs. I will however allow myself the pleasure of referring to the first occasion on

which I saw him.   It was about the year 1837, when he called
on me in Carlton Gardens.   This was an unexpected honour,
for I had no other tie with him than having been in earlier life
the friend of his friend, to whom he afterwards erected so
splendid a literary monument.   I cannot now remember particulars, but I still retain the liveliest impression of both the
freedom and kindness with which he conversed with me during
a long interview.

I am greatly pleased to hear that you have undertaken the
"Life," — doubtless an arduous task, but one to which your titles
are multiple as well as clear.

Believe me most sincerely yours,

W. E. GLADSTONE.

The years spent in strenuous labour and self-educa-
tion, and his engagement to Emily Sellwood, had again
braced my father for the struggle of life.   The current of
his mind no longer ran constantly in the channel of mournful memories and melancholy forebodings.   During this
autumn of 1838 he sought out "fresh woods and pastures
new" in Torquay, where he wrote his "Audley Court."
His friends had not yet grasped the change in the tenor
of his thoughts and still tried to cheer him.   "Go and live
at Cambridge," said Venables   "You might perceive, if
you had any doubt about it, when you were last there
how great a pleasure it was to us all to see you, and
how little trouble to provide for you.   Now you would
be more at home there than you were then after so long
an absence, and you can get books innumerable, and
smoke and talk, or not talk; and make poetry and
commit it to surer records than the leaves of which so
many are lost.   Do not continue to be so *careless of
fame, and of influence.*"   Or again he advised my father
to go and work in Prague, where he would receive new
impressions and a new stimulus to the imagination.

"I almost wonder that you with *your love of music
and tobacco* do not go and live in some such place."

Yet my father paid heed to none of these invitations, but went his own way. He had abundant materials now for publication. He had made friends in London, and when he published again he would start as a well-known man, with the certainty that he could not be overlooked and that by many he would be appreciated. He was on the whole happy in his life, and looked forward to still better days.

> Hope, a poising eagle, burnt
> Above the unrisen morrow.

He must earn a livelihood on which to marry. He would arrange his material and give as perfect a volume as he could to the world. "I felt certain of one point then," he said: "if I meant to make any mark at all, it must be by shortness, for the men before me had been so diffuse, and most of the big things except 'King Arthur' had been done." Another fact also began to dawn upon him, that if he never published again, even that which he had published "would be taken out of its napkin and would be given to him who had published ten volumes."

CHAPTER VII.*

EXTRACTS FROM LETTERS TO EMILY SELLWOOD.

[These extracts, that follow chronological order, are made from a series of letters from my father to my mother extending over three years. I have not felt able to include the many passages which would show the intensity of feeling expressed in these letters, but have burnt the correspondence according to my father's directions.]

1838–1840.

1838. I saw from the high road thro' Hagworthingham the tops of the elms on the lawn at Somersby beginning to kindle into green. Do you remember sitting with me there on the iron garden chair one day when I had just come from London? It was earlier in the year than now. I have no reason for asking except that the morning three years back seems fresh and pleasant; and you were in a silk pelisse, and I think I read some book with you.

I dare not tell how high I rate humour, which is generally most fruitful in the highest and most solemn human spirits. Dante is full of it, Shakespeare, Cervantes, and almost all the greatest have been pregnant with this glorious power. You will find it even in the Gospel of Christ.

167

1839. " The stern daughter of the Voice of God," unclothed with the warmth of the feelings, is as impotent to convert as the old Stoicism.

Wells. The light of this world is too full of refractions for men ever to see one another in their true positions. The world is better than it is called, but wrong and foolish. The whole framework seems wrong, which in the end shall be found right.

Bitterness of any sort becomes not the sons of Adam, still less pride, for they are in that talk of theirs for the most part but as children babbling in the market-place.

High Beech. I have been at this place (High Beech in Epping Forest) all the year, with nothing but that muddy pond in prospect, and those two little sharp-barking dogs.

Perhaps I am coming to the Lincolnshire coast, but I scarcely know. The journey is so expensive and I am so poor.

The far future has been my world always.

I shall never see the Eternal City, nor that dome, the wonder of the world; I do not think I would live there if I could, and I have no money for touring.

Mablethorpe. I am not so able as in old years to commune *alone* with Nature. I am housed at Mr Wildman's, an old friend of mine in these parts: he and his wife are two perfectly honest Methodists. When

I came, I asked her after news, and she replied: "Why, Mr Tennyson, there's only one piece of news that I know, that Christ died for *all* men." And I said to her: "That is old news, and good news, and new news"; wherewith the good woman seemed satisfied. I was half-yesterday reading anecdotes of Methodist ministers, and liking to read them too...and of the teaching of Christ, that purest light of God.

That made me count the less of the sorrows when I caught a glimpse of the sorrowless Eternity.

A good woman is a wondrous creature, cleaving to the right and the good in all change; lovely in her youthful comeliness, lovely all her life long in comeliness of heart.

London. There is no one here but John Kemble with whom I dined twice; he is full of burning indignation against the Russian policy and what he calls the moral barbarism of France; likewise he is striving against what he calls the "mechanic influence of the age and its tendency to crush and overpower the spiritual in man," and indeed what matters it how much man knows and does if he keeps not a reverential looking upward? He is only the subtlest beast in the field.

We must bear or we must die. It is easier perhaps to die, but infinitely less noble. The immortality of man disdains and rejects the thought, the immortality of man to which the cycles and the æons are as hours and as days.

"Why has God created souls knowing they would sin and suffer?" a question unanswerable. Man is greater than all animals because he is capable of moral good and evil, tho' perhaps dogs and elephants, and some of the higher mammalia have a little of this capability. God might have made me a beast; but He thought good to give me power, to set Good and Evil before me that I might shape my own path. The happiness, resulting from this power well exercised, must in the end exceed the mere physical happiness of breathing, eating, and sleeping like an ox. Can we say that God prefers higher happiness in some to a lower happiness in all? It is a hard thing that if I sin and fail I should be sacrificed to the bliss of the Saints. Yet what reasonable creature, if he could have been askt beforehand, would not have said, "Give me the metaphysical power; let me be the lord of my decisions; leave physical quietude and dull pleasure to lower lives." All souls methinks would have answered thus, and so had men suffered by their own choice, as now by the necessity of being born what they are, but there is no answer to these questions except in a great *hope* of universal good: and even then one might ask, why has God made one to suffer more than another, why is it not meted equally to all? Let us be silent, for we know nothing of these things, and we trust there is One who knows all. God cannot be cruel. If he were, the heart could only find relief in the wildest blasphemies, which would cease to be blasphemies. God must be all powerful, else the soul could never deem Him worthy of her highest worship. Let us leave it therefore to God, as to the wisest. Who knows whether revelation be not itself a veil to hide the glory of that Love which we could not look upon without marring our sight, and our onward progress? If it were proclaimed as a truth "No man shall perish: all shall live, after a certain time shall have gone by, in bliss with God"

such a truth might tell well with one or two lofty spirits,
but would be the hindrance of the world.

High Beech, July 10th.   What a thunderstorm we had
the other night! I wonder whether it was so bad at H—.
It lasted the whole night and part of the previous afternoon.   Lewis Fytche, who was with us then, was looking
out of my window about half-past 11 o'clock, and saw a
large fireball come up the valley from Waltham till it
seemed to come quite over our pond: it then according
to his account grew on a sudden amazingly large.   How
large? I askt him: he said, "like a great balloon, and
burst with an explosion like fifty batteries of cannon." I
was so sorry not to have seen it, for it was a thing to
remember; but I had just gone to my mother's room:
she was grovelling on the floor in an extremity of fear
when the clap came; upon which she cried out, "Oh!
I will leave this house: the storms are very bad here,"
and F— who is here burst out weeping.   Such a scene,
almost ludicrous in its extremes.

I have been engaged in packing books.   I have a
good many.   I am afraid I shall be obliged to sell them,
for I really do not know where to stow them and the
house at Tunbridge is too small, a mere mouse-trap.

All life is a school, a preparation, a purpose: nor can
we pass current in a higher college, if we do not undergo
the tedium of education in this lower one.

Annihilate within yourself these two dreams of Space
and Time.   To me often the far-off world seems nearer

than the present, for in the present is always something unreal and indistinct, but the other seems a good solid planet, rolling round its green hills and paradises to the harmony of more steadfast laws. There steam up from about me mists of weakness, or sin, or despondency, and roll between me and the far planet, but it is there still.

Dim mystic sympathies with tree and hill reaching far back into childhood. A known landskip is to me an old friend, that continually talks to me of my own youth and half-forgotten things, and indeed does more for me than many an old friend that I know. An old park is my delight, and I could tumble about it for ever.

Sculpture is particularly good for the mind: there is a height and divine stillness about it which preaches peace to our stormy passions. Methinks that, in looking upon a great statue like the Theseus (maim'd and defaced as it is), one becomes as it were Godlike, to feel things in the Idea.

There is the glory of being loved, for so have we "laid great bases for Eternity."

Thro' darkness and storm and weariness of mind and of body is there built a passage for His created ones to the gates of light.

That world of perfect chrysolite, a pure and noble heart.

Aberystwith.   I cannot say I have seen much worth
the trouble of the journey, always excepting the Welsh-
women's hats which look very , comical to an English eye, being in truth men's hats, beavers, with the
brim a little broad, and tied under the chin with a
black ribband.   Some faces look very pretty in them.
It is remarkable how fluently the little boys and girls
can speak Welsh, but I have seen no leeks yet, nor shot
any cheeses.   This place, the Cambrian Brighton, pleases
me not,...a sea certainly to-day of a most lovely blue,
but with scarce a ripple.   Anything more unlike the
old Homeric " much-sounding " sea I never saw.   Yet
the bay is said to be tempestuous.   O for a good
Mablethorpe breaker!   I took up this morning an unhappy book of English verse by a Welshman, and read
therein that all which lies at present swampt fathom-
deep under the bay of Carnarvon was long ago in the
twilight of history a lovely lowland, rich in woods, thick
with cities.   One wild night a drunken man, who was
a sort of clerk of the drains and sewers in his time,
opened the dam-gates and let in the sea, and Heaven
knows how many stately palaces have ever since been
filled with polyps and sea-tangle.   How many gentlemen
discussing after-dinner politics of that day were surprised
by the precocious entrance of lobster before supper!
How many young ladies playing at their pre-historic
pianos ended some warm love-song of life in a quavering
swan-song of death!

I require quiet, and myself to myself, more than any
man when I write.

Barmouth.   Barmouth is a good deal prettier place
than Aberystwith, a flat sand shore, a sea with breakers,
looking Mablethorpelike, and sand hills, and close behind

them huge crags and a long estuary with cloud-capt hills running up as far as Dolgelly, with Cader Idris on one side.

The most beautiful thing I saw this time in Wales — Llanberis lakes. ("Edwin Morris" was written there.)

In *letters*, words too often prove a bar of hindrance instead of a bond of union.

London. My friends have long since ceased to write, knowing me to be so irregular a correspondent. A brief and terse style suits the man, but the woman is well when she deals in words.

So much to do and so much to feel in parting from the house. Such a scene of sobbing and weeping was there on Monday morning among the servants at Beech Hill, and cottagers' daughters, as that cockney residence has seldom witnessed, perhaps never since its stones were cemented and trowelled. There were poor Milnes wringing her hands and howling, Ann Green swallowing her own tears with exclamations of such pathos as would have moved the heart of a whinstone, and other villagers all joining in the chorus, as if for some great public calamity. Finding we had human hearts, though we lived in a big house, they thought it all the harder that they were to lose us so soon. We drove the other day to see a Captain Pellew, who had drawn several sketches of the Himala mountains. Capt. P. said that in the early morning when all the hills were wrapt in blackness, the sharp snow-peaks shine out like rosy lamps hung high up in heaven, and apparently having no connection with this earth. A man who had just visited the Alps was with him there, and he said " the Himala was just twice as magnificent."

Warwick. 1840. I got into the third class of carriages in the train to Leicester. It is a carriage entirely open, without seats, nothing but a rail or two running across it, something like pens of cattle....Tho' we did not move very quickly, yet it was liker flying than anything else....I learnt some curious lessons in perspective, e.g. the two rails on the road were always drawn together with the greatest rapidity. I stopt last night at Leicester, and came on here (to Warwick) this morning by a slow mail. On driving into Warwick, by great chance I happened to have my glass in my eye and perceived my friend, Edward Fitzgerald, taking his walk on the pavé towards Leamington. I stopt the coach, and he got up, and we drove to the George here, and had an evening together. Kenilworth looked grand in the distance. I think of going over with Fitz to-morrow. Warwick not to be seen till Saturday as the family are there. Almost afraid I cannot stop as long, as it is very expensive being at an inn. Warwick Castle looked grand and black among its woods from the bridge this evening, a nightingale was singing, and rooks were cawing, and there was moreover the noise of a waterfall.

London. I went thro' Warwick Castle. It is certainly a noble specimen of old feudalism, and the views from the windows would be of unrivalled loveliness if the river were only clearer. I and Fitzgerald also (climbed) up Guy's tower, and had " large prospect " of the surrounding country : but nothing pleased me better on the whole than two paintings I saw in the castle : one, an Admiral van

Tromp by Rembrandt, the other Macchiavelli by Titian, both wonderful pictures, but the last grand beyond all words. We strayed about the gardens....Afterwards we went to Stratford and saw Shakespeare's monument. I should not think it can be a good likeness. That foolish fellow painted it white all over, and served poor Johnny Combe, who lies on a monument near, in the same way. I suppose from a notion that so painted they would look more classic, but the monuments all about were gilded and painted, and so were theirs. By which fancy of Malone we have in all probability lost the colour of Shakespeare's hair and eyes, which perhaps would do the world very little good to know, but would have been a little satis-faction to poor physiognomists like myself. We went also into the room where they say he was born. Every part of it is scribbled over with names. I was seized with a sort of enthusiasm, and wrote mine, tho' I was a little ashamed of it afterwards : yet the feeling was genuine at the time, and I did homage with the rest. I forgot Kenilworth. We tumbled about the ruins for three hours, but I was rather disappointed. I had expected to find them larger and more august. (My father came from Coventry to London and wrote " Godiva." He encloses " a virgin-ballad never yet written down," " Sweet Emma Morland " — " simple enough at any rate," he writes of it.)

After this date all correspondence between Alfred Tennyson and Emily Sellwood was forbidden; since there seemed to be no prospect of their ever being married, owing to that unfortunately

> " Eternal want of pence
>   Which vexes public men."

Letters to and from friends, 1840–1842

This letter to Tennant, without date or address, I have found among the letters received from his friends at this period:

To Reverend R. J. Tennant[1].

MY DEAR ROBERT,

It is about three centuries since I heard from you. I suppose you did not calculate on my sending you any answer, had you written. I think it just possible that I might: however my regard for you has thriven as lustily as ever in the silence, and I have had, now and then, certain memorials of you from different quarters: not indeed altogether grateful, for I am told that your wife has been ill almost the whole time you have been in Italy, also that you had lost great part of your library by shipwreck, also that you hated the land of the sun, where men, according to Alfieri, come up more vigorously than in other latitudes. Often have I intended to come over and pay you a visit, and as often my empty purse has gaped in my face and broken my dream of you and the Pitti palace together. Well, I suppose we shall meet somewhere or other on this side of the grave, and that our friendship at Cambridge has not been only to cease to be. How many puns have we made together! how many walks have we taken arm in arm in the dark streets of the old University and on the Trumpington

---

[1] Since Cambridge days Tennant had been in an unsettled frame of mind. He had been a frequenter of Coleridge's famous gatherings at Highgate, had been shaken in his belief and had hesitated, like many others then, to take orders. Subsequently he was ordained and became curate to J. C. Hare, at Hurstmonceux (a post afterwards filled by John Sterling), then he lived for several years as English chaplain at Florence, where he died.

road! and how you used to scepticize till we both ran away!

My people are located at a place which is my abomination, viz. Tunbridge Wells in this county; they moved thither from Essex by the advice of a London physician, who said it was the only place in England for the Tennyson constitution: the sequel is that they are half killed by the tenuity of the atmosphere and the presence of steel more or less in earth, air and water. I have sometimes tried to persuade them to live abroad but without effect, and I dare say you in your exile agree with them that there is no place like an English home.

I came over to this place about a fortnight back.

A. T.

To Edward Fitzgerald.

MABLETHORPE, ALFORD, 1841.

DEAR OLD FITZ,

Not on the Western, on the Eastern coast. Mablethorpe near Alford in the fat shire of Lincoln is the place where I am. I walk about the coast, and have it all to myself, sand and sea. You bore me about my book; so does a letter just received from America, threatening, tho' in the civilest terms, that, if I will not publish in England, they will do it for me in that land of freemen. I *may* curse, knowing what they will bring forth. But I don't care. I am in a great haste writing for the muffin-man, my only communication with the world, who comes once a week bringing the produce of his art, also what letters may be stagnating at the Alford post, waits five minutes and then returns.

Always yours, A. T.

To Edmund Lushington.

OTLEY, *September 19th,* 1841.

MY DEAR EDMUND,

This is to let you know that I am at present in the classic neighbourhood of Bolton Abbey whither I was led the other day by some half-remembrance of a note to one of Wordsworth's poems, which told with me (to speak the truth) more than the poem itself: said Wordsworth having stated, (as far as I recollect) that everything which the eyes of man could desire in a land-skip was to be found at and about the Abbey aforesaid. I, coming with an imagination inflamed, and working upon this passage, was at first disappointed, but yesterday I took a walk of some seven or eight or, by our Lady, nine miles, to left and right of the Wharfe, and you may conjecture that no ordinary charms of nature could get nine miles walk out of legs (*at present*) more familiar with armchair and settle than rock and greensward, so that I suppose there is something in what Wordsworth asserts, and that something will probably keep me here some time, and whether I shall see you or no before you return to Glasgow is thereby rendered uncertain. I suppose there is no chance of your coming here, is there? that would be a Godsend I have no right to expect, but Harry at High Beech was a Godsend I did not expect. Poor fellow, he was very nervous, very uncomfortable too about his Italian journey, but in that respect I found it hard to sympathize with him.

Ever yours, A. TENNYSON.

To Edmund Lushington.

BOXLEY, *Early in* 1842.

DEAR EDMUND,

I was very glad to hear of the reconvalescence of your " Geschwister " for I had some fancy (as I told you) that all was not right. Your lines[1] I liked. Some doubt I had about " πολυπίδακε " but Venables set me right: not that I believed *you* could be out of your Greek, but the " πολυπίδακος Ἴδης " ran in my head. " Νασμῷ ἐν ἀμφιρύτῳ " is a wrong translation, the rest good. I have no news. I have not yet taken my book to Moxon. Spedding's going to America has a little disheartened me, for some fop will get the start of him in the *Ed. Review* where he promised to put an article and I have had abuse enough. Moreover Spedding was just the man to do it, both as knowing me, and writing from clear conviction. However I intend to get it out shortly, but I cannot say I have been what you professors call " working " at it, that indeed is not my way. I take my pipe and the muse descends in a fume, not like your modern ladies who shriek at a pipe as if they saw a " splacknuck ": do you know what a splacknuck is[2]? I have been once into your grounds, the house looked very unhappy. Charles and I went together: he admired the place much, tho' everything was deep in snow.

Yours ever, A. TENNYSON.

---

[1] A translation of " Œnone " in Greek hexameters.

[2] " His Majesty, a Prince of much Gravity, and austere Countenance, not well observing my shape at first view, asked the Queen after a cold manner, how long it was since she grew fond of a *Splacknuck*? for such it seems he took me to be, as I lay upon my breast on her Majesty's Right hand." Swift's *Voyage to Brobdingnag.*

From John Sterling.

SOUTH PLACE, KNIGHTSBRIDGE, *Oct. 26th.*

MY DEAR TENNYSON,

Your note afflicted us, and others too. I have long wished to be allowed to see something of you, and now that you would be kind enough to permit it we are both invalids, and I in London only for two or three days. For my part however I will not give the thing up and shall either call on you or write to you again in a day or two. Carlyle was here yesterday evening, growled at having missed you, and said more in your praise than in any one's except Cromwell and an American backwoodsman who has killed thirty or forty people with a bowie knife and since run away to Texas.

I learn from Americans who were also here that a certain Wheeler (known to you I think by name) is dead: whether he has carried your dollars with him and paid them by mistake to Beelzebub or Orpheus I know not.

For the moment farewell.

Believe me truly yours, JOHN STERLING [1].

.

[1] Before his death at Ventnor in September, 1844, Sterling reviewed the 1842 volume favourably in the *Quarterly*, classing my father's poems "among the richest of our recent literature."

CHAPTER VIII.

LONDON LIFE AND THE 1842 VOLUMES.

It is long since we have had so good a lyrist; it will be long before we have his superior. "Godiva" is a noble poem that will tell the legend a thousand years... "Locksley Hall" and "The Two Voices" are meditative poems, which were slowly written to be slowly read. "The Talking Oak," though a little hurt by its wit and ingenuity, is beautiful, and the most poetic of the volume. "Ulysses" belongs to a high class of poetry, destined to be the highest, and to be more cultivated in the next generation. "Œnone" was a sketch of the same kind.

EMERSON.

Tunbridge Wells was not liked by my grandmother, so she and the family migrated to Boxley not far from Maidstone in order to be near the Lushingtons at Park House; Edmund Lushington, the accomplished Greek and German scholar and Egyptologist, having married Miss Cecilia Tennyson. The park round the house is described in the prologue to "The Princess." My father had a particularly high regard not only for Edmund and Franklin Lushington but also for their brother Harry, and would say, "Others may find faults in a poem, but Harry finds *the* fault and tells you how to mend it." He is one of the three [1] friends mentioned in the poem " In the Garden at Swainston." His memory was surprising and his criticism always of the finest. " His taste was perhaps rendered more exquisite by his personal anxiety for the perfection and success of works which could scarce have interested him more if they had been his own composition." At

[1] Arthur Hallam, Henry Lushington, Sir John Simeon.

Park House my father met many friends, old and new;
Monckton Milnes, Venables, Chapman, Savile Morton,
Lear, and William Thomson (now Lord Kelvin).   With
one of these friends, or more generally by himself, he
would take long walks either on the Pilgrim's Road, or
to some one of the picturesque villages in the neighbourhood.

From time to time he stayed in town and mingled
with all sorts and conditions of men.   He always delighted in the "central roar" of London.   Whenever he
and I went to London, one of the first things we did
was to walk to the Strand and Fleet Street.   "Instead
of the stuccoed houses in the West End, this is the
place where I should like to live," he would say.   He
was also fond of looking at London from the bridges
over the Thames, and of going into St Paul's, and
into the Abbey.   One day in 1842 Fitzgerald records
a visit to St Paul's with him when he said, "Merely as
an inclosed space in a huge city this is very fine," and
when they got out into the open, in the midst of the
"central roar," "This is the mind; that is a mood of it."

He writes, "My lodgings are the last house, Norfolk
Street, Strand, at the bottom of the street on the left;
the name is Edwards which you will see projecting from
the door on a brass plate."   Generally he would stay
at the Temple or in Lincoln's Inn Fields; dining
with his friends at The Cock, and other taverns[1].

---

[1] Savile Morton, for some years the brilliant Paris correspondent of the
Daily News, wrote of one of these dinners : "Thackeray gave the dinner —
Tennyson, Forster (the literary critic of the *Examiner*), Emerson Tennant,
M.P., Crowe an author, and Maclise were the party.   Lever, the ballad
and Irish story man, came at the beginning, and told Alfred he was greatly
delighted to meet a *brother-poet*, the cool impudence of which amused
the party greatly, at Lever's expense....The largeness of Alfred's proportions,
both physical and poetical, were universally the theme of admiration.
Maclise admired him excessively, and fell quite in love with him." (*From
an unpublished letter (undated) to Mary Brotherton, author of "Rosemary
for Remembrance" and "Old Acquaintance."*)

A perfect dinner was a beef-steak, a potato, a cut of
cheese, a pint of port, and afterwards a pipe (never a
cigar). When joked with by his friends about his liking
for cold salt beef and new potatoes, he would answer
humorously, "All fine-natured men know what is good
to eat." Very genial evenings they were, with plenty
of anecdote and wit and " thrust and parry of bright
monostich." At good sayings my father would sit laughing away, " laughter often interrupted by fits of sadness."
He would take off the voices and expressions of well-
known public characters, protesting that " The oddities
and angularities of *great* men should never be hawked
about," or he would dramatically give parts of Shakespeare
or of Molière, or " enact with grim humour Milton's ' So
started up in his foul shape the fiend,' from the crouching
of the toad to the explosion [1].

He used also to do the sun coming out from a cloud, and
retiring into one again, with a gradual opening and shutting of
the eyes, and with a great fluffing up of his hair into full wig and
elevation of cravat and collar; George IV. in as comical and
wonderful a way. 'The plump head-waiter of The Cock,' by
Temple Bar, famous for chop and porter, was rather offended
when told of the poem (' Will Waterproof '). 'Had Mr Tennyson dined oftener there, he would not have minded it so much,'
he said. I think A. T.'s chief dinner resort in these ante-laureate
days was Bertolini's at the Newton's Head, close to Leicester
Square. We sometimes called it Dirtolini's, but not seriously;
for the place was clean as well as very cheap and the cookery
good for the price. Bertolini himself, who came to take the
money at the end of the feast, was a grave and polite man. He
retired with a fortune I think [2]."

My father was a member of the Sterling Club, a
literary Society of those days named in Sterling's honour,
where he met many of his old fellow "Apostles." He

[1] " Depend upon it," my father said, " Milton shot up into some grim
Archangel, Fitz." (1842.)

[2] MS Note, Edward Fitzgerald.

also often saw Carlyle, Rogers, "Barry Cornwall," Thackeray, Dickens, Forster, Savage Landor, Maclise, Leigh Hunt, and Tom Campbell. I have heard that he always showed an eager interest in the events and in the great scientific discoveries and economic inventions and improvements of the time[1]. His talk largely touched upon politics[2], philosophy and theology, and the new speculations rife on every side. Upon the projects of reform, or the great movements of philanthropy he reflected much.

> Yearning for the large excitement that the coming
>   years would yield,
> Eager-hearted as a boy when first he leaves his
>   father's field.

The Chartist and Socialist agitations were then alarming the country. My father thought they should be met not by universal imprisonment and repression, but by a widespread National education, by more of a patriotic and less of a party spirit in the Press, by partial adoption of Free Trade principles, and by an increased energy and sympathy among those who belonged to the different forms of Christianity. He was sometimes described as advancing opposite opinions at different times. This was because from his firm sense of justice he had a dramatic way of representing an opinion adverse to his own in a favourable light, in order that he might give it the most generous interpretation possible.

[1] Alluding to one such improvement he said: "Before the Penny Post a wretched review from the Continent followed me all over England, and I had to pay one pound eight shillings for it."

[2] I have heard him speak of his feelings at that time about the Afghan campaign: he thought that we ought to stand no trifling in Afghanistan; and that the English Cabinet was neglectful of the advice of Polonius: "Beware of entrance to a quarrel, but, being in, bear't that the opposer may beware of thee." Speaking of Canadian affairs, he gloried in the work done by Lord Durham and in the form of Colonial Government initiated by him in Canada.

These indeed were years rich in social and political movement: it may be enough to name Bright and Cobden, Carlyle, Thackeray, and Dickens, each with his exposure of abuses, or efforts for amendment. The atmosphere of the time inspired such lines as the following:

Ah, tho' the times when some new thought can bud
Are but as poets' seasons when they flower,
Yet seas that daily gain upon the shore
Have ebb and flow conditioning their march,
And slow and sure comes up the golden year,
When wealth no more shall rest in mounded heaps,
But smit with freer light shall slowly melt
In many streams to fatten lower lands,
And light shall spread, and man be liker man
Thro' all the season of the golden year.

*   *   *   *   *   *   *

Fly, happy happy sails, and bear the Press;
Fly happy with the mission of the Cross;
Knit land to land, and blowing havenward
With silks, and fruits, and spices, clear of toll,
Enrich the markets of the golden year[1].

Theology, always a deep interest to him, shared in this advance. The Oxford movement had been begun by a band of saintly and devoted churchmen, and the Vice-Chancellor of Oxford with the heads of houses had already censured the author of *Tract No. XC*[2]. Meanwhile Maurice, Kingsley and the Cambridge men were striving to make thought more tolerant, and to impress all men with a sense of brotherhood. Both efforts in a few years effected a mighty change in

[1] "The Golden Year" was first published in 1846 in the *Poems* (4th ed.).
[2] Published February 1841.

the spirit of the National Church by broadening its borders and deepening its spirituality.

The biographies of friends and acquaintances, recently published, are full of allusions to my father at this period. Perhaps the most life-like portrait[1] is that drawn by Carlyle for Emerson in America.

Alfred is one of the few British and foreign figures (a not increasing number I think) who are and remain beautiful to me, a true human soul, or some authentic approximation thereto, to whom your own soul can say, " Brother ! " However, I doubt he will not come [to see me] ; he often skips me, in these brief visits to town ; skips everybody, indeed ; being a man solitary and sad, as certain men are, dwelling in an element of gloom, carrying a bit of Chaos about him, in short, which he is manufacturing into Cosmos......He had his breeding at Cambridge, as if for the Law or Church ; being master of a small annuity on his father's decease, he preferred clubbing with his mother and some sisters, to live unpromoted and write Poems. In this way he lives still, now here, now there ; the family always within reach of London, never in it ; he himself making rare and brief visits, lodging in some old comrade's rooms. I think he must be under forty, not much under it. One of the finest looking men in the world. A great shock of rough dusky dark hair ; bright, laughing, hazel eyes ; massive aquiline face, most massive yet most delicate ; of sallow brown complexion, almost Indian looking, clothes cynically loose, free-and-easy, smokes infinite tobacco. His voice is musical, metallic, fit for loud laughter and piercing wail, and all that may lie between ; speech and speculation free and plenteous ; I do not meet in these late

[1] On Sept. 5th, 1840, Carlyle had sketched another portrait of my father for his brother John : " Some weeks ago, one night, the poet Tennyson and Matthew Allen were discovered here sitting smoking in the garden. Tennyson had been here before, but was still new to Jane, — who was alone for the first hour or two of it. A fine, large-featured, dim-eyed, bronze-coloured, shaggy-headed man is Alfred ; dusty, smoky, free and easy ; who swims, outwardly and inwardly, with great composure in an articulate element as of tranquil chaos and tobacco-smoke ; great now and then when he does emerge ; a most restful, brotherly, solid-hearted man. Allen looked considerably older ; speculative, hopeful, earnest-frothy as from the beginning." (See for Allen, p. 220.)

decades such company over a pipe! we shall see what he will grow to.

Mrs. Carlyle also gives a characteristic portrait:

Three of the autographs which I send you to-day are first-rate. A Yankee would almost give a dollar apiece for them. Entire characteristic letters from Pickwick, Lytton Bulwer and Alfred Tennyson; the last the greatest genius of the three, though the vulgar public have not as yet recognized him as such. Get his poems if you can, and read the " Ulysses," " Dora," the " Vision of Sin," and you will find that we do not overrate him. Besides, he is a very handsome man, and a noble-hearted one, with something of the gypsy in his appearance, which for me is perfectly charming. Babbie never saw him, unfortunately, or perhaps I should say fortunately, for she must have fallen in love with him on the spot, unless she be made absolutely of ice; and then men of genius have never anything to keep wives upon.

Carlyle did not, I believe, become intimate with my father until after 1842, " being naturally prejudiced against one whom everyone was praising, and praising for a sort of poetry which he despised. But directly he saw and heard the Man, he knew there was a man to deal with and took pains to cultivate him; assiduous in exhorting him to leave Verse and Rhyme, and to apply his genius to Prose[1]." Indeed he told him then that he was " a life-guardsman spoilt by making poetry."

When the 1842 volumes were published the literary world in London accepted them at once, and Milnes[2] and Sterling led the chorus of favourable reviews.

My father's comprehension of human life had grown: and the new poems dealt with an extraordinarily wide range of subjects, chivalry, duty, reverence, self-control, human passion, human love, the love of country, science,

[1] MS Note, Edward Fitzgerald.
[2] *Westminster Review*, October, 1842.

philosophy, simple faith and the many complex moods of the religious nature; whilst they were free from the brooding self-absorption into which modern poetry is liable to lapse, and from what Arthur Hallam called "the habit of seeking relief in idiosyncrasies."

It was the heart of England even more than her imagination that he made his own. It was the Humanities and the truths underlying them that he sang, and he so sang them that any deep-hearted reader was made to feel through his far-reaching thought that those Humanities are spiritual things, and that to touch them is to touch the garment of the Divine. Those who confer so deep a benefit cannot but be remembered. The Heroic is not greatly appreciated in these days; but on this occasion the challenge met with a response [1].

With a selection from the early poems, some of them almost rewritten, appeared a number of English Idyls and Eclogues, pictures of English home and country life, quite original in their form. Upon the sacredness of home life he would maintain that the stability and greatness of a nation largely depend; and one of the secrets of his power over mankind was his true joy in the family duties and affections. Among these new poems were "The Gardener's Daughter," "Dora," "Audley Court," "Walking to the Mail," "The Talking Oak," "Locksley Hall," "Godiva," "Edward Gray," "Lady Clare," "The Lord of Burleigh," "Will Waterproof," and the conclusion of "The May Queen." Then there were the more general poems, "Morte d'Arthur," "St Simeon Stylites," "Love and Duty," "Ulysses," "The Two Voices," "The Day-Dream[2]," "Amphion," "St Agnes' Eve," "Sir Galahad," "Sir

[1] Aubrey de Vere (in letter to me).

[2] The Prologue and Epilogue were added after 1835, when we first heard it in Cumberland; I suppose for the same reason that caused the Prologue of the "Morte d'Arthur," giving a reason for telling an old-world tale. MS Note, E. F. G.

In 1842 he had eight of the blank verse poems printed for his private use.

Launcelot and Queen Guinevere," " A Farewell," " The Beggar Maid," " The Vision of Sin," " Move eastward, happy Earth," " Break, Break " (made in a Lincolnshire lane at 5 o'clock in the morning between blossoming hedges), " The Poet's Song," and his three political poems.

On the other side of the Atlantic these volumes were also welcomed; Hawthorne, Margaret Fuller, Emerson, Edgar Allan Poe were notably enthusiastic.

The popular German poet Ferdinand Freiligrath writes to Mary Howitt from Frankfort, Oct. 1842 : " Tennyson is indeed a true poet, though perhaps sometimes a little too transcendental. ' Mariana in the Moated Grange,' and some other of his poems are superb; and breathe such a sweet and dreamy melancholy that I cannot cease to read and admire them[1]."

The most remarkable review of these volumes was by Spedding in the *Edinburgh* for April 1843 (reprinted in *Reviews and Discussions*), from which I subjoin extracts, as these give accurately the growth of his friend's mind.

The decade during which Mr Tennyson has remained silent has wrought a great improvement. The handling in his later pieces is much lighter and freer; the interest deeper and purer; there is more humanity with less image and drapery; a closer adherence to truth; a greater reliance for effect upon the simplicity of Nature. Moral and spiritual traits of character are more dwelt upon, in place of external scenery and circumstance. He addresses himself more to the heart and less to the ear and eye. This change which is felt in its results throughout the second volume, may in the latter half of the first be traced in

because he always liked to see his poems in print some months and sometimes some years before publication, " for," as he said, " poetry looks better, more convincing, in print."   This little volume was entitled *Morte d'Arthur; Dora, and other Idyls*.

[2] From private letter lent by Miss Howitt.

its process. The poems originally published in 1832 are many
of them largely altered; generally with great judgment, and
always with a view to strip off redundancies, to make the expression simpler and clearer, to substitute thought for imagery
and substance for shadow. "The Lady of Shalott," for instance,
is stripped of all her finery; her pearl garland, her velvet bed,
her royal apparel and her "blinding diamond bright," are all
gone; and certainly in the simple white robe which she now
wears, her beauty shows to much greater advantage.

"The Miller's Daughter," again, is much enriched by the
introduction of the mother of the lover; and the following
beautiful stanzas (which many people, however, will be ill
satisfied to miss) are displaced to make room for beauty of a
much higher order :

> Remember you the clear moonlight
>   That whiten'd all the eastern ridge,
> When o'er the water dancing white
>   I stepp'd upon the old mill bridge?
> I heard you whisper from above,
>   A lute-toned whisper, "I am here!"
> I murmur'd "Speak again, my love,
>   The stream is loud : I cannot hear!"
>
> I heard, as I have seem'd to hear,
>   When all the under air was still,
> The low voice of the glad New Year
>   Call to the freshly-flower'd hill.
> I heard, as I have often heard,
>   The nightingale in leafy woods
> Call to its mate when nothing stirr'd
>   To left or right but falling floods.

These, we observe, are away; and the following graceful and
tender picture, full of the spirit of English rural life, appears in
their place. (The late squire's son, we should premise, is bent
on marrying the daughter of the wealthy miller :)

> And slowly was my mother brought
>   To yield consent to my desire:
>
> *   *   *   *   *   *

And rose, and, with a silent grace
Approaching, press'd you heart to heart.

> Vol. i. p. 109.

Mr Spedding goes on to say that in the song of
"The Lotos-Eaters," which "hardly admitted of improvement," my father had added "some touches of deeper
significance, indicating the first effects of the physical
disease upon the moral and intellectual nature:

Dear is the memory of our wedded lives,

*   *   *   *   *   *   *

And eyes grown dim with gazing on the pilot stars."

> Vol. i. p. 182.

Then at the end of the poem there is found an alteration of
a like kind : where for the flow of triumphant enjoyment, in
the contemplation of merely sensual ease and luxurious repose,
with which it originally closed, a higher strain is substituted,
which is meant apparently to show the effect of lotos-eating
upon the religious feelings.   The gods of the Lotos-eaters, it
is worth knowing, are altogether Lucretian.

"The May Queen[1]" too was made "more deeply
and tragically interesting" by the third and concluding
part.   But the four poems, in which "the work is at the
highest level," and from which we may gather some
hints concerning "his moral theory of life and its issues
and of that which constitutes a sound condition of the
soul," are " The Palace of Art," the dramatic monologue
of " St Simeon Stylites," " The Two Voices," and " The
Vision of Sin."

"The Palace of Art" represents allegorically the condition
of a mind which, in the love of beauty, and the triumphant
consciousness of knowledge, and intellectual supremacy, in the
intense enjoyment of its own power and glory, has lost sight

---

[1] "The May Queen" is all Lincolnshire inland, as "Locksley Hall" its
sea-board.   MS Note, E. F. G.

of its relation to man and God. * * * As "The Palace of Art" represents the pride of voluptuous enjoyment in its noblest form, the "St Simeon Stylites" represents the pride of asceticism in its basest [1].

Of "The Two Voices [2]" Spedding says:

In "The Two Voices" we have a history of the agitations, the suggestions and counter-suggestions of a mind sunk in hopeless despondency, and meditating self-destruction; together with the manner of its recovery to a more healthy condition.... Others would have been content to give the bad voice the worst of the argument; but, unhappily, all moral reasoning must ultimately rest on the internal evidence of the moral sense; and where this is disordered, the most unquestionable logic can conclude nothing, because it is the first principles which are at issue; the *major* is not admitted. Mr Tennyson's treatment of the case is more scientific.... "The Vision of Sin" touches upon a more awful subject than any of these; the end, here and hereafter, of the merely sensual man.

In conclusion Spedding adds, that these poems show that the author's art is no trick of these versifying times, born of a superficial sensibility to beauty and a turn for setting to music the current doctrines and fashionable feelings of the day; but a genuine growth of nature, having its root deep in the pensive heart, a heart accustomed to meditate earnestly and feel truly upon the prime duties and interests of man.

Some notes on the second volume have been left me by my father, the first of which is on the "Morte d'Arthur." This particular note I wrote down from what

---

[1] This is one of the poems A. T. would read with grotesque grimness, especially such passages as "coughs, aches, stitches," etc., laughing aloud at times. MS Note, E. F. G.

[2] My father told me, "When I wrote 'The Two Voices' I was so utterly miserable, a burden to myself and to my family, that I said, 'Is life worth anything?' and now that I am old, I fear that I shall only live a year or two, for I have work still to do." The last part, E. F. G. writes, was probably made in the fields about Dulwich.

he said; but he gave it his approval, as expressing his own view correctly.

" How much of history we have in the story of Arthur is doubtful. Let not my readers press too hardly on details whether for history or for allegory. Some think that King Arthur may be taken to typify conscience. He is anyhow meant to be a man who spent himself in the cause of honour, duty and self-sacrifice, who felt and aspired with his nobler knights, though with a stronger and a clearer conscience than any of them, 'reverencing his conscience as his king.' 'There was no such perfect man since Adam' as an old writer says. 'Major præteritis majorque futuris Regibus.'"

Edward Fitzgerald writes:

The " Morte d'Arthur" when read to us from manuscript in 1835 had no introduction or epilogue; which was added to anticipate or excuse the "faint Homeric echoes," etc. (as in the "Day-Dream"), to give a reason for telling an old-world tale.

Again:

Mouthing out his hollow oes and aes, deep-chested music, this is something as A. T. reads, with a broad north country vowel, except the u in such words as "mute," "brute," which he pronounces like the thin French "u." His voice, very deep and deep-chested, but rather murmuring than mouthing, like the sound of a far sea or of a pine-wood, I remember greatly struck Carlyle when he first came to know him. There was no declamatory showing off in A. T.'s recitation of his verse; sometimes broken with a laugh, or a burlesque twist of voice, when something struck him as quaint or grim. Sometimes Spedding would read the poems to us; A. T. once told him he seemed to read too much as if bees were about his mouth, all in good humour as in sincerity. Of the Chivalry Romances he said to me, "I could not read 'Palmerin of England' nor 'Amadis,' nor any other of those Romances through. The 'Morte d'Arthur' is much the best: there are very fine things in it, but all strung together without Art[1]."

[1] MS Note.

In "Locksley Hall" my father annotates the line "Let the great world spin for ever down the ringing grooves of change." "When I went by the first train from Liverpool to Manchester (1830), I thought that the wheels ran in a groove. It was a black night and there was such a vast crowd round the train at the station that we could not see the wheels. Then I made this line."— Further: "'Locksley Hall' is an imaginary place (tho' the coast is Lincolnshire) and the hero is imaginary. The whole poem represents young life, its good side, its deficiencies, and its yearnings. Mr Hallam said to me that the English people liked verse in Trochaics, so I wrote the poem in this metre."

In the first unpublished edition of "Locksley Hall," after "*knots of Paradise*," came the following couplet, which was omitted lest the description should be too long:

All about a summer ocean, leagues on leagues of
    golden calm,
And within melodious waters rolling round the knolls
    of palm.

I remember my father saying that Sir William Jones' prose translation of the *Moâllakât*, the seven Arabic poems (which are a selection from the work of pre-Mahommedan poets) hanging up in the temple of Mecca, gave him the idea of the poem.

When these volumes were published my father was often in the habit of breakfasting with Rogers, for whom he had a real affection, but who "rather bored him with attentions, very generous and amiable from the old poet." Rogers would praise "Locksley Hall," and would say "Shakespeare could not have done it better." "I should have thought," observed my father, "that such a poem as 'Dora' was more in Rogers' line:

perhaps it was too much in his line. 'Dora,' being
the tale of a nobly simple country girl, had to be told in
the simplest possible poetical language, and therefore
was one of the poems which gave most trouble."
"Ulysses," my father said, "was written soon after
Arthur Hallam's death, and gave my feeling about the
need of going forward, and braving the struggle of life
perhaps more simply than anything in 'In Memoriam.'"

My father's note on "Audley Court" runs thus:

"This poem was partially suggested by Abbey Park
at Torquay.   Torquay was in old days the loveliest
sea village in England and now is a town.   In those
old days I, coming down from the hill over Torquay,
saw a star of phosphorescence made by the buoy appearing and disappearing in the dark sea, and wrote
these lines.

> But ere the night we rose
> And saunter'd home beneath a moon, that, just
> In crescent, dimly rain'd about the leaf
> Twilights of airy silver, till we reach'd
> The limit of the hills; and as we sank
> From rock to rock upon the glooming quay,
> The town was hush'd beneath us: lower down
> The bay was oily calm; the harbour-buoy,
> Sole star of phosphorescence in the calm,
> With one green sparkle ever and anon
> Dipt by itself, and we were glad at heart."

However he never cared greatly for this sea on the
south coast of England, "not a grand sea," he would
say, "only an angry curt sea.   It seems to shriek as
it recoils with the pebbles along the shore; the finest
seas I have ever seen are at Valencia, Mablethorpe and
in (West) Cornwall.   At Valencia the sea was grand,
without any wind blowing and seemingly without a wave:

but with the momentum of the Atlantic behind, it dashes up into foam, blue diamonds it looks like, all along the rocks, like ghosts playing at hide and seek. When I was in Cornwall it had blown a storm of wind and rain for days, and all of a sudden fell into perfect calm; I was a little inland of the cliffs: when, after a space of perfect silence, a long roll of thunder, from some wave rushing into a cavern I suppose, came up from the distance, and died away. I *never* felt silence like that[1]."

The seas at Mablethorpe he would describe as "interminable waves rolling along interminable shores of sand."

In working at "The Gardener's Daughter" he said: "The centre of the poem, that passage describing the girl, must be full and rich. The poem is so, to a fault, especially the descriptions of nature, for the lover is an artist, but, this being so, the central picture must hold its place.

> One arm aloft —
> Gown'd in pure white, that fitted to the shape —
> Holding the bush, to fix it back, she stood.
> A single stream of all her soft brown hair
> Pour'd on one side: the shadow of the flowers
> Stole all the golden gloss, and, wavering
> Lovingly lower, trembled on her waist —
> Ah, happy shade — and still went wavering down,
> But, ere it touch'd a foot, that might have danced
> The greensward into greener circles, dipt,
> And mix'd with shadows of the common ground!
> But the full day dwelt on her brows, and sunn'd
> Her violet eyes, and all her Hebe bloom,
> And doubled his own warmth against her lips,
> And on the bounteous wave of such a breast
> As never pencil drew."

---

[1] MS Note by E. F. G.

I remember too my father's telling me that Fitzgerald had said that the autumn landscape, which in the
first edition was described in the lines beginning " Her
beauty grew," was taken from a background of a Titian
(Lord Ellesmere's *Ages of Man*); and that perhaps in
consequence they had been omitted. They ran thus:

Her beauty grew: *till drawn in narrowing arcs*
The southing Autumn touch'd with sallower gleams
The granges on the fallows. At that time,
Tired of the noisy town I wander'd there;
The bell toll'd four; and by the time I reach'd
The Wicket-gate, I found her by herself.

The correction of the proofs of this poem and of this volume
took place in Spedding's chambers at 60 Lincoln's Inn Fields,
in the forepart of 1842. The poems to be printed were nearly
all, I think all, in a foolscap folio parchment-bound blank book
such as accounts are kept in (only not ruled), and which I used
to call "The Butcher's Book." The poems were written in
A. T.'s very fine hand (he once said, not thinking of himself,
that great men generally wrote "terse" hands) toward one side
of the large page; the unoccupied edges and corners being often
stript down for pipe-lights, taking care to save the MS, as A. T.
once seriously observed. The pages of MS from the Butcher's
Book were one by one torn out for the printer, and, when
returned with the proofs, were put in the fire. I reserved two
or three of the leaves; and gave them to the Library of Trinity
College (Cambridge[1]).

I insert here an unpublished poem which was originally intended as a prologue to " The Gardener's Daughter" and was called " The Ante-Chamber." My father
wished it never to be printed in front of "The Gardener's
Daughter" because this is already full enough. It is
however too good to be lost. The portrait in " The

---

[1] E. F. G., MS notes on A. T.

Ante-Chamber" might be himself at the period, — so his
friends say, — but that was by no means his intention[1].

The Ante-Chamber.[*]   (*Unpublished.*)

That is his portrait painted by himself.
Look on those manly curls so glossy dark,
Those thoughtful furrows in the swarthy cheek;
Admire that stalwart shape, those ample brows,
And that large table of the breast dispread,
Between low shoulders; how demure a smile,
How full of wisest humour and of love,
With some half-consciousness of inward power,
Sleeps round those quiet lips; not quite a smile;
And look you what an arch the brain has built
Above the ear! and what a settled mind,
Mature, harbour'd from change, contemplative,
Tempers the peaceful light of hazel eyes,
Observing all things.   This is he I loved,
This is the man of whom you heard me speak.
  My fancy was the more luxurious,
But his was minted in a deeper mould,
And took in more of Nature than mine own;
Nor proved I such delight as he, to mark
The humours of the polling and the wake,
The hubbub of the market and the booths:
How this one smiled, that other waved his arms,
These careful and those candid brows, how each —
Down to his slightest turns and attitudes —
Was something that another could not be,
How every brake and flower spread and rose,
A various world! which he compell'd once more
Thro' his own nature, with well mingled hues,

---

[1] Samuel Laurence painted the earliest portrait of my father about 1838.

Into another shape, born of the first,
As beautiful, but yet another world.
    All this so stirr'd him in his hour of joy,
Mix'd with the phantom of his coming fame,
That once he spake: " I lift the eyes of thought,
I look thro' all my glimmering life, I see
At the end, as 'twere athwart a colour'd cloud,
O'er the bow'd shoulder of a bland old Age,
The face of placid Death." Long, Eustace, long
May my strong wish, transgressing the low bound
Of mortal hope, act on Eternity
To keep thee here amongst us! Yet he lives;
His and my friendship have not suffer'd loss,
His fame is equal to his years: his praise
Is neither overdealt, nor idly won.
    Step thro' these doors, and I will show to you
Another countenance, one yet more dear,
More dear, for what is lost is made more dear;
" More dear " I will not say, but rather bless
The All-perfect Framer, Him, who made the heart,
Forethinking its twinfold necessity,
Thro' one whole life an overflowing urn,
Capacious both of Friendship and of Love.

CHAPTER IX.

REMINISCENCES OF TENNYSON (ABOUT 1842).

[At this time there seems to have been an almost total cessation of correspondence between my father and his intimate friends; and I accordingly asked Edmund Lushington, the present Dean of Westminster, and Aubrey de Vere to give me some reminiscences of those days.]

Edmund Lushington writes:

During my first two years at Cambridge I had no acquaintance with A. T. ; the first occasion I can remember of knowing him by sight was when Arthur Hallam read in the College Chapel his essay which gained the first declamation prize. The place where the reader stood was slightly raised above the aisle of the chapel; A. T. sat on the bench just below, listening intently to the spoken words.

At this time, and indeed for several years later, copies of numerous poems of his were widely circulated about Cambridge in MS, and I remember one debate in a Society called the " Fifty," on the rank to which his poetry was entitled, in the course of which numerous passages were quoted from poems as yet not publicly known— " The Gardener's Daughter " in particular.

I believe the first time he visited me in my own house was in the summer of 1840 when he came to stay a few days. He was then habitually residing with his mother and sisters at Tunbridge Wells, where, beautiful as the neighbourhood was, the site was found not healthy for all of the family, and they were wishing to meet with some other place to settle in. A day or two later I went over with him to pay a short visit to his mother's house at Tunbridge Wells, where among other notabilities we saw an old lady famous for cherishing memories of the great Dr Samuel Johnson, whose likeness graced an expansive medallion which she wore about her neck, Miss L.[1] Not long after this visit he came over with his mother and two younger sisters to stay some days at Park House, which they partly spent in looking round the neighbouring country at any such houses as might appear to be suitable for a settled residence in preference to Tunbridge Wells.

They eventually settled before long upon engaging a house belonging to Colonel Best in Boxley Parish, to which they removed before the winter of 1841–42. The house was nearly two miles by the road, rather less by the fields, from our residence at Park House, which is nearer Maidstone. Early in October we drove up in an open phaeton to London by the old coach-road which knew no railways in that time. Whether A. T. went up with us I am not sure: at any rate the next day he was in London and came to take leave of us at the station where we left by train for the north. I remember how some one out of a crowd of lookers on, just before the train was starting, after a long gaze at his dark features uttered an emphatic " foreign."

At Xmas 1841 I went for a few days' holiday from Glasgow to Kent and spent the time mostly at Boxley, where A. T. was now settled with his mother and sisters. We had sometimes dance and song in the evening, where, tho' no one spoke of it, assuredly many a heart was filled "with an awful sense of one mute Shadow watching all," as his own undying words record of an earlier occasion. In the meantime the number of the memorial poems had rapidly increased since I had seen the poet, his book containing many that were new to me. Some I heard him repeat before I had seen them in writing, others I learnt to know first from the book itself which he kindly allowed me to look through without stint. I remember one particular night when we were sitting up together late in his bedroom. He began to recite the poem that stands sixth in " In Memoriam," "One writes, that ' Other friends remain,' " and I do not know that the deep melodious thunder of his voice with all its overwhelming pathos, often and often as I have heard it, ever imprest me more profoundly. On one other occasion he

---

[1] She observed that Dr Johnson " often stirred his lemonade with his finger and that often dirty." My father was very angry with her for relating such a story about a great man, and said, " The dirt is in her own heart."

came and showed me a poem he had just composed, saying he liked it better than most he had done lately, this was No. LI., "Do we indeed desire the dead."

He was present on July 6th, 1842, at a festival of the Maidstone Mechanics' Institute held in our Park, of which he has introduced a lively description in the beginning of "The Princess."

In the course of that summer appeared the collection of his poems published in two vols.; the first contains, with some exceptions, the poems published under the title *Poems, chiefly Lyrical*, in 1830, and as a second division, with various changes, those which first appeared in 1832. The second volume had all new poems, already known to many in private circulation, but not as yet openly given to the world.

He went with me once or twice to London to make arrangements such as are required by the law with reference to the marriage of his youngest sister Cecilia. The marriage ceremony was performed by his elder brother, the Rev. Charles Tennyson Turner, who had come to spend some time with his mother and with whom I then first became acquainted.

*   *   *   *   *   *

In the hottest part of the summer (1845) A. T. had gone down to Eastbourne, and was lodging in one of two or three cottages prettily grouped together, bearing the well-deserved name of Mount Pleasant. A little garden lay in front of the cottages, beyond that a cornfield extended some way till it was stopt by a path on the edge of the cliff, which overlooked the sea, and continued its course on to Holywell. Mount Pleasant and all in front of it has now vanished through the encroachment of the sea. Its last vestige I saw many years since as a brick fragment in the yard of a grand new hotel built just above the parade to which the present sea-line reaches. I went down there to see him and remained a few days. He had then completed many of the cantos in "In Memoriam" and was engaged on "The Princess," of which I had heard nothing before. He read or showed me the first part, beyond which it had then hardly advanced. He said to me, "I have brought in your marriage at the end of 'In Memoriam,'" and then showed me those poems of "In Memoriam" which were finished and which were a perfectly novel surprise to me.

The Dean of Westminster writes:

In 1841 and 1842 I paid two visits in the month of August to Park House near Maidstone, the property of your father's brother-in-law Edmund Lushington, who in those days made it his southern residence during the many months of the long vacation that set him free from his laborious work in Scotland. I found there not only a bright, charming and happy group of his brothers and sisters, four sisters and two brothers, the Henry Lushington who died at Malta in the year 1855, and my own friend and contemporary Franklin, but one or two visitors, Mr George Venables, and Mr Chapman, a Fellow I think then of Jesus College, Cambridge. I shall never forget the impression made on me by coming in contact with men so striking at once in character and ability, and yet a circle so wholly, so widely, different from that which had gathered round Arnold at Rugby, or with which I was familiar, so far as was possible for one so young, at my own University. The questions that stirred so deeply our seniors and ourselves at Oxford, the position of J. H. Newman and his friends, the course of the "Oxford movement," the whole Tractarian Controversy, were scarcely mentioned, or, if mentioned, were spoken of as matters of secondary or remote interest: while on the other hand the Lushington brothers, especially the Professor, "uncle Edmund" as I have always heard you term him, seemed as much at home in the language of the Greek dramatists as if it was their native tongue, while of Henry I remember his friend Chapman saying that it was difficult to quote or read a line of Shakespeare, to which he could not at once give the reference and the context. Of Mr Venables and the position which he had long held among his Cambridge friends and which he was already gaining in London literary society, I need not speak. How many of that group, whose wide and varied attainments, unstudied but suggestive conversation, so impressed the young Oxford undergraduate, fresh from so different an atmosphere, have passed beyond the veil!

It was in the midst of these, all his warm friends and associates, that I first saw your father. I feel sure that I saw him during my first visit; on the second occasion he and his mother and sisters had been living for some months in Boxley Hall, the parish in which Park House is situated. The Professor was

already engaged to your aunt Cecilia Tennyson, and the wedding
followed soon after my return home. Your father was I need
hardly say constantly at Park House, and there were few days
on which I did not see him. The year was marked by the recent
publication of the two-volume edition of his poems. The first
volume, a copy of which during my visit was given me by Frank
Lushington, is still a treasured possession. The second alas!
is lost. I try to look back through the mist of years and see
your father as I saw him then; I remember watching him as
he sat on a garden seat on the grass, in a brown suit, looking
somewhat grave and silent, and wondering whether my friends at
Oxford would feel as I did the poems which I had already read,
" Mariana," " The Gardener's Daughter," " Œnone," " Locksley
Hall," and " The Two Voices." Of his conversation I can only
recall one or two fragments. We, the younger members of the
party, as well as the older guests and your father, were in the
garden employed, some of the party in gathering, some in
eating wall-fruit, peaches and apricots. Some one made a
remark about the fruit being liable to disagree with himself or
others, to which another (it was Chapman) replied with a
jocular remark about "the disturbed districts," alluding of
course to some disorders apprehended or existing in the
centres of industry. I remember being startled by your father's
voice and accent, " I can't joke about so grave a question," and
thinking to myself that it was exactly what one so different
as Dr Arnold, who had died some two months earlier, might
have said under similar circumstances.

Again, I was greatly struck by his describing to us on one
singularly still starlit evening, how he and his friends had once
sat out far into the night having tea at a table on the lawn
beneath the stars, and that the candles had burned with steady
upright flame, disturbed from time to time by the inrush of a
moth or cockchafer, as tho' in a closed room. I do not know
whether he had already written, or was perhaps even then
shaping, the lines in " In Memoriam," which so many years
afterwards brought back to me the incident.

As one looks back to the years previous to 1842 it is curious
to notice the immense change caused by the publication of those
two volumes. On my return to Oxford in October 1842 his
name was on everyone's lips, his poems discussed, criticised,
interpreted; portions of them repeatedly set for translation

into Latin or Greek verse at schools and colleges; read and re-read so habitually that there were many of us who could repeat page after page from memory. At one of the earliest meetings which I remember at a small debating Society, "The Decade," well known at Oxford in those days, I think it was in 1844, was a discussion as to the relative merits of Wordsworth and Tennyson, in which I especially recall the speeches of J. C. Shairp, A. H. Clough, and I think I may add of the future Chief Justice John Coleridge.

It was a great change; though no doubt a small, I should think a very small, circle of Oxford residents may have been more or less acquainted with his published poems at an earlier date. In a letter from Arthur Stanley, written from Hurstmonceux Rectory in the September of 1834, he says to his friend W. C. Lake (afterwards Dean of Durham), still at Rugby, that Julius Hare, with whom he was staying, " often reads to us in the evening things quite new to me, for instance (tell it not in Gath) A. Tennyson's *Poems*," and he goes on to name some which had greatly pleased him, and to advise his friend to get the volume and read it. The expression " tell it not," etc. is no doubt a reference to the acrid and contemptuous article in the *Quarterly* of 1833.

The readings at Hurstmonceux were not forgotten by the young scholar of Balliol. In Stanley's very striking prize poem " The Gipsies," written in 1837, he adapted to the heroic measure a line from the introduction in blank verse to " The Palace of Art," and quoted the words without the author's name in a note.

In a paper on John Keble he tells us how as the Professor of Poetry went thro' the poem before recitation with him, he noticed the quotation and passed on, saying " Shakespeare I suppose."

In the three or four terms which I had spent at Oxford I remember also myself translating into Latin Elegiacs in February 1841, from a printed copy, the last three stanzas of the lines to J. S. beginning with " Words weaker than your grief," etc. They were in the possession of my private tutor E. Massey of Wadham, a distinguished Shrewsbury scholar, whose Cambridge friends may possibly have suggested their use for such a purpose. Otherwise I cannot recall anyone at Oxford before the publication of the two volumes ever mentioning your father's poems. We talked much of Keble on the one hand, Shelley and Byron on the other, and some of us I need not say were strong Words-

worthians and were half-amused, half-indignant at the tendency
of some of our undergraduate friends to depreciate Milton as a
Puritan poet; but the intense interest called out by the two
volumes seems to me, on looking back, to have taken my young
contemporaries at Oxford as well as the outside world of readers
as it were by storm. I seem still to hear voices that have long
since been silent repeating line after line, which I can hardly
read even now without recalling the very accent and the faces of
friends of "days that are no more."

Aubrey de Vere writes:

It was in 1841 or 1842 that I first met the Poet[1] on whom
and on whose works my imagination had rested so often during
the preceding ten years; and I lost nothing when the living man
stood before me. The large dark eyes, generally dreamy but
with an occasional gleam of imaginative alertness, the dusky,
almost Spanish complexion, the high-built head and the massive
abundance of curling hair like the finest and blackest silk, are still
before me, and no less the stalwart form, strong " with the certain
step of man," though some years earlier it might have moved

> Still hither thither idly sway'd
> Like those long mosses in the stream.

Whenever we were both in London, I met him as often as
I could, sometimes at the rooms of James Spedding, or at some
late smoking-party consisting of young men, their intimates at
the University, the well-known Cambridge "Apostles." That
was a society unvexed by formalities ; and I do not remember
that my new friend and I ever called each other otherwise
than by our Christian names. He was thus always called by
many of his intimates beside; for their affection for him partook
largely of domestic affection in its character. He was preeminently a *man*, as well as a genius, but not the least the
man of the world. He was essentially refined; but convention
fled before his face. At none of those reunions did I meet any
of his brothers, though in later years I knew Frederick, many
of whose poems were much admired by Henry Taylor as
well as by myself. Unfortunately I never met his brother

---

[1] See Appendix, p. 501, for "The Reception of the Early Poems," by
Aubrey de Vere.

Charles, who early published a slender volume of Sonnets warmly praised by Coleridge. My father had greatly admired one on the sea —

"The lightest murmur of its seething foam," etc.

The entire simplicity and unconventionality of Alfred Tennyson was part of the charm which bound his friends to him. No acquaintance, however inferior to him in intellect, could be afraid of him. He felt that he was not in the presence of a critic, but of one who respected human nature wherever he found it free from unworthiness, who would think his own thoughts whether in the society of ordinary or extraordinary men, and who could not but express them plainly if he spoke at all. That perfect transparency of mind, like the clearness of air in the finest climates, when it is nearness not distance that "lends enchantment to the view," I have seen only in three men beside him, Wordsworth, Sir William Rowan Hamilton and one other. His unguardedness, in combination with his unworldliness, made his friends all the more zealous to help him; and perhaps their emulous aid was more useful to him than self-help could have been. His friends' appreciation of his poetry too was an enthusiasm ardent enough to carry with it a healthful infection. It forced others to give his works an earlier attention than would otherwise have been their lot, and consequently an earlier recognition; but it was the genuine merit of his poetry which produced that enthusiasm and prevented it from cooling while the wise were forming their judgments, and the wiseacres were depreciating minor poets and confounding him with them. Friends could but raise the sail high enough to catch what breeze might be stirring. The rest depended on the boat. It seems strange however that his larger fame made way so slowly. For many a year, we, his zealots, were but zealots of a sect. Seventeen years after the publication of his first volume, and five more after that of his third, "The Princess," came out, I wrote a critique in one of our chief *Quarterlies*, and called him a "great poet." The then Editor struck out "great" and substituted "true." He considered that the public would not tolerate so strong an eulogium.

Alfred Tennyson's largeness of mind and of heart was touchingly illustrated by his reverence for Wordsworth's poetry, notwithstanding that the immense merits which he recognised in

it were not, in his opinion, supplemented by a proportionate amount of artistic skill.   He was always glad to show reverence to the "Old Poet," not then within ten years of the age at which the then younger one died.   "Wordsworth," he said to me one day, "is staying at Hampstead in the house of his friend Mr. Hoare; I must go and see him; and you must come with me; mind you do not tell Rogers, or he will be displeased at my being in London and not going to see him."   We drove up to Hampstead, and knocked at the door; and the next minute it was opened by the Poet of the World, at whose side stood the Poet of the Mountains.   Rogers' old face, which had encountered nearly ninety years, seemed to double the number of its wrinkles as he said, not angrily but very drily : " Ah, you did not come up the hill to see me! "   During the visit it was with Tennyson that the Bard of Rydal held discourse, while the recluse of St James' Place, whom " that angle " especially delighted, conversed with me.   As we walked back to London through grassy fields not then built over, Tennyson complained of the old Poet's coldness.   He had endeavoured to stimulate some latent ardours by telling him of a tropical island where the trees, when they first came into leaf, were a vivid scarlet; —
"Every one of them, I told him, one flush all over the island, the colour of blood!   It would not do.   I could not inflame his imagination in the least!"   During the preceding year I had had the great honour of passing several days at Rydal Mount with Wordsworth, walking on his mountains and listening to him at his fireside.   I told him that a young poet had lately risen up.   Wordsworth answered that he feared from the little he had heard that if Crabbe was the driest of poets, the young aspirant must have the opposite fault.   I replied that he should judge for himself, and without leave given, recited to him two poems by Tennyson : viz. "You ask me, why, tho' ill at ease," and "Of old sat Freedom on the heights."   Wordsworth listened with a gradually deepening attention.   After a pause he answered, "I must acknowledge that these two poems are very solid and noble in thought.   Their diction also seems singularly stately[1]."

[1] Some of the critics state that before these poems appeared, no modern poet had undertaken the hard task of setting forth with poetic fire and glow the golden mean of politics.   Tennyson's view was that a poet ought to love his own country, but that he should found his political poems on what was

There was another occasion on which the Poet whose great work was all but finished, and the youthful compeer whose chief labours were yet to come, met in my presence. It was at a dinner given by Mr Moxon. The ladies had withdrawn, and Wordsworth soon followed them. Several times Tennyson said to me in a low voice, "I must go: I cannot wait any longer." At last the cause of his disquiet revealed itself. It was painful to him to leave the house without expressing to the old Bard his sense of the obligation which all Englishmen owed to him, and yet he was averse to speak his thanks before a large company. Our host brought Wordsworth back to the dining-room; and Tennyson moved up to him. He spoke in a low voice, and with a perceptible emotion. I must not cite his words lest I should mar them; but they were few, simple and touching. The old man looked very much pleased, more so indeed than I ever saw him look on any other occasion; shook hands with him heartily, and thanked him affectionately. Wordsworth thus records the incident in a letter to his accomplished American friend, Professor Reed: "I saw Tennyson when I was in London several times. He is decidedly the first of our living poets, and I hope will live to give the world still better things. You will be pleased to hear that he expressed in the strongest terms his gratitude to my writings. To this I was far from indifferent[1]."

Our many conversations, in those pleasant years, turned chiefly on Poetry, a subject on which Tennyson could say nothing that was not original. It was easy to see that to discern the Beautiful in all around us, and to reveal that beauty to others, was his special poetic vocation. In these conversations he never uttered a word that was disparaging, or tainted with the spirit of rivalship. One of the Poets least like himself, Crabbe, was among those whose merits he affirmed most unequivocally, especially his gift of a *hard* pathos. The only poet I heard him criticise roughly or unfairly was himself. "Compare," he once said to me, "compare the heavy handling of my workmanship with the exquisite lightness of touch in Keats!" Another time he read aloud a song by one of the chivalrous Poets of Charles the First's time, perhaps Lovelace's "Althea," which Wordsworth also used to *croon* in the woods, and said, "There! I would give

noble and great in the history of all countries, and that his utterances should be outspoken, yet statesmanlike, without any colour of partizanship.

[1] *Prose Works of William Wordsworth*, Vol. III., p. 391. Dr Grosart.

all my poetry to have made one song like that!" Not less ardent was his enthusiasm for Burns. And here an incident with no small significance recurs to me. "Read the exquisite songs of Burns," he exclaimed. " In shape, each of them has the perfection of the berry; in light the radiance of the dewdrop: you forget for its sake those stupid things, his serious pieces!" The same day I met Wordsworth, and named Burns to him. Wordsworth praised him, even more vehemently than Tennyson had done, as the great genius who had brought Poetry back to Nature; but ended, "Of course I refer to his serious efforts, such as the 'Cotter's Saturday Night'; those foolish little amatory songs of his one has to forget." I told the tale to Henry Taylor that evening; and his answer was: "Burns' exquisite songs and Burns' serious efforts are to me alike tedious, and disagreeable reading!" So much for the infallibility of Poets in their own art!

CHAPTER X.

LETTERS.

1842–1845.

From Samuel Rogers.

St James' Place, *August 17th,* 1842.

My dear Tennyson,

Every day have I resolved to write and tell you with what delight I have read and read again your two beautiful volumes; but it was my wish to tell you so *face* to *face.* That wish however remains unfulfilled and write I must, for very few things, if any, have ever thrilled me so much.

Yours ever, S. Rogers.

To Edmund Lushington.

Sept. 8th, 1842.

My dear Edmund,

*   *   *   *   *

I called on Moxon, not at home, gone to the Pyrenees with W. Wordsworth's two sons. 500 of my books are sold: according to Moxon's brother I have made a sensation! I wish the wood-works[1] would make a sensation! I expect they will. I came here this morning by the Liverpool packet. I go to Limerick

---

[1] This was Dr Allen's manufactory for carving wood, in which my father had invested all his little money. Full details of this are given on p. 220.

to-night. I hope you are all blooming. What with ruin in the distance and hypochondriacs in the foreground God help all. Pray write to me at P. O.

Love to all yours and mine.

Yours ever, A. T.

From Thomas Carlyle.

CHEYNE ROAD, CHELSEA.
7th Dec. 1842.

DEAR TENNYSON,

Wherever this find you, may it find you well, may it come as a friendly greeting to you. I have just been reading your Poems; I have read certain of them over again, and mean to read them over and over till they become my poems: this fact, with the inferences that lie in it, is of such emphasis in *me*, I cannot keep it to myself, but must needs acquaint you too with it. If you knew what my relation has been to the thing call'd English "Poetry" for many years back, you would think such fact almost surprising! Truly it is long since in any English Book, Poetry or Prose, I have felt the pulse of a real man's heart as I do in this same. A right valiant, true fighting, victorious heart; strong as a lion's, yet gentle, loving and full of music: what I call a genuine singer's heart! there are tones as of the nightingale; low murmurs as of wood-doves at summer noon; everywhere a noble sound as of the free winds and leafy woods. The sunniest glow of Life dwells in that soul, chequered duly with dark streaks from night and Hades: everywhere one feels as if all were fill'd with yellow glowing sunlight, some glorious golden Vapour; from which form after form bodies itself; naturally, *golden* forms. In one word, there seems to be a note of "The Eternal Melodies" in this man; for which let all other men be thankful and joyful! Your "Dora" reminds me of the *Book of Ruth;* in the "Two Voices," which I am told some Reviewer calls "trivial morality," I think of passages in *Job.* For truth is quite *true* in Job's time and Ruth's as now. I know you cannot read German: the more interesting is it to trace in your "Summer Oak" a beautiful kindred to something that is best in Goethe; I mean his "Müllerinn" (Miller's daughter) chiefly, with whom the very Mill-dam gets in love; tho' she proves a flirt after all and the thing ends in satirical lines! very strangely too in the "Vision of Sin" I am reminded of my friend Jean Paul. This is not babble, it is speech; true deposition of a volunteer witness. And so I say let us all rejoice somewhat. And so let us all smite rhythmically, all in concert, "the sounding furrows"; and sail forward with new cheer, "beyond the sunset," whither we are bound —

> It may be that the gulfs will wash us down,
> It may be we shall touch the happy Isles
> And see the great Achilles whom we knew!

These lines do not make me weep, but there is in me what would fill whole Lachrymatories as I read. But do you, when you return to London, come down to me and let us smoke a pipe together. With few words, with many, or with none, it need not be an ineloquent Pipe!

Farewell, dear Tennyson; may the gods be good to you. With very great sincerity (and in great haste) I subscribe myself

Yours, T. CARLYLE.

My father tells his sister Emily to copy this letter and enclose it to my mother. Emily writes as follows:

I like this letter, dost not thou? I asked Alfred what Carlyle meant by saying he could not read German, and he said, when the poems he (i.e. Carlyle) alluded to were written he knew little or nothing of German. He must have told Carlyle this who has made a jumble. Moreover Alfred says, "Carlyle is mistaken about the satirical lines, concluding the 'Müllerinn.' They are in another poem."

Thy very affectionate EMILY.

From Sara Coleridge[1] to Edward Moxon (enclosed to my father in a letter from Moxon).

1842.

MY DEAR SIR,

My husband and I have very often had to thank you for additions to our library most kindly made. Your last gift is a most acceptable one and supplies me with a rich treat for

---

[1] The only and highly-gifted daughter of S. T. Coleridge.

days to come, and one which I need not devour too greedily, but can recur to from time to time with fresh pleasure. It is a compliment (as far as admiration of mine can be complimentary) to Mr Tennyson, that having laid hold of the first volume, containing poems which I had read over and over again a few years ago, I could not part with it for the new productions, much as my curiosity had been excited about them, but fell to reading my old favourites with even greater admiration than ever.

What I have read of the second volume will sustain the author's reputation, which is much to say. The Epic is what might have been expected, not epical at all but very beautiful, in Tennyson's old manner.

"The Gardener's Daughter" is most highly wrought and still more to be admired I think than the "Morte d'Arthur."

Accept best thanks both from Mr Coleridge and myself and believe me

Very sincerely yours, SARA COLERIDGE.

To the Rev. H. D. Rawnsley.

1842.

MY DEAR RAWNSLEY,

Your note dated the 5th only reached me last night (eleven days after date) at this place, Torquay, Devon. Dr Allen did not forward it immediately as he ought to have done, in fact in the multiplicity of his business and his 40 letters a day I believe he had quite forgotten my direction, until I refresht his memory by sending it. How the wood-scheme goes on you ask. The concern I believe is going on very well; there are as many orders as can be executed by our old presses; we have been modelling presses all this time. They sent one from Brummagem, wretched thing! split as soon as put into action (I hear that all Brummagem machinery is of the worst description: let Brummagem look to it or she will ruin her reputation), but Wood has succeeded in making really quite a beautiful press which will do as much work in the same time as two of the old ones.

And now (as we have it on the pattern) we are going to have one made a week, till we have enough. We shall go on swimmingly. The presses have been modelling, and the men educating up till now, for after all (simple as it seems) it is a very delicate process to manage properly, and we want a great many workmen.

I have written in great haste, and I know not whether your queries are answer'd; if not, write again and ask me what you wish to know. We have dropt the name "Pyroglyph" as too full of *meaning* (a singular reason for rejecting a word!), and call ourselves "The Patent Decorative Carving and Sculpture Company!" Be *careful!* I told you all about it on the score of old friendship and auld lang syne. Poor Sophy! I am deeply grieved to hear of her illness.

Drummond's affair [1] is no secret to me for I accused him of it in your little study and the sort of denial he made was as good as a confession, and I have since heard of it from other quarters: these things never are secrets in the country.

You never heard the word "ivy-tod"; but you have heard of "tods of wool," and I take it they are the same words originally, a certain weight or mass of something.

Kindest love to all your party,

Ever yours in great haste, A. T.

TORQUAY, DEVON.

I shall most likely leave this place for town in a few days. You had better, therefore, if you write again write to London. Farewell. I have had so little time, I am afraid I have written a very confused letter.

---

[1] Drummond Rawnsley's engagement to Catherine Franklin, daughter of Sir Willingham Franklin, and niece of Sir John Franklin.

To Aubrey de Vere.

EASTBOURNE.
Saturday, July 30th, 1842.

MY DEAR AUBREY,

As for dining with your uncle, that, you see, is out of the question, as your note has just been delivered to me at this place, Eastbourne, on the Sussex coast. I shall account myself *highly honoured* in receiving a copy of " Edwin the Fair " from Henry Taylor; these are not empty words: therefore I underscore them: likewise your edited book will, I have no doubt, yield me much pleasure. I shall be about a week longer at this place, and if you send the parcel hither directed 22 Seahouses, Eastbourne, it will go far to relieve the tedium of a watering-place.

Ever yours, A. T.

To Aubrey de Vere.

VICTORIA HOTEL, KILLARNEY.
September, 1842.

MY DEAR AUBREY,

I am sorry you had the fruitless trouble of calling at the Temple[1]. I tried hard to find you out in London but did not succeed. Partly from indisposition and partly from business and that of a nature the most unpleasant[2], I was kept at Boxley far longer than I wished or expected, so long indeed that I have hardly any time left for Ireland, as in a day or two I must again set out for Boxley. I have only just got your letter to me out of the Killarney Post Office. Christie, the member, found it in L.'s rooms, and brought it to Chapman, who sent it to Edmund Lushington, who sent

---

[1] 1 Mitre Court Buildings: F. Lushington's rooms where he often lodged.
[2] When the wood-carving company had begun to fail.

it to my people who sent it to me.   Now if that sentence has not taken away your breath, make my apologies to your cousin and beg her not to hate me because I never seem to accept an invitation of hers.   I suppose you are yet in Blandford Square, to which accordingly I send this note.   I do not know that, if you were here, I should have time to come.

I have been to your Ballybunion caves but could not get into the finest on account of the weather.   I was obliged to give Dingle up from want of time, tho' I much wished to see it, and I am afraid I must forgo Glengarry likewise.

A. T.

I can find no further account of this visit to Ireland, except that my father then made the following lines, which occur in " Merlin and Vivien," within one of the caves of Ballybunion :

So dark a forethought roll'd about his brain,
As on a dull day in an Ocean cave
The blind wave feeling round his long sea-hall
In silence.

To James Spedding.

January 25th, 1843.

DEAR JAMES,

I send you a sketch of Mablethorpe.   I was wrong about the muffin-man, he comes o' Saturdays and I can likewise get letters on Tuesdays, those being market-days at Alford and churls going.   Don't forget the *Athenæum*.   I send the sketch to melt your heart. Impart what booksellers' news there may be and re-member me to Fitz, if in town.

Ever yours, A. T.

He also writes to Moxon from Mablethorpe: "There is nothing here but myself and two starfish; therefore, if you have any stray papers which you do not know what to do with, as you once told me, they would be manna in the wilderness to me."

From Charles Dickens, sent with a copy of his "Works."

DEVONSHIRE TERRACE,
March 10*th*, 1843.

MY DEAR TENNYSON,

For the love I bear you as a man whose writings enlist my whole heart and nature in admiration of their Truth and Beauty, set these books upon your shelves; believing that you have no more earnest and sincere homage than mine.

Faithfully and Gratefully your Friend,

CHARLES DICKENS.

To Aubrey de Vere.

ST LEONARD'S, *Sept.* 17*th*, 1843.

MY DEAR AUBREY,

I received your letter, but not in time to answer by return of post, and as you purposed setting out next day, I do not know whether it were worth while writing to you at all: perhaps you may get my note somewhere in Italy; as it contains nothing, you will be hurt at sight of an English postmark on a pithless scrawl. I am sorry to hear of Henry Taylor's ill-health, but I have good faith in warm suns and leisure. You are quite unforgiveable in your perpetual assumption of my nonchalance as to whatever you write. Why you do always so assume, and what reason I can have given you for such an error on your part, is to me hidden in black cloud. You should have sent your proofs. It is quite true that you have heard me say that I was sometimes bored by Mr E—— and others; but why you should be so ultra-humble as to mass yourself along with these, and dream you range no higher in my andrometer, is beyond my following. Peace be with such fancies, that is, I hope they are dead and over them the " hic jacent " of all futurity. Thank you however for the book.

I am down here at St Leonard's with the Lushingtons; there are smooth seas and hot weather, and I wish you were with me. Good-bye, and don't be angry at this scrapling.

Ever yours, A. TENNYSON.

On July 13th, 1844, Moxon wrote that Tom Campbell had died at Boulogne. My father missed him, for he was a kind-hearted man and a brilliant talker in a tête-à-tête; and very good-natured whenever they met, as not unfrequently chanced, at the different clubs.

That the following letter should be understood, it is necessary to explain why my father had fallen ill. Dr Allen, who has been already mentioned, was a physician near Beech Hill, with whom the Tennyson family had become acquainted, and who had either conceived, or had adopted, the idea of wood-carving by machinery. At all events he inspired the Tennysons with so great an enthusiasm for it, that by degrees he persuaded my father to give him the money for which, wearied by a careless agent, he had sold his little estate in Grasby, Lincolnshire, and even the £500 left him as a legacy by Arthur Hallam's aunt. Not merely this however, — since, but for my father's intervention apparently, all the property of such of the family as were at Beech Hill would have been merged in this philanthropic undertaking; so fascinating was the prospect of oak panels and oak furniture carved by machinery, thus brought by its cheapness within the reach of the multitude.

The confidence my father had placed in the "earnest-frothy" Dr Allen proved to be misplaced. The entire project collapsed: my father's worldly goods were all gone, and a portion of the property of his brothers and sisters. Then followed a season of real hardship, and many trials for my father and mother, since marriage seemed to be further off than ever. So severe a hypochondria set in upon him that his friends despaired of his life. "I have," he writes, "drunk one of those most bitter draughts out of the cup of life, which go near to make men hate the world they move in." My uncle Edmund Lushington in 1844 generously insured Dr Allen's life for part of the debt due to my father; the Doctor died in January 1845.

To Edmund Lushington.

CHELTENHAM, *July 29th*, 1844.

MY DEAR EDMUND,

I ought certainly to have written before, but I don't know how it is, I cannot abide letter writing. Many letters have I conceived to you tho' brought forth none. In the first stages of Hydropathy (under Dr Jephson) I found it quite impossible to write, I could not turn my hand to anything and now I am not much better. I shall have to go into the system again and carry it out to the end. It is true I had ten crisises but I am not cured, tho' I do not doubt of the efficiency of the treatment in most cases, having *seen* most marvellous cures performed. I am going to town to-morrow for two or three days. I want among other things to see the exhibition and this is its last week. I have seen no Art, and my soul thirsts for it, for a year. I fear it would be too expensive to come on to Eastbourne, and you are not at Park House, and will not be perhaps for a fortnight or three weeks. At any rate I shall hope to see you at Cheltenham. Perhaps with Harry's leave I shall try to get Geraldine to give me a bed in his rooms. I have walked thrice up Snowdon which I found much easier to accomplish than walking on level ground.

London. I arrived last night at the old Hummums at 11 o'clock: called on Spedding, to my great disappointment he had left town; called on Chapman, door sported, no answer to repeated applications at his no-knockered portal.

Love to Cissy and the rest.

Ever yours, A. T.

During this visit to London Savile Morton wrote to Mrs Brotherton that he had "come across Alfred Tennyson." "We looked out some Latin translations of his poems by Cambridge men, and read some poems of Leigh Hunt's, and some of Theocritus and Virgil. It is delightful to have a passage picked out for one to admire by him. Seeing through his eyes much enlarges one's view. He has the power of impressing you with the greatness of what he admires and bringing out its meaning. I had no idea Virgil could ever sound so fine as it did by his reading....Yesterday I went to see him again. After some chat we sat down in two separate rooms to read *Ellen Middleton*, by Lady Georgiana Fullerton — very highly spoken of." In another letter he says: "Seeing Alfred has been a diversion to me.... I never met a heart so large and full of love."

In November my father was again at Cheltenham, and wrote to Edward Moxon:

I want you to get me a book which I see advertised in the *Examiner:* it seems to contain many speculations with which I have been familiar for years, and on which I have written more than one poem. The book is called *Vestiges of the Natural History of Creation*[1], and published by J. Churchill, Princes St. Soho; the price 7s. 6d., but you can get it cheaper.

Another book I long very much to see is that on the superiority of the modern painters to the old ones, and the greatness of Turner as an artist, by an Oxford under-graduate I think[2]. I do not much wish to buy it, it may be dear; perhaps you could borrow it for me out of the London Library, or from Rogers. I saw it lying on his table. I would promise to take care of it, and send it back in due time. At any rate let me have the other. Kind remembrances to Mrs and Miss Moxon and the little one to boot.

To Edward Fitzgerald.

Tuesday Night.
10 St James' Square, Cheltenham,
Jan. 14th, 1845.

My dear Fitz,

I *had* heard the news[3]. No gladness crossed my heart but sorrow and pity: that's not theatrical but the truth; wherefore bear with me, tho' perhaps it may seem a little out of the tide of things. Now will you be at 19 C. S. to-morrow or the day after? I am coming up to see you, and shall arrive most probably between

[1] The sections of "In Memoriam" about Evolution had been read by his friends some years before the publication of the *Vestiges of Creation* in 1844. Of natural selection Romanes writes, "In 'In Memoriam' Tennyson noted the fact, and a few years later Darwin supplied the explanation." *Darwin and after Darwin*, Romanes.

[2] Ruskin's first volume of *Modern Painters*.

[3] The reference in this letter is to the death of Dr Allen.

9 and 10 p.m., when I trust I shall find you well and thriving.

Ever yours, A. T.

From Henry Hallam (enclosing Sir Robert Peel's letter).

WRAXALL LODGE, near BRISTOL.
Sept. 24th, 1845.

MY DEAR TENNYSON,

You will believe that it is with the greatest pleasure I enclose to you the letter I have this day received from Sir R. Peel.

I think you will have no hesitation about answering it to *him*, nothing can be more flattering or delicate.

We want to learn more about Emily *herself*. Can she not ever *write* herself? The last we heard was that she had left Cheltenham, yet this can hardly be.

We have been for some months here and shall continue till the beginning of December; if you ever wander this way, we shall be very glad to give you a dinner and bed; and I have both glades and distant views to show you.

Believe me yours very truly,

H. HALLAM.

From the Right Honourable Sir Robert Peel to Alfred Tennyson.

I rejoice that you have enabled me to fulfil the intentions of Parliament by advising the Crown to confer a mark of Royal Favour[1] on one who has devoted to worthy purposes great intellectual powers.

The Queen has cordially approved of the recommendation which on the receipt of your letter I humbly offered to Her Majesty.

---

[1] Pension of £200 annually.

I have more than once heard Lord Houghton and my father talk together of Peel as a man and a statesman; and on those occasions Lord Houghton would invariably relate the story of his interview with Carlyle about the pension, given in Wemyss Reid's *Life* and here reprinted.

"Richard Milnes," said Carlyle one day, withdrawing his pipe from his mouth, as they were seated together in the little house in Cheyne Row, "when are you going to get that pension for Alfred Tennyson?"

"My dear Carlyle," responded Milnes, "the thing is not so easy as you seem to suppose. What will my constituents say if I do get the pension for Tennyson? They know nothing about him or his poetry, and they will probably think he is some poor relation of my own, and that the whole affair is a job."

Solemn and emphatic was Carlyle's response. "Richard Milnes, on the Day of Judgment, when the Lord asks you why you didn't get that pension for Alfred Tennyson, it will not do to lay the blame on your constituents; it is *you* that will be damned."

The question arose whether Sheridan Knowles or my father should be placed on the pension list. Peel knew nothing of either of them. Houghton said that he then made Peel read "Ulysses," "whereupon the pension was granted to Tennyson."

My father wrote then to his old friend, Rawnsley:

CHELTENHAM, 1845.

MY DEAR RAWNSLEY,

I was delighted to see your handwriting again. I thought you had given me up as a bad job, for I remember that I once very flagitiously did not answer a very kind letter of yours long long ago: and truly my love for my friends must not be measured by the quantity of black and white into which I put it: for, however

appearances are against me, I *have* a love for old
Lincolnshire faces and things which will stick by me as
long as I live.   As to visiting you I wish I could, but I
am engaged to Hallam, who has a country house in the
neighbourhood of Bristol, and it is an engagement of
some standing, and thither am I going as soon as ever
I recover from the worst cold I ever caught since I was
a Somersby suckling.   It has kept me half-deaf for a
month.   I got it one wet night at Chelsea, when I went
to see Mr. Carlyle.   The better half of the Carlyle was
then in Scotland.   He, by the bye, is about to publish a
book which you had better get in your book club — all the
letters of Oliver Cromwell that can be got at, connected
with a short narration or commentary of his own.   Oliver
is Carlyle's [1] God, the greatest of great men, and he
intends if he can to sweep off all the royalist cobwebs
that have hitherto obscured his fair fame.

I am glad to hear of your quadrilling at Horncastle.
There is something pleasant in the notion of your figur-
ing in L'Été with all your hood fluttering about you,
and I respect a man who can keep his heart green when
the snows of Time begin to whiten his head: not that I
mean to say your head is white, but the silver hair *may*
intrude " obiter," tho' as far as I recollect you had a very
stout black crop when I saw you last.   I should like to
have been amongst you as in old times but

> " The days are awa that we hae seen,"

and I begin to feel an old man myself.   I have gone
thro' a vast deal of suffering (as to money difficulties in
my family etc.) since I saw you last, and would not live
it over again for quadruple the pension Peel has given
me and on which you congratulate me.   Well, I suppose
I ought in a manner to be grateful.   I have done nothing

---

[1] My father would rally Carlyle on his " might is right " and " one man "
theories.

slavish to get it: I never even solicited for it either by myself or thro' others. It was all done for me without word or hint from me, and Peel tells me I "need not by it be fettered in the public expression of any opinion I choose to take up"; so, if I take a pique against the Queen, or the Court, or Peel himself, I may, if I will, bully them with as much freedom, tho' not perhaps quite so gracefully, as if I were still unpensioned. Something in that word "pension" sticks in my gizzard; it is only the name, and perhaps would "smell sweeter" by some other. I feel the least bit possible Miss Martineauish about it. You know she refused one, saying she "should be robbing the people who did not make laws for themselves": however that is nonsense: her non-acceptance of the pension did not save the people a stiver, and meantime (what any one would have thought must have been more offensive to her feelings) her friends subscribed for her and kept her from want. If the people *did* make laws for themselves, if these things went by universal suffrage, what literary man ever would get a lift, it being known that the mass of Englishmen have as much notion of poetry as I of fox-hunting? Meantime there is some meaning in having a gentleman and a classic at the head of affairs, who may now and then direct the stream of public bounty to us, poor devils, whom the Grundyites would not only not remunerate, but kick out of society as barely *respectable;* for Calliope herself, as I have heard, never kept a *gig* but walks barefoot about the sacred hill, no better than an Irishwoman.

I wish the causelessly bitter against me and mine no worse punishment than that they could read the very flattering letter Peel wrote me; let us leave them in their limbo

"Non ragionam di lor, ma guarda e passa."

Peel's letter I would send you if I had it, but I have sent it to Hallam, and told him to keep it till I see him. I wrote to Rogers thanking him for his kindness. I thought he must have been mentioning me to Peel. He wrote me back a very pretty answer which I send Sophy for an autograph of the old Bard ; would any one think that pretty little hand was written by a man somewhere between eighty and ninety?

Now, Sophy, if as a matron you do not care for autographs, or intend to lose it or give it away, why let me have it back again for I have some value for it ; particularly as the old man and I fell out one wet day in Pall Mall about half a year ago, when I said something that offended him, and his face flushed and he plucked his arm out of mine and told me I was " affecting the smart," and since then I haven't seen him. How is " Mamma," you do not say a word about her health and I want to know, for she was always like a mother to me? I wonder whether she recollects my playing the drunken son at Bristol. Many a pleasant talk have I had with her, and I much regret that I cannot come and see you now. Tell Mundy I retain a lively recollection of his puns ; and remember me to Coltman (George I mean), who always seemed to me a real good fellow. I recollect his sending me, when I lived at Boxley, a book of poems by a friend. I forget now what my answer was, but I hope I said nothing to hurt him or his friend's feelings. If you knew what a nuisance these volumes of verse are! Rascals send me their's per post from America, and I have more than once been knocked up out of bed to pay three or four shillings for books of which I can't get thro' one page, for of all books the most insipid reading is second-rate verse. Blue books, red books, almanacks, peerages, anything is better. See! how I keep chattering, just as if I were sitting by your fireside, in the little book-room, pipe in hand.

I shall not be in London in November, for I have only just returned from thence, but do you never by any chance mean to come and visit us? Are we in these days, who live East and West, to be as badly off as if we lived one at each Ind, or in the heart of the eighteenth century? Come and see us, you can do it some time, going to or from the Hallidays, and we shall be at least as glad to see you as they. Why don't you clip a few days from them and let us have the advantage? Here is a handsome town of thirty-five thousand inhabitants, a polka-parson-worshipping place, of which the Rev. Francis Close is Pope, besides pumps and pumprooms, chalybeates, quadrilles (as you have taken to them again), and one of the prettiest countries in Great Britain. My mother would be delighted to see you, and the girls would coax you, and make so much of you, you would feel yourself in a new planet. Edmund Lushington and Cissy have been with us and have just gone on to Glasgow. Their little one looks like a young Jupiter with his head full of Greek: but she, poor thing, was out of health, and dreaded the winter in Glasgow, which does not agree with her.

Tell Edward and Drummond that I expected them to have called on me the day after I met them at Moxon's, and I was very savage. Remember me to them with all kindness and to " Mamma " and Sophy ; and not *me* only but all of us here to all of you there (if that's sense).

Now dinner's ready and I must say Good bye.

Ever yours affectionately,

A. TENNYSON.

CHAPTER XI.

Journal kept in Manuscript-book of "Princess."

("Come down, O maid, from yonder mountain height" was written during this tour among the Alps.)

1846. Went on a tour to the Isle of Wight and in August to Switzerland with Edward Moxon.

August 2nd. Up at 4 to go by "Princess Maude." Picturesque sunrise from the pier. Bruges. Englishman with moustache told us of festival at Bruges. I go down into fore-cabin and get the very worst breakfast I ever had in my life. Arrival at Ostend. Order from Belgian king that no passports need be shown. Inhuman conduct and supererogatory fury of porters. We lose our presence of mind and run for it, but there is plenty of time. Arrive at Bruges, walk to Hôtel de Blé, recommended by moustached Englishman, missing the conveyance thitherward, which, marked with gilt letters Fleur de Blé, rolls by us as we near our hotel. Great rejoicings of the people and hero-worship of Simon

Stevin [1], S on the banners, and names, busts and statues
of all the Flanders great men, statesmen, sculptors, poets,
etc. in an inner square within the great square. Horse-
men riding in a circle for prize. High tower and clock
in great square, picturesque groups in Cathedral, motioned
from the seats we had taken opposite pulpit, depart to
F. de Blé, dinner in salle — affected Englishwoman whom
I took for Belge or German opposite, hot nervous night
with me. Man "hemmed" overhead enough to shake
the walls of Jericho.

August 3rd. Off to Grand Hôtel de Flandre, monkey,
pleasant folk, commissionaire, pharmacien and opticien.
J. Arteveld's house, town-hall very fine, musée not good,
go to Louvain, Hôtel de Suède, new town-hall, old café,
row of poplars, nervous night.

August 4th. Off to Liège, two sons of Sir Robert
Peel, Hôtel d'Angleterre good, money changed, too
soon for rail which came very late, pretty scenery,
Chaudefontaine, old man and little boy, railway bordered
with young acacias. Cologne, Hôtel de Cologne, rooms
overlooking moonlit Rhine, hotel full of light and festival,
pillaring its lights in the quiet water, bridge of boats,
three steamers lying quietly below windows, not quite
four hours' sleep.

August 5th. Woke at 5 or earlier, clash and clang
of steamboat departure under me, walk on the quay,
Cathedral splendid but to my mind too narrow for its
length.

"Gaspar and Melchior and Balthazar
　　Came to Cologne on the broad-breasted Rhine
　　And founded there a temple which is yet
　　A fragment, but the wonder of the world."

---

[1] Born in the sixteenth century at Bruges, and a great mathematician and
mechanic.

Embark, the bore of the Rhine, three Hyde Park drawling snobs, deck very hot, Nonnenwerth and Drachenfels, sad recollections; Coblentz, horrid row, king of Holland, shuffled off to the Rheinischerhof, stupid hotel. Coblentz as hateful as it was long years before, over the bridge to the Cheval Blanc, coffee there, back again, the bridge opening islanded us in the river.

August 6th. Off again by boat, three drawlers departed at Mainz, talk about language with Germans, sad old city of Worms among poplars, reach Mannheim, Hôtel de l'Europe, take a dark walk among shrubberies with M.

August 7th. Early next morning off by rail to Kehl, confusion about the two railways, douane, stop and see Cathedral, nave magnificent, rail to Basle, Three Kings, green swift Rhine roaring against the piers, Swiss fountain.

August 8th. Café in room, off by diligence to Lucerne, vines, agreeable Swiss young lady to whom I quoted Goethe and she spouted *William Tell*, sorry to lose her, see Righi and Pilatus in the distance, walk before diligence but get in again, pass bridge over swift green stream, bureau, go to Schweizerhof, room at top of house, look out in the night and see the lake marbled with clouds, gabble of servants, bad night.

August 9th. Walk up the hill above the town, churchyard, innumerable gilt crosses, go to a villa, lie on the grass, return a different way from M., cross a part of the lake, walk back.

August 10th. Strolled about the painted bridges, M. met his friend, we bought Keller's map, off by 2 o'clock steamer to Weggis, hired a horse up the Righi, looked over and saw the little covers and wooded shores and villages under vast red ribs of rock, very fine, dismissed my horse at the Bains where we entered with an Englishman and found peasants waltzing, gave two francs to boy who had ordered beds, summit, crowd of people, very feeble sunset, tea, infernal chatter as of innumerable apes.

August 11*th.*　Sunrise, strange look of clouds packed on the lake of Egeri, far off Jungfrau looking as if delicately pencilled. Rossberg, Küssnacht, breakfast, began to descend at 9, strange aspect of hill, cloud, and snow, as if the mountains were on fire, watch the clouds opening and shutting as we go down, and making framed pictures of the lake, etc., long hot descent, dined at Weggis, landlady takes me out to select live fish for dinner, I am too tender-hearted so we go without fish, boat touches, off to Fluelen, very sleepy, carriage road to Italy, Tell's chapel, go in to church, return to Sweizerhof.

August 12*th.*　Lake, guide and boat to Alpnach, hire voiture up the vale of Sarnen, walk a little before, get in, nothing very remarkable, arrive at Lungern, pretty green Alpine " thal " shut in with steep cliffs, one long waterfall, jolly old Radical who abused Dr Arnold, over the hills to Meyringen, home (after having seen Lauterbrunnen and the Bernese Alps, the best things in the tour).

To Edward Fitzgerald.

CHELTENHAM, *Nov.* 12*th*, 1846.

Well, Moxon went to Switzerland; saw Blanc, he was very sulky, kept his nightcap on, doff'd it one morning when I was knocked up out of bed to look at him at four o'clock, the glance I gave did not by any means repay me for the toil of travelling to see him. Two other things I *did* see in Switzerland, the stateliest bits of landskip

I ever saw, one was a look down on the valley of Lauterbrunnen while we were descending from the Wengern
Alp, the other a view of the Bernese Alps: don't think
that I am going to describe them.   Let it suffice that
I was so satisfied with the size of crags that (Moxon being
gone on before in vertigo and leaning on the arm of the
guide) I *laughed* by myself.   I was satisfied with the size
of crags, but mountains, great mountains disappointed
me.   * * * *   I called on Dickens at Lausanne who
was very hospitable, and gave us biscuits (a rare luxury
on the Continent, not such as are sweet and soft, but
hard and unsweet) and a flask of Liebfraumilch, which
is being interpreted " Virginis lac," as I dare say you
know.

I have just got *Festus;* order it and read.   You will
most likely find it a great bore, but there are really *very
grand* things in *Festus.*

Ever thine, A. T.

*Letters to Mrs Burton (the wife of the patron of
Dr Tennyson's living of Somersby).*

1846.

My dear Mrs Burton,

Nothing could be sweeter than Cathy's
Somersby violets, and doubt not but that I shall keep
them as a sacred treasure.   The violets of one's native
place gathered by the hands of a pure innocent child
must needs be precious to me, and indeed I would have
acknowledged the receipt of them and sent her a thousand loves and kisses before now, but there were several

reasons why I did not write which it is of no use troubling you with; only I pray you kiss her for me very sweetly on lip and cheek and forehead, and assure her of my gratitude. I love all children, but I loved little Cathy par excellence by a kind of instinct when I saw her first. Do as you choose about the miniatures, but I am told that you have had illness in your house and it would make me uncomfortable to cause you any kind of trouble. I am here in London on a visit to a friend of mine at 6 Michael's Grove, Brompton. People fête and dine me every day but I am somewhat unwell and out of spirits: meanwhile I trust that your own health is improved, and that you are prosperous and happy. Farewell and believe me

Ever yours truly, A. Tennyson.

My dear Mrs Burton,

The miniatures which you have sent me we will treasure as precious memorials of our shortlived acquaintanceship: not that they do either you or the child full justice. Nature without doubt has been much more bountiful to you both than the artist: however the portraits are not unlike and moreover well-painted. I am sorry to learn from some fragments of your letter to Emily, which she read to me, that you are not altogether satisfied with the world about you. Pray keep up your spirits in the wilderness of Lincolnshire. I trust that we shall all meet again, and meanwhile may your New Year be happy. Truly do I wish it may be so. You know wise men say that our happiness lies in our own hands: and therefore do you make the best of things about you, not only for the sake of husband and children, but of your friends here, who live in the hope of re-seeing you, among whom count upon myself as ever yours truly,

A. TENNYSON.

MY DEAR MRS BURTON,

I am very much grieved that your letter reached me so late. I had left Umberslade and was visiting at two or three places in Warwickshire, and as I had given orders for any letter that came to be forwarded to Cheltenham, I have only just now on arriving received yours. I shall be very happy to be god-father to your little one, and so I am sure will Charles; he is not here but in town, but he shall be written to to-day, and there is no doubt of his compliance with your kind and flattering proposal: only you must take his consent for granted, as it is impossible for us or you to receive an answer before the time specified: nor for many reasons can either he or I attend in person: I am sorry that all this has so happened. Call your child Alfred if you will: he was born in the same house, perhaps the same chamber, as myself, and I trust he is destined to a far happier life than mine has been, poor little fellow! Give him a kiss for his god-father, and one to Cathy for her violets which I received and cherished: or if one do not seem enough, give them by the dozen. I am glad that you like the miniature. The papers spoke the truth about Umberslade but they fibbed when they said I was about to publish. What would be the use of that in a general election? I am writing in a great hurry to save the Northern post, so I bid you good-bye,

A. TENNYSON.

2 St James' St., Buckingham Gate.
Wednesday, *May 17th.*

My dear Mrs Burton,

I have sent a silver cup for my little godson.
I had intended to have sent it many a long month ago,
but somehow or other I let the days slip on without doing
so; for this I beg his pardon, which he must grant me
as soon as he can babble. I trust that you will receive
the cup at the same time with this letter. I hope that
you are well and happy during this fine weather which
makes me wish myself far away out of smoky London.
Best love to my dear little violet-girl, and believe me
always, dear Mrs Burton,

Yours truly, A. Tennyson.

Letters to Mrs Howitt.

[1846.]

My dear Mrs Howitt,

The day you mention was at least as pleasant
to myself as to you; one, indeed, not easily to be forgotten. Clapton is henceforth to be remembered with
higher and other than cockney associations, it is no
longer the London suburb but the home of Mary Howitt.
As for the morning dresses, did I notice them? if I did,
what matter? they were a compliment to myself.

Your book from Longman has not yet arrived; but
when it does, since (however you may please to depreciate beforehand) it must have something of you

about it, I will give it a hearty welcome and my best attention.

I got your letter yesterday, and I have had so much to do in the interim that I have merely glanced over the extracts. They seem to me to be very clever and full of a noble 19th century-ism (if you will admit such a word), but whether not too fantastic, if considered as an explanation of the Mosaic text, may I think admit of doubt. Meanwhile I hail all such attempts as heralding a grander and more liberal state of opinion, and conse-quently sweeter and nobler modes of living. There was no more *sea*, says St John in Revelation. I wonder your friend did not quote that: perhaps he does in some other part of his book. I remember reading that when a child, and not being able to reconcile myself to a future when there should be no more sea.

I am going up to Cambridge to-morrow to be present at the commemoration of the founding of Trinity College 300 years ago. There is to be a great dinner in Hall, and as I have got a special invitation from my old Tutor, now the Master, I am going; the 22nd is the dinner-day. I have just left myself time to get there; think of me to-morrow night as passing within two or three miles of you on the Eastern C. R., perhaps not so far, and again sweeping back a day or two after on my return yet not able to stop, divers duties calling me home with voices of undeniable authority. I ought not to go at all but old recollections drag me. However sometime betwixt the death of Spring and the birth of Summer I do hope to see you once more.

I partly guess your mysterious request. Mr Howitt's surprise at the hyacinths is a very pretty household picture. I wish that we Englanders dealt more in such symbols, that we drest our affections up in a little more poetical costume; real warmth of heart would lose nothing, rather gain by it. As it is, our manners are as cold as the walls of our churches.   Good-bye, dear Mrs Howitt, say everything kind for me to husband and daughter and trust me

Yours ever, A. TENNYSON.

10 ST JAMES' SQUARE, CHELTENHAM.
Nov. 19th.

DEAR MRS HOWITT,

Your kind letter gave me very sincere pleasure, and I shall be most happy to meet Mr Dempster under your roof when I come to town.   I did not hear the Hutchinsons [1] when they were in England and I regret it.   I am sure Abby must have sung divinely for everyone says she did.   I can scarce help fancying that the female voice is more suited by nature to the singing of such poems than any man's, but I am wrong, for you tell me that Mr Dempster sings quite as exquisitely as Abby.   I should have been in town before now but several little matters have occurred to hinder me. Among other things I sent an invitation to the German poet, Freiligrath: he has translated some of my poems and he sent me his book thro' my publisher: the letter to Moxon was dated from Mrs Leigh's, Clapton Pond; do you know such a person?   I have got no answer and I am puzzled by his silence.   Perhaps he may not be in England, after all, but every time the postman knocks I expect to hear from him and that he is coming.   I will send you word of my arrival in town.

A. T.

---

[1] American ladies who were noted singers.

Letters to Edward Moxon.

(*After the tour in Switzerland.*)

1846.

MY DEAR MOXON,

I got your parcel and bluebell this morning and a letter from a man who seems deserving and in difficulties; he has asked me to lend him four pounds, which I have promised to *give* him, and referred him to you. So let him have that sum if he calls with my letter: his name is R. C. W.

Ever yours, A. TENNYSON [1].

Second visit to Dr Gully's watercure.

UMBERSLADE HALL, BIRMINGHAM, 1847.
Tuesday afternoon.

MY DEAR MOXON,

I wish you would make up your mind to come down on Saturday and see me here. You could come down by the express as I did in three hours to Birmingham, and any of the cabs at the station would bring you on: here is a Hall in a pleasant park, and you would be all the better for a Sunday's mouthful of fresh air. We can give you a bed here and you should do just as you like. I want to talk with you. I find it very

---

[1] Whenever any literary man " deserving and in difficulties " applied to him for money, he always endeavoured to help him. To the day of his death he continued this practice.

difficult to correct proofs under the treatment [1], but you shall have them all back with you on Monday; don't show them to people. I have not at all settled whether I shall publish them now or in the Autumn, yet an Edinburgh paper mentions that I have a poem in the press. Confound the publicities and gabblements of the 19th century! Now, I hope you will come. If you do, bring two copies of my poems with you, two persons in this house want them; if you don't come (but I hope you will) send two. The printers are awful zanies, they print erasures and corrections too, and other sins they commit of the utmost inhumanity. Come! Send a line first.

Yours ever,

A. TENNYSON.

To Rev. H. Rawnsley.

PARK HOUSE, MAIDSTONE.
April 16th, 1847.

MY DEAR RAWNSLEY,

Many thanks for your very kind letter, which was grateful to me as showing that I am not forgotten

---

[1] From Umberslade my father writes to Mrs Russell: "They tell me not to read, not to think; but they might as well tell me not to live. I lack something of the woman's long-enduring patience in these matters. It is a terribly long process, but then what price is too high for health, and health of mind is so involved with health of body... I wish you could find time in the course of the summer to come over and see us. We should be so happy to see you. We expect my mother from Scotland in a few days' time. She comes as far as Birmingham with Cecilia and the Professor (Lushington). The latter go on to Park House, Lushington's seat near Maidstone; and Charles goes to bring my mother here. Of *her* kindness and true-heartedness I am sure you never had any doubt, and therefore I need not say anything of the joyful welcome she would give you. She has been much grieved just now with the loss of her cousin, Mr Wheeldon of Market Street near St Albans. A purer Christian, a better man, never lived. He was like her, for he had not a touch of gall in his whole nature. Peace be with him."

amongst you; not that I wanted any proof of that, but still it is pleasant to have assurance doubly sure. You would have been answered before had I not been away from home, lying sick of more than one ailment at a friend's chamber in the Temple, from whence the other day I came on here partly for change of air and partly because I had promised to pay a farewell visit to my brother-in-law's brother, Harry Lushington. He is going out to Malta as secretary to the Maltese government, a post of (I believe) about £1500 a year and one which he is quite clever enough to occupy with credit to himself; but being a man of feeble stamina he is afraid of the climate and altogether down in the mouth about it, so I came to see the last of him before he went, and do my best to set him up. I am much grieved to hear of your rheumatism. I fear this bitter April is very unfavourable and the east wind which comes sweeping from the sea over your marshes to Halton. H. L. goes some time next week, and till then I must be here, so that I fear that what with this and my illness a journey into Lincolnshire so as to catch all your "clan" in full conclave is quite impossible. Well, I can't help it, I love my old friends as much as ever; recent friendships may be broken thro' but old ones early-made are a part of one's blood and bones. I say my old friendships are as dear as ever, but that you must accept this protestation in lieu of my personal presence and not be hard of faith but believing.

Give my kindest love to each and all of the "old familiar faces," and

Believe me always yours truly,

A. TENNYSON.

To Mrs Russell.

10 St James' Square, Cheltenham.
Saturday evening. [*Undated.*]

My dearest Aunt,

I have received your welcome note and cheque and had hoped to have a better account of your eyes. Those "animals[1]" you mention are very distressing and mine increase weekly : in fact I almost look forward with certainty to being blind some of these days. I have however no sort of inflammation to complain of, it is all failing nerve. I have no great opinion of the salubrity of Leamington, and as for this place it is often as muggy and turbid as London itself. "Much company" and after-dinner "talk of roads," etc. are not much in your favour, but why do all English country gentlemen talk of dogs, horses, roads, crops etc.? It is better after all than affecting Art and Feeling: they would make a poor hand of that, though *you* tried to help them out. I wish they would be a little kinder to the poor. I would honour them then and they might talk what they would. But I am rambling and moreover getting personal on the squires, which perhaps I have no business to do, for, as Hamlet says, "use every man after his deserts and who shall scape whipping?" With respect to the non-publication of those poems[2] which you mention, it is partly occasioned by the considerations you speak of, and partly by my sense of their present imperfectness; perhaps they will not see the light till I have ceased to be. I cannot tell but I have no wish to send them out yet. Emily wished us to remember her kindly to you

---

[1] *Muscæ volitantes.*
[2] Probably "In Memoriam."

when she was here. She has been visiting the Lushingtons in Kent, and is now with the Hallams at Clifton.
I wonder whether you can read this scrawl, my pen is an
old steel one in a state of hopeless splittage and divari-
cation. You must forgive me for not answering you
before[1]. I have no excuse to offer and I fling myself on
your mercy. Do you know, I don't write even a note
once in three months. I never can get myself set down
to write, and I am in arrears of correspondence with all
the world. Goodbye, dearest Aunt. Mother, sisters
etc. send lots of love to you and Emma.

Always affectionately yours,

A. Tennyson.

P.S. Have you read Miss Martineau on Mesmerism
in the *Athenæum* (two of them)? I have got them and
if you like I will send them to you. They are very
wonderful.

In 1846 the fourth edition of the Poems was published: and, having been bitterly attacked by Lytton
Bulwer because Peel had placed him on the Pension
list, my father contributed to *Punch* the only personal
satire he ever wrote, "The New Timon and the Poets,"
February 28th; followed by an "After-thought[2]," March
7th. About these poems he left a note:

"I never wrote a line against anyone but Sir Edward
Lytton Bulwer. His lines did not move me to do so.
But at the very time he was writing or had written these
he was visiting my cousins, the d'Eyncourts, and said to
them, 'How much I should like to know your cousin

---

[1] He said he could not devote himself to his work and write letters also,
so he gave up writing to friends and relations.

[2] Published afterwards under the title of "Literary Squabbles."

Alfred'; and I, going into a book-club in the town where I was then living, found a newspaper turned up and folded so that I could not miss, 'See how Sir Edward tickles up the poetasters and their patrons.' The stupid insignificant paper, and the purpose with which it had been set before me, provoked me. I saw afterwards a letter which he wrote to my friend John Forster. Moreover, he stated in a note that I belonged to a very rich family. The younger son, his friend, who had inherited was rich enough, but the elder branch was shut out in the cold, and at that time I had scarce anything. Moreover, I remembered that he had said 'If a man be attacked, let him attack.'

Wretched work. Odium literarium."

My father added: " I never sent my lines to *Punch*. John Forster did. They were too bitter. I do not think that I should ever have published them."

. Then she 'let some one' sing to us. lightlier move

The minutes fledged with music.' & as maid

Of those behind her smote her harp & sang

~~Tears, idle~~ Tears, I know not what they mean.

Tears from the depth of some divine despair

Rise in the heart & gather to the eyes

In looking on the happy Autumn fields

And thinking of the days that are no more.

Fresh as the first beam glittering on a sail

That brings our friends up from the underworld

Sad as the last which reddens over one

That sinks with all we love below the verge

So sad, so fresh the days that are no more

Ah sad & strange as in dark summer-dawns

The earliest pipe of half awaken'd birds

To dying ears when unto dying eyes

The casement slowly grows a glimmering square

So sad, & strange the days that are no more

Dear as remember'd kisses after death

And sweet as those by hopeless fancy feign'd

On lips that are for others; deep as love

Deep as first love, & wild with all regret

O death in life, the days that are no more

From the Original MS.

CHAPTER XII.

"THE PRINCESS."

Maybe wildest dreams
Are but the needful preludes of the truth.

O lift your natures up:
Embrace our aims: work out your freedom!

There are thousands now
Such women, but convention beats them down;
It is but bringing up; no more than that.

"I say God made the woman for the man,
And for the good and increase of the world."
"Parson," said I, "you pitch the pipe too low."

What someone called the "herald-melody" of the
higher education of women, "The Princess," mostly
written in Lincoln's Inn Fields, was published in 1847,
and at this time "The Golden Year" was added to the
Poems. The subject of "The Princess," my father
believed, was original, and certainly the story is full of
original incident, humour and fancy[1].

It may have suggested itself when the project of

---

[1] Sir William Rowan Hamilton, the great mathematician, said: "It
deeply presses on my reflection how much wiser a book is Tennyson's
Princess than my *Quaternions*."

a Women's College was in the air[1], or it may have
arisen in its mock-heroic form from a Cambridge joke,
such as he commemorated in these lines, which I found
in one of his old MS books :

The Doctor's Daughter. (*Unpublished.*)

Sweet Kitty Sandilands,
   The daughter of the doctor,
We drest her in the Proctor's bands,
   And past her for the Proctor.

All the men ran from her
   That would have hasten'd to her,
All the men ran from her
   That would have come to woo her.

Up the street we took her
   As far as to the Castle,
Jauntily sat the Proctor's cap
   And from it hung the tassel.

As for the various characters in the poem, they give
all possible views of Woman's higher education ; and as
for the heroine herself, the Princess Ida, the poet who
created her considered her as one of the noblest among
his women.   The stronger the man or woman, the more
of the lion or lioness untamed, the greater the man or
woman tamed.   In the end we see this lioness-like
woman subduing the elements of her humanity to that
which is highest within her, and recognizing the relation
in which she stands towards the order of the world and
toward God —

A greater than all knowledge beat her down.

---

[1] He talked over the plan of the poem with my mother in 1839.

His friends report my father to have said, that the two great social questions impending in England were "the housing and education of the poor man before making him our master, and the higher education of women"; and that the sooner woman finds out, before the great educational movement begins, that "woman is not un-developt man, but diverse," the better it will be for the progress of the world[1].

There have not been wanting those who have deemed the varied characters and imagery of the poem wasted on something of a fairy tale without the fairies[2]. But, in this instance as in others involving the supreme meaning and guidance of life, a parable is perhaps the teacher that can most surely enter in at all doors.

It was no mere dramatic sentiment, but one of my father's strongest convictions of the true relation between man and woman, which impelled him to write:

Let this proud watchword rest
Of equal; seeing either sex alone
Is half itself, and in true marriage lies
Nor equal, nor unequal: each fulfils
Defect in each, and always thought in thought,
Purpose in purpose, will in will, they grow,
The single pure and perfect animal,
The two-cell'd heart beating, with one full stroke,
Life.

[1] Dawson, the Canadian editor of "The Princess," writes: "At the time of the publication of 'The Princess' the surface-thought of England was intent solely upon Irish famines, corn-laws and free-trade. It was only after many years that it became conscious of anything being wrong in the position of women... No doubt such ideas were at the time 'in the air' in England, but the dominant, practical Philistinism scoffed at them as 'ideas' banished to America, that refuge for exploded European absurdities."

[I believe the *Vindication of the Rights of Woman* by Mary (Wollstone-craft) Godwin (1792) first turned the attention of the people of England to the "wrongs of women."]

[2] The following paragraphs are based on what my father said about the poem.

And if woman in her appointed place "stays all the fair young planet in her hands," she may be well content. She has space enough to

> Burgeon out of all
> Within her — let her make herself her own
> To give or keep, to live and learn and be
> All that not harms distinctive womanhood.

She must train herself to do the large work that lies before her, even though she may not be destined to be wife or mother, cultivating her understanding not her memory only, her imagination in its highest phases, her inborn spirituality and her sympathy with all that is pure, noble and beautiful, rather than mere social accomplishments; then and then only will she further the progress of humanity, then and then only men will continue to hold her in reverence.

On the other hand one of the poet's main tests of manhood is "the chivalrous reverence" for womanhood.

> To love one maiden only, cleave to her,
> And worship her by years of noble deeds,
> Until they win her; for indeed I know
> Of no more subtle master under heaven
> Than is the maiden passion for a maid,
> Not only to keep down the base in man,
> But teach high thought and amiable words,
> And courtliness and the desire of fame,
> And love of truth, and all that makes a man.

He would say, "I would pluck my hand from a man even if he were my greatest hero, or dearest friend, if he wronged a woman or told her a lie."

After 1847 "The Princess" underwent considerable alterations. The second edition was published in 1848 with a few amendments, and dedicated to Henry

Lushington, but in 1850 a third edition appeared with omissions and many additions, and notably six songs were introduced, which help to express more clearly the meaning of "the medley."

These songs

> The women sang
> Between the rougher voices of the men,
> Like linnets in the pauses of the wind.

In 1851 the "weird seizures" of the Prince were inserted. His too emotional temperament was intended from an artistic point of view to emphasize his comparative want of power. "Moreover," my father writes, "the words 'dream-shadow,' 'were and were not' doubtless refer to the anachronisms and improbabilities of the story: compare the prologue,

> Seven and yet one, like shadows in a dream,

and v. 466,

> And like a flash the weird affection came,
>
>   *   *   *   *   *   *   *
>
> I seem'd to move in old memorial tilts,
> And doing battle with forgotten ghosts,
> To dream myself the shadow of a dream."

"It may be remarked that there is scarcely anything in the story which is not prophetically glanced at in the prologue." My father added: "It is true that some of the blank verse in this poem is among the best I ever wrote"—such passages as:

> Not peace she look'd—the Head: but rising up
> Robed in the long night of her deep hair, so
> To the open window moved, remaining there
> Fixt like a beacon-tower above the waves

Of tempest, when the crimson-rolling eye
Glares ruin, and the wild birds on the light
Dash themselves dead. She stretch'd her arms and
     call'd
Across the tumult and the tumult fell;

and as this description of a storm seen from Snowdon:

As one that climbs a peak to gaze
O'er land and main, and sees a great black cloud
Drag inward from the deeps, a wall of night,
Blot out the slope of sea from verge to shore,
And suck the blinding splendour from the sand,
And quenching lake by lake, and tarn by tarn,
Expunge the world;

and as these lines from the last canto:

Look up, and let thy nature strike on mine,
Like yonder morning on the blind half-world;
Approach and fear not; breathe upon my brows;
In that fine air I tremble, all the past
Melts mist-like into this bright hour, and this
Is morn to more, and all the rich to-come
Reels, as the golden Autumn woodland reels
Athwart the smoke of burning weeds. Forgive me,
I waste my heart in signs: let be. My bride,
My wife, my life. O we will walk this world,
Yoked in all exercise of noble end,
And so thro' those dark gates across the wild
That no man knows.

For *simple* rhythm and vowel music he considered
his " Come down, O maid, from yonder mountain height,"
written in Switzerland (chiefly at Lauterbrunnen and
Grindelwald), and descriptive of the waste Alpine heights
and gorges, and of the sweet, rich valleys below, as
amongst his "*most successful work.*" But by this phrase

he meant no more than that he felt he had done his best: there was no tinge of vanity in it. To put his own poetry in favourable comparison with that of others was never in his mind.

He said that "The passion of the past, the abiding in the transient, was expressed in 'Tears, idle Tears,' which was written in the yellowing autumn-tide at Tintern Abbey, full for me of its bygone memories. Few know that it is a blank verse lyric." He thought that my uncle Charles' sonnet of "Time and Twilight" had the same sort of mystic, *dämonisch* feeling.

The only song in "The Princess" approved by Fitzgerald was "Blow, Bugle, Blow," commemorating the echoes at Killarney[1].

"That is one of Fitz's crotchets," Fitzgerald said to me in 1876, "and I am considered a great heretic, because like Carlyle I gave up all hopes of him after 'The Princess.'" He wrote once, and repeated for me in his MS notes, that none of the songs had "the old champagne flavour," adding, "Alfred is the same magnanimous, kindly delightful fellow as ever, uttering by far the finest prose-sayings of anyone." Nothing either by Thackeray or by my father met Fitzgerald's approbation unless he had first seen it in manuscript.

The following notes on "The Princess" were left by my father:

In the Prologue the "Tale from mouth to mouth" was a game which I have more than once played when I was at Trinity College, Cambridge, with my brother undergraduates. Of course, if he "that inherited the tale" had not attended very carefully to his predecessors, there were contradictions; and if the story were historical, occasional anachronisms. In defence of what

---

[1] When my father was last there a boatman said to him, "So you're the gentleman that brought the money to the place?"

some have called the too poetical passages, it should
be recollected that the poet of the party was requested
to " dress the tale up poetically," and he was full of the
" gallant and heroic chronicle."   Some of my remarks
on passages in the " Princess " have been published by
Dawson of Canada, who copied them from a letter
which I wrote to him criticizing his study of the
" Princess[1]."   The child is the link thro' the parts as
shown in the songs which are the best interpreters of
the poem[2].   Before the first edition came out, I deliber-
ated with myself whether I should put songs between
the separate divisions of the poem; again I thought
that the poem would explain itself, but the public did not
see the drift.   The first song I wrote was named " The
Losing of the Child."   The child is sitting on the bank
of the river and playing with flowers; a flood comes
down; a dam has been broken thro'— the child is borne
down by the flood; the whole village distracted; after
a time the flood has subsided; the child is thrown safe
and sound again upon the bank; and there is a chorus
of jubilant women.

[1] The letter is printed on pp. 256–259 of this volume.

[2] "At the end of the first canto, fresh from the description of the female
college, with its professoresses, and hostleresses, and other Utopian monsters,
we turn the page, and —

> As through the land at eve we went.
> *   *   *   *   *   *
> O there above the little grave,
> We kissed again with tears.

Between the next two cantos intervenes the well-known cradle song, perhaps
the best of all; and at the next interval is the equally well-known bugle-
song, the idea of which is that of twin-labour and twin-fame in a pair of
lovers.   In the next the memory of wife and child inspirits the soldier on
the field; in the next the sight of the fallen hero's child opens the sluices of
his widow's tears; and in the last,...the poet has succeeded, in the new
edition, in superadding a new form of emotion to a canto in which he
seemed to have exhausted every resource of pathos which his subject
allowed."   Charles Kingsley, in *Fraser's Magazine*, September, 1850.

(Unpublished fragment.)

The child was sitting on the bank
　Upon a stormy day,
He loved the river's roaring sound;
The river rose and burst his bound,
Flooded fifty leagues around,
Took the child from off the ground,
　And bore the child away.
O the child so meek and wise,
　Who made *us* wise and mild!

＊　　＊　　＊　　＊　　＊

Two versions of "Sweet and Low" were made, and were sent to my mother to choose which should be published. She chose the published one in preference to that which follows, because it seemed to her more song-like.

(Unpublished version.)

Bright is the moon on the deep,
Bright are the cliffs in her beam,
　Sleep, my little one, sleep!
Look he smiles, and opens his hands,
He sees his father in distant lands,
And kisses him there in a dream,
　　　Sleep, sleep.

Father is over the deep,
Father will come to thee soon,
　Sleep, my pretty one, sleep!
Father will come to his babe in the nest,
Silver sails all out of the West,
Under the silver moon,
　　　Sleep, sleep!

"The notices of "The Princess" that I know interested my father were those by Aubrey de Vere[1], Charles Kingsley, Robertson (the Brighton preacher), and Dawson of Montreal. To the last[2] he wrote a letter (Nov. 21st, 1882) which may be quoted in full:

I thank you for your able and thoughtful essay on "The Princess." You have seen amongst other things that if women ever were to play such freaks, the burlesque and the tragic might go hand in hand. * * * Your explanatory notes are very much to the purpose, and I do not object to your finding parallelisms. They must always occur. A man (a Chinese scholar) some time ago wrote to me saying that in an unknown, untranslated Chinese poem there were two whole lines[3] of mine almost word for word? Why not? Are not human eyes all over the world looking at the same objects, and must there not consequently be coincidences of thought and impressions and expressions? It is scarcely possible for anyone to say or write anything in this late time of the world to which, in the rest of the literature of the world, a parallel could not somewhere be found. But when you say that this passage or that was suggested by

---

[1] *Edinburgh Review*, No. CLXXXII. October, 1849.

[2] In Dawson's *Study of the Princess* I find that I have written, after a talk with my father *à propos* possibly of the battle at the end of the poem : — "A. T. observed : 'Macpherson's 'Ossian' is poor in most parts, but this is a grand image — After saying that the beam of battle was bright before the spectral warrior, he goes on somehow like this : ' But behind thee was the Shadow of Death, like the darkened half of the moon behind its other half in growing light.'' A. T. talked of ' the beautiful picture that the girl graduates would have made ; the long hall glittering like a bed of flowers with daffodil and lilac.' Then he touched on the old religions and the ' old god of war '; 'the Norse mythology,' he said, ' is finer than the Greek with its human gods, though the Greek has more beauty. The Norsemen thought that there was something better in the way of religion that would dawn upon the earth after the Ragnarok or twilight of the gods.'"

[3] The Peak is high, and the stars are high,
And the thought of a man is higher.
"The Voice and the Peak."

Wordsworth or Shelley or another, I demur; and more, I wholly disagree. There was a period in my life when, as an artist, Turner for instance, takes rough sketches of landskip, etc. in order to work them eventually into some great picture, so I was in the habit of chronicling, in four or five words or more, whatever might strike me as picturesque in Nature. I never put these down, and many and many a line has gone away on the north wind, but some remain: e.g.

A full sea glazed with muffled moonlight.

Suggestion.

The sea one night at Torquay, when Torquay was the most lovely sea-village in England, tho' now a smoky town. The sky was covered with thin vapour, and the moon behind it.

A great black cloud
Drags inward from the deep.

Suggestion.

A coming storm seen from the top of Snowdon.

In the " Idylls of the King,"
With all
Its stormy crests that smote against the skies.

Suggestion.

A storm which came upon us in the middle of the North Sea.

As the water-lily starts and slides.

Suggestion.

Water-lilies in my own pond, seen on a gusty day with my own eyes. They did start and slide in the sudden puffs of wind till caught and stayed by the tether of their own stalks, quite as true as Wordsworth's simile and more in detail.

> A wild wind shook, —
> Follow, follow, thou shalt win.

Suggestion.

I was walking in the New Forest. A wind did arise and

> Shake the songs, the whispers and the shrieks
> Of the wild wood together.

The wind I believe was a west wind, but because I wished the Prince to go south, I turned the wind to the south, and naturally the wind said "follow." I believe the resemblance which you note is just a chance one. Shelley's lines are not familiar to me tho' of course, if they occur in the *Prometheus*, I must have read them. I could multiply instances, but I will not bore you, and far indeed am I from asserting that books as well as Nature are not, and ought not to be, suggestive to the poet. I am sure that I myself, and many others, find a peculiar charm in those passages of such great masters as Virgil or Milton where they adopt the creation of a bygone poet, and re-clothe it, more or less, according to their own fancy. But there is, I fear, a prosaic set growing up among us, editors of booklets, book-worms, index-hunters, or men of great memories and no imagination, who *impute themselves* to the poet, and so believe that *he*, too, has no imagination, but is for ever poking his nose between the pages of some old volume in order to see what he can appropriate. They will not allow one to say ' Ring the bell ' without finding that we have taken it from Sir P. Sidney, or even to use such a simple expression as the ocean "roars," without finding out the precise verse in Homer or Horace from which we have plagiarised it (fact !).

I have known an old fish-wife, who had lost two sons
at sea, clench her fist at the advancing tide on a stormy
day, and cry out, " Ay! roar, do! how I hates to see thee
show thy white teeth." Now if I had adopted her ex-
clamation and put it into the mouth of some old woman
in one of my poems, I daresay the critics would have
thought it original enough, but would most likely have
advised me to go to Nature for my old women and not
to my own imagination [1]; and indeed it is a strong figure.

Here is another anecdote about suggestion. When
I was about twenty or twenty-one I went on a tour to
the Pyrenees. Lying among these mountains before a
waterfall [2] that comes down one thousand or twelve
hundred feet I sketched it (according to my custom
then) in these words:

Slow-dropping veils of thinnest lawn.

When I printed this, a critic informed me that " lawn "
was the material used in theatres to imitate a waterfall,
and graciously added, " Mr T. should not go to the
boards of a theatre but to Nature herself for his suggestions." And I *had* gone to Nature herself.

I think it is a moot point whether, if I had known
how that effect was produced on the stage, I should have
ventured to publish the line.

I find that I have written, quite contrary to my
custom, a letter, when I had merely intended to thank
you for your interesting commentary.

Thanking you again for it, I beg you to believe me

Very faithfully yours,

A. TENNYSON.

---

[1] He used to compare with this the Norfolk saying which we heard when
we were staying with the Rev. C. T. Digby at Warham: " The sea is
moaning for the loss of the wind."

[2] In the Cirque de Gavarnie.

Letters after the publication of "The Princess."

To Edward Fitzgerald.

1847.

MY DEAR FITZ,

Ain't I a beast for not answering you before? not that I am going to write now, only to tell you that I have seen Carlyle more than once, and that I have been sojourning at 42 Ebury Street for some twenty days or so, and that I am going to bolt as soon as ever I can, and that I would go to Italy if I could get anybody to go with me which I can't, and so I suppose I shan't go, which makes me hate myself and all the world; for the rest I have been be-dined usque ad nauseam. A pint of pale ale and a chop are things yearned after, not achievable except by way of lunch. However, this night I have sent an excuse to Mrs Procter and here I am alone, and wish you were with me. How are you getting on? Don't grow quite into glebe before I see you again.

My book is out and I hate it, and so no doubt will you.

Never mind, you will like me none the worse, and now good-night. I am knocked up and going to bed.

Ever yours, A. TENNYSON.

To Aubrey de Vere.

1847.

MY DEAR AUBREY,

I have ordered Moxon to send you the new edition [1] of "The Princess." You will find that I have in some measure adopted your suggestions, not entirely.

---

[1] Not published till 1848.

Many thanks for your critique in the *Edinburgh*. There were only one or two little things in it which I did not like; for instance that about the " dying and the dead " which is quite wide of the mark[1], and you will see that I have inserted a line to guard against such an interpretation in future; however I have every reason to be grateful to you, both for the ability of the article and for the favourable view you take of me in general; too favourable surely. I dare not believe such good things of myself. I have seen no papers for an age, and do not know how your poor are going on. I fear this bitter weather is very hard upon them.

A. T.

To Mrs Howitt.

42 EBURY STREET.

MY DEAR MRS HOWITT,

I got your beautiful book of Ballads the other day at Moxon's. It contains (as far as I have seen it) much that is sweet and good and reminds me of yourself. I have however been myself so much engaged with proof-sheets for the few days since I received it that I have not had leisure to do it justice by a fair perusal. Accept in return a book[2] of mine which I have sent to Longmans' for you. I don't believe you will like it — not at least till after three readings, if you will honour it so far. Best remembrances to husband and daughter, not forgetting the younglings and

Believe me always yours,

A. TENNYSON.

[1] See p. 282.
[2] " The Princess."

For the sisters Brontë my father had the highest admiration. He received the following letter from Currer Bell (Charlotte Brontë):

June 16th, 1847.

SIR,

My relatives, Ellis and Acton Bell, and myself, heedless of the repeated warnings of various respectable publishers, have committed the rash act of printing a volume of poems.

The consequences predicted have of course overtaken us; our book is found to be a drug; no man needs it nor heeds.

In the space of a year the publisher has disposed but of two copies; and by what painful efforts he succeeded in getting rid of these two, himself only knows.

Before transferring the edition to the trunkmakers, we have decided on distributing as presents a few copies of what we cannot sell. We beg to offer you one in acknowledgement of the pleasure and profit we have often and long derived from your works.

I am, Sir, yours very respectfully,

CURRER BELL.

CHAPTER XIII.

CHELTENHAM, LONDON, CORNWALL, SCOTLAND AND IRELAND, 1846-1850.

The headquarters of the Tennysons were now at Cheltenham, Bellevue House in St James' Square. I am indebted to Dr Ker, brother of Judge Alan Ker, who married Miss Mary Tennyson, for some details of my father's life at this time.

From 1846 to 1850 he was often with his mother and family, but cannot be said to have moved in the society of the place: still he made some new acquaintances. The names I can recall are those of Dobson [1], afterwards Principal of Cheltenham College; Boyd, afterwards Dean of Exeter; Foxton, author of *Popular Christianity*; Sydney Dobell, the poet; Dr Acworth; Rashdall, Vicar of Malvern; Reece; and the well-known and "much beloved" Frederick Robertson, then Boyd's curate, afterwards incumbent of Trinity Chapel, Brighton.

There was a little room at the top of the house in St James' Square, not kept in very orderly fashion, for books and papers were to be seen quite as much on the floor and the chairs as upon the table. Here my father, pipe in mouth, discoursed to his friends more unconstrainedly than anywhere else on men and things and what death means. When the talk was on religious

---

[1] Dobson was third classic in the same year that Edmund Lushington was senior classic and Thompson fourth.

questions, which was not often, he spoke confidently of a future existence. Of Christianity he said, "it is rugging at my heart[1]."

My father would say: "The first time I met Robertson I felt that he expected something notable from me because I knew that he admired my poems, that he wished to pluck the heart from my mystery; so for the life of me from pure nervousness I could talk of nothing but beer."

Dr Ker says:

Sydney Dobell did not see much of your father in Cheltenham; but in Malvern, some years after your family left this place, Dobell, as he afterwards told me, saw a good deal of him. Dobell, as you know, was not a popular poet, and the number of his readers does not increase as the years go on, but that he was no commonplace poet your father heartily allowed. Frederick Foxton could only be brought to speak on one subject, Carlyle, whose companion and caretaker he had been during a journey on the Continent. Rashdall and Dr Acworth were men of cultivation and high social qualities whom your father met occasionally and much liked.

One acquaintance would keep on assuring my father that it was the greatest honour of his life to have met him. My father's answer to such praise was, " Don't talk d—d nonsense."

His chief companion, when in Cheltenham, for the best part of two years, was Dr Ker's brother Alan. Both were great walkers, and few near or distant places in this beautiful neighbourhood were left unvisited by them.

A year or two before, my father had lived some weeks in a Hydropathic Establishment at the very primitive village of Prestbury, and the village boys were in the habit of following him and the other inmates whenever they showed themselves on the roads and shouting,

[1] Dr Ker, MS Notes.

"Shiver and shake." This made him very nervous at the time, and the thought even of passing through Prestbury revived the feeling.

Dr Ker writes:

Two wishes I used to hear him express; one was to see the West Indies, the other to see the earth from a balloon.

Few things delighted me more than to see the mother and son together. You cannot remember your grandmother, I think. She was a perfect picture, a beautiful specimen of the English gentlewoman, loving and loveable, "no angel but a dearer being," and so sensitive that touch her feelings ever so lightly and the tears rushed to her eyes. Then it was we used to hear your father say, "Dam your eyes, mother, dam your eyes!" and then she smiled and applied the white pocket-handkerchief and shook her head at her son. He often jested with her about Dr Cumming and his "bottles," the bottles being the seven vials of St John's Revelation! You have heard, I dare say, that your grandmother confined her reading at that time to two books, the *Bible* and Dr Cumming's work on *Prophecy*. He used to jest with his mother about her monkey, a clever little black thing that was generally seen in the garden perched on the top of a pole. Your father naturally christened it St Simeon Stylites. I once ventured to ask him whether his mother had not sat for the picture of the Prince's mother in "The Princess," and he allowed that no one else had.

> Happy he
> With such a mother! faith in womankind
> Beats with his blood, and trust in all things high
> Comes easy to him, and tho' he trip and fall
> He shall not blind his soul with clay.

Your father's estimate of Wordsworth's poetry was a very high one as you must know, and I dare say you know that Wordsworth's opinion of your father was also very high. On one of the occasions of their meeting Wordsworth said to him: "Mr Tennyson, I have been endeavouring all my life to write a pastoral like your 'Dora' and have not succeeded." That was great praise from one who honestly weighed his words and was by no means lavish of his praise.

From Cheltenham my father made expeditions to London to see his old friends. One day Savile Morton writes that he has called on Alfred, and found Thackeray there, and "a stack of shag tobacco with Homer and Miss Barrett on the table." " Both Thackeray and Alfred," he adds, " praise Miss Barrett." My father grew to know Thackeray well and would call him a "loveable man." A story which he told illustrates the character of both the friends. They had been dining together and my father said, " I love Catullus for his perfection in form and for his tenderness, he is tenderest of Roman poets," and quoted the lines about Quintilia's death ending with

"Quo desiderio veteres renovamus amores
Atque olim amissas flemus amicitias " —

lines which he would translate by four lines from one of Shakespeare's Sonnets,

"Then can I drown an eye, unused to flow
For precious friends hid in death's dateless night,
And weep afresh Love's long since cancell'd woe,
And moan the expense of many a vanish'd sight,"

and the stanza from the " Juliæ et Mallii Epithalamium,"

"Torquatus, volo, parvulus
Matris e gremio suæ
Porrigens teneras manus
Dulce rideat ad patrem,
Semihiante labello."

Thackeray answered, " I do not rate him highly, I could do better myself." Next morning my father received this apology:

My dear Alfred,

I woke at 2 o'clock, and in a sort of terror at a certain speech I had made about Catullus. When I have dined, sometimes I believe myself to be equal to the greatest painters and poets. That delusion goes off; and then I know what a small fiddle mine is and what small tunes I play upon it. It was very generous of you to give me an opportunity of recalling a silly speech : but at the time I thought I was making a perfectly simple and satisfactory observation. Thus far I must *unbus'm* myself : though why should I be so uneasy at having made a conceited speech ? It is conceited not to wish to seem conceited. With which I conclude,

Yours, W. M. T.

"It was impossible," said my father, "to have written in a more generous spirit. No one but a noble-hearted man could have written such a letter."

During the "forties" he was in the habit of walking with Carlyle at night, and Carlyle would rail against the "governments of Jackasserie which cared more for commerce than for the greatness of our empire"; or would rave against the stuccoed houses in London as "acrid putrescence," or against the suburbs as a "black jumble of black cottages where there used to be pleasant fields"; and they would both agree that it was growing into "a strange chaos of odds and ends, this London." They were not in the least afraid of one another although many were afraid of them, and they had long and free discussions on every conceivable subject, and once only almost quarrelled, when Carlyle asserted that my father talked of poetry as "high art," which he flatly contradicted, "I never in my whole life spoke of 'high art.'"

They had — both of them — lost MSS of their works; Carlyle his *French Revolution*, my father *Poems, chiefly Lyrical.* When my father asked Carlyle how he felt after the disappearance of his MS, he answered, "Well, I just felt like a man swimming without water."

My uncle Frederick writes :

I am sure I could not perform such a feat as I know Alfred to have done, any more than raise the dead. The earliest MS of the *Poems, chiefly Lyrical* he lost out of his great-coat pocket one night while returning from a neighbouring market town.

This was enough to reduce an ordinary man to despair, but the invisible ink was made to reappear, all the thoughts and fancies in their orderly series and with their entire drapery of words arose and lived again. I wonder what under such circumstances would become of the "mob of gentlemen who write with ease." Of course it would not much matter as they could easily indite something new.

My father's poems were generally based on some single phrase like "Someone had blundered": and were rolled about, so to speak, in his head, before he wrote them down: and hence they did not easily slip from his memory.

In these London days among his friends were the Kembles, Coventry Patmore, Frederick Pollock, Alfred Wigan, and Macready; and he enjoyed "turning in" at the theatres. Macready he thought not good in "Hamlet" but fine in "Macbeth": yet said that his "Out, out, brief candle!" was wrong, "not vexed and harassed as it ought to be, but spoken with lowered voice, and a pathos which I am sure, Shakespeare never intended."

One evening, at Bath House, Milnes wished to introduce my father to the Duke of Wellington. "No," my father said, "why should the great Duke be bothered by a poor poet like me?" He only once saw the Duke, when he was riding out of the Horse Guards at Whitehall: and took off his hat. The Duke instantly made his usual military salute, commemorated in the "Ode on the death of the Duke of Wellington" in the well-known lines:

> No more in soldier fashion will he greet
> With lifted hand the gazer in the street.

Rogers continued to be intimate with my father, and would ask him privately his opinion on literary matters [1].

---

[1] My father asked him why he did not write a sonnet. "I never could dance in fetters," he answered. My father himself preferred the Shakespearian form of sonnet to the Italian, as being less constrained.

At one of the famous breakfasts, wishing to do my father honour before the company, and expecting praise, Rogers enquired whether he approved of a particular poem by himself. My father told him frankly that a certain emendation would be an improvement. "It shall be attended to," answered Rogers, but very stiffly. Then, because my father went to the Water-Cure, Rogers had an erroneous idea that he "suffered from many infirmities." When I showed my father this statement in a published letter, he wrote down: "No truer comment could be made on this than my favourite adage, 'Every man imputes himself.' My good old friend had many infirmities. What mine were I know not unless short-sight and occasional hypochondria be infirmities. I used, from having early read in my father's library a great number of medical books, to fancy at times that I had all the diseases in the world, like a medical student. I dare say old Rogers meant it all for the best. Peace be with him! often bitter, but very kindly at heart. We have often talked of death together till I have seen the tears roll down his cheeks."

About this time there was a dinner given at Hampstead by a Society of Authors, Sergeant Talfourd in the chair. My father accepted an invitation to the dinner on condition that he should not be asked to make a speech. Many speeches were made, each author praising every other author. My father seems to have said to his neighbour, "I wonder which of us will last 500 years?" Upon which Talfourd jumped up and burst forth into "A speech about Tennyson," affirming that he was "sure to live." Then Douglas Jerrold seized my father's hand and said, "I haven't the smallest doubt that you will outlast us all, and that you are the one who will live." The subject of these enthusiastic words disclaimed his sureness of lasting, and told his friends that while thanking them all he felt his inability to make

a speech and so on.   Talfourd shouted out, "Why you are
making a speech."   "Yes," answered my father, "but not
upon my legs."

Letters, 1847.

To Mrs Howitt.

May 22nd, [1847?].

MY DEAR MRS HOWITT,

I got your letter three or four days ago and
if I did not answer immediately you must lay it to the
account of the water-cure which I am undergoing and
which renders letter-writing or anything, except washing
and walking, more difficult than those who have not past
thro' the same ordeal would easily believe.

At this moment my own family do not know where I
am: I have not written home, nor shall write I dare say
for some time; to be sure I am not at any time much in
the habit of writing home, and so my people know my
ways and forgive them; but to you I feared to seem
unkind and forgetful of the pleasant day I spent under
your roof if I kept silence; so I write to tell you that my
visit to Clapton though necessarily postponed will really
if I live and thrive sometime take place; "sunshine"
and "flowers" will go on for a long time yet, and before
they are all gone I hope to see you and to find you
wholly recovered from the effects of that sad and anxious
winter you speak of; to me it is not permitted to be
either sad or anxious if I am to get better. I must,
like Prince Hal, "doff the world aside and let it pass,"
so says my doctor tho' he does not quote Shakespeare
for it.

Good-bye and give my best remembrances to all yours whom I know, and

Believe me, my dear Mrs Howitt,

Yours very truly, A. TENNYSON.

To F. Freiligrath.

10 ST JAMES' SQUARE, CHELTENHAM.
Nov. 5*th*, [1847?].

MY DEAR SIR,

I had long ago heard of you : I knew that you were a celebrated German Poet and lover of Liberty : therefore was my satisfaction great to receive (as I did this morning) a copy of your works with your own friendly autograph. I need not say how much I feel the honour you have done me in translating some of my poems into your own noble and powerful language. Would that my acquaintance were more perfect with German [1], then would my tribute of approbation be of more value and less incur the charge of presumption. I have not yet had time and leisure sufficient to read your translations from myself carefully, but from what I have seen and if I may be permitted to judge, I should say that they are not dry bones, but seem full of a living warmth, in fact a *Poet's* translation of Poetry. I could wish however that you had taken the 2nd edition of " Mariana in the South ": the old poem was so imperfect as to be wholly unworthy your notice.

Accept my friendship and my regrets that I am not at present able to come up to town and shake you by the hand. How long do you stop in England ? Is there any hope that you could be prevailed upon to come to

[1] He could read German with ease at this time.

Cheltenham? I should be most happy to see you.
Write to me and tell me, and

Believe me, my dear Sir, ever yours,

A. Tennyson.

1848–49.

In February the Tennysons received a letter from
Emily in Paris. The Revolution against Louis Philippe
had begun. She had been looking out of her window,
and was shot at by one of the Revolutionists, the bullet
missing her and going through the ceiling. The account
continues, written but not signed by her:

31, Rue Tronchet.
Feb. 25th, 1848.

*   *   *   *   *   *   *   *   *

It would be impossible to attempt any description of the
horrors of yesterday. However, the public events are better
recorded, and will have reached you by means of the paper.
But I will at once satisfy your anxiety as to the safety of myself
and all our friends. Instead of retiring to the Convent as I had
intended on Wednesday, I could not make up my mind to leave
my friends at a moment of such imminent danger, and the only
moment past in which I could have crossed the Bridges. I have
remained the last two nights with Madame Marthion, sleeping
in her room, unable to procure any clothes but those I brought
on my back from the Convent on Tuesday. Yesterday past
like a fearful dream. In the morning it was hoped the resignation of Guizot would satisfy the people, but their triumph
only made them the more exorbitant, and while the General who had gone to his post at the Tuileries was breakfasting at 11 o'clock, the Deputation came to the King, and
everything was immediately in disorder. The King, after
recommending to the National Guard the safety of the citizens,
started for St Cloud in a carriage, with all his family, except the
Duchess of Orleans and her children. The General was ap-
prised of Sophie's arrival at the Tuileries, and went downstairs
to see her, and on returning to his post by the Duchess of

Orleans as quickly as he could, was met by her. "Mon cher Général, suivez-moi" was all she was able to say to him in passing. The poor man was unable to obey, and his feelings can be better understood than described, as he saw her crossing the Tuileries Gardens on foot, escorted by a few friends amidst this infuriated mob to the Chamber of Deputies. There she was at first well received, but some of the mob penetrated and surrounded her, and one man applied a gun to her cheek. This however was happily turned off by a Deputy, and Jules Lasteyre, another of the Opposition Deputies, aided by many of his brother Deputies, defended her and contrived to get her into a fiacre which he drove to the Invalides. She was separated from her children for some time, but at length they joined her in disguise, and she is at this moment not at the Invalides, but in a secret place of safety, of which the General himself is ignorant. After the departure of the King, the Tuileries was thoroughly invaded by the mob, and every article of furniture completely destroyed. The poor General stayed to defend the property of the Duchess as long as he thought he could be of use, and then he with Sophie left the Tuileries, he, almost lifted downstairs by a man whom he had had an opportunity of serving, and his infirmities were respected by the mob, till he got to the Rue du 29 Juillet, towards 2 o'clock; from thence, as soon as he could be removed, to the Rue des Capucines where he is now. Of course his place and position are gone, but you may conceive the anxiety of our minds to know what had become of him and Sophie during the fearful hours they were in the Tuileries, where it was impossible to attempt any communication. * * * You never saw such a set of ruffians as infest the streets, armed with every weapon with which they could furnish themselves, shouting and singing the "Marseillaise," etc. About half an hour ago a gang went by shouting "Au chemin de fer"; and we fear that the passage out of Paris will be completely cut off. The streets are all barricaded so that no carriage can pass, and though Madame Marthion and Sophie consider the wisest plan would be to leave the town we fear it will scarcely now be possible. * * * The Palais Royal is burnt down. * * * We were obliged to illuminate for safety's sake last night, and such a host of villains have taken advantage of this tumult, that you may imagine our rest was scarcely so to be called. The fear of pillage, and the anxiety lest this infuriated mob might even turn against our only security, the National Guard, at a moment of no existing government (for the provisional government could not yesterday come to any measures), kept our minds awake, while our eyes were closed, though fatigue of mind and body overcame our anxiety in a great measure. The situation of the General's house, next to Guizot's, also keeps us in constant alarm. The noise of firing also all night, in the uncertainty of its being merely rejoicing, or with murderous objects, contributed its share to add to our anxiety. * * *

Provisions are growing very scarce, and the cry for bread is now strong. Yesterday half the mob were drunk.

My father's journal of his Tour in Cornwall, 1848 (when he thought of again taking up the subject of Arthur).

Tuesday, May 30th. Arrived at Bude in dark, askt girl way to sea, she opens the back door...I go out and in a moment go sheer down, upward of six feet, over wall on fanged cobbles[1]. Up again and walked to sea over dark hill.

June 2nd. Took a gig to Rev. S. Hawker at Morwenstow, passing Comb valley, fine view over sea, coldest manner of Vicar till I told my name, then all heartiness. Walk on cliff with him, told of shipwreck.

Sunday. Rainy and bad, went and sat in Tintagel ruins, cliff all black and red and yellow, weird looking thing.

---

[1] " At one place," writes Miss Fox, " where he arrived in the evening, he cried, ' Where is the sea? Show me the sea.' So after the sea he went stumbling in the dark, and fell down and hurt his leg so much that he had to be nursed six weeks by a surgeon there, who introduced some friends to him, and thus he got into a class of society totally new to him ; and when he left they gave him a series of introductions, so that instead of going to hotels he was passed on from town to town, and abode with little grocers and shopkeepers along his line of travel. He says that he cannot have better got a true impression of the class, and thinks the Cornish very superior to the generality. They all knew about Tennyson, and had read his poems, and one miner hid behind a wall that he might see him. Thus he became familiarized with the thoughts and feelings of all classes of society."

5*th*. Clomb over Isle, disappointed, went thro' the sea-tunnel-cavern over great blocks. Walls lined with shells, pink or puce jellies. Girls playing about the rocks as in a theatre.

6*th*. Slate quarries, one great pillar left standing; ship under the cliff loading ; dived into a cavern all polished with the waves like dark marble with veins of pink and white. Follow'd up little stream falling thro' the worn slate, smoked a pipe at little inn, dined, walked once more to the old castle darkening in the gloom.

7*th*. Camelford, Slaughter Bridge, clear brook among alders. Sought for King Arthur's stone, found it at last by a rock under two or three sycamores, walked seaward, came down by churchyard. Song from ship.

8*th*. Walked seaward. Large crimson clover; sea purple and green like a peacock's neck. " By bays, the, peacock's neck in hue."

14*th*. Read part of *Œdipus Coloneus.*

19*th*. Finished reading *Fathom* [1]. Set off for Polperro, ripple-mark, queer old narrow-streeted place, back at 9. Turf fires on the hills; jewel-fires in the waves from the oar, which Cornish people call " bryming."

July 1*st*. Museum. After dinner went to Perranzabuloe. Coast looked gray and grand in the fading light. Went into cave, Rembrandt-like light thro' the opening.

6*th*. Went to Land's End by Logan rock, leaden-backed mews wailing on cliff, one with two young ones. Mist. Great yellow flare just before sunset. Funeral. Land's End and Life's End.

8*th*. The Lizard, rocks in sea, two southern eyes of England [2]. Tamarisk hedge in flower. Round Pentreath beach, large crane's bill near Kynance, down to cove. Glorious grass-green monsters of waves. Into caves of Asparagus Island. Sat watching wave-rainbows.

---

[1] Doubtless Smollett's *Ferdinand Count Fathom.*   [2] Lighthouses.

11*th.* Down to Lizard Cove. Smoked with workmen. Boat to several places. Saw the further ships under Penzance like beads threading the sunny shore.

12*th.* Polpur. Bathed, ran in and out of cave. Down to Caerthillian, lovely clear water in cove. Lay over Pentreath beach, thunder of waves to west. Penaluna's *Cornwall.*

13*th.* Bathed in Polpur Cove. Bewick-like look of trunk, cloak and carpet bag, lying on rock. Sailed, could not land at Kynance. Saw the long green swell heaving on the black cliff, rowed into Pigeonthugo, dismal wailing of mews. To St Ives.

Mrs Rundle Charles[1], who was then Miss Rundle, allowed me to publish the following account, from her private diary, of my father's visit (during this tour) to her uncle's house near Plymouth.

We were staying at Upland, a country house belonging to an uncle of mine four miles from Plymouth. Whilst there we were walking on the Hoe at Plymouth one day, when to my delight we were told that my father was to drive Mr Tennyson from Tavistock to pay us a visit at Upland. The clergyman's wife and other friends came to tea that afternoon, but Mr Tennyson did not appear. We went out for a ramble in the wood, were caught in a shower and ran home. Mr Tennyson was there, in the hall, just arrived: my father introduced me to him, and he came into the drawing-room, and said to my mother, "You have a party," which he did not seem to like. My father then called me in to make tea for Mr Tennyson in the dining-room, and we had a quiet talk; a powerful, thoughtful face, kind smile, hearty laugh, extremely near-sighted[2]. He spoke of travelling; Dresden, unsatisfactoriness of picture-gallery seeing; the first time he was in Paris he "went every day for a fortnight to the

---

[1] Author of *The Schönberg-Cotta Family*; she died in 1896.

[2] He talked then with his friends of Sir Charles Napier and of his battle of Meeanee (1843), about which he half thought of making a poem, and said that Westley the optician had told him that Sir Charles Napier and he were the two most short-sighted men in England.

Louvre, saw only one picture, 'La Maîtresse de Titien,' the second time looked only at 'Narcissus lying by a stream, Echo in the distance and ferocious little Love.'" Mr Ruskin set his own thought against the united admiration of centuries, but he spoke of a "splendid chapter on Clouds" in *Modern Painters.*

Then he turned to Geology, Weald of Kent, Delta of a great river flowing from as far as Newfoundland. "Conceive," he said, "what an era of the world that must have been, great lizards, marshes, gigantic ferns!" Fancied, standing by a railway at night, the engine must be like some great Ichthyosaurus. I replied how beautiful Hugh Miller's descriptions of that time are: he thought so too: then spoke of Peach, the Cornish geologist on the Preventive Service, maintaining a wife and seven children on £100 a year, whilst we in one annual dinner, champagne, turtle, etc. spend £25.

He spoke of the Italians as a great people (it was in 1848, the year of revolutions [1]) "twice matured." He had read a poem of mine on Italy: said he felt "great interest in the Italian movement as in all great movements for freedom"; that perhaps all looked equally disorderly as they arose; that the German revolutions (of 1848) were miserable plagiarisms. We went into the drawing-room, I played Mendelssohn. Mr Tennyson came and talked to me about Schiller, — "Schwärmerisch, yet Schwärmerei better than mere kalter Verstand, not dramatic; knew by heart Goethe's Gedichte 'Summer breathings.' Felt the grand intellectual power of *Faust*, but threw it aside in disgust at the first reading!" Then he spoke of Milton's Latinisms, and delicate play with words, and Shakespeare's play upon words. At supper he spoke of Goethe's *Tasso:* he felt with Tasso, did not care for anything else in the play. "Leonora, discreet, prudential young lady, could not of course care for the poor

---

[1] He used to tell with infinite humour the following story, illustrating the love of a row in the hot-blooded South. "Edward Lear, the painter, had been living at a hotel in a small town in Southern Italy, but had gone on a tour leaving his room locked up. On his return he found the place in the uproar of a mushroom revolution, the inhabitants drunk with *chianti* and shouting *libertà* and *la patria* through the streets. 'Where is my *chiave*,' said he to the waiter, 'of my *camera* to get at my *roba*?' 'O,' replied the waiter, not liking to be let down from his dream of a golden age, '*O che chiave!* O che camera! O che roba! Non c' è più chiave! Non c' è più camera! Non c' è più roba! Non c' è più niente! Tutto è amore e libertà! O che bella revoluzione!'"

poet — it would not have been the thing, it would not have done: remembered only these lines:

> ' Es bildet ein Talent sich in der Stille,
> Sich ein Charakter in dem Strom der Welt.' "

Said he had talked of me last night and heard from Dr Beale, a clergyman of Tavistock, brother-in-law of W. H. Smith, that I knew Greek, and he said he only disliked *pedantry* in women. He said, "Wordsworth was great, but too one-sided to be dramatic." He spoke of the "snobbery of English society." It was getting late, so my aunt asked him to stay the night, but he said he had breakfasted alone for a dozen years; then he said to me, "Ich kann nicht hier schlafen." I said, "Warum?" He said, "Ich kann nicht rauchen." I translated aloud, he laughed, declared he "had never been played such a trick before, chose the disguise of an obscure northern dialect, and was betrayed to everyone"; then he said, "German has great fine words: every language is really untranslateable." Then the carriage came to take him into Plymouth : he asked to take my poems (manuscript) with him, and said, "Good-night not Good-bye." Next morning (Tuesday, July 25th) Mr Tennyson came again : he talked about lower organisms feeling less pain than higher, but would not fish : could not comprehend the feeling of animals with ganglia, little scattered knots of nerves and no brain; spoke of wonderful variety of forms of life, instinct of plants, etc., told the story of "a Brahmin destroying a microscope because it showed him animals killing each other in a drop of water"; "significant, as if we could destroy facts by refusing to see them." We walked into the garden, sat on chairs at entrance of avenue; then he laughed about some tremendous "duty-woman," clergyman's wife, now Low, now High Church, "always equally vehement, little brains, much conscientiousness; husband preached one thing in the church, she another in the parish." He said it was right to "enjoy leisure," spoke of Miss Martineau's *Eastern Life*, did not like her, said he supposed we were not Unitarians or Pagans, although it was the fashion with literary ladies. Then he spoke of my poems, said he liked some very much, especially some lines on the gentianella : then he kindly made one or two verbal criticisms in one called "The Poet's Daily Bread." "Have you printed?" he said. "Do not publish too early, you cannot retract." I ventured to thank him for his poems, in which we delighted. "I thank you for yours," he said graciously. We went into the kitchen garden, he talked of flowers and cabbages, picked gooseberries, he "used as a boy to lie for hours under a gooseberry bush reading a novel, finishing his gooseberries and novel together"; he liked the kitchen garden, "so wholesome." "I would rather stay with you bright girls than dine with Mr W.," he said. He sent away his fly, then we went into my cousin Helen's garden, and he told us stories of "an African woman, who asked to *be breakfasted upon* (by white men)," etc. etc. Afterwards we drove him into Plymouth. "You would not think me a shy man, but I am always shy with false or conventional people; people are sometimes affected from shyness, and *grow* simple." Then we talked of Carlyle: "You would like him for one day," he said, "but get tired of him, so vehement and destructive"; he gave by way of a specimen of his talk in a deep tragic voice, "For God's sake away with gigs, thousand million gigs in the world, away with them all in God's name, spoke and axle, the world will never be right until they are all swept into the lowest pit of Tophet." He often smokes with Carlyle; "Goethe once Carlyle's hero, now Cromwell his epitome of human excellence. Carlyle spoke once as if he wished poets to be our statesmen; fancy Burns Prime Minister!" Then he said to me, "Do you know the *Odyssey?* I like it better as a whole than the *Iliad:* I should have met you before; why didn't you write? I could teach you Greek in a month, then perhaps (quoting my poem called 'The Poet's Daily Bread') you would scorn me with bitter scorn." I laughed. "I will send you the *Odyssey*, I have two copies in my portmanteau; I will be grave when next I meet you; I vary." In the course of conversation he said, "Some parts of *The Book of Revelation* are finer in English than in Greek, e.g. 'And again they said "Alleluia"' and their smoke went up for ever and ever[1],' — magnificent conception, darkness and fire rolling together, for ever and ever."

[1] He would quote the tenth chapter with boundless admiration: "And I saw another mighty angel come down from heaven, clothed with a cloud... and he set his right foot upon the sea, and his left foot on the earth... And the angel which I saw stand upon the sea and upon the earth lifted up his hand to heaven, and sware by him that liveth for ever and ever, who created heaven, and the things that therein are, and the earth, and the things that therein are, and the sea, and the things that are therein, that there should be time no longer," or, as he translated it, "that time should be no more."

Letters, 1848–9.

To Aubrey de Vere (after a visit to Scotland in 1848).

CHELTENHAM, *Oct.*

MY DEAR AUBREY,

  I have just now on my return to Cheltenham got two letters from you, for I am one, as you know, who wander to and fro for months careless of P. O. and correspondences. I am grieved to have occasioned you so much trouble about the article, but let it pass, excuses will not mend it: neither will I mention the money[1] troubles I have had, for they are dead and buried, tho' you bribe with your " great piece of news," which I take it must mean that you are going to be married! is it so? if so, joy to you. I am glad that you have thought of me at Kilkee by the great deeps. The sea is my delight, tho' Mr Chretien in the *Christian Examiner* says that I have no power upon him and always represent him dead asleep. I have seen many fine things in Scotland, and many fine things did I miss seeing, rolled up as they were tenfold in Scotch mists. Loch Awe too, which you call the finest, I saw. It is certainly very grand, tho' the pass disappointed me. I thought of Wordsworth's lines there, and, approving much, disapproved of much in them. What can be worse than to say to old Kilchurn Castle,

" Take then thy seat, vicegerent unreproved "?

Surely, master Aubrey, that is puffed and false. I steamed from Oban to Skye, a splendid voyage, for the whole day, with the exception of three hours in the

---

[1] His friends tried to persuade him to write popular short poems in magazines, but, however poor he might be, he never could or would write a line for money offered.

morning, was blue and sunny; and I think I saw more outlines of hills than ever I saw in my life; and exquisitely shaped are those Skye mountains.   Loch Corusk, said to be the wildest scene in the Highlands, I failed in seeing.   After a fatiguing expedition over the roughest ground on a wet day we arrived at the banks of the loch, and made acquaintance with the extremest tiptoes of the hills, all else being thick wool-white fog.   Dunkeld is lovely, and I delighted in Inverary, tho' there likewise I got drenched to the skin, till my very hat wept tears of ink.   I rejoiced in Killeen, but on the whole perhaps I enjoyed no day more than the one I spent at Kirk Alloway by the monument of poor Burns, and the orchards, and " banks and braes of bonny Doon."   I made a pilgrimage thither out of love for the great peasant; they were gathering in the wheat and the spirit of the man mingled or seemed to mingle with all I saw.   I know you do not care much for him, but I do, and hold that there never was immortal poet if he be not one. Farewell.   Give my best love and remembrances to all yours, and

Believe me ever yours,

A.

To Aubrey de Vere.

[*Undated.*]

MY DEAR AUBREY,

I have just returned to this place whence I think I wrote to you last, and hither your letter after travelling Cheltenhamward and otherwhere followed me. I assure you I experienced a very lively gratification in finding that my recent alterations [1] had met your approval and not your's only but your mother's and sister's.   I am still not quite satisfied with it, and I think that one or two of the ballads might be improved or others substituted, but I have done with it at present.   I gave it up

[1] In " The Princess."

to the printer in a rage at last and left London, not having revised the last proofs, and so I see there is a mistake or two, for instance "marbled stairs" which is vile. Don't you think too that the Dedication to Harry Lushington looks very queer, dated "January, '48," the French row taking place in the February following, and such allusions and the subsequent ones made in the Epilogue! Well, I suppose that does not much matter, and I am as I said vastly gratified with your good opinion of the improvements.

I wrote so far — now I am in town for a week or so. Now for your two queries.

I have not the *Edinburgh* with me, and so cannot give you the exact passage in the critique; but I know there is mention made therein of "The Princess" coming out among the dying and the dead. Now I certainly did not mean to kill anyone, and therefore I put this new line into the old king's mouth,

I trust that there is no one hurt to death,

and in the old tourneys it really did happen now and then that there was only a certain amount of bruises and bangs and no death. Perhaps the Editor, not you, inserted the passage. With respect to the "Elegies[1]," I cannot say that I have turned my attention to them lately. I do not know whether I have done anything new in that quarter since you saw them, but I believe I am going to print them, and then I need not tell you that you will be perfectly welcome to a copy, on the condition that when the book is published, this avant-courier of it shall be either sent back to me, or die the death by fire in Curragh Chase. I shall print about twenty-five copies, and let them out among friends under the same condition of either return or cremation. The review in the *Westminster* was not one of "The Princess," but of two or three of the old Poems.

---

[1] "In Memoriam."

I have sent you a most shabby note in return for your long and agreeable one, but pray forgive me : I have such a heap of correspondence just now, half of which will never get answered at all.

Love to your brother and his wife, your mother and sister. I don't know, but I feel quite sorry that Caroline (Standish) is married. She did so well unmarried, and looked so pure and maidenly that I feel it quite a pity that she should have changed her state.

Ever yours, dear Aubrey,

A. TENNYSON.

The following *four* letters refer to what my father called " the highest honour I have yet received."

(1) From Mrs Gaskell to John Forster.

MANCHESTER, Oct. 8th, 1849.

I want to ask for your kind offices. You know Tennyson, and you know who Samuel Bamford is, a great, gaunt, stalwart Lancashire man, formerly hand-loom weaver, author of *Life of a Radical*, age nearly 70, and living in that state which is exactly decent poverty with his neat little apple-faced wife. They have lost their only child. Bamford is the most hearty (and it's saying a good deal) admirer of Tennyson I know. I dislike recitations exceedingly, but he repeats some of Tennyson's poems in so rapt and yet so simple a manner, utterly forgetting that anyone is by in the delight of the music and the exquisite thoughts, that one can't help liking to hear him. *He* does not care one jot whether people like him or not in his own intense enjoyment. He says when he lies awake at night, as in his old age he often does, and gets sadly thinking of the days that are gone when his child was alive, he soothes himself by repeating T.'s poems. I asked him the other day if he had got them of his own. "No," he said rather mournfully : he had been long looking out for a second-hand copy, but somehow they had not got into the old book-shops, and 14*s.* or 18*s.* (which are they ?) was too much for a poor man, and then he brightened up and said, Thank God he had a good memory, and whenever he got into a house where there were Tennyson's poems he learnt as many as he could by heart. He thought he knew better than twelve, and began " Œnone," and then the " Sleeping Beauty." Now I wonder if you catch a glimpse of what I want. I thought at first of giving him the poems this Xmas, but then I thought you would perhaps ask Tennyson if he would give Bamford a copy *from himself*, which would be glorious for the old man. Dear, how he would triumph.

(2) *To John Forster.*

MABLETHORPE, ALFORD,
LINCOLNSHIRE. 1849.

MY DEAR FORSTER,

I got both your notes almost at the same time. I have been flying about from house to house for a long time, and yours was delivered to me at a place called Scremby Hall in this county where I was making a morning call. All that account of Sam. Bamford is very interesting indeed. I reckon his admiration as the highest honour I have yet received. A lady was so charmed with the relation that I gave her the letter. Of course I will give him a copy but I shall not be in town for a fortnight. The first thing I do will be to call at Moxon's and get him one. I am here on this desolate sea-coast. My friends have fêted me in this county so long that I think it high time to move, but they will not let me go yet. How have you been, my dear boy? I trust well. In the hope of seeing you as soon as possible,

I am, yours as ever,

A. TENNYSON[1].

(3) *From Mrs Gaskell to John Forster.*

FRIDAY, *Dec. 7th*, 1849.

I have not yet taken my bonnet off after hunting up Bamford. First of all we went to Blakeley to his little white-

---

[1] He inclosed to Forster for the *Examiner*, March 24th, " You might have won the poet's fame ": reprinted in the *Poems* (sixth ed.), 1850.

washed cottage. His wife was cleaning, and regretted her
"master" was not at home. He had gone into Manchester,
where she did not know. I shan't go into the details of the
hunting of this day. At last we pounced upon the great gray
stalwart man coming out of a little old-fashioned public-house
where Blakeley people put up. When I produced my book he
said, "This is grand." I said, "Look at the title-page," for I saw
he was fairly caught by something he liked in the middle of the
book, and was standing reading it in the street. "Well, I am a
proud man this day!" he exclaimed. Then he turned it up and
down and read a bit (it was a very crowded street) and his gray
face went quite brown-red with pleasure. Suddenly he stopped.
"What must I do for him back again?" "Oh! you must write
to him, and thank him." "I'd rather walk 20 mile than write a
letter any day." "Well, then, suppose you set off this Christmas,
and walk and thank Tennyson." He looked up from his book,
right in my face, quite indignant. "Woman! walking won't
reach him. We're on the earth don't ye see, but he's there, up
above. I can no more reach him by walking than if he were an
eagle or a skylark high above my head." It came fresh, warm,
straight from the heart, without a motion or making a figurative
speech, but as if it were literal truth, and I were a goose for not
being aware of it. Then he dipped down again into his book,
and began reading aloud the "Sleeping Beauty," and in the
middle stopped to look at the writing again. And we left him
in a sort of sleep-walking state, and only trust he will not be run
over.

(4) *From Samuel Bamford to Alfred Tennyson.*

BLAKELEY, *Dec.* 13*th*, 1849.

DEAR SIR,

Mrs Gaskell a few days since presented to me your
poems, with your autograph, in kind terms, and I can only say,
as to the present, that I am very greatly obliged; and that you
could not have done anything that would have pleased me
better. Accept my most sincere thanks.

Your poems, I cannot forget them. I cannot put them away
from my thoughts; the persons and the scenes they represent

haunt me.   I have read them all over and over, and I have not
awakened once this night without

> Thy heart, my life, my love, my bride

immediately recurring to my thoughts.

Oh! your " Oriana " has started the tears into my eyes, and
into those of my dear wife, many a time.   It is a deep thing.
Your "Locksley Hall" is terribly beautiful; profoundly impressive.   The departure of your " Sleeping Palace " is almost my
favourite, and your "·Gardener's Daughter," ah! it brings early
scenes to my mind.

> The story of my early love that haunts me now I'm old,
> And broods within my very heart altho' 'tis well-nigh cold.

My wife, bless her! I never feel my sensibilities gushing
over, but when I look I find hers are doing the same.   And it
has frequently been the case since I was so fortunate as to have
your poems.

But your English! why it is almost unlimitedly expressive.
This language of ours, what can it not be made to say ?   What
height, what depth filled with all glorious hues, terrible glooms,
and vivid flashes does it not combine and your poems exhibit all?

Are you well?   Are you happy?   I hope you are both.
Accept my kindest wishes, and believe me to be

> Yours most truly,
>
> SAMUEL BAMFORD.

To Miss Holloway (of Spilsby) my father wrote
about her cousin Miss Jean Ingelow's poems, *A
Rhyming Chronicle of Incidents and Feelings.*

My DEAR MISS HOLLOWAY,

Many thanks for your very kind note.   I
have only just returned to town, and found the *Rhyming
Chronicle.*   Your Cousin must be worth knowing: there
are some very charming things in her book, at least it
seems so to me, tho' I do not pique myself on being
much of a critic at first sight, and I really have only

skimmed a few pages. Yet I think I may venture to pronounce that she need not be ashamed of publishing them. Certain things I saw which I count abominations, tho' I myself in younger days have been guilty of the same, and so was Keats. I would sooner lose a pretty thought than enshrine it in such rhymes as "Eudora" "before her," "vista" "sister." She will get to hate them herself as she grows older, and it would be a pity that she should let her book go forth with these cockneyisms. If the book were not so good I should not care for these specks, but the critics will pounce upon them, and excite a prejudice. I declare I should like to know her.

I have such a heap of correspondence to answer that I must bid you good-bye. What the German lady says is very gratifying. I shall perhaps see you again in the autumn. My best remembrances to each and all of your circle.

Ever yours truly, A. TENNYSON.

P.S. Strange! that I did not see it. I turn to the title-page, and find the book *is* published. I fancied it had only been printed. Forgive my hurry! Well, your cousin will amend, perhaps, the errors I have mentioned, in her next edition.

On the invitation of Aubrey de Vere, my father paid his second visit to Ireland; but he has left no record of his tour. At my request Mr de Vere has kindly written the following account: to which he has added some reminiscences of his first hearing "In Memoriam" read in 1850.

In the year 1848 Alfred Tennyson had felt a craving to make a lonely sojourn at Bude: "I hear," he said, "that there are larger waves there than on any other part of the British coast: and must go thither and be alone with God." I persuaded him to come also to Ireland where the waves are far higher and the cliffs often rise to 800 feet and in one spot, Slieve League, to 2000 : while at the mountain's landward side are still shown the "prayer-stations" of Saint Columbkill.   He passed five weeks with us at Curragh Chase, to us delightful weeks.   The day before our arrival we visited the celebrated "fall" of the Shannon at Castleconnel; over it there hung a full moon, the largest I have ever seen.   The aspect might well have shaken weak nerves.   It looked as if the "centrifugal" force had ceased, and the vast luminary might come down upon the earth in another hour.   That night we slept in my sister's house, and she had the satisfaction of conversing with the Poet whose works she had fed on since her girlhood.

The weeks passed by only too rapidly.   We drove our guest to the old Castles and Abbeys in the neighbourhood : he was shocked at the poverty of the peasantry, and the marks of havock wrought through the country by the great potato-famine: he read in the library ; and worked on a new edition of "The Princess," smoking at the same time without hindrance in our most comfortable bedroom, and protected as far as possible from noise ; he walked where he pleased alone, or in company through woods in which it was easy to lose oneself, by a cave so deep that Merlin might have slept in it to this day unawakened.   In the evenings he had vocal music from Lady de Vere and her sister, Caroline Standish, and Sonatas of Mozart or Beethoven played by my eldest brother, with a power and pathos rare in an amateur.   Later, he read poetry to us with a voice that doubled its power, commonly choosing pathetic pieces ; and on one occasion after finishing "A Sorrowful Tale" by Crabbe, glanced round reproachfully and said, "I do not see that any of you are weeping !"   One night we turned his poem of "The Day-Dream" into an acted charade ; a beautiful girl whom he used to call "that stately maid," taking the part of the Sleeping Beauty; and the poet himself that of the Prince who broke the spell of her slumber.   Another night there was a dance which he denounced as a stupid thing, while a brilliant and amusing person, Lady G., who was accustomed to speak her mind to all alike, scolded him sharply.   "How would the world get on if others went about it growling at its amusements in a voice as deep as a lion's ?   I request that you will go upstairs, put on an evening coat, and ask my daughter Sophia to dance."   He did so, and was the gayest of the gay for several hours, turning out moreover an excellent dancer. He was liked all the better for always saying what came into his head. One day a young lady who sat next him at dinner, spoke of a certain marriage just announced, as a very *penniless* one. He rummaged in his pocket, extracted a penny, and slapped it down loudly close to her plate saying, "There, I give you that, for that is the God you worship." The girl was a little frightened, but more amused: they made friends; and he promised to send her a pocket copy of Milton. Some months later she received one from England, beautifully bound.

It was a time of political excitement, and Ireland was on the brink of that silly attempt at rebellion which put back all her serious interests for a quarter of a century. Half Europe was in revolt and the prophets of the day averred that England might any day find herself involved in a general war. Some one remarked that an invasion would be more practicable in these days of steamships than in those of Nelson and Napoleon. Tennyson was a Patriot-poet like Shakespeare, who gave us the glorious dying speech of "Old John of Gaunt, time-honoured Lancaster," the Patriot-prince. His reply was, "Don't let them land on England's coast, or we will shatter them to pieces."

We took care that our guest should see or hear something of Ireland's quaint humours: I must find room for one story which especially amused him, and which he often retold. Returning home recently after a fortnight's absence, I had visited our old Parish Priest, Father Tim, and found him at dinner with his curate. It had been a time of great disturbance: many houses had been attacked by night, many guns borne off in triumph, and much blood shed. In answer to my enquiries he said: "The country has been quiet enough, much as usual, except one disgraceful outrage, such as no one ever heard of before in Ireland. What would you think, Sir, of a girl being carried off by night, and no car sent for her?" It had long been a traditional usage in Ireland, when parents on unreasonable grounds resisted their daughter's marriage, for her lover and his friends to carry her off, apparently by force, but in reality with her connivance. After a few days the parents had to accept what they could not then avert; but the abduction was a ceremonial in which the Sabine Maid was always treated with entire respect. "Sir, I ask you," said Father Tim to his

curate, laying down his knife and fork, and his old face flushing
up, "as long as you are on the mission, did you ever hear of
a girl being carried off, and no car sent for her?" "Never,
Sir," was the answer, "and it would not be a common car,
but a side-car." "Yes," Father Tim rejoined, "and moreover
a woman would be sent for her with the party, to keep her
in courage." "To be sure there would," the curate replied;
"and a most respectable woman." For several minutes the
affirmation and the response were alternated more and more
loudly and with stronger gesticulations; "A car would be sent!"
"Aye, and a side-car!" "A woman would be sent!" "Aye,
and a most respectable woman!" The old priest ended, "I am
afraid old Ireland is going to the bad! Well, thank Heaven
it did not happen in my parish; but it happened within a
hundred yards of it! A girl of the Molonys, one of the old
stock!" Neither priest finished his poor dinner of bacon and
cabbage that day. This violation of traditional etiquette led
to consequences which justified Father Tim's last words, "Well,
God is good! it did not happen in my parish!" For more
than two years that parish had been the prey of eight marauders
who roamed at large, plundering or making the farmers pay
black-mail. They defied alike magistrate, police and country-
gentlemen; for though everyone knew who they were, no one
dared to give information. Not so that daughter of the old
stock. The rogues had carried her to the house of an old
woman in complicity with the enterprise, but who, on recognizing in the girl a fifth cousin of her aunt's, placed her in her
own bed and sent off the adventurers without a glass of whisky.
At the risk of her life the girl went to a magistrate, gave information against the gang, and promised to swear to it in Court,
on one condition. It was that one man should not be proceeded against. The other seven, she affirmed, were blackguards,
who had not so much as given her time to dress herself "anyway
tidy"; and who had dragged her without a shoe on her feet
through three muddy fields; but there was one man of a better
sort who had "behaved mighty polished" to her, hoisting her
up on his shoulders once when they crossed a bog. The
"polished" man was forgiven, and probably begged pardon
of Father Tim, and returned to his duties: the other seven were
transported, and probably made their fortunes in the Colonies;
and the parish had peace.

Alfred Tennyson's desire to see cliffs and waves revived, and we sent him to our cousin, Maurice FitzGerald, Knight of Kerry, who lived at Valencia where they are seen at their best. On his way thither he slept at Mount Trenchard, the residence of Lord Monteagle, and I led him to the summit of Knock Patrick, the farthest spot in the South West to which Ireland's Apostle, Patriarch and Patron, advanced. There while from far and near from both sides of the Shannon the people flocked round him, Saint Patrick preached his far-famed sermon and gave his benediction to the Land, its mountains and its plains, its pastures, its forests, its rivers and the sands under the rivers. The sunset was one of extraordinary but minatory beauty. It gave, I remember, a darksome glory to the vast and desolate expanse with all its creeks and inlets from the Shannon, lighted the green islands in the mouth of the Fergus, fired the ruined Castle of Shanid, a stronghold of the Desmonds, one of a hundred which they were said to have possessed. The western clouds hung low, a mass of crimson and gold; while, from the ledge of a nearer one, down plunged a glittering flood empurpled like wine. The scene was a thoroughly Irish one; and gave a stormy welcome to the Sassenach Bard. The next morning he pursued his way alone to Valencia. He soon wrote that he had enjoyed it. He had found there the highest waves that Ireland knows, cliffs that at one spot rise to the height of 600 feet, tamarisks and fuchsias that no sea-winds can intimidate, and the old " Knight of Kerry," who, at the age of nearly 80, preserved the spirits, the grace and the majestic beauty of days gone by — as chivalrous a representative of Desmond's great Norman House as it had ever put forth in those times when it fought side by side with the greatest Gaelic Houses, for Ireland's ancient faith, and the immemorial rights of its Palatinate[1]. Afterwards Tennyson visited Killarney but

[1] On his eighty-second birthday my father received the following letter:

CALVERLEY PARK, TUNBRIDGE WELLS,
August 6th, 1891.

"Long life to your honour," as Irish peasants used to say, and so say I, the man who was working the State quarry, on the Island of Valencia, when you spent a few days there in 1848, Chartist times in London and Fenian times in Ireland. I remember your telling us, not without some glee, how a Valencian Fenian stealthily dogged your footsteps up the

remained there only a few days; yet that visit bequeathed a memorial. The echoes of the bugle at Killarney on that loveliest of lakes inspired the song introduced into the second edition of his " Princess," beginning

The splendour falls on castle walls.

It is but due to Killarney that *both* the parents of that lyric should be remembered in connection with " that fair child between them born"; and through that song, Killarney will be recalled to the memory of many who have seen yet half forgotten it. When they read those stanzas, and yet more when they hear them fittingly sung, they will see again, as in a dream, the reach of its violet-coloured waters where they reflect the " Purple Mountain," the "Elfland" of its Black Valley, " Crooma-doof," the silver river that winds and flashes through wood and rock, connecting the mystic " Upper Lake," and the beetling rock of the " Eagle's Nest" with the two larger and sunnier but not lovelier lakes. Before them again will rise Dinis Island, with its embowered coves and their golden sands, the mountain gardens of Glena haunted by murmurs of the cascade, not distant, but shrouded by the primeval oak-woods. They will look again on that island, majestic at once and mournful, Inisfallen, its grey-stemmed and solemn groves, its undulating lawns,

mountain and coming at last close to your ear, whispered, "Be you from France?"

Your sonorous reading to us after dinner sundry truculent passages in Daniel O'Connell's *History of Ireland*, which happened to be lying on my table, has lingered in my ears ever since. Seeing among my few books all that your friend Carlyle had up to that time published, you told me you thought he had nothing more to say. I was often reminded of this whilst reading his subsequent *Cromwell* and *Frederick* and *Latter Days*, and how near that was to the truth. You will hardly have forgotten the old Knight of Kerry, the owner of the Island, his dignified presence and his redolence of Grattan and Curran and Castlereagh and the Irish Parliament in which he sat for many years. I don't know whether "the rude imperious surge" which lashes the sounding shore of the Island ever drew from you, as I had hoped, some "hoarse rough verse," some of that roar, which tells us, as "music tells us, of what in all our life we have never known, and never will know."

With the "troops of friends" this day wishing you long life, heartily joins the ci-devant quarryman and

Yours truly, BEWICKE BLACKBURNE.

(*Now also Octogenarian.*)

which embosom the ruins of that Abbey, the shelter from century to century of Ireland's Annalists.   They will muse again in the yew-roofed cloister of Muckross, and glide once more by its caverned and fantastic rocks, and promontories fringed by arbutus brakes, with their dark yet shining leaves, their scarlet berries and their waxen flowers.   Whatever is fairest in other lakes they will see here combined, as if Nature had amused herself by publishing a volume of poetic selections from all her works.   As the vision fades, their eyes will rest long on the far mountains that girdle all that beauty, mountains here and there dark with those yew-forests through which the wild deer of old escaped from the stag-hounds of MacCarthymore.   It is marvellous that so many of the chief characteristics of Killarney should have found place in a poem so short.

We met next in London.   Few of the hours I spent with Alfred survive with such a pathetic sweetness and nearness in my recollection as those which are associated with that time and with " In Memoriam," which, as he told me, he once thought of entitling " Fragments of an Elegy."   Soon after this he published the poem.

I went to him very late each night, and he read many of the poems to me or discussed them with me till the early hours of the morning.   The tears often ran down his face as he read, without the slightest apparent consciousness of them on his part.   The pathos and grandeur of these poems were to me greatly increased by the voice which rather intoned than recited them, and which, as was obvious, could not possibly have given them utterance in any manner not thus musical.   Sometimes towards the close of a stanza his voice dropped; but I avoided the chance of thus losing any part of the meaning by sitting beside him, and glancing at the pieces he read.   They were written in a long and narrow manuscript book, which assisted him to arrange the poems in due order by bringing many of them at once before his eye.   As I walked home alone in the early mornings, the noises had ceased in each " long unlovely street "; and the deep voice which had so long charmed me followed me still, and seemed to waft me along as if I had glided onward half-asleep in a gondola.   I have ever regarded " In Memoriam " as the finest of the Poet's works.   As in the case of Dante, a great sorrow had been the harbinger of a song greater still : Dante had vowed to celebrate Beatrice as no other

woman had ever been celebrated; and he kept that vow. The
Northern Poet had also in early youth lost his chief friend, and
after the lapse of seventeen years commended him to a fame such
as neither "Lycidas" nor "Adonais" had ever inherited. Many
of Tennyson's poems are "of imagination all compact." In "In
Memoriam" imagination claims less, comparatively, to win more.
In this work each successive feeling and thought ascend from
the depths of the Poet's heart, as the fountain's bubbles mount
from the gold sands beneath it, and pass thence through the
imagination, in progress to the sympathies of mankind. Natural
description is here too invested with its finest function, for
throughout it blends itself most subtly with the human affections,
now adding to their sorrow, and now assuaging it: and here
Poetic Art finds its aptest opportunities, for each of the pieces,
while it constitutes part of a great whole, is itself so brief that
it admits of the highest, most palpable perfection of shape.
Tennyson was a true artist because he was not an artist only.
He understood the relations in which Art stands to Nature and
to fact. An incident will illustrate this remark. It had often
seemed to me that though "In Memoriam" had been designed
by its author chiefly as a monument raised to his friend, it
was also regarded by him as a work which carried a spiritual
teaching with it: it taught that the history of a great sorrow
is the history of a soul; and that a soul which passes bravely
through the dark shadow of the planet of grief must, on emerging
thence, meet the sunrise at its remoter side. Long after the publication of "In Memoriam" I reminded him of what he had let
fall on that subject, and added that such a scheme of poetic thought
if carried out to the full, would create, in a lyrical form, a work
not without much analogy to Dante's *Divina Commedia*, the
first part of which is all woe, though the latter cantos of the
second part, the "Purgatorio," abound in consolation and peace;
while the third part, the "Paradiso," is the song of triumph and
of joy. I remarked that many of the later pieces in the second
part of "In Memoriam" were also songs of consolation and
peace, and suggested that perhaps he might at some later time
give to the whole work its third part, or Paradise. The poet's
answer was this: "I have written what I have felt and known;
and I will never write anything else."

CHAPTER XIV.*

"IN MEMORIAM."

Break, break, break,
  On thy cold gray stones, O Sea!
And I would that my tongue could utter
  The thoughts that arise in me.

O well for the fisherman's boy,
  That he shouts with his sister at play!
O well for the sailor lad,
  That he sings in his boat on the bay!

And the stately ships go on
  To their haven under the hill;
But O for the touch of a vanish'd hand,
  And the sound of a voice that is still!

Break, break, break,
  At the foot of thy crags, O Sea!
But the tender grace of a day that is dead
  Will never come back to me.

Half a mile to the south of Clevedon in Somerset-shire, on a lonely hill, stands Clevedon Church, "obscure and solitary," overlooking a wide expanse of water, where the Severn flows into the Bristol Channel. It is dedicated to St Andrew, the chancel being the original fishermen's chapel.

From the graveyard you can hear the music of the tide as it washes against the low cliffs not a hundred yards away. In the manor aisle of the church, under

---

* Copyright, 1897, by The Macmillan Company.

which is the vault of the Hallams, may be read this epitaph to Arthur Hallam, written by his father:

TO

THE MEMORY OF

ARTHUR HENRY HALLAM

ELDEST SON OF HENRY HALLAM ESQUIRE
AND OF JULIA MARIA HIS WIFE
DAUGHTER OF SIR ABRAHAM ELTON BARONET
OF CLEVEDON COURT

WHO WAS SNATCHED AWAY BY SUDDEN DEATH
AT VIENNA ON SEPTEMBER 15TH 1833
IN THE TWENTY-THIRD YEAR OF HIS AGE
AND NOW IN THIS OBSCURE AND SOLITARY CHURCH
REPOSE THE MORTAL REMAINS OF
ONE TOO EARLY LOST FOR PUBLIC FAME
BUT ALREADY CONSPICUOUS AMONG HIS CONTEMPORARIES
FOR THE BRIGHTNESS OF HIS GENIUS
THE DEPTH OF HIS UNDERSTANDING
THE NOBLENESS OF HIS DISPOSITION
THE FERVOUR OF HIS PIETY
AND THE PURITY OF HIS LIFE

VALE DULCISSIME
VALE DELECTISSIME DESIDERATISSIME
REQUIESCAS IN PACE
PATER AC MATER HIC POSTHAC REQUIESCAMUS TECUM
USQUE AD TUBAM

In this part of the church there is also another tablet to the memory of Henry Hallam, the epitaph written by my father: who thought the simpler the epitaph, the better it would become the simple and noble man, whose work speaks for him:

HERE WITH HIS WIFE AND CHILDREN RESTS

HENRY HALLAM THE HISTORIAN

It was not until May 1850 that "In Memoriam" was printed and given to a few friends. Shortly afterwards it was published, first of all anonymously, but the authorship was soon discovered.

The earliest jottings, begun in 1833, of the "Elegies" as they were then called, were nearly lost in a London lodging, for my father was always careless about his manuscripts.

Mr Coventry Patmore wrote to me about this:

The letter from your father concerning the MS of "In Memoriam" I gave to the late Sir John Simeon, thinking that he ought to have it, as he had the MS[1] itself. This letter asked me to visit the lodging in Mornington Place, Hampstead Road, which he had occupied two or three weeks before, and to try to recover the MS, which he had left in a closet where he was used to keep some of his provisions. The landlady said that no such book had been left, but I insisted on looking for it myself, and found it where your father said it was.

The letter alluded to is given below:

BONCHURCH, I. W.,
Feb. 28*th*, 1850.

MY DEAR COVENTRY,

I went up to my room yesterday to get my book of Elegies: you know what I mean, a long, butcher-ledger-like book. I was going to read one or two to an artist here: I could not find it. I have some obscure remembrance of having lent it to you. If so, all is well, if not, will you go to my old chambers and institute a vigorous inquiry? I was coming up to-day on purpose to look after it, but as the weather is so furious I have yielded to the wishes of my friends here to stop till to-morrow. I shall be, I expect, in town to-morrow at 25 M. P. when I shall be glad to see you. At 9.10 p.m. the train in which I come gets into London. I shall be

---

[1] This MS, given to Sir John Simeon by my father, has been generously returned to me by Lady Simeon.

in Mornington Place about 10 o'clock I suppose. Perhaps you would in your walk Museum-ward call on Mrs Lloyd and tell her to prepare for me. With best remembrances to Mrs Patmore,

Believe me ever yours,

A. TENNYSON.

At first the reviews of the volume were not on the whole sympathetic. One critic in a leading journal, for instance, considered that " a great deal of poetic feeling had been wasted," and " much shallow art spent on the tenderness shown to an Amaryllis of the Chancery Bar." Another referred to the poem as follows : " These touching lines evidently come from the full heart of the widow of a military man." However, men like Maurice and Robertson thought that the author had made a definite step towards the unification of the highest religion and philosophy with the progressive science of the day ; and that he was the one poet who " through almost the agonies of a death-struggle " had made an effective stand against his own doubts and difficulties and those of the time, "on behalf of those first principles which underlie all creeds, which belong to our earliest childhood, and on which the wisest and best have rested through all ages ; that all is right ; that darkness shall be clear ; that God and Time are the only interpreters ; that Love is King ; that the Immortal is in us ; that, which is the keynote of the whole, 'All is well, tho' Faith and Form be sundered in the night of Fear[1].' " Scientific leaders like Herschel, Owen, Sedgwick and Tyndall regarded him as a champion of Science, and cheered

---

[1] Robertson goes so far as to say : " To my mind and heart the *most* satisfactory things that have been ever said on the future state are contained in this poem."

The best analysis of " In Memoriam " is by Miss Chapman (Macmillan and Co.).

him with words of genuine admiration for his love of
Nature, for the eagerness with which he welcomed
all the latest scientific discoveries, and for his trust
in truth. Science indeed in his opinion was one of the
main forces tending to disperse the superstition that
still darkens the world. A review which he thought
one of the ablest was that by Mr Gladstone. From
this review I quote the following to show that in Gladstone's opinion my father had not over-estimated Arthur
Hallam.

In 1850 Mr Tennyson gave to the world under the title of
"In Memoriam," perhaps the richest oblation ever offered by the
affection of friendship at the tomb of the departed. The memory
of Arthur Henry Hallam, who died suddenly in 1833, at the age
of twenty-two, will doubtless live chiefly in connection with this
volume. But he is well known to have been one who, if the
term of his days had been prolonged, would have needed no
aid from a friendly hand, would have built his own enduring
monument, and would have bequeathed to his country a name
in all likelihood greater than that of his very distinguished
father. The writer of this paper was, more than half a century
ago, in a condition to say

> "I marked him
> As a far Alp; and loved to watch the sunrise
> Dawn on his ample brow[1]."

There perhaps was no one among those who were blessed
with his friendship, nay, as we see, not even Mr Tennyson[2], who
did not feel at once bound closely to him by commanding
affection, and left far behind by the rapid, full and rich development of his ever-searching mind; by his

> "All-comprehensive tenderness,
> All-subtilising intellect."

It would be easy to show what in the varied forms of human
excellence, he might, had life been granted him, have accomplished; much more difficult to point the finger and to say, "This

[1] De Vere's *Mary Tudor* IV. I.
[2] See "In Memoriam," CIX., CX., CXI., CXII., CXIII.

he never could have done." Enough remains from among his early efforts, to accredit whatever mournful witness may now be borne of him. But what can be a nobler tribute than this, that for seventeen years after his death a poet, fast rising towards the lofty summits of his art, found that young fading image the richest source of his inspiration, and of thoughts that gave him buoyancy for a flight such as he had not hitherto attained[1].

Bishop Westcott and Professor Henry Sidgwick have written me interesting letters which respectively give the impressions the poem made on Cambridge men in 1850, and in 1860, and I quote them *in extenso.*

The Bishop writes:

When "In Memoriam" appeared, I felt (as I feel if possible more strongly now) that the hope of man lies in the historic realization of the Gospel. I rejoiced in the Introduction, which appeared to me to be the mature summing up after an interval of the many strains of thought in the "Elegies." Now the stress of controversy is over, I think so still. As I look at my original copy of "In Memoriam," I recognise that what impressed me most was your father's splendid faith (in the face of the frankest acknowledgment of every difficulty) in the growing purpose of the sum of life, and in the noble destiny of the individual man as he offers himself for the fulfilment of his little part (LIV., LXXXI., LXXXII. and the closing stanzas). This faith has now largely entered into our common life, and it seems to me to express a lesson of the Gospel which the circumstances of all time encourage us to master.

Professor Sidgwick writes:

After thinking over the matter, it has seemed to me better to write to you a somewhat different kind of letter from that which I originally designed: a letter not primarily intended for publication, though I wish you to feel at liberty to print any part of it which you may find suitable, but primarily intended to serve rather as a "document" on which you may base any statements you may wish to make as to the impression produced by "In Memoriam." I have decided to adopt this course:

[1] Gladstone's *Gleanings of Past Years*, Vol. II., pp. 136–37.

because I want to write with rather more frank egotism than I should otherwise like to show. I want to do this, because in describing the impression made on me by the poem, I ought to make clear the point of view from which I approached it, and the attitude of thought which I retained under its influence. In what follows I shall be describing chiefly my own experiences : but I shall allow myself sometimes to say " we " rather than " I," meaning by " we " my generation, as known to me, through converse with intimate friends.

To begin, then : our views on religious matters were not, at any rate after a year or two of the discussion started in 1860 by *Essays and Reviews*, really in harmony with those which we found suggested by " In Memoriam." They were more sceptical and less Christian, in any strict sense of the word : certainly this was the case with myself : I remember feeling that Clough *represented* my individual habits of thought and sentiment more than your father, although as a poet he *moved* me less. And this more sceptical attitude has remained mine through life ; while at the same time I feel that the beliefs in God and in immortality are vital to human well-being.

Hence the most important influence of " In Memoriam " on my thought, apart from its poetic charm as an expression of personal emotion, opened in a region, if I may so say, deeper down than the difference between Theism and Christianity : it lay in the unparalleled combination of intensity of feeling with comprehensiveness of view and balance of judgment, shown in presenting the *deepest* needs and perplexities of humanity.   And this influence, I find, has increased rather than diminished as years have gone on, and as the great issues between Agnostic Science and Faith have become continually more prominent. In the sixties I should say that these deeper issues were somewhat obscured by the discussions on Christian dogma, and Inspiration of Scripture, etc. You may remember Browning's reference to this period —

> " The Essays and Reviews debate
>   Begins to tell on the public mind
>   And Colenso's words have weight."

During these years we were absorbed in struggling for freedom of thought in the trammels of a historical religion : and perhaps what we sympathize with most in " In Memoriam " at this time, apart from the personal feeling, was the defence of "honest doubt," the reconciliation of knowledge and faith in the introductory poem, and the hopeful trumpet-ring of the lines on the New Year —

> Ring out the thousand wars of old,
> Ring in the thousand years of peace,

and generally the *forward* movement of the thought.

Well, the years pass, the struggle with what Carlyle used to call "Hebrew old clothes" is over, Freedom is won, and what does Freedom bring us to? It brings us face to face with atheistic science: the faith in God and Immortality, which we had been struggling to clear from superstition, suddenly seems to be *in the air:* and in seeking for a firm basis for this faith we find ourselves in the midst of the "fight with death" which "In Memoriam" so powerfully presents.

What "In Memoriam" did for us, for me at least, in this struggle was to impress on us the ineffaceable and ineradicable conviction that *humanity* will not and cannot acquiesce in a godless world: the "man in men" will not do this, whatever individual men may do, whatever they may temporarily feel themselves driven to do, by following methods which they cannot abandon to the conclusions to which these methods at present seem to lead.

The force with which it impressed this conviction was not due to the *mere intensity* of its expression of the feelings which Atheism outrages and Agnosticism ignores: but rather to its expression of them along with a reverent docility to the lessons of science which also belongs to the essence of the thought of our age.

I remember being struck with a note in *Nature*, at the time of your father's death, which dwelt on this last-mentioned aspect of his work, and regarded him as preeminently the Poet of Science. I have always felt this characteristic important in estimating his effect on his generation. Wordsworth's attitude towards Nature was one that, so to say, left Science unregarded: the Nature for which Wordsworth stirred our feelings was Nature as known by simple observation and interpreted by religious and sympathetic intuition. But for your father the physical world is always the world as known to us through physical science: the scientific view of it dominates his thoughts about it; and his general acceptance of this view is real and sincere, even when he utters the intensest feeling of its inadequacy to satisfy our deepest needs. Had it been otherwise, had he met the atheistic tendencies of modern Science with more confident defiance, more confident assertion of an Intuitive Faculty of theological knowledge, overriding the results laboriously reached by empirical science, I think his antagonism to these tendencies would have been far less impressive.

I always feel this strongly in reading the memorable lines:

"If e'er, when faith had fallen asleep" down to "I have felt [1]."

At this point, if the stanzas had stopped here, we should have shaken our heads and said, "Feeling must not usurp the function of Reason. Feeling is not knowing. It is the duty of a rational being to follow truth wherever it leads."

But the poet's instinct knows this; he knows that this usurpation by Feeling of the function of Reason is too bold and confident; accordingly in the next stanza he gives the turn to humility in the protest of Feeling which is required (I think) to win the assent of the "man in men" at this stage of human thought.

These lines I can never read without tears. I feel in them the indestructible and inalienable minimum of faith which humanity cannot give up because it is necessary for life; and which I know that I, at least so far as the man in me is deeper than the methodical thinker, cannot give up.

If the possibility of a "godless world" is excluded, the faith thus restored is, for the poet, unquestionably a form of Christian faith: there seems to him then no reason for doubting that the

> Sinless years
> That breathed beneath the Syrian blue,

and the marvel of the life continued after the bodily death, were a manifestation of the "immortal love" which by faith we embrace as the essence of the Divine nature. "If the dead rise not, Christ is not risen": but if we may believe that they rise, then it seems to him, we may and must believe the main drift of the Gospel story; though we may transiently

[1] See pp. 314-15.

wonder why the risen Lord told his disciples only of life, and nothing of "what it is to die [1]."

From this point of view the note of Christian faith struck in the introductory stanzas is in harmony with all that follows. And yet I have always felt that in a certain sense the effect of the introduction does not quite represent the effect of the poem. Faith, in the introduction, is too completely triumphant. I think this is inevitable, because so far as the thought-debate presented by the poem is summed up, it must be summed up on the side of Faith. Faith must give the last word : but the last word is not the whole utterance of the truth : the whole truth is that assurance and doubt must alternate in the moral world in which we at present live, somewhat as night and day alternate in the physical world. The revealing visions come and go ; when they come we *feel* that we *know:* but in the intervals we must pass through states in which all is dark, and in which we can only struggle to hold the conviction that

> Power is with us in the night
> Which makes the darkness and the light
> And dwells not in the light alone.

"It must be remembered," writes my father, " that this is a poem, *not* an actual biography. It is founded on our friendship, on the engagement of Arthur Hallam to my sister, on his sudden death at Vienna, just before the time fixed for their marriage, and on his burial at Clevedon Church. The poem concludes with the marriage of my youngest sister Cecilia. It was meant to be a kind of *Divina Commedia*, ending with happiness. The sections were written at many different places, and as the phases of our intercourse came to my memory and suggested them. I did not write them with any view of weaving them into a whole, or for publication, until I found that I had written so many. The different moods of sorrow as in a drama are dramatically given, and my conviction that fear, doubts, and suffering

---

[1] See Browning's "Epistle containing the Strange Medical Experience of Karshish."

will find answer and relief only through Faith in a
God of Love. 'I' is not always the author speaking
of himself, but the voice of the human race speaking
thro' him. After the Death of A. H. H., the divisions
of the poem are made by First Xmas Eve (Section
XXVIII.), Second Xmas (LXXVIII.[1]), Third Xmas Eve
(CIV. and CV. etc.). I myself did not see Clevedon till
years after the burial of A. H. H. Jan. 3rd, 1834, and
then in later editions of 'In Memoriam' I altered the
word 'chancel,' which was the word used by Mr Hallam
in his Memoir, to 'dark church.' As to the localities in
which the poems were written, some were written in
Lincolnshire, some in London, Essex, Gloucestershire,
Wales, anywhere where I happened to be[2]."

"And as for the metre of 'In Memoriam' I had no
notion till 1880 that Lord Herbert of Cherbury had

---

[1] No. LXXII. refers to the first anniversary of the death Sept. 15th, 1833.
No. C. to the farewell of the family to Somersby in 1837.

[2] In a letter to Mr Malan written at the same time as the above note,
in reply to enquiries as to whether, in "In Memoriam," he has copied
Statius, or Ovid's "Epicedion," or the "Sorrow of Arcadius Etruscus," or
"Spring Stanzas to Domitian," etc. etc. my father writes:

Nov. 14th, 1883.

DEAR SIR,

I am sorry that your letter has gone so long unanswered, but my
eyes are so bad, and I have such a large correspondence that I find it
impossible to answer everybody. It is news to me that the remains of
A. H. H. were landed at Dover. I had always believed that the ship which
brought them put in at Bristol. As to his being buried in the chancel,
Mr Hallam in a printed memoir of his son, states that it was so. * * * * I
can assure you I am innocent as far as I am aware of knowing one line of
Statius; and of Ovid's "Epicedion" I never heard. I have searched for it
in vain in a little three volume edition of Ovid which I have here, but that
does not contain this poem; nor have I ever heard of the "Sorrow of
Arcadius Etruscus," nor of the "Spring Stanzas to Domitian." The memoir
of his son by Mr Hallam, to which I allude, was printed merely for private
circulation: and whether he repeated the statement of the chancel burial in
the published Memoir I do not know.

Yours very truly,
A. TENNYSON.

written his occasional verses in the same metre. I believed myself the originator of the metre, until after 'In Memoriam' came out, when some one told me that Ben Jonson and Sir Philip Sidney had used it. The following poems were omitted from 'In Memoriam' when I published, because I thought them redundant[1]."

The Grave (originally No. LVII.). (*Unpublished*.)

I keep no more a lone distress,
  The crowd have come to see thy grave,
  Small thanks or credit shall I have,
But these shall see it none the less.

The happy maiden's tears are free
  And she will weep and give them way;
  Yet one unschool'd in want will say
"The dead are dead and let them be."

Another whispers sick with loss:
  "O let the simple slab remain!
  The 'Mercy Jesu' in the rain!
The 'Miserere' in the moss!"

"I love the daisy weeping dew,
  I hate the trim-set plots of art!"
  My friend, thou speakest from the heart,
But look, for these are nature too.

To A. H. H. (originally No. CVIII.). (*Unpublished*.)

Young is the grief I entertain,
  And ever new the tale she tells,
  And ever young the face that dwells
With reason cloister'd in the brain:

[1] "O Sorrow, wilt thou live with me" was added in 1851.

Yet grief deserves a nobler name:
　　She spurs an imitative will;
　　'Tis shame to fail so far, and still
My failing shall be less my shame:

Considering what mine eyes have seen,
　　And all the sweetness which thou wast
　　In thy beginnings in the past,
And all the strength thou wouldst have been:

A master mind with master minds,
　　An orb repulsive of all hate,
　　A will concentric with all fate,
A life four-square to all the winds.

The Victor Hours (originally No. CXXVII.).
(*Unpublished.*)

Are those the far-famed Victor Hours
　　That ride to death the griefs of men?
　　I fear not; if I fear'd them, then
Is this blind flight the winged Powers.

Behold, ye cannot bring but good,
　　And see, ye dare not touch the truth,
　　Nor Sorrow beauteous in her youth,
Nor Love that holds a constant mood.

Ye must be wiser than your looks,
　　Or wise yourselves, or wisdom-led,
　　Else this wild whisper round my head
Were idler than a flight of rooks.

Go forward! crumble down a throne,
　　Dissolve a world, condense a star,
　　Unsocket all the joints of war,
And fuse the peoples into one.

That my father was a student of the Bible, those who have read " In Memoriam " know. He also eagerly read all notable works within his reach relating to the Bible, and traced with deep interest such fundamental truths as underlie the great religions of the world. He hoped that the Bible [1] would be more and more studied by all ranks of people, and expounded simply by their teachers ; for he maintained that the religion of a people could never be founded on mere moral philosophy: and that it could only come home to them in the simple, noble thoughts and facts of a Scripture like ours [2].

Soon after his marriage he took to reading different systems of philosophy [3], yet none particularly influenced him. The result I think is shown in a more ordered arrangement of religious, metaphysical and scientific thought throughout the " Idylls " and his later works. " In Poems like ' De Profundis ' and the 'Ancient Sage,' " Jowett said, " he often brings up metaphysical truths from the deepest depths." But as a rule he knew that poetry must touch on metaphysical topics rather by allusion than systematically. In the following pages I shall not give any of his subtler arguments ; but only attempt to illustrate from " In Memoriam," with some of the other poems, and from his conversation, the *general* everyday attitude of his mind toward the highest problems that confront us. In dealing with these none was readier in the discovery of fallacies, none was more resolute in proclaiming what seemed to him realities.

His creed, he always said, he would not formulate, for people would not understand him if he did; but he

---

[1] He also said : " The Bible ought to be read, were it only for the sake of the grand English in which it is written, an education in itself."

[2] See Nos. XXXVI., LII., LXXXIV. last stanza but one.

[3] Spinoza, Berkeley, Kant, Schlegel, Fichte, Hegel, Ferrier, were among the books added to his library.

considered that his poems expressed the principles at the foundation of his faith.

He thought, with Arthur Hallam, "that the essential feelings of religion subsist in the utmost diversity of forms," that "different language does not always imply different opinions, nor different opinions any difference in *real* faith." " It is impossible," he said, "to imagine that the Almighty will ask you, when you come before Him in the next life what your particular form of creed was : but the question will rather be, ' Have you been true to yourself, and given in My Name a cup of cold water to one of these little ones?'"

"This is a terrible age of unfaith," he would say. " I hate utter unfaith, I cannot endure that men should sacrifice everything at the cold altar of what with their imperfect knowledge they choose to call truth and reason. One can easily lose all belief, through giving up the continual thought and care for spiritual things."

And again, " In this vale of Time the hills of Time often shut out the mountains of Eternity."

My father's friend, the Bishop of Ripon, writes:

With those who are impatient of *all* spiritual truth he had no sympathy whatever ; but he had a sympathy with those who were impatient of the formal statement of truth, only because he felt that all formal statements of truth must of necessity fall below the greatness and the grandeur of the truth itself. There is a reverent impatience of forms, and there is an irreverent impatience of them. An irreverent impatience of formal dogma means impatience of all spiritual truth ; but a reverent impatience of formal dogma may be but the expression of the feeling that the truth must be larger, purer, nobler than any mere human expression or definition of it. With this latter attitude of mind he had sympathy, and he expressed that sympathy in song ; he could understand those who seemed

To have reach'd a purer air,
Whose faith has centre everywhere,
Nor cares to fix itself to form.

He urged men to "cling to faith, beyond the forms of faith [1]." But while he did this he also recognised clearly the importance and the value of definitions of truth, and his counsel to the very man who prided himself upon his emancipation from forms was:

> Leave thou thy sister when she prays,
> 　Her early Heaven, her happy views;
> Nor thou with shadow'd hint confuse
> 　A life that leads melodious days.

> Her faith thro' form is pure as thine,
> 　Her hands are quicker unto good:
> Oh, sacred be the flesh and blood
> 　To which she links a truth divine [2]!

He warned the man proud of his emancipation from formal faith, that in a world of so many confusions he might meet with ruin, "Ev'n for want of such a type." And we are not surprised, knowing how insidious are the evil influences which gather round us:

> Hold thou the good; define it well,
> 　For fear Divine Philosophy
> 　Should push beyond her mark, and be
> Procuress to the lords of Hell.

And thus he had sympathy with those who feel that faith is larger and nobler than form, and at the same time he had tenderness and appreciation for those who find their faith helped by form. To him, as to so many, truth is so infinitely great that all we can do with our poor human utterances is to try and clothe it in such language as will make it clear to ourselves,

---

[1] Cf. Vol. II. chap. XXIII. 1st paragraph.

[2] Jowett wrote about my father's "defence of honest doubt" as compared with this passage: "Can we find any reconciliation of these varying utterances of the same mind? I think that we may. For we may argue that truth kept back is the greatest source of doubt and suspicion: that faith cannot survive without enquiry, and that the doubt which is raised may be the step upward to a higher faith. And so we arrive at the conclusion that truth is good, and to be received thankfully and fearlessly by all who are capable of receiving it. But on the other hand it is not always to be imparted in its entirety to those who cannot understand it, and whose minds would be puzzled and overwhelmed by it."

and clear to those to whom God sends us with a message, but
meanwhile, above us and our thoughts — above our broken
lights — God in His mercy, God in His love, God in His
infinite nature is greater than all.

Assuredly Religion was no nebulous abstraction for
him. He consistently emphasized his own belief in what
he called the Eternal Truths; in an Omnipotent, Omnipresent and All-loving God, Who has revealed Himself
through the human attribute of the highest self-sacrificing
love; in the freedom of the human will; and in the
immortality of the soul. But he asserted that " Nothing
worthy proving can be proven," and that even as to the
great laws which are the basis of Science, " We have but
faith, we cannot know." He dreaded the dogmatism of
sects and rash definitions of God. " I dare hardly name
His Name " he would say, and accordingly he named
Him in " The Ancient Sage " the " Nameless." " But
take away belief in the self-conscious personality of God,"
he said, " and you take away the backbone of the world."
" On God and God-like men we build our trust." A
week before his death I was sitting by him, and he talked
long of the Personality and of the Love of God, " That
God, Whose eyes consider the poor," " Who catereth even
for the sparrow." " I should," he said, " infinitely rather
feel myself the most miserable wretch on the face of the
earth with a God above, than the highest type of man
standing alone." He would allow that God is unknow-
able in " his whole world-self, and all-in-all," and that
therefore there was some force in the objection made by
some people to the word " Personality," as being " anthropomorphic," and that perhaps " Self-consciousness " or
" Mind " might be clearer to them: but at the same
time he insisted that, although " man is like a thing of
nought " in " the boundless plan," our highest view of
God must be more or less anthropomorphic: and that

" Personality," as far as our intelligence goes, is the widest definition and includes " Mind," " Self-conscious-ness [1]," " Will," " Love " and other attributes of the Real, the Supreme, " the High and Lofty One that inhabiteth Eternity Whose name is Holy."

Jowett asked him to write an anthem about God for Balliol Chapel and he wrote " The Human Cry ":

We feel we are nothing — for all is Thou and in Thee;
We feel we are something — *that* also has come from
    Thee;
We know we are nothing — but Thou wilt help us to be.
Hallowed be Thy name — Hallelujah!

When his last book was in proof, we spoke together of the ultimate expression of his own calm faith at the end of his life:

That Love which is and was
My Father and my Brother and my God [2].

Everywhere throughout the Universe he saw the glory and greatness of God, and the science of Nature was particularly dear to him. Every new fact which came within his range was carefully weighed. As he exulted in the wilder aspects of Nature (see for instance sect. xv.) and revelled in the thunderstorm; so he felt a joy in her orderliness; he felt a rest in her steadfast-ness, patient progress and hopefulness; the same seasons ever returned; the same stars wheeled in their courses;

[1] " A. T. thinks it ridiculous to believe in a God and deny his con-sciousness, and was amused at someone who said of him that he had versified Hegelianism." Jowett, MS Note.

[2] To enquiries as to the meaning of the words " Immortal Love " in the Introduction to " In Memoriam," he explained that he had used " Love " in the same sense as St John (1 John, chap. iv.). " The Word " also in No. xxxvi. was " The Word " as used by St John, the Revelation of the Eternal Thought of the Universe.

the flowers[1] and trees blossomed and the birds sang
yearly in their appointed months; and he had a triumphant appreciation of her ever-new revelations of beauty.
One of the " In Memoriam " poems, written at Barmouth[2], gives preeminently his sense of the joyous peace
in Nature, and he would quote it in this context along
with his Spring and Bird songs:

> Sweet after showers, ambrosial air,
>   That rollest from the gorgeous gloom
>   Of evening over brake and bloom
> And meadow, slowly breathing bare
>
> The round of space, and rapt below
>   Thro' all the dewy-tassell'd wood,
>   And shadowing down the horned flood
> In ripples, fan my brows and blow
>
> The fever from my cheek, and sigh
>   The full new life that feeds thy breath
>   Throughout 'my frame, till Doubt and Death,
> Ill brethren, let the fancy fly
>
> From belt to belt of crimson seas
>   On leagues of odour streaming far,
>   To where in yonder orient star
> A hundred spirits whisper " Peace[3]."

But he was occasionally much troubled with the intellectual problem of the apparent profusion and waste
of life and by the vast amount of sin and suffering
throughout the world, for these seemed to militate against
the idea of the Omnipotent and All-loving Father.

No doubt in such moments he might possibly have

---

[1] Picking up a daisy as we walked, and looking close to its crimson-tipt
leaves he said: " Does not this look like a thinking Artificer, one who wishes
to ornament ? "   MS Note, E. F. G.

[2] He notes this in his own hand.

[3] See also Nos. LXXXVIII., LXXXIX., XCI., CXV., CXVI., CXXI., CXXII.

been heard to say what I myself have heard him say:
"An Omnipotent Creator Who could make such a painful world is to me *sometimes* as hard to believe in as to
believe in blind matter behind everything. The lavish
profusion too in the natural world appals me, from the
growths of the tropical forest to the capacity of man to
multiply, the torrent of babies."

"I can almost understand some of the Gnostic here-
sies, which only after all put the difficulty one step further
back ":

> O me! for why is all around us here
> As if some lesser god had made the world,
> But had not force to shape it as he would,
> Till the High God behold it from beyond
> And enter it, and make it beautiful?[1]

After one of these moods in the summer of 1892
he exclaimed: "Yet God *is* love, transcendent, all-
pervading! We do not get *this* faith from Nature or
the world. If we look at Nature alone, full of perfection
and imperfection, she tells us that God is disease, murder
and rapine. We get this faith from ourselves, from
what is highest within us, which recognizes that there
is not one fruitless pang, just as there is not one lost
good."

> That which we dare invoke to bless;
>   Our dearest faith; our ghastliest doubt;
>   He, They, One, All; within, without;
> The Power in darkness whom we guess;

> I found Him not in world or sun,
>   Or eagle's wing, or insect's eye;
>   Nor thro' the questions men may try,
> The petty cobwebs we have spun:

[1] He would sometimes put forward the old theory that "The world is
part of an infinite plan, incomplete because it is a part. We cannot therefore
read the riddle."

If e'er when faith had fall'n asleep,
  I heard a voice "believe no more"
  And heard an ever-breaking shore
That tumbled in the Godless deep;

A warmth within the heart would melt
  The freezing reason's colder part,
  And like a man in wrath the heart
Stood up and answer'd "I have felt."

No, like a child in doubt and fear;
  But that blind clamour made me wise;
  Then was I as a child that cries,
But, crying, knows his father near;

And what I am beheld again
  What is, and no man understands;
  And out of darkness came the hands
That reach thro' nature, moulding men.

He had been reading the eighth chapter of Romans, and said that he thought that St Paul fully recognized in the sorrows of Nature and in the miseries of the world a stumbling-block to the divine idea of God, but that they are the preludes necessary as things are to the higher good[1]. "For myself," he said, "the world is the shadow of God," and then he referred to Jowett's commentary on this chapter:

As we turn from ourselves to the world around us, the prospect on which we cast our eyes seems to reflect the tone and colour of our own minds, and to share our joy and sorrow. To the religious mind it seems also to reflect our sins. We cannot indeed speak of the misery of the brute creation, of whose constitution we know so little; nor do we pretend to discover in the loveliest spots of earth indications of a fallen world. But when we look at the vices and diseases of mankind, at the life of labour in which animals are our partners, at the aspect in modern

[1] Cf. St John xvi. 21, 22.

times of our large towns, as in ancient, of a world given to idolatry, we see enough to explain the Apostle's meaning, and to understand how he could say that "The whole creation groaneth and travaileth till now." He is not speaking, of course, of the conscious feeling of degradation, but of the world, as it seemed to the eye of faith; not as it appeared to itself, but as we may imagine it to appear in the sight of God when compared with the divine idea.... But the Spirit helps us, and God has chosen us according to his purpose, and in all things God is working with us for good [1].

My father invariably believed that humility [2] is the only true attitude of the human soul, and therefore spoke with the greatest reserve of what he called "these unfathomable mysteries," as befitting one who did not dogmatise, but who knew that the Finite can by no means grasp the Infinite: "Dark is the world to thee [3], thyself is the reason why"; and yet, he had a profound trust that when all is seen face to face, all will be seen as the best. "Fear not thou the hidden purpose of that Power which alone is great." "Who knows whether Revelation be not itself a veil to hide the Glory of that Love which we could not look upon, without marring the sight and our onward progress?"

This faith was to him the breath of life, and never, I feel, really failed him, or life itself would have failed.

Free-will and its relation to the meaning of human life and to circumstance was latterly one of his most common subjects of conversation. Free-will was undoubtedly, he said, the "main miracle, apparently an act of self-limitation by the Infinite, and yet a revelation by

---

[1] Jowett, *Epistle to the Romans.*

[2] "Almost the finest summing up of Religion is 'to do justice, to love mercy, and to walk humbly with God.'" A. T.

He often quoted Newton's saying that we are like children picking up pebbles on the shore of the Infinite Ocean.

[3] The real mysteries to him were Time, life, and "finite-infinite" space: and so he talks of the soul "being born and banish'd into mystery."

Himself of Himself." " Take away the sense of individual responsibility and men sink into pessimism and
madness." He wrote at the end of the poem " Despair ":
" In my boyhood I came across the Calvinist Creed,
and assuredly however unfathomable the mystery, if one
cannot believe in the freedom of the human will as of
the Divine, life is hardly worth having." The lines that
he oftenest repeated about Free-will were,

> This main miracle that thou art thou
> With power on thine own act and on the world.

Then he would enlarge upon man's consequent moral
obligations, upon the Law which claims a free obedience,
and upon the pursuit of moral perfection (in imitation of
the Divine) to which man is called.

> οὐ γὰρ ἔχω ἔγωγε οὐδὲν οὕτω μοι ἐναργὲς ὄν, ὡς τοῦτο,
> τὸ εἶναι ὡς οἷόν τε μάλιστα καλόν τε καὶ ἀγαθόν.

" For I hold nothing so clear as this, that I must be as
good and noble as a man can be."

I cannot refrain from setting down the drift of his
talk to a young man who was going to the University.—
" If a man is merely to be a bundle of sensations,
he had better not exist at all. He should embark on
his career in the spirit of selfless and adventurous
heroism; should develop his true self by not shirking
responsibility, by casting aside all maudlin and introspective morbidities, and by using his powers cheerfully
in accordance with the obvious dictates of his moral
consciousness, and so, as far as possible, in harmony
with what he feels to be the Absolute Right.

> Self-reverence, self-knowledge, self-control,
> These three alone lead life to sovereign power.
> Yet not for power (power of herself
> Would come uncall'd for) but to live by *law*,

Acting the law we live by without fear;
And, because right is right, to follow right
Were wisdom in the scorn of consequence.

It is motive, it is the great purpose which consecrates life[1]. The real test of a man is not what he knows, but what he is in himself and in his relation to others. For instance, can he battle against his own bad inherited instincts, or brave public opinion in the cause of truth? The love of God is the true basis of duty, truth, reverence, loyalty, love, virtue and work. I believe in these although I feel the emptiness and hollowness of much of life. ' Be ye perfect as your Father in heaven is perfect.' " Then he added characteristically: " But don't be a prig. Most young men with anything in them make fools of themselves at some time or other."

One of the last passages I heard him recite about Free-will was:

But ill for him who, bettering not with time,
Corrupts the strength of Heaven-descended Will,
And ever weaker grows thro' acted crime,
Or seeming-genial venial fault,
Recurring and suggesting still!
He seems as one whose footsteps halt,
Toiling in immeasurable sand,
And o'er a weary sultry land,
Far beneath a blazing vault,
Sown in a wrinkle of the monstrous hill,
The city sparkles like a grain of salt.

And he wrote for me as to man's will being free but only within certain limits: " Man's Free-will is but a bird in a cage; he can stop at the lower perch, or he can

---

[1] St Paul's expression "The temple of the Holy Ghost" he thought had had a powerful effect on the Christian appreciation of the meaning of life.

mount to a higher.   Then that which is and knows will
enlarge his cage, give him a higher and a higher perch,
and at last break off the top of his cage, and let him out
to be one with the Free-will of the Universe." Then
he said earnestly: " If the absorption into the divine
in the after-life be the creed of some, let them at all
events allow us many existences of individuality before
this absorption; since this short-lived individuality seems
to be but too short a preparation for so mighty a
union[1]."

> Death's truer name
> Is " Onward," no discordance in the roll
> And march of that Eternal Harmony
> Whereto the worlds beat time.

In the same way, " O living will that shalt endure "
he explained as that which we know as Free-will, the
higher and enduring part of man.   He held that there
was an intimate connexion between the human and the
divine, and that each individual will had a spiritual and
eternal significance with relation to other individual wills
as well as to the Supreme and Eternal Will.

Throughout his life he had a constant feeling of a
spiritual harmony existing between ourselves and the
outward visible Universe, and of the actual Immanence
of God in the infinitesimal atom as in the vastest system[2].
" If God," he would say, "were to withdraw Himself for
one single instant from this Universe, everything would
vanish into nothingness."   When speaking on that subject he said to me: " My most passionate desire is to

---

[1] " In Memoriam," No. XLVII.

[2] He would point out the difficulties of materialism, and would propound
to us, when we were boys, the old puzzle: " Look at the mystery of a grain
of sand; you can divide it for ever and for ever.   You cannot conceive
anything material of which you cannot conceive the half."   He disliked
the Atomic theory: and was taken by the theory of *aboriginal centres of
force*.

have a clearer and fuller vision of God. The soul seems to me one with God, how I cannot tell. I can sympathize with God in my poor little way." In some phases of thought and feeling his idealism tended more decidedly to mysticism. He wrote : "A kind of waking trance I have frequently had, quite up from boyhood, when I have been all alone. This has generally come upon me thro' repeating my own name two or three times to myself silently, till all at once, as it were out of the intensity of the consciousness of individuality, the individuality itself seemed to dissolve and fade away into boundless being, and this not a confused state, but the clearest of the clearest, the surest of the surest, the weirdest of the weirdest, utterly beyond words, where death was an almost laughable impossibility, the loss of personality (if so it were) seeming no extinction but the only true life[1]." " This might," he said, " be the state which St Paul describes, ' Whether in the body I cannot tell, or whether out of the body I cannot tell.' "

He continued: " I am ashamed of my feeble description. Have I not said the state is utterly beyond words? But in a moment, when I come back to my normal state of ' sanity,' I am ready to fight for *mein liebes Ich*, and hold that it will last for æons of æons."

In the same way he said that there might be a more intimate communion than we could dream of between the living and the dead, at all events for a time.

> May all love,
> His love, unseen but felt, o'ershadow Thee,
> Till God's love set Thee at his side again!

---

[1] Cf. "The Ancient Sage," and the smaller partial anticipation in " In Memoriam," xcv. st. 9.

" Yet it appeared that he distinguished himself from external things." Jowett, MS Note.

And —

> The ghost in Man, the ghost that once was Man,
> But cannot wholly free itself from Man,
> Are calling to each other through a dawn
> Stranger than earth has ever seen; the veil
> Is rending, and the Voices of the day
> Are heard across the Voices of the dark.

I need not enlarge upon his faith in the Immortality of the Soul as he has dwelt upon that so fully in his poems[1]. " I can hardly understand," he said, " how any great, imaginative man, who has deeply lived, suffered, thought and wrought, can doubt of the Soul's continuous progress in the after-life." His poem of " Wages " he liked to quote on this subject.

He more than once said what he has expressed in " Vastness ": " Hast Thou made all this for naught! Is all this trouble of life worth undergoing if we only end in our own corpse-coffins at last? If you allow a God, and God allows this strong instinct and universal yearning for another life, surely that is in a measure a presumption of its truth. We cannot give up the mighty hopes that make us men."

> My own dim life should teach me this,
>   That life shall live for evermore,
>   Else earth is darkness at the core,
> And dust and ashes all that is.
> What then were God to such as I?

I have heard him even say that he " would rather know that he was to be lost eternally than not know that the whole human race was to live eternally "; and when he speaks of " faintly trusting the larger hope " he means by " the larger hope " that the whole human race would

---

[1] He said to Bishop Lightfoot: " The cardinal point of Christianity is the Life after Death " (2 Tim. chap. i.).

through, perhaps, ages of suffering, be at length purified and saved, even those who now "better not with time"; so that at the end of "The Vision of Sin" we read

God made Himself an awful rose of dawn.

One day towards the end of his life he bade me look into the Revised Version and see how the Revisers had translated the passage "Depart from me, ye cursed, into everlasting fire." His disappointment was keen when he found that the translators had not altered "everlasting" into "æonian[1]" or some such word: for he never would believe that Christ could preach "everlasting punishment."

> "Fecemi la divina potestate
> La somma sapienza, e 'l primo amore,"

were words which he was fond of quoting in this relation, as if they were a kind of unconscious confession by Dante that Love must conquer at the last.

Letters were not unfrequently addressed to him asking what his opinions were about Evolution, about Prayer, and about Christ.

Of Evolution he said: "That makes no difference to me, even if the Darwinians did not, as they do, exaggerate Darwinism. To God all is present. He sees present, past, and future as one."

> To your question now
> Which touches on the workman and his work.
> "Let there be light and there was light": 'tis so:
> For was and is and will be are but is:
> And all creation is one act at once,
> The birth of light; but we that are not all,
> As parts, can see but parts, now this, now that,
> And live perforce from thought to thought, and make
> The act a phantom of succession: there
> Our weakness somehow shapes the shadow, Time.

[1] "Eternal" in R. V.

In the poem "By an Evolutionist," written in 1888 when he was dangerously ill, he defined his position; he conceived that the further science progressed, the more the Unity of Nature, and the purpose hidden behind the cosmic process of matter in motion and changing forms of life, would be apparent. Someone asked him whether it was not hard to account for genius by Evolution. He put aside the question, for he believed that genius was the greatest mystery to itself [1].

To Tyndall he once said, "No evolutionist is able to explain the mind of Man or how any possible physiological change of tissue can produce conscious thought [2]." Yet he was inclined to think that the theory of Evolution caused the world to regard more clearly the "Life of Nature as a lower stage in the manifestation of a principle which is more fully manifested in the spiritual life of man, with the idea that in this process of Evolution the lower is to be regarded as a means to the higher [3]."

[1] "People," he once said, "do not consider that every human being is a vanful of human beings, of those who have gone before him, and of those who form part of his life."

[2] Cf. Tyndall's *Scientific Materialism*: "But the passage from the physics of the brain to the corresponding facts of consciousness is unthinkable, granted that a definite thought and a definite molecular action in the brain occur simultaneously; we do not possess the intellectual organ, nor apparently any rudiment of the organ, which would enable us to pass, by a process of reasoning, from the one to the other. They appear together, but we do not know why."

[3] In a letter from the present Master of Balliol to me.

And in "In Memoriam" he had written thus:

> They say,
> The solid earth whereon we tread
>
> In tracts of fluent heat began,
>   And grew to seeming-random forms,
>   The seeming prey of cyclic storms,
> Till at the last arose the man;
>
> Who throve and branch'd from clime to clime
>   The herald of a higher race,

In " Maud " he spoke of the making of man:

As nine months go to the shaping an infant ripe for
    his birth,
So many a million of ages have gone to the making
    of man:
He now is first, but is he the last?

The answer he would give to this query was: " No,
mankind is as yet on one of the lowest rungs of the
ladder[1], although every man has and has had from
everlasting his true and perfect being in the Divine
Consciousness."

About prayer he said: " The reason why men find it
hard to regard prayer in the same light in which it was
formerly regarded is, that *we* seem to know more of the
unchangeableness of Law: but I believe that God
reveals Himself in each individual soul.   Prayer is, to
take a mundane simile, like opening a sluice between the
great ocean and our little channels when the great sea
gathers itself together and flows in at full tide."

" Prayer on our part is the highest aspiration of the
soul."

And of himself in higher place,
If so he type this work of time

Within himself, from more to more;
    Or, crown'd with attributes of woe
    Like glories, move his course, and show
That life is not an idle ore,

But iron dug from central gloom,
    And heated hot with burning fears,
    And dipt in baths of hissing tears,
And batter'd with the shocks of doom

To shape and use.   Arise and fly
    The reeling Faun, the sensual feast;
    Move upward, working out the beast,
And let the ape and tiger die.

[1] " The herald of a higher race."

A breath that fleets beyond this iron world
And touches Him who made it.

And

Speak to Him thou for He hears, and Spirit with
Spirit can meet —
Closer is He than breathing, and nearer than hands
and feet.

And
More things are wrought by prayer
Than this world dreams of.

He said that "O Thou Infinite, Amen," was the
form of prayer which he himself used in the time of
trouble and sorrow: and that it was better to suffer
than to lose the power of suffering.

When questions were written to him about Christ,
he would say to me: "Answer for me that I have given
my belief in ' In Memoriam [1].'"

As the Master of Balliol wrote:

The "In Memoriam" records most of his inner nature. It
was the higher and prevailing temper of his mind. He used to
regard it as having said what he had to say on religion.

The main testimony to Christianity he found not in
miracles but in that eternal witness, the revelation of
what might be called "The Mind of God," in the
Christian morality, and its correlation with the divine
in man.

He had a measureless admiration for the Sermon on
the Mount; and for the Parables — "perfection, beyond
compare," he called them. I heard a talk on these between him and Browning, and Browning fully agreed with
my father in his admiration. Moreover my father expressed
his conviction that " Christianity with its divine Morality

[1] "In Memoriam," XXXVI.

but without the central figure of Christ, *the* Son of Man, would become cold[1], and that it is fatal for religion to lose its warmth "; that "*The* Son of Man " was the most tremendous title possible; that the forms of Christian religion would alter; but that the spirit of Christ would still grow from more to more " in the roll of the ages."

> Till each man find his own in all men's good,
> And all men work in noble brotherhood.

" This is one of my meanings," he said, " of

> Ring in the Christ that is to be:

when Christianity without bigotry will triumph, when the controversies of creeds shall have vanished, and

> Shall bear false witness, each of each, no more,
> But find their limits by that larger light,
> And overstep them, moving easily
> Thro' after-ages in the Love of Truth,
> The truth of Love[2]."

" The most pathetic utterance in all history," he said, " is that of Christ on the Cross, ' It is finished,' after that passionate cry, ' My God, My God, why hast Thou forsaken Me ? ' " Nevertheless he also recognized the note of triumph in " It is finish'd[3]." " I am always amazed when I read the New Testament at the splendour of Christ's purity and holiness and at His infinite pity[4]." He disliked discussion on the Nature of Christ, "seeing that such discussion was mostly unprofitable, for none knoweth the Son but the Father." " He went about doing good " he would say: and one of the

---

[1] " He did not preach His opinions; He preached Himself." Renan's *Vie de Jésus*. " The spiritual character of Christ," my father would say, "is more wonderful than the greatest miracle."

[2] " Akbar's Dream."

[3] See *The Death of Œnone, and other Poems*, p. 80. Westcott writes: "I always think that the tense ἐγκατέλιπες marks the crisis as past."

[4] What he called "the man-woman " in Christ, the union of tenderness and strength.

traditional and unwritten sayings of Christ which oftenest came home to him was, " He that is near Me is near the fire," the baptism of the fire of inspiration. For in " In Memoriam " the soul, after grappling with anguish and darkness, doubt and death, emerges with the inspiration of a strong and steadfast faith in the Love of God for man, and in the oneness of man with God, and of man with man in Him —

, That God, which ever lives and loves,
    One God, one law, one element,
    And one far-off divine event,
To which the whole creation moves.

I cannot end this chapter on " In Memoriam " more fitly than by quoting Henry Hallam's letter on receiving in 1850 what he calls " the precious book."

I know not how to express what I have felt. My first sentiment was surprise, for, though I now find that you had mentioned the intention to my daughter, Julia, she had never told me of the poems. I do not speak as another would to praise and admire : few of them indeed I have as yet been capable of reading, the grief they express is too much akin to that they revive. It is better than any monument which could be raised to the memory of my beloved son, it is a more lively and enduring testimony to his great virtues and talents that the world should know the friendship which existed between you, that posterity should associate his name with that of Alfred Tennyson.

CHAPTER XV.

MARRIAGE (1850–51).

Like perfect music unto noble words.

My father and mother had met in the spring of 1850 at Shiplake on the Thames; where they had both stayed with the Rawnsleys, Mrs Rawnsley being my mother's cousin.

If "In Memoriam" were published, Moxon had promised a small yearly royalty on this and on the other poems, and so my father had decided that he could now honourably offer my mother a home.

Accordingly after ten years of separation their engagement was renewed.

Early in those ten years my grandmother had suggested dividing her jointure with them, so that they might marry, but this, of course, they could not allow. Moxon now advanced £300 — so my Uncle Charles told a friend, — at all events £300 were in my father's bank in his name; and with this and their united small incomes, and all household furniture given them by my mother's father, they decided that they could brave life together and that the marriage should take place at Shiplake on the 13th of June, the month which saw the publication of "In Memoriam."

Of the Vicarage with its terraced garden, and of the fine old church Miss Mitford gives the following picturesque description:

A few miles further, and a turn to the right conducts us to one of the grand old village churches, which give so much of character to English landscape. A large and beautiful pile it is. The tower, half clothed with ivy, stands with its charming vicarage and its pretty vicarage-garden on a high eminence, overhanging one of the finest bends of the great river. A woody lane leads from the church to the bottom of the chalk-cliff, one side of which stands out from the road below, like a promontory, surmounted by the laurel hedges and flowery cedar of Lebanon. This is Shiplake church, famed far and near for its magnificent oak carving, and the rich painted glass of its windows, collected, long before such adornments were fashionable, by the fine taste of the late vicar, and therefore filled with the very choicest specimens of mediæval art, chiefly obtained from the remains of the celebrated Abbey of St Bertin near St Omer, sacked during the first French Revolution. In this church Alfred Tennyson was married.

The wedding was of the quietest (even the cake and dresses arriving too late), which made my father say, to the amusement of those who were present, that it was " the nicest wedding " he had ever been at. In after-life he said: "The peace of God came into my life before the altar when I wedded her."

The marriage party consisted of the bride's father[1], Henry Sellwood, Edmund and Cecilia Lushington, Charles Weld, husband of Anne, one of the Sellwood sisters, and Mr Greville Phillimore. The two child bridesmaids were Mary and Margaret Rawnsley.

[1] He was a stately, courteous gentleman, kindly, cultivated, unaffected, and above all a good friend. His family had come in old days from Somersetshire into Berkshire. He himself was a solicitor at Horncastle. Greatly to his honour he had taken up this profession when his family was on the road to ruin. In 1812 he had married Sarah Franklin, sister of the "heroic sailor" Sir John Franklin, but she had died in 1816, aged 28, leaving three daughters, Emily, Anne, and Louisa.

My uncle Charles and Louisa Tennyson Turner could not join the party, and my uncle wrote accordingly :

Oh what a queer world it is! I hope however it has done a brace of amiable and remarkable people some genuine good, whirligig as it is — this time at least. Well! The thing is to come off on the 13th, daddy says. Good wishes in crowds from me. I despatch a dove's wing to you. I am going to keep pigeons, would they were carrier pigeons! then would I trouble their wings with missives of congratulation to arrive more swiftly than the railroad.

Coo! coo! coo! Your affectionate brother,

CHARLES.

My father made and repeated the following poem, as my mother and he drove from Shiplake to Pangbourne; enclosing it to Drummond Rawnsley through Mrs Rawnsley.

MY DEAR KATE,

You managed it all very well yesterday. Many thanks.

Ever yours, A. T.

P.S. Dubbie's [1] fees must be come at as he can best manage. The clerk and shirts are owing.

The poem would be more perfect without the third stanza, but I do not think you would like to miss it.

To the Vicar of Shiplake. (Unpublished.)

Vicar of this pleasant spot
    Where it was my chance to marry,
Happy, happy be your lot
    In the Vicarage by the quarry.
You were he that knit the knot!

[1] Short for *Drummond*.

Sweetly, smoothly flow your life.
　Never tithe unpaid perplex you,
Parish feud, or party strife,
　All things please you, nothing vex you,
You have given me such a wife!

Live and prosper! Day by day
　Watch your standard roses blowing,
And your three young things at play,
　And your triple terrace growing
Green and greener every May!

Sweetly flow your life with Kate's,
　Glancing off from all things evil,
Smooth as Thames below your gates,
　Thames along the silent level,
Streaming thro' his osier'd aits!

And let me say here — although, as a son, I cannot
allow myself full utterance about her whom I loved as
perfect mother and "very woman of very woman," —
"such a wife" and true helpmate she proved herself.
It was she who became my father's adviser in literary
matters; "I am proud of her intellect," he wrote. With
her he always discussed what he was working at; she
transcribed his poems : to her and to no one else he
referred for a final criticism before publishing. She,
with her "tender, spiritual nature [1]," and instinctive nobility of thought, was always by his side, a ready, cheerful,
courageous, wise, and sympathetic counsellor. It was she
who shielded his sensitive spirit from the annoyances and
trials of life, answering (for example) the innumerable
letters addressed to him from all parts of the world. By
her quiet sense of humour, by her selfless devotion, by
"her faith as clear as the heights of the June-blue
heaven," she helped him also to the utmost in the hours

[1] My father's words.

of his depression and of his sorrow; and to her he wrote two of the most beautiful of his shorter lyrics, " Dear, near and true," and the dedicatory lines which prefaced his last volume, *The Death of Œnone*.

The day after the wedding they went to Weston-super-Mare, on their way to Clevedon. " It seemed a kind of consecration to go there." They saw Arthur Hallam's resting-place, and were received by Sir Abraham Elton in the beautiful old Manor House, Clevedon Court ; and thence they went to Lynton. In that country, more solitary then than now, they enjoyed long rambles through the woods and over the heather and rode to the Valley of Rocks and Exmoor, in spite of " the weeping Devonshire climate."

Glastonbury, one of the reputed " island valleys of Avilion," followed : where they lunched in what had been the Refectory of the old Hospital for Pilgrims, built by an Abbot, John de Selwode, of the same name and race as my mother. This Abbot alone, as they were told, is buried beside the tomb of King Arthur, in the chancel of that famous Abbey, — once the wonder of the world, now but a few ruins in a garden. My father was greatly interested by the legend that Joseph of Arimathea came there in 63 A.D. and founded the first Christian colony in England :

> From our old books I know
> That Joseph came of old to Glastonbury,
> And there the heathen Prince, Arviragus,
> Gave him an isle of marsh whereon to build ;
> And there he built with wattles from the marsh
> A little lonely church in days of yore.

Clifton was the next halting-place ; thence they went to Bath, and on to Cheltenham to visit his mother. Many honeymoon houses were offered ; among others Brancepeth by his cousins, Fryston by R. M. Milnes,

Tent Lodge, Coniston, by Mrs James Marshall, a sister
of my father's college friend, Stephen Spring Rice.
They selected Tent Lodge, and set off for Patterdale
and Ullswater, then to "the little villa on Coniston
water." On their arrival my father writes to Mrs
Russell:

DEAREST AUNT,

Have you yet received the bound copy of
" In Memoriam " which I purposed for you? If not,
will you or Emma drop me a line to this place, and I
will take care that you have it immediately? We have
been making a little tour about these lakes, and have
spent the last few days with my friends the Speddings
at Bassenthwaite Water. We only arrived here last night.
Mr Marshall's park looked as lovely as the Garden of
Eden, as we descended the hill to this place. We have
a very beautiful view from our drawing-room windows,
crag, mountain, woods and lake, which look especially
fine as the sun is dropping behind the hills. I wish you
could see it. The Marshalls themselves are not here
but expected daily. We found the seat of a Marshall
on almost every lake we came to, for it seems there
are several brothers who have all either bought or been
left estates in this country; and they are all, report says,
as wealthy as Crœsus. I send you this little note just
to tell you where we are, and how much your bounty
has enabled us to enjoy ourselves among the mountains.
We have been on the whole fortunate in weather, tho'
this climate has a bad name. I do not know whether
you are at Cheltenham or Burwarton, but wherever you
are, dearest aunt, God bless and preserve you from all
ill. My wife desires her kindest love to you. Good-bye.

Ever yours affectionately,

A. TENNYSON.

The drives and walks over the mountains, the boating on the lake among the water-lilies and by the islands where the herons built, he rowing, she steering, are noted in their diary.

Here for the first time my mother saw Carlyle, who was staying with the Marshalls. The meeting was characteristic; he slowly scanned her from head to foot, then gave her a hearty shake of the hand. Next day he called at Tent Lodge; and, hearing her cough, "with his invariable kindness" stole round, while the others were talking, and shut the window which was open behind her[1].

One evening Mr Venables and Mr de Vere called. They talked for about an hour with my father — my mother having already retired to rest. At last, after puffing at his pipe for some moments in silence, my father spoke "like one thinking aloud": "I have known many women who were excellent, one in one way, another in another way, but this woman is the noblest woman I have ever known[2]." As Aubrey de Vere writes to me: "No friend who had then heard him could have felt any further anxiety as to his domestic happiness."

The Marshalls offered my father and mother Tent Lodge as a permanent home, and the Ashburtons a house near Croydon, but these kind offers they thought it best to decline and went for a time to Park House, to find a residence of their own.

On November 19th my father was appointed Poet Laureate, owing chiefly to Prince Albert's admiration for "In Memoriam." Wordsworth had been now dead

[1] Another story of his concern for others my father would tell. "Having heard that Henry Taylor was ill, Carlyle rushed off from London to Sheen with a bottle of medicine, which had done Mrs Carlyle good, without in the least knowing what was ailing Henry Taylor, or for what the medicine was useful."

[2] MS, Aubrey de Vere.

some months; and my father, as he has assured me, had not any expectation of the Laureateship, or any thought upon the subject: it seemed to him therefore a very curious coincidence, that the night before the offer reached him he dreamt that Prince Albert came and kissed him on the cheek, and that he said in his dream, " Very kind, but very German."

In the morning this letter about the Laureateship was brought to his bedroom:

WINDSOR CASTLE, Nov. 5th, 1850.

By the death of the late lamented Wm. Wordsworth the Office of Poet Laureate to the Queen became at Her Majesty's disposal.

The ancient duties of this Office, which consisted in laudatory Odes to the Sovereign, have been long, as you are probably aware, in abeyance, and have never been called for during the Reign of Her present Majesty. The Queen however has been anxious that the Office should be maintained ; first on account of its antiquity, and secondly because it establishes a connection, through Her Household, between Her Majesty and the poets of this country as a body.

To make however the continuance of this Office in harmony with public opinion, the Queen feels that it is necessary that it should be limited to a name bearing such distinction in the literary world as to do credit to the appointment, and it was under this feeling, that Her Majesty in the first instance offered the appointment to Mr Rogers, who stated to Her Majesty, in his reply, that the only reason which compelled him gratefully to decline Her Majesty's gracious intention, was, that his great age rendered him unfit to receive any new office.

It is under the same desire that the name of the poet appointed should adorn the Office, that I have received the commands of the Queen to offer this post to you, as a mark of Her Majesty's appreciation of your literary distinction.

I have the honour to be, Sir,

Your obedient humble servant,

C. B. PHIPPS.

He took the whole day to consider and at the last wrote two letters, one accepting, one refusing, and determined to make up his mind after a consultation with his friends at dinner. He would joke and say, " In the end I accepted the honour, because during dinner Venables told me, that, if I became Poet Laureate, I should always when I dined out be offered the liver-wing of a fowl. '

After accepting the Laureateship he writes to the Rev. H. Rawnsley:

My dear Rawnsley,

You do ill to seem as though you blamed me for forgetfulness of you and yours; you know it is not so, and can never be so, but I confess that in the matter of letter-writing I am in arrear to everybody. I have dozens of letters to write this afternoon, and I cannot help wishing that I could hire the electric telegraph once a month, and so work off my scores with the wires at whatever expense. This old-world, slow pen and ink operation is behind the age. I thank you for your congratulations touching the Laureateship. I was advised by my friends not to decline it * * *. I have no passion for courts, but a great love of privacy. It is, I believe, scarce £100 a year, and my friend R. M. Milnes tells me that the price of the patent and court dress will swallow up all the first year's income. I have mislaid your letter, and so cannot tell whether you asked me any questions. Let me ask *you* one. I have been looking out for an unfurnished house, with good rooms, for £60 a year or thereabouts: do you know of any such near you? If you do, please communicate with me and I will come and see it. I expect an heir to nothing about next March or April. I suppose I must lay by the Laureate's hire for him as Southey did. Pray give

my kindest love to Mrs R. and my best remembrances
to all friends, particularly G. Coltman, and

Believe me yours affectionately,

A. TENNYSON.

The immediate result of becoming Poet Laureate
was that poems and letters poured in, and my father
writes: "I get such shoals of poems that I am almost
crazed with them; the two hundred million poets of
Great Britain deluge me daily with poems: truly the
Laureateship is no sinecure. If any good soul would
just by way of a diversion send me a tome of prose!"
In answer to an appeal from Moxon for a fresh volume
of new poems, he said, "We are correcting all the
volumes for new editions [1]."

My parents' first venture in the choice of a home
was not encouraging. The house that they took was at
Warninglid in Sussex, pleasant and sunny, with large
airy rooms from which there was a Copley-Fielding-
like view of the South Downs. "The full song of the
birds delighted us as we drove up to the door," and the
home seemed at first in every way suitable. But one night
soon after their arrival a tremendous storm blew down
part of the wall in their bedroom, and through the gap
the wind raved and the water rushed. Then they learnt
that their dining-room and bedroom had been a Roman
Catholic Chapel, that a baby was buried somewhere on
the premises, and later that one of a notorious gang of
thieves and murderers known as "The Cuckfield Gang"
had lived in their very lodge.

Besides they discovered that no postman came near

[1] In the *Keepsake* for 1851 were published:

What time I wasted youthful hours,

and

Come not when I am dead.

This last poem, "Edwin Morris," "The Eagle," and the Dedication
"To the Queen," were included in the *Poems*, seventh edition, 1851.

the house, that the nearest doctor and butcher lived at Horsham, seven miles off; and that there was not even a carrier who passed anywhere within hail. Altogether everything was so uncanny and so uncomfortable, that they took a speedy departure, my father drawing my mother in a Bath chair over a very rough road to Cuckfield.

Finally, by the kind aid of Mrs Henry Taylor, they took up their abode at Chapel House, Montpelier Row, Twickenham; a house which overlooked the parks of General Peel and of the Duc d'Aumale. It was entered through a square hall, and on the fine old staircase stood the carved figure of a mitred bishop "as if to bless the passers by."

On the 21st February their diary says: "We read *Alton Locke*, drove about in search of a Court dress for Levée, could not find one and had to give up Levée on the 26th. Rogers, hearing of this, offer'd his own dress, which had been also worn by Wordsworth and had been promised to the Wordsworth family as an heirloom. The coat did well enough, but about other parts of the dress there was some anxiety felt for the Levée on March 6th, as they had not been tried on."

He was meditating his first Laureate poem, " To the Queen," and was especially thinking of a stanza in which " the empire of Wordsworth should be asserted: for he was a representative Poet Laureate, such a poet as kings should honour, and such an one as would do honour to kings;— making the period of a reign famous by the utterance of memorable words concerning that period." Spedding wrote to my father: " Those potentates stand highest in the estimation of succeeding ages, not who have been best praised in their own time, but who have in their own time done honour and given aid and encouragement to that which remains great and memorable in all time."

Later in March he stayed at Sir Alexander Duff Gordon's; and whilst there, at an evening party given by Lord John Russell, was introduced to Bunsen and to the Duke of Argyll. The Duke in after days and to the end of my father's life was one of his most valued friends.

On April 5th he received from Mr Macready a letter of thanks for the sonnet addressed to him on leaving the stage.

Farewell, Macready, since to-night we part;
Full-handed thunders often have confessed
Thy power, well used to move the public breast.
We thank thee with our voice, and from the heart.
Farewell, Macready, since this night we part,
Go, take thine honours home; rank with the best,
Garrick and statelier Kemble, and the rest,
Who made a nation purer thro' their art.
Thine is it that our drama did not die,
Nor flicker down to brainless pantomime,
And those gilt gauds men-children swarm to see.
Farewell, Macready; moral, grave, sublime;
Our Shakespeare's bland and universal eye
Dwells pleased, thro' twice a hundred years, on thee.

From W. C. Macready.

SHERBORNE, DORSET, *April 4th,* 1851.

My DEAR MR TENNYSON,

If I had obeyed the impulse of my feelings, I should have written to you long since, when our friend Forster first communicated to me the kindness you had shown me in honouring my name with the glory of your verse. This was some days before the publication of your lines, and he may have told you that the emotion they excited in me was a manifestation of my grateful appreciation beyond what words can render you.

You have indeed embalmed my perishable name, which will not so soon be lost in the long night, as "carens vate sacro," and I may truly assure you, of no testimony have I felt more proud, and on none have I reflected with more grateful pleasure, than on that which bears your name.

I remain, dear Mr Tennyson,

Always and sincerely yours,

W. C. MACREADY.

On the 20th of April my parents' first child, a boy, was born, and, owing to my mother's having fallen down a step, died in the birth.   At the time my father wrote:

"It was Easter Sunday and at his birth I heard the great roll of the organ, of the uplifted psalm (in the Chapel adjoining the house).... Dead as he was I felt proud of him. To-day when I write this down, the remembrance of it rather overcomes me; but I am glad that I have seen him, dear little nameless one that hast lived tho' thou hast never breathed, I, thy father, love thee and weep over thee, tho' thou hast no place in the Universe. Who knows? It may be that thou hast...... God's Will be done."

In the summer they met the Carlyles again. About this time he described my father to Sir J. Simeon as "sitting on a dung-heap among innumerable dead dogs." Carlyle meant that he was apt to brood over old-world subjects for his poems. Once many years after, when we called upon him, my father teazed him about this utterance, and Carlyle replied, "Eh! that was not a very luminous description of you."

This was the year of the first great Exhibition, and what seems to have most delighted my father was the building itself and the great glass fountain.

On July 15th they left for Boulogne on their way to Italy. "The Daisy" gives the journey better than any prose of mine can give it. Jowett writes, "He always had a living vision of Italy, Greece and the Mediterranean." He was proud of the metre of "The Daisy" which he called a far-off echo of the Horatian Alcaic [1]. Among the many metres he invented, this he ranked among his best, together with some of the anapæstic movements in "Maud," and the long-rolling rhythm of his "Ode to Virgil." On their journey he took with him his usual travelling companions, Shakespeare, Milton, Homer, Virgil, Horace, Pindar, Theocritus, and probably the *Divina Commedia* and Goethe's *Gedichte.*

Italy was in such a disturbed state that they did not go to Rome as they had intended. The fever was prevalent in Venice, so this had also to be given up. They stayed three weeks at the Baths of Lucca in the house of one Giorgio Basantino, opposite a wood where they would sit watching the green lizards at play. There were delightful evening drives over the mountains; and they rejoiced in "the glorious violet colouring of the Apennines, and the picturesqueness of the peasants beating out their flax or spinning with their distaffs at their cottage doors." Thence they journeyed to Florence to stay with my uncle Frederick at the Villa Torregiani, which had been for many years his home. On September 24th they left Florence, returning by way of the "snowy Splügen" to Paris. Here the Brownings called on them at their hotel. Mr Browning, already my father's friend, was affectionate as ever. Mrs Browning was "fragile-looking, with great spirit eyes," and met my mother "as if she had been her own sister." Savile Morton came too, and the diary says: "His wild laugh sounded through the corridors. The Brownings gave us, before parting, two beautiful Paris nosegays (the flowers arranged in a sort of Grecian

---

[1] He was pleased with the slightly different effect of (substantially) the same metre in the invitation "To the Rev. F. D. Maurice," gained by the dactyl which in those verses begins each fourth line (see p. 429).

pattern) and both alike." On their return home to Chapel House, my father quotes Catullus as he enters the door:

"O, quid solutis est beatius curis!
Cum mens onus reponit, ac peregrino
Labore fessi venimus larem ad nostrum,
Desideratoque acquiescimus lecto.
Hoc est, quod unum est pro laboribus tantis!"

Soon after he wrote the following letter to his old friends Mr and Mrs Brookfield, who were on their way to Madeira:

MY DEAR WILLIAM AND JANE,

I have only just got back to England and heard of you in calling on Mrs Taylor at Mortlake. Grieved I was to hear so ill an account, that you are forced to leave England and that I may not see you again for a long time; yet I do not know why I should write except to tell you that my sympathies go with you and to wish that you, William, may soon be better and that God's blessing may be with you on the winter seas, and in the fair island which I have so often longed to see. If my wife could stand the sea nothing would have pleased me better than to have accompanied you thither, but I hear that one friend at least has preceded you, and is there now, Stephen Spring Rice. That we may soon see you back in renewed health is the wish and prayer of

Yours affectionately,

A. TENNYSON.

Spedding was consulted as to some " National Songs for Englishmen " published in the *Examiner* in 1852, " since

Easy patrons of their kin
Have left the last free race with naked coasts."

He replies:

I will send £5 to Coventry Patmore for the Rifles, thinking that the more noise we make in that way the better, and the more we practise the less likely are we to be called upon to perform. I answered your summons to the Thatched House and found a room full of people not one of whom I knew; all sufficiently zealous, and at the same time rational, and (so far as the preliminaries went) of one mind. I suppose they know one another, or some know some; and as there seemed to be no want of volunteers for the Committee and Sub-committee to arrange details, I thought I might, without abandoning my country in her extremity, leave that part of the business to them and join some club when it is organized. I think I could hit a Frenchman at 100 yards, if he did not frighten me.

Forster sent for me yesterday to look at the new poems, which I highly approve, and by no means allow of the objection suggested against the stanza[1]. America is our daughter but the men of America are our sons. Forster wants a name for the poet, which I think very desirable; and no great matter what name is chosen so it be short and pronounceable, Alfred, Arthur, Merlin, Tyrtæus, Edward Ball, Britannicus, Honved, Hylax, anything. Amyntor would sound well, is not hackneyed, and is good Greek for defender or protector.

Your note though dated the 2nd did not arrive yesterday till I had gone out.

National Songs (1852).

When " Britons, guard your own," and " Hands all round " were written, my father along with many others regarded France under Napoleon as a serious menace to the peace of Europe. Although a passionate patriot, and a true lover of England, he was not blind to her faults, and was unprejudiced and cosmopolitan in seeing the best side of other nations; and in later years after the Franco-German war, he was filled with admiration at the dignified way in which France was gradually

[1] About America (p. 346).

gathering herself together. He rejoiced whenever England and France were in agreement, and worked together harmoniously for the good of the world.

Britons, guard your own.

This version was given to my mother many years afterwards, so that she might publish it with her musical setting.

Rise, Britons, rise, if manhood be not dead;
The world's last tempest darkens overhead:
    All freedom vanish'd —
    The true men banish'd —
He triumphs! maybe we shall stand alone!
      Britons, guard your own.

Call home your ships across Biscayan tides,
To blow the battle from their oaken sides.
    Why waste they yonder
    Their idle thunder?
Why stay they there to guard a foreign throne?
      Seamen, guard your own.

We were the best of marksmen long ago,
We won old battles with our strength, the bow.
    Now practise, yeomen,
    Like those bowmen,
Till your balls fly as their true shafts have flown,
      Yeomen, guard your own.

Should they land here and but one hour prevail,
There must no man go back to bear the tale;
    No man to bear it,
    Swear it! We swear it!
Although we fought the banded world alone,
      We swear to guard our own.

Hands all round[1]!

First drink a health, this solemn night,
 A health to England, every guest;
That man's the best cosmopolite,
 Who loves his native country best.
May Freedom's oak for ever live
 With stronger life from day to day;
That man's the true Conservative
 Who lops the moulder'd branch away.
  Hands all round!
  God the tyrant's hope confound!
To this great cause of Freedom drink, my friends,
And the great name of England round and round.

A health to Europe's honest men!
 Heaven guard them from her tyrant jails!
From wrong'd Poerio's noisome den,
 From iron'd limbs and tortured nails!
We curse the crimes of southern kings,
 The Russian whips and Austrian rods,
We, likewise, have our evil things;
 Too much we make our Ledgers Gods,
  Yet hands all round!
  God the tyrant's cause confound!
To Europe's better health we drink, my friends,
And the great name of England round and round.

What health to France, if France be she,
 Whom martial prowess only charms?
Yet tell her — Better to be free
 Than vanquish all the world in arms.

---

[1] Feb. 9th, 1852. I must send you what Landor says in a note this morning: "'Hands all round! is incomparably the best (convivial) lyric in the language, though Dryden's 'Drinking Song' is fine."

        JOHN FORSTER to MRS TENNYSON.

Her frantic city's flashing heats
  But fire to blast the hopes of men.
Why change the titles of your streets?
  You fools, you'll want them all again.
        Yet hands all round!
        God the tyrant's cause confound!
To France, the wiser France, we drink, my friends,
And the great name of England round and round.

Gigantic daughter of the West,
  We drink to thee across the flood,
We know thee most, we love thee best,
  For art thou not of British blood?
Should war's mad blast again be blown,
  Permit not thou the tyrant powers
To fight thy mother here alone,
  But let thy broadsides roar with ours.
        Hands all round!
        God the tyrant's cause confound!
To our great kinsmen of the West, my friends,
And the great name of England round and round.

O rise, our strong Atlantic sons,
  When war against our freedom springs!
O speak to Europe thro' your guns!
  They *can* be understood by kings.
You must not mix our Queen with those
  That wish to keep their people fools;
Our freedom's foemen are her foes,
  She comprehends the race she rules.
        Hands all round!
        God the tyrant's cause confound!
To our great kinsmen of the West, my friends,
And the great cause of freedom round and round [1].

---

[1] " The third of February, 1852," is not printed here because it was included in the *Poems* (ed. 1872). Other contributions appeared in the *Examiner*, but my father did not think them good enough to be reprinted.

CHAPTER XVI.

CHELTENHAM AND WHITBY (1852).

My father's letter-diary [1].

CHELTENHAM, *Jan.* 18*th*, 1852.

Alan Ker has taken four copies of my Ode " My Lords " to send to papers here and there. Mother was delighted beyond measure to see me, making me remorseful that I had not been here before. Alan and Mary seem well and hopeful: they say it is only a fortnight's steam to Jamaica (where he is appointed a judge), and they will not take a large outfit because at any time they can have things from England. Dobson says we could live here much better and cheaper than at Twickenham I find the air much fresher.

(*Apparently answering a query as to Count D'Orsay* [2].)

Jan. 1852.

Count D'Orsay is a friend of mine, co-godfather to Dickens' child with me. He is Louis Napoleon's

---

[1] This he habitually wrote to my mother when absent from home.

[2] My father said that before this he had dined with Count D'Orsay and other friends at John Forster's. The Count was a glorious, handsome fellow, generally dressed in tight-fitting blue coat with gilt buttons. So carried away by D'Orsay's splendour was Forster that he was heard shouting out above the hubbub of voices to his servant Henry: " Good heavens, sir, butter for the Count's flounders ! "

347

intimate friend and secretary, and moreover I am told a man who has wept over my poems. See how strangely things are connected. Just put the things together. Wonderful are these times, and no one knows what may arise from the smallest things. I the poet of England with the secretary of Louis Napoleon whom I have abused.

CHELTENHAM, *Jan. 22nd.*

A note from Charles Weld this morning. He sent my poem to the *Times*, but the *Times* ignores it. Alan Ker says it is not their custom to put in poems except they are allowed to subscribe the author's name. I have told him to try the *Morning Chronicle:* he seems for *Fraser*, tho' it is so long before *Fraser* comes out that my poem will be half superannuated like the musket. I see that here and there people are really beginning to be awake to their danger * * * *. In this horrible age of blab I can scarce trust aright.

Jan. 23rd.

I have been out every day dining. The readers of the *Examiner* will no doubt guess the authorship from knowing Forster's friendship for me. The military letters in the *Times* are very interesting. The hills here have fine lights on them as seen from my windows. John Rashdall wants us to go and spend three weeks with him at Malvern.

YORK, *July 7th,* 1852.

Slept at Spedding's where I found they expected me. Started this morning 11 a.m. Hay fever atrocious with irritation of railway, nearly drove me crazed, but could not complain, the other only occupant of the carriage having a curiously split shoe for his better ease, and his eyes and teeth in a glare at me with pain of gout the whole way, and finally helped out by his servant, going to drink Harrogate waters. Came here to the Black Swan, ordered dinner, went out and bought weed, having left mine at Spedding's with gloves (ay me!). Enquired of tobacconist state of parties here, "Never was anything so satisfactory, all purity of Election, no row, no drunkenness, Mr Vincent will come in without any bother." While he was yet speaking arose a row, innumerable mob raging, housekeepers all down the street rushed out with window-shutters to prevent windows being broken. My dinner waiting for me, I having to plunge thro' mob to get at it, essayed the fringes of the crowd, very dense nucleus of enormous brawl somewhere within. Presently the glazed hats of policemen, like sunshine striking here and there at the breaking up of a storm, showed me an issue of hope. I plunged through in the wake of the bluecoats and got home. To-morrow to Whitby. Vincent after all not returned. When I got to Waterloo the roses had snapt off short and lay at the bottom of the carriage. The porter opened the door, picked up one, snuffed at it with vast satisfaction, and never so much as "by your leave."

5, NORTH TERRACE, WEST CLIFF, WHITBY,
July 8th, 1852.

I am set down here for a week at least in lodgings. It is rather a fine place, a river running into the sea between precipices, on one side new buildings and a very handsome royal hotel belonging to Hudson the railway king, on the other at the very top a gaunt old Abbey, and older parish Church hanging over the town amid hundreds of white gravestones that looked to my eye something like clothes laid out to dry. Moreover there is the crackiness of an election going on and lots of pink and blue flags, and insane northland boatmen of Danish breed, who meet and bang each other for the love of liberty, foolish fellows. In the midst of the row yesterday came a funeral followed by weeping mourners, a great hearse, plumes nodding and mourning coach, and the gaunt old Abbey looked down with its hollow eyes on the life and death, the drunkenness and the political fury, rather ironically as it seemed to me, only that it was too old to have much feeling left about anything. No bathing men were to be had, so I e'en walked into the sea by myself and had a very decent bathe. Hay fever was much better yesterday and is bad again this morning. I could not write yesterday for I came in after the post had started by a very pretty rail which curves like a common road between great wolds, the Esk, which is the stream that debouches here, running below. Then we really went down a considerable hill with a rope. The same thing I think occurs at Liége, but this seemed to me much steeper. I am told there are very fine views in the neighbourhood, though most probably I shall not get out far enough to see them as it is pestilent hot.

WHITBY, *July* 13*th*.

I want to go to Redcliffe Scar which old Wordsworth once told me of, or perhaps to Bolton Abbey. I think it a great pity that your "Sweet and low" hadn't the start of all these musical jottings. I have had two very good days coasting, I mean walking along on and under the cliffs. Very singular they are with great bivalve shells sticking out of them. They are made of a great dark slate-coloured shale (is it to be called?) that comes showering down ever and anon from a great height; and on the hard flat rock which makes the beach on one side of the town (for on the other side are sands), you see beautiful little ammonites which you stoop to pick up but find them part of the solid rock. You know these are the snakes which St Hilda drove over the cliff and falling they lost their heads, and she changed them into stone. I found a strange fish on the shore with rainbows about its wild staring eyes, enclosed in a sort of sack with long tentacula beautifully coloured, quite dead, but when I took it up by the tail it spotted all the sand underneath with great drops of ink, so I suppose it was a kind of cuttle-fish. I found too a pale pink orchis on the sea bank and a pink vetch, a low sort of shrub with here and there a thorn. I am reading lots of novels. The worst is they do not last longer than the day. I am such a fierce reader I think I have had pretty well my quantum suff.: Venables' anecdotes are very interesting indeed. One cannot help wishing that such a man as Gladstone may come to sit on the top branch of the tree.

WHITBY, *July* 19*th.*

I have ordered a carriage and am going to see Lord Normanby's park near here, tho' I am half afraid of it, a carriage so excites my hay fever. I met an old smuggler on the coast yesterday who had been in Lord N.'s service (not as smuggler of course !), and he took me for Lord Normanby at first, a likeness I have been told of more than once before. I got into conversation with him and I am going to call for him to-day and he is to show me the caves and holes in the coast where they used to land their kegs. I am going from here to-morrow, I think I shall go by the Scarboro' packet but I am not certain. I shall most likely pop down on Charles at Grasby, but if I go to Scarboro' I hardly think I shall go out of my way again to Leeds. I shall like much to see the Brownings again, Mrs B. particularly. I suppose when I come back the Lushingtons will want me to spend some days at Park House. I have seen no houses here to be sold, but then I have not looked out for them. A tailor who sewed me on some buttons, told me Whitby was remarkable for longevity, the healthiest place in England except some place (he said) near Cheltenham, he had forgotten the name. I dare say he meant Malvern.

GRASBY, *July 22nd.*

I came by the packet boat to Scarborough where I stopt the night and came on here yesterday. The train only stopt at Moortown, and I was obliged to walk through the fields to Grasby when I admired the deep long-stemmed Lincolnshire wheat which I had not seen for many a day.

I find Charles and Louisa very well, only Charles rather low as it seems to me. It is a nice little place they have and the country really looks pretty at this time of year. I shall stop a few days.

GRASBY, *July 27th.*

Pray take drives every day. The school children have a feast here to-morrow for which I am going to stay. They run in sacks and do all manner of queer things. Our parson-party went off well. Agnes I suppose will be triumphant to-morrow. I think when I leave here I shall go round by Grimsby to see the new docks and perhaps get a bathe at Cleethorpes.

We went over to drink tea the other afternoon with Mr Maclean, the Vicar of Caistor, where I made fun for the children, and saw a young cuckoo which a boy had found in a sparrow's nest, a rather rare circumstance so late in July; but the boy had had him for three weeks and fed him with worms. He was a good deal duskier than the adult cuckoo, and with a white band on his head and very voracious, would have swallowed anything.

HULL, *July* 31*st.*

I am going out of the way to see Crowland Abbey and maybe shall stop a day or so there. I write this in vast haste at the Mason Arms, Louth. Daddy [1] drove me over last night to Grimsby to see the new dock, truly a great work.

When he reached home, Monckton Milnes asked him to dinner. He wrote:

MY DEAR MILNES,

I have never dined in town (except once with Hallam en famille when I met him by chance in Lear the painter's rooms looking at his picture of the Syracusan Quarries [2], and once or twice with my brother-in-law en famille also) since I dined with you, Heaven knows how long ago, and met Doyle and others. I have given up dining out and am about to retire into utter solitude in some country house, but if you feel aggrieved at sending one invitation after another to me, unaccepted, I will come. You have not mentioned your hour 6? 7? 8? let me know. Do not bother yourself about giving me a bed, I can get one (and my own way too in the matter of smoke) better at Spedding's. Really I am very unwell and, tho' hay fever sometimes lets me alone for a whole day together, yet it sometimes makes me quite unfit to sit at table. Send me a line to say what your hour is and what Maurice's hour is and I will see if I can come in time for Maurice.

Ever yours,

A. TENNYSON.

[1] Henry Sellwood.
[2] Now in the drawing-room at Farringford.

To James Spedding.

DEAR J. S.

Can you let me have your attic next Saturday night and Sunday? I am going to dine with Milnes on Sunday, he has offered me a bed but I am more at mine ease in mine inn (smoking-room I should say) with you.

*   *   *   *   *

Go and see (and having seen, if you can interest yourself in) Thomas Woolner's design for the W. W.[1] Westminster monument. I am told it is good and I promised to say a good word for him.

Ever yours, A. TENNYSON.

[1] Wordsworth, now in the drawing-room at Farringford.

CHAPTER XVII.

TWICKENHAM (1852–53).

Early in 1852 my father and mother went on a visit to one of his old College friends, Mr. Rashdall the clergyman of Malvern, and met the Carlyles and Sydney Dobell[1]. Rashdall was a man so beloved by his parishioners, and so simple and direct in his language from the pulpit, that he had emptied the Dissenting Chapels for miles round. He would often hold his Church services in the fields. A flowery record of Spring follows in my mother's journal, about the beauty of the daffodils, wood anemones, primroses, and violets; the pear trees throughout the country in bloom "like springing and falling fountains." While they were there my father read Dr Wordsworth's *Apocalypse* to my mother. On their return to Twickenham, he visited the Exhibition, and was delighted with Millais' "Ophelia" and "The Huguenot," but liked "The Huguenot" much the best. They came to know the Peels at Marble Hill, and Archibald Peel (the General's son) pointed out the avenue in which Sir Walter Scott placed the interview between Jeanie Deans and Queen Caroline. Happy days were spent in the

---

[1] Mr Briton Rivière writes to me: "I asked my brother-in-law, Sydney Dobell, to describe your father to me, and he said: 'If he were pointed out to you as the man who had written the *Iliad*, you would answer, "I can well believe it."'"

little Twickenham garden, my father reading aloud passages of any book which struck him. Layard's *Nineveh* and Herschel's *Astronomy* were read at this time. Numerous friends called from London: Spedding, Venables, Patmore, Edmund and Franklin Lushington, Temple, Palgrave, Jowett, the Welds and others. He writes, "lots of callers, I expect I shall be inundated." The Diary continues, "Hallam born on the 11th of August."

To John Forster.

August 11*th*, 1852.

My DEAR JOHN FORSTER,

I did not tell you of my marriage which you took rather in dudgeon. Now I will tell you of the birth of a little son this day. I have seen beautiful things in my life, but I never saw anything more beautiful than the mother's face as she lay by the young child an hour or two after, or heard anything sweeter than the little lamblike bleat of the young one. I had fancied that children after birth had been all shriek and roar; but he gave out a little note of satisfaction every now and then, as he lay by his mother, which was the most pathetic sound in its helplessness I ever listened to. You see I talk almost like a bachelor, yet unused to these things: but you — I don't hear good reports of you. You should have been better by this. Get better quickly if you would have me be as I always am

Yours most truly, A. TENNYSON.

My DEAR JOHN FORSTER,

I have only time for one word of bulletin. Everything, I believe, is going on well, tho' the mother suffers from an almost total want of sleep, and the little monster does anything but what Hamlet says Osric did in his nursery-days. I found him lying alone on the third day of his life, and, while I was looking at him, I saw him looking at me with such apparently earnest, wide-open eyes, I felt as awe-struck as if I had seen a spirit. I hope you are mending.

God bless you, A. Tennyson.

To Mrs Browning.

CHAPEL HOUSE, TWICKENHAM,
August 11th, 1852.

MY DEAR MRS BROWNING,

I wrote to you once before this morning. I now write again to tell you what I am sure your woman's and poet's heart will rejoice in, that my wife was delivered of a fine boy at 9.30 a.m. this day, and that both she and the child are doing well. I never saw any face so radiant with all high and sweet expression as hers when I saw her some time after.

Ever yours truly, A. Tennyson.

Mrs Browning's reply was the first congratulatory letter.

58 WELBECK STREET,
Wednesday night.
August 12th, 1852.

MY DEAR MR TENNYSON,

Thank you and congratulate you indeed from my heart. May God bless you all three.

Robert said, when I was writing the note of enquiry which has gone to the post, "Tell him we will hope still for a joyful meeting," but I had not courage at that moment of crisis to mention a word of "joy."

Now I may, thank God. Will you say to dear Mrs Tennyson

when she is able to think of anything so far off as a friend, how deeply I sympathise in her happiness, with the memory of all that ecstasy as I felt it myself, still thrilling through me?

And there are barbarians in the world who dare to call the new little creatures not pretty, ugly even!!

Will you after a day or two send me a " line of bulletin "? See how I encroach upon your kindness!

Most truly yours,

ELIZABETH BARRETT BROWNING.

P.S. by Robert Browning.

I can't help saying too, how happy I am in your happiness and in the assurance that it is greater than even you can quite know yet. God bless, dear Tennyson, you and all yours.

R. B.

Saturday.

MY DEAR MRS BROWNING,

Here is one word of bulletin as you desired. All is doing as well as can be.

To this one word, let me add another, that is how very grateful your little note and Browning's epilogue made me. I began to read it to my wife but could not get on with it, so I put it away by her bedside, and she shall read it as soon as she reads anything.

Ever yours and your husband's,

A. TENNYSON.

" From the first," my mother writes, "Alfred watched Hallam with interest; some of his acquaintances would have smiled to see him racing up and down stairs and dandling the baby in his arms." The poem " Out of the Deep " was begun then and finished long afterwards. The christening was at Twickenham, the godfathers being Henry Hallam and F. D. Maurice.

From Henry Hallam.

WILTON CRESCENT, *August 25th*, 1852.

MY DEAR ALFRED TENNYSON,

I returned from a three weeks' tour in France late last night. Of your paternal dignity, lately accrued, I had had no information. This is my excuse for delay in acknowledging your letters of the 16th and in expressing at once my sincere congratulations on the event, and my most willing acceptance of the office which you desire me to undertake. That the names of Hallam and Tennyson should be united in the person of this infant will be to me a gratifying reflection for the remainder of my days. You have already made those names indissoluble. I beg you to give my kind regards to Mrs A. Tennyson. My daughter is at her own house at Hayes in Kent; I shall soon go down.

Yours most truly, H. HALLAM.

From Rev. F. D. Maurice.

BODINGTON RECTORY, nr. SHREWSBURY,
August 30th, 1852.

MY DEAR SIR,

I am almost ashamed to confess the pleasure which your note of this morning caused me. It does not look like the proper feeling of responsibility of the office with which the kindness of Mrs Tennyson and you would invest me, to have experienced such delight, and I am afraid you will think very differently and much more truly of my Christianity when you hear of it. But I have so very much to thank you for, especially of late years since I have known your poetry better and I hope I have been somewhat more in a condition to learn from it, that I cannot say how thankful I feel to you for wishing that I should stand in any nearer and more personal relation to you. I beg you to express to Mrs Tennyson how very much I value this proof of her confidence and how much I hope I may not prove utterly unworthy of it.

Very truly yours, F. D. MAURICE.

From Mrs Browning.

58 WELBECK STREET, *Sept.* 1852.

MY DEAR MRS TENNYSON,

It is delightful always to have kind words, most delightful to have them from *you*.

We had resolved on leaving England on the fifth, but you offer us an irresistible motive for staying, in spite of fogs and cold. So you will see us on Tuesday, and we shall come in time for the ceremony : we would not miss the christening for the world.

And I must tell you, a baby has screamed in this house ever since we have been in England, much to my sympathy...only, as the child grows fatter and fatter I have come to consider the screaming to be a sign of prosperity. Still, it is very painful to hear a young child : when he cried I was always near crying myself. Only the fact is that these little creatures *will* make much ado about nothing sometimes, and we are wrong in reading their ills too large through our imagination. I hope to find your darling well and serene on Tuesday, and yourself stronger than you seem to be now.

Let me be (why not ?)

Affectionately yours always,

ELIZABETH BARRETT BROWNING.

From Charles Dickens.

DOVER, 1*st Oct.* 1852.

MY DEAR TENNYSON,

I have received your note here only to-day. It would have given me the heartiest pleasure to have welcomed a young Tennyson to this breathing world wherein he is much wanted, on so good an occasion as his christening, but that I have engaged to go to Boulogne on Sunday for a fortnight. I shall drink his health on the fifth.

As your letter bears no address and as I cannot call your address to mind, I send this to Moxon's care.

Ever yours, CHARLES DICKENS.

From Frederick Tennyson.

Having duly received the bulletins announcing an autumnal shoot of the old Laurel in the shape of Hallam Tennyson (is this his only name?) I write not only to wish you joy of your new acquisition but to have more particulars from you on that all engrossing subject. Is he to turn out a dove or an eagle? Has he a hawking eye and the aquiline supremacy of the Cæsars in his nose or is there a classical type of head, a Belvederino with strong ideality? Will the pencils of the rays of the ancestral Intellectualities converge into a focus in the concavity of his cranium and be reflected therefrom in redoubled warmth and light, or will they neutralize one another and become common sense, a very good thing? You will probably be better enabled to answer these questions some ten years hence than now, but it is astonishing how early children begin to exhibit distinctive qualities. In my three little girls I fancy I detect strong marks of Individualities.

Your affectionate brother, F. T.

There was some question as to the name, whether it should be Arthur or Hallam. My father called out in a clear voice, that rang through the church, "Hallam," which pleased Henry Hallam, though jokingly he said in London: "They would not name him Alfred lest he should turn out a fool, and so they named him 'Hallam.'" Thinking that in future it would be an interesting link with a former age[1], his parents took him with them to old Samuel Rogers, and Rogers, bowing to my mother, said in his courtly and diplomatic way, "Mrs Tennyson, I made one great mistake in my life, I never married."

In November was the burial of the Duke of Wellington. The Ode was published on the morning of

---

[1] Rogers, my father told me, had had his hand on Dr Johnson's knocker, but was too shy to knock and had run away without seeing the great man.

the funeral, but some additions were made to it afterwards[1].

My father wrote: *Nov. 18th.* " Have seen the procession at the Duke of Wellington's funeral: very fine; hope to see the interior of St Paul's before I leave." To Edward Fitzgerald he observed: "At the funeral I was struck with the look of sober manhood in the British soldier." " In the midst of the solemn silence," said my father, " Magdalene Brookfield whispered to her mother when she saw the Duke's boots carried by his charger, ' Mama, when I am dead shall I be that?' meaning the boots."

It is interesting to note that while the Ode was being abused in all directions by the Press my father wrote thus to his publishers: " If you lose by the Ode, I will not consent to accept the whole sum of £200, which you offered me. I consider it quite a sufficient loss if you do not gain by it."

Henry Taylor wrote:

MORTLAKE, *Nov. 17th,* 1852.

I have read your ode (" Death of the Duke of Wellington "), and I believe that many thousands at present, and that many hundreds of thousands in future times, will feel about it as I do, or with a yet stronger and deeper feeling; and I am sure that every one will feel about it according to his capacity of feeling what is great and true. It has a greatness worthy of its theme and an absolute simplicity and truth, with all the poetic passion of your nature moving beneath.

And here is my father's reply:

SEAFORD HOUSE, SEAFORD,
Nov. 23rd, 1852.

Thanks, thanks! I have just returned from Reading and found your letter. In the all but universal depre-

---

[1] The Ode was written in the " Green Room," Chapel House, Twickenham.

ciation of my ode by the Press, the prompt and hearty appreciation of it by a man as true as the Duke himself is doubly grateful.

Ever, my dear Taylor, yours,

A. TENNYSON.

This autumn the Twickenham meadows were so much flooded that my father and mother moved to Seaford, Brighton and Farnham. At the last place Charles Kingsley came to see them, fresh and vivacious as ever.

At the beginning of next year (1853) my father was asked whether he would allow himself to be nominated as Rector of the University of Edinburgh. He replied:

To Appleby Stephenson, M.D.

LONDON, *March 1st*, 1853.

SIR,

Your letter of the twenty-fourth of February has reached me only this morning. I trust that yourself and those other gentlemen, whom you speak of as being willing to give their vote for me as President of your University, will forgive me when I say that however gratefully sensible of the honour intended me, I must beg leave with many thanks to decline it. I could neither undertake to come to Edinboro' nor to deliver an inaugural address at the time specified. You will doubtless find another and worthier than myself to fill this office.

I am, Sir, your obliged and obedient servant,

A. TENNYSON.

My father then went off house-hunting and wrote from Farnham to my mother:

FARNHAM.

"I saw Elstead Lodge yesterday, dry soil but quite flat, with view of distant hills, and one hill very near:

splendid lawn but house looking north. The park here is delicious and the little house to be sold has a large garden......As for the house, you would find the rooms too low. If I buy, there is plenty of room for building two good additional rooms. I saw the lawyer here and he has given me the refusal. It is quite retired, just under the Bishop's palace. What an air after Twickenham! I walked over to Hale and looked into the old premises[1]."

In the summer my father and mother took a tour to York[2], Whitby, Redcar, Richmond and Grasby. He left her at Richmond to return to Grasby, and went with Palgrave to Glasgow. From Glasgow the change was very pleasant when the travellers found themselves at Carstairs, the home of my father's old college friend, Robert Monteith. " The Daisy " was written in Edinburgh; and " To Edward Lear, on his Travels in Greece " was printed at this time among the collected poems.

Farringford[3].

Later my father paid a visit to Bonchurch. There he heard of Farringford as a place that might possibly be suitable for his home, as it was beautiful and far

---

[1] Where my grandfather, Henry Sellwood, lived with my mother after leaving Horncastle.

[2] My father wrote from Tait's Hotel, July 29th, 1853: "A Roman epitaph in the Museum at York touched me:

> D. M. Simpliciae Florentine
> Anime innocentissime
> Que vixit menses decem.
> Felicius Simplex Pater Fecit.
> Leg. VI. V."

[3] The name *Farringford* is old. I have in my possession deeds of the fourteenth century signed by Walter de Ferringford. Prior's Manor, attached to Farringford, belonged to the Abbey of Lyra in Normandy. Many of the fields retain the old names of that time, the Prior's Field, Maiden's Croft (dedicated to the Virgin Mary), the Clerks' Hill, Abraham's Mead, etc.

from the haunts of men. " If society were what it is
not," wrote Lady Taylor to Aubrey de Vere, "it might
be well to give up something for it." Society being
what it is, he determined to quit Twickenham and to
live a country life of earnest work, only seeing his
many friends from time to time. When my mother
and he went down to look at Farringford, they crossed
the Solent in a rowing boat on a still November evening,
and " One dark heron flew over the sea, backed by a
daffodil sky."

Next day, as they gazed from the drawing-room
window out through the distant wreath of trees towards
a sea of Mediterranean blue, with rosy capes beyond, the
down on the left rising above the foreground of undulating park, golden-leaved elms and chestnuts, and red-
stemmed pines, they agreed that they must if possible
have that view to live with.

Nov. 14*th*, 1853. My father writes: " I wrote on
Friday to accept [1] the house (Farringford), I also wrote
to-day to Moxon to advance one thousand pounds, four
hundred pounds he owes me, the odd six hundred to
be paid if he will in March when I get my moneys in.
Why I did it? Because by buying safe debentures in
the East Lincolnshire Line for two thousand five hundred
pounds, with that and five hundred [2] a year I think we
ought to get on...Venables and Chapman agree in the
propriety of the investment. Seymour has sent no
papers yet. I don't know what is to be done with
Laurence: it would be in the highest degree inconvenient
for me to come back from the Isle of Wight to sit for
him. Fitz would, I have no doubt, let him have his
old sketch of me."

Accordingly on November the 24th, having taken
the house on trial, they left Twickenham, and on the

---

[1] To lease the house with the option of buying it.
[2] The sum which since 1850 he had made from his books.

25th entered into possession of Farringford, which was to be a home to them for forty years, and where some of my father's best-known works were written. Mrs Thackeray Ritchie describes the place in her pleasant *Records*, as she saw it when it had become their own.

For the first time I stayed in the Island, and with the people who were dwelling there, and walked with Tennyson along High Down, treading the turf, listening to his talk, while the gulls came sideways, flashing their white breasts against the edge of the cliffs and the Poet's cloak flapped time to the gusts of the west wind. The house at Farringford itself seemed like a charmed palace, with green walls without, and speaking walls within. There hung Dante with his solemn nose and wreath; Italy gleamed over the doorways; friends' faces lined the passages, books filled the shelves, and a glow of crimson was everywhere; the oriel drawing-room window was full of green and golden leaves, of the sound of birds and of the distant sea.

My father and mother settled to a country life at once, looking after their little farm, and tending the poor and sick of the village. In the afternoons they swept up leaves, mowed the grass, gravelled the walks, and he built what he called "a bower of rushes" in the kitchen garden. The primroses and snowdrops and other flowers were a constant delight, and he began a flower dictionary. He also bought spy-glasses through which he might watch the ways and movements of the birds in the ilexes, cedar and fir trees. Geology too he took up, and trudged out with the local geologist, Keeping, on many a long expedition.

He wrote to Charles Kingsley about *Hypatia*:

1853.

MY DEAR KINGSLEY,

I hope your wife got my books which mine ordered Moxon to send. In the conclusion of the " Princess " the compositors have made a slight mistake.

Gray halls alone among their massive groves.

They have printed "their" "the" which somewhat weakens the line.

Hypatia never came; but I cannot afford to be without it. Part of the conclusion seems to me particularly valuable. I mean the talk of the Christianized Jew to the classic boy. Hypatia's mistreatment by the Alexandrians I found almost too horrible. It is very powerful and tragic; but I objected to the word "naked." Pelagia's nakedness has nothing which revolts one... but I really was hurt at having Hypatia stript, tho' I see that it adds to the tragic, and the picture as well as the moral is a fine one.

Will you lay your hand on my Adam Smith and send it per post? I enclose you six Queen's heads for that purpose.

Believe me, dear Kingsley,

Ever yours, A. TENNYSON.

CHAPTER XVIII.

FARRINGFORD (1853–1855).

Throughout the following chapters I have, with my mother's leave, made free use of her private journal. Most of it however has been necessarily compressed; and the numerous anecdotes about our childhood have been eliminated.

Here however I may perhaps be allowed to note my father's attitude toward children. This has best been given in his baby-songs, "Sweet and Low," "What does little birdie say?" "Minnie and Winnie," "Dainty Little Maiden," and his dedicatory poem to "Ally." I will however endeavour to set down briefly what I myself have known of some of his ways with children, and to begin with, what I have heard of his love for them in days before my own.

When he was a young man, living at Somersby, I have been told by those of the family younger than himself that "Alfred was their delight." They would sit upon his knee, or cling about his feet, while he told them stories of his own invention that enthralled them, long stories of hair-breadth escapes, and of travels ranging over all parts of the world. For the boys he would make himself a Colossus of Rhodes, the fun being that they should brave a "thwack" from his open hand, or escape it if they could, while rushing under the archway of his legs.

Of babies he would say: "There is something gigantic about them. The wide-eyed wonder of a babe has a grandeur in it which as children they lose. They seem to me to be prophets of a mightier race."

To his own children he was devoted. From the first he would, when my mother and he were alone, carry me in my bassinet into the drawing-room that he might watch my baby-gestures; and one of the very early things which I remember is that he helped the Master of Balliol to toss my brother and myself in a shawl. Later, he made us, though still very young, as much as possible his little companions. My mother was not strong enough to walk as far as we did, and so my father would harness my brother and myself to her garden carriage, and himself push from behind; and in this fashion we raced up hill and down dale. When the days were warm enough, perhaps we sat together on a bank in one of our home-fields, and he would read to us, or in cold weather would play football with us boys in an old chalk-pit, or build castles of flint on the top of the "Beacon Cliff," and we all then cannonaded from a distance, or he would teach us to shoot with bow and arrow. Some days we went flower-hunting, and on our return home, if the flower was unknown, he would say, " Bring me my Baxter's *Flowering Plants*," to look it out for us.

If it was rainy or stormy, and we were kept indoors, he often built cities for us with bricks, or played battledore and shuttlecock; or sometimes he read Grimm's *Fairy Stories* or repeated ballads to us. I remember his emphatic recitation in those far-off years of

> " Malbrouck s'en va-t'en guerre,
>   Mironton, mironton, mirontaine,"

and of " Si le roi m'avait donné
       Paris sa grand' ville,"

and of   " Ye Mariners of England,"

and of   " The Burial of Sir John Moore."

On feast days he would blow bubbles and then grow
much excited over the "gorgeous colours and landscapes, and the planets breaking off from their suns,
and the single star becoming a double star," which he
saw in these bubbles; or if it were evening he would
help us to act scenes from some well-known play.
He enjoyed superintending our boy-charades, and if
a prologue had to be written would make the most
amusing part of it.

In the autumn we had frequent brushing up of leaves
from the lawns, and he would employ us in helping to
make new glades through the shrubs or in re-shingling
old paths. It was a red-letter day when an Italian
organ-grinder came, as he did more years than one, and
was asked to warm himself by our bonfire of leaves and
wood, while my father and he told stories of Savoy,
Piedmont and Lombardy. My father was always interested in the imaginative views which we children took
of our surroundings. Of these I may give one instance:
how Lionel had been brought from his bed at night,
wrapt in a blanket, to see the great comet, and suddenly
awaking and looking out at the starry night, asked, " Am
I dead? "

The chief anxiety of my parents, I remember, was
that we should be strictly truthful, and my father's words,
spoken long ago, still dwell with me, " A truthful man
generally has all virtues." He was very particular about
our being courteous to the poor. The severest punishment he ever gave me, though that was, it must be
confessed, slight, was for some want of respect to one of
our servants.

The first Latin I learnt from him was Horace's
O fons Bandusiæ, and the first Greek the beginning of

the *Iliad*. Before this he liked to make us learn
and repeat ballads, and simple poems about Nature, but
he would never teach us his own poems, or allow us
to get them by heart.

In the summer as children we generally passed
through London to Lincolnshire, and he would take
us for a treat to Westminster Abbey, the Zoological
Gardens, the Tower of London, the Elgin Marbles at
the British Museum, or the National Gallery. In the
last he much delighted and would point us out the
various excellences of the different masters; he always
led the way first of all to the " Raising of Lazarus "
by Sebastian del Piombo and to Titian's " Bacchus and
Ariadne."

A favourite saying was, " Make the lives of children
as beautiful and as happy as possible." In the later
years of his life his grandchildren loved a romp with him,
and enjoyed their drives when he would fight them with
newspapers or play " pat-a-cake " with them. To the end
he liked a "frolic with young things," and when on one
of his last walks he met the village school-children, he
pointed his stick at them, barking like a dog to make
them laugh. In 1889, after he had turned eighty, he
wrote the lullaby in " Romney's Remorse," partly for his
little grandson Lionel:

> Father and mother will watch you grow,
> And gather the roses whenever they blow,
> And find the white heather wherever you go,
>   My sweet.

These anecdotes about him and his children, as I
read them over, seem trivial enough, yet I preserve them,
as testifying in their way to the " eternal youth of the
poet."

The year 1854 opened with the booming of cannon from Portsmouth, where the artillery were practising for the Crimean war. On March 16th Lionel was born. My father when he heard of the birth was looking through the study window at the planet Mars "as he glowed like a ruddy shield on the Lion's breast," and so determined to give the name Lionel.

After Lionel's birth he writes to Mrs Cameron and to John Forster:

March 22nd, 1854.

MY DEAR MRS CAMERON,

In my first batch of letters, sent off in all directions, when the new babe was born, I omitted to write to you, not willingly, but of necessity, not knowing your " Terrace," and my wife, who did know, not being to be spoken to....But I hope that this day, the sixth from her confinement, will, ere it fade (a very brilliant one over cape and sea), see her well, except for weakness. I have been mesmerizing her, which, she says, has done her a great deal of good. If she could but get a sleepful night, I have no doubt it would be all right by the morrow. As for the little fellow, he is as jolly as can be, and hardly cries at all yet. Little Hallam watches him, awe-struck, cannot make him out, and occasionally wails over him. I daresay that these are phenomena which you have often tenderly watched in your own family. You have not written, which I would far rather impute to the fact of my not having written than to the possibility of your being unwell. Pray Heaven the last be not the case with you; neither has Mary Marshall answered, which makes me anxious about her. God bless you, dear Julia Cameron, and

Believe me affectionately yours,

A. TENNYSON.

FARRINGFORD HOUSE, ISLE OF WIGHT,
March 29th, 1854.

MY DEAR FORSTER,

I understand from Archibald Peel that you are aggrieved at my not writing to you: that is wrong, morbid I think. I almost never write except in answer. Why, if you wished to know of me did you not write to me and you would have heard? Pray don't be distrustful. I love you all the same, tho' I should not write for 100 years.

Now it happens that a letter was half written to you partly to condole with you on the loss of dear good genial Talfourd, partly to announce the birth of another son of mine. I had dozens of letters to indite at that time to female cousins, etc., and I put this by to finish another day, and I cannot find it, or I would send it to prove that you are not forgotten, but you *must* be more trustful of me, or how can we get on? You must at any rate try the effect of a small note addrest to *me* before you find fault with me.

A reason for my not writing much is the bad condition of my right eye which quite suddenly came on as I was reading or trying to read small Persian text. You know perhaps how very minute in some of those Eastern tongues are the differences of letters: a little dot more or less: in a moment, after a three hours' hanging over this scratchy text, my right eye became filled with great masses of floating blackness, and the other eye similarly affected tho' not so badly. I am in a great fear about them, and think of coming up to town about them, for (whatever you may conjecture) I have not been in town for many months, not ever since I came here — did not even pass thro' town on my way here but went by Kingston.

I beseech your and all my friends' most charitable interpretation of whatever I do or may be said to do.

Our post only allows us from 11 o'clock to 1 o'clock to receive and answer letters which is (I think) another reason why I write so few.

I have been correcting my brother Frederick's proofs[1]. I dare say you may have seen notice of their approaching publication. He is a true poet, though his book (I think) ought to have been a shorter one.

Farewell, my dear fellow, God bless you and keep you.

Yours affectionately and unchangingly,

A. TENNYSON.

My wife's kind regards to you: she has been in a great state of suffering and sleeplessness for nine days, but at last I set her right by mesmerizing, — the effect was really wonderful.

In April the diary says that he drew my mother out in her garden chair to see the "wealth of daffodils" and the ruby sheaths of the lime leaves. At this time Edward Fitzgerald stayed at Farringford for a fortnight; he sketched and my father carved in wood. One day Fitzgerald brought home bunches of horned poppies and yellow irises over which like a boy he was ecstatic. In the evenings he played Mozart, or translated Persian Odes for my father, who, as has been said in the letter to Forster, had hurt his eyes by poring over a small-printed Persian Grammar: until this with Hafiz and other Persian books had to be hidden away, for he had seen "the Persian letters stalking like giants round the walls of his room." My father observed that his best working days were "in the early spring, when Nature begins to awaken from her winter sleep."

[1] *Days and Hours.*

To this date belongs the following letter to a friend:

You will not often see anything so sweet as my little, not quite two years old boy, who is toddling up and down the room, and saying, " Da, date," and "dada," meaning "give" in a very respectable Italian lingo, pointing to everything that strikes his fancy. Singularly enough the very day when I despatched my note to you another boy was born at 9 p.m., a lusty young fellow, who strikes the elder one with awe, sometimes into sympathetic tears, sometimes into a kind of mimic bleating, when he hears the younger one's inarticulate cooings. The first we had was born dead (a great grief to us), really the finest boy of the three; and I nearly broke my heart with going to look at him. He lay like a little warrior, having fought the fight, and failed, with his hands clenched, and a frown on his brow....If my latest born were to die to-night, I do not think that I should suffer so much as I did, looking on that noble little fellow who had never seen the light. My wife, who had had a most terrible time lasting near the whole of one Easter Sunday, never saw him. Well for her.

Yours, A. TENNYSON.

In May my father stayed in London and in August visited Glastonbury, Wells and the Cheddar Cliffs.

My father's letter-diary.

May 18*th*, 1854. 60 *Lincoln's Inn Fields.* I called on Moxon to arrange the " Illustrated Edition of Poems," and we went round to the artist Creswick, a capital broad genial fellow; Mulready, an old man, was full of vivacity and showed me lots of his drawings and one or two of his pictures. Then on to Horsley who was likewise very amiable and said that I was the painter's poet, etc., then on to Millais, who has agreed to come down in a month's time and take little Hallam as an illustration of " Dora." Sir E. Landseer I did not call upon and Holman Hunt was out of town.

Went to Forster's, and am going now to dine with Spedding somewhere, and then going to the Exhibition.

May 21*st.* Grove called and will be ready to show us the Crystal Palace. On Friday I dine with Frederick Locker, on Saturday with Forster.

May 22*nd.* I went to the Crystal Palace yesterday with Weld: certainly a marvellous place, but yet all in confusion. I do not think that it will be worth while to go up on the 10th for the opening, as it will be by no means so striking an affair as the last opening, 1851. I was much pleased with the Pompeian house and with the Iguanodons and Ichthyosaurs. I dined with Frank Lushington at the Oxford and Cambridge Club afterwards; Horatio dined with us. Tom Taylor came to Spedding's in the evening and gave me a book of Breton ballads, exceedingly beautiful, many of them.

May 23*rd.* I called on Hallam yesterday, he looks very well.

August.

I came to Glastonbury after parting from Grant[1], then to Yeovil in a fly, 17 miles, which rather jarred against my paternity when I thought that little Hallam and Lionel had to be educated. I went to the Abbey. As soon as I got there, there rose an awful thunderstorm, and I took shelter over Arimathæan Joseph's bones in

---

[1] Sir Alexander Grant who was first head of the University of Bombay, afterwards Principal of the University of Edinburgh.

the crypt of his chapel for they say (credat Judæus) he lies there.   Only one arch remains.

Walked over to Wells.   To Wookey Hole this morning, a cave; it was not quite what I wanted to see, tho' very grim.   Am at the Swan Hotel, shall go over to Cheddar to-morrow.

Arrived at Cheddar to-day and have just seen a stalactite cavern, a thing I had never seen before.

August 17*th*.   Corfe Castle, Christchurch, very well worth seeing: Bournemouth fashionable, not at all a place to buy a house in.   We found an old Waterloo soldier on the coast.

When my father had returned to Farringford, he and my mother "saw a great deal of the Simeons, Aubrey de Vere and Baron de Schroeter from Swainston, and lengthy were the discussions on Roman Catholicism." My father was much impressed by the deeply felt religious enthusiasm of the Baron, who was like an old ascetic monk, and anxious to convert my parents.

Of Sir John Simeon's first visits his daughter, Mrs Richard Ward, writes:

On the day of Lionel's christening my father paid his first visit to Farringford, and found the family party just returning from church.   During these early years, it was one of my father's greatest pleasures to ride or drive over from Swainston in the summer afternoons.   He and the Tennysons would go long expeditions through the lanes and over the downs: then back through the soft evening air to dinner and to the long evening of talk and of reading, which knit "that fair companionship" and made it "such a friendship as had mastered time."

It was then that my father worked at "Maud," morning and evening, sitting in his hard high-backed wooden chair in his little room at the top of the house. His "sacred pipes," as he called them, were half an hour after breakfast, and half an hour after dinner, when no one was allowed to be with him, for then his best thoughts came to him. As he made the different poems he would repeat or read them. The constant reading of the new poems aloud was the surest way of helping him to find out .any defects there might be. During his "sacred half-hours" and his other working hours and even on the Downs, he would murmur his new passages or new lines as they came to him, a habit which had always been his since boyhood, and which caused the Somersby cook to say "What is master Awlfred always a praying for?"

Aubrey de Vere writes of this year:

In 1854 I went from Swainston, the residence of Sir John Simeon, my friend, and the friend no less of Alfred Tennyson, in whose elegiac lines his memory is embalmed for ever, to Farringford, where the poet then made abode with his wife and two children. The eldest was about two years old; the other an infant in arms; and I was so much struck by his eyes, the most contemplative which I had ever seen, that I exclaimed, "When that child grows to be a man he must be a Carthusian monk!" "Nothing of the sort," was the answer I received; "but a happy husband, and a happy father, in a happy home." The home I stood in was a happy home; and the fortnight I spent in it was one I can never forget. The recollection of it is all the more delightful because it carries with it little sense of variety, "So like, so very like was day to day." The year had reached its zenith: the sky was almost always blue, and the lovely gleam of sea was a somewhat darker blue, while the healthful breezes of Freshwater prevented even the noontide from feeling sultry. The earlier part of the day I spent chiefly in reading and writing: in the afternoon we sometimes read aloud in the open air, or rather we listened to the Poet's reading, with such distractions alone as were caused by a bird-note louder than the rest or a distant sea-gleam more bright. On one occasion our book, which we agreed in greatly admiring, was Coventry Patmore's *Angel in the House*, then recent. Alfred and I had many a breezy walk along the Downs and as far as The Needles, sometimes with distant views of the coast flushed by sunset, sometimes with a nearer

one of the moonbeams " marbling " the wet sea-sands, as the
wave recoiled, which last always reminded me of Landor's
lines,

> " And the long moonbeam on the hard wet sands
> Lay like a jasper column half uprear'd."

Tennyson was engaged on his new poem " Maud." Its origin
and composition were, as he described them, singular. He had
accidentally lighted upon a poem of his own which begins, " O
that 'twere possible," and which had long before been published
in a selected volume got up by Lord Northampton for the aid of
a sick clergyman. It had struck him, in consequence, I think, of
a suggestion made by Sir John Simeon, that, to render the poem
fully intelligible, a preceding one was necessary. He wrote it;
the second poem too required a predecessor; and thus the
whole work was written, as it were, *backwards*. The readers of
" Maud " seldom observe that in the love-complexities of that
poem the birds take a vehement part. The " birds in the high
Hall-garden" are worldly birds, factious for the young Lord and
the millionaire Brother :

> Where is Maud, Maud, Maud,
> One is come to woo her ?

The " birds in our wood " are as ardent partizans of the
lovers. I remarked to the Poet on this circumstance; but his
answer was as vague as the "mowt a beän " of the " Northern
Farmer."

This summer my father wrote of Freshwater to a
friend : " Ours is by far in my opinion the most note-
worthy part of the island, with an air on the Downs
' worth,' as somebody said, ' sixpence a pint.' "

Through the autumn and winter evenings he translated aloud to my mother the sixth *Æneid* of Virgil and
Homer's description of Hades, and they read Dante's
Inferno together. Whewell's *Plurality of Worlds* he
also carefully studied. " It is to me anything," he writes,
" but a satisfactory book. It is inconceivable that the
whole Universe was merely created for us who live in
this third-rate planet of a third-rate sun."

The excitement about the Crimean War was intense. On October 10th the papers were full of the particulars of the battle of the Alma [1]. The journal says: "Looking from the Beacon and seeing the white cliffs and the clear sea, their violet gray shading seemed to us tender and sad; perhaps the landscape seemed so sad because of the sorrowful news of the death-roll in the Crimea and of the death of our neighbour Colonel Hood in the trenches."

In November an unknown friend sent an account of the charge of the Heavy Brigade at Balaclava on October 25th, — how the Scots Greys and the Inniskilleners flung themselves against the solid Russian column. The writer says: "Our ears were frenzied by the monotonous incessant cannonade going on for days together."

On November 22nd Millais' long promised visit was paid. He was "beguiled into sweeping up leaves and burning them [2]. He made sketches of Hallam and his mother, Hallam appearing in the illustration to 'Dora.'" There were talks with Millais "as to the limits of realism in painting." My father hated the modern realism in painting and literature, notably as shown by the French schools. With regard to certain English pictures he said to Millais that from his point of view, "if you

---

[1] My father wrote the first stanza of a song entitled "The Alma River," which my mother finished and set to music:

Frenchman, a hand in thine!
    Our flags have waved together!
Let us drink to the health of thine and mine
    At the battle of Alma River.

Our flags together furl'd,
    Henceforward no other strife —
Than which of us most shall help the world,
    Which lead the noblest life.

Then pledge we our glorious dead,
    Swear to be one for ever,
And God's best blessing on each dear head
    That rests by the Alma River.

[2] Perhaps this suggested his fine early picture upon the subject.

have human beings before a wall, the wall ought to be picturesquely painted, and in harmony with the idea pervading the picture, but must not be made obtrusive by the bricks being *too* minutely drawn, since it is the human beings that ought to have the real interest for us in a dramatic picture."

When Millais left, my parents read together Souvestre's account of the Bretons. The fact that their most popular songs are religious and that, when the cholera was among them, they would not listen to the doctors until they put their advice in song, set to national airs, struck my father. On Dec. 2nd he wrote " The Charge of the Light Brigade [1] " in a few minutes, after reading the description in the *Times* in which occurred the phrase " some one had blundered," and this was the origin of the metre of his poem. Christmas Eve is kept by his " blowing bubbles for the children, and making fun for them by humping up his shoulders high, and pretending to be a giant."

At the end of the year he received Professor Ferrier's *History of Philosophy*, with the following letter:

St Andrews, Dec. 17th, 1854.

Dear Sir,

You were among the very first to whom my book was to be sent and I supposed that you had received it some six weeks ago. Possibly Blackwood did not know your address and therefore sent it to your publisher.

If anything strikes you as inconsecutive in the reasoning you will do me a favour by pointing it out.

One eminent authority has given it as his opinion that there is a non sequitur in the passage from Prop. I. to Prop. II. To me this seems odd. I esteem it a high honour to have now made your acquaintance and a great privilege to be allowed to subscribe myself

Very truly yours, F. Ferrier.

[1] Published in the *Examiner*, Dec. 9th.

Frederick Tennyson wrote from Florence :

Dec. 30th, 1854.

MY DEAR E. AND A.,

Browning comes in occasionally, but poor Mrs B. never stirs out during the winter. Under the rose, they are both preparing new poems, Browning a batch of Lyrics which are to be the real thing, Mrs B. a kind of Metrical Romance. Though I have the highest esteem for Browning, and believe him to be a man of infinite learning, jest and bonhommie, and moreover a sterling heart that reverbs no hollowness, I verily believe his school of poetry to be the most grotesque conceivable. With the exception of the " Blot on the 'Scutcheon," through which you may possibly grope your way without the aid of an Ariadne, the rest appear to me to be Chinese puzzles, trackless labyrinths, unapproachable nebulosities. Yet he has a very Catholic taste in poetry, doing justice to everything good in all poets past or present, and he is one who has a profound admiration of Alfred. I hear from Palgrave that A. has a new poem on the stocks ; a few of the best stanzas in your next letter I should prize highly, and the Brownings would be delighted to see a specimen of it. I suppose the poem on the " Charge of the Six Hundred " in the *Examiner*, signed A. T., is really by Alfred. Browning sent me the paper but I could give him no information on the subject.

Your affectionate brother, F. TENNYSON.

On Jan. 10th, 1855, my father had " finished, and read out, several lyrics of ' Maud.' " The weather in January and February was arctic and the waves froze on the beach.

The news of the loss of Sir John Franklin, my mother's uncle, in the Arctic Regions was at this time " a great shock [1]." It is interesting to note that Dr Kane, who was on the second Grinnell Expedition in search of Sir John, honoured my father by naming a natural rock

[1] My mother thought that her uncle's last words to her were : " If I am lost, remember, Emily, my firm belief that there is open sea at the North Pole. "

column 480 feet high, on a pedestal 280 feet high, to the
north of latitude 79 degrees, " Tennyson's Monument."

Dr Kane wrote:

I remember well the emotions of my party as it first broke
upon our view.   Cold and sick as I was, I brought back a sketch
of it, which may have interest for the reader, though it scarcely
suggests the imposing dignity of this magnificent landmark.
Those who are happily familiar with the writings of Tennyson
and have communed with his spirit in the wilderness, will apprehend the impulse that inscribed the scene with his name.

In February my father " translated aloud three Idylls
of Theocritus, *Hylas*, *The Island of Cos*, and *The Syracusan Women*."   In March " Woolner made a medallion
of him (the best likeness that had yet been made)."

On March 22nd my father received this letter from
Ruskin:

DENMARK HILL, CAMBERWELL,
21st March, 1855.

DEAR MR TENNYSON,

I venture to write to you, because as I was talking
about you with Mr Woolner yesterday, he gave me more pleasure than I can express by telling me that you wished to see my
" Turners."

By several untoward chances I have been too long hindered
from telling you face to face how much I owe you   So you see
at last I seize the wheel of fortune by its nearest spoke, begging
you with the heartiest entreaty I can, to tell me when you are
likely to be in London and to fix a day if possible that I may
keep it wholly for you, and prepare my " Turners " to look
their rosiest and best.   Capricious they are as enchanted opals,
but they must surely shine for you.

Any day will do for me if you give me notice two or three
days before, but please come soon, for I have much to say to
you and am eager to say it, above all to tell you how for a
thousand things I am gratefully and respectfully yours,

J. RUSKIN.

In April my father walked to Bonchurch, and wrote
to my mother: " If I stop another day here, I may have

a chance of seeing double stars thro' a telescope of
Dr Mann's, a very clever interesting doctor with whom
I spent two hours this morning.   He showed me things
thro' his microscope."

He was home again on April 25th, and "copied out
'Maud' for the press, and read 'The Lady of the Lake,'
having just finished Goethe's 'Helena.'"

On June 6th he writes: "I have strangely enough
accepted the Oxford Doctorship.   Friends told me I
ought to accept it, so I did."   Temple [1] had suggested my
father for that degree.   My parents stayed at Balliol ; and
my father said, as he sat in the Balliol gardens, "The
shouts of the Undergraduates from the theatre are
like the shouts of the Roman crowd, 'Christiani ad
Leones!'"   He was very nervous before going, but
entered the theatre quite calmly with Sir John Burgoyne,
the stately-looking Montalembert, and Sir de Lacy Evans.
He sat on the steps nearly under Lord Derby, then there
was one great shout for "In Memoriam," one for "Alma"
and one for "Inkermann."   The sea of upturned faces was
very striking, and my father had a "tremendous ovation"
when he received his degree.   The new doctor ordinarily
borrows a doctor's robes from a tailor and just wears
them in the Sheldonian Theatre for the ceremony.   But
my father after luncheon asked the Master of Balliol
whether it would be against rule and propriety if he
might have a smoke, as it was his fancy to do so, among
the green trees when clad in his red doctorial robes.
The Master said that he might do so, and he smoked in
the then walled-in Master's garden, now open to the
college.   "In the evening at Magdalen he had long
talks with Mr Gladstone and Montalembert."   Next
day Arthur Butler and Max Müller took my father and
mother about Oxford, and to the Bodleian, to see the

---

[1] Now Archbishop of Canterbury.

Illuminated Missals, and Dr Wellesley showed them the Raffaelle sketches. At night they had tea with Professor Johnson and Professor Adams, and looked at the Nebulæ in Cassiopeia through the big telescope, the Ring Nebula in Lyra and also some double stars.

On July 7th they reached home, and the last touch was put to " Maud," before giving it to the publisher. Up to the time of my father's death, when his friends asked him to read aloud from his own poetry, he generally chose " Maud," the " Ode on the Duke of Wellington," or " Guinevere."

Translations into French of " Ring out, wild bells," and " Mariana in the Moated Grange," were sent him from France.

He pointed out "what a poor language French is for translating English poetry, although it is the best language for delicate *nuances* of meaning. How absurd ' Ring out, wild bells ' sounds in the translation 'Sonnez, Cloches, Sonnez,' and what a ridiculous rendering of ' He cometh not, she said ' is ' Tom ne vient pas '!¹ "

August 6th. " The Balaclava Charge " with the following short preface was forwarded to John Forster to be printed on a fly-leaf for the Crimean Soldiers.

---

¹ About this time he wrote a letter to the Breton poet Hippolyte Lucas:
Une Lettre inédite d'Alfred Tennyson à Hippolyte Lucas.

CHER MONSIEUR,
  Ce m'est véritablement une douce chose que d'avoir trouvé une âme poétique qui puisse fraterniser avec la mienne de l'autre côté de la grande mer. Les poètes, comme vous le dites fort bien, sont ou plutôt devraient être reliés ensemble par une chaîne électrique, car ils ne doivent pas parler seulement pour leurs compatriotes. J'ai lu vos vers plusieurs fois, et ils m'ont causé plus de plaisir à chaque nouvelle lecture. Je suis particulièrement flatté de leur ressemblance avec mon propre poème.
  Si jamais je fais un voyage en Bretagne, j'aurai l'honneur et le plaisir de vous faire une visite. Votre province est riche en légendes poétiques de toute espèce, et par cela même particulièrement chère aux Anglais. J'espère la voir un jour, et vous en même temps.
  En attendant, croyez-moi, cher monsieur, votre tout dévoué
                                              ALFRED TENNYSON.

August 8th, 1855.

Having heard that the brave soldiers before Sebastopol, whom I am proud to call my countrymen, have a
liking for my ballad on the charge of the Light Brigade
at Balaclava, I have ordered a thousand copies of it to
be printed for them.   No writing of mine can add to the
glory they have acquired in the Crimea; but if what I
have heard be true they will not be displeased to receive
these copies from me, and to know that those who sit
at home love and honour them.

ALFRED TENNYSON.

To John Forster.

[*Undated.*]

MY DEAR FORSTER,

In the first place thanks for your critique
which seems to me good and judicious.   Many thanks,
my wife will write to you about it; but what I am writing
to you now about is a matter which interests me very
much.   My friend Chapman of 3, Stone Buildings,
Lincoln's Inn, writes to me thus: — "An acquaintance
of mine in the department of the S.P.G. as he calls it
(Society for the Propagation of the Gospel) was saying
how a chaplain in the Crimea sent by the Society
writes to the Society — (neither he nor the Society being
suspected of any Tennysonian prejudices) — ' The *greatest
service you can do*[1] just now is to send out on printed
slips Mr A. T.'s ' Charge at Balaclava.'   It is the greatest
favourite of the soldiers — half are singing it, and all
want to have it in black and white, so as to read what
has so taken them.' "

Now, my dear Forster, you see I cannot possibly be
deaf to such an appeal.   I wish to send out about 1000
slips, and I don't at all want the S.P.G. or any one to

[1] Thus underscored in the original.

send out the *version last printed*: it would, I believe, quite disappoint the soldiers. Don't you live quite close to the S.P.G.? Could you not send Henry over to say that *I* am sending over the soldiers' version of my ballad, and beg them not to stir in the matter? The soldiers are the best critics in what pleases them. I send you a copy which retains the "Light Brigade," and the "blunder'd"; and I declare it is the best of the two, and that the criticism of two or three London friends (not yours) induced me to spoil it. For Heaven's sake get *this* copy fairly printed at once, and sent out. I have sent it by this post likewise to Moxon, but you are closer to your printer. Concoct with him how it is all to be managed: I am so sorry that I am not in town to have done it at once. I have written a little note to the soldiers which need not be sent — just as you like. It might be merely printed "From A. Tennyson." Please see to all this: and see that there are *no mistakes;* and I will be bound to you for evermore, and more than ever yours in great haste,

A. TENNYSON.

P.S. I am convinced now after writing it out that this *is* the best version.

The following tribute was received from Scutari :

We had in hospital a man of the Light Brigade, one of the few who survived that fatal mistake, the Balaclava charge ; but which, deplorable as it was, at least tended to show the high state of discipline attained in the British army. I spoke to several of those engaged in that deadly conflict, and they could describe accurately the position of the Russian cannon ; were perfectly aware when obeying that word of command, that they rode to almost certain death. This patient had received a kick in the chest from a horse long after the battle of Balaclava, while in barracks at Scutari. He was depressed in spirits, which prevented him from throwing off the disease engendered by the blow. The doctor remarked that he wished the soldier could be roused. Amongst other remedies leeches were prescribed. While watching them I tried to enter into a conversation with him, spoke of the charge, but could elicit only monosyllabic replies. A copy of Tennyson's poems having been lent me that morning, I took it out and read it. The man, with kindling eye, at once entered upon a spirited description of the fatal gallop between the guns' mouths to and from that cannon-crowded height. He asked to hear it again, but, as by this time a number of convalescents were gathered around, I slipped out of the ward. The chaplain who had lent me the poem, understanding the enthusiasm with which it had been received, afterwards procured from England a number of copies for distribution. In a few days the invalid requested the doctor to discharge him for duty, being now in health; but whether the cure was effected by the leeches or the poem it is impossible to say. On giving the card the medical man murmured, "Well done, Tennyson!"

On one of the anniversaries of the Balaclava charge a banquet was given in London, and my father was pressed to attend. Being unable to do so, he sent the following letter to the chairman of the committee:

FARRINGFORD, FRESHWATER.

DEAR SIR,

I cannot attend your banquet, but I enclose £5 to defray some of its expenses, or to be distributed as you may think fit among the most indigent of the survivors of that glorious charge. A blunder it may have been, but one for which England should be grateful, having thereby learnt that her soldiers are the most honest and most obedient under the sun. I will drink a cup of wine on the 25th to the health and long life of all your fine fellows; and, thanking yourself and your comrades heartily for the cordial invitation sent me, I pray you all to believe me, now and ever, your admiring fellow-countryman,

A. TENNYSON.

He had intended to write a poem on the soldiers' battle of Inkermann, but only got as far as the first line: "Strong eight thousand of Inkermann."

At this time my father's friend Harry Lushington, who with his brother Franklin had published some stirring poems on the Crimean war, died in Paris.

My father's letter-diary of days in the New Forest.

August 31*st.*   Haven't had the heart to get further than Winchester and Salisbury.   I am going to-day to take a gig across country to Lyndhurst.

Lyndhurst, Sept. 1*st.*   Tho' I had said that the New Forest, for didn't I expect that it was disforested, would not do again; tho', when I started this morning, I got on the wrong track for four miles or so out of the way of the great timber; the vast solemn beeches delighted me, but my soul was not satisfied, for I did not meet with any so very large beech as I had met with before.   Yet I rejoiced in the beeches and have resolved to stay till Monday and see them twice again. I have lost the tobacco case which Simeon gave me; I am grieved, but it was so like the colour of last year's beech leaves that I did not see it when I turned to leave the spot where I had smoked.

Crown Hotel, Lyndhurst. Sept. 2*nd.*   I lost my way in the Forest to-day, and have walked I don't know how many miles.   I found a way back to Lyndhurst by resolutely following a track which brought me at last to a turnpike.   On this I went a mile in the wrong direction, that is towards Christchurch, then met a surly fellow who grudgingly told me I was four miles from Lyndhurst, whereby I turned and walked to Lyndhurst. My admiration of the Forest is great: it is true old wild English Nature, and then the fresh heath-sweetened air is so delicious.   The Forest is grand.

London, Sept. 28th. I dined yesterday with the Brownings and had a very pleasant evening. Both of them are great admirers of poor little " Maud." The two Rossettis came in during the evening[1].

October 1st. I dined at Twickenham, my mother looking very well and intending to keep the house on another year. I also dined with the Camerons last night, she is more wonderful than ever I think in her mild-beaming benevolence. I read " Maud " to five or six people at the Brownings (on Sept. 28th).

Mrs Browning writes thereupon to my mother:

13 DORSET STREET, *October*, 1855.

MY DEAR MRS TENNYSON,

If I had not received your kindest of letters I had yet made up my mind not to leave England without writing to you to thank you (surely it would have been your due) for the deep pleasure we had in Mr Tennyson's visit to us. He didn't come back as he said he would to teach me the " Brook " (which I persist nevertheless in fancying I understand a little), but he did so much and left such a voice (both him " and a voice! ") crying out " Maud " to us, and helping the effect of the poem by the personality, that it's an increase of joy and life to us ever. Then may we not venture to think now of Alfred Tennyson *our friend*? and was it not worth while coming from Italy to England for so much? Let me say too another thing, that though I was hindered (through having women friends with me, whom I loved and yet could not help wishing a little further just then) from sitting in the smoke and hearing the talk of the next room, yet I heard some sentences which, in this materialistic low-talking world, it was comfort and triumph to hear from the lips of such a man. So I thank you both, and my husband's thanks go with mine.

As to a visit to you, how pleasant that you should ask us!

---

[1] Gabriel Rossetti wrote to William Allingham about this evening in an unpublished letter: " He is quite as glorious in his way as Browning in his, and perhaps of the two even more impressive on the whole personally."

This year we could not have gone, next year perhaps we shall not be able any more * * * but every year of our lives it will be pleasant to think that you have wished it. Dear Mrs Tennyson, you do not mind the foolish remarks on " Maud " * * * do you? These things are but signs of an advance made, of the tide rising. People on the shore are troubled in their picking up of shells a little.

Kiss your children for me: I hope my child may play with them before long. My husband's " Men and Women " shall go to Mr Tennyson on the publication, not to trouble him (understand) with exaction of a letter or opinion, but simply as a sign of personal regard and respect.

Dear Mrs Tennyson and dear Mr Tennyson, believe us *both* very affectionately yours, though I have but the name of

ELIZABETH BARRETT BROWNING.

P.S. (We leave England to-morrow.) God bless you, dear and admirable friends. My wife feels what she says, and I feel with her.

Affectionately yours,

ROBERT BROWNING.

On his return the evening books were Milton, Shakespeare's *Sonnets*, Thackeray's *Humourists*, some of Hallam's *History* and of Carlyle's *Cromwell*.

This Christmas " Mr. Lear paid us a visit and sang his settings of ' Mariana,' ' Lotos-Eaters,' ' Let not the solid earth,' and ' Oh that 'twere possible.' "

One day my father received " an interesting letter telling him of a man who had been roused from a state of suicidal despondency by ' The Two Voices.' "

At the end of the year an unknown Nottingham artizan came to call. My father asked him to dinner and at his request read " Maud." It appears that the poor man had sent his poems beforehand. They had been acknowledged, but had not been returned, and had been forgotten. He was informed that the poems,

thus sent, were always looked at, although my father
and mother had not time to pass judgment on them.
A most pathetic incident of this kind, my father told
me, happened to him at Twickenham, when a Waterloo
soldier brought twelve large cantos on the battle of
Waterloo. The veteran had actually taught himself
in his old age to read and write that he might thus
commemorate Wellington's great victory. The epic lay
for some time under the sofa in my father's study, and
was a source of much anxiety to him. How could he go
through such a vast poem? One day he mustered up
courage and took a portion out. It opened on the
heading of a canto: "The Angels encamped above the
field of Waterloo." On that day, at least, he "read no
more." He gave the author, when he called for his
manuscript, this criticism: "Though great images loom
here and there, your poem could not be published as a
whole." The old man answered nothing, wrapt up each
of the twelve cantos carefully, placed them in a strong
oak case and carried them off. He was asked to come
again but he never came.

CHAPTER XIX.

"MAUD[1]."

After reading "Maud":

Leave him to us, ye good and sage,
Who stiffen in your middle age.
Ye loved him once, but now forbear;
Yield him to those who hope and dare,
And have not yet to forms consign'd
A rigid ossifying mind.

Ionica.

Pure lyrical poetry of every form had been essayed by my father before 1855, but a monodramatic lyric, like "Maud," was a novelty. In consequence its meaning and drift were widely misunderstood even by educated readers, which partly accounts for the outburst of hostile criticism that greeted its appearance. It is a "Drama of the Soul," set in a landscape glorified by Love, and according to Lowell, "The antiphonal voice to 'In Memoriam[2].'" Nothing perhaps more justified what has been said of my father, that had he not been a poet, he might have been remarkable as an actor, than his reading of "Maud," with all its complex contrasts of motive and

---

[1] The volume contained "Maud" (*written at Farringford*), "The Brook," "The Letters," "Ode on the death of the Duke of Wellington," "The Daisy," "To the Rev. F. D. Maurice," "Will," "The Charge of the Light Brigade."

[2] My father sometimes called "In Memoriam," "The Way of the Soul."

action. He generally prefaced his reading with an explanation, the substance of which has been given by Dr Mann in his *Maud Vindicated*.

[1] "At the opening of the drama, the chief person or hero of the action is introduced with scenery and incidents artistically disposed around his figure, so as to make the reader at once acquainted with certain facts in his history, which it is essential should be known. Although still a young man, he has lost his father some years before by a sudden and violent death, following immediately upon unforeseen ruin brought about by an unfortunate speculation in which the deceased had engaged. Whether the death was the result of accident, or self-inflicted in a moment of despair, no one knows, but the son's mind has been painfully possessed by a suspicion of villainy and foul play somewhere, because an old friend of his family became suddenly and unaccountably rich by the same transaction that had brought ruin to the dead. Shortly after the decease of his father, the bereaved young man, by the death of his mother, is left quite alone in the world. He continues thenceforth to reside in the retired village in which his early days have been spent, but the sad experiences of his youth have confirmed the bent of a mind constitutionally prone to depression and melancholy. Brooding in loneliness upon miserable memories and bitter fancies, his temperament as a matter of course becomes more and more morbid and irritable. He can see nothing in human affairs that does not awaken in him disgust and contempt. Evil glares out from all social arrangements, and unqualified meanness and selfishness appear in every human form, so he keeps to himself and chews the cud of cynicism and discontent apart from his kind. Such in rough outline is the figure the poet has sketched as the foundation and centre of his

[1] My father desired that the passage by Dr Mann, here quoted, should be inserted among his notes 1891–92.

plan * * *. Since the days of his early youth up to
the period when the immediate action of the poem is
supposed to commence, the dreamy recluse has seen
nothing of the family of the man to whom circumstances
have inclined him to attribute his misfortunes. This
individual, although since his accession to prosperity
the possessor of the neighbouring hall and of the
manorial lands of the village, has been residing abroad.
Just at this time however there are workmen up at the
dark old place, and a rumour spreads that the absentees
are about to return. This rumour, as a matter of course,
stirs up afresh rankling memories in the breast of the
recluse, and awakens there old griefs. But with the
group of associated recollections that come crowding
forth, there is one of the child Maud, who was in
happier days his merry playfellow. She will now
however be a child no longer. She will return as the
lady mistress of the mansion (being the only daughter
of the Squire, who is a widower). What will she be
like? He, who wonders, has heard somewhere that
she is singularly beautiful. But what is this to him?
Even while he thinks of her, he feels a chill presentiment,
suggested no doubt by her close relationship to one who
he considered had already worked him so much harm,
that she will bring with her a curse for him."

I shall never forget his last reading [1] of " Maud," on
August 24th, 1892. He was sitting in his high-backed
chair, fronting a southern window which looks over the
groves and yellow cornfields of Sussex toward the long
line of South Downs that stretches from Arundel to
Hastings (his high-domed Rembrandt-like head outlined
against the sunset-clouds seen through the western
window). His voice, low and calm in everyday life,
capable of delicate and manifold inflection, but with

---

[1] He owned that " Some of the passages are hard to read because they
have to be taken in one breath and require good lungs."

"organ-tones" of great power and range, thoroughly brought out the drama of the poem. You were at once put in sympathy with the hero. As he said himself, "This poem is a little *Hamlet*," the history of a morbid poetic soul, under the blighting influence of a recklessly speculative age. He is the heir of madness, an egotist with the makings of a cynic, raised to sanity by a pure and holy love which elevates his whole nature, passing from the height of triumph to the lowest depth of misery, driven into madness by the loss of her whom he has loved, and, when he has at length passed through the fiery furnace, and has recovered his reason, giving himself up to work for the good of mankind through the unselfishness born of his great passion. My father pointed out that even Nature at first presented herself to the man in sad visions.

And the flying gold of the ruin'd woodlands drove
    thro' the air.

The "blood-red heath" too is an exaggeration of colour; and his suspicion that all the world is against him is as true to his nature as the mood when he is "fantastically merry." "The peculiarity of this poem," my father added, "is that different phases of passion in one person take the place of different characters."

The passion in the first Canto was given by my father in a sort of rushing recitative through the long sweeping lines of satire and invective against the greed for money, and of horror at the consequences of the war of the hearth.

Then comes the first sight of Maud, and "visions of the night," and in Canto IV. a longing for calm, the reaction after a mood of bitterness, and yearning for

A philosopher's life in the quiet woodland ways.

But the clarion call of the " voice by the cedar tree " singing

> A passionate ballad gallant and gay,

awakens a love in the heart which revolutionizes and inspires the whole life. In Canto XI. my father expressed the longing for love in

> O let the solid ground
> Not fail beneath my feet:

in Canto XVII. the exultation of love, knowing that it is returned:

> Go not, happy day,
> From the shining fields.

But this blessedness is so intense that it borders on sadness, and my father's voice would break down when he came to

> I have led her home, my love, my only friend.
> There is none like her, none.

Joy culminates in " Come into the garden, Maud," and my father's eyes, which were through the other love-passages veiled by his drooping lids, would suddenly flash as he looked up and spoke these words, the passion in his voice deepening in the last words of the stanza.

> She is coming, my own, my sweet;
>   Were it ever so airy a tread,
> My heart would hear her and beat,
>   Were it earth in an earthy bed;
> My dust would hear her and beat,
>   Had I lain for a century dead;
> Would start and tremble under her feet,
>   And blossom in purple and red.

Then we heard after the duel the terrible wail of agony and despair in

> The fault was mine,

and the depth of forlorn misery in

> Courage, poor heart of stone!

when the man feels that he is going mad, both read with slow solemnity: then the delirious madness of

> O me, why have they not buried me deep enough?

The lyrics in "Maud" which my father himself liked best were

> I have led her home,

and   O that 'twere possible,

and   Courage, poor heart of stone!

About the mad-scene one of the best-known doctors for the insane wrote that it was "the most faithful representation of madness since Shakespeare."

It is notable that two such appreciative critics as Mr Gladstone and Dr Van Dyke wholly misapprehended the meaning of "Maud" until they heard my father read it, and that they both then publicly recanted their first criticisms. "No one but a noble-minded man would have done that" my father would say of Mr Gladstone. Dr Van Dyke's recantation he did not live to read[1].

Mr Gladstone's recantation runs thus:

I can now see, and I at once confess, that a feeling, which had reference to the growth of the war-spirit in the outer world at the date of this article (*Quarterly Review*, 1855), dislocated my

---

[1] When Fanny Kemble heard that my father read his "Maud" finely, she wrote: "I do not think any reading of Tennyson's can ever be as striking and impressive as that 'Curse of Boadicea' that he intoned to us, while the oak trees were writhing in the storm that lashed the windows and swept over Blackdown the day we were there." (Unpublished MS.)

frame of mind, and disabled me from dealing even tolerably with the work as a work of imagination.   Whether it is to be desired that a poem should require from common men a good deal of effort in order to comprehend it; whether all that is put into the mouth of the Soliloquist in "Maud" is within the lines of poetical verisimilitude, whether this poem has the full moral equilibrium which is so marked a characteristic of the sister-works; are questions open, perhaps, to discussion.   But I have neither done justice in the text to its rich and copious beauties of detail, nor to its great lyrical and metrical power.   And what is worse, I have failed to comprehend rightly the relation between particular passages in the poem and its general scope. This is, I conceive, not to set forth any coherent strain, but to use for poetical ends all the moods and phases allowable under the laws of the art, in a special form of character, which is impassioned, fluctuating and ill-grounded.   The design, which seems to resemble that of the Ecclesiastes in another sphere, is arduous; but Mr Tennyson's power of execution is probably nowhere greater.   Even as regards the passages devoted to war-frenzy, equity should have reminded me of the fine lines in the *latter* portion of x. 3 (Part I), and of the emphatic words v. 10 (Part II):

> I swear to you, lawful and lawless war
> Are scarcely even akin.

W. E. G. 1878 [1].

Among the few who recognized merit in "Maud" were Henry Taylor, Jowett and the Brownings.

From Henry Taylor.

COLONIAL OFFICE, LONDON,
31st July, 1855.

MY DEAR TENNYSON,

I thank you much for sending me "Maud."   I have only read it twice, but I have already a strong feeling of what it is.   I say a feeling and not an opinion, for I am always disposed to have as little as possible to say to opinions in matters poetical.

[1] Gladstone's *Gleanings*, Vol. II.

I felt the passion of it and the poetic spirit that is in it, and the poetic spirit that it seemed in some measure to bring back unto me. I am glad that there is some one living who can do me that service and glad that you are he.

Ever yours sincerely, H. TAYLOR.

In December Jowett writes:

I want to tell you how greatly I admire "Maud." No poem since Shakespeare seems to show equal power of the same kind, or equal knowledge of human nature. No modern poem contains more lines that ring in the ears of men. I do not know any verse out of Shakespeare in which the ecstasy of love soars to such a height.

He adds that the critics have "confused the hero with the author[1]."

Some of the reviews accused him of loving war,

[1] I take from Dr Mann, with some condensation, the following remarks about "Maud," because in the light of present criticism they are curious. "One member of the fraternity of critics immediately pronounced the poem to be a 'spasm,' another acutely discovered that it was a 'careless, visionary, and unreal allegory of the Russian War.' A third could not quite make up his mind whether the adjective 'mud' or 'mad' would best apply to the work, but thought, as there was only one small vowel redundant in the title in either case, both might do. A fourth found that the 'mud' concealed 'irony'; and the fifth, leaning rather to the mad hypothesis, nevertheless held that the madness was only assumed as an excuse for pitching the tone of the poetry in 'a key of extravagant sensibility.' Others of the multifold judgments were of opinion that it was 'a political fever,' an 'epidemic caught from the prevalent carelessness of thought and rambling contemplativeness of the time'; 'obscurity mistaken for profundity,' 'the dead level of prose run mad'; 'absurdity such as even partial friendship must blush to tolerate,' 'rampant and rabid bloodthirstiness of soul.' These are but a few of the pleasant suggestions which critical acumen brought forward as its explanations of the inspiration of numbers that must nevertheless be musical."

Maud Vindicated.

One of the anonymous letters my father received he enjoyed repeating with a humorous intonation:

SIR, I used to worship you, but now I hate you. I loathe and detest you. You beast! So you've taken to imitating Longfellow.

Yours in aversion * * *.

and urging the country to war, charges which he sufficiently answered in the "Epilogue to the Heavy Brigade," ending with these lines:

> And here the singer for his Art
>   Not all in vain may plead,
> The song that nerves a nation's heart
>   Is in itself a deed.

The truth is that though he advocated the war of defence and of liberty, and often said, " Peace at all price implies war at all cost," no one loathed war more than he did, or looked forward more passionately to the

Parliament of man, the Federation of the world,

. when the earth at last should be one.

> A warless world, a single race, a single tongue,
> I have seen her far away, for is not Earth as yet so
>   young?
> Every tiger madness muzzled, every serpent passion
>   kill'd,
> Every grim ravine a garden, every blazing desert till'd,
> Robed in universal harvest up to either pole she
>   smiles,
> *Universal ocean softly washing all her warless isles*[1].

What even his hero in " Maud " says is only that the sins of the nation, " civil war" as he calls them, are deadlier in their effect than what is commonly called war, and that they may be in a measure subdued by the war between nations which is an evil more easily recognized.

At first my father was nettled by these captious remarks of the " indolent reviewers," but afterwards would take no notice of them, except to speak of them in a half-pitiful, half-humorous, half-mournful manner. About

---

[1] This line he held to be one of the best of the kind he had ever written.

"Maud" and other monodramatic poems (the stories of which were his own creation) he said to me: "In a certain way, no doubt, poets and novelists, however dramatic they are, give themselves in their works. The mistake that people make is that they think the poet's poems are a kind of 'catalogue raisonné' of his very own self, and of all the facts of his life, not seeing that they often only express a poetic instinct, or judgment on character real or imagined, and on the facts of lives real or imagined. Of course some poems, like my 'Ode to Memory,' are evidently based on the poet's own nature, and on hints from his own life."

The poem was first entitled "Maud or the Madness." My father thought that part of the misunderstanding of "Maud" had arisen from a misconception of the story, so left me the following MS headings and notes.

Part I.

Sections

I.   Before the arrival of Maud.

II.   First sight of Maud.

III.   Visions of the night. The broad-flung ship-wrecking roar. In the Isle of Wight the roar can be heard nine miles away from the beach. (Many of the descriptions of Nature are taken from observations of natural phenomena at Farringford, although the localities in the poem are all imaginary.)

IV.   Mood of bitterness after fancied disdain.

V.   He fights against his growing passion.

VI.   First interview with Maud.

VII. He remembers his own and her father talking just before the birth of Maud.

VIII. That she did not return his love.

IX. First sight of the young lord.

X. The *Westminster Review* said this was an attack on John Bright. I did not know at the time that he was a Quaker. (It was not against Quakers but against peace-at-all-price men that the hero fulminates.)

XI. This was originally verse III. but I omitted it.

> Will she smile if he presses her hand,
> This lord-captain up at the Hall?
> Captain! he to hold a command!
> He can hold a cue, he can pocket a ball;
> And sure not a bantam cockerel lives
> With a weaker crow upon English land,
> Whether he boast of a horse that gains,
> Or cackle his own applause....
>
> What use for a single mouth to rage
> At the rotten creak of the State-machine;
> Tho' it makes friends weep and enemies smile,
> That here in the face of a watchful age,
> The sons of a gray-beard-ridden isle
> Should dance in a round of an old routine.

XII. Interview with Maud.

> "Maud, Maud, Maud" is like the rook's caw.
> "Maud is here, here, here" is like the call of the little birds.

XIII. Mainly prophetic. He sees Maud's brother who will not recognize him.

XVI. He will declare his love.

XVII.   Accepted.

XVIII. Happy. The sigh in the cedar branches seems to chime in with his own yearning.

"Sad astrology" is modern astronomy, for of old astrology was thought to sympathize with and rule man's fate.

Not die but live a life of truest breath. This is the central idea, the holy power of Love.

XXI.   Before the Ball.

XXII.   In the Hall-Garden.

PART II.

Sections

I.   The Phantom (after the duel with Maud's brother).

II. In Brittany. The shell undestroyed amid the storm perhaps symbolizes to him his own first and highest nature preserved amid the storms of passion.

III. He felt himself going mad.

IV. Haunted after Maud's death.

" O that 'twere possible " appeared first in the *Keepsake.* Sir John Simeon years after begged me to weave a story round this poem and so " Maud " came into being.

V.   In the mad-house.

The second corpse is Maud's brother, the lover's father being the first corpse, whom the lover thinks that Maud's father has murdered.

Part III.

VI. Sane but shattered. Written when the cannon
was heard booming from the battle-ships in
the Solent before the Crimean War.

Letters to and from friends, 1854–55.

To Gerald Massey.

FRESHWATER, I. OF WIGHT,
April 1st, 1854.

MY DEAR SIR,

In consequence of my change of residence I
did not receive your captivating volume till yesterday.
I am no reader of papers and Reviews and I had not
seen, nor even heard of any of your poems: my joy was
all the fresher and the greater in thus suddenly coming
on a poet of such fine lyrical impulse, and of so rich
half-oriental an imagination. It must be granted that
you make our good old English tongue crack and sweat
for it occasionally, but time will chasten all that. Go on
and prosper, and believe me grateful for your gift, and

Yours most truly, A. TENNYSON.

Letters to Dr Mann, author of "Maud Vindicated."

1855.

Thanks for your *Vindication*. No one with this
essay before him can in future pretend to misunderstand
my dramatic poem, "Maud": your commentary is as
true as it is full, and I am really obliged to you for
defending me against the egregiously nonsensical imputation of having attacked the Quakers or Mr Bright:
you are not aware, perhaps, that another wiseacre accused me of calling Mr Layard an "Assyrian Bull!"

Yours very truly, A. TENNYSON.

Without the prestige of Shakespeare, *Hamlet* (if it came out now) would be treated in just the same way, so that one ought not to care for their cackling, not that I am comparing poor little "Maud" to the Prince, except as, what's the old quotation out of Virgil, *sic parvis componere, etc.* Would it not be better that all literary criticisms should be signed with the name or at least the initials of the writer? To sign political articles would be perhaps unadvisable and inconvenient, but my opinion is that we shall never have a good school of criticism in England while the writer is anonymous and irresponsible.

Believe me yours ever, A. T.

I am delighted with Miss Sewell's gift[1], tho' yet unseen. I should like as I have told her to learn something of the history of the naming of it: can you tell me anything? Please get it framed, we shall be half a year getting it done here. I think it should not have a great white margin except the artist herself desires it. Perhaps the lake was not called after your humble servant but another. I enclose you the note to Miss Sewell which please deliver and read if you choose.

A. T.

I wished for you much yesterday. Merwood[2] brought me a lump of snake's eggs, and I picked carefully out two little embryo snakes with bolting eyes and beating hearts. I laid them on a piece of white paper. Their hearts or blood-vessels beat for at *least* two hours after extraction. Does not that in some way explain why it is so very difficult to kill a snake? I was so sorry not to have you and your microscope here.

A. T.

[1] Miss Sewell had painted a picture of Lake Tennyson in New Zealand, so named by Sir Frederick Weld.
[2] Tenant at Farringford farm.

From Mrs Vyner, a stranger[1].

RIVER, NEW SOUTH WALES, 1855.

DEAR FRIEND,

I know that the poet's life must have its common-place daily sorrows and toils and that there must be moments when he even doubts his own gift, but I fancy a poet's heart must be so large and loving that he can feel for and forgive even folly. Folly it may be, and yet I *must* write and thank you with a true and grateful heart for the happy moments your thoughts and your pen have given me. I am in the wildest bush of Australia, far away from all that makes life beautiful and endurable excepting the strong and stern sense of duty, the consciousness that where God has placed us is our lot to be, and that our most becoming posture is to accept our destiny with grateful humility. You must let me tell you how in a lonely home among the mountains, with my young children asleep, my husband absent, no sound to be heard but the cry of the wild dog or the wail of the curlew, no lock or bolt to guard our solitary hut, strong in our utter helplessness I have turned (next to God's book) to you as a friend, and read far into the night till my lot seemed light and a joy seemed cast around my very menial toils: then I have said, "God bless the poet and put still some beautiful words and thoughts into his heart," and the burthen of life became pleasant to me or at least easy. If you are the man I feel you must be you will forgive this address: there are certain impulses which seem irresistible, and I believe these are the genuine, truthful moments of our life, and such an impulse has urged me to write to you, and I know that the blessing of a faithful heart cannot be bootless: and may He who seeth not as man seeth spare you to plead the cause of truth and to spurn foolish saws and sickly conventionalities. Farewell.

God bless you: always your friend,

MARGARET ANNA VYNER.

My father's aunt Mrs Russell was vexed at what she thought an attack on coal-mine owners in "Maud,"

---

[1] My father was deeply touched by this letter: and kept it among the things he most prized.

and so he writes: " I really could find it in my heart
to be offended with such an imputation, for what
must you think of me if you think me capable of such
gratuitous and unmeaning personality and hostility?
I am as sensitive a person as exists, and sooner than
wound anyone in such a spiteful fashion, would consent
never to write a line again; yea, to have my hand cut
off at the wrist. Why, if you had the least suspicion
that I had acted in this way, did you not inquire of me
before? Now see, you the kindliest and tenderest of
human beings, how you have wronged me, and cherished
in your heart this accusation as baseless, no, more
baseless, than a dream, for dreams have some better
foundation in past things: but pray put it all out of
your head."

To George Brimley.

FRESHWATER, I. W.
Nov. 28th, 1855.

SIR,

I wish to assure you that I quite close with
your commentary on " Maud." I may have agreed with
portions of other critiques on the same poem, which have
been sent to me; but when I saw your notice I laid my
finger upon it and said, " There, that is my meaning."
Poor little " Maud," after having run the gauntlet of so
much brainless abuse and anonymous spite, has found a
critic. Therefore believe her father (not the gray old
wolf) to be

Yours not unthankfully, A. TENNYSON.

P.S. But there are two or three points in your
comment to which I should take exception, e.g. " The
writer of the fragments, etc.," surely the speaker or the
thinker rather than the writer; again, as to the character

of the love, do any of the expressions "rapturous," "painful," "childish," however they may apply to some of the poems, fully characterize the 18th? is it not something deeper? but perhaps some day I may discuss these things with you, and therefore I will say no more here, except that I shall be very glad to see you if ever you come to the Isle of Wight.

To F. G. Tuckerman.

1855.

DEAR MR TUCKERMAN,

I have just returned home (i.e. to Farringford) from a visit to London, during which I called on Moxon, and found your kind present of books waiting for me. I fear that you must have thought me neglectful in not immediately acknowledging them: and so I should have done had I not been waiting to send along with my thanks a small volume of my own, containing some of the things I repeated to you in my little smoking-attic here. These poems, when printed, I found needed considerable elision and so the book has hung on hand.

When I arrived here I found that my small smoking-room did not smell of smoke at all, nay was even fragrant. I could not at first make it out. At last I perceived it was owing to the Russian leather on your Webster which you made mine. Even so (as some one says),

"The actions of the just
Smell sweet and blossom in the dust"—

and there was dust enough on the table almost to justify the application.

You will find in my little volume "The Charge of the Light Brigade." * * * * It is not a poem on which

I pique myself, but I cannot help fancying that, such as it is, I have improved it.

Farewell and forgive my silence hitherto. I shall always remember with pleasure your coming to see me in the frost and our pleasant talk together. Did you see in your paper that the Oxford University would make me a Doctor the other day, and how the young men shouted?

I am, dear Mr Tuckerman,

Ever yours, A. Tennyson.

To the Rev. G. G. Bradley[1].

FARRINGFORD,
August 25th, 1855.

Dear Mr Bradley,

Many thanks for the Arnold: nobody can deny that he is a poet. "The Merman" was an old favourite of mine, and I like him as well as ever. "The Scholar Gipsy" is quite new to me, and I have already an affection for him, which I think will increase. There are several others which seem very good, so that altogether I may say that you have conferred a great boon upon me. I have received a Scotch paper, in which it is stated that poor "Maud" is to be slashed all to pieces by that mighty man, that pompholygous, broad-blown Apollodorus, the gifted X. Her best friends do not expect her to survive it!

I am yours very truly,

A. Tennyson.

[1] Dean of Westminster.

From J. Ruskin.

DENMARK HILL, 12*th November*, 1855.

MY DEAR SIR,

I hear of so many stupid and feelingless misunderstandings of " Maud " that I think it may perhaps give you some little pleasure to know my sincere admiration of it throughout.

I do not like its versification so well as much of your other work, not because I do not think it good of its kind, but because I do not think that wild kind quite so good, and I am sorry to have another cloud put into the sky of one's thoughts by the sad story, but as to the general bearing and delicate finish of the thing in its way, I think no admiration can be extravagant.

It is a compliment to myself, not to you, if I say that I think with you in *all* things about the war.

I am very sorry you put the " Some one had blundered " out of the " Light Brigade [1]."

It was precisely the most tragical line in the poem. It is as true to its history as essential to its tragedy.

Believe me sincerely yours, J. RUSKIN.

From Herbert Spencer (about "The Two Voices").

7 MARLBOROUGH GARDENS,
ST JOHN'S WOOD, LONDON, 1855.

SIR,

I happened recently to be re-reading your Poem " The Two Voices," and coming to the verse

Or if thro' lower lives I came —
Tho' all experience past became
Consolidate in mind and frame —

it occurred to me that you might like to glance through a book which applies to the elucidation of mental science, the hypothesis to which you refer. I therefore beg your acceptance of *Psychology* which I send by this post.

With much sympathy yours,

HERBERT SPENCER.

[1] Some friends of excellent critical judgment prevailed upon him to omit this phrase which was however soon re-inserted: for it was originally the keynote of the poem.

With the proceeds of the sale of " Maud " Farringford was bought, and my mother's journal says :

April 24th, 1856.   This morning a letter came from Mr G. S. Venables saying that Mr Chapman pronounced the title of Farringford good.   We have agreed to buy, so I suppose this ivied home among the pine-trees is ours.   Went to our withy holt : such beautiful blue hyacinths, orchises, primroses, daisies, marsh-marigolds and cuckoo-flowers.   Wild cherry trees too with single snowy blossom, and the hawthorns white with their " pearls of May."   The park has for many days been rich with cowslips and furze in bloom.   The elms are a golden wreath at the foot of the down ; to the north of the house the mespilus and horse-chestnut are in flower and the apple-trees are covered with rosy buds.   A. dug the bed ready for the rhododendrons.   A thrush was singing among the nightingales and other birds, as he said " mad with joy."   At sunset, the golden green of the trees, the burning splendour of Blackgang Chine and St Catharine's, and the red bank of the primeval river, contrasted with the turkis-blue of the sea (that is our view from the drawing-room), make altogether a miracle of beauty.   We are glad that Farringford is ours.

CHAPTER XX.

HOME LIFE AND "IDYLLS OF THE KING."

1856–1859.

A thousand thanks for your charming letter from the Isle of Wight with suggestive date of Bonchurch (the only church you went to that day), and the spirited outline sketch of the Idyllic Poet serenely ploughing his windy acres. How must you have enjoyed!... The "Idylls (of the King)" are a brilliant success. Rich tapestries, wrought as only Tennyson could have done them, and worthy to hang by the *Faerie Queen*. I believe there is no discordant voice on this side of the water.

(From H. W. Longfellow to James T. Fields, 1854.)

1856.

My father went to the Grange (Lord Ashburton's) in January, and met the Carlyles, Venables, Brookfields, Tom Taylors, Goldwin Smith and Spedding. Brookfield wrote: "Alfred has been most cheerful and the life of the party." The note by my father is: "It seems a house not uneasy to live in, only I regret my little fumitory at Farringford. Here they smoke among the oranges, lemons, and camellias....I cannot see in Lady Ashburton a touch of the haughtiness which fame attributes to her. She is most perfectly natural, tho' like enough she sometimes snubs her own grade now and then, when she sees presumption and folly. But as Brookfield said this morning, 'She is very loyal to her *printers*.'"

During the winter evenings of 1855 my father would translate the *Odyssey* aloud into Biblical prose to my mother, who writes, "Thus I get as much as it is possible to have of the true spirit of the original."

He had been evolving the main scheme of the
" Idylls of the King" at different periods during the last
twenty years and more: the Morte d'Arthur episode had
appeared in the volume of 1842. He resumed the plan
with " Merlin and Nimue" (called " Vivien ") in February;
and in the " Forest of Broceliande" are many reminiscences of what was now the near scenery of the New
Forest[1]. This Idyll was finished by March 31st, and
" Geraint and Enid " begun on April 16th.

Meantime for daily exercise he planted trees and
shrubs; rolled the lawn and dug in the kitchen garden,
taking all the while a loving note of Nature. Thus as
he was digging one day a well-known line formed itself:

As careful robins eye the delver's toil.

Farringford being now his property, the Twickenham
furniture was brought over to the new home. As it
was unpacked, my father's eye was struck by a certain
crimson-covered sofa and some oak chairs grouped together in the farmyard in front of the old thatched
farmstead and the ivy-covered wall through which the
kitchen garden is entered. " What a picture it would
make!" he said; repeating his new song in " Enid,"
that then for the first time came to him:

Turn fortune, turn thy wheel and lower the proud.

Presently, within doors, while the books were being
sorted and rearranged, all imaginable things strewed over
the drawing-room floor, and the chairs and tables in wild
disarray, Prince Albert called. He had driven over
suddenly from Osborne. The parlour-maid went to the
front door, heard the Prince's name announced, and, being
bewildered and not knowing into what room to show him,
stood stock still; so the Equerry, I have been told, took

---

[1] On one occasion he stayed in the New Forest with his friend, the well-
known ornithologist, Lord Lilford, in order to observe the bird-life there.

her by the shoulders and turned her round, bidding her lead them in.   The Prince expressed great admiration of the view from the drawing-room window, and one of the party gathered a bunch of cowslips which H. R. H. said he must take to the Queen.

From the first the Prince was very cordial, and impressed my father as being a man of strong and self-sacrificing nature.

In June news came that R.'s bank would probably break and that all my father's little savings might be lost. On July 2nd my mother wrote: " A. showed a noble disregard of money, much as the loss would affect us." That evening, so as to give her courage, he asked her to play and sing the grand Welsh national air, " Come to battle ": and afterwards, to divert themselves from dwelling on the possible loss, they hung their Michael Angelo engravings round the drawing-room.

In July and August my father and mother took us children to Wales, and here " Enid " was all but finished. We stayed at Llangollen, then at Dolgelly, and at Barmouth.   My father spoke of " the high rejoicing lines of Cader Idris."   My mother wrote: *"Sept. 8th.*   A. climbed Cader Idris.   Pouring rain came on.   I and the children waited a long time for him.   I heard the roar of waters, streams and cataracts, and I never saw anything more awful than that great veil of rain drawn straight over Cader Idris, pale light at the lower edge.   It looked as if death were behind it, and made me shudder when I thought he was there.   A message came from him by the guide that he had gone to Dolgelly."

It was near Festiniog that he heard the roar of a cataract above the roar of the torrent, and wrote that Virgilian simile:

For as one,

That listens near a torrent mountain-brook,
All thro' the crash of the near cataract hears

The drumming thunder of the huger fall
At distance, were the soldiers wont to hear
His voice in battle.

He particularly admired the still pools of the torrent
in the "Torrent Walk" at Dolgelly, and the mysterious
giant steps of Cwn Bychan.   Harlech, Festiniog, Llanid-
loes, Builth, Caerleon were the next halting-places; and
on September 16th he wrote: "The Usk murmurs by
the windows, and I sit like King Arthur in Caerleon.
This is a most quiet, half-ruined village of about 1500
inhabitants with a little museum of Roman tombstones
and other things."   From Caerleon he made expeditions
to Caerphilly, Merthyr Tydvil, Raglan; and then we
all returned by Brecon, Gloucester and Salisbury home.
With the help of local schoolmasters in Wales my
parents had learned some Welsh, and now read together
the *Hanes Cymru* (Welsh History), the *Mabinogion* and
Llywarch Hen.

On Dec. 31st a characteristic letter was sent to a
stranger who had forwarded a volume of verse:

I have as you desired considered your poem, and
though I make it a rule to decline passing any judgment
on poems, I cannot in this instance refrain from giving
you a word of advice.

Follow your calling diligently, for be assured, work,
far from being a hardship, is a blessing, and if you are
a poet indeed, you will find in it a help not a hindrance.
You might, if you chose, offer these lines to some magazine, but you must not be surprised if they are refused,
for the poetic gift is so common in these days that
hundreds must have to endure this disappointment, and
I should not be an honest friend if I did not prepare you
for that.

I should by no means recommend you to risk the
publication of a volume on your own account.   The

publication of verse is almost always attended with loss. As an amusement to yourself and your friends, the writing is all very well. Accept my good wishes and believe me,

Your obedient servant,

A. TENNYSON.

1857.

An invitation was sent in January to Mr and Mrs Carlyle. The latter answered:

5 CHEYNE ROAD, CHELSEA,
21st January, 1857.

MY DEAR MRS TENNYSON,

You *are* a darling woman to have gone and written to me on the "voluntary principle" such a kind little note! *You* to have been at the trouble to know that *I* was ill! *You* to express regret at *my* illness. I feel both surprised and gratified, as if I were an *obsolete* word that some great Poet (Alfred Tennyson for example) had taken a notion to look up in the Dictionary.

In *London*, when one is sick, especially when one continues sick for three months, one falls so out of thought! it is much if even your female friend, in the next street, do not weary of you and then forget you! I say female advisedly for, to give the Devil his due, I find that men hold out longer than women against the loss of one's "powers of pleasing."

Now however I begin to be about: and have no longer the pretext of illness for straining what Mr Carlyle calls " the inestimable privilege of being as ugly and stupid and disagreeable as ever one likes!" and my friends drop in more frequently and sit much longer!

The heartiest thanks for your invitation to Freshwater.

Wouldn't I like to go and visit you if that man would leave his eternal *Frederick* and come along! nay wouldn't I like to go on my own small basis, if only I had the *nerve* for it, which I have not yet! *He* goes nowhere, sees nobody, only for two hours a day he rides, like the wild German Hunter, on a horse he has bought, and which seems to like the sort of thing! Such a horse! he (not the horse) never wearies, in the intervals of *Frederick*, of celebrating the creature's "good sense, courage and sensibility!" "Not once," he says, "has the creature shown the slightest disagreement from *him* in *any question of Intellect*" (more than can be said of most living Bipeds)! I wrote to a relation in Scotland, "If this horse of Mr C.'s dies, he will certainly write its biography," and that very day he said to me, " My dear, I wish I could find out about the genealogy of that horse of mine! and some particulars of its life! I am beginning to feel sure it is a Cockney."

Poor Lady Ashburton has made nothing by leaving the Grange deserted this winter, she has been quite ill ever since she went to Nice.

May I offer my affectionate regards to your husband? And may I give yourself a kiss?

Yours very truly,

JANE WELSH CARLYLE.

In April a report reached us that Tom Moore was dying. A friend writes: " This darling old poet is only just alive, mind and body. X goes over frequently to see him and read him your poems, which he cries over and delights in."

"Enid" and "Nimue, or The True and the False" were put into print this summer.

In June the American translator of *Faust*, Bayard Taylor, stayed at Farringford and was full of talk. Among other things he told my father that the most beautiful sight in the world was a Norwegian forest in winter, sheathed in ice, the sun rising over it and making the whole landscape one rainbow of flashing diamonds.

Taylor published the following account of his visit to us:

As we drew near Freshwater, my coachman pointed out Farringford, a cheerful gray country mansion with a small thick-grassed park before it, a grove behind, and beyond all, a deep shoulder of the chalk downs, a gap in which, at Freshwater, showed the dark blue horizon of the Channel. Leaving my luggage at one of the two little inns, I walked to the house, with lines from "Maud" chiming in my mind. "The dry-tongued laurel" shone glossily in the sun, the cedar "sighed for Lebanon" on the lawn, and "the liquid azure bloom of a crescent of sea" glimmered afar. I had not been two minutes in the drawing-room before Tennyson walked in. So unlike are the published portraits of him, that I was almost in doubt as to his identity. The engraved heads suggest a moderate stature, but he is tall and broad-shouldered as a son of Anak, with hair, beard and eyes of southern darkness. Something in the lofty brow and aquiline nose suggests Dante, but such a deep mellow chest-voice never could have come from Italian lungs. He proposed a walk, as the day was wonderfully clear and beautiful. We climbed the steep comb of the chalk cliff, and slowly wandered westward till we reached the Needles, at the extremity of the Island and some three or four miles from his residence. During the conversation with which we beguiled the way, I was struck with the variety of his knowledge. Not a little flower on the downs, which the sheep had spared, escaped his notice, and the geology of the coast, both terrestrial and submarine, was perfectly familiar to him. I thought of a remark I once heard from the lips of a distinguished English author (Thackeray), that "Tennyson was the wisest man he knew," and could well believe that he was sincere in making it.

July 9th. My mother writes in her journal: "A. has brought me as a birthday present the first two lines that he has made of 'Guinevere' which might be the nucleus of a great poem. Arthur is parting from Guinevere and says:

> 'But hither shall I never come again,
>   Never lie by thy side; see thee no more:
>   Farewell!'"

July 25th. The following letter was received from Mr Ruskin about the edition of the *Poems* illustrated by Dante Gabriel Rossetti, Millais, Holman Hunt and others, in which my father had taken great interest, having called on most of the artists so as to give them his views of what the illustrations ought to be.

EDINBURGH,
July 24th, 1857.

MY DEAR SIR,

It is a long time since I have heard from you and I do not like the mildew to grow over what little memory you may have of me.

It is however no excuse for writing to say that I wanted to congratulate you on the last edition of your poems. Indeed it might be and I hope will be some day better managed, still many of the plates are very noble things, though not, it seems to me, illustrations of your poems.

I believe in fact that good pictures never can be; they are always another poem, subordinate but wholly different from the poet's conception, and serve chiefly to show the reader how variously the same verses may affect various minds. But these woodcuts will be of much use in making people think and puzzle a little; art was getting quite a matter of form in book-illustrations, and it does not so much matter whether any given vignette is right or not, as whether it contains thought or not, still more whether it contains any kind of plain facts. If people have no sympathy with St Agnes, or if people as soon as they get a distinct idea of a living girl who probably got scolded for dropping her candle-wax about the convent-stairs, and caught cold by looking too long out of the window in her bedgown, feel no true sympathy with her, they can have no sympathy in them.

But we P. R. B.'s [1] must do better for you than this some day : meantime I do congratulate you on " The wind is blowing in turret and tree," and Rossetti's Sir Galahad and Lady of Shalott, and one or two more.

[1] Pre-Raphaelite Brotherhood.

Please send me a single line to Denmark Hill, Camberwell, and believe me

Faithfully yours,
J. RUSKIN.

This summer the tour was to Manchester, Coniston, Inverary Castle, and Carstairs (the home of my father's college friend Monteith). On this journey he read aloud *Tom Brown's School-Days* to my mother, enjoying it thoroughly.

When at Manchester my parents heard Dickens recite his *Christmas Carol*.

A visit was made to the Exhibition held there, and much time spent in studying Holman Hunt's pictures, the Turner sketches, Mulready's drawings, and various fine Gainsboroughs and Reynolds.

Hawthorne was in the same room, and my father afterwards expressed great regret that he had not been introduced to the author of *The Scarlet Letter*. Hawthorne wrote: " Gazing at him with all my eyes I liked him well, and rejoiced more in him than in all the wonders of the Exhibition."

After the tour Mrs Browning wrote to enquire after his health :

ALLA VILLA TOSCANA,
BAGNI DI LUCCA.
September 6th, 1857.

MY DEAR MRS TENNYSON,

We see in the *Galignani* that Mr Tennyson is not well, by the side of threats of fall of our Indian empire and other disasters; and it disquiets us to the point that I must write to ask you whether it is true or not and how far? The trade of newspapers is to blow bubbles, and a little breath more or less determines the size of the bubble.

May this be a mere bubble ! write one word to say so. Oh may you be able to smile at my question from over the sea !

But remember we have lost our friend, your brother Frederick, from whom we could always hear about you! He has devastated our Florence for us by going to live at Pisa; and now he is farther off still, at Genoa, while we are mountain-locked here with no news from anybody.

The spring and summer have been heavy to me from a family grief [1], but we three are well, thank God, living quietly in the shade till the sun shall have done his worst and best alas! in this beautiful Italy. Little Penini [2] is very happy, gossiping with the Contadini, among whom he passes for un Vero Fiorentino, though he talks English inside the house as fast as Italian out of it. I hope that one day he may know your boys. How sorry I was to leave England last year without seeing them or you, or "King Arthur"!

My husband made me envious by the advantage he had over me in having listened to a certain exquisite music of which I could only dream.

Just before we left Florence to come hither, we saw your brother Frederick who went there for a day or two. We thought we never saw him looking so well. It was provoking to hear, very provoking; but he maintained that he *slept* at Pisa as he never could at Florence. I was very cross, and inclined to retort that at Pisa one slept by day as well as by night, the place was so dull.

Think of our loss having to lose him!

Dear Mrs Tennyson, will you send me just a few words? Really we are anxious. Being in all affection to both of you, his and yours,

ELIZABETH BARRETT BROWNING

& R. B.

A letter came about this time from Colonel Phipps, saying that the Queen desired that a stanza should be added to *God save the Queen* for a concert to be given at Buckingham Palace on the evening of the Princess Royal's wedding-day. These two stanzas were sent in answer, and published in the *Times*, January 26th, 1858:

[1] Death of her father.
[2] Familiar name of their son.

God bless our Prince and Bride!
God keep their lands allied,
　God save the Queen!
Clothe them with righteousness,
Crown them with happiness,
Them with all blessings bless,
　God save the Queen.

Fair fall this hallow'd hour,
Farewell our England's flower,
　God save the Queen!
Farewell, fair rose of May!
Let both the peoples say,
God bless thy marriage-day,
　God bless the Queen.

For the last few months the Indian Mutiny had excited the profoundest interest throughout the country, and on Christmas Day the account of the relief of Lucknow arrived. Havelock's death, which had occurred on Nov. 25th, was not then known. When this sad news came, my father wrote the following lines:

Havelock.　Nov. 25th, 1857.　(*Unpublished.*)
　Bold Havelock march'd,
　Many a mile went he,
　Every mile a battle,
　Every battle a victory.

　Bold Havelock march'd,
　Charged with his gallant few,
　Ten men fought a thousand,
　Slew them and overthrew.

　Bold Havelock march'd,
　Wrought with his hand and his head,
　March'd and thought and fought,
　March'd and fought himself dead.

Bold Havelock died,
Tender and great and good,
And every man in Britain
Says " I am of Havelock's blood ! "

1858.

In January "The Parting of Arthur and Guinevere"
was finished and my mother records her first impression
— " It is awe-inspiring." On March 8th the entry in
her journal is: " To-day he has written his song of
'Too Late,' and has said it to me"; and on March
15th, "'Guinevere' is finally completed."

My father then occasionally wrote in his new summer-
house looking towards the down and the sea; and on
the windows of which he was painting marvellous
dragons and sea-serpents. " One day" (she says),
"while writing his 'Guinevere,' A. spoke of 'the want
of reverence now-a-days for great men, whose brightness,
like that of the luminous bodies in the Heaven, makes
the dark spaces look the darker.'"

At this time he sent a letter to Dr Mann in Natal:

Our winter has been the mildest I have ever known.
I read of ripe pomegranates hanging on a houseside at
Bath, and I myself counted scores of our wild summer
roses on a hedge near, flourishing in December and lasting
on into January, tho' now gone, for the temperature has
changed. They were perfectly fragrant, and I brought
home a bouquet of them and put them in water. You
ask after the farm? I cannot say that * * is going on
satisfactorily, very niggard of manure in the fields and
ever doing his best to 'reave me of my rent by working
at little odd jobs as a set off, so that at the end of the
year, all things deducted, I get almost nothing. I am
now building a little summer-house to catch the southern

sun in Maiden's Croft, if you remember what field that
is. I shall sit there and bask in the sunbeams and think
of you far south. How I should love to rove about that
parklike scenery of which you give such a fascinating
account!

Yours ever, A. TENNYSON.

P.S. I may tell you however that young Swinburne
called here the other day with a college friend of his,
and we asked him to dinner, and I thought him a very
modest and intelligent young fellow. Moreover I read
him what you vindicated[1], but what I particularly admired
in him was that he did not press upon me any verses of
his own. Good-bye. How desolate No. 7 B. T. must
feel itself!

Several friends urged the immediate publication of
the newly-written Idylls, among them Jowett, who says:

I have great pleasure in sending some books which I hope
you will accept, the best books in the world (except the Bible),
Homer and Plato.

I take the opportunity also of enclosing Lemprière's *Dictionary*. The price is 1*s.* 6*d.* The bookseller valued it so little that
he offered to give me the book. I have added two or three
other books which I thought you might like to see, the translation of the Vedas as a specimen of the oldest thing in the
world, Hegel's *Philosophy of History*, which is just "the increasing purpose that through the ages runs" buried under a
heap of categories. If you care to look at it will you turn to the
pages I have marked at the beginning? It is a favourite book
of mine. I do not feel certain of the impression it will make on
anyone else.

I also send you the latest and best work on Mythology, and
Bunsen's new *Bibelbuch*, which, from the little I have read, seems
to be an interesting and valuable introduction to Scripture. What

---

[1] Later Swinburne writes: "'Maud' is the poem of the deepest charm and
fullest delight, pathos and melody ever written, even by Mr Tennyson."

a cartload of heavy literature! Do not trouble yourself to read or to send it back to me: I will carry it away some day myself.

I fear I have no news to tell you, and "the art of letter-writing" Dr Johnson says "consists solely in telling news."

May I say a word about "mosquitoes[1]"? Anyone who cares about you is deeply annoyed that you are deterred by them from writing or publishing. The feeling grows and brings in after years the still more painful and deeper feeling that they have prevented you from putting out half your powers. Nothing is so likely to lead to misrepresentation. Persons don't understand that sensitiveness is often combined with real manliness as well as great intellectual gifts, and they regard it as a sign of fear and weakness.

A certain man on a particular day has his stomach out of order and the stomach "getteth him up into the brain," and he calls another man "morbid." He is morbid himself and wants soothing words, and the whole world is morbid with dissecting and analysing itself and wants to be comforted and put together again. Might not this be the poet's office, to utter the "better voice" while Thackeray is uttering the worse one? I don't mean to blame Thackeray, for I desire to take the world as it is in this present age, crammed with self-consciousness, and no doubt Thackeray's views are of some value in the direction of anti-humbug.

But there is another note needed afterwards to show the good side of human nature and to condone its frailties which Thackeray will never strike. That note would be most thankfully received by the better part of the world.

Give my love to Hallam and Lionel. Tell Hallam I have put his letter "where I can always see it," and that I read every day about "Louise."

No more about "mosquitoes," I have bored you enough. With most kind regards to Mrs Tennyson,

Ever yours truly,

B. Jowett.

At this time Lord Dufferin wrote from Highgate, with a copy of his *Letters from High Latitudes.*

---

[1] Spiteful critics.

My dear Mr Tennyson,

I am going to do a very bold thing, but in asking you to accept the accompanying book I hope you will consider I am only obeying an impulse I have felt for many many years, but to which until now I have never had any excuse for giving way.

For the first 20 years of my life I not only did not care for poetry, but to the despair of my friends absolutely disliked it, at least so much of it as until that time had fallen in my way. In vain my mother read to me Dryden, Pope, Byron, Young, Cowper and all the standard classics of the day, each seemed to me as distasteful as I had from early infancy found Virgil: and I shall never forget her dismay when at a literary dinner I was cross-examined as to my tastes, and blushingly confessed before an Olympus of poets that I rather disliked poetry than otherwise.

Soon afterwards however I fell in with a volume of yours, and suddenly felt such a sensation of delight as I never experienced before. A new world seemed open to me, and from that day, by a constant study of your works, I gradually worked my way to a thorough appreciation of what is good in all kinds of authors.

Naturally enough I could not help feeling very grateful to the Orpheus whose music had made the gate of poet-land fly open, and for years I longed to make your acquaintance. Now that I have done so I cannot help wishing to make you a little thank-offering as a token of my sense of what I owe to you, and however insignificant, I trust you will accept it as being the best and only thing I have to give.

Ever yours sincerely, Dufferin.

April 5th. Professor Tyndall, Mr Newman and Mr Dicey called: my father said of Tyndall: "He is such a good fellow, so unscornful and genial, so full of imagination and of enthusiasm for his work!"

In July we stayed at Little Holland House, Kensington, with the Prinseps: and here my father began

"The Fair Maid of Astolat," and read aloud "The Grandmother."

Watts was at work on what his friends called "the great moonlight portrait" of the Bard.

It was then that my father met Ruskin again. A voice from the corner of the room exclaimed: "Jones, you are gigantic." This was Ruskin apostrophizing Burne Jones as an artist.

From Little Holland House my father started on a trip to Norway, and he wrote in his Letter-Diary:

Started from Hull on July 23rd. Saw E. on board the little New Holland Steamer, and waved my hand-kerchief as both our boats were moving off: watched the two lights of Spurn Point till they became one star and then faded away. Next day very fine but in the night towards morning storm arose and our topmast was broken off. I stood next morning a long time by the cabin door and watched the green sea looking like a mountainous country, far off waves with foam at the top looking like snowy mountains bounding the scene; one great wave, green-shining, past with all its crests smoking high up beside the vessel[1]. As I stood there came a sudden hurricane and roared drearily in the funnel for twenty seconds and past away.

Christiansand. Went up into the town and saw the wooden houses.

---

[1] They couch'd their spears and prick'd their steeds, and thus,
   Their plumes driv'n backward by the wind they made
   In moving, all together down upon him
   Bare, as a wild wave in the wide North-sea,
   Green-glimmering toward the summit, bears, with all
   Its stormy crests that smoke against the skies,
   Down on a bark, and overbears the bark,
   And him that helms it, so they overbore
   Sir Lancelot and his charger.
                                    "Lancelot and Elaine."

August 1st. Christiania. Magnificent seas on the way here. At Christiansand called on a Mr Murch, and the Frau Murch gave me a splendid bouquet of flowers : arrived here at 6 this afternoon. I write this at the house of Mr Crowe, consul, looking over the Sound — very pretty in the evening light. Am not quite certain whether I shall join Barrett and the other.

August 2nd. Christiania. I let Barrett and Tweedie go by themselves to Bergen. I am starting to-day to see the Riukan Foss with Mr Woodfall, a very quiet sensible man, and we shall take our time. I have had great kindness from the Crowes. Yesterday a Norwegian introduced himself at the hotel, and began to spout my own verses to me ; and I likewise rather to my annoyance found myself set down in the Christiania papers as " Den berömte engelske Digter."

I have seen the Riukan Foss. Magnificent power of water ; weird blue light behind the fall.

On his return the Frederick Maurices visited us at Farringford. Mr Maurice read family prayers in the morning, and my mother notes : "A. rejoiced as much as I did in his reading — ' the most earnest and holiest reading,' A. said, ' he had ever heard.' "

In the evenings my father recited his new poems " The Grandmother " and " Sea Dreams [1]," saying that the rascal in " Sea Dreams " was drawn from a man who had grossly cheated him in early life. Mr Maurice was charmed with the place :

> Groves of pine on either hand,
> To break the blast of winter, stand ;
> And further on, the hoary Channel
> Tumbles a billow on chalk and sand.

[1] First published in *Macmillan's Magazine*, Jan. 1860.

If his doctrine had been somewhat more within ordinary comprehension, my father was of opinion that he would have taken his place as foremost thinker among the Churchmen of our time. Consequently the following dedication of Maurice's *Theological Essays* gave him great pleasure.

MY DEAR SIR,

I have maintained in these *Essays* that a Theology which does not correspond to the deepest thoughts and feelings of human beings cannot be a true Theology. Your writings have taught me to enter into many of these thoughts and feelings. Will you forgive me the presumption of offering you a book which at least acknowledges them and does them homage?

As the hopes which I have expressed in this volume are more likely to be fulfilled to our children than to ourselves, I might perhaps ask you to accept it as a present to one of your name, in whom you have given me a very sacred interest[1]. Many years, I trust, will elapse, before he knows that there are any controversies in the world into which he has entered. Would to God that in a few more he may find that they have ceased! At all events, if he should look into these *Essays*, they may tell him what meaning some of the former generation attached to words, which will be familiar and dear to his generation, and to those that follow his, how there were some who longed that the bells of our churches might indeed

> Ring out the darkness of the land,
> Ring in the Christ that is to be.

Believe me, my dear Sir,

Yours very truly and gratefully,

F. D. MAURICE.

Two ideas which Maurice expressed my father would quote with approbation, that the "real Hell was the

[1] See p. 358.

absence of God from the human soul, and that all religions seemed to him to be imperfect manifestations of the true Christianity."

I remember too his reading with admiration this passage from Maurice's *Friendship of Books*. " If I do not give you extracts from any of Milton's specially controversial writings, it is not that I wish to pass them over because the conclusions in them are often directly opposed to mine, for I think that I have learnt most from those that are so."

Oct. 4th. " To-day," my mother says, " A. took a volume of the *Morte d'Arthur* and read a noble passage about the battle with the Romans. He went to meet Mr and Mrs Roebuck at dinner at Swainston : and the comet was grand, with Arcturus shining brightly over the nucleus. At dinner he said he must leave the table to look at it and they all followed. They saw Arcturus seemingly dance as if mad [1] when it passed out of the comet's tail. He said of the comet's tail, ' It is like a besom of destruction sweeping the sky.' " When he returned next night he " observed the comet from his platform [2], and, when he came down to tea, read some *Paradise Lost.*"

Oct. 17th. He read aloud " The Rape of the Lock," and noted the marvellous skill of many of the couplets.

November. My father writes : " I have just seen Ruskin : he says that the Signor's (G. F. Watts') portrait of me is the grandest thing he has seen in that line, but so he said of (Woolner's) bust [3]."

During these last months of the year he was full of the Queen's wise proclamation to India after the transference of the government from the Company to the

[1] Alluded to in " Harold."

[2] The platform on the top of the house was a favourite place with him at night, and there he continually observed the stars.

[3] Now in the Library of Trinity College, Cambridge.

Crown.   The Indian Mutiny had stirred him to the
depths.

Letters from the Rev. B. Jowett.

Dec. 1858.

DEAR MRS TENNYSON,

We shall long remember your kind hospitality, which
made the Easter Vacation a very happy time to us.

You asked me whether I could suggest any subjects for
poetry.   I have been so presumptuous as to think of some.   I
don't believe that poetical feelings and imagery on subjects can
ever be exhausted.   That is only a fancy which comes over us
when our minds are dry or in moments of depression.   This
generation is certainly more poetical and imaginative than the
last, and perhaps in spite of the critics the next may be more
poetical than our own.

And as to the critics their power is not really great.   Waggon-
loads of them are lighting fires every week or on their way to the
grocers.

I often fancy that the critical form of modern literature is
like the rhetorical one which overlaid ancient literature and will
be regarded as that is, at its true worth in after times.   One drop
of natural feeling in poetry or the true statement of a single new
fact is already felt to be of more value than all the critics put
together.

I suggested "old age" to Mr Tennyson, a sort of "In
Memoriam" over a lost child, wandering in soothing strains over
all the thoughts and feelings of the aged.   It always seems to
me that "old age" has been badly treated by poets notwithstanding Burns' beautiful ballad.   Its beauty, its sadness, its
peace, its faded experience of life are good elements of poetry.
An old lady once said to me quite simply, "The spirits of my
children always seem to hover about me[1]."   Might not something of the kind be expressed in verse?   If it could, like "The
May Queen," it would touch the chords of many hearts.

The 2 Sam. xix. 34, 35 is to me a very affecting passage.

---

[1] My father had heard this saying before, and it was the germ of "The
Grandmother."

I wish Mr Tennyson could be persuaded to put the "Dogma of Immortality" to verse, not the fanciful hope of Immortality from "recollections of childhood," nor the conceptions of a future life derived from the imagery of Scripture such as are common in devotional poetry, but an heroic measure suited to manly minds embodying the deep ethical feeling which convinces us that the end of the Maker though dark is not here. I believe such a poem might be a possession for the world and better (what a bathos!) than ten thousand sermons.

Subjects like blackberries seem to me capable of being gathered off every hedge. (That shows the folly of suggesting what anybody can find for themselves anywhere.) I do not see why the Greek Mythology might not be the subject of a poem; not Wordsworth's "Lively Grecian," but such as it is in the philosophical idea of it as the twilight of the human mind, which lingers still among forms of sense and is unable to pierce them.

Have not many sciences such as Astronomy or Geology a side of feeling which is poetry? No sight touches ordinary persons so much as a starlight night.

I think you once said to me that "Whole philosophies might be contained in a line of verse." Is it not true also that whole periods of history, seen by the light of modern ideas, admit of being described in short passages of poetry? Representative men such as Charlemagne or Hildebrand seem to me safer than the shadowy personages of the legends of romance. The Coronation of Charlemagne, and the scene of Hildebrand and the Emperor might help to form the situation. New friends or foes with old faces might occasionally peep out.

A representative from one of the Monastic orders similar in idea to St Simeon Stylites and to be called St Francis of Assisi, more Christian and less barbarous, would perhaps be possible.

Painters like to teach new lessons in nature. The successive phases of the human mind in different ages are subjects for poetry even more than for philosophy. Might not the poet teach many lessons of that sort, not in the æsthetical, artistic manner of Goethe but with simpler English poetic feeling?

Now I have said enough foolish things and will conclude. You will do me a great favour if you will let me know of any books that I can send Mr Tennyson which you think may be useful or suggestive. Almost anything can be got here, or if you will tell me the subjects, I can find the books.

I hold most strongly that it is the duty of everyone who has the good fortune to know a man of genius, to do any trifling service they can to lighten his work.

I will write to Mr Tennyson in a few days. Remember me to him and

> Believe me most truly yours,
>
> B. JOWETT.

> BALL. COLL.
> *Dec.* 12*th*, 1858.

DEAR MRS TENNYSON,

I cannot but feel greatly ashamed of my ingratitude and disrespect in not having answered your last kind letter which gave me great pleasure at the time I received it. I believe that ingratitude is not the real cause (for that I could not possibly feel) but inveterate indolence about certain things, among which I fear come some of the duties of friendship.

You return me good for evil by sending me the two sweet letters of the children; which I recognize as most genuine productions. Give my love to the two "little birds." Lionel's epistle especially is just a picture of a child's mind.

I hope Mr Tennyson is well and has good success in his great work [1]. Authors great and small have some trials in common and some joys when a "book is born into the world."

I think I have read somewhere a description of Burns' wife and child coming to meet him when he was in a sort of ecstasy, "with the tears rolling down his cheeks," writing "Tam o' Shanter" at the side of a stream. That must be a great alleviation. I am sure it is only success (in the higher sense) and not resignation or philosophy that can make an author happy.

I do not doubt that the world will be charmed with the "Arthur Idylls." No malice will be able to prevent people from seeing that they are most beautiful poems. I have more

---

[1] The "Idylls of the King."

hesitation (shall I go on ?) about the other poem respecting the clerk and wife [1], and could wish that the fortunes of it were tried alone so as not to interfere with the good-will towards " Arthur."

The scene and the satirical passage appear to me the doubtful points.   It seems to me quite as fine as the " Idylls," but I speak with reference to its effect on the public.

You told me that I might suggest to you any subjects that I dreamed of.   Did I mention " Jupiter Olympius," the statue of Phidias ?   The subject could partly be the Olympic games and the interest the Classical Greek feeling of the poem.   But now I want to suggest something that would " express the thoughts of many hearts," which I must always think to be the highest excellence of poetry, and afford a solace where it is much needed.   The subject I mean is " In Memoriam " for the dead in India.   It might be done so as to include some scenes of Cawnpore and Lucknow ; or quite simply and slightly, " Relatives in India," the schemings and hopings and imaginings about them, and the fatal missive suddenly announcing their death. They leave us in the fairness and innocence of youth, with nothing but the vision of their childhood and boyhood to look back upon, and return no more.

Perhaps you know what sets my thoughts upon this, the death of my dear brother, the second who has died in India.   It matters nothing to the world, for they had never the opportunity of distinguishing themselves, but it matters a great deal to me. They were dear good disinterested fellows, most unselfish in their ways, and as grateful to me for what I did for them when they were boys, as if it had been yesterday.   I like to think of them in the days of their youth busying themselves with engineering which was their great amusement.   They were wonderfully attached to each other.   The younger one especially, who died first about five years ago, was one of the sweetest dispositions I ever knew.

If I did not venture to look upon you and Mr Tennyson as something like friends, I should not venture to trouble you with this sorrow about persons whom you have never seen or heard of.

I hope to have the pleasure of coming to see you about the

[1] " Sea Dreams."

6th or 7th of January for a few days.   But I could come at any other time if more convenient.

Ever truly yours, B. Jowett.

1859.

The sudden death of Henry Hallam was a great grief to my father, for the historian had been a good friend through thirty years.   On hearing of Mr Hallam's last days he read some " In Memoriam " aloud and dwelt on those passages which most moved him.   Generally when he was asked to read the poem he would refuse, saying: " It breaks me down, I cannot."   In the spring of the year the four " Idylls of the King," " Enid," " Vivien," " Elaine," " Guinevere," were prepared for publication.

" Boadicea " was also written, the metre being " an echo of the metre in the 'Atys' of Catullus[1]": he wished that it were musically annotated so that it might be read with proper quantity and force.

" Riflemen, Form !" appeared in May in the *Times* after the outbreak of war between France, Piedmont, and Austria; when more than one power seemed to be prepared to take the offensive against England; and it rang like a trumpet-call through the length and breadth of the Empire.   It so happened that three days later an order from the War Office came out, approving of the formation of Volunteer rifle corps.   To Colonel Richards, who was one of the prominent promoters of the movement, my father wrote: " I must heartily congratulate you on your having been able to do so much for your country; and I hope that you will not cease from your labours until it is the law of the land that every male child in it shall be trained to the use of arms."   On the same day that " Riflemen, Form !" was forwarded for

[1] A. T. MS.

publication, the proofs of the last "Idyll" ("Elaine") were finally corrected for press[1].

He made too a song for sailors:

Jack Tar. (*Unpublished.*)

They say some foreign powers have laid their heads
    together
  To break the pride of Britain, and bring her on
    her knees,
There's a treaty, so they tell us, of some dishonest
    fellows
  To break the noble pride of the Mistress of the
    Seas.
      Up, Jack Tars, and save us!
      The whole world shall not brave us!
      Up and save the pride of the Mistress of the
      Seas!

We quarrel here at home, and they plot against us
    yonder,
  They will not let an honest Briton sit at home
    at case:
Up, Jack Tars, my hearties! and the d—l take the
    parties!
  Up and save the pride of the Mistress of the Seas!
      Up, Jack Tars, and save us!
      The whole world shall not brave us!
      Up and save the pride of the Mistress of the
      Seas!

[1] Mr Coventry Patmore wrote to my father in May 1859: "It will please you to hear that 'Riflemen, Form!' is being responded to. I hear that four hundred clerks of the War Office alone have at once answered to the Government invitation, and on my proposing that our department should send a contingent, almost every man in the place put his name down, although a large cost will be incurred, and we are nearly all poor. If things go through the country at that rate, there never will be an invasion."

The lasses and the little ones, Jack Tars, they look to
    you!
The despots over yonder, let 'em do whate'er they
    please!
God bless the little isle where a man may still be
    true!
God bless the noble isle that is Mistress of the
    Seas!
    Up, Jack Tars, and save us!
    The whole world shall not brave us!
    If *you* will save the pride of the Mistress of
    the Seas.

In *Once a Week*, July 16th, was published "The
Grandmother's Apology" with a beautiful illustration by
Millais.

With a view to some new "Idylls of the King" my
father was studying "Pelleas and Ettarre" and "La
belle Isoude"; and, after working at those already in
print, went for a holiday in August with Mr Palgrave to
Portugal.

My father's letter-diary. Journey to Portugal
with F. T. Palgrave and F. C. Grove[1].

August 16*th*.   Radley's Hotel, Southampton.   Have
been over the Vectis, the name of the vessel, not Tagus,
Tagus being repaired, or running alternately with the
Vectis.   She is very prettily got up and painted, and
apparently scrupulously clean.   Brookfield[2] keeps up my
spirits by wonderful tales, puns, etc.   I find that neither
Palgrave nor Grove wants to move except as I will and
they are quite content to remain at Cintra.

August 17*th*.   Have passed a night somewhat broken
by railway whistles.

[1] Eldest son of Judge Sir W. Grove.
[2] Brookfield had come to see his friends off from Southampton.

[This — writes Palgrave — was Tennyson's second voyage (so far as I know) of more than Channel length. It was strange, that sensation of the little moving island, the vessel which was bridging for us the ocean between England and Iberia : "like a world hung in space," as Tennyson called it. Tennyson's flow and fertility in anecdote, such as I have elsewhere tried to sketch it, was wonderful.

No need to dwell on the few incidents which broke the pleasant monotony of the voyage : porpoises plunging and re-appearing round the ship, like black wheels ploughing the gray-blue waters : small whales spouting their fountains on the near horizon : the meridian observations ; the rocks of Ushant : the beacon light on Finisterre : I name them only because of the vivid interest with which they were studied by Tennyson. But we desired nothing better than the *far niente* of those cloudless days. Presently, however, that craving for "the palms and temples of the South" which he was never to gratify, fell upon Tennyson ; and he began to long in vain to push onward to Teneriffe.]

August 21st. Braganza Hotel, Lisbon. Just arrived at Lisbon and settled at the Braganza Hotel after a very prosperous voyage tho' with a good deal of rolling. We merely touched at Vigo which looked fruitful, rolled up in a hot mist, and saw Oporto from the sea, looking very white in a fat port-wine country. It is here just as hot as one would wish it to be but not at all too hot. There was a vast deal of mist and fog all along the coast as we came. Lisbon I have not yet seen except from the sea, and it does not equal expectation as far as seen [1]. Palgrave and Grove have been helpful and pleasant companions, and so far all has gone well. We shall go to Cintra either to-morrow or next day. It is said to be Lisbon's Richmond and rather cockney tho' high and cool. The man who is landlord here is English and an Englishman keeps the hotel at Cintra. I hope with good hope that I shall not be pestered with the plagues of Egypt. I cannot say whether we shall stick at Cintra or go further on. Brookfield gave a good account of the cleanliness of Seville.

[1] Except the convent chapel at Belem.

August 23*rd*. Cintra. We drove over Lisbon yesterday in a blazing heat and saw the Church of St Vincent, and the Botanical Gardens where palms and prickly pears and huge cactuses were growing, and enormous oleanders covered all over with the richest red blossom, and I thought of our poor one at Farringford that won't blossom. There were two strange barbaric statues at the gate of the garden, which were dug up on the top of a hill in Portugal : some call them Phœnician but no one knows much about them. I tried to see the grave of Fielding the novelist, who is buried in the Protestant cemetery, but could find no one to let me in ; he lies among the cypresses. In the evening we came on here : the drive was a cold one, and the country dry, tawny, and wholly uninteresting. Cintra disappointed me at first sight, and perhaps will continue to disappoint, tho' to southern eyes from its ever green groves, in contrast to the parched barren look of the landscape, it must look very lovely. I climbed with Grove to the Peña, a Moorish-looking castle on the top of the hill, which is being repaired, and which has gateways fronted with tiles in pattern ; these gates look like those in the illustrated *Arabian Nights* of Lane [1].

August 26*th*. It is, I think, now decided that we are to go on to Cadiz and Seville on the 2nd, and then to Gibraltar and possibly to Tangiers, possibly to Malaga and Granada. The King's Chamberlain has found me out by my name : his name is the Marquis of Figueros or some such sound ; and yesterday even the Duke of Saldanha came into the *salle à manger*, described himself as " having fought under the great Duke, and having been in two and forty combats and successful in all, as having married two English wives, both perfect women," etc., and ended with seizing my hand and crying out

---

[1] Then they strolled to the Bay of Apples.

" Who does not know England's Poet Laureate ?   I am the Duke of Saldanha." I continue pretty well except for toothache ; I like the place much better as I know it better. A visit to Santarem (the city of convents) was greatly enjoyed.

[The town itself proved a labyrinth of narrow and filthy streets, though here also were many large ecclesiastical buildings, ending in a vast ruined castle, which from an immense height commanded the river valley. Here we two (for our pleasant comrade had now left us) sat long, and beneath us saw miles on miles of level land, forest and vineyard, dotted with unknown villages, and lighted up by the long curves of the Tagus. This undoubtedly is one of the great panoramic landscapes of Europe, and I suppose the least visited. Nearer the city, thorny lines of glaucous aloe, here and there throwing out lofty flower-stems, ran up the hill-sides planted thick with olive-trees, beneath which the sun now cast down long separate shadows, and illuminated the Tagus flowing right below our eyes between wide tawny sandbanks to the deepest fold of its green and sinuous channel[1].]

Sept. 2nd. Lisbon. The heat and the flies and the fleas and one thing or another have decided us to return by the boat to Southampton which starts from this place on the 7th. We propose on arriving at Southampton to pass on to Lyndhurst to spend two or three days in the Forest.

[Our visit, we gradually found, was not at the most favourable season : the fields browned and burnt by heat, the mosquitoes afflicting. Against the latter, Tennyson had provided himself with an elaborate tent (first contrived, I believe, by Sir C. Fellowes for use in Asia Minor, during the night-time) : a sheet formed into a large bag, but ending in a muslin canopy, which was distended by a cane circle, and hung upwards, to accommodate head and shoulders, from a nail which I took the freedom to run into his bedroom wall. Into this shelter the occupant crept by a narrow sheet-funnel, which he closed by twisting ; and once in, he was unable to light a match outside for fear lest the action should set the muslin on fire. Hence one night Tennyson, able to command the bell, summoned the waiter. I brought him in through my (contiguous) room with a light ; and the man's terror at the spectacle of the great ghost, looking spectral within its white canopy, was

[1] Palgrave MS.

delightful.   He almost ran off.   But I think that after this experience
Tennyson abandoned the tent and took his chances : only pretending
to wish that he had a little baby in bed with him, as a whiter and more
tempting morsel to the insect world.

More serious than the mosquito was the sun.   This so wrought
upon and disturbed Tennyson, in a manner with which many English
travellers to Italy during the heat will be unpleasantly familiar, that he
now began gravely to talk about leaving his bones by the side of the
great novelist Fielding, who died and was buried at Lisbon in 1754 [1].]

Sept. 13*th.* Southampton.   Arrived, and going on
to-morrow to Lyndhurst, where I shall stop two or three
days, then I am going on to Cambridge with Palgrave
from a longing desire that I have to be there once
more.

Crown Hotel, Lyndhurst.   Palgrave has been as
kind to me as a brother, and far more useful than a valet
or courier, doing everything.   His father is away at Spa,
he (Palgrave) is horrified at being alone.   I gave him
hopes of his being with me till his father returned and I
do not therefore like to leave him.

Sept. 20*th.* Cambridge.   I have been spending the
evening with my old tobacconist in whose house I used
to lodge, and to-morrow I am to dine with Macmillan.
I admire Jesus Chapel which is more like a Church than
a Chapel.

[Palgrave writes : Cambridge was in Long Vacation, but Munro, the
great Latin scholar, and W. G. Clark, then charming and gay, and
unforeseeing the shadow destined to eclipse his later days, feasted us ;
welcoming Tennyson once again back to Trinity.   He showed me,
with pathos in his voice of memories distant and dear, Arthur Hallam's
rooms ; the " Backs," to which Oxford (he would have it) " has no rival,"
and the curious Jacobean brickwork of Queens' College, where in his
time the " Combination room " had yet a sanded floor, and the table
was set handsomely forth with long " church-wardens."]

In the autumn my father returned to Farringford
and entertained the American statesman, Charles Sumner.

[1] Palgrave MS.

In November he was reading with intense interest an early copy of Darwin's *Origin of Species*, sent him by his own desire; and was finishing his "Tithonus," which he forwarded to Thackeray for the *Cornhill Magazine*[1]. A letter came from Charles Kingsley:

EVERSLEY, 1859.

MY DEAR TENNYSON,

I wrote for *Fraser*, September 1850, a review of you, and especially of "In Memoriam." I am now going to publish a set of Miscellanies and thought of including that review. But when I read it through I thought I ought to ask your leave. I felt it almost too personal toward you in its expression of admiration and gratitude for your influence, and in its expression about "In Memoriam." It was necessary to be so then; for, while penny-a-liners were talking vulgar and unkind personalities, I felt bound to tell all whom I could make listen, what a gentleman and a Christian ought to think of you and your work; but I am not sure that you would like all I said there republished now that the bubble is over. Will you say "Yes" or "No"? and if you will say "Yes," you will deeply gratify me; for I wish to leave behind me some record of what I owe you. Pray remember me to Mrs Tennyson and to your children, whom I do not know alas! I seem destined never to see you. Here I live, as busy as a bee in my parish, and never leave home but for urgent business.

Believe me your devoted C. KINGSLEY.

Soon after this the Kingsleys paid us a visit. "Charles Kingsley," so my father told me, "talked as usual on all sorts of topics and walked hard up and down the study for hours smoking furiously, and affirming that tobacco was the only thing that kept his nerves quiet." Among the topics discussed were the "Idylls" which Kingsley admired only less than "In Memoriam." Ten thousand copies had been sold in the first week of publication, and hundreds more were selling monthly. The reviews that were best in my father's estimation appeared

[1] February, 1860.

in the *Spectator*, the *Edinburgh* and the *Quarterly*, the last by Mr Gladstone [1].

Letters to and from friends about the "Idylls."

From Henry W. Longfellow.

MY DEAR MR TENNYSON,

I have requested my publishers in London, Messrs Routledge, to send you a copy of a translation of the *Divina Commedia*, which I have had the temerity to make, and which they are now publishing. In the notes I have taken the liberty to quote your beautiful song of Fortune (from " Enid "), and also part of " Ulysses," at which, I hope, you will not be displeased, as you are in very good company. Many thanks for your kind letter acknowledging the (Red Indian) red stone pipe of peace. To a civilized human being I fancy it can never be of any practical use. But it is pretty, and has a certain value as coming from those far-away Western mountains.

Always with great regard yours truly,

HENRY W. LONGFELLOW.

From W. M. Thackeray.

FOLKESTONE, *September.*
36 ONSLOW SQUARE, *October.*

MY DEAR OLD ALFRED,

I owe you a letter of happiness and thanks. Sir, about three weeks ago, when I was ill in bed, I read the " Idylls of the King," and I thought, " Oh I must write to him now, for this pleasure, this delight, this splendour of happiness which I have been enjoying." But I should have blotted the sheets, 'tis ill writing on one's back. The letter full of gratitude never went as far as the post-office and how comes it now?

D'abord, a bottle of claret. (The landlord of the hotel asked me down to the cellar and treated me.) Then afterwards sitting here, an old magazine, *Fraser's Magazine*, 1850, and I come on a poem out of " The Princess " which says " I hear the horns of

[1] For chapter on the " Idylls," see Vol. II., p. 121.

Elfland blowing blowing," no, it's "the horns of Elfland faintly
blowing " (I have been into my bedroom to fetch my pen and it
has made that blot), and, reading the lines, which only one man
in the world could write, I thought about the other horns of
Elfland blowing in full strength, and Arthur in gold armour, and
Guinevere in gold hair, and all those knights and heroes and
beauties and purple landscapes and misty gray lakes in which
you have made me live.　They seem like facts to me, since about
three weeks ago (three weeks or a month was it?) when I read
the book.　It is on the table yonder, and I don't like, somehow,
to disturb it, but the delight and gratitude!　You have made me
as happy as I was as a child with the *Arabian Nights*, every step
I have walked in Elfland has been a sort of Paradise to me.
(The landlord gave *two* bottles of his claret and I think I drank
the most) and here I have been lying back in the chair and
thinking of those delightful " Idylls," my thoughts being turned to
you : what could I do but be grateful to that surprising genius
which has made me so happy?　Do you understand that what
I mean is all true and that I should break out were you sitting
opposite with a pipe in your mouth?　Gold and purple and
diamonds, I say, gentlemen and glory and love and honour, and
if you haven't given me all these why should I be in such an
ardour of gratitude?　But I have had out of that dear book the
greatest delight that has ever come to me since I was a young
man ; to write and think about it makes me almost young,
and this I suppose is what I'm doing, like an after-dinner
speech.

P.S.　I thought the " Grandmother " quite as fine.　How can
you at 50 be doing things as well as at 35 ?

October 16*th*. (I should think six weeks after the writing of
the above.)

The rhapsody of gratitude was never sent, and for a peculiar
reason ; just about the time of writing I came to an arrangement
with Smith and Elder to edit their new magazine, and to have a
contribution from T. was the publishers' and editor's highest
ambition.　But to ask a man for a favour, and to praise and
bow down before him in the same page seemed to be so like
hypocrisy, that I held my hand, and left this note in my desk,
where it has been lying during a little French-Italian-Swiss tour
which my girls and their papa have been making.

Meanwhile S. E. and Co. have been making their own

proposals to you, and you have replied not favourably I am
sorry to hear: but now there is no reason why you should not
have my homages, and I am just as thankful for the "Idylls,"
and love and admire them just as much, as I did two months
ago when I began to write in that ardour of claret and gratitude.
If you can't write for us you can't.   If you can by chance some
day, and help an old friend, how pleased and happy I shall be!
This however must be left to fate and your convenience : I don't
intend to give up hope, but accept the good fortune if it comes.
I see one, two, three quarterlies advertized to-day, as all bringing
laurels to laureatus.   He will not refuse the private tribute of an
old friend, will he ?   You don't know how pleased the girls were
at Kensington t'other day to hear you quote their father's little
verses, and he too I daresay was not disgusted.   He sends you
and yours his very best regards in this most heartfelt and
artless

(note of admiration)!

Always yours, my dear Alfred,

W. M. THACKERAY.

To W. M. Thackeray.

FARRINGFORD.

MY DEAR THACKERAY,

Should I not have answered you ere this 6th
of November? surely: what excuse? none that I know
of: except indeed, that perhaps your very generosity and
boundlessness of approval made me in a measure shame-
faced. I could scarcely accept it, being, I fancy, a
modest man, and always more or less doubtful of my
own efforts in any line. But I may tell you that your
little note gave me more pleasure than all the journals
and monthlies and quarterlies which have come across
me: not so much from your being the Great Novelist I
hope as from your being my good old friend, or perhaps
from your being both of these in one. Well, let it be.
I have been ransacking all sorts of old albums and scrap
books but cannot find anything worthy sending you.

Unfortunately before your letter arrived I had agreed to give Macmillan the only available poem I had by me (" Sea Dreams ") [1]. I don't think he would have got it (for I dislike publishing in magazines) except that he had come to visit me in my Island, and was sitting and blowing his weed vis-à-vis. I am sorry that you have engaged for any quantity of money to let your brains be sucked periodically by Smith, Elder & Co.: not that I don't like Smith who seems from the very little I have seen of him liberal and kindly, but that so great an artist as you are should go to work after this fashion. Whenever you feel your brains as the " remainder biscuit," or indeed whenever you will, come over to me and take a blow on these downs where the air as Keats said is " worth sixpence a pint," and bring your girls too.

Yours always, A. TENNYSON.

From the Duke of Argyll.

LONDON, *July* 14*th*, 1859.

MY DEAR MR TENNYSON,

I think my prediction is coming true, that your " Idylls of the King " will be understood and admired by many who are incapable of understanding and appreciating many of your other works.

Macaulay is certainly not a man incapable of *understanding* anything but I knew that his tastes in poetry were so formed in another line that I considered him a good test, and three days ago I gave him " Guinevere."

The result has been as I expected, that he has been *delighted with it.* He told me that he had been greatly moved by it, and admired it exceedingly. Altho' by practice and disposition he is eminently a critic, he did not find one single fault. Yesterday I gave him the " Maid of Astolat " with which he was delighted also.

I hear the article in the *Edin. Review* is not to contain

---

[1] " Tithonus " was sent to Thackeray for the *Cornhill*, February, 1860.

much criticism, it consists to a great extent of long extracts. But I have not seen it myself, nor am I sure who wrote it.

How are you standing this tropical heat, and Mrs Tennyson? Let us have a good account of yourselves.

This Peace is abominable, and you should be perpetually, telescope in hand, watching for the "Liberator of Italy," who has proclaimed to his soldiers that he stops because the contest is no longer in the *interests of France!*

Yours most sincerely, ARGYLL.

To the Duke of Argyll.

FARRINGFORD,
Monday, July 18th, 1859.

MY DEAR DUKE,

Doubtless Macaulay's good opinion is worth having and I am grateful to you for letting me know it, but this time I intend to be thick-skinned; nay, I scarcely believe that I should ever feel very deeply the pen-punctures of those parasitic animalcules of the press, if they kept themselves to what I write, and did not glance spitefully and personally at myself. I hate spite.

*   *   *   *   *   *

Yours ever, A. TENNYSON.

Best remembrances to the Duchess.

From the Rev. B. Jowett.

19 GLOUCESTER TERRACE,
July 17th, 1859.

MY DEAR TENNYSON,

Thank you many times for your last: I have read it through with the greatest delight, the "Maid of Astolat" twice over, and it rings in my ears. "The Lily Maid" seems to me the fairest, purest, sweetest love-poem in the English language. I have not seen any criticisms nor do I care about them. It moves me like the love of Juliet in Shakespeare (though that is not altogether parallel), and I do not doubt whatever opinions are expressed about it that it will in a few years be above criticism.

There are hundreds and hundreds of all ages (and men as well as women) who, though they have not died for love (have no intention of doing so), will find there a sort of ideal consolation of their own troubles and remembrances.

Of the other poems I admire "Vivien" the most (the naughty one), which seems to me a work of wonderful power and skill.

It is most elegant and fanciful.   I am not surprised at your Delilah reducing the wise man, she is quite equal to it.

The allegory in the distance *greatly strengthens, also elevates, the meaning of the poem.*

I shall not bore you with criticisms.   It struck me what a great number of lines —

> He makes no friends, who never made a foe — [1]
> Then trust me not at all, or all in all —

will pass current on the lips of men, which I always regard as a great test of excellence, for it is saying the thing that everybody feels.

I am sure that the "Grandmother" is a most exquisite thing.

I hope you will find rest after toil and listen to the voice that says " Rejoice, Rejoice."

Next week I shall probably be in London.   I am afraid that I shall not be able to manage going abroad.   But I should like to come and look in upon you if you are at any house where it would be convenient to you to see me.

With most kind regards to Mrs Tennyson and love to the children,

Believe me ever most truly yours,

B. JOWETT.

---

[1] This line my father generally wrote in autograph albums.

From Arthur H. Clough.

COUNCIL OFFICE,
18*th July*, 1859.

DEAR MRS TENNYSON,

The Welsh books appeared suddenly one morning, by what agency I do not know, and I have already appeased my uncle's bibliomaniac fears by communicating the fact of their arrival.

The reception of the "Idylls of the King" will I hope satisfy all Farringford.

I have heard no words of dispraise: and in my own opinion they are just what we had a right to hope for, better, because more fully given, without any disparagement to what went before.

Faithfully yours, A. H. CLOUGH.

From the Duke of Argyll.

July 20th, 1859.

MY DEAR MR TENNYSON,

I hope you will give me note of your arrival in town.

The applause of the "Idylls" goes on crescendo, and so far as I can hear without exception. Detractors are silenced.

Macaulay has repeated to me several times an expression of his great admiration. Another well-known Author, himself a Poet, whom I shall not name, who heretofore could go no further than a half unwilling approval of the "Lotos-Eaters," has succumbed to the "Idylls," has laid down his arms, without reserve. I consider him a test and index of a large class of minds. I have heard of several other obdurate sinners who have been converted from the error of their ways.

Gladstone, who is not one of the class, has spoken to me, and has written to the Duchess of Sutherland that the impression of the power and beauty of these Poems increases daily in reading them.

I am delighted, specially from my love of natural history, with some of your imagery from natural things.

The passage comparing the voice of Enid to the first heard song of the nightingale is singularly beautiful in expression. So is that passage comparing the dispersion of Geraint's foes to the shoals of fish among the " crystal dykes of Camelot."

By the bye I have always omitted to ask you what you mean in one of your old poems by " The Red-Cap [1] whistled." I know of no such bird : don't you mean the *Black*-Cap, which does whistle beautifully? The Golden-crested Wren is never called " Red-Cap," nor can it be said to whistle, tho' it has a loud song.

L. Nap.'s explanation of the Peace is, I have no doubt, a tolerably correct account. But it will seem a bitter mockery to those whose "illusions" he encouraged, and now contemns.

Can you send me a copy of your song " The Great Name of England round and round "? Do.

Yours ever, ARGYLL.

To the Duke of Argyll.

E. L. Lushington's,
PARK HOUSE, MAIDSTONE,
July 29th, 1859.

MY DEAR DUKE,

Your last note was very welcome to me and if I did not answer it earlier, why, I was all the more to blame; answered partly it was by my wife's copy of the song [2] requested, which I hope arrived safely. She has set it to music far more to the purpose than most of Master Balfe's.

" Red-cap " is, or was when I was a lad, provincial for " Gold-finch "; had I known it was purely provincial I should probably not have used it. Now the passage has stood so long that I am loth to alter it.

Ever yours, A. TENNYSON.

---

[1] Provincial name for the goldfinch.
[2] " Riflemen, Form! "

From my father's mother.

ROSE MANOR, WELL WALK.
Monday, Jan. 10th, 1860.

DEAREST ALLY,

I received a nice kind note from Alan Ker a short time since, which I now enclose, thinking it will give thee pleasure to know what he says about thy last beautiful and interesting poems. It does indeed (as he supposes it would) give me the purest satisfaction to notice that a spirit of Christianity is perceptible through the whole volume. It gladdens my heart also to perceive that Alan seems to estimate it greatly on that account. O dearest Ally, how fervently have I prayed for years that our merciful Redeemer would intercede with our Heavenly Father, to grant thee His Holy Spirit to urge thee to employ the talents He has given thee, by taking every opportunity of endeavouring to impress the precepts of His Holy Word on the minds of others. My beloved son, words are too feeble to express the joy of my heart in perceiving that thou art earnestly endeavouring to do so. Dearest Ally, there is nothing for a moment to be compared to the favour of God: I need not ask thee if thou art of the same opinion. Thy writings are a convincive proof that thou art. My beloved child, when our Heavenly Father summons us hence, may we meet, and all that are dear to us, in that blessed state where sorrow is unknown, never more to be separated. I hope Emmy and thyself continue well, also the dear little boys. All here join me in kindest love to both.

Ever, dearest Ally,

Thy attached and loving mother,

E. TENNYSON.

From J. Ruskin.

STRASBURG.

DEAR MR TENNYSON,

I have had the "Idylls" in my travelling desk ever since I could get them across the water, and have only not written about them because I could not quite make up my mind about that increased quietness of style. I thought you would like a little to know what I felt about it, but did not quite know myself what I did feel.

To a certain extent you yourself of course know better what the work is than anyone else, as all great artists do.

If you are satisfied with it, I believe it to be right. Satisfied with bits of it you must be, and so must all of us, however much we expect from you.

The four songs seem to me the jewels of the crown, and bits come every here and there, the fright of the maid for instance, and the "In the darkness o'er her fallen head," which seem to me finer than almost all you have done yet. Nevertheless I am not sure but I feel the art and finish in these poems a little more than I like to feel it[1]. Yet I am not a fair judge quite, for I am so much of a realist as not by any possibility to interest myself much in an unreal subject to feel it as I should, and the very sweetness and stateliness of the words strike me all the more as *pure* workmanship.

As a description of various nobleness and tenderness the book is without price: but I shall always wish it had been nobleness independent of a romantic condition of externals in general.

"In Memoriam," "Maud," "The Miller's Daughter," and such like will always be my own pet rhymes, yet I am quite prepared to admit this to be as good as any, for its own peculiar audience. Treasures of wisdom there are in it, and word painting such as never was yet for concentration, nevertheless it seems to me that so great power ought not to be spent on visions of things past but on the living present. For one hearer capable of feeling the depth of this poem I believe ten would feel a depth quite as great if the stream flowed through things nearer the hearer. And merely in the facts of modern life, not

---

[1] So far as the word *art*, as used here by Mr Ruskin, suggests that these Idylls were carefully elaborated, the suggestion is hardly in accordance with the fact. The more imaginative the poem, the less time it generally took him to compose. "Guinevere" and "Elaine" were certainly not elaborated, seeing that they were written, each of them, in a few weeks, and hardly corrected at all. My father said that he often did not know why some passages were thought specially beautiful, until he had examined them. He added: "Perfection in art is perhaps more sudden sometimes than we think; but then the long preparation for it, that unseen germination, *that* is what we ignore and forget."

drawing-room formal life, but the far away and quite unknown growth of souls in and through any form of misery or servitude, there is an infinity of what men should be told, and what none but a poet can tell. I cannot but think that the intense masterful and unerring transcript of an actuality, and the relation of a story of any real human life as a poet would watch and analyze it, would make all men feel more or less what poetry was, as they felt what Life and Fate were in their instant workings.

This seems to me the true task of the modern poet. And I think I have seen faces, and heard voices by road and street side, which claimed or conferred as much as ever the loveliest or saddest of Camelot. As I watch them, the feeling continually weighs upon me, day by day, more and more, that not the grief of the world but the loss of it is the wonder of it. I see creatures so full of all power and beauty, with none to understand or teach or save them. The making in them of miracles and all cast away, for ever lost as far as we can trace. And no "in memoriam."

I do not ask when you are likely to be in London for I know you do not like writing letters, and I know you will let Mrs Prinsep or Watts send me word about you, so that I may come and see you again, when you do come; and then on some bright winter's day, I shall put in my plea for Denmark Hill.

Meanwhile believe me always

Faithfully and gratefully yours, J. RUSKIN.

Part of a letter from Aubrey de Vere.

1860.

Love to Alfred, from whom I hope to have more of those glorious chivalrous legends. * * *

Alfred seems to be founding a school just as Raffaelle and Titian founded their respective Roman and Venetian schools. There cannot be a truer tribute to genius than this. It proves that it has struck roots in the national mind.

From H.R.H. Prince Albert.

BUCKINGHAM PALACE,
17th May, 1860.

MY DEAR MR TENNYSON,

Will you forgive me if I intrude upon your leisure with a request which I have thought some little time of making, viz. that you would be good enough to write your name in the accompanying volume of your "Idylls of the King"? You would thus add a peculiar interest to the book, containing those beautiful songs, from the perusal of which I derived the greatest enjoyment. They quite rekindle the feeling with which the legends of King Arthur must have inspired the chivalry of old, whilst the graceful form in which they are presented blends those feelings with the softer tone of our present age.

Believe me always yours truly, ALBERT.

From the Rev. Charles Kingsley.

EVERSLEY RECTORY, WINCHFIELD,
Nov. 10th, 1859.

MY DEAR TENNYSON,

I was amused to-night at a burst of enthusiasm in your behalf from a most unenthusiastic man (though a man of taste and scholarship), Walter the proprietor of the *Times*. He confest to having been a disbeliever in you, save in "Locksley Hall," which he said was the finest modern lyric; but he considered you had taken liberties, and so forth. But the "Idylls," he confest, had beaten him. He thought them the finest modern poem. There was nothing he did not or would not say in praise of them. He now classed the four great English poets as Shakespeare, Spenser, Byron, Tennyson, and so on, and so on, very pleasant to me though little worth to you. But I like to tell you of a "jamjam efficaci do manus scientiæ" from anyone who has not as yet appreciated you, to his own harm. He did not write the disagreeable review of you in the *Times* some years back. It was, I believe, a poor envious, dyspeptic, poetaster parson, ——. I tell you this for fear you should think Walter, who is really a fine fellow, had anything to do with it.

God bless you, C. KINGSLEY.

To the Duke of Argyll.

FARRINGFORD,
Oct. 3rd, 1859.

MY DEAR DUKE,

We are delighted to hear that your Duchess has added another scion to your race, and that mother and child are both prospering. I had fancied that the event would have come off while I was in Portugal (for in Portugal I have been), and made enquiries thereanent of Mr Henry Howard [1] but he could tell me nothing.

If I came back with "bullion" in the "Tagus," it was nowhere in my packages. I went to see that Cintra which Byron and Beckford have made so famous : but the orange-trees were all dead of disease, and the crystal streams (with the exception of a few sprinkling springlets by the wayside) either dried up, or diverted thro' unseen tunnels into the great aqueduct of Lisbon. Moreover the place is cockney, and, when I was there, was crammed with Lisbon fashionables and Portuguese nobility; yet Cintra is not without its beauties, being a mountain of green pines rising out of an everywhere arid and tawny country, with a fantastic Moorish-looking castle on the peak, which commands a great sweep of the Atlantic and the mouth of the Tagus : here on the topmost tower sat the king (they say) day by day in the old times of Vasco da Gama watching for his return, till he saw him enter the river : there, perhaps, was a moment worth having been waited for. I made some pleasant acquaintances, but I could not escape autograph hunters; a certain Don Pedro Something even telegraphed for one after I had returned to Lisbon.

As to Macaulay's suggestion of the Sangreal, I doubt whether such a subject could be handled in these days, without incurring a charge of irreverence. It would be

[1] English Minister at Lisbon in 1859.

too much like playing with sacred things. The old writers *believed* in the Sangreal. Many years ago I did write " Lancelot's Quest of the Grail " in as good verses as I ever wrote, no, I did not write, I made it in my head, and it has now altogether slipt out of memory.

My wife, I am sorry to say, has been very unwell.

Yours ever, A. TENNYSON.

UNPUBLISHED POEM OF THIS PERIOD.

The Philosopher.

He was too good and kind and sweet,
 Ev'n when I knew him in his hour
 Of darkest doubt, and in his power,
To fling his doubts into the street.

Truth-seeking he and not afraid,
 But questions that perplex us now —
 What time (he thought) have loom or plough
To weigh them as they should be weighed?

We help the blatant voice abroad
 To preach the freedom of despair,
 And from the heart of all things fair
To pluck the sanction of a God.

CHAPTER XXI.

TOUR IN CORNWALL AND THE SCILLY ISLES.

1860.

So great had been the success of the first four "Idylls of the King" that my father's friends begged him to "continue the epic." He received a letter from the Duke of Argyll again urging him to take up as his next subject the Holy Grail, but he said he shunned handling the subject, for fear that it might seem to some almost profane. He answered:

1860.

My dear Duke,

I sympathised with you when I read of Macaulay's death in the *Times*. He was, was he not, your next-door neighbour? I can easily conceive what a loss you must have had in the want of his brilliant conversation. I hardly knew him: met him once, I remember, when Hallam and Guizot were in his company: Hallam was showing Guizot the Houses of Parliament then building, and Macaulay went on like a cataract for an hour or so to those two great men, and, when they had gone, turned to me and said, "Good morning, I am happy to have had the pleasure of making your acquaintance," and strode away. Had I been a piquable man I should have been piqued, but I don't think I was, for the movement after all was amicable.

Of the two books I should, I think, have chosen the
Crabbe, though Macaulay's criticisms on poetry would
be less valuable probably than his historical ones. Peace
be with him !

As to the *Sangreal,* as I gave up the subject so
many long years ago I do not think that I shall resume
it. You will see a little poem of mine in the *Cornhill
Magazine.* My friend Thackeray and his publishers
had been so urgent with me to send them something,
that I ferreted among my old books and found this
" Tithonus," written upwards of a quarter of a century
ago, and now queerly enough at the tail of a flashy
modern novel. It was originally a pendent to the
" Ulysses " in my former volumes, and I wanted Smith
to insert a letter, not of mine, to the editor stating this,
and how long ago it had been written, but he thought
it would lower the value of the contribution in the
public eye. Read in Browning's *Men and Women*
"Evelyn Hope" for its beauty, and "Bishop Blougram's
Apology " for its exceeding cleverness, and I think that
you will not deny him his own. The *Cornhill Magazine* gives a very pleasant account of Macaulay.

                              Yours ever, A. TENNYSON.

The Duke and the Duchess spent some days at
Farringford, and were most emphatic that the " Grail "
ought to be written forthwith. My father said that he
was not " at present in the mood for it," and read aloud
his " Boadicea," which he had now quite finished. He
gloried in his new English metre, but he "feared
that no one could read it except himself, and wanted
someone to annotate it musically so that people could
understand the rhythm." " If they would only read
it straight like prose," he said, " just as it is written,
it would come all right." Among other guests was

Lord Dufferin, full of Cyril Graham's discoveries of the white marble cities in the black basaltic land of the Hauran with their inscriptions in an unknown tongue. Then the missionary Dr Wolff stayed with us, recounting his hairbreadth escapes in Central Asia, and giving an awe-inspiring description of an earthquake in Bokhara.

It was not until August that my father was able to go on his summer tour to Cornwall and the Scilly Isles, in company with Woolner, Palgrave, Holman Hunt and Val Prinsep.

My father's letter-diary.   Tour in Cornwall and the Scilly Isles.

August 18*th.*   All Souls' Reading Room, Oxford. Before my departure Palgrave called with his Syrian brother, a very interesting man in an Eastern dress with a kind of turban, having just escaped from his convent in the Syrian Deserts where several of his fellow monks were massacred.   Palgrave is obliged to stop for a week at Hampstead till the brother goes to Paris, where he will have an interview with the Emperor on the affairs of the East.   I started off alone, and I believe that in a week's time Holman Hunt, Val Prinsep and Frank Palgrave will join me at Penzance. Woolner, like a good fellow, followed me here yesterday that I might not feel lonely, and this morning we breakfasted with Max Müller, and are going to dine with him at 7.

August 21*st.*   Bideford.   We came here last night at 7 o'clock.   I and Woolner are going down the coast to Tintagel, where we shall stop till the others join us.

August 23*rd.*   Bude.   Fine sea here, smart rain alternating with weak sunshine.   Woolner is very kindly. We go off to-day to Boscastle which is three miles from Tintagel.

August 23rd. Arrived at Tintagel, grand coast, furious rain. Mr Poelaur would be a good name to direct to me by.

August 25th. Tintagel. Black cliffs and caves and storm and wind, but I weather it out and take my ten miles a day walks in my weather-proofs. Palgrave arrived to-day.

To Hallam.

TINTAGEL,
Aug. 25th, 1860.

MY DEAR HALLAM,

I was very glad to receive your little letter. Mind that you and Lionel do not quarrel and vex poor mamma who has lots of work to do; and learn your lessons regularly; for gentlemen and ladies will not take you for a gentleman when you grow up if you are ignorant. Here are great black cliffs of slate-rock, and deep, black caves, and the ruined castle of King Arthur, and I wish that you and Lionel and mamma were here to see them. Give my love to grandpapa and to Lionel, and work well at your lessons. I shall be glad to find you know more and more every day.

Your loving papa, A. TENNYSON.

August 28th. Tintagel. We believe that we are going to-morrow to Penzance or in that direction. We have had two fine days and some exceedingly grand coast views. Here is an artist, a friend of Woolner's (Inchbold), sketching now in this room. I am very tired of walking against wind and rain.

[Mr Palgrave writes: Following the publication of the first four "Idylls of the King" in 1859, when he was intending to write further Idylls, this was, perhaps, specially entitled to be named Tennyson's Arthurian journey.

At a sea inlet of wonderful picturesqueness, so grandly

modelled are the rocks which wall it, so translucently purple the
waves that are its pavement, — waves whence the " naked babe "
Arthur came ashore in flame, — stand the time-eaten ruins of
unknown date which bear the name Tintagel. To these of course
we climbed, — descending from "the castle gateway by the
chasm," and at a turn in the rocks meeting that ever graceful,
ill-appreciated landscapist, Inchbold: whose cry of delighted
wonder at sight of Tennyson still sounds in the sole survivor's
ear. Thence, after some delightful wandering walks, by a dreary
road (for such is often the character of central Cornwall), we
moved to Camelford on the greatly-winding stream which the
name indicates. Near the little town, on the edge of the river, is
shown a large block of stone upon which legend places Arthur,
hiding or meditating, after his last fatal battle. It lay below the
bank; and in his eagerness to reach it and sit down (as he
sat in 1851 on that other, the *Sasso di Dante* by Sta. Maria del
Fiore), Arthur's poet slipped right into the stream, and returned
laughing to Camelford.

The next halting-place I remember was Penzance; whence,
by Marazion, we crossed to and saw our English smaller but
yet impressive and beautiful St Michael's Mount [1].]

August 31*st.* Union Hotel, Penzance. I am so
very much grieved for poor Simeon's loss of his wife;
it casts a gloom on my little tour: what will he do
without her and with all those children? I have now
walked 10 miles a day for 10 days, equal 100, and
I want to continue doing that for some time longer. I
am going to-morrow to Land's End and then I must
return here, and then I go to the Scilly Isles and then
again return here.

Sept. 5*th.* Land's End Inn. I will write to Simeon
to-day, tho' I rather shun writing to him on such a
subject, for what can one say, what comfort can one
give? We are here at this racketty, rather dirty inn,
but we have had four glorious days and *magnificently
coloured seas.* To-day the Scilly Isles look so dark and
clear on the horizon that one expects rain.

[1] Palgrave MS.

[I was struck — Mr Palgrave notes again — on the plateau of Sennen by the likeness between the masses of rock, piled up by Nature only, and those cromlechs which also occur in Cornwall; "Do you not remember that Wordsworth has a sonnet on this point?" Tennyson said, alluding to that beginning

"Mark the concentred hazels..."

adding, "He seems to have been always before one in observation of Nature [1]."]

Sept. 6th. Penzance. I start in an hour by the boat for the Scilly Islands. The weather is splendid, and the sea as calm as any lake shut in on all sides by hills. Woolner goes back to London and Palgrave continues with me.

Sept. 9th. St Mary's, Scilly Isles. Captain Tregarthen, who has the packet and the hotel here, has brought me my letters: the packet only goes three times a week. I shall stop here till Wednesday; there are West Indian aloes here 30 feet high, in blossom, and out all the winter, yet the peaches won't ripen; vast hedges of splendid geraniums, a delight to the eye, yet the mulberry won't ripen. These Islands are very peculiar and in some respects very fine. I never saw anything quite like them.

Sept. 11th. Three Tuns, Lizard. At the Lizard; and intend coming on to Falmouth. Hope to be at Brockenhurst next Saturday, but if not there, I shall have turned aside to see Avebury and Silbury Hill.

Sept. 20th. Falmouth. Have not found it easy to write every day in the bustle and bother of travellers' inns. I am now writing on my knees in my bedroom at a fishmonger's, there being no room at the hotel, and the whole town mad with a bazaar for riflemen, who get drunk every night and squabble and fight and

[1] Palgrave MS.

disgrace themselves and their corps.   We left Hunt and
Val Prinsep hard at work at the Lizard, sketching on
a promontory.

[Mr Palgrave concludes his notes on this tour thus: From
Falmouth [1] a little river-steamer was to carry us to Truro.
We sat on deck enjoying the fresh air and sight of the
fine estuary. But upon *l'incognito* Tennyson had reckoned too
soon. Our captain presently came forward with a tray and a
squat bottle, and said with unimpeachable good manners that
" he was aware how distinguished a passenger, etc., and that
some young men sitting opposite, and he, would be much
honoured if Mr Tennyson would take a tumbler of stout with
them." With as much courteous ease as if he had been a royal
prince he stepped forward, said a few words of graceful thanks,
pleased, and looking so; bowed to the hospitable party; and
drank off his glass to their good health.

Presently the Captain reappeared, and this time it was the
ladies in the cabin who begged that the Laureate would only
step down among them. But the height of that small place of
refuge, Tennyson declared, would render the proposed exhibition impossible; might he not be kindly excused? The good
women however were not to be baulked; and one after another
presented her half-length above the little hatchway before us,
gazed, smiled and retreated. " It was like the crowned figures
who appear and vanish in *Macbeth*," he said; and so, talking
with our fellow-passengers and the captain, in due time we
disembarked at Truro.

Next day a long and pleasant walk took us to Perran-
porth, a little village on the coast, which here was a stretch
of level golden sands, barred at each end by fine rocks. Some
way hence, we were directed through a little labyrinth of dunes

---

[1] Caroline Fox described my father on this tour in *Memories of Old
Friends*: " Tennyson is a grand specimen of a man, with a magnificent
head set on his shoulders like the capital of a mighty pillar. His hair is
long and wavy, and covers a massive head. He wears a beard and
moustache, which one begrudges, as hiding so much of that firm, forceful,
but finely chiselled mouth. His eyes are large, gray (?), and open wide when
a subject interests him; they are well shaded by the noble brow, with its
strong lines of thought and suffering. I can quite understand Sam. Laurence
calling it the best balance of head he had ever seen."

to the famous buried church of Perranzabuloe. Only a few sand-heaped lines of wall remain. But St Piran is assigned to the fifth century, and the church might be of Arthur's age, if we place him about that period [1].]

A vivid picture of my father, from a letter addressed to my mother (23rd Sept. 1860) by Woolner, may be added:

"I expect idling about so long will make his brain so fertile that when he gets back to Farringford he will do an immense deal of work. He was physically better, there can be no question, for he actually ate breakfasts! and partook of tarts not once but *twice* at dinner! which he had not done before for many years: and his face had grown a reddish bronze, a very healthy colour; and he was perpetually making jokes at expense of Palgrave, or at mine, and taking long walks, and swimming, and not smoking much, and drinking scarcely any wine. So you may consider all this as flourishing."

In my father's note-book are written as below the following Verse-Memoranda of tours in Cornwall, Isle of Wight and Ireland [2].

(*Babbicombe.*) Like serpent-coils upon the deep.
(*Torquay.*) As the little thrift
Trembles in perilous places o'er the deep.
(*From the Old Red Sandstone.*)
As a stony spring
Blocks its own issue (tho' it makes a fresh one of course).
(*Fowey.*) A cow drinking from a trough on the hill-side. The netted beams of light played on the wrinkles of her throat.

---

[1] Palgrave MS.

[2] When I was walking with my father almost for the last time, he said to me: "I generally take my nature-similes direct from my own observation of nature, and sometimes jot them down, and if by chance I find that one of my similes is like that in any author, my impulse is not to use that simile." If he was in the vein during a walk, he would make dozens of similes that were never chronicled.

(*Cornwall.*) The wildflower, called lady's finger, of a golden yellow when open'd, is, unopen'd, of a rich orange red, frequently at least in Cornwall when I observed it.

The open sea.)   Two great ships
          That draw together in a calm.

(*Bonchurch.*) A little salt pool fluttering round a stone upon the shore.

(*I. of Wight.*)
     As those that lie on happy shores and see
     Thro' the near blossom slip the distant sail.

(*Park House.*)   Before the leaf,
     When all the trees stand in a mist of green.

After his tour in Ireland he had written on the same page :

(*Valencia.*)   Claps of thunder on the cliffs
          Amid the solid roar.

(*Bray Head.*)
     O friend, the great deeps of Eternity
     Roar only round the wasting cliffs of Time.

(*The river Shannon, on the rapids.*)
          Ledges of battling water.

CHAPTER XXII.

FARRINGFORD FRIENDS.

THE PYRENEES. DEATH OF THE PRINCE CONSORT.

1860–1862.

Some of the journals of this period have been mislaid, and Mrs Bradley has allowed me to make use of the Reminiscences written by her during the visits which she and the present Dean of Westminster paid to us at Farringford. They begin with the first impression of my father:

Here is Farringford, Tennyson's home, with its "careless ordered garden close to the ridge of a noble down" buried in trees. He invited Granville to dine with him to meet "Lear the artist, not the king," at Farringford two or three times, and Granville has had walks and talks with him and brings away memories full of pleasure and interest. To have come near the *man* and found in him all one could have desired in a great poet! I must write down my first sight of him. I was on the top of the stack in the yard having a birthday feast, very gay under a blue tent with decorations of flowers, etc. A carriage drove up to the little gate of the yard, I could not see who it was but guessed it was he. He came to the stack and looked up. I saw a tall large figure, cloak and large black wide-awake. He had no beard or moustache, I recollect being impressed with the beauty and power of his mouth and chin.

His face is full of power and thought, a deep furrow runs from nose to chin on either side, and gives a peculiar expression to the face, a lofty forehead adds to this. I remember the splendour of his eyes. He asked me who I was and told me

467

to "throw the little maid into his arms" promising to catch her. He asked Edith how old she was, she said "thwee to-day." He said, "Then you and I have the same birthday, August 6th." He did not say much, but walked into the little parlour. Granville came in and they talked a little. Mr Tennyson took up the books on the table and remarked to himself about them.

He and Granville have been on an expedition to Brooke Bay, geologising, botanising, poetising, talking of everything great and small, of life inward and outward, at home and abroad, of religious and social difficulties; they talked from 12 noon to 10 p.m. almost incessantly this day, Mr Tennyson walking back with him to the Warren Farm still talking; Granville says that beneath all the slight allusions to various subjects in his poems lies a mine of knowledge. "He speaks of poetry as a great master only can do."

1860. Mr Tennyson has read "Maud" to us. He is a little vexed at the reception of "Maud." He said: "You must always stand up for 'Maud' when you hear my pet bantling abused. Perhaps that is why I am sensitive about her. You know mothers always make the most of a child that is abused." He commented on the poem as he read, pointed out certain beauties of metre and meaning which he admired himself. He excuses all that people pronounce sardonic in his poems, by saying, he does not cry out against the age as hopelessly bad, but tries to point out where it is bad in order that each individual may do his best to redeem it; as the evils he denounces are individual, only to be cured by each man looking to his own heart. He denounced evil in all its shapes, especially those considered venial by the world and society.

Speaking of Alexander Smith: "He has plenty of promise, but he must learn a different creed to that he preaches in those lines beginning 'Fame, fame, thou art next to God.' Next to God — next to the Devil say I. Fame might be worth having if it helped us to do good to a single mortal, but what is it? only the pleasure of hearing oneself talked of up and down the street."

[*Death's Jest-Book* by Thomas Lovell Beddoes he also praised.] He tells stories very well, ghost and other stories, and has plenty of humour. Amongst others he told us several stories of queer letters he has had from all sorts of people, companies, associations, etc. One young lady wrote imploring him to write some poetry for her to produce at a picnic when everyone was to recite an original poem! He said the deceit of passing off his poem as her own disgusted him, on the other hand he thought it plucky to tell him what she meant to do, and he would have written it for her, but unfortunately she signed her note "Kate" and sent no address.

Those evenings when the poet, sitting in his old oak arm-chair after dinner in the drawing-room, talked of what was in his heart, or read some poem aloud, with the landscape lying before us like a beautiful picture framed in the dark-arched bow-window, are never to be forgotten. His moods are so variable, his conversation so earnest, his knowledge of all things he writes about is so wide and minute. It is a rare treat to be in his domestic circle, where he talks freely and brightly without shyness or a certain morbidity which oppresses him occasionally in society. Crabbe, Gray and Keats were the chief poets he read to us.

There is a look in his face like a bright burning light behind it, like an inward fire that might consume his very life.

The reference in the following letter from my father is to an article on "English Metrical Critics" contributed by Mr Patmore to the *North British Review* for 1857 (Vol. XXVII. pp. 127–161).

This is the passage referred to:

The six-syllable "iambic" is the most solemn of all our English measures. It is scarcely fit for anything but a dirge; the reason being, that the final pause in this measure is greater, when compared with the length of the line, than in any other verse. Here is an example, which we select on account of the peculiar illustration of its nature as a "dimeter brachy-catalectic," which is supplied by the *filling up* of the measure in the seventh line:

> How strange it is to wake
>   And watch, while others sleep,
> Till sight and hearing ache
>   For objects that may keep
> The awful inner sense
>   Unroused, lest it should mark
> The life that haunts the emptiness
>   And horror of the dark.

We have only to *fill up* the measure in every line as well as the seventh, in order to change this verse from the slowest and most mournful, to the most rapid and high-spirited of all English metres, the common eight-syllable quatrain; a measure particularly recommended by the early critics, and continually chosen by poets of all times for erotic poetry, on account of its joyous air.

It will be seen that my father's second specimen is constructed by "filling up" Mr Patmore's lines in the manner that he suggests.

My DEAR C. P.

Specimen of the "most solemn" English metre.

> How glad am I to walk
>   With Susan on the shore!
> How glad am I to talk!
>   I kiss her o'er and o'er.
> I clasp her slender waist,
>   We kiss, we are so fond,
> When she and I are thus embraced,
>   There's not a joy beyond.

Is this C. P.'s most solemn?

Specimen of the "most high-spirited" metre.

> How strange it is, O God, to wake,
>   To watch and wake while others sleep,
> Till heart and sight and hearing ache
>   For common objects that would keep
> Our awful inner ghostly sense
>   Unroused, lest it by chance should mark
> The life that haunts the emptiness
>   And horrors of the formless dark.

Is this C. P.'s rapid and high-spirited?   A. T.

1861.

January. The Bensons[1] and Bradleys here. My
father spoke of seeing Freshwater cliffs and the Needles
from Bournemouth, and said, " The Isle of Wight
looked like a water-lily on a blue lake." Talking of
some poems published by an advanced young lady,
which were instantly suppressed and the edition bought
up by her friends, he quoted two or three passages to
show how she had poetic perception rendered worthless
by bad taste. One line ran : " whose looks were well-
manured with love[2]."

January 22nd. My father said on the evening
when the Bradleys were leaving : " You are going away
— it is taking away a bit of my sunshine : I've been
cutting down trees to let in some, and now you are
taking away a bit of it." He continued : " All that
sounds like flattery : there is no need for us to make
fine speeches. By this time you know I never do, and
it is just a plain truth that your going takes away some
of my sunshine."

On Feb. 17th my father told my mother about his
plan for a new poem, " The Northern Farmer."

By the evening of Feb. 18th he had already written
down a great part of " The Northern Farmer " in one of
the MS books bound in blue and red paper (which my
mother always made for him herself). They also read of
Sir Gareth in the *Morte d'Arthur.* About this time we
went with my father to the National Gallery to see what
he called " some of the great pictures of the world," the

---

[1] The late Archbishop of Canterbury and his wife.

[2] I may observe that my father was by no means a severe critic of the
poems sent him. I remember his saying to Millais (about 1879) : — " The
average poems which I get are not at all bad, but there is just the something,
I suppose, wanted, that I cannot explain." Millais assured him that he found
the same difficulty in criticizing pictures by young painters, that there was a
good level of performance throughout their work, yet somehow falling short
of excellence.

" Titians," the new " Veronese[1]," and the portrait of Ariosto.

In March my mother received a letter from Mr Jowett, a passage in which refers to some advice my father had given him with regard to the manner of expressing his theological opinions.

BALLIOL.

I had not the courage to follow Mr Tennyson's advice about the Essay[2]. It was, however, of great use to me, for I have modified the objectionable passages. I will send you a copy in a few days.

Believe me ever most truly yours,

B. JOWETT.

In May it was decided that my father should receive a degree at Cambridge, but we were unable to go further than Oatlands Park Hotel, for he had such a bad attack of palpitation of the heart that Cambridge had to be given up. After a few days spent in walking to Hampton Court and about the country round, we returned to Farringford, my father stopping at Winchester and Lyndhurst on the way.

Auvergne and the Pyrenees (July and August).

In the summer of 1861 we travelled in Auvergne and the Pyrenees. Some things we could not but be glad to have seen, but the difficulty of getting rooms, carriages, or even donkeys to ride in those days, and the impossibility of finding food not soaked in garlic, took away much of our pleasure.

The Cathedral at Bourges, its great pillars and its gorgeous windows, was what struck my father most on the journey out. On our arrival at Clermont, the comet

---

[1] The great picture, " Darius and his family before Alexander," brought from the Pisani Palace, Venice, in 1857.

[2] The famous essay in *Essays and Reviews*.

was flaring over the market-place. Here we should have been content to stay, had it not been for the bad drainage.

My father and Mr Dakyns [1] climbed the Puy de Dôme and several of the extinct volcanoes in the neighbourhood. Afterwards we drove to Mont Dore and La Bourboule; the plain of Clermont, where Peter the Hermit preached the First Crusade, and over which we looked during the drive, is very fine. At Mont Dore, while my father was reading some of the *Iliad* out aloud to us, little boys came and stood outside the window in open-mouthed astonishment. He took long walks there by the Dordogne, and one day when he came in from his walk we heard him call " Clough, come upstairs," and in walked Mr Clough. My father, Mr Clough and Mr Dakyns made many expeditions to waterfalls and up mountains, Mr Clough riding. We were delighted with the gorgeous meadows of forget-me-nots, and yellow anemones. We left Mr Clough at Mont Dore and drove to Tulle and Perigueux, a quaint place with its old Roman Tower and Cathedral with grass-grown tower, church of St Etienne, and city walls. Thence to Bordeaux, Tarbes, Bagnères de Bigorre where there was a magnificent thunderstorm at night, forked lightning of different colours striking the mountains on either hand. From this place my father and Mr Dakyns made an expedition up the Pic du Midi. When the climbers reached the summit, three great eagles, they said, kept swooping round without any perceptible movement of wing. On our drive from Bigorre to Bagnères de Luchon, a brigand cut one of our trunks from behind the carriage and was making off with it, when our driver looked round and caught sight of him, whereat the rascal ran off into the mountains, our driver cracking his whip at him and shouting out volleys of break-jaw oaths. At Bagnères

[1] Mr Dakyns had recently come to be our tutor; previously my mother had taught my brother and myself.

dc Luchon we lodged in a house among the maize fields, and one night there was in the town a grand puppet show, a sham fight between the French and the Chinese, illustrating some of the incidents in the Chinese war of 1860. The English were conspicuous by their absence. My father walked with Mr Dakyns to the Port de Venasque and into Spain, and to see the Cascade d'Enfer and other cascades, and the Lac D'Oo, and the Lac Vert, and up several mountains : or sometimes he would ride on a white pony about the mountain valleys, one of these being the Vallée de Lys, which he much admired. Mr Clough joined us again at Luchon. He and my father went together to the Cascade des Demoiselles. He was with us too at Luz. My father was enchanted with the torrent of the Gave de Pau, he "sat by it and watched it, and seemed to be possessed by the spirit of delight." Mr Dakyns and he climbed toward the Brèche de Roland, Mr Clough meeting them on their return in the Cirque de Gavarnie, where my father said that the phrase " slow dropping veils of thinnest lawn" was taken from the central cataract which pours over the cliff. He observed that Gavarnie did not impress him quite so much this time as when he was here before. It seemed to him " different, but still the finest thing in the Pyrenees." Mr Clough noticed how silent my father was, and how absorbed by the beauty of the mountains. On August 6th, my father's birthday, we arrived at Cauteretz, — his favourite valley in the Pyrenees. Before our windows we had the torrent rushing over its rocky bed from far away among the mountains and falling in cataracts. Patches of snow lay on the peaks above, and nearer were great wooded heights glorious with autumnal colours, bare rocks here and there, and greenest mountain meadows below. He wrote his lyric " All along the Valley[1] " " after hear-

---

[1] Extract from Clough's *Journal*: "Sept. 1st. The Tennysons arrived here at 6.30 yesterday. Tennyson was here with Arthur Hallam thirty-one

ing the voice of the torrent seemingly sound deeper as the night grew" (in memory of his visit here with Arthur Hallam).

And all along the valley, by rock and cave and tree,
The voice of the dead was a living voice to me.

My father, Mr Clough and Mr Dakyns climbed to the Lac de Gaube, a blue, still lake among fir woods, where my father quoted to Mr Clough the simile of the "stately pine" in "The Princess," which he made from a pine here on an island in mid-stream between two cataracts. More pines he found had grown by the side of this solitary pine that he remembered years ago.

> And standing like a stately Pine
> Set in a cataract on an island-crag,
> When storm is on the heights, and right and left
> Suck'd from the dark heart of the long hills roll
> The torrents, dash'd to the vale: and yet her will
> Bred will in me to overcome it or fall.

My father clambered on to the Lac Bleu; he said that the water was marvellously blue except where the shadow of the mountains made parts of the lake purple. My mother writes in her journal:

"We had a sad parting from Mr Clough at Pau. There could not have been a gentler, kinder, more unselfish or more thoughtful companion than he has been. Among other kind things he corrected the boys' little journals for them; we called him the 'child-angel.'

years ago; and really finds great pleasure in the place: they stayed here and at Cauteretz. He is very fond of this place evidently."

"Clough," said my father, "had great poetic feeling: he read me then his 'In Mari Magno' and cried like a child over it."

My father was vexed that he had written "two and thirty years ago" in his "All along the Valley" instead of "one and thirty years ago," and as late as 1892 wished to alter it since he hated inaccuracy. I persuaded him to let his first reading stand, for the public had learnt to love the poem in its present form: and besides "two and thirty" was more melodious.

After stopping at Pau for a few days we journeyed home by Dax, St Emilion, Libourne, Tours and Amiens : and on our return A. said to me : ' I have seen many things in this tour I shall like to remember.'"

My father wrote to the Duke of Argyll on his return :

THE TEMPLE, LONDON, 1861.

MY DEAR DUKE,

I had intended to write yesterday so that my answer might have reached Cliveden on the 10th, and I scarce know why I did not : perhaps because in these chambers I had lighted on an old and not unclever novel *Zohrab the Hostage ;* partly perhaps because I had fallen into a muse about human vanities and " the glories of our blood and state " (do you know those grand old lines of Shirley's ?). This must have been suggested by the progress of His Majesty the Mayor down the Strand, where I was entangled for half an hour in a roaring crowd and hardly escaped unbruised ; — however, what with the novel and what with the musing fit, I let the post slip ; but this morning let me say that I am grateful for the enquiring after myself and mine : of myself indeed I have no good account to render, being very far from well, living at a friend's rooms here in the Temple, and dancing attendance on a doctor. France, I believe overset me, and more especially the foul ways and unhappy diet of that charming Auvergne : no amount of granite craters or chestnut-woods, or lava-streams, not the Puy de Dôme which I climbed, nor the Glen of Royat, where I lived, nor the plain of Clermont seen from the bridge there, nor the still more magnificent view of the dead volcanoes from the ascent to Mont Dore could make amends for those drawbacks : so we all fell sick by turns : my wife is better since our return, and the boys are well enough, tho' they suffered too at the time ; but I remain with a torpid liver, not having much pleasure in anything: yet I can still grieve with my friends' griefs, and therefore I am sorry for the occasion which exiles your good and kind Duchess, tho' it be but for this December. I am sure the Duchess will sympathise with my disgust at having my Freshwater (where I had pitched my tent, taken with its solitariness) so polluted and defiled with brick and mortar, as is threatened; they talk of laying out streets and crescents, and I oscillate between my desire of purchasing land at a ruinous price in order to keep my views open, and my wish to fly the place altogether. Is there no millionaire who will take pity on the wholesome hillside and buy it all up?

"Boadicea," no, I cannot publish her yet, perhaps never, for who can read her except myself? I have half consented to write a little ode on the opening of the International Exhibition. The commissioners prest me: I should never have volunteered; for I hate a subject given me, and still more if that subject be a public one. Present my best remembrances to your Duchess and to [her mother] the Duchess of Sutherland. I am half afraid to inquire after her Grace's eyesight lest I should hear ill news.

Yours, my dear Duke, always,

A. TENNYSON.

In September Lord Dufferin wrote:

CLANDEBOY, BELFAST, Sept. 24th, 1861.

MY DEAR MR TENNYSON,

I wonder if you will think me very presumptuous for doing what at last, after many months' hesitation, I have determined to do.

You must know that here in my park in Ireland there rises a high hill, from the top of which I look down not only on an extensive tract of Irish land, but also on St George's Channel, a long blue line of Scotch coast, and the mountains of the Isle of Man.

On the summit of this hill I have built an old-world tower which I have called after my mother "Helen's Tower."

In it I have placed on a golden tablet the birthday verses which my mother wrote to me on the day I came of age, and I have spared no pains in beautifying it with all imaginable devices. In fact my tower is a little "Palace of Art." Beneath is a rough outline of its form and situation.

Now there is only one thing wanting to make it a perfect little gem of architecture and decoration and that is "*a voice.*" It is now ten years since it was built and all that time it has stood silent. Yet if he chose there is one person in the world able to endow it with this priceless gift, and by sending me some little short distich for it to crown it for ever with a glory it cannot otherwise obtain, and render it a memorial of the personal friendship which its builder felt for the great poet of our age.

Yours ever, DUFFERIN.

In answer my father sent the following lines, and annotated, as below, the words "recurring Paradise":

Helen's Tower.

Helen's Tower, here I stand,
Dominant over sea and land.
Son's love built me and I hold
Mother's love engrav'n in gold.
Love is in and out of time,
I am mortal stone and lime.
Would my granite girth were strong
As either love to last as long!
I should wear my crown entire
To and thro' the Doomsday fire,
And be found of angel eyes
In earth's recurring Paradise[1].

[1] The fancy of some poets and theologians that Paradise is to be the renovated earth, as, I dare say, you know.

The death of the Prince Consort in December my

father felt was a great loss to Britain and the Empire. He sent the first copies of his *Dedication* of the " Idylls " to the Princess Alice with the following letter:

MADAM,

Having heard some time ago from Sir C. B. Phipps that your Royal Highness had expressed a strong desire that I should in some way " idealize " our lamented Prince, and being at that time very unwell, I was unwilling to attempt the subject, because I feared that I might scarce be able to do it justice; nor did I well see how I should idealize a life which was in itself an ideal.

At last it seemed to me that I could do no better than dedicate to his memory a book which he himself had told me was valued by him. I am the more emboldened to send these lines to your Royal Highness, because having asked the opinion of a lady who knew and truly loved and honoured him, she gave me to understand by her reply that they were true and worthy of him: whether they be so or not, I hardly know, but if they do not appear so to your Royal Highness, forgive me as your Father would have forgiven me.

Though these lines conclude with an address to our beloved Queen I feel that I cannot do better than leave the occasion of presenting them to the discretion of your Royal Highness.

Believe me, as altogether sympathizing with your sorrow,

Your Royal Highness'

faithful and obedient servant,

A. TENNYSON.

1862.

Jan. 9th. My father recited in a rolling voice his new Ode for the opening of the Exhibition in the summer [1]. He explained that the rhythm and composition were hampered by the necessity of arranging it for a choir of 4000 voices: " I think for that kind of Ode the wild irregular bursts are an addition to its effectiveness." The lines on the death of the Prince Consort had to be put in after the first draft was written. My father was deeply grieved, not only by the death of the Prince, but also by the deaths of his two friends Clough and Godley. He wrote: " We have lost Clough: he died at Florence of a relapse of malaria-fever: it gave me a great shock. I see that Godley too has gone: so we fall, one by one."

Jan. 19th. Princess Alice wrote to my father about the *Dedication* of the " Idylls " to the Prince Consort:

If words could express *thanks* and *real* appreciation of lines so beautiful, so truly worthy of the great pure spirit which inspired the author, Princess Alice would attempt to do it; — but these failing, she begs Mr Tennyson to believe how much she admires them, and that this just tribute to the memory of her beloved Father touched her deeply. Mr Tennyson could not have chosen a more beautiful or true testimonial to the memory of him who was so really good and noble, than the dedication of the ' Idylls of the King ' which he so valued and admired. Princess Alice transmitted the lines to the Queen, who desired her to tell Mr Tennyson, with her sincerest thanks, how much moved she was on reading them, and that they had soothed her aching, bleeding heart. She knows also how *he* would have admired them.

[1] Sung May 1, 1862; set by Sterndale Bennett. One newspaper reported that the poet-laureate was present, " clothed in his green *baize* " (probably a misprint for " bays ").

The Crown Princess of Prussia also wrote:

February 23rd, 1862.

The first time I ever heard the " Idylls of the King " was last year, when I found both the Queen and Prince quite in raptures about them. The first bit I ever heard was the end of " Guinevere," the last two or three pages: the Prince read them to me, and I shall never forget the impression it made upon me hearing those grand and simple words in his voice! He did so admire them, and I cannot separate the idea of King Arthur from the image of him whom I most revered on earth!

I almost know the " Idylls of the King " by heart now: they are really sublime!

Surely it must give the Author satisfaction to think that his words have been drops of balm on the broken and loving hearts of the widowed Queen and her orphan children.

VICTORIA,

Crown Princess of Prussia, Princess Royal.

Even the " calm Spedding " wrote enthusiastically about the " Dedication ":

The thing I had to say was merely that the Dedication was, and continues to be, the most beautiful and touching thing of the kind that I ever read, to which I have nothing to add except that I find *that* to be the general opinion of men and women within my small circle of acquaintance. Not that I have heard it much talked of. But I think that is because people are afraid of not meeting with the sympathy they require in such a case. With some of my most intimate friends, whom I was frequently meeting, not a word passed about it for weeks, till at last some accident brought it shyly out, and we found we had been all the time thinking exactly alike.

Hitherto I have enjoyed the quiet dignity belonging to the editor of a book of good repute which everybody is willing to be thought familiar with, but nobody reads, so the critics have taken their information from the preface, and passed me to the respectable shelf with compliments. But now I come on ground [the *Life of Francis Bacon*] where they have opinions of their own, and must be prepared for the rougher side of the critic tongue.

Of all creatures that feed upon the earth, the professional critic is the one whose judgment I least value for any purpose except advertisement, but of all writers, the one whom he sits in judgment on is also the one whom he is least qualified to assume a superiority over. For is it likely that a man, who has written a serious book about anything in the world, should not know more about that thing than one who merely reads his book for the purpose of reviewing it? But so it must be: and a discreet man must just let it be. What I want to know is whether men and women and children who care nothing about me, but take an intelligent interest in the subject, find the book readable. What its other merits are nobody knows so well as [I].

Letters to the Duke of Argyll.

FARRINGFORD, *Feb.* 1862.

MY DEAR DUKE,

Many thanks for your very interesting letter. Very touching is what you tell me about the Queen. I am of course exceedingly gratified that anything which I have written should have the power to console one whom we all love; strange that a book[1] which, when it first appeared, was pronounced by more than one clergyman as Pantheistic, if not, as (I think) one wiseacre commented on it, Atheistic, should have such a power, but after all it is very little that words can do. Time, time!

I have written out for the Princess Royal a morsel from " Guinevere." I do so hate rewriting my own things that my pen refuses to trace the " Dedication."

Her critique on the " Idylls " is enthusiastic, and mingled up with the affection of her father, as I would wish it to be. As to joining these with the " Morte d'Arthur," there are two objections, — one that I could scarcely light upon a finer close than that ghostlike passing away of the king, and the other that the " Morte "

[1] " In Memoriam."

is older in style [1]. I have thought about it and arranged all the intervening Idylls, but I dare not set to work for fear of a failure, and time lost. I am now about my " Fisherman," which is heroic too in its way.

Yours ever, A. TENNYSON.

If you call me Mr Tennyson any longer, I think that I must Your-grace you till the end of the chapter.

MONDAY, *March 3rd,* 1862.

MY DEAR DUKE,

I have been out on a visit (a very unusual proceeding on my part), and on returning found your letter, which a little dismayed me, for, as you in the prior one had bound me by no promise of secrecy, I, in talking of Her Majesty and her sorrow, did say to two friends, whom I bound by such a promise, that she had found comfort in reading " In Memoriam," and had made the private markings therein.

I don't suppose much harm would result even if these broke their promise, for that is all that could be reported; still I am vexed, because if the Queen heard of the report she might fancy that her private comments were public prey. As to those very interesting ones communicated in your last, whether you had bound me to secrecy or not, I should not have dreamt of repeating them: they are far too sacred; and possibly your caution of silence only refers to these.

I hope so. I think it *must* be so. I wrote off the very day I returned to both my friends, urging them to abide by their promise, for in these days of half-unconscious social treachery and multitudinous babble I felt that I ought to make assurance doubly sure. You can scarce tell how annoyed I have been. I hope the

---

[1] " ' The Coming and the Passing of Arthur ' are simpler and more severe in style, as dealing with the awfulness of Birth and Death." A. T.

Princess Royal got my note and inclosure, but she has not acknowledged it. My letters, I believe, have ere this been opened and stopt at our little Yarmouth P. O. but not in the present Postmaster's time.

My best remembrances to the Duchess.

Yours ever, A. TENNYSON.

March 26th, 1862.

MY DEAR DUKE,

I am a shy beast and like to keep in my burrow. Two questions, what sort of salutation to make on entering Her[1] private room? and whether to retreat backward? or sidle out as I may?

I am sorry to hear that you were the worse for your journey. I myself am raven-hoarse with cold.

Yours ever, A. TENNYSON.

April, 1862.

MY DEAR DUKE,

As you were kind enough to say that you would mention Woolner's name to the Queen, I send a photograph of a work of his, which Gladstone, who saw it the other day, pronounced the first thing he had seen after the antique. The children are Thomas Fairbairn's, deaf and dumb, not pretty certainly, but infinitely pathetic.

I do not say, show this to her Majesty, you know best, but admit that myself and Gladstone are justified in our admiration.

Yours ever, A. TENNYSON.

[1] The Queen's.

My father's first visit to the Queen, April, 1862[1],
after the death of the Prince Consort.

A. was much affected by his interview with the
Queen. He said that she stood pale and statue-like
before him, speaking in a quiet, unutterably sad voice.
" There was a kind of stately innocence about her." She
said many kind things to him, such as " Next to the
Bible ' In Memoriam ' is my comfort." She talked of
the Prince, and of Hallam, and of Macaulay, and of
Goethe, and of Schiller in connection with him, and said
that the Prince was so like the picture of Arthur Hallam
in " In Memoriam," even to his blue eyes. When A.
said that he thought that the Prince would have made a
great king, she answered, " He always said that it did
not signify whether *he* did the right thing or did not, so
long as the right thing was done."

A. said, " We all grieve with your Majesty," and the
Queen replied, " The country has been kind to me, and
I am thankful."

When the Queen had withdrawn, Princess Alice
came in with Princess Beatrice.

After the interview my father wrote to Lady Augusta
Bruce[2]:

FARRINGFORD, *April 17th*, 1862.

MY DEAR LADY AUGUSTA,

Accept my very best thanks for your kind
letter. I perceive that it was written on the evening of
that day when I called at Osborne, but I received it
only yesterday; then I thought that I would wait till

---

[1] This account was written down by my mother immediately after my
father's return from Osborne.

[2] Afterwards the wife of Dean Stanley, then Lady-in-Waiting to the
Queen.

the prints [1] arrived, but as they have not, I will not delay my answer.

I was conscious of having spoken with considerable emotion to the Queen, but I have a very imperfect recollection of what I did say. Nor indeed — which perhaps you may think less excusable — do I very well recollect what Her Majesty said to me: but I loved the voice that spoke, for being very blind I am much led by the voice, and blind as I am and as I told Her I was, I yet could dimly perceive so great an expression of sweetness in Her countenance as made me wroth with those imperfect cartes de visite of H.M. which Mayall once sent me. Will you say, as you best know how to say it, how deeply grateful I am to Her Majesty for the prints of Herself and of Him which She proposes to send me, and how very much I shall value Her Gift? I was charmed with Princess Alice. She seemed to me what Goethe calls *eine Natur*. Did he not say that was the highest compliment that could be paid to a woman? and the little Beatrice with her long tresses was very captivating. Thank you also for what you tell me of your own family. True, as you write, I often receive similar communications, but the value of these depends on the value of those from whom they come. I often scarce believe that I have done anything, especially when I meet with too flowery compliments: but when I know that I am spoken to sincerely, as by your Ladyship, I lift my head a little, and rejoice that I am not altogether useless.

Believe me, yours very truly,

A. TENNYSON.

[1] Portraits of the Queen and Prince Consort.

CHAPTER XXIII.

DERBYSHIRE AND YORKSHIRE.

LETTERS.

1862–1864[1].

During this summer, after finishing his "Enoch Arden[2]," or "The Fisherman" as he called it then, my father went with Palgrave for a tour to Derbyshire and Yorkshire. On his return I remember hearing him express delight at the beauties of Haddon Hall, and at the glories of the Peak cavern. The guide had asked the travellers, before entering the cavern, at what scale they would wish to see the Great Hall illuminated, for when the Emperor of Russia had been there, he had chosen the most magnificent of the illuminations offered. My father answered : " Let us be as grand as Emperors for once ": and Palgrave and he were amply rewarded by the wonderful colour-effects produced, and especially by the display of the crimson fire. From Castleton they went to Ripon, Leyburn, Middleham, Wensleydale, Bolton, and Skipton. My father told me that it was at Middleham Castle he had made the lines in " Geraint and Enid ":

And here had fall'n a great part of a tower,
Whole, like a crag that tumbles from the cliff,
And like a crag was gay with wilding flowers.

[1] See Appendix, p. 511, for Reminiscences by Thomas Wilson and William Allingham, 1863–64.
[2] See Fitzgerald's " Hints for ' Enoch Arden ' " in Appendix, p. 515.

At Christmas a greeting from Edward Fitzgerald came:

MARKET RISE, WOODBRIDGE,
1862.

Let me hear how you both are and your boys, and where you have been this summer.

I have as usual, nothing to tell of myself: boating all the summer and reading *Clarissa Harlowe* since; you and I used to talk of the book more than 20 years ago. I believe I am better read in it than almost any one in existence now. No wonder, for it is almost intolerably tedious and absurd. But I can't read the *Adam Bedes, Daisy Chains*, etc. at all: I look at my row of Sir Walter Scott, and think with comfort that I can always go to him of a winter evening, when no other book comes to hand.

I think you must come over here one summer-day, not till summer, but before more summers are gone. Else, who knows? Do you smoke? I sometimes talk with seafaring men who come from Boston in billyboys, and from Goole, and other places in the Humber, and then I don't forget the coast of Locksley Hall.

1863.

In January my father wrote to Frederick Locker, sending at the same time a volume of his poems for his daughter Eleanor:

FARRINGFORD,
Jan. 31*st*, 1863.

DEAR MR LOCKER,

I am glad that your young lady approves of my little book. Why wouldn't you let me give it to her? As to this canard of a Baronetcy, I remember the same foolish rumour arising some years ago, and with some little trouble I put it down, or it died down of itself. In this instance the notice had been out in the *Athenæum* several days before I heard of it, but I answered the first letter which alluded to it, by declaring that the rumour was *wholly* unfounded; so that, as no Baronetcy has been offered, there is less reason for considering your friendly pros and cons as to acceptance or refusal; if it had, I trust that I should have had grace and loyalty enough to think more of the Queen's feelings than my own in this matter. I mean whichever way I answered. Both myself and my wife have been somewhat vexed, and annoyed, by all this chatter.

Kind regards to Lady Charlotte. I shall be glad to see you here, whenever you like to come our way. Froude promised me he would come in January, but January is breathing his last to-day.

Yours very truly,

ALFRED TENNYSON.

On March 6th my father sent off his "Welcome to Alexandra." He would like to have seen the pageant at the Prince of Wales' wedding, but his ticket for the Chapel only arrived on the 10th, having been mis-sent.

After the arrival of the Princess of Wales in England, Lady Augusta Bruce wrote:

WINDSOR CASTLE,
March 8th, 1863.

DEAR MR TENNYSON,

Last night, a few minutes after the advent of the lovely Bride, while I felt my heart still glowing from seeing the look of inexpressible brightness, confidence, and happiness, with which she alighted on the threshold of Windsor Castle and threw herself into the arms of her new family, your letter, and the beautiful lines of welcome it enclosed, were put into my hands.

I cannot convey to you the impression they made on me, or how I longed to put them into the hands of our beloved Queen, how I longed that the heart of the nation should be moved and touched by them, as mine had been, that the noble, soul-inspiring feeling of which we have witnessed the outburst, should find itself so expressed. The Queen's response to your words was all that I had expected. Her Majesty desires me to thank you very warmly, and to tell you with how much pleasure she has read the lines [1], and how much she rejoices that the sweet and charming Princess should be thus greeted.

One looks at her with trembling hope, but every expression, every act, word, and gesture more than justifies one's most sanguine expectations and desires. God grant it for the sake of the Prince, the Country, and I am tempted to feel above all, for the sake of that sorrowing heart, which is ever more and more being lifted up to the divine height of which you speak. Truly the royal mourner is bearing this joy as she has borne the sorrow, and it is a spectacle that would move a heart of stone. I should have liked you and dear Mrs Tennyson to see the light on Her Majesty's countenance, as she read your lines and as she speaks of the young joyous bride, so joyous but so tender and gentle to the widowed mother; also when Her Majesty speaks of the feeling manifested by her people, realizing as she does all that is contained in it.

I remain yours truly,

AUGUSTA BRUCE.

At this time my father's indignation against Russia for her treatment of Poland was boundless. He was filled with horror too at the gigantic civil war in America, although he had always looked forward anxiously to the total abolition of slavery [2] : but he had hoped that it might have been accomplished gradually and peacefully.

In May the Queen asked my father what she could do for him, and he said : " Nothing, Madam, but shake my two boys by the hand. It may keep them loyal in the troublous times to come." So on the 9th Her Majesty sent for us all to Osborne. We lunched with

---

[1] "A Welcome," published by Moxon (March, 1863).

[2] He would sing with enthusiasm the great chorus of the " Battle-hymn of the Republic":

" Singing 'Glory, Glory, Hallelujah!'
His soul goes marching on..."

Lady Augusta Bruce, and drove with her in the grounds.

After returning to the Palace we waited in the drawing-room, and the Queen came to us. All the Princesses came in by turns, Prince Leopold also.

My mother wrote :

The Queen is not like her portraits, her face is full of intelligence and is very mobile and full of sympathy. A. was delighted with 'the breadth and freedom of her mind.' We talked of everything in heaven and earth. Shades of pain and sadness often passed over the Queen's face.

On the 11th a Queen's messenger rode over, bringing from Her Majesty Guizot's edition of Prince Albert's *Speeches*, *In der Stille* by Karl Sudhoff, *Lieder des Leides* by Albert Zeller, and an Album of the Queen's, in which A. was to write something." He wrote out " All along the Valley," and the next day sent the following letter to Lady Augusta Bruce :

May 12th, 1863.

DEAR LADY AUGUSTA,

I had no time yesterday to overlook the volume which Her Majesty sent me. I did but see the inscription in the beginning by the Duchess of Kent and Goethe's " Edel sei der Mensch " in the Prince's handwriting — a poem which has always appeared to me one of the grandest things which Goethe or any other man has written. Perhaps some time or other the Queen will allow me to look at the book again.

The little song which I inserted in it was repeated to H.M. last year by the Duke of Argyll who told me that she approved of it, and I thought it more graceful to give an unpublished than an already printed one.

Cauteretz, which I had visited with my friend before

I was twenty, had always lived in my recollection as a sort of Paradise; when I saw it once more, it had become a rather odious watering-place, but the hills wore their old green, and the roaring stream had the same echoes as of old. Altogether I like the little piece as well as anything I have written: I hope I wrote it out correctly — for I was very much hurried — and I feel sure that in my note to yourself I somewhere or other made pure nonsense of a sentence by putting an 'of' for an 'a' or 'and.'

I have read Guizot's Preface, which is just what it ought to be — compact, careful, reverential: I have also dipt slightly into the *Meditations* and what I have read of them I can quite approve of: their one defect to me being that I discern the German through the translation. Passages here and there which would look quite natural in the original read a little too quaintly in our English: yet I find my appreciation of these essays scarce lessened by feeling that they are a translation. They are true-hearted, tender, and solacing, and contrasting advantageously with our disquisitions on these subjects. Does H.M. know the sermons of Robertson of Brighton? he died young, not very long ago. These have always appeared to me the most spiritual utterances of any minister of the church in our times.

I am glad that the Queen remembers my visit with pleasure, and refers to the conversation she held with us, not without interest.

It was very good of you to think of bringing the book: we were sorry, it could not be.

Believe me, dear Lady Augusta,

Yours very truly,

A. TENNYSON.

My father wrote to the Duke of Argyll:

FARRINGFORD,
May 28th, 1863.

MY DEAR DUKE,

I have delayed so long granting the " absolution[1]," that like enough by this time you may have forgotten that you desired it.

However it is granted.

Only do not, after absolution, begin sinning the sin again with a greater gusto.

Of course I am glad to have given a moment's satisfaction to our poor Queen, glad too that you give a somewhat better account of her.

I had a very pleasant two days' visit to Cliveden. I sat in your favourite seat which looks over the reach of the river, and regretted that you were not at my side. Gladstone was at C. with me. I had met him before, but had never seen him so nearly. Very pleasant, and very interesting he was, even when he discoursed on Homer, where most people think him a little hobbyhorsical: let him be. His hobby-horse is of the intellect and with a grace.

Yours ever, A. TENNYSON.

In the summer we went on a tour to York, Harrogate, Ripon and Fountains Abbey: my father was busy with his translation of Homer, and with his Alcaics to Milton.

O mighty-mouth'd inventor of harmonies,
O skill'd to sing of Time and Eternity,
 God-gifted organ-voice of England,
  Milton, a name to resound for ages.

---

[1] Because the Duke had repeated to the Queen " All along the Valley."

After the different experiments in Classical metre had been published in the *Cornhill* for December, my uncle Frederick wrote as follows:

I got a letter from Fitzgerald yesterday, in reply to a note from me communicating to him poor Thackeray's sudden death, which I thought it very possible he might never have learnt in his solitude and indifference to newspapers. He tells me he has been ill with his old complaint, blood to the head, and expects to be taken off by it in the end; he hopes it may be suddenly, that he may not linger after an attack in a paralysed state. But there is "a Providence that shapes our *ends*," and whatever those ends may be, whether apoplexy, paralysis, or the painless separation of the *man* from his integuments, or natural death, not a very different thing from putting off your clothes to go to bed, no doubt (tho' poor Fitz cannot see a hand's breadth before him in these matters) all is for the best. I read Alfred's experiments in Classical metres in the *Cornhill*, and think them clever, though I prefer the translation from Homer. I send him an Italian sonnet which I am rather proud of, though Petrarch would stand aghast at it, and Dante would tell me to mind my own business.

At Christmas, Mr Jowett, Mr W. G. Clark (Public Orator at Cambridge), Dr and Mrs Butler, and the Bradleys visited us. The flow of my father's jests and stories, when he had sympathetic listeners, was inexhaustible: and this party was particularly sympathetic.

One evening they were talking of repartee, and my father said, laughing: "I would give all my poems to have made the two following retorts courteous. (1) A certain French king, seeing at Court a man said to be very like him, blurted out, 'You are very like our family: is it possible that your mother was much at Court?' 'No! sire,' said the man, 'but my father was.' (2) The Prince Regent, being in Portsmouth one day and seeing Jack Towers across the street, shouted out in his royal way, 'Hulloa, Towers, I hear you are the greatest blackguard

in Portsmouth!' Towers replied with a low bow, 'I
hope your Royal Highness has not come here to take
away my character!'"

He also thought that two of the neatest repartees
were (1) the reply of Margaret More to a Lady
Manners, both having had honours conferred on their
families. To the satirical remark of Lady Manners
"Honores mutant Mores," Margaret More replied:
"That goes better in English, Madam,—'Honours
change Manners.'" (2) The reply of the Italian lady
to Napoleon who said to her, "Tutti Italiani sono
perfidi." "Non tutti, ma Buona parte."

At the end of December my father was finishing
"Aylmer's Field." He said "The story is incalculably
difficult to tell, the dry facts are so prosaic in themselves."
He often pointed out how hard he had found such and
such a passage, how much work and thought it had cost
him; for instance, the lawyer at work in chambers; the
pompous old Aylmer in his wrath; the suicide. He
liked his own descriptions of English landscape, and
of cottages covered with creepers; and especially the
passage about the Traveller's Joy.

The following letter was written by my father to
a stranger who questioned him as to his belief in a
hereafter.

SIR,

I have been considering your questions, but
I am not a God or a disembodied spirit that I should
answer them. I can only say that I sympathize with
your grief, and if faith mean anything at all it is trusting
to those instincts, or feelings, or whatever they may be
called, which assure us of some life after this.

A. TENNYSON.

He also wrote to Mr Swinburne about "Atalanta in Calydon":

My dear Sir,

Accept my congratulations on the success of your Greek play. I had some strong objections to parts of it, but these I think have been modified by a re-perusal, and at any rate I daresay you would not care to hear them; here however is one. Is it *fair* for a Greek chorus to abuse the Deity something in the *style* of the Hebrew prophets?

Altogether it is many a long day since I have read anything so fine; for it is not only carefully written, but it has both strength and splendour, and shows moreover that you have a fine metrical invention which I envy you.

Yours very truly, A. Tennyson.

APPENDIX.

(P. 7.) *Professor Hales' account of Louth School.*

They (the masters) were not cruel-hearted men; to make ears tingle, bones ache, life generally a burden and a misery, was no extreme pleasure to them. Small specimens of humanity leaping and dancing, and wringing their hands, and shrieking as if engaged in the worship of some Baal who perchance slept, and must needs be awakened, could scarcely have been agreeable objects of contemplation; but they knew not of any other method in which instruction might possibly be imparted.... To shew how completely we lay at the mercy of the head-master, I perhaps ought to state that we generally sat when "up" to him upon one long form, opposite to which stood a chair, on which was seated the particular boy who was "going on." Our master adopted for himself the peripatetic, or, more strictly perhaps, the ana- or kata-patetic method; his beat was immediately in front of the form on which we sat, so that he could get at the centre class as he paced up and down. He very frequently availed himself of his opportunities; and with the masterly dexterity and quickness which distinguished him, often succeeded in "touching up" each one of us in the course of a single promenade. But most pitiable was the position of the poor boy on the chair on the other side of the master's line of walk. That chair was a sort of altar on which boy-sacrifices were offered. There the youth sat, exposed on every side to the blast of blows and boxes that might descend on him at any moment, which were sure to descend upon him sooner or later in a hideous hurricane.

(P. 43.) *Ghosts.* (*Prologue of my father's paper written for the "Apostles."*)

He who has the power of speaking of the spiritual world, speaks in a simple manner of a high matter. He speaks of life and death, and the things after death. He lifts the veil, but the form behind it is shrouded in deeper obscurity. He raises the cloud, but he darkens the prospect. He unlocks with a golden key the iron-grated gates of the charnel house, he throws them wide open. And forth issue from the inmost gloom the colossal Presences of the Past, *majores humano*; some as they lived, seemingly pale, and faintly smiling; some as they died, still suddenly frozen by the chill of death; and some as they were buried, with dropped eyelids, in their cerements and their winding sheets.

The listeners creep closer to each other, they are afraid of the drawing of their own breaths, the beating of their own hearts. The voice of *him* who speaks alone like a mountain stream on a still night fills up and occupies the silence. He stands as it were on a vantage ground. He becomes the minister and expounder of human sympathies. His words *find* the heart like the arrows of truth. Those who laughed long before, have long ago become solemn, and those who were solemn before, feel the awful sense of unutterable mystery. The speaker pauses :

"Wherefore," says one, "granting the intensity of the feeling, wherefore this fever and fret about a baseless vision?" "Do not assume," says another, "that any vision *is* baseless."

(P. 108.) LETTERS ABOUT ARTHUR HALLAM (AFTER HIS DEATH).

From R. J. Tennant to my father.

Nov. 26th, 1833.

MY DEAR ALFRED,

I wish I were gifted with a far sight to reach over hills and towns even as far as Somersby and thro' the windows of the house, that I might see you, how you look when you come down to breakfast, and after breakfast whether you sit reading, writing or musing, whether you are gloomy or cheerful ; I hope the latter ; and that you can look back upon the mournful past without that bitterness of spirit which you felt when I saw you. I would rather not allude to this ; but I wish to talk to you of what has been much in my thoughts since you were in town, and on which I have spoken to many of our friends. It appears to be a universal wish among them, that whatever writings Arthur has left should be collected and published ; that there may be some memorial of him among us, which, tho' it will fall very far short of what was hoped and expected of him, will yet be highly gratifying to his friends, and as we think will not be without interest and value to many others. A great number of his poems are such as everyone will delight in, and there are several essays that will do honour to his powers of original thought and expression. It seemed the most proper way to cause this to be done if you were to intimate it to Mr Hallam as the general wish of his friends. His desire that you would suggest to him whatever you think that Arthur would have wished to be done, gives you ample opportunity to do this without being in the least obtrusive. I asked Spedding's opinion and he entirely agreed with me ; and he is one whose opinion on such a matter is of great weight. It is possible that Mr Hallam may himself intend to do this ; but even if it be so, it will probably be a great satisfaction to him to learn that this feeling and wish prevails so generally among us, and that such a wide circle of men are unanimous in seeking to pay honour to one who by his nearer friends was so deeply loved. You are not perhaps aware how widely his loss is felt ; one circumstance will show it ; *many* of his *less intimate* acquaintance have been exerting themselves to cause a tablet to be placed in Trinity Chapel to his memory : the intention failed only because he was in fact not on the foundation. I hope you will not think it ill-timed in me to recall your memory to what I fear you already dwell too much upon. To me the remembrance of Arthur is full of delight, looking back upon the days when he gave light and life to my spirit ; it is only when I need his counsels and know that I cannot any more receive them, or when I think upon you and your sorrow, that regret is mixed with bitterness. God bless you all. You are all in my thoughts night and day.

Ever your affectionate

R. J. TENNANT.

From Robert Monteith to my father.

1833.

MY DEAR ALFRED,

I assure you I have never been quite easy without having had some communication between us since the news of the loss sustained by you. I say *you* because, though it was and still is to myself one of those dreadful things which at moments one cannot bring oneself to believe, yet the sorrow of all others combined cannot be supposed equal to that of you and your family. I assure you all with whom I have spoken about it have been full of sympathy with you, and all wish, as I do, for still stricter friendship with you, if it might be

(which is all but impossible) that together we might help to fill up the
gap. One feeling that remains with me is a longing to preserve all
those friends whom I know Hallam loved and whom I learnt to love
through him. He was so much a centre round which we moved that
now there seems a possibility of many connections being all but
dissolved. Since Hallam's death I almost feel like an old man looking
back on many friendships as something bygone. I beseech you, do not
let us permit this, you may even dislike the interference of common
friendship for a time, but you will be glad at length to gather together
all the different means by which you may feel not entirely in a different
world from that in which you knew and loved Hallam. I will write
you a long letter some day which I daresay will trouble you : if it does I
shall be sorry, but it will rather prove the propriety of our not leaving
you alone. I wish you were abroad with us and am revolving some
schemes for seeing the south together. All Mr Garden's family desire
to be most kindly remembered to you.

Believe me your very sincere friend,

R. MONTEITH.

(P. 117.) MARIANA IN THE SOUTH.

Arthur H. Hallam to W. B. Donne[1].

TRINITY,
Sunday. [1831.]

MY DEAR DONNE,

          I rejoice exceedingly at the admiration you express for
Alfred Tennyson in general, and the Indian ditty[2] in particular.

I expect you to be properly grateful to me for sending you by these
presents another poem, of which to say that I love it would be only
saying that it is his. It is intended, you will perceive, as a kind of
pendant to his former poem of "Mariana," the idea of both being the
expression of desolate loneliness, but with this distinctive variety in
the second, that it paints the forlorn feeling as it would exist under the
influence of different impressions of sense. When we were journeying
together this summer through the South of France we came upon a
range of country just corresponding to his preconceived thought of a
barrenness, so as in the South, and the portraiture of the scenery in
this poem is most faithful. You will, I think, agree with me that the

---

[1] Afterwards "Examiner of plays." This hitherto unpublished letter has been
kindly given to me by his son Mr Mowbray Donne.
[2] "Anacaona," p. 56.

essential and distinguishing character of the conception requires in the
"Southern Mariana" a greater lingering on the outward circumstances,
and a less palpable transition of the poet into Mariana's feelings, than
was the case in the former poem. Were this not implied in the subject
it would be a fault : "an artist," as Alfred is wont to say, "ought to be
lord of the five senses," but if he lacks the inward sense which reveals
to him what is inward in the heart, he has left out the part of Hamlet
in the play. In this meaning I think the objection sometimes made to
a poem, that it is too picturesque, is a just objection ; but according to
a more strict use of words, poetry cannot be too pictorial, for it cannot
represent too truly, and when the object of the poetic power happens to
be an object of sensuous perception it is the business of the poetic
language to paint.

It is observable in the mighty models of art, left for the worship of
ages by the Greeks and those too rare specimens of Roman production
which breathe a Greek spirit, that their way of imaging a mood of the
human heart in a group of circumstances, each of which reciprocally
affects and is affected by the unity of that mood, resembles much
Alfred's manner of delineation, and should therefore give additional
sanction to the confidence of our praise.

I believe you will find instances in all the Greek poems of the
highest order, — at present I can only call into distinct recollection
the divine passage about the sacrifice of Iphigenia in Lucretius and
the desolation of Ariadne in Catullus, and the fragments of Sappho,
in which I see much congeniality to Alfred's peculiar power. I beg
pardon for this prose, here comes something better.

(Here the "Southern Mariana" is copied at length.)

Your very sincere friend,

A. H. HALLAM.

(P. 207.) THE RECEPTION OF THE EARLY POEMS, BY AUBREY DE VERE.

1832–1845.

There are moments when the day on which I first made acquaintance with Alfred Tennyson's poetry seems to me less remote than
those days upon which events comparatively recent took place. It
is more clearly marked in my memory than the day on which I first
met the poet himself. My acquaintance with him as a poet had been
so long and familiar, that to have made acquaintance with him as a
man would have been to me something remarkable only if the man

and the poet had been in striking contrast. On the contrary they were very like each other.

The mode in which I first made acquaintance with Alfred Tennyson's poetry is recorded in a letter which was written by me after the death of the late Lord Houghton and published in his recent biography by Mr Wemyss Reid. Lord Houghton, then Richard Monckton Milnes, a Cambridge friend of my eldest brother's, drove up to the door of our house at Curragh Chase one night in 1832, and in a few days had quite won our hearts by his pleasant ways, his wit, and his astonishing acquaintance with all the modern European Literatures. He had brought with him the first number of a new magazine entitled *The Englishman* containing Arthur Hallam's essay on Tennyson's *Poems, chiefly Lyrical.* The day on which I first took the slender volume into my hands was with me a memorable one. Arthur Hallam's essay had contrasted two different schools of modern poetry, calling one of these classes Poets of Reflection, and the other class Poets of Sensation, the latter represented by Shelley and Keats. Of Keats I knew nothing, and of Shelley very little ; but the new poet seemed to me, while he had about him a touch of both the classes thus characterized, to have yet little in common with either. He was eminently original, and about that originality there was for me a wild, inexplicable magic and a deep pathos, though hardly as simple as Wordsworth's pathos, and with nothing of its homeliness ; and the character of its language was nearly the opposite of that which Wordsworth had, at least in his youth, asserted to be the true poetic diction, viz. the language of common life among the educated. The diction of the new poet was elaborate in accordance with a certain artificiality belonging to the time, that is, whenever strange combinations of words were needed in order to produce a corresponding exactitude of significance. The youthful poet very soon afterwards discarded that elaborateness, perceiving that the loss of simplicity caused by it could not be compensated for by any degree of expressiveness, and adopted a style especially marked by its purity. But the subtle exquisiteness of his imagination remained unchanged and had never required any such artificial aid. It had ever "fed among the lilies" of a " Fairy Land," which to it had ever been a native land. With the bleating of the lamb or the lowing of the herd there mingled from afar " the horns of Elfland faintly blowing." I remember my dear friend, Sara Coleridge, daughter of the poet, once remarking to me that, however inferior the bulk of a young man's poetry may be to that of the poet when mature, it generally possesses some passages with a special freshness of their own, and an inexplicable charm to be found in them alone. Such was the charm with which many of those early poems

captivated me, a charm which they have never lost. Still, as in that
old time, the old oak-tree, "thick-leaved, ambrosial," sighs over the
grave of "Claribel." The new interpretation of Nature given to me
then remains, and the beauty mingled with the pathos, when the scene
described is one of Nature's forlornest, as in "The Dying Swan," or
in the weird lines

> Low-flowing breezes are roaming
> The broad valley dimm'd in the gloaming —

never cease to possess me as they did the day that I read them first.
The sea beside which the minstrel lover chanted the ballad of "Oriana"
seemed to me to uplift a clamour of woe such as no sea had ever
uttered before, and reminded me of the "sad prophet's" cry, "Magnum
sicut mare lamentatio mea." Another image of grief, if in a form less
terrible, yet more drearily desolate, was presented to me by "Mariana
in the Moated Grange," with the blackened pool close by, and the
poplar that "shook alway" above it. The "Recollections of the
Arabian Nights" seemed all the more wonderful because the picture
presented with such truthfulness was one taken less from Nature's page
than that of art, because its very excess of magnificence precluded
that effect of tawdriness which commonly characterizes descriptions of
Oriental splendours ; and also because the harmony of the poem's
metre so fully sustained the brilliancy of its imagery. It was

> "A world of bright vision set floating in sound[1]."

Many of the other poems impressed me not less vividly, and I remember most of them by heart still. Day after day my sister and
I used to read them as we drove up and down the "close green ways"
of our woods. Our pony soon detected our abstracted mood. Several
times he nearly upset us down a bank ; and often choosing his path
according to his private judgment, stood still with his head hanging
over a gate. We sometimes sketched an imaginary likeness of the unknown poet. We determined that he must be singularly unlike Shelley ;
that his step must not be rapid but vague, that there would be on his
face less of light, but more of dream ; that his eye would be that of
one who saw little where the many see much, and saw much where
the many see little. Wholly unlike the young poet we thought must
be the countenance of him who had long been the chief object of our
poetic veneration, the great contemplative Bard who had forsaken "the
fortunate Isles of the Muses" for his "Tower of Speculation on the
mountain top," Coleridge.

[1] Leigh Hunt.

In two years more Alfred Tennyson met us again in the gift of a new volume : it had been eagerly waited for and it was eagerly read. The second volume was in several particulars a decided advance upon the earlier ; yet we enjoyed it less at first. Though its subjects were more important and were also treated with more skill, a something seemed to be wanting. That something was probably the spontaneity and unconsciousness which belongs to very youthful poetry in its most felicitous specimens ; for its failures are more numerous than its successes. A third and maturer period comes, in which the best qualities that mark the first and the second period are found united. A few poems in the later volume touched us nearly in the same way as those in the earlier. One of these was "The Lady of Shalott," destined to reappear at the interval of many years in a nobler, ampler and richer form, but not one which challenged more vividly the youthful imagination. Another was "Margaret," to which might be added "The Death of the Old Year," and "The Miller's Daughter"; but most of them were remoter themes, characteristic of memorable epochs, or involving some metaphysical problems. Those poems were written with very great power and skill: they were unlike each other ; they showed that the author's genius possessed an extraordinary versatility, and that besides what was most characteristic in that genius he possessed an exquisite taste and a high art. "Mariana in the South" breathes the air of Southern France ; and its sadness is touched by an amenity which never mitigates the wintry dreariness of "Mariana in the Moated Grange." "Œnone" is thoroughly Greek in spirit, though far richer in detail than the Greek art, a severe thing, as this commonly is. "The May Queen" is an enchanting Idyl of English Rural Life, not rendered dull by its moral but ennobled by it. The "Dream of Fair Women" does not illustrate any particular country or period ; but it is a marvellous specimen of one especial class of poetry, that of Vision, which reached its perfection in Dante, whose verse the young aspirant may have been reading with a grateful desire to note by this poem the spot on which his feet had rested for a time. There is however nothing of plagiarism in it. "The Lotos-Eaters" is not more admirable for its beauty than for its unity ; everywhere the luxuriously lovely scenery corresponds with the voluptuous sentiment ; though voluptuous only in the way of enervate thought, not of passion. I remember the poet's pointing out to me the improvement effected later by the introduction of the last paragraph setting forth the Lucretian Philosophy respecting the Gods, their aloofness from all human interests and elevated action, an Epicurean and therefore hard-hearted repose, sweetened not troubled by the endless wail from the earth. The sudden change of metre in the last paragraph has a highly artistic effect, that of throwing the bulk of the poem as it were into a remote distance. This poem should be contrasted with another and later one, "Ulysses," which illustrates the same lesson in a converse form. It shows us what Heroism may be even in old age, though sustained by little except the love of knowledge, and the scorn of sloth. Carlyle said that it was "Ulysses" which first convinced him that "Tennyson was a true poet." I remember hearing that Bishop Thirlwall made the same statement respecting "St Simeon Stylites."

Another poem in the second volume, which, if it has not the spontaneousness of many in the first, at least illustrates a great theme with a great and manifold mastery, is "The Palace of Art." In its extreme subjectivity it reminds us of German genius; but though its scope is a philosophical and spiritual one, its handling is as strikingly objective; and it consists almost wholly of images which though subordinated to moral, not material ends, yet possess a vividness and a concentrated power rarely found elsewhere, and reminds us of Matthew Arnold's assertion that German Literature, however profound it may be in thought, is cumbrous and clumsy in style compared with English. Its theme is the danger resulting from that "Art Heresy" of modern times, which substitutes the worship of Art for its own sake in place of that reverence which man should feel for it, only when it knows its place, and is content to minister at the altars of Powers greater than itself, viz. Nature and Religion. In this poem nearly every stanza is a picture condensed within four lines. It describes a Palace not a Temple, one created by the imagination exclusively for its own delight, an imagination so great that it refuses all human sympathy, "O God-like isolation which art mine," and yet so small that it can dream of nothing greater than itself.

> I sit as God, holding no form of Creed,
> But contemplating all.

The root of the evil, as the poet clearly intimates, is to be found not in the Sense, but in Pride, a greater crime, the sole expiation of which is Humility.

> "Make me a cottage in the vale," she said,
> "Where I may mourn and pray."

This poem is far greater in thought and in power than any of those in the earlier volume, though less attractive to some, perhaps on account of an apparently didactic purpose. I remember a legend about it, whether authentic or not. Alfred Tennyson and Richard Chenevix Trench had been friends at Cambridge, and had a common love of poetry. Soon after his ordination the future Archbishop paid a visit to the future Laureate. He spoke about the new heresy which substituted Art for Faith and Beauty for Sanctity. His brother-poet, it is said, contested nothing, but simply listened, occasionally replenishing his pipe. When Trench had taken his departure the auditor took up his pen, and the single thought became a poem. Later the same thought was illustrated by Trench in two poems, viz. "The Prize of Song," one of the stateliest lyrics of modern times, and a noble representative of Hellenic Song: and, secondly, in a sonnet, beginning, "What good soever in thy heart or mind."

Two short poems of an extraordinary strength and majesty were written at this time: one would have thought that they had been written at a maturer period; but, if I remember right, they were suggested by some popular demonstrations connected with the Reform Bill of 1832, and its rejection by the House of Lords. Their political teaching shows that when but twenty-three years of age Tennyson's love of Liberty, which at all periods so strongly characterized his poetry, was accompanied by an equally strong conviction that Liberty must ever be a Moral Power beginning upon the spiritual "heights" of wisdom, mutual respect and self-control; and that no despotism could be more fatal than that *tyranny of a majority* in which alone a material omnipotence is united with a legal one. These two poems begin respectively with the lines, "You ask me, why, tho' ill at ease," and "Of old sat Freedom on the heights." Their massive grandeur results mainly from their brevity, and the austere simplicity of their diction, which belongs to what has sometimes been called the "lapidary" style. Each might indeed have been carved upon the entablature of a temple; and I remember hearing an aged statesman exclaim that they reminded him of what he felt when, driving across the lonely plain of Paestum, he found himself confronted by its two temples. Their power consists largely in that perfection of poetic form with which each of them is invested. In this respect they may be profitably contrasted with a third poem which begins "Love thou thy land, with love far-brought." In thought and imagination that poem is equal to the former two; yet it bears no comparison with them as regards weight and effectiveness, because the same perfection of form was forbidden to it by the extent and complexity of its theme. It could not have been caused by want of pains on the part of the poet. An anecdote will illustrate his solicitude on the subject of poetic form, the importance of which was perhaps not as much appreciated by any other writer since the days of Greek poetry. One night, after he had been reading aloud several of his poems, all of them short, he passed one of them to me and said, "What is the matter with that poem?" I read it and answered, "I see nothing to complain of." He laid his fingers on two stanzas of it, the third and fifth, and said, " Read it again." After doing so I said, " It has now more completeness and totality about it ; but the two stanzas you cover are among its best." " No matter," he rejoined, " they make the poem too longbacked ; and they must go, at any sacrifice." " Every short poem," he remarked, " should have a definite shape, like the curve, sometimes a single, sometimes a double one, assumed by a severed tress or the rind of an apple when flung on the floor."

In 1842, twelve years after the publication of Alfred Tennyson's first volume, a new edition of his poems appeared in two volumes, the earlier of which included his poems previously published, with a few exceptions, while the second was wholly new. It was this edition which carried his poetry beyond a narrower circle and fixed it in the heart of the nation : but in winning the many the poet did not cease to delight the " fit and few." They gladly recognised the progress which his art had made, a progress the result of well-directed pains, as well as of the poet's moral characteristics and peculiarities.

Genius is often frittered away by the social popularity which greets its earlier achievements, one among the worst forms of adulation. Henry Taylor amusingly describes his own immunity from such perils. He was, he tells us,

> " From social snares with ease
> Saved by that gracious gift, inaptitude to please."

The younger poet was as little open to such snares. He was proof against them through the absence of vanity, even more than through shyness, indolence, or any other peculiarity. He was born a poet ; and had no ambition except the single one of first meriting and then receiving the poet's crown, an ambition the unselfish character of which is so asserted by Shelley in the expression " Fame is Love disguised." No matter how much courted he might be, no attraction, whether of wit, beauty or fashion, could prevail on him to frequent any society except that of those whom he cordially liked ; and in none did he ever talk for effect. Neither did he allow himself, as so many of our best modern poets have done, to be diverted from poetry by inferior forms of labour ; though the loss very frequently sustained by poetry is doubtless much compensated by the signal aptitude which the poetic faculty sometimes shows for tasks not properly its own, whether literary or practical. He delighted in all forms of knowledge, but he was faithful to his own gift, and drew all things beside into the service of poetry, as their Suzerain. For this task the largeness of his sympathies specially qualified him, though it might have produced the opposite effect if he had not possessed a great unity of purpose as well as a great imaginative versatility.

Another gift contributed to make these twelve years fruitful to him, that of a singular common sense. This gift, often regarded as but an humble one, is in reality nothing less than a form of inspiration, for, like the loftier inspiration, it works it knows not how, and spontaneously. It is often, as obviously in the case of Shakespeare, united with the highest genius; and it is as often signally defective in men of high abilities, but men who in genius have no part. The gift of common sense united with that of imagination attracted Alfred Tennyson to the humorous side of things as well as to the pathetic, and thus made him learned in Life, the Life of the Humanities. All those things in them which others see but in their accidents, the mind thus dowered with a twofold inspiration sees in their essence.

Those English Idyls[1] were a gift such as no other writer of Idyls had ever given to his countrymen. No Englishman can read them in far lands without the memory coming back to him of the days when he sat on an English stile, and watched English lambs at play, or walked beneath hedgerow trees in " a land of ancient peace " listening to the last note of the last bird-song as the twilight deepened into night. He will see an English Ruth adorning with flowers the hat of the child that is not hers, in the hope of winning his grandfather's heart, or sitting on the poppied ground amid the wheat, while

> The reapers reap'd
> And the sun fell and all the land was dark.

He will see " The Gardener's Daughter," and her garden described, to quote Henry Taylor's words, " as only Tennyson could describe it," that Garden bordered by

> A league of grass, wash'd by a slow broad stream
> That stirr'd with languid pulses of the oar,
> Waves all its lazy lilies, and creeps on,
> Barge-laden, to three arches of a bridge
> Crown'd with the minster towers.

It would be hard to find two Idyls more perfect than " Dora " and " The Gardener's Daughter," or more unlike each other — the former so Hebraic in its stern and unadorned simplicity; the latter so pure in its richness, sweetness and pathos, a pathos not of sorrow, but of joy, one that delights, not wounds. I remember an incident connected with " The Gardener's Daughter." The poet had corrected

---

[1] My father used to spell Idyls then with one " l " for these shorter Idyls, and Idylls with two " l's " for the epic " Idylls of the King."

it as carefully as he had originally composed it in his head, where he was in the habit of keeping more than one poem at a time before he wrote down any of them. I found him one day in James Spedding's rooms. He shewed me the MS and said, "The corrections jostled each other, and the poem seemed out of gear. Spedding has just now remarked that it wants nothing but that this passage, forty lines, should be omitted. He is right." It was omitted.

Few of these Idyls are more perfect than "Audley Court," short as it is. What can be more vigorous than these lines illustrative of simple aversion, as distinguished from hatred or resentment?

> Oh! who would love? I woo'd a woman once.
> But she was sharper than an eastern wind,
> And all my heart turned from her, *as a thorn*
> *Turns from the sea ;* but let me live my life.

Those descriptions of nature owe half their charm to the circumstance that the illustrations of men and manners are in entire harmony with them. In them material nature and human life are mirrors that mutually reflect each other. There exist pictures in which the landscape is by one artist and the figures by another. Compared with these poems they are failures.

Among the Idyls none are more delightful than those which illustrate the life of young Englishmen and Englishwomen. Such are "Edwin Morris," "Locksley Hall," "The Day-Dream," and "Will Waterproof's Lyrical Monologue." To me the most delightful of these is "The Talking Oak." It is more difficult to make the Manor House poetical than the Cottage ; but here as in "The Princess" and elsewhere that arduous problem is solved. In it the poet's gift of expressive, harmonious and richly coloured language reaches its highest :

> O rock upon thy towery top
> All throats that gurgle sweet !
> All starry culmination drop
> Balm-dews to bathe thy feet !
>
> All grass of silky feather grow —
> And while he sinks or swells
> The full south-breeze around thee blow
> The sound of minster bells.

Very remarkable is the skill with which "The Talking Oak," while depicting the country life of England, connects with it a series of sketches illustrating, each in but a few happy touches, many of her past historical periods. Its author told me that this poem was an experiment meant to test the degree in which it is within the power

of poetry to *humanize* external nature. The *subtlety* of his own sympathies with Nature probably rendered it easier for him than for any
other poet to invest tree or stream with human affections and sympathies. He mentioned that he had written, as a companion to this
poem, another one, dealing in similar fashion with a rivulet, but that
it was lost: and he repeated a line the syllables of which imitated
the sound of a stream running over a stony bed, "I babble with my
pebbles." The lost poem seems to survive in "The Brook," the
most artistic, I think, of that kind of Idyl. To this Idyl series many
were added in later volumes, such as "The First Quarrel," "The
Sisters," "The Village Wife," "The Spinster's Sweet-'arts," "The
Children's Hospital," and "Rizpah," among the strongest of the
series.

In this series Idylic Poetry was raised to a height after which it
had never before aspired. In most of the old Idyls, and the modern
imitations of them, a couple of shepherds piped their loves in rivalry.
One of them gained his prize, and thanked Faunus; another lost it,
as he had already lost the treacherous object of his affections, and
went home seriously distressed but not without hope of "better luck
the next time." There was in them no attempt at descriptive poetry:
the trees and the pastures were generally as like each other as sheep
is like sheep. It was otherwise with these new Idyls. In them there
was room for the whole range of human affections, passions and
interests; and their descriptive passages delineated nature in all her
moods and aspects, the humblest as well as the greatest. Had those
poems included nothing but their descriptive portions they would hence
still have possessed a great charm: but they were yet more remarkable
for the dramatic skill with which the characters were discriminated,
whether they belonged to the cultured or the humbler classes of society.
How unlike are the self-satisfied and harmless babbler of "Philip's
Farm," and the sturdy yeoman who starves his son because he will
not marry Dora, and who later weeps over that son's orphan child!
How different from both is that Northern farmer of "the old style,"
with a heart hard as a stone, and a mind that seems but animated
matter, and yet with a single spot of tenderness in him, one for the
soil itself, from which he seems to have risen full-grown, on which
he has laboured so long, and over which he cannot bear that the
new-fangled steam-plough and the hiss of the "kettle" should ever
pass! Many a year before Tennyson wrote drama, his Idyls had
proved that in his poetic gift there lived a latent but admirable
dramatic insight.

The volume of 1842 was welcomed not only with gratitude for
all that it bestowed, but as an augury of gifts greater yet sure to follow

whenever a genius so potent and so various measured itself with a theme worthy of it, and capable of testing all its powers. That augury was fulfilled by the publication of " In Memoriam " and the " Idylls of the King." " In Memoriam " showed how great a thing man's love is, by revealing the greatness of that love, that grief and that deliverance from grief, of which it is capable. The "Idylls of the King," more of a complete great Epic than any of the great Epics, showed how high is that aim which every commonwealth of men is bound to propose to itself; and it showed not less that that high aim, political at once and spiritual, when frustrated, owes its doom not to mischance, or external violence chiefly, but to moral evil that saps the State's foundations.

(P. 487.) Reminiscences by Thomas Wilson and William Allingham.

1863–64.

Mr Wilson writes :

We used frequently to walk together with the boys, sometimes drawing Mrs Tennyson in her little four-wheeled carriage along the Downs, towards the Needles, through Maiden's Croft over the little rustic bridge across the lane, where sometimes inquisitive strangers used to lie in wait to catch a sight of the Poet.

Maiden's Croft reminds me of Mr Tennyson's resentment of Mr Ruskin's criticising his line in " Maud " as a " pathetic fallacy " :

And left the daisies rosy.

" Why," he said, " the very day I wrote it, I saw the daisies rosy in Maiden's Croft, and thought of enclosing one to Ruskin labelled ' A pathetic fallacy.' " I remember asking him if unselfishness was the essence of virtue? his reply was " Certainly."

Not unfrequently I used to have evening talks with him on the way up to bed, looking at the many pictures that adorned the staircase : these he said he looked at far more frequently than pictures in the room. On one of these occasions, as he was holding a candle to examine some book or picture (for he was very near-sighted), his wavy dark hair took fire ; I was for putting it out : " Oh, never mind," he said, " it depends upon chance burnings."

He spoke of " the wind torturing the roof," and used often to mount outside the roof from his attic-chamber, to admire the moonlight, and the sound of the breakers in the Bay. He was so short-sighted that the moon, without a glass, seemed to him like a shield across the sky[1].

He came into my room one day looking for any new book to feed upon : he took down one by Stevenson called *Praying and Working*, an account of German Ragged Schools ; he told me afterwards he had read it with great pleasure ; he was keen to get De Morgan's *From Matter to Spirit*.

On Lionel's birthday we acted a little Play or Charade: the first scene, to represent the word 'lion,' was the interlude of Pyramus and Thisbe from *Midsummer Night's Dream ;* the servants were admitted to the performance, and laughed heartily at Wall, the Moon, and other grotesque characters. Tennyson remarked that this confirmed his opinion of the enduring popularity of broad Comedy in England.

Tennyson always said that his childhood had been at times very unhappy ; and his desire was to make Hallam and Lionel's childhood as happy as possible : he encouraged Lionel, who had some talent for drawing, to copy natural objects.

He used sometimes to read aloud in the evening, in a deep sustained sonorous voice. I remember little Hallam warning me not to trouble him when he was smoking his first morning pipe, when he used to think that his best inspirations came.

At the time of these Recollections I was not in good health, sometimes suffering from fits of melancholy ; on one such occasion he said, "If you wish to kill yourself don't do it here : go to Yarmouth and do it decently" ; on another occasion he said, "Just go grimly on." I once spoke of Christ as an example of failure. "Do you," said he, "call that failure which has altered the belief and the social relations of the whole world?"

Mr Allingham writes :

Oct. 3rd, 1863. Saturday. We drove to Farringford (Mrs A., Clough and W. A.), picking up on the way Pollock and his son. Drawing-room tea, Mrs Tennyson in white, I can sometimes scarcely hear her low tones. Mrs Cameron, dark, short, sharp-eyed, one hears very distinctly. I wandered to the book-table where Tennyson joined me. He praised Worsley's *Odyssey*. In a book of Latin versions from his own poetry he found some slips in Lord Lyttelton's Latin *Cytherea Venus*, etc. "Did I find Lymington very dull?" I told him that

---

[1] He said that he never saw the two end stars in the tail of "Ursa Major" separate. To his eyes they intersected one another.

since coming there I had heard Cardinal Wiseman lecture (on Self-culture), Spurgeon preach, and seen Tom Sayers spar. "More than I have," he remarked. In taking leave he said, "Come to-morrow."

Oct. 4th. I walked over alone to Farringford, found first Mrs Tennyson, the two boys and their tutor. Tennyson at luncheon. "What do we know of the feelings of insects? Nothing." Tennyson takes me upstairs to his "den" on the top storey, and higher, up a ladder, to the leads. He often comes up here at night to look at the heavens....Then we went down and walked about the grounds, looking at a cedar, a huge fern, an Irish yew. The dark cedar in "Maud," "sighing for Lebanon," he got at Swainston, Sir John Simcon's....We went down the garden, past a large fig-tree growing in the open, "like a breaking wave." Contradictions *from him* are no way disagreeable: and so to the farmyard. "Have you a particular feeling about a farm-yard?" he asked, "a special delight in it? I have. The first time I read Shakespeare was on a hay-stack, *Othello*. I said, 'This man's overrated.' Boys can't understand Shakespeare." We spoke a little of the Shakespeare "Tercentenary," next year. "Most people pronounce 'Arbutus' wrong, with the second syllable long. 'Clematis' too, which should be 'Clē-mătis.'" In the passage, or somewhere near it, I noticed a dusty phial hanging up with some dried brown stuff in it (left by the last owners of Farringford). "It is a Lar," he said, with a twinkle in his eyes. "And what else is it?" I asked. "An old bottle of Ipecacuanha." We looked at the great magnolia stretching up to the roof; then into the hall and saw some fossils. "Man is so small!" he said, "but a fly on the wheel." Mrs Clough was in the house, and she and I now departed, Tennyson coming with us as far as the little south postern opening on the lane....In parting he said to me, "We shall see you sometimes?" which gladdened me.

Later. We (W. A. and Rev. W. Barnes, the Dorsetshire poet) drove in a fly to Farringford, where Tennyson, Mrs Tennyson, Miss Tennyson, met us in the hall. Tennyson and Barnes at once on easy terms, having simple poetic minds and mutual good-will. Talk of "Ancient Britons, barrows, roads," etc. I to upper room to dress, Tennyson comes in to me, and we go down together. Dinner: stories of Ghosts and Dreams. To drawing-room as usual, where Tennyson had his port. Barnes no wine. Tennyson said, "Modern fame is nothing: I'd rather have an acre of land. I shall go down, down! I'm up now. Action and reaction." Tennyson went upstairs by himself. Tea. Enter Mrs Cameron (in a funny red open-work shawl) with two of her boys. Tennyson reappeared, and Mrs Cameron showed a small firework toy called "Pharaoh's Serpents," a kind of pastille which when lighted twists about in a wormlike shape. Mrs Cameron said they were poisonous, and forbade us all to touch. Tennyson in defiance put out his hand. "Don't touch 'em," shrieked Mrs Cameron. "You shan't, Alfred!" But Alfred did. "Wash your hands then!" But Alfred wouldn't, and rubbed his moustache instead, enjoying Mrs Cameron's agonies. Then she said to him, "Will you come to-morrow to be photographed?" He, very emphatically, "No!" Then she turned to me, "You left a Great Poet out of *Nightingale Valley*, and have been repenting ever since in sackcloth and ashes, eh?" She meant Henry Taylor. I tried to say that the volume was not a collection of specimens of poets, but she did not listen. Then she said graciously, "Come to-morrow and you shall be taken, and (whispers) you shall see Madonna, eh?" Madonna, otherwise called Island Mary, being one of her pretty servants whom she photographs as the Virgin, etc. This eh! and hm! makes a droll little finish to many of Mrs Cameron's sentences. She is extremely clever, and good-natured. Tennyson and I went out to the porch with Mrs Cameron, where her donkey-chair was waiting in the moonlight. We looked at some of her own photographs on the walls, and at one of Henry Taylor. Tennyson said to one of the Cameron boys, "All your mother's geese are swans and all her Taylors are gods!" "What's that?" says Mrs Cameron, who only heard part; upon which Tennyson repeated the words, introducing them with "Your son says," at which we all laughed, whether the lady enjoyed it or not. But she was candid enough on her part. Tennyson asked her would she photograph Mr Barnes? But she said "No." She objected to the top of his head.

Tennyson now took Barnes and me to his top room. "Darwinism, Man from Ape, would that really make any difference?" "Time is nothing (said T.) : are we not all part of Deity?" "Pantheism," hinted Barnes, who was not at ease in this sort of speculation. "Well," says Tennyson, "I think I believe in Pantheism, of a sort." Barnes to bed, Tennyson and I up ladder to the roof and looked at Orion; then to my room, where more talk. He liked Barnes, he said, "but he is not accustomed to strong views theologic." We talked of Browning, for whom Tennyson had a very strong personal regard. "I can't understand how he should care for my poetry. His new poem has 15,000 lines: there's copiousness! Good night." Bed about 1.

(P. 487.) *Hints for "Enoch Arden" from Edward Fitzgerald* (1862), *in a letter to my mother.*

How is it that your note has been unanswered this month or more? Why, a fortnight of the month I didn't see it at all : being away with a sister in Norfolk ; and the remaining fortnight? Why I kept thinking I might tell you something about the *fishing* questions you ask me : I mean, about telling you "*anything*" about fishermen, etc. Well, somehow, what little I know on such matters won't turn up on demand : perhaps it would undemanded if you and A. T. were in my boat one summer day on this poor river, or plunging over its bar into the German Seas. Ah ! Alfred should never have left his old county with its Mablethorpe sea. As to the definite questions you ask on the subject, I can only answer for the customs in such matters *hereabout*.

1. There is no *apprenticeship* to fishing : anyone takes anyone who comes handy, etc., even in the *Deep-Sea* fishing, i.e. not along the coast, but out to the Dogger bank, Scotland, Ireland, etc. (for cod-fish) ; anyone *may* go who *can* get a berth. Only a little while ago, a lad was telling me at Aldbro' how *he* first went, as a boy of 13 : he *hid* himself in the *stern* of the boat that was pushing off to the *smack :* and when they were well off shore, he pushed up his head from under ropes, etc., and the "Master" only said, "What ! is thee that devil of a boy? You'll be glad enough to be at home again before along !" and so took him out to sea ; and now the lad has his 14*s.* a week (grown to 19 years old) like the rest.

2. "May *fishermen* act as pilots, or must they be of a *Guild* of pilots?" *Yes*, properly : no one is *authorized* to become a pilot, unless he has served his time as *mate* in a *square-rigged vessel* (i.e. nothing under *a brig :* even a *schooner* won't do). When he has so served a certain time, he has to pass examinations before (I *think*) the *Trinity Board* and so is admitted or not to be of the Guild. But, when all the authorized pilots in a place are exhausted (as will happen when many foreign ships pass, etc.), then a *fisherman* or other *un*authorized sailor will go : being called a "*Brummagem Pilot.*"

Oh dear ! this is very learned, very useless, I dare say. But you ask me and I tell my best. I have been almost tempted to write you out some morsels of Dampier's *Voyages* which I copied out for myself : so fine as they are in their way I think, but they would be no use unless A. T. fell upon them by chance : for, of all horses, Pegasus least likes to be dragged to drink. I love Captain Cook too : what fine English his, in the Johnsonian days ! I remember, 10 years ago, telling Alfred at Brighton of some poor little verses found in the Prayer-Book of a seafaring son of our old coachman, who died at sea: and Alfred took the pipe out of his blessed old lips to remurmur one, which *Thackeray* pooh-poohed. Along the coast here are many peculiar and fine Scandinavian words, which are not registered even by our provincial glossarists (who have dealt chiefly with the inland husbandman people).

Well, I shan't go on more about this unless you desire some more. About the photographs of A. T., thank you for them: as *you* think one of them very good, I have no doubt it is so: but what becomes of the eyes? I had seen some bigger ones, which made a sort of Rembrandt Burgomaster of him: but in reality I don't much love photographs: though I asked you for one, because I knew they were always going on: and I sincerely thank you for sending me (I dare say) the best.

This is vile weak scribbling, after two glasses of b-r-n-d-y and water too (Sunday evening).

I saw (in Norfolk) that Yarrell does give that human note to the plover: so I dare say he is right, and my friends on the river here wrong. I see too that Yarrell writes the word "Curlew" as French "*Couvre lieu*" (*I think*), supposed to be from its *cry*. (Query. Will A. T. say anything better than an Aldbro' fisherman said of *a* boat — (Humph) "Ah! — She go like *a Wiolin*, she do!")

Some Summer — some Summer day send the old wretch here, where nobody scarce knows his name (don't be angry, Mrs A. T.), though a duller place is not! but an ugly river

(and a dirty sea)
(and E. F. G.)

which is my poem Q. E. D.

(P.S. Leave the scrap of *Cook* on the floor, in Alfred's way: don't give it him.)

TENNYSON

VOL. II

CHAPTER I.

THE "ENOCH ARDEN" VOLUME, WITH NOTES BY MY FATHER.

Spedding, the calm philosopher, glowed with delight, and said "Enoch Arden" was the finest story he had ever heard[1], and was more especially adapted for Alfred than for any other poet.

Letter from Thomas Woolner to Mrs Tennyson.

1864.

My father was always an enthusiast for Italian freedom. Hence the great event of the year at Farringford was Garibaldi's visit. My mother wrote in April:

We went to the Seelys of Brooke to pay our respects to Garibaldi. A most striking figure in his picturesque white poncho lined with red, his embroidered red shirt and coloured tie over it. His face very noble, powerful, and sweet, his forehead high and square. Altogether he looked one of the great men of our Elizabethan age. His manner was simple and kind. A. and I went out to fix a spot in our garden where the Wellingtonia should be planted by him (given to A. by the Duchess of Sutherland, and raised by her from a cone that had been shot from a tree three hundred feet high in California). Poor Philip Worsley's[2] poems had just arrived — the thought of

---

[1] Adelaide Procter wrote a poem on a similar subject, but this my father did not know until after "Enoch Arden" had been published.

[2] The author of the well-known translation of the *Odyssey*.

him, dying of consumption in the lodging near the bay, mingled strangely with the feeling of this moment and the sounds of welcome as Garibaldi passed thro' the village to Farringford. People on foot and on horseback and in carriages had waited at our gate two hours for him. Some rushed forward to shake hands with him. He stood up and bowed. A. and I and the boys were in the portico awaiting his arrival. On entering the house Garibaldi admired the primroses with which the rooms were decked, and liked the view of our park, and said to A., " I wish I had your trees in Caprera." A. and he went up to A.'s study together, and they talked on politics, A. advising the General not to talk politics in England. They repeated Italian poetry to each other.

He told A. that he "could never doubt his country — that he loved her." "*She* never alters!" he said. " Next to God I never cease to have faith in *her*." We introduced Garibaldi to Sir Henry Taylor [1] and to other friends. It was pleasant to see how his face lighted up when he recognized his old acquaintance Mrs Franklin (wife of Colonel Franklin stationed here): and he greeted the Colonel warmly too. Mrs Cameron wanted to photograph Garibaldi, and dropped down on her knees before him, and held up her black hands, covered with chemicals. He evidently thought that she was a beggar until we had explained who she was.

Then we went to plant the Wellingtonia. A. had the large screen put up to protect Garibaldi from the cold east wind. Several strangers were there, and when the tree was planted they gave a shout. On going away Garibaldi shook hands with all and kissed the boys. A. was charmed with his simplicity, but thought that in worldly matters he seemed to have the " divine stupidity of a hero." A. also saw Mazzini, and was

---

[1] Henry Taylor wrote of Garibaldi's visit to Farringford :

> "And there was he, that gentle hero, who,
>   By virtue and the strength of his right arm,
> Dethroned an unjust king, and then withdrew
>   To tend his farm.
>
> To whom came forth a mighty man of song,
>   Whose deep-mouth'd music rolls thro' all the land,
> Voices of many rivers, rich or strong,
>   Or sweet or grand."

struck with his keen intellectual face, and quoted with approval what he had said, " Nothing in this world is so contemptible as a literary coterie."

My father wrote then to the Duke of Argyll :

MY DEAR DUKE,

Did you hear Garibaldi repeat any Italian poetry? I did, for I had heard that he himself had made songs and hymns: and I asked him, " Are you a poet?" "Yes," he said quite simply, whereupon I spouted to him a bit of Manzoni's great ode, that which Gladstone translated. I don't know whether he relished it, but he began immediately to speak of Ugo Foscolo and quoted, with great fervour, a fragment of his " I Sepolcri," beginning with " Il navigante che veleggio," etc. and ending with " Delle Parche il canto," which verses he afterwards wrote out for me : and they certainly seem to be fine, whatever the rest of the poem may be. I have not yet read it but mean to do so, for he sent me Foscolo's *Poesie* from London ; and in return I sent him the " Idylls of the King," which I do not suppose he will care for. What a noble human being! I expected to see a hero and I was not disappointed. One cannot exactly say of him what Chaucer says of the ideal knight, "As meke he was of port as is a maid"; he is more majestic than meek, and his manners have a certain divine simplicity in them, such as I have never witnessed in a native of these islands, among men at least, and they are gentler than those of most young maidens whom I know. He came here and smoked his cigar in my little room and we had a half hour's talk in English, tho' I doubt whether he understood me perfectly, and his meaning was often obscure to me. I ventured to give him a little advice: he denied that he came with any political purpose to England, merely to thank the English for their kindness to him, and the interest they had taken in himself and all Italian matters, and also to consult Ferguson about his leg. Stretching this out he said, "There's a campaign in me yet." When I asked if he returned thro' France he said he would never set foot on the soil of France again. I happened to make use of this expression, "That fatal debt of gratitude owed by Italy to Napoleon." "Gratitude," he said; "Hasn't he had his pay? his reward? If Napoleon were dead I should be glad, and if I were dead he would be glad." These are slight chroniclings, but I thought you would like to have them. He seemed especially taken with my two little boys.

As to "sea-blue birds" &c. defendant states that he was walking one day in March by a deep-banked brook, and under the leafless bushes he saw the kingfisher flitting or fleeting underneath him, and there came into his head a fragment of an old Greek lyric poet, " ἀλιπόρφυρος εἶαρος ὄρνις," " The sea-purple or sea-shining bird of Spring," spoken of as the halcyon. Defendant cannot say whether the Greek halcyon be the same as the British kingfisher, but as he never saw the kingfisher on this particular brook before March, he concludes that in that country at least, they go down to the sea during the hard weather and come up again with the Spring, for what says old Belon:

> " Le Martinet-pescheur fait sa demeure
> En temps d'hiver au bord de l'océan,
> Et en esté sur la rivière en estan,
> Et de poisson se repaist à toute heure."

You see he puts "esté," which I suppose stands for all the warmer weather. Was not the last letter in *The Field* written by yourself?

Ever, my dear Duke, with all kind things from myself and wife to the Duchess,

Yours, A. TENNYSON.

We are sorry not to have seen you at Farringford in the time of flowers; let us know when you can come. I hope the Queen is well and able to enjoy this fine weather.

Just before the publication of " Enoch Arden " we made a pilgrimage into Brittany, where we unearthed many wild " Enoch Arden " stories and ballads. The Breton sailors are fine, simple, religious fellows, many of whom join the Iceland fishery and the French navy. My mother wrote:

There are many pleasant things in our pleasant journey to think of, not the least those weird stones[1]. Carnac owes much less to them than we expected: the Morbihan district interested us much more. Mont St Michel, the old churches, and the Bayeux tapestry, to say nothing of our drives about the country, were very interesting too. From Quimper to Morlaix is wild Wales in miniature. We did not see as much as we ought to have done of the Western and Northern coasts. We drove by a road near the coast, not on the coast, having foolishly omitted to get a good map in Paris, and not having been able to find one afterwards. The people we found very uncommunicative, and, as far as we could discover, totally ignorant of the past history of their country, and of the Arthur legends. We went to Lannion on purpose to see Keldthuen (where Arthur is said to have held his court) and Avalon: but Keldthuen we found a moated and not ancient chateau, and tho' our driver showed us Avalon, the sailors declared it was not Avalon.

Nevertheless the hostess of the Hôtel de l'Europe at Lannion somehow discovered who my father was, and proclaimed everywhere that he was the poet of "notre grand roi Arthur."

The joy of my father in heroism, whether of a past age or of the present, and his delight in celebrating it, are more than ever apparent throughout this volume of

---

[1] The dolmens and cromlechs.

1864. He was especially happy when writing of his " Old Fisherman." In these " Idylls of the Hearth[1] " he had worked at the same vein which he opened in his 1842 poems. — Here he writes with as intimate a knowledge, but with greater power, on subjects from English life, the sailor, the farmer, the parson, the city lawyer, the squire, the country maiden, and the old woman who dreams of her past life in a restful old age.

He said that, excepting the poems suggested by the simple, old-world classical subjects, he had mostly drawn his scenes in England, because he could not truly pourtray the atmosphere of foreign lands. He added that he thought *Romola* a mistake ; because George Eliot had not been able to enter into the complex Italian life and character, however much she might have studied them in books.

Sixty thousand copies of " Enoch Arden " were sold in a very short time, and after this he was not infrequently called " The Poet of the People," a title which could not but be appreciated by one who wrote:

Plowmen, shepherds have I found, and more than
    once, and still could find,
Sons of God and kings of men in utter nobleness
    of mind.

Indeed, judging by the countless letters from all conditions of men all over the world, and from the many translations into foreign languages, this volume — which contained, besides " Enoch Arden," " Aylmer's Field," " The Grandmother," " Sea Dreams," " The Northern Farmer," " Tithonus," " The Sailor Boy," " The Flower," the " Welcome to Alexandra " and the " Dedication " — is, perhaps with the exception of " In Memoriam," the most popular of his works.

---

[1] The first title in the proof-sheets of the " Enoch Arden " volume.

" I can always write when I see my subject whole," he said; but he was fastidious in his choice of subjects, which were selected according to his mood. It took him only about a fortnight to write " Enoch Arden," within a little summer-house in the meadow called Maiden's Croft, looking over Freshwater Bay and toward the downs. In this meadow he paced up and down, making his lines; and then wrote them in his MS book on the table of the summer-house, which he himself had designed and painted.

He loved the sea as much as any sailor, and knew all its moods whether on the shore or in mid-ocean. He loved it for its own sake and also because English heroism has ever been conspicuous on ship-board: he felt in himself the spirit of the old Norsemen. This delight in the sea more especially comes out in such poems as " Enoch Arden," " Ulysses," " The Revenge," " The Voyage," " The Sailor Boy," " Sea Dreams," " Maud," " Break, break," and " Crossing the Bar," and I remember well his glory in having made these lines in " Boadicea " —

Fear not, isle of blowing woodland, isle of silvery
    parapets !
Thine the liberty, thine the glory, thine the deeds to
    be celebrated,
Thine the myriad-rolling ocean, light and shadow
    illimitable;

and,

Roar'd as when the roaring breakers boom and blanch
    on the precipices.

His MS notes written for me on " Enoch Arden " are as follows: " ' Enoch Arden ' (like 'Aylmer's Field ') is founded on a theme given me by the sculptor Woolner. I believe that this particular story came out of Suffolk, but something like the same story is told in Brittany and elsewhere."

Englishmen living in the tropics often assured him that, in his description of the isle, the splendours of those regions were faithfully depicted; also the sense of weariness which weighs upon an Englishman doomed to live long among them.   On the lines which follow —

> Once likewise, in the ringing of his ears,
> Tho' faintly, merrily — far and far away —
> He heard the pealing of his parish bells,

he wrote: "Mr Kinglake told me that he had heard his own parish bells in the desert on a Sunday morning when they would have been ringing at home: and added, 'I might have had a singing in my ears, and the imaginative memory did the rest.'"

About the line

> There came so loud a calling of the sea,

he observed: "The calling of the sea is a term used, I believe, chiefly in the Western parts of England, to signify a ground swell.   When this occurs on a windless night, the echo of it rings thro' the timbers of the old houses in a haven."

His similes in "Enoch Arden," he said, were all such as might have been used by simple fisher-folk, quoting this as one of the tenderest (he thought) he had written:

> She heard,
> Heard, and not heard him; as the village girl,
> Who sets her pitcher underneath the spring,
> Musing on him that used to fill it for her,
> Hears and not hears, and lets it overflow.

Among many stories as to the effect of "Enoch Arden" on the uneducated, I will quote one.

A district visitor was distributing tracts among a large meeting of some poor folk to whom she had lately read part of "Enoch Arden." "Thank you, ma'am," one old lady said, "but I'd give all I had for that other beautiful tract which you read t'other day (a sentiment which was echoed by the others), it did me a power of good." This pleased him; he "was glad to have done any good to anyone."

The opening lines of "Aylmer's Field" unfold the moral of that poem. The sequel describes the Nemesis which fell upon Sir Aylmer Aylmer in his pride of wealth. My father always felt a prophet's righteous wrath against this form of selfishness; and no one can read his terrible denunciations of such pride trampling on a holy human love, without being aware that the poet's heart burnt within him while at work on this tale of wrong.

He notes that "Tithonus" had been begun years ago, at the same date that "Ulysses" was written, and that Professor Jebb's translation of the poem into Latin hexameters was a work of real genius.

About the "Northern Farmers," old and new style, my father writes: "Roden Noel calls these two poems 'photographs,' but they are imaginative. The first is founded on the dying words of a farm-bailiff, as reported to me by a great uncle of mine when verging upon 80, — 'God A'mighty little knows what He's about, a-taking me. An' Squire will be so mad an' all.' I conjectured the man from that one saying."

"The 'Farmer, new style' (in 'The Holy Grail' volume), is likewise founded on a single sentence, 'When I canters my 'erse along the ramper (highway) I 'ears proputty, proputty, proputty.' I had been told that a rich farmer in our neighbourhood was in the habit of saying this. I never saw the man and know no more of him. It was also reported of the wife of this worthy that, when she entered the *salle à manger* of a sea bathing-place, she slapt her pockets and said, 'When I married I brought him £5000 on each shoulder.'"

My father was fond of telling stories of this kind in Lincolnshire dialect. The three following are examples:

A housemaid, who was born in the fen country, and accustomed to drink the strong fen water, went to Caistor on the Wolds, famous for its splendid springs. However, she soon gave warning for this reason— "She liked Caistor, but could not abear the watter, for that taästed o' nowt [nothing]." Another story was of a Lincolnshire farmer coming home on Sunday after a sermon about the endless fires of hell and talking to his wife— "Noä, Sally, it woän't do, noä constitootion cud stan' it." A third was of a Lincolnshire minister praying for rain: "O God, send us rain, and especially on John Stubbs' field in the middle marsh, and if Thou doest not know it, it has a big thorn-tree in the middle of it."

The Lincolnshire dialect poems are so true in dialect and feeling, that when they were first read in that county a farmer's daughter exclaimed: "That's Lincoln labourers' talk, and I thought Mr Tennyson was a gentleman."

"The Flower [1]," one of the shorter poems in this volume, is described in the manuscript notes as "an universal apologue." On the subject he quoted: "In

---

[1] *To J. B. Selkirk.*

FRESHWATER, I. W.

DEAR SIR,

Accept my best thanks for your volume of Essays, one of which I had read before, in the *Cornhill* I think. The world, and especially the schools of our younger poets, would be none the worse for lending you an attentive ear. I may remark that you have fallen into a not uncommon error with respect to my little fable "The Flower," as if "I" in the poem meant A. T. and "the flower" my own verses. And so you have narrowed into personality an universal apologue and parable. I once had a letter from a stranger asking whether Christianity were not intended by it. You see by this that I have more than dipt into your book.

Pray believe me yours in all sincerity,

A. TENNYSON.

this world there are few voices and many echoes." A friend writes:

However absorbed Tennyson might be in earnest talk, his eye and ear were always alive to the natural objects around him. I have often known him stop short in a sentence to listen to a blackbird's song, to watch the sunlight glint on a butterfly's wing, or to examine a field flower at his feet. The lines on "The Flower" were the result of an investigation of the "love-in-idleness" growing at Farringford — he made them nearly all on the spot and said them to me (as they are) next day. Trees and plants had a special attraction for him and he longed to the last to see the vegetation of the Tropics [1].

Among the experiments in classical quantity [2], the Alcaic "Ode to Milton" was annotated thus: "My Alcaics are not intended for Horatian Alcaics, nor are Horace's Alcaics the Greek Alcaics, nor are his Sapphics, which are vastly inferior to Sappho's, the Greek Sapphics. The Horatian Alcaic is perhaps the stateliest metre in the world except the Virgilian hexameter at its best; but the Greek Alcaic, if we may judge from the two or three specimens left, had a much freer and lighter movement: and I have no doubt that an old Greek if he knew our language would admit my Alcaics as legitimate, only Milton must not be pronounced Mil*ton*."

His hexameters directed against the translation of Homer into accentual English hexameters are well known. German hexameters he disliked even more than English. He once said — "'Was die Neugier nicht thut': What a beginning of an hexameter!" and "What a line 'Hab' ich den Markt und die Strassen, doch nie so einsam gesehen!'"

Indeed he thought that even quantitative English

[1] Mrs Richard Ward.
[2] First published in the *Cornhill Magazine*, December, 1863.

hexameters were as a rule only fit for comic subjects[1] "tho' of course you might go on with perfect hexameters of the following kind, but they would grow monotonous:

> High woods roaring above me, dark leaves falling
>   about me."

I remember a comic end of an Alcaic in quantity, which he made at this time:

> Thine early rising well repaid thee,
>   Munificently rewarded artist.

The well-known unquantitative couplet by Coleridge he altered into

> Up springs hexameter with might, as a fountain
>   arising,
> Lightly the fountain falls, lightly the pentameter.

I have heard him say, "Englishmen *will* spoil English verses by scanning when they are reading, and they confound accent and quantity[2]."

Virgil's finest hexameters, he thought, occurred in the *Georgics*, and in that noble sixth book of the *Æneid*: for instance for descriptive beauty and fine sound he would quote:

> "Fluctus ut, in medio cœpit quum albescere ponto,
>   Longius, ex altoque sinum trahit; utque volutus

---

[1] Some of the hexameters in my "Jack and the Beanstalk," and some of those in my "Bluebeard" (Mrs Thackeray Ritchie's *Bluebeard's Keys*), were made by him. Throughout these hexameters by his advice quantity, except here and there for the sake of variety, coincides with accent. "Twice," my father would say, "in the first two lines of the first *Æneid*, and elsewhere perpetually, quantity is contradicted by accent."

[2] As an illustration of a quantitative line regardless of accent he suggested the following pentameter:

> All men alike hate slops, particularly gruel.

Ad terras, immane sonat per saxa, neque ipso
Monte minor procumbit: at ima exæstuat unda
Vorticibus, nigramque alte subjectat arenam ” ;

and,

“ Romanos rerum dominos gentemque togatam ” ;

and,

“ Demens qui nimbos et non imitabile fulmen
Ære et cornipedum pulsu simularat equorum. ”

The single Homeric hexameters that he was fondest
of quoting for examples of sounding lines, were

“ ἐξ ἀκαλαρρείταο βαθυρρόου ὠκεάνοιο, ”

and

“ βῆ δ’ ἀκέων παρὰ θῖνα πολυφλοίσβοιο θαλάσσης. ”

“ These are,” he would say, “ grander in our modern
broad Northern pronunciation than in the soft Southern
talk of the Greeks, with a difference as between the roar
of the Northern sea and the hissing of the Mediterranean.”

I need not dwell on my father's love of the perfection
of classical literary art, on his sympathy with the temper
of the old world [1], on his love of the old metres, and on
his views as to how the classical subject ought to be
treated in English poetry.

He purposely chose those classical subjects from
mythology and legend, which had been before but
imperfectly treated, or of which the stories were slight,
so that he might have free scope for his imagination,
“ The Lotos-Eaters,” “ Ulysses,” “ Tithonus,” “ Œnone,”
“ The Death of Œnone,” “ Tiresias,” “ Demeter and
Persephone,” “ Lucretius.” A modern feeling was to
some extent introduced into the themes, but they were

---

[1] Shown especially in such poems as “ Lucretius,” “Frater ave atque
vale,” and “ To Virgil.”

dealt with according to the canons of antique art. The blank verse was often intentionally restrained [1].

About his blank verse he said something of this kind to me: "The English public think that blank verse is the easiest thing in the world to write, mere prose cut up into five-foot lines; whereas it is one of the most difficult. In a blank verse you can have from three up to eight beats [2]; but, if you vary the beats unusually, your ordinary newspaper critic sets up a howl. The varying of the beats, of the construction of the feet, of the emphasis, of the extra-metrical syllables and of the pauses, helps to make the greatness of blank verse. There are many other things besides, for instance a fine ear for vowel-sounds, and the kicking of the geese out of the boat (i.e. doing away with sibilations); but few educated men really understand the structure of blank verse. I never put two 'ss' together in any verse of mine. My line is not, as often quoted,

And freedom broadens *slowly* down —

but

And freedom slowly broadens down.

---

[1] "As a metrist, he is the creator of a new blank verse, different both from the Elizabethan and from the Miltonic. He has known how to modulate it to every theme, and to elicit a music appropriate to each; attuning it in turn to a tender and homely grace, as in 'The Gardener's Daughter'; to the severe and ideal majesty of the antique, as in 'Tithonus'; to meditative thought, as in 'The Ancient Sage,' or 'Akbar's Dream'; to pathetic or tragic tales of contemporary life, as in 'Aylmer's Field,' or 'Enoch Arden'; or to sustained romantic narrative, as in the 'Idylls.' No English poet has used blank verse with such flexible variety, or drawn from it so large a compass of tones; nor has any maintained it so equably on a high level of excellence. In lyric metres Tennyson has invented much, and has also shown a rare power of adaptation. Many of his lyric measures are wholly his own; while others have been so treated by him as to make them virtually new." *The English Poets*, edited by T. H. Ward, Preface by Professor Jebb.

[2] As an example of rapid blank verse he would give the passage in "Balin and Balan" from "He rose, descended, met" to "face to ground."

People sometimes say how 'studiedly alliterative' Tennyson's verse is. Why, when I spout my lines first, they come out so alliteratively that I have sometimes no end of trouble to get rid of the alliteration."

The note by my father, that originally headed his blank verse translation from the *Iliad* beginning

He ceased, and sea-like roar'd the Trojan host,

ran: "Some, and among these one at least of our best and greatest[1], have endeavoured to give us the *Iliad* in English hexameters, and by what appears to me their failure have gone far to prove the impossibility of the task. I have long held by our blank verse in this matter, and now after having spoken so disrespectfully here of these hexameters, I venture or rather feel bound to subjoin a specimen (however brief and with whatever demerits) of a blank verse translation."

The passages in the *Iliad* which most struck him for their beauty of poetic feeling and diction were those two which he translated into blank verse: and the parting of Paris at the end of the sixth book of the *Iliad*, which he translated *vivâ voce* to me as follows:

" Nor did Paris linger in his lofty halls, but when he had girt on his gorgeous armour, all of varied bronze, then he rushed thro' the city, glorying in his airy feet. And as when a stall-kept horse, that is barley-fed at the manger, breaketh his tether, and dasheth thro' the plain, spurning it, being wont to bathe himself in the fair-running river, rioting, and reareth his head, and his mane flieth back on either shoulder, and he glorieth in his beauty, and his knees bear him at the gallop to the haunts and meadows of the mares; so ran the son of Priam, Paris, from the height of Pergamus, all in arms,

---

[1] This was written after reading Sir John Herschel's " Book I. of the *Iliad* translated in the Hexameter Metre," *Cornhill Magazine*, May 1862.

glittering like the sun, laughing for light-heartedness, and his swift feet bare him."

Letter from Robert Browning about "Enoch Arden."

19 WARWICK CRESCENT,
Oct. 13th, 1864.

DEAR TENNYSON,

I have been two months away, and only just find your book now. (It ought to show " From A. T." on the fly-leaf for my son's sake hereafter.) " Enoch " continues the perfect thing I thought it at first reading; but the " Farmer," taking me unawares, astonished me more in this stage of acquaintanceship. How such a poem disproves the statement in that strange mistake of yours, the Flower-apologue! " Steal your seed? " as if they want flower-seed in a gum-flower manufactory! One might cabbage out a tolerable rose, by adroit scissor-work on starched calico, after studying in your gardens of Gul, but the seed for the phenomenon itself comes from a place that was never reached from the top of a wall, you may be sure. " Boadicea," the new metre, is admirable, a paladin's achievement in its way. I am thinking of Roland's Pass in the Pyrenees, where he hollowed a rock that had hitherto blocked the road, by one kick of his boot: so have you made our language undergo you.

Do but go on, and I won't mind adding, may I continue to see and hear you, it is reason enough for being ready to do so.

Good-bye and God bless you! Give my congratulations to Mrs Tennyson. I looked a long look three days ago at the Hôtel de Douvres where I met her first; and of you I was thinking particularly at Amiens station next afternoon when somebody clapped me on the shoulder, Grant Duff, if you know him.

Ever yours, on the various stations of this life's "line," and, I hope, in the final refreshment-room ere we get each his cab and drive gaily off " Home," where call upon

ROBERT BROWNING.

Unpublished Epigram of this Period.

Sadness.

Eternal illimitable darkness is brother to eternal silence.

Immeasurable sadness!
And I know it as a poet,
And I greet it, and I meet it,
Immeasurable sadness!
And the voice that apes a nation —
Let it cry an affectation,
Or a fancy or a madness, —
But I know it as a poet,
And I meet it, and I greet it,
And I say it, and repeat it,
Immeasurable sadness!

The Queen having asked for some lines to be inscribed on the Duchess of Kent's statue in the Mausoleum at Frogmore, these were sent:

Her children rise up and call her blessed.

Long as the heart beats life within her breast,
    Thy child will bless thee, guardian mother mild,
And far away thy memory will be bless'd
    By children of the children of thy child.

CHAPTER II.

MY MOTHER'S JOURNAL AND MY FATHER'S LETTER–DIARIES.

[Throughout Chapters II, III, IV and VI, for the greater clearness of the text, I have printed all extracts from my mother's journal in small print; and my father's diary and letters, as well as my own paragraphs, in large print.]

1865–1869.

My father's letter-diary. (The death of his mother.)

1865. *Feb. 21st.* Rosemount, Hampstead. Mother had gone before I came, she went at 10 p.m., age 84.

I dare not see her. I shall have to stop over the funeral. She did not ask for me especially, which is one comfort.

Feb. 25th. Hampstead. I am going to put up at Arthur's. We are all I think *pretty* cheerful. I hope Woolner will make himself quite at home (at Farringford) and have an attic for smoking, for he enjoys his pipe.

Monday, Hampstead. We are going to the funeral to-day. The departure of so blessed a being, almost whose last words were, when asked how she felt, "very quiet," seems to have no sting in it and she declared that she had no pain. We all of us hate the pompous funeral we have to join in, black plumes, black coaches and nonsense.   We should like all to go in white and gold rather, but convention is against us.

(After the funeral[1].)   All has gone off very quietly. A funeral came before us and a funeral followed.   I could have wished for the country churchyard[2].

My mother's journal.—*The Club, "Aylmer's Field," Mesmerism, Winchester, Professor Owen.*

The following Preface was written by A. for the "Selection from his Poems" (sold in threepenny numbers), in which were included six new poems, "The Captain," "On a Mourner," "Home they brought him slain with spears," and "Three sonnets to a coquette":

"I have been assured that a selection from my poems would not be unacceptable to the people.

It is true that there are some who cry out against selections, and perhaps not unjustly when these are fragments, but I have inserted nothing here which is not whole in itself, and such as I have been led to believe would be most popular.

Therefore not without the hope that my choice may be sanctioned by their approval I dedicate this volume to the 'Working Men of England.'"

The Queen sent her thanks for the "Selection from the Poems," expressing her cordial satisfaction on hearing that this "admirable selection from your poems will thus be brought within the reach of the poorest amongst the subjects of Her Majesty."

A. wrote the following letters to the Duke of Argyll about his election to The Club (Dr Johnson's Club), and with reference to the two lines which ended "Aylmer's Field" in the first edition:

There the thin weasel with faint hunting-cry
Follows the mouse, and all is open field.

[1] A plain cross marks the grave at the entrance to Highgate cemetery.
[2] My mother writes: "All was so painless and peaceful, and she was so much like an angel, there is all the comfort that can be in her end, and in her memory."

FARRINGFORD,
Feb. 17*th*, 1865.

MY DEAR DUKE,

Before answering definitely, I should like
to know something about expenses. " The Club "?
It is either my fault or my misfortune that I have
never heard of it. I suppose one has not to pay some
25 guineas entrance and some 7 ditto a year, because
then, I would not say that the game is not worth the
candle, but that the candle is too dear for me. Does
one only pay for one's dinner when eaten, or how is it?

Ever yours not ungratefully,

A. TENNYSON.

I have ascertained that weasels *have* a hunting-cry.

FARRINGFORD,
Feb. 20*th*, 1865.

MY DEAR DUKE,

Propose me: I agree: yours be the shame if
I'm blackballed!!!

Weasels.

I have not heard of any weasels crying in the chase
after a *mouse*, nor where it is a *solitary* hunter of *anything*. But I am assured by those who have heard them
that when they join in the chase after *great* game, such
as a rabbit (even tho' there should be no more than two),
they not unfrequently utter their faint hunting-cry. I
suppose the size of their victim excites them.

I never see *The Field*. Would it be worth while
writing thereto on this matter?

Yours ever, A. TENNYSON.

From the Duke of Argyll.

PRIVY SEAL OFFICE,
March 16th, 1865.

MY DEAR TENNYSON,

You were last night unanimously elected a member of "The Club," and you will probably receive by this post the usual formal invitation to that effect from Dean Milman, who was chairman at last night's dinner.

The form of intimation was drawn up as a joke by Gibbon and has been adhered to ever since [1]. You will be amused by its terms. The Duc d'Aumale was elected along with you. There were four vacancies and we think we have filled them up to our credit.

1. Poet Laureate. 2. Duc D'Aumale. 3. Froude. 4. Dean Stanley. You will have to send £7 (£5 entrance and £2 for the year's subscription) to the credit of the Club account with, — I forget the banker's name but I will send it to you.

Ever yours, ARGYLL.

During the end of March and beginning of April the Alexander Grants, Annie Thackeray, Mr. G. F. Watts, Mrs and Miss Marsden visited us.

About Mrs Marsden A. recalled how through his mesmerism before her marriage she had recovered her health : — " We were staying at Malvern. Dr Marsden was attending my wife and said to me, 'Instead of paying me my fee, I wish you would grant me a favour. Come and mesmerize a young lady who is very ill.' I said, 'I can't mesmerize, I never mesmerized anyone in my life.' But the doctor would take no refusal and said, 'Pooh! look at your powerful frame!' So I mesmerized her according to the doctor's instructions. The first day it took me about an hour to send her to sleep; afterwards only a few seconds. Once she had a pain over her eye, and the doctor said, 'Breathe upon her eye!' I did so, then begged her pardon, saying that I had forgotten I had been smoking. Dr Marsden said, 'She cannot hear you, that one breath has sent

---

[1] "I have to intimate to you that *you have had the honour of being elected* a member of 'The Club.'"

her off into the deepest of slumbers.' In a little while the lady grew better, and we moved to Cheltenham. A week or two afterwards I returned to Malvern for a few hours, but I had not thought of telling anyone that I was coming. I met Dr Marsden in the street, who at once went and told the lady. Before the doctor had said more to her than ' I have good news for you,' the lady said, ' I know what you have come to tell me, I have felt Mr Tennyson here for half an hour.' " This lady eventually married Dr Marsden.

May 7th. Last evening, in answer to a letter from Florence asking for lines on Dante, he made six and sent them off to-day in honour of Dante's six hundredth centenary.

He wrote to Aubrey de Vere about the death of his friend Stephen Spring Rice (father of the present Lord Monteagle) as follows :

FARRINGFORD, *May* 15*th*, 1865.

MY DEAR AUBREY,

The death of my good friend Stephen has not taken me in any way by surprise. I had even expected to hear of it some weeks ago. Death is, I should hope, to most of us a " deliverance," and to him especially, suffering as he did continually from these attacks, it must have been a " great " one. I have had such dear and near losses this year, that — I do not say I can on that account sympathise more fully with his wife and children, but I do most fully feel for and with them : and tell them so whenever an opportunity occurs. I hope they are all well, and you also.

Ever yours, A. TENNYSON.

P. S.   He was one of the five of his friends I knew before our marriage, and the third (the other two Arthur Hallam and Henry Lushington) who has left us. No new friends can be like the old to him or to any, I suppose, and few of the old were so dear to him as

he.   May I too say all that is kind and sympathising?
How does his father bear his loss?   It seems a long
time since we met.

Ever yours, EMILY TENNYSON.

May 22nd.   We started with the boys for their private tutor's,
Mr Paul, at Bailie in Dorsetshire.   We visited the Minster
at Wimborne on the way.   Saw the monument of Margaret
Beaufort with her hand in her husband's.   A sorrowful sight
to us both — our two boys on the Bailie platform, alone for the
first time in their lives as our train left.

June 8th.   We went home by Winchester and slept there,
and lunched with the Warburtons.   He took us into the Dean's
garden to see the fine view of the Cathedral, and the wonderfully clear stream.   A. told a story of his driving into Winchester on the coach when a young man, and asking the coachman,
"What can you tell me about Winchester?" and his answer,
"Debauched, sir, like all cathedral cities."   He and Mr Warburton compared notes, for A. had been reading *Job* in Hebrew,
a book in which he had always rejoiced.

June 12th.   Mrs Woolner, speaking of a party at Oxford at
which A. had been expected, wrote:

Everyone was regretting Mr Tennyson's absence from the
party, above the rest Bishop Colenso who had been very desirous to meet him.   Indeed he said that your husband was the
only man he had wished to see before leaving England, as he
thought him the man who was doing more than any other to
frame the Church of the future.

July 23rd.   Farringford.   Professor Owen arrived.   A. went
with him to Brightstone.   They spread out their luncheon on
Mr Foxe's lawn and looked at the great dragon (a Saurian
reptile dug up at Brooke) which was new to the Professor, and
which quite answered his expectations.   He never saw one
so sheathed in armour, and thought of calling it Euacanthus
Vectianus.   Most interesting he was.   The story of his medical
student days, of the negro's head which he had been carrying

slipping from under his arm, bounding down the hill and bursting through a window into the midst of a quiet family at tea :
their horror: his rushing in after the head without a word, and
clutching at it and "bolting," was very ghastly.

Tour to Waterloo, Weimar and Dresden.

Aug. 12*th.* Drove through the forest of Soigny to Waterloo.
The high pillared beeches delighted A., "making a grand aisle,
their leaves dappled with sunlight, — a wonderful fawn-coloured
carpet of sward beneath." At one spot they were burning
charcoal: there was a clearing in the wood, and the seed of
innumerable willow-herbs made a silver mist. At Waterloo we
lunched at the top of the Lion Mound, which has spoilt the field.
A. and the boys went to Hougoumont, looked at the red wall
that the French charged, mistaking it for our redcoats, and saw
the famous gateway. They took a bullet out of the wall. We
stayed at the Hôtel du Musée, and made a careful tour of the
whole field with maps and Siborne's volumes.

Next day we accomplished the circuit of the field, going over
the French position. A. was impressed with the "wailing of the
wind" at night, as if the dead were lamenting; and with the
solemn feeling that all around us were the graves of so many
thousand men. We saw the bank behind which our Guards lay
when the last French attack was made by the "Old Guards."
Sergeant Mundy, who showed us round Hougoumont, assured
us that the Duke of Wellington did not say "Up, guards, and at
them," but merely put his hand to his head and said "Ready."
As A. observed, "That is infinitely more like him." One of the
old French Imperial Guards visited the place afterwards, and said
that it seemed on that day and at that hour as if our men had
"risen out of the earth." The sergeant told A. a striking fact,
that he sat all night on horseback in rain and thunder and
lightning without anything to eat, not even tasting food till next
night, yet so great was the excitement that he neither felt wet nor
hunger, but that the whole time seemed to him five minutes.

We spent a week at the Hotel, A. enjoying his study of the
battlefield and his long walks.

Thence we went to Luxembourg and Trèves. The last is an
enchanting place — the Cathedral, the river, the Porta Nigra, the
Basilica and the Palace of Constantine, and the Amphitheatre,

where so many thousands of Christians have fought with beasts, or have been bidden to slay each other.   A. called the Basilica "The ideal Methodist Chapel"; outside the proportions are grand and simple.   There are fine old MSS in the Museum.

We drove to Mülheim, and rowed down the Moselle in a little boat by Berncastel and Zell to Coblentz.   A lovely row between hills of all shapes, sometimes clothed with vines, sometimes with forest.

Weimar.

A. disliked Coblentz as much as ever ; we left this (going by Eisenach and seeing the Wartburg) for Weimar.   The people there seemed to be rather stupid about Goethe and Schiller, and in vain we tried to impress upon our driver that we wanted to see all which concerned them.   Thanks to the kindness of a soldier we got inside the palace, and saw the rooms where Goethe lived so much with the Grand Duke and Duchess. Next morning we secured a commissionaire, who took A. and the boys inside the Fürstengruft, where they saw Goethe's and Schiller's coffins lying with those of the Royal Family.   Lionel had a leaf of bay given him for A. from Goethe's coffin.   We were very much pleased by the cheerfulness and simplicity of Goethe's gartenhaus, which we visited.   Afterwards we drove to Schiller's house, three rooms pleasant enough in spite of their bareness.   His wife's guitar lay near his bed ; on it a portrait of himself, said to be good, taken soon after death.   The "other-world" peace of it struck A. and me.   Then we went to the Church to see Lucas van Cranach's altar-piece, so interesting from the portraits of Luther and himself.   The portrait of Luther as a monk I liked best.   We drove to Tréport, charmingly situated on the Ilm which babbles pleasantly along.

Sept. 1*st.*   Went with Mr Marshall — secretary to the Grand Duchess — to Goethe's town-house.   No key there for the rooms. The old woman said that she was alone in the house, and could not possibly go and fetch it.   A. was touched by seeing the "Salve" on the door-mat, and all Goethe's old boots at the entrance.   Mr Marshall brought the Herr Direktor, for eight years Goethe's secretary, who courteously left his dinner to come.   Mr Marshall expressed his regret that there was no time to write to Madame von Goethe for an order to see the study.

The Director made no remark at the time, but, when he had shown us the busts and gems and statuettes, and Goethe's own drawings, he took us into the sacred study. One cannot explain in words the awe and sadness with which this low dark room filled A. The study is narrow, and in proportion long. In the middle was a table with a cushion on it where Goethe would lean his arms, and a chair with a cushion where he sometimes sat, but his habit was to pace up and down and dictate to his secretary. On one side of the room was a bookcase about two-thirds up the wall, with boxes for his manuscripts. There were also visiting cards, strung like bills together, and Goethe's old, empty, wine bottles, in which the wine had left patterns like frost patterns. On the other side of the room was a calendar of things that had struck him in newspapers. Here a door opened to his bedroom. Such a melancholy little place! By the bed was an arm chair, to which at last he used to move from his bed for a little change. All round the wall, by the bed and the chair, a dark green leafy carpet or tapestry was fastened half-way up the wall of the room. On the washing-stand was some of the last medicine he took. The one window at the foot of the bed was partly boarded up. It looked I think into the garden.

Dresden.

After seeing Goethe's house Mr Marshall met us at the station, and saw us off for Leipzig. Next day we left Leipzig for Dresden. On our arrival at Dresden we went to the gallery. The Madonna and Child by Raffaelle struck A. and me as wonderfully "human and Divine." We seemed to see the trouble of the world in the Virgin's eyes, and the Child made A. "marvel at His majesty." Indeed there is a still majesty in the whole picture. Afterwards A. and the boys visited the Zoo-logical Gardens and A. saw the great aurochs which interested him. Next day to the gallery, to see the Raffaelle Madonna again; we also looked at the Holbein Holy Family, which is very great, Titian's Tribute-money, and Correggio's Magdalene, etc. The day after A. and the boys went to the Green Vaults, and the splendour of the diamonds struck A. much. A German professor suddenly discovered A. and made him a long com-plimentary speech, which was trying. A. took us to the gallery again, and showed us the Titians, also Correggio's Virgin, La

Notte, and the Spanish pictures, and again the two great Madonnas.

Sept. 6th. A. and the boys went to the armoury, to the picture-gallery once more, and then to Saxon Switzerland.

Sept. 7th. After a very pleasant week at Dresden, we went by train to Brunswick. At night we heard tremendous crashing, as if all the windows in the house were being smashed. We asked what it meant, and were told that to-morrow a very rich young lady was to be married, and that it was the custom on the eve of a marriage to break all sorts of dishes and bottles against the bride's door. Was this the Polternacht for good luck? The houses are quaint. A. and the boys went to the crypt of the church to look at the coffins of the nine Dukes of Brunswick, who all fell in battle.

Sept. 11th. Aix-la-Chapelle. A. had been here before. The city looked magical as we swept through the old gates last evening, when the domes and hills stood out gold and blue in the rich sunset.

Farringford, Queen Emma, G. F. Watts, London.

Sept. 28th. Farringford. Queen Emma of the Sandwich Islands arrived, Major Hopkins and a huge native, Mr Hoapili, in attendance. Aunt Franklin came [1]. The Queen's maid and her luggage lost on the road: they arrived at midnight. We had had a throne chair made out of our Ilex wood. It was first used by the Queen. She, poor lady, wanted to stay quietly here, but she had to go to banquets, etc. about the Island. I collected money for the projected cathedral in Honolulu.

A. went with the Queen up the Down. John Welsh, the Queen's servant, said nothing would induce him to leave her, she was so good. There was a wailing thro' the seven Sandwich Islands for the Queen when she left, because the natives thought she never would return. Endless guests came in to tea. A. took her out that she might read her letters; and hid her from the guests in the summer-house in the kitchen garden ("among the cabbages" she said). A. and I were pleased with her sweet dignity of manner, and a calmness that made one think of an Egyptian statue; her voice was musical. Mr and Mrs Hoapili

[1] Lady Franklin.

sang Hawaiian songs. They sat on the ground and acted the song while they sang. They then chanted an ode to the young Prince, a wild monotonous chant. All great people's children in Hawaii have odes made to them on the day of their birth, a kind of foreshadowing of their lives. When a bard meets the hero of any ode so made he has to sing it to him.

Oct. 2nd. A. gave her two large magnolia blossoms on her leaving. She has an affectionate nature; something very pathetic about her.

Oct. 6th. A. read me some Lucretius, and the 1st Epistle of St Peter. (At work at his new poem of "Lucretius.")

This letter accompanied Robert Browning's own small selection from his poems:

19 WARWICK CRESCENT, *Oct. 10th,* 1865.

MY DEAR TENNYSON,

When I came back last year from my holiday I found a gift from you, a book; this time I find only the blue and gold thing which, such as it is, you are to take from me. I could not even put in what I pleased, but I have said all about it in the word or two of preface, as also that I beg leave to stick the bunch in your button-hole. May I beg too that Mrs Tennyson will kindly remember me?

Ever affectionately yours,

ROBERT BROWNING.

To Robert Browning.

FARRINGFORD.

MY DEAR BROWNING,

Very welcome is the nosegay, not only for "the *love* in the gift," which makes me, who am physically the most unbumptious of men and authors, proud: but also for its own very peculiar flowerage and fructification, for which I think I have as high a respect as any man in Britain. I stick it into my buttonhole and feel * * *'s cork heels added to my boots.

My wife always remembers you, and another.

I too, when last in Paris, took a long look at the Hôtel de Douvres, thinking of the former time[1].

Ever yours affectionately,

A. TENNYSON.

A. and I went to our ploughman, to congratulate him on his having won the first ploughman's prize in the Isle of Wight. All the family radiant with the prize-money. The wife went off with it to buy winter shoes for her husband and the children.

Mr G. F. Watts, with his accustomed munificence, gave us the pictures that he had made of me and of the boys, and wrote to A. of the boys' picture : " If there had been any correspondence between my will and power, the picture would have been worth acceptance for itself, but I can only hope that it may have some small value as a token of friendship, and an expression of profound admiration and respect."

Mayall came with the photographs. That of A. very fine.

My father's letter-diary from London.

Yesterday I called with Woolner on Froude, and then we all walked to Carlyle's. Mrs C. seemed feeble, but was very glad to see me, then Carlyle walked a mile or two with us, and was agreeable and amusing as usual.

Dec. 5*th.* I called on Queen Emma twice yesterday. Our Queen had been very kind and cordial to Queen Emma, and had given her a rich gold bracelet with a serpent onyx, and a portrait of herself, and a lock of her hair. Queen Emma was off for the Continent this morning at 8 o'clock. The great man Gladstone is coming to dine with me here on Friday; a compliment; but how he can find time from the mighty press of business amazes me. I go over to Palgrave's to-morrow.

[1] See p. 16.

Dec. 6th. 29 Welbeck Street. I go to Palgrave's to-day, 5 York Gate, Regent's Park. I dined there yesterday and met Joseph Hooker, who told me my tropical island (in "Enoch") was all right; but X— in his illustrations has made it all wrong, putting a herd of antelopes upon it, which never occur in Polynesia.

Dec. 7th. York Gate. I am installed here, having come from Woolner's last night, where I dined with Mr Jenner, who has ordered my bust[1] from W. and who is going to leave it to the National Portrait Gallery; an amiable and reverential man he seems. I called on the Guests yesterday, for Schreiber saw me walking in the Green Park, and shouted to me thro' the rails, as he was riding down the street, and begged me to call. Enid was in and he; Lady Charlotte out. I must go and call on Forster to-day. I saw old Procter yesterday, better than he was, but very feeble.

Dec. 8th. York Gate. I was inducted into the Royal Society last night, after dining with W. White, whither Woolner accompanied me. We had a merry dinner with lots of anecdotes; there were very few people, and I went thro' it without nervousness.

Dec. 9th. York Gate. Yesterday at Woolner's, Gladstone, Holman Hunt, and Dr Symonds and his son. Dr S. is a famous physician at Bristol, who had come all the way to dine with Gladstone and myself. I like him much. The great man was infinitely agreeable, and delivered himself very eloquently and freely on Homer, etc. I asked him to speak to Lord Russell about Allingham's little pension, which he promised to do. He spoke too about Jamaica, and seems, tho' he suspends his judgment, to think that Eyre was so terribly in the wrong that he may have to be tried for his life.

After this dinner my father wrote to Gladstone:

[1] Mr Jenner gave this bust to me in 1893 to place in Westminster Abbey.

MY DEAR MR GLADSTONE,

As you were kind enough to say that you would forward to Lord Russell Mr Allingham's application for an increase of pension together with my petition that it might be taken into consideration, I send you A.'s letter to myself, wherein he sets forth at full what his claims are, and why he wishes them to be attended to. As I said to you at the time — the man has a true spirit of song in him, I have no doubt of it: and my opinion, I am happy to say, is confirmed by Carlyle in his letter to A. which I only do not forward because, from his letter, it does not appear that I am at liberty so to do. Carlyle also mentions some work of Allingham's (I have not seen it myself — it is possibly some preface to his projected work on Ireland) in these following terms — "Your pleasant and excellent historical introduction might, if its modesty would permit, boast itself to be the very best ever written perhaps anywhere for such a purpose. I have read it with real entertainment and instruction on my own behoof, and with real satisfaction on yours — so clear, so brief, definite, graphic; and a fine genially human tone in it." I think you will agree with me, that this testimonial from one who is a great name in Britain, and who has won his own laurels chiefly in the field of History, does go some way in establishing a case for Allingham. And for myself I really believe that, if he were set free as he says by his pension being raised to the amount required, he might do good to Ireland, and thro' Ireland to England, by accomplishing a work which under his present circumstances seems all but impossible. I may add that I have known him for years, that he is very industrious, and in his life sober and moral: — his age somewhere between 40 and 50.

Believe me, my dear Mr Gladstone,

Ever sincerely yours, A. TENNYSON.

Dec. 12*th.* I dine at the Deanery of St Paul's to-morrow. Sir John Lubbock has just sent me his *Prehistoric Times*, which I shall find greatly interesting. Dean Milman was very agreeable yesterday. The Stanleys did not come. Browning was here.

Dec. 13*th.* York Gate. The Palgraves go into the country on Monday and I leave this house, but whether I shall get beyond Winchester the first day is, I should think, doubtful. I don't much care for Lionel's sporting propensities, but then you know man is naturally "a beast of prey."

Dec. 14*th.* Dined at Milman's yesterday. Milman told me that Her Majesty's household do not serve on juries, and if ever I am asked again so to do, to state this, Her Majesty being supposed to be always requiring their services. I called on Tyndall yesterday and had a long chat with him about mind and matter, etc. He is coming to see me to-night at Woolner's where I dine and meet Dr Woolley the Australian and Froude.

Dec. 15*th.* A great gathering last night at Woolner's. Dr Woolley seems altogether of the higher class of man [1]. Thompson the Confederate was there and Browning, and innumerable anecdotes were told. To-day I dine here; nobody asked, at my request.

The following note about "The Northern Farmer" arrived from W. G. Clark:

Thompson has been staying at Fryston, where he met a Mr Creyke, a Yorkshireman, with a talent for recitation. This Mr Creyke had been staying at a farmhouse in Holderness, where in the evening the neighbouring farmers used to come and smoke. One evening he repeated "The Northern Farmer." When it was done, one of them said, "Dang it, that caps owt.

---

[1] Dr Woolley, the Principal of Sydney College, went down in the "London," which was wrecked during a storm in the Bay of Biscay, Jan. 11, 1866.

Now, sur, is that i' print, because if it be I'll buy t' book, cost what it may?" Creyke said, "The book contains things you mayn't like as well, so I'll write it out for you."

This he did: the farmer put it in his breast-pocket; and next day when out shooting Creyke saw him from time to time taking it out to read.

After this Mr Tennyson may claim to have rivalled Orpheus.

Dec. 31*st.* " 1865–66[1]" was written. The last two lines give the monotony of the storm — the only answer to the question as to what the future will bring forth.

1866.

My mother's journal. — London, Marlborough, New Forest, "Song of the Wrens," Governor Eyre.

London. *Feb.* 4*th.* We found an invitation to luncheon at the Deanery (Westminster). Mr Vaughan[2] came in, and we had a delightful talk before luncheon and also at luncheon, when the Carlyles joined us. A. is fond of the Abbey and of strolling about it by himself. "How dreamlike it looks!" he said. We went to see Thackeray's bust. The Dean remarked at luncheon: "Having to do with artists and sculptors about statues and busts of great men gives fresh cause to lament their death."

Feb. 10*th.* Mr Browning[3] gave me an affectionate greeting after all these years. In the evening the Brookfields joined us, and their daughter Magdalen, with her white, gold-bordered dress, seemed, A. said, "as if she had come out of a fairy-story."

---

[1] Printed in *Good Words*, 1868. My father wrote to Mr Palgrave: "What a season! The wind is roaring here like thunder, and all my ilexes rolling and whitening. Indeed we have had whole weeks of wind."

[2] Brother-in-law to Dean Stanley, afterwards Dean of Llandaff.

[3] Browning writes on Feb. 19th:

I go out a great deal; but have enjoyed nothing so much as a dinner last week with Tennyson, who, with his wife and one son, is staying in town for a few weeks, and she is just what she was, and always will be, very sweet and dear; he seems to me better than ever. I met him at a large party on Saturday, also Carlyle, whom I never met at a "drum" before. *Life and Letters of Robert Browning,* p. 273.

April 20th. A. wrote to the Duke of Argyll:

April 20th, 1866.

MY DEAR DUKE,

The son's [1] sonnet is I think creditable to him both as regards feeling and execution. I read and grieved to hear of his illness in the *Times*, but he is it seems all right again now. I know nothing of politics here except from the newspapers, but I suppose the [Reform] Bill is looking up, as they say, since I left town, and that you are not going to Switzerland as you threatened.

I see that Mr Lowe did me the honour of quoting me the other night. If anyone on your side wished to make his speech culminate in a quotation which may be a prophecy, he might possibly produce an effect by quoting the last two stanzas of my address to the Queen, in the preface to my poems —

And statesmen at her councils met
Who knew the season when, etc.

which really would seem *à propos.*

Ever, my dear Duke, yours,

A. TENNYSON.

My mother wrote: *May 1st,* 1866. Farringford. To-day I was to have gone with A. to take Hallam to Marlborough [2], but could not.

Marlborough.

" I sent him to Marlborough," said my father, " because Bradley is a friend of mine, and Stanley has told me that it is the best school in England."

May 2nd. Marlborough. We drove to Avebury and Silbury, my father suggesting that Silbury was a

---

[1] Marquis of Lorne.   [2] See Appendix, p. 518, for talk on Milton.

monument after some great battle. In the evening the
Bradleys had a large dinner-party. Someone spoke of
Dīplŏmăcy and Prŏgress. " Oh ! " said my father,
" why do you pronounce the word like that? pray give
the ō long." Then turning to an excellent scholar :
" You, so-and-so," he said jokingly, "you never open
your mouth without making a grammatical blunder."

Bradley knowing my father's love of science had
asked masters interested in geology, botany and archæology to meet him. He conversed with all of them : and
praised the organist's (W. S. Bambridge's) settings of
" Thou art gone to the grave " and " Lead, kindly light."
At the request of Mrs Bradley he read " The Northern
Farmer," and then criticised amusingly some of the boys'
Prize Poems which Bradley had begged him to look
through. Later in the evening he was talking on death,
and quoting a Parisian story of a man having deliberately
ordered and eaten a good dinner, and having afterwards
committed suicide by covering his face with a chloro-
formed handkerchief. " That's what I should do," my
father said, " if I thought there was no future life."

May 3rd. In view of the old cut yews (opposite his
window) he began to write his ballad of " The Victim."
He expressed great delight at the choir of birds in the
trees here. In the afternoon we drove through Savernake
Forest, ablaze with golden beeches.

After dinner the Upper Sixth came in, and at their
petition he read " Guinevere," refusing however enthrone-
ment in a large arm-chair, and asserting it was " too
conspicuous."

May 4th. My father walked about the garden,
finishing " The Victim." He was full of fun, and at
luncheon told the following story about Dr Abernethy :

" A farmer went to the great doctor complaining of
discomfort in the head, weight and pain. The doctor
said, ' What quantity of ale do you take?' 'Oh, I taaks

ma yaale pretty well.' Abernethy (with great patience
and gentleness), 'Now then, to begin the day, breakfast.
What time?' 'Oh at haafe-past seven.' 'Ale then?
How much?' 'I taakes my quart.' 'Luncheon?' 'At
11 o'clock I gets another snack.' 'Ale then?' 'O yees,
my pint and a haafe.' 'Dinner?' 'Haafe-past one.'
'Any ale then?' 'Yees, yees, another quart then.'
'Tea?' 'My tea's at haafe-past five.' 'Ale then?'
'Noa, noa.' 'Supper?' 'Noine o'clock.' 'Ale then?'
'Yees, yees. I taakes my fill then. I goes asleep
arterwards.' Like a lion aroused Abernethy was up,
opened the street door, shoved the farmer out and
shouted out, 'Go home, sir, and let me never see your
face again: go home, drink your ale and be damned.'
The farmer rushed out aghast, Abernethy pursuing him
down the street with shouts of 'Go home, sir, and be
damned.'"

The Bradley children brought in some wild cherry
blossoms, and my father said, "You have ruthlessly
picked the future fruit: do you remember Wordsworth's
poem about picking strawberry-blossoms?" He never
much liked flowers being gathered: he would say he
preferred "to see them growing naturally."

In the afternoon we drove to Martinsell and walked
over the mounds, and looked at the relics of the British
village.

After dinner my father was again asked to read by
Mrs Bradley: "Will it be too cruel to ask you to read
'The Grandmother'?" "No, I can't read to-night, and
I must be in a proper mood for that and I am not."
"Oh well, do give us all the pleasure of hearing you
read, only choose something else." "How can you ask
me when you know I only read to my intimate friends?"
"I know you don't, but I know you will read to *our*
intimate friends. No others are here to-night." "Well,
well, but not 'The Grandmother.'" A Belgian governess,

Mdlle. Stapps, was on the chair just behind him. He said, " I can't read ' The Grandmother ' properly except after breakfast, when I am weak and tremulous; fortified by dinner and a glass of port I am too vigorous." "Well, read ' The Northern Farmer' then." So he did: and asked Mdlle. how much she understood. " Pas un mot, Monsieur."

Then he read " The Grandmother," and after that four pieces out of Hood's *Whims and Oddities*, " Faithless Nelly Gray," " Faithless Sally Brown," " Tim Turpin " and " Ben Battle." He explained the play on words in them to Mdlle. who was " excessivement enchantée." He laughed till the tears came at some things he read. This went on till 11.50, and then we separated.

May 5th. My father returned home, leaving me at school [1].

Letters from friends.

Letter from Rev. J. Waite (my father's schoolmaster at Louth), thanking him for a set of his books.

MANBY RECTORY, near LOUTH,
May 8th, 1866.

MY DEAR SIR,

I return you my best thanks for your immortal works forwarded to me by your bookseller, which I shall not fail to have placed on a shelf in the library of the new Grammar School in Louth with the works of your two elder brothers, as a contribution more precious than gold or silver, being really Aurea Carmina; in memory of the elementary part of your education received by all of you in that royal institution. Had I been asked in your boyish days which of the three would probably scale the highest summit of Parnassus, I almost fancy I should have awarded the palm to primogeniture, and I am still almost disposed to say

"Arcades omnes, Et cantare pares et respondere parati."

[1] This account is mainly taken from Mrs Bradley's diary.

The two seniors have been however far distanced in the quantity, if not in the quality of their productions. I am ashamed to confess that I had never before seen all your works ; but they will now form a portion of my daily reading, as an agreeable dessert after my more plain repast of Divinity and my old school books.

Your sincere friend,

J. WAITE (in his 86th year).

June 9th. A letter from Mr Twisleton arrived, asking A. to sign an application for a Memorial to Keble in Westminster Abbey.

3 RUTLAND GATE, LONDON,
June 8th, 1866.

DEAR MR TENNYSON,

I thank you for your note and I am very glad that you consent to sign the application for a Memorial in Westminster Abbey to Mr Keble. The application shall be duly forwarded to you for your signature.

I may add that I was acquainted with your friend A. H. Hallam, and that I never met a man whom on a short acquaintance I liked so much. The last time I saw him could not have been long before the fatal event in 1833. I had been at Vienna and had been travelling with my mother in what is called the Austrian Switzerland. On a very fine day we had left Ischl on our way to Salzburg, and just as we were arriving at the brow of the hill whence travellers from Salzburg have the first view of the lake of Ischl I met him in a carriage with his father. We both left our carriages and I had about five minutes' conversation with him, each telling the other what he might expect to see. He was in the highest spirits, expressing himself delighted with the beauty of the country which could be visited from Salzburg, and he seemed to me in the florid health of one embrowned by exercise in the sun. It was only afterwards that it struck me as possible that the supposed signs of health might have been owing to fatal fulness of blood. I relate these facts thinking they may interest you, as it is not likely that many Englishmen who knew him previously could have seen him later than myself.

Yours very truly, EDWARD TWISLETON.

New Forest. *July* 15*th.* An enchanting drive through glades and lawns : grand groups of trees and ferns, and a rich smell of heather. The wild ponies formed very pretty groups on knolls backed by forest. We saw brilliant woodpeckers, and strange birds flashed here and there across the open spaces "with vibratory wings." We went to Mark Ash (where the biggest beeches are): the " green gloom " as A. called it very fine under the old and huge trees.

July 17*th.* Two mornings A. wandered alone. One day the forest was " mystical and sad, wrapped in cloud."

These lines (in " The Last Tournament ") were made on an old oak here :

A stump of oak half-dead,
From roots like some black coil of carven snakes,
Clutch'd at the crag, and started thro' mid air
Bearing an eagle's nest.

July 18*th.* A. and Hallam set out to walk to Romsey Church. A. thought that it was one of the simplest and finest churches in England; it reminded us of William's church at Caen. Lionel and I followed, driving, and found them, as I thought we should, near the river Test. Part of it higher up A. said was " every square inch a ripple," and at Romsey he was charmed with the swift clear stream gliding over its rushy bed.

July 19*th.* A. walked to Beaulieu Abbey thro' the woods, Lionel and I drove over the heath. A postman of the Stony Cross district told A. that all the great yew trees, which A. had been looking for, had been cut down and sold to a cabinet-maker. " They offered them to me for a few pounds," he said.

Farringford. *August* 6*th.* A.'s birthday : we gave a dinner to the farm men. Lincolnshire " frumenty " caused great amusement among them, many not having the courage to touch it.

August 17*th.* We took Lionel to school at Hastings. A. walked twice back along the road with him to comfort him at parting. We then left for Park House, Maidstone, by Battle Abbey and Tunbridge Wells. In the evening, at the Lushingtons' request, A. read " The Victim, or The Norse Queen," " The Voyage," and "All along the Valley." A. and Edmund talked metaphysics : they have engrossed A. much of late.

Mr (now Sir) George Grove wrote asking A. to make a cycle of songs for music:

Mr Payne tells me he has communicated to you a little proposal of mine for a Book of Songs [1], and at his request I send you Heine's *Lieder* because I alluded to them in my letter as being often used by the German musicians to set to music. Those I was more particularly thinking of are the Songs I to VIII, p. 36–45, which Schumann has set as *Liederkreis*, and those beginning p. 106, out of which he has made a similar selection. But why one should send you patterns of songs when your own " Little Birdie " (to name but one) is a perfect model, I don't know. It was more because of the way the Germans have of connecting several songs together. If the idea of the first song could be brought back again in the last it would help the composer very much, for nothing is so charming in music as to wind off a composition in that way. Beethoven (as great in small things as in the greatest) has done it with masterly effect in a Liederkreis called " An die ferne Geliebte [2]." If you like I will write that out for you with the greatest pleasure.

We have subscribed to the defence of Governor Eyre. A. was anxious about the facts in Jamaica, not knowing whether to accede to the request of the Committee that he would place his name on it; as he could not approve of all the late proceedings. The question of course was, " Could Governor Eyre have prevented revolution and massacre otherwise? "

To the Secretary of Governor Eyre's Defence Committee.

October, 1866.

SIR,

I thank you and the Committee for the honour done to me.

I sent my small subscription as a tribute to the nobleness of the man, and as a protest against the spirit in which a servant of the State, who has saved to us one

---

[1] The result was " The Song of the Wrens."

[2] My father often asked that these songs, and *Molly's Abschied*, might be sung to him: he was fond of Beethoven's music.

of the Islands of the Empire, and many English lives, seems to be hunted down.

But my entering my name on your Committee might be looked upon as pledge that I approve of all the measures of Governor Eyre. I cannot assert that I do this, neither would I say that he has erred, my knowledge of the circumstances not being sufficient.

In the meantime, the outbreak of our Indian Mutiny remains as a warning to all but madmen against want of vigour and swift decisiveness.

I have the honour to be

Your most obedient servant,

A. TENNYSON.

1867.

My mother's journal. — Bayard Taylor, Hallam's illness, Blackdown, Lyme Regis, and South Devon.

A. has written a letter to Longfellow, "We English and Americans should all be brothers as none other among the Nations can be; and some of us, come what may, will always be so I trust."

Feb 21st. Mr and Mrs Bayard Taylor came. A. gave them some of Mr Ellis' sherry made in 1815, called "Waterloo Sherry," and some of Mr Ellis' yet more "gorgeous wines." She (a charming German lady) told A. the striking story of her uncle, now an old man of 70 or 80, the son of the late Duke of Saxe-Gotha's chief huntsman. He was at the time of Napoleon's highest power about fifteen, and was so wrought upon by hearing Napoleon continually called by his countrymen "the chief enemy of the human race," that he determined to shoot the great man while he was passing alone down one of the long corridors of the palace, as he often did when he visited the Duke, of whom he was fond. One day accordingly the youth posted himself in a corner of one of the bay windows of the corridor, rifle in hand. He heard the Emperor's footstep in the distance coming nearer and nearer. As Napoleon approached, he put his hand to the trigger. But Napoleon, without stopping, just turned and fixed his great eagle eye upon him, in such a terrible fashion that the youth was paralysed with fear, trembled from head to foot, almost swooned away, and let his rifle drop with a clang upon the ground. No notice was taken of this incident.

Then A. spoke of Napoleon coming in hot and dusty from battle, and seeing the Duchess of Weimar, and saying, " Êtes-vous la Duchesse de Weimar?" of her simple answer, " Oui, Sieur "; and of his thereupon shouting savagely, " J'écraserai votre mari." " Wellington said of Napoleon," A. added, " that he was ' emphatically *not* a gentleman.' "

March 1*st*. A telegram arrived, telling of Hallam's serious attack on his lungs. We started off by the next boat to Marlborough.

We telegraphed for Dr Symonds at Bristol.

This is all I could record about the terrible time. A. was very calm, but deeply moved. At the crisis he said humbly, "I have made up my mind to lose him : God will take him pure and good, straight from his mother's lessons. Surely it would be better for him than to grow up such a one as I am." He was wrapped up in the boy. He talked a great deal about " our all being gathered up somehow into the all-absorbing love of God, into a state infinitely higher than we can now conceive of [1]."

He wrote to Sir John Simeon :

March, 1867.

MY DEAR SIMEON,

He is better to-day, yesterday we thought he was going, for the pulse stopt and he was seized with a coup de nerfs. We telegraphed for Dr Symonds of Bristol, who gave us good hope that he is past the worst and will recover; it was an attack of pneumonia with low symptoms.

Yours ever, A. T.

We returned to Farringford where Hallam speedily recovered, thence went to Hindhead, and before going A. wrote to F. T. Palgrave.

[1] These words of my father's are quoted from the Bradley diary.

23rd March, 1867.

DEAR PALGRAVE,

I suppose I may come up to town some time after we are settled in our farm-house, where I have taken rooms for ourselves and three servants for two years, and can have them for six if I choose. We go there in about a week, more or less: there will be one room for a guest.

I don't give the name of the place because I wish it to be kept secret: I am not flying from the cockneys here to tumble in among the cockneys there I hope: tho' some of my friends assert that it will be so, and that there will be more cockneys and of a worse kind, but I don't believe them, for the house is quite solitary and five miles from town or village. You ask whether Doré's illustrations are a success. I liked the first four I saw very much, tho' they were not quite true to the text, but the rest not so well; one I hate, that where the dead lady[1] is stuck up in a chair, with her eyes open, as if her father had forgotten to close them, or as if she had opened them again, for they are closed in the voyage down the river. On the whole I am against illustrators, except one could do with them as old Mr Rogers did, have them to breakfast twice a week and explain your own views to them over and over again.

My wife (thanks for your enquiries) had been shut up in the house for nearly three months, with cough and cold. The Queen sent her an invitation to go with me to Osborne, but I was obliged to make her excuses, and went alone. You say that you expect another little one in June: ought I to congratulate you or condole? Love to Mrs Palgrave from both.

Believe me yours ever,

A. TENNYSON.

[1] Elaine.

April 29*th*.   We arrived at Grayshott farm, where we were
to spend the early summer.   In the copses the nightingales were
singing; the anemones were out in all the woods.

May 18*th*.   A. has bought Morris' *British Birds*.   One
evening we heard the fern owl quite close to us, and the snap,
snap of the wings as it flew away.   The boys had been that day
with their father to White's Selborne, and climbed the "Hanger."
He liked the pretty village, and the Bells who lived in White's
house.

He read the new version of one of the "Window Songs,"
"Take my Love"; Heine's "Songs"; and some of the *Reign
of Law* [1].   The chapter on "Law in Politics" was specially interesting to us.   The quotations from A. expressed some of the
deepest truths.   Seeing these, I felt that perhaps I had been
wrong in not having fulfilled my half-formed purpose of making
a book of "Great Thoughts and Sayings of Tennyson."   Perhaps
not, for I always think great thoughts and sayings lose so much
of their life and point when drawn from their natural context.
With the boys he was reading *Flodden Field*, the *Prometheus* of
Æschylus, and the 1st *Georgic*.

June 5*th*.   Mrs Gilchrist and Mr Simmons having taken
endless trouble in communicating with Mr Lucas about Black-
horse Copse on Blackdown [2], we went there in an odd procession,
Lionel on a donkey with a lady's saddle, I driving in the basket-
carriage, the rest walking.   The wheels spun round on the axles
without touching ground in some of the deep ruts, and the
carriage had to be lifted over, William leading the pony carefully.   At last we reached the charming ledge on the heathery
down.   This looks over an immense view bounded by the South-
downs on the south, by Leith Hill on the north.   Copse-wood
surrounds the ledge, and the hill protects it from the north-west.
The foxglove was in full bloom.   A. helped me down the
mountain-path.   We all enjoyed the day thoroughly.

Mr Lear came from Liphook: he liked our neighbourhood so

---

[1] By the Duke of Argyll.

[2] Now Aldworth.   My mother, writing this June of our home-life, says:
"I think it is a thing to be very thankful for, having a home of one's very
own, especially taking in the hope that one's children may live on there
when we are gone, and have it made still more a home by the memories of
childhood."

much that he said we were to look out for some land for him
hereabouts.

He told an excellent story about a misquotation of a
passage in "You ask me, why." A friend of his remarked to
him: "It is a well-known fact that Tennyson hates travelling."
"Nonsense," answered Lear, "he loves it." "On the contrary,"
the friend retorted, "he hates it, and he says so himself somewhere:

> 'And I will *die* before I see
> The palms and temples of the South.' "

Among other letters at this time A. wrote the following to
an unknown correspondent, a Mr Tennyson of Chester, who had
named his child "Alfred."

June 13th, 1867.

DEAR SIR,

I have not been at home for many weeks
or your kindly letter would not have remained so long
without an answer, notwithstanding the multitude of
letters, which really make it impossible for me to answer
all. You have paid me a great compliment, nay, it is
more than a compliment— in naming your son after
me.

I wish him a useful and happy career, and only hope
that he will take a better model than his namesake to
shape his life by.

It is doubtless a pleasure to know that I have had
sometimes the power to cheer the soldier, whose life of
devotion to his country I honour;· and few things in the
world ought to gratify me so deeply as the assurance
that anything I may have written has had an influence
for good.

Believe me, dear sir, yours truly,

A. TENNYSON.

He also wrote to the Duke of Argyll:

STOATLEY FARM, HASLEMERE,
1867.

MY DEAR DUKE,

I shall be very glad to read your book
[*The Reign of Law*], which I suppose is waiting for
me at Farringford. We are at present lodging at a
farmhouse here in the neighbourhood of Haslemere.
My wife has always had a fancy for the sandy soil
and heather-scented air of this part of England, and
we are intending to buy a few acres, and build a
little home here, whither we may escape when the
cockneys are running over my lawns at Freshwater. I
am sorry that I did not see Lord Lorne, but I will call
for the calumet[1] when I go to town. It is odd that the
Americans always send me pipes, or tobacco, as if I cared
for nothing else in this world; and their tobacco is not
my tobacco, nor their pipes my pipes: bird's-eye and a
Milo-cutty being more according to my fancy than
costlier things. I don't however mean to undervalue
Longfellow's gift. I envy you your journey. I have
been along the Corniche, as you may read in my little
poem " The Daisy." I don't suppose that Europe, or
Asia perhaps, has a more splendid piece of coast-scenery,
but at this time of year you will hardly see it in perfection. Perhaps however if the Autumn tints remain they
may more than make up for the loss of that opulence of
summer, which seemed to satiate heart and eye when
I looked from the hill above Nice, over rock and ruin
and down-streaming vineyard, to the many coloured
Mediterranean. We did not get further than Florence,
and Rome is only a dream to me and not a very distinct
one.

[1] Sent by Longfellow.

Mine and my wife's love to the Duchess, and all joy to you both. You must feel like the starling that has got out, and the sweets of office outsweetened by the sweets of out of office. Hallam is at Marlborough and flourishing; Lionel with Dr Hunt near Hastings. Lady Edith is, we trust, quite recovered, and enjoying her tour.

Ever yours,

A. TENNYSON.

June 16*th.* The Blackdown land was bought: Mr Estcourt being most kind and helpful. A. met Mr Knowles at the station; he did not recognize him; but, when Mr Knowles had called at Farringford, A. had said to him as he does to most strangers, "I am so short sighted that I shall not know you if I meet you unless you speak to me." Mr Knowles accordingly spoke to him, reminding him of this; and A. (knowing that Mr Knowles was an architect) said, "You had better build me my house (on Blackdown)."

Mr Knowles came to luncheon and looked at our sketch and plans, and took them home to put them in "working form," as he said.

Lyme and South Devon.

On August 23rd my father left for Bridport.

He was led on to Lyme by the description of the place in Miss Austen's *Persuasion*, walking thither the nine miles over the hills from Bridport. On his arrival he called on Palgrave, and, refusing all refreshment, he said at once: "Now take me to the Cobb, and show me the steps from which Louisa Musgrove fell." Palgrave and he then walked to the undercliff, "a noble natural terrace, edging the sea and tossed into endless small mounds and valleys."

Palgrave writes:

Tennyson said, "this exactly represents some of the romantic landscape before my mind's eye in the 'Idylls': little winding glades, closed all round with grassy mounds and wild shrubs, where one might fancy the sudden appearance of a knight riding, or a spell-bound damsel." This peculiar character (which was partly suggested to him by the backgrounds of mediæval illuminations) he also once pointed out in a certain field of his own (called Pathacre) beyond his summer-house at Farringford.

After this the friends went to Princetown and Dartmoor. Palgrave writes:

Our way lay right across Dartmoor, desolate and eerie even under the brightest sun, to Princetown: a village gloomy in itself from its high wind-exposed site, and more so from the great convict-prison, whose inhabitants we saw working in sad files and guarded by rifles from escaping. The inn, rough and small but clean, was in accord with the surroundings. One bedroom with two huge four-posters was allotted us: and Tennyson lay in his with a candle, reading hard the book which on this trip he had taken for his novel-companion, and at every disengaged moment opened whilst rambling over the Moor. This chanced to be one of Miss Yonge's deservedly popular tales, wherein a leading element is the deferred Church Confirmation of a grown-up person. On Tennyson read, till I heard him cry with satisfaction, "I see land! Mr * * is just going to be confirmed!" after which, darkness and slumber.

Thence they made their way to Tavistock, Dartmouth, Salcombe and Exeter.

My mother's journal.

Dec. 1*st.* "The Song of the Wrens" ("Window Songs") and "The Victim," printed at the Canford Press, received from Sir Ivor Guest. A. is reading Hebrew (*Job* and the *Song of Solomon* and *Genesis*): he talked much about his Hebrew, and about all-pervading Spirit being more understandable by him than solid matter. He brought down to me his psalm-like poem, "Higher Pantheism." Louie [daughter of Sir John Simeon], who was with us a day or two later, said: "As I sat at breakfast, he came behind me, and in fun dropped on my plate the MS of 'Wages [1],' which he had perfected during the night."

"Vivien" and "Guinevere," illustrated by Doré, were brought out at Christmas.

A. wrote to the Master of Trinity (answering an invitation which was accepted in Feb. 1868):

1867.

A smoking room!

If I put pipe to mouth *there*, should I not see gray Elohim ascending out of the earth, him whom we capped among the walks in golden youth, and hear a voice, "Why hast thou disquieted me to bring me up?" I happened to say to Clark that, from old far-away undergraduate recollections of the unapproachable and august seclusion of Trinity Lodge, Cambridge, I should feel more blown out with glory by spending a night under your roof, than by having lived Sultanlike for a week in Buckingham Palace. Now, you see, I was not proposing a visit to you, but speaking as after wine and over a pipe, and falling into a trance with my eyes open. At the same time, your invitation and that of Mrs Thompson (to whom present all my best thanks) is so kindly and hearty, that I may, I can't say when at this moment, try to realize this vision, and if I do I will let you know some time beforehand. Meantime, my dear T., with my wife's best regards,

I am yours ever, A. TENNYSON.

And to J. Kenward:

FARRINGFORD, 1867.

My dear Sir,

I am much obliged to you for the first volume of *Barddas*, which I have not yet seen, but which will arrive in due time from Moxon's. I envy

[1] Printed in *Macmillan's Magazine*, Feb. 1868.

your visit to Villemarqué. When I was in Brittany, — stopping at Auray, I think, — I asked the landlord how far off he lived, and I found it was some 14 or 15 miles, a long way to post, and it was not certain whether he were at home or not. Believe me, dear Sir, in great haste, for (substitute "letters" for "bairns") I am like the old woman who lived in a shoe.

Yours truly, A. TENNYSON.

1868.

My mother's journal. — "*The Lover's Tale,*" *Hebrew Studies, Longfellow, Darwin, building of Aldworth, Tintern, Irish Church Bill.*

January 11*th.* A. read the article on the Talmud by Deutsch. He talked of publishing "The Lover's Tale," because someone was sure to publish it some day. I urged this. We heard that written copies were being circulated. He said : "Allowance must be made for redundance of youth. I cannot pick it to pieces and make it up again. It is rich and full, but there are mistakes in it." For instance he pointed out one in the passage beginning : "Even as the all-enduring camel, etc." "There could not have been a crimson colouring in the middle of the moonlight night. The poem is the breath of young love [1]."

January 24*th.* Canon Warburton and the Bradleys visited us. Mrs Bradley writes :

Mr Tennyson said to us that it would not be easy to understand the allusions in "The Lover's Tale," unless we knew the story in Boccaccio from which it was taken ; that it was the tale of a lover, whose mistress became the wife of another man. She fell ill, died apparently, and was buried. The old lover went to her tomb : on opening her coffin he found her heart beating : he took her home to his mother's house, where she gave birth to a child. Afterwards the lover invited his friends

[1] My father had some copies of the poem printed to see what it was like.

and neighbours to a feast, among these the husband of the lady. In the middle of the feast the lover brought in a veiled figure, and asked the guests: "To whom would belong by right a dog, whose master turned him out to die, and which was rescued and restored to life and health by another?" The unanimous opinion was given that "the man who saved the dog had a right to him." The lover unveiled the lady with her babe, and said to the husband, "I restore you your own." He then rode away and was seen no more.

Jan. 25th. Mr Tennyson told us how much better he felt spiritually, mentally, and bodily, while engaged on some long poem; and how often in the intervals he found time hang heavily, and a longing came for regular work. He said to my husband: "I envy you your life of hard, regular, useful, important work."

He told us that he taught himself Italian by writing all the words and sentences he wanted especially to remember (making a kind of private grammar) on the sides of a large old-fashioned mantelpiece, in his Somersby bedroom. He wrote them in a fine small hand, very elaborately; and he got them up whilst he was dressing and smoking: but he went away for a few days, and when he came back the writing had all vanished. He blamed the housemaid, who answered "contemptuously," that she "had washed off the nasty, dirty mess and cleaned the mantelpiece nicely for him." He is full of the *Song of Solomon*, reading it in Hebrew: and he said that most people knew nothing about it, that in the coarsely-painted, misrepresented, ununderstandable story, given in the Bible translation, there is hardly a trace of what he calls "The most perfect Idyl of the faithful love of a country girl for her shepherd, and of her resistance to the advances of a great king, that ever was written." The study of Hebrew was a great pleasure to him: it occupied his whole mind and time.

He told us that he was always puzzled by that expression in the *Song of Solomon*, chap. iv., "Thy teeth are like a flock of sheep . . . whereof every one bears twins, and none is barren among them," but that in his present study of Hebrew he had discovered its meaning. "Every tooth corresponds to its fellow, and there are no gaps among them."

Jan. 28th. A Play in the evening. Play over, the drawing-room was cleared for dancing. Mr Tennyson led off Lady

Simeon, Sir John was my partner. Mr Tennyson thoroughly gave himself up to the enjoyment of waltzing, and did not sit down once ; he was very merry and full of fun.

Jan. 31*st.* Mr Tennyson left for Haslemere, to fix the site of the new house on Blackdown. The name of the plot of land, "Black-horse Copse," was changed to "Aldworth." Some of Mrs Tennyson's family came from a village of that name near Streatley in Berks : where there is a curious old church with the old tombs of her Sellwood ancestors.

My father received the following letter from the Reverend W. Warburton (afterwards Canon of Winchester):

WINCHESTER, *Jan.* 14*th,* 1868.

MY DEAR TENNYSON,

On the chance of your having found it "tanti" to make your way through the outworks of Hebrew Grammar, etc.[1], I send you a little book which seems to me to be helpful. If you want a nice book to read with *Solomon's Song,* I recommend you Ginsburg's *Coheleth.* He is of course a German, but writes in English. *Solomon's Song* is only eight short chapters, and

---

[1] Canon Warburton writes the following note on this letter :

This belongs to a passage in your dear and honoured father's life not generally known, namely, his beginning the study of Hebrew with a view to making a metrical version, or failing this a new prose version, at once poetical and correct, of the *Book of Job.* In connection with this undertaking (which was found, unfortunately, to present fatal difficulties) I remember him one day turning over the pages of Renan's wonderful translation of *Job,* in my house at Winchester, and coming upon the famous passage about the War-horse — " Hast thou clothed his neck with thunder ? " " Qui revêt son cou d'une crinège flottante? " " Why, that is downright prose! I think I could do better than that." " He saith among the trumpets Ha! Ha! " " Au premier bruit de la trompette il dit 'Allons !' " " What a very French horse! " Also in connection with this project, I may remind you that he one day asked the late Master of Balliol (then staying at Farringford) to give him a literal translation of one of the verses. " But I can't read Hebrew," faltered the Master. " What," he exclaimed, " you the Priest of a religion, and can't read your own sacred Books! "

W. WARBURTON.

very nearly comes up to *Job* in interest, when properly translated, and has a much more curious history.

With kindest remembrances to Mrs Tennyson,

Believe me ever sincerely yours,

W. WARBURTON.

P.S.   Ginsburg is barely half an inch thick.

In answer to Mr Warburton's letter my father wrote:

Jan. 21*st*, 1868.

MY DEAR WARBURTON,

No Ginsburg yet; and I looked rather reckoningly for it every morning. What is the publisher's name? will you write again? or shall I tell mine to get it for me? I flatter myself that I have hit upon something like the right sound of the ע. I can produce a sound in the throat (for is it not a guttural?) something between a *y* and a *g*, and easily melting into a vowel, where the ע is supposed to be soft.

Ever yours, A. TENNYSON.

My mother's journal. — Farringford.

April.   There has been a great deal of smoke in the yew-trees this year. One day there was such a cloud that it seemed to be a fire in the shrubbery. [It was then that he wrote the speech of Ambrosius, etc. in "The Holy Grail" with the lines about this "smoke," that is, the pollen of the yew blown and scattered by the wind.

O brother, I have seen this yew tree smoke,
Spring after spring, for half a hundred years.

He would say: "I made most of 'The Holy Grail' walking up and down my field 'Maiden's Croft.'"   "In Memoriam," Section XXXIX., was also written at this time.]

Many pirated editions of the poems having been smuggled into England, a letter is written to Mr Disraeli, begging him to try and stop this illicit trade.

He answered as follows:

HUGHENDEN MANOR, *April 15th*, 1868.

DEAR MR TENNYSON,

I have sent your papers up to town, that the matter may be examined and reported on to me by competent persons. You will hear officially in due course, and may rely upon your interests being not neglected.

I would not, however, have you answered only by a secretary, and therefore I trouble you with this to say that I remember our acquaintance, and am proud of it, and am always

Faithfully yours, B. DISRAELI.

April 23rd. Shakespeare's birthday. A. laid the foundation stone of Aldworth. Mrs Gilchrist had seized the few minutes before post after the laying of the stone to write to me. Weather glorious, Sir John and Lady Simeon and Louie and Mr Knowles there. Sir John said a few simple and appropriate words when the stone was laid. A. in excellent spirits; he was pleased with the inscription on the stone — "Prosper thou the work of our hands, O prosper thou our handiwork."

He wrote to Baron von Tauchnitz about his edition of the poems:

FARRINGFORD, *April 29th*, 1868.

MY DEAR SIR,

I pray your pardon for not having answered you earlier. I scarce know by what carelessness, or fatality, I have omitted, till now, to acknowledge yours of February 25th; but finding your letter lately at the bottom of my pocket, I was struck with my own ungraciousness, and, as I say, pardon my negligence. I am quite aware that I made rather a bad bargain with you, in selling the continental copyright for so small a sum, and my publisher affirms (whether rightly or not) that I annually lose some hundreds of pounds by this transaction. I am also aware that the royalty you offer me now is all of your free grace, and that I have no claim upon you. I can only hope that my accepting this offer will not be made a pretext by sellers (of course I am not including yourself) and buyers for introducing more copies into England. Accept my thanks therefore.

Believe me, my dear sir, yours very truly,

A. TENNYSON.

I hope your son I had the pleasure of seeing once at Farringford is well and prospering.

Part of a letter from Mr Jowett.

May, 1868.

I am glad that Alfred is thinking of Hildebrand. I remember a long time ago reading Bowden's Life of him, and either the man or the book struck me greatly.

Hildebrand's dying in exile might give an opportunity of drawing first the Roman Catholic Ideal, secondly, the impossibility of it, notwithstanding its grandeur.

     *   *   *   *   *   *

I thought " Lucretius[1] " a most noble poem, and that is the universal impression.

I cannot see any reason why Alfred should not write better and better as long as he lives, and as Mr Browning says that he hopes and intends to do

I know that a poet is an inspired person, who is not to be judged by ordinary rules, nor do I mean to interfere with him. But I can never see why some of the dreams of his youth should not still be realized[2].

With love to him and the boys,

Believe me, dear Mrs Tennyson,

affectionately yours,

B. JOWETT.

July 15*th.* Mr Longfellow arrived with a party of ten. Very English he is, we thought. A. considered his " Hiawatha " his most original poem, and he quoted his translation, " Though

---

[1] Printed in *Macmillan's Magazine*, May, 1868.
[2] The completion of the " Idylls."

the mills of God grind slowly, yet they grind exceeding small."
Both poets admired Platen's *In der Nacht*.

July 16th. The Longfellows and he talked much of spiritualism, for he was greatly interested in that subject, but he
suspended his judgment, and thought that, if in such manifestations there is anything, " Pucks, not the spirits of dead men,
reveal themselves." We invited forty or fifty neighbours to tea.
Mr Longfellow spoke kindly and graciously to each guest : Mrs
Fraser Tytler and her daughters were among them, and Mr
Longfellow said, in his old-fashioned, courteous way, " It was
worth while coming to England to see such young ladies [1]."

The Longfellows were all charmed with our Down. Indeed
I believe the ladies wished to remain on the Island [2].

July 18th. Poor little Alamayu, King Theodore of Abyssinia's
son, came with Captain Speedy. The Captain said that Alamayu
would not sleep without both his (Captain Speedy's) arms round
him lest the Evil One should take him. Alamayu's nerves had
been greatly shaken by the siege of Magdala, and the knowledge
of his father's fate. King Theodore had killed himself, when
the English had scaled the rock of Magdala, and his body had
been found just inside the gate of the city. Captain Speedy
tried to put the boy off when he began to speak of this, but
he said " Oh, I know it is so, I heard them tell all about it."
He exclaimed that our English bread was the best thing he had
ever tasted. When he drove past the large ilex here, he said,
" Take care : there will be an elephant in that jungle."

July 20th. To Eton, to enter Lionel there, as his health
could not endure the cold climate of Marlborough. We went to
St George's Chapel. A. and Hallam rowed in Mr Warre's boat
to the boat-race.

July 25th. We drove to Tintern. A pleasant little cottage
inn. We saw the golden cornfields thro' the windows of the
beautiful Abbey, "the happy autumn fields [3]." We climbed up
the Wind Cliff, a glorious view of the Wye joining the Severn,.
bounded by dark woods crowning the cliffs.

[1] Afterwards Mrs G. F. Watts and Mrs Edward Liddell.

[2] Longfellow writes (July 19th) to Mrs Fields : "We came last night from
Freshwater, where we had passed two happy days with Tennyson, not at his
house, but mostly with him. He was very cordial and amiable ; and gave
up his whole time to us. At Farringford your memory is fresh and fragrant."

[3] Cf. Vol. I. p. 252.

To Chepstow, thence to the Castle of Caerphilly.

Aug. 17th. Farringford. Mr Darwin called, and seemed to be very kindly, unworldly, and agreeable. A. said to him, " Your theory of Evolution does not make against Christianity " : and Darwin answered, " No, certainly not." In the afternoon the Dean of Chichester and Sir William Wood (afterwards Lord Hatherley) called. It was very interesting to see the old friends together. Dr Hook asked A. to read " Enoch Arden." He replied he could not to-day. Dr Hook thereupon began in fun to read it so badly that A. clutched the book, " No, I cannot stand that," and read it all to them.

Sept. 9th. A. read me a bit of his " San Graal," which he has now begun.

Sept. 11th. He read me more of the " San Graal " : very fine. We drove on the Down. Kingfishers and oyster-catchers ~~en. Last night he went to Mr Pritchard's to look thro' his telesc, and was charmed with the Nebula in Hercules, " that mighty firmament " ; and with Jupiter and his four moons " filling all the field," and as he said " more *homey* " — the planet seeming so much more akin to earth.

Sept. 14th. He has almost finished the " San Graal " in about a week (he had seen the subject clearly for some time). It came like a breath of inspiration. I was pleased to think that the Queen and the Crown Princess wished him to write it.

Sept. 23rd. We took Lionel to Eton, and left him in Mr Stone's house. At Mr Warre's request A. read the " San Graal " MS complete in the garden.

Of his views on the Irish Church Bill I wrote to Mr W. C. Bennett :

" We look with anxiety to the Irish Church Bill, feeling that the only wise course, as far as we see, is to retain the Endowment, apportioning part to the English Church in Ireland, part to Educational purposes, or any other equally sacred for the good of the Roman Catholics.

Any severance of Church and State is, we think, above all things to be deprecated, as fostering the common tendency to look upon parts of man as man instead of the whole being. I write this seeing how much interest you take in politics, and feeling how much we all ought to take."

Oct. 10*th.* _A. wrote to Mr Gladstone about the alleged bad treatment of the Fenians in prison, enclosing *Lays of a Convict:*

MY DEAR MR GLADSTONE,

The enclosed has been sent to me, possibly to you also: if not, read it now; it seems to me a terrible cry. I don't much believe in the accuracy of the Irishman generally: — but I wish you, who enlightened us formerly on the Neapolitan prisons, to consider whether here too there be not a grievous wrong to be righted.

Yours ever, A. TENNYSON.

An unpublished Epigram by A. (*written about this time*).

By a Darwinian.

How is it that men have so little grace,
When a great man's found to be bad and base,
    That they chuckle and chatter and mock?
We come from apes — and are far removed —
But rejoice when a bigger brother has proved
    That he springs from the common stock.

November. A. went to stay with Mr Knowles at Clapham Common.

My father's letter-diary.

November. The Hollies, Clapham Common. I have sent the "Grail" to be *printed*, and I will send a copy when it comes. I read it last night to Strahan and Pritchard, who professed themselves delighted. I am grieved for the poor old shepherd losing his wife. Jowett's letter is very kind, but I do not like Lionel's going by rail alone to Oxford. I went to Miss Eden's, where we tried to move a table mesmerically. Browning came in, and returned with me and Knowles to dinner, where again I read the "Grail," and Browning said it was my "best and highest." B. is coming again to-night to read part of his new poem [1], also Macmillan.

Nov. 21*st.* I do not think I can possibly come down while this business [2] is yet pending, for it is not yet finished. In the meantime I have written to Pritchard (who is on the election committee on the other side — Conservative) to pair off with me; and, if he be not going to vote, to get Mr Cotton, who is I suppose against Simeon, to pair off with me.

Browning read his Preface [3] to us last night, full of strange vigour and remarkable in many ways; doubtful whether it can ever be popular.

I am not going as yet to Palgrave's: if I go, it will be on Monday afternoon, but I rather want to come home again as soon as I can, to work at the other "Idylls of the King."

Nov. 23*rd.* I have sent the whole of "The Lover's Tale" to the press, and am to have it back on Thursday. I stop here till Friday morning, when Gifford Palgrave comes with his bride. The agreement (with Strahan) is now all ready for signature. Woolner is out in the country, doing Darwin's bust.

[1] "The Ring and the Book."
[2] Leaving the Moxons.
[3] To "The Ring and the Book."

To Sir John Simeon.

November 17th, 1868.

MY DEAR SIR JOHN,

I return you the voting-paper duly signed, whereby you will see that I intend to give you my vote; but, in case the business that brought me to town should unavoidably detain me, I take this occasion to say, that I should think it quite a misfortune for us if you are not again returned as our member.

It is in my opinion no small advantage to the House of Commons to have a Liberal Catholic Christian among them, who may stand up in his place to refute the bigotries both of Roman and Protestant.

I cannot but trust that your well-earned personal popularity will carry you successfully through the present Election, in spite of this invasion of the "*Over-ers*" as we call them in the Island.

Believe me, my dear Sir John,

Yours ever, A. TENNYSON.

My mother's journal.

A. went abroad with Mr Locker to Paris, and, when he returned to Farringford, found the following letter from the Rev. Charles Cockin:

24 PARLIAMENT STREET, HULL.
Nov. 1868.

SIR,

In reading an old translation of Du Bartas[1] I was struck with the following verse from the " Woodman's Beare," Stanza 55:

[1] The passage quoted is not the work of Du Bartas but of Joshua Sylvester, the translator of Du Bartas, and is in a poem called "The Woodman's Beare," appended to the *Divine Weekes and Workes* of Du Bartas.

"But her slender virgin waste
Made me beare her girdle spight,
Which the same by day imbraste
Though it were cast off at night:
That I wisht, I dare not say,
To be girdle night and day."

May I be pardoned for my curiosity in wishing to know whether these lines suggested the two last stanzas in the song in the "Miller's Daughter"?

I am, Sir, yours faithfully,

Charles E. Cockin.

To this he replied:

Farringford, *Dec.* 31*st*, 1868.

Sir,

I never saw the lines before: and the coincidence is strange enough, and until I saw the signature I fully believed them to be a hoax.

Yours faithfully, A. Tennyson.

He wrote to Mr Palgrave about "The Holy Grail":

Farringford, 24*th December*, 1868.

My dear Palgrave,

You distress me when you tell me that, without leave given by me, you showed my poem to Max Müller: not that I care about Max Müller seeing it, but I do care for your not considering it a sacred deposit. Pray do so in future; otherwise I shall see some boy in some Magazine making a lame imitation of it, which a clever boy could do in twenty minutes — and, though his work would be worth nothing, it would take away the bloom and freshness from mine.

I can't conceive how the Grail M. M. mentions can well be treated by a poet of the 13th century from a similar point of view to mine, who write in the 19th, but, if so, I am rather sorry for it, as I rather piqued myself on my originality of treatment.

If Max Müller will give you or me the name of the book, which contains all the Mediæval literature about the Grail, I will order it of the London Library; though, if it be in German prose, I fear I shan't have the patience to wade thro' a tenth of it.

The " Grail " is not likely to be published for a year or two, and certainly not along with the other thing which you hate so much (too much it seems to me). I shall write three or four more of the " Idylls," and link them together as well as I may. Jowett comes on Saturday, and I will give him your message. The boys are both here and well, not at Farringford which is getting scoured and cleaned, but at a house at Alum Bay (Headon Hall) where Nature, in winter at least, seems always in a rage.

Please attend to my request about the " Grail " and the " Lover's Tale," and show them to no one, or if you can't depend upon yourself, forward them to me.

Always yours,

A. TENNYSON.

Publications 1868 :

" The Victim," *Good Words* (January).
" On a Spiteful Letter," *Once a Week* (January)[1].
" Wages," *Macmillan's Magazine* (February).
" 1865–66," *Good Words* (March).
" Lucretius," *Macmillan's Magazine* (May).

[1] My father wrote to *Once a Week*, December 24th, 1867: " It is no particular letter that I meant. I have had dozens of them from one quarter or another."

1869.

My mother's journal. — "The Holy Grail," Switzerland.

January. A. read "The Holy Grail" to the Bradleys, explaining the realism and symbolism, and how the natural, if people cared, could always be made to account for the supernatural.

He pointed out the difference between the five visions of the Grail, as seen by the Holy Nun, Sir Galahad, Sir Percivale, Sir Lancelot, Sir Bors, according to their different, their own peculiar natures and circumstances, and the perfection or imperfection of their Christianity. He dwelt on the mystical treatment of every part of his subject, and said the key[1] is to be found in a careful reading of Sir Percivale's vision and subsequent fall and nineteenth century temptations.

Jan. 15*th.* To-day the Moxon connection of 37 years ceased. A. however anonymously still allows the widow (Mrs Moxon) and her daughters a cor~iderable sum a year. We would that the necessity for leaving had not arisen[2].

Feb. 13*th.* A. read what he had done of the birth and marriage of "Arthur."

The agreement with Mr Strahan came for signature. Mr Strahan had offered to publish for A. for nothing, but that A. would not allow. A letter arrived from Mr Gladstone in answer to one about our proposal for increasing the post-office percentage on the small deposits of the poor.

11 CARLTON HOUSE TERRACE,
Feb. 16*th*, 1869.

DEAR MRS TENNYSON,

Taxation and all that belongs to it form rather a painful chapter in human affairs. For good nine years and over I had to pore over that chapter night and day. I am now in a measure emancipated from that and inducted into another and

[1] See p. 90.
[2] Virtually through the death of Mr E. Moxon.

more varied servitude. But the best answer I can make to your note is to claim upon the strength of it that you should within no long time give me an opportunity of conversing upon it with you by a visit to or better still a sojourn in London. My kindest remembrances to your husband.

Sincerely yours, W. E. GLADSTONE.

Before the end of February A. had read me all "The Coming of Arthur" finished, and was reading at night Browning's "Ring and the Book" — "Pompilia" and "Caponsacchi" are the finest parts.

Mr Fitzgerald wrote about Mr Browning:

MY DEAR OLD ALFRED,

I have been thinking of you so much for the last two or three days, while the first volume of Browning's *Poems* has been on my table, and I have been trying in vain to read it, and yet the *Athenæum* tells me it is wonderfully fine. And so sometimes I am drawn to write to you (with only one eye, the other scorched by reading with a paraffin lamp these several winters), and, whether you care for my letter or not, you won't care to answer; and yet I want to know what you yourself think of this poem; you, who are the one man able to judge of it, and magnanimous enough to think me capable of seeing what is fine in it. I never could read Browning. If Browning only gave a few pence for the book he drew from, what will posterity give for his version of it, if posterity ever find it on a stall? If Shakespeare, Milton, Dryden, Pope and Tennyson survive, what *could* their readers make out of this Browning a hundred years hence? Anything so utterly unlike the *Ring* too which he considers he has wrought out of the old gold — this shapeless thing. "You are unjust, Fitz" — that is what you will say or think, I fancy. I wish you *would* say as much; and also that you are not angry with me for the use I made of your name, which I am rather afraid of. And I don't at all wish to give you any such offence, and never thought, till too late, that you were jealous of such liberties — even in such a local trifle as I took it in. For you have no more loyal follower than

E. F. G.
Who can hardly see.

May 7th. A. said " Leodogran's Dream " to me, just made, giving the drift of the whole poem.

May 18th. A. read the " San Graal." I doubt whether the " San Graal " would have been written but for my endeavour, and the Queen's wish, and that of the Crown Princess. Thank God for it. He has had the subject on his mind for years, ever since he began to write about Arthur and his knights.

May 25th. Mr and Mrs Fields and Miss Lowell (daughter of James Russell Lowell) came. A. took them to the Needles. Miss Lowell said that her grandmother, Mrs Spence, used to shut her shutters and put crape on her knocker every 4th of July. Her grandfather was even banished for his love of England. A. assured her that he would drink a "cup of wine" to her grandmother's memory. Miss Lowell saw her first cowslips here. Very pleasant guests.

June 14th. A. left Folkestone with Mr Locker for Munich and Switzerland. Mr Eardly joined them. Before starting, A. had written to Mr Locker : "We will go by the Brussels route : we might possibly be detained at Paris, which seems ready to break out into fire."

Notes made by A. in Switzerland.

" The last cloud clinging to the peak when all the mists have risen." " Snow and rock thro' cloud unbelievably high." " The top of the Jungfrau rich saffron colour at dawn, the faded moon beside it." " The vision over the valley of Schwarenbach." " Splendour of sunlit clouds passing over the shadowed peak of the Eiger."

CHAPTER III.*

TOUR IN SWITZERLAND (1869); ALSO SOME OPINIONS
ON POETRY.

Mr Frederick Locker-Lampson kindly gave me the following account of his travels with my father:

I am proud to have won the friendship of Alfred Tennyson, "quella fonte che spande di parlar si largo fiume." I first met him in Publisher Moxon's Dover Street parlour. Shortly afterwards, I think about 1864 or 1865, I stayed with him at Grayshott Hall, near Haslemere. We were cordial, we soon became intimate. I rejoice to think we have always remained so. I have often visited Tennyson at Farringford and at Aldworth, and not seldom he has been my guest. We have not met so constantly of late years. Before Hallam and Lionel Tennyson grew up, I used to see a good deal of him in London, for to be near us at 91 Victoria Street he secured a pied-à-terre in Albert Mansions opposite. It was from there that we sallied forth together to see many of his old friends, among others Carlyle, Froude and Mr Gladstone, and we often took morning walks in the Parks and Kensington Gardens.

Tennyson and I have made two successful little tours together, to Paris in December, 1868, and through France to Switzerland in June and July, 1869. We also met at St Moritz in 1870. I found him an exceedingly amiable and most interesting travelling companion.

It was thus that the first tour came about.

Tennyson had not been out of England for eight years or more, and we agreed that it would be very pleasant to go abroad together, if only for a week; so without more ado, we arranged that on the coming Saturday, the 28th November, he should pick me up at 91 Victoria Street, that we should catch the 4.30 p.m. train at Victoria Station (you see we were precise), and that we should sleep at Dover.

At four o'clock on the day appointed, when I was sitting ready packed and expectant, a message arrived that Tennyson's cold was so severe he could not possibly start, and further that he was to be heard of at Mr Knowles'. I swallowed my disappointment, went to church next day, forgave Tennyson his cold, and on the Monday drove down to Clapham.

It was then and there that we solemnly agreed to set off on Wednesday, the 2nd December, which we actually did.

Shortly after quitting the wind-swept cliffs of Dover, as we were looking down on the tumbling waves, and enjoying the salt smell and keen spray that flew up towards the bows of the steamer, Tennyson said: "They are swift, glittering deeps, sharp like the back fin of a fish," and so they were.

We took life easily in Paris, went to the Louvre, especially to see the Venus of Milo and a Demosthenes seated; then there was a little picture by Nicolas Poussin, which Tennyson on the journey had spoken of with pleasure. The subject was the death of Narcissus, Echo slightly in the background, fading slowly away, and Cupid holding a torch. Tennyson said: "Standing over the dead body he looks like a little god of the world." He gazed at this picture with delight, but I confess I saw little to admire; the colour was disappointing, — indeed I did not consider it a typical specimen of the learned Frenchman.

We again saw this Poussin in 1869. I venture to think that Tennyson's vivid imagination had something to do with his admiration.

We strolled on the Boulevards, we visited the churches, museums and markets, and we went to the theatres; one representation must have been very popular, for we could only get places in a shallow little box, a mere ledge, at the very top of the house, almost touching the ceiling, and cheek-by-jowl with an enormous gas chandelier; it was a beetling precipice; what with the dizzy height, our short sight and the glare, we could distinguish nothing. The stage seemed in shadow, and Tennyson turning to me said gloomily, and I did not want to differ from him, "Locker, this is like being stuck on a spike over Hell." Altogether we got a good deal of discomfiture for our money.

5—2

We also paid a visit to the Couvent des Oiseaux; the Sœur Louise Marie was an old friend of the Tennysons, and we saw her under interesting circumstances.

We dined with my old friends Mons. and Madame Mohl, in the Rue du Bac, also at the Maison Dorée, when Mr and Mrs Charles Perkins, of Boston, old Roman friends, were our guests. I think all I have said up to this point took place during our first visit to Paris; what follows will refer to the second.

Tennyson was an excellent travelling companion; he endured, good-humouredly endured, many annoyances, some of them irritating enough, and which I might relate, if the doing so would not be making myself and my companion somewhat ridiculous. I will here jot down any disjointed scraps of our talk, or aught else that occurs to me.

We know that Tennyson's power of expressing himself in his writings is remarkable, and it is equally so in his conversation; he always, and without effort, uses the most felicitous epithets; they light up his sentences and are never pedantic.

Dear reader, while reading these cheerful notes, you must always please to remember that my many-sided travelling companion was a humourist.

Mürren, 19*th June*. We were looking towards the higher Alps, and Tennyson said that perhaps this earth and all that is on it — storms, mountains, cataracts, the sun and the skies — are the Almighty: in fact, that such is our petty nature, we cannot see Him, but we see His shadow, as it were, a distorted shadow: he added that possibly, at that moment, there might be beings invisible to us, who see the Almighty more clearly than we do, and he illustrated his meaning by saying that we have five senses, but that if we had been born with only one of these, our ideas of Nature would have been very different, much more limited.

Tennyson went on to say that supposing there were creatures who instead of having five senses had five hundred, how far they would be in advance of anything we could conceive of! that a worm or an oyster, as compared with ourselves, had a very limited mental vision, and he added how very small the earth must appear to worms and oysters!

I think Tennyson justly recognised the bounds of our knowledge. He said that "whatever is the object of Faith cannot be the object of Reason. In fine, Faith must be our guide, — *that* Faith which we believe comes to us from a Divine Source."

We talked of the Materialists. "After all," said he, "what is matter?" He added, "I think it is merely the shadow of something greater than itself, and which we poor shortsighted creatures cannot see. If the rationalists are in the right, what is the meaning of all the mosques and temples and cathedrals, spread and spreading over the face of the earth? They will not easily beat the character of our Lord, that union of man and woman, sweetness and strength."

He spoke with great regard of X—, then he added : "I think that I believe more of revealed religion than X— does. He believes in a God, but knows nothing more." I said : "I wonder if he is happy." He replied : "So good a man must be happy." Then he added : "I am not blasé, I see the nothingness of life, I know its emptiness, but I believe in Love, and Virtue, and Duty. Perhaps, thanks to Byron, I was more blasé at fourteen than I am now."

We talked of Byron and Wordsworth. "Of course," said Tennyson, "Byron's merits are on the surface. This is not the case with Wordsworth. You must love Wordsworth ere he will seem worthy of your love. As a boy I was an enormous admirer of Byron, so much so that I got a surfeit of him, and now I cannot read him as I should like to do. I was fourteen when I heard of his death. It seemed an awful calamity; I remember I rushed out of doors, sat down by myself, shouted aloud, and wrote on the sandstone : ' *Byron is dead !* ' "

He said that as a boy he had "delighted in Pope's *Homer*," but he added, though "Pope is a consummate artist, in the lower sense of the term," he could not now read him. I suppose he meant "lower" as compared with the supreme power and sublime music of *Paradise Lost*, about which I have often heard him quote *Polixenes* in *The Winter's Tale:*

> "This is an art
> Which does mend nature, change it rather, but
> The art itself is nature."

Tennyson went on to say that there was a great wind of words in a good deal of Shelley, but that as a writer of blank

verse he was perhaps the most skilful of the moderns [1].   He
said : " Nobody admires Shelley more than I once did, and I still
admire him.   I think I like his ' Epipsychidion ' as much as
anything by him."   He said that Keats had " a keen physical
imagination ; if he had been here (at Mürren) he would, in one
line, have given us a picture of that mountain."   (The Mönch, etc.
opposite.)

We often talked of Wordsworth.   I remember his saying
something to this effect : " You must not think because I speak
plainly of Wordsworth's defects as a poet that I have not a very
high admiration of him.   I shall never forget my deep emotion
the first time I had speech with him.   I have a profound
admiration for ' Tintern Abbey.' "   And yet even in that poem
he considered the old poet had shown a want of literary instinct,
or whatever it may be called.   He thought it too long.   He
pointed out that the word " again " occurs four times in the first
fourteen lines, that the sixth and seventh lines might have been
more terse.   " Something like this," said he, extemporising on
the spur of the moment :

That makes a lone place lonelier.

He pencilled these and some other remarks in my volume of
Wordsworth.   Of course he greatly praised the famous line
" Whose dwelling is the light of setting suns " — " the permanent
in the transitory " ; — he ended by saying, and saying emphatically, that, putting aside a great deal that Wordsworth had
written which was not by any means first rate, he thought that
" Wordsworth's very best is the best in its way that has been
sent out by the moderns."   I think that those were his exact
words.   I understood him to mean since Milton.

I spoke with admiration of his " Ulysses "; he said, " Yes,
there is an echo of Dante in it."   He gave " Tithonus " the
same position as " Ulysses."   He said that if Arthur Hallam
had lived he would have been " one of the foremost men of his
time, *but not as a poet.*"

He talked of " The Princess " with something of regret, of its
fine blank verse, and the many good things in it : " but," said

[1] At the same time my father always spoke of " Wordsworth's best blank
verse as being on the whole the finest since Milton."

he, "though truly original, it is, after all, only a medley." He
added that it was very difficult in blank verse to give descriptions,
such as "So that sport * * * the patron with his curls," and
at the same time to retain poetical elevation. Tennyson insisted
that the employment of rhyme would have made it much easier.
He went on to say that Wordsworth attempted this sort of
thing in "The Excursion," but not successfully; for instance,
"And sitting on the grass partook The fragrant beverage drawn
from China's herb." "Why could he not have said 'And sitting
on the grass had tea'? There is no doubt that Wordsworth
injured fine passages by the introduction of flat and essentially
prosaic phrases, such as 'for several hours,' which occurs in his
Prelude in the description of the Simplon."

My first sight of Tom Moore was at the Athenæum Club,
where, as a boy, I had been taken by my father; we were
talking to Lord Monteagle, when a very little man, eyeglass in
hand, entered the room for an instant, raised himself on the tips
of his toes, and glanced around, presumably to see if some
person he was in quest of were there, and my father said to me,
"That's Tom Moore, the poet." He pronounced it *More*. I told
all this to Tennyson, and he said he had first seen Moore at
Mr Rogers' and that "he had a George the Fourth look." Then
I hazarded the remark that Rogers' best short poems were
as good as Moore's. "No," said Tennyson, "Rogers is not
as good as Moore. Moore had a wilder fancy, but still hardly
anything that Moore wrote is altogether what it should be." He
gave as an instance: "She is far from the land where her young
hero sleeps." He also quoted with mingled merriment and
contempt a passage or two of Little's poems, and said "How
fat that is!" meaning how material, and how fleshly. He did
this with remarkable finesse of expression. Tennyson exceedingly admired "Oft in the stilly night." I suggested that
Byron's "Isles of Greece" might have been admitted into
the *Golden Treasury:* he also thought so, but he supposed
that the editor had discovered some defect in it, of which he
(Tennyson) was not aware — but he had not read it for years.
He then repeated the first stanza, and said, "That's very fine,
but Thackeray tells me that Samian wine is very wretched
stuff."

We talked of Rogers, and of 22 St James' Place. I told
him that one morning my father had taken me, when quite a boy

to see the poet-wit: he was an ugly little man, a wrinkled Mæcenas, in a brown coat. Henry Luttrell happened to be there, also in a brown coat. He was also little and ugly, and as my father had a little brown coat too, I suppose there were three of them. Rogers was calm and kind; he showed me a china coffee cup which had belonged to General Washington, who he knew had been a friend of my maternal grandfather. Neither then nor afterwards did I detect in him any of that quiet venom which his particular friends seemed so anxious to discover in him.

All this talk interested Tennyson; he said: "When I first knew Rogers, he more than once asked me to go and see him; for a long time I refused, but at last I went, and was fully repaid. I knew him well, and often breakfasted with him, and spent long half days in his society." He said he was once walking down Bond Street with Rogers, and they met a hearse, and Rogers said, in his very quiet, deliberate and slightly sardonic tones : "You know they call me a *tête morte;* the other day I was walking out of St James' Place, and I saw three hearses turning in there, and I said to myself, 'perhaps these hearses are coming for *me,*' and I kept out of the way for the whole day, and when I returned at night, I found that St James' Place had been full of hearses — a trick of that rascal Theodore Hook's."

Tennyson went on to say that perhaps some of Rogers' shorter poems would last longer than the ambitious efforts of more important writers. Rogers used often to read to him passages of his writings, and to consult him about the notes to his *Italy.* "He liked me," Tennyson said, "and thought that perhaps I might be the coming poet, and might help to hand his name down to future ages. One day we were walking arm in arm, and I spoke of what is called Immortality and remarked how few writers could be sure of it. Upon this, Rogers squeezed my arm and said: 'I am sure of it.'" Tennyson was fond of Rogers and told me this with no unamiable intention, but, on the contrary, in all kindliness and good faith. Most poets have felt at times as Rogers felt on this occasion, but with this difference, that they had not an Immortal's arm to squeeze.

After these conversations, he would often end with "Rogers was a kindly old man, excepting when he was bilious"; now, the same might have been said of Bede, the Venerable Saint.

Tennyson was greatly impressed by the deadly-earnest and savagery, and let me say *sadness*, of Swift's *Legion Club*. He has more than once read it to me; on the last occasion, Houghton and George Venables, two great friends (than whom none were more warmly regarded by the circle that met fitfully at Farringford and Aldworth), were present, and they were also impressed by it.

Tennyson admired Samuel Johnson's grave earnestness, and said that certain of his couplets, for these qualities and for their "high moral tone," were not surpassed in English satire. However, he ventured to make merry over:

> "Let observation, with extensive view,
> Survey mankind, from China to Peru."

"Why did he not say ' Let observation, with extended observation, observe extensively ' ? "

He spoke of Mr Ruskin and the *Pathetic Fallacy*. He thought Wordsworth was justified in saying that "The moon looked round her with delight when the heavens were bare," but that the late Alexander Smith, "a poet of considerable promise," went too far when he spoke of "the wave, a bride wooing the shore." He said the same of Kingsley, that "the cruel, crawling wave" was too much like a live creature.

Tennyson liked Jonson's "It is not growing like a tree," and Marvell's "To a Prude," "but," he added, "I can't read Ben Jonson, especially his comedies. To me he appears to move in a wide sea of glue." I said, "Do you like Goldsmith's 'When lovely woman stoops to folly'?" And he replied: "I love it." He also greatly praised the *Vicar of Wakefield*.

He told me that he was moved to write "Tears, idle Tears" at Tintern Abbey; and that it was not real woe, as some people might suppose; "it was rather the yearning that young people occasionally experience for that which seems to have passed away from them for ever." That in him it was strongest when he was quite a youth. He said, "Old Carlyle, who is never moved by poetry, once quoted those lines of mine, while we were out walking." Carlyle had written to him in praise of " Ulysses," and to his regret he had lost the letter[1]. He valued Carlyle's opinion.

Tennyson said that the " Bugle Song" was written at

[1] See Vol. I. p. 213.

Killarney, and "O Swallow, Swallow," was first composed in rhyme. He had been told that

> Come down, O Maid, from yonder mountain height —

to   Myriads of rivulets hurrying thro' the lawn,
> The moan of doves in immemorial elms,
> And murmuring of innumerable bees,

was as felicitous as Theocritus.

He spoke of "The Brook," and the pauses in that passage "'Run Katie!' Katie never ran * * * blushing for a boon," and of the whole spirit of the poem, as not having been appreciated; and he said the same of some of his similes, such as in "Vivien" the blood of Merlin likened to an opal, and in "Enid" the serpent compared to a worm dragging the leaf under the soil.

Tennyson spoke to me several times, almost with horror, of the way people who have won fame are likely to be maligned after their death. I have an old commonplace book, into which, with many other scraps of prose and verse, I had copied an epigram by Thomas Hood. It runs as follows:

A joke.   "What is a modern poet's fate?
> To write his thoughts upon a slate;
> The critic spits on what is done,
> *Gives it a wipe* — and all is gone."
>
>   T. HOOD.

This quatrain amused Tennyson, and he said: "It is a good joke, and now I'll write you a grave *truth*." Which he did as follows, adding the words "a joke" by the side of Hood's lines.

A truth.   While I live, the owls!
> When I die, the GHOULS!!!

In his dedication of the "Idylls" to the Prince Consort at line 15, after the words, "We know him now: all narrow jealousies," he originally had said:

> The fume and babble of a petulant hour.

He left out this line when the passage was published. I have many such notes by him.

In the first issue of "The Princess," edition 1875, King & Co., vol. IV. p. 120, line 8 runs thus:

And followed by a hundred *h*airy does.

Was not this unkind of the printer? I was with the unlucky author when the proof reached him. He gazed at it with horror and gave a very prolonged and remarkable groan, which not having been set to music, I cannot do justice to here.

It was exceedingly sultry at the falls of Schaffhausen. These were very impressive, but to escape the sun we were glad to take refuge in a shed pervaded by an atrocious odour of decayed cheeses, or some such horror. "This is my usual luck," says Tennyson, "I never go to see anything which is very impressive, without encountering something mean or repulsive. Now, this sublime cataract, and this disgusting stench, will for ever dwell together in my memory." He went on to say that the unpleasant odours of London were as offensive as those of Paris, but that the latter were more pungent, piercing like the point of a lance; and then he added with grave emphasis, "It is an age of lies, and also an age of stinks."

Grindelwald, Aigle, *26th June* [1]. To-day we bought two large carved wood bears, for which, after breaking a good deal of French over the dealer, we agreed that Tennyson should pay one hundred francs. These bears are now in the entrance hall at Aldworth, keeping watch and ward, quite ready to welcome the arriving guest with a friendly hug.

In the evening we played battledore and shuttlecock in the pension attached to the *Aigle*. He said that he had once kept up two thousand. This *Aigle* is a huge hungry-looking caravansary, with curiously uncomfortable beds. Tennyson's, especially, had none of the caressing and consenting softness of that to which he had been accustomed; suggestive of anything but sleep, it was hard and lumpy, and of the pronounced German type—the kind of bed that Gray, the poet, must have had in his mind's eye when he said:

"That hush'd in grim repose, expects its ev'ning prey."

[1] F. Locker-Lampson wrote to F. T. Palgrave, June 24th, 1869: "I think A. T. is happy and quite well. He walks excellently, and is ready for a walk now (2 o'clock), having been at it since 8 A.M."

Just now the *Aigle* would be entirely deserted, but for ourselves and a young, lately-married and superlatively happy couple. This pair much interest my poet. We sit opposite to them at breakfast and again at dinner, at the extreme end of a vast expanse of bare, cold tablecloth. They nestle close to each other like love-birds on one perch, that perch being a short one. She is a bouncing *blonde*, frankly blue in her eyes, and there is a coquetry, uncalculated or calculated, in her dimples, her boots and her parasol; she has also an exasperating little hat and feather. Sad to say, none of these allurements seem lost on my gifted companion. As often as she addresses her swain, she gazes with innocent rapture into his mild eyes, and every now and again, as if asserting her right of possession, with sympathetic fingers arranges and re-arranges the bow of his cravat, and then sends a pretty appealing glance across the table in our direction. These lovers take pastoral walks together, and are often to be met in twilight intervals, steeped in honeymoon-shine. On such occasions they deem it expedient to affect an exquisite confusion.

Excepting for this, and you will allow this is a large exception, our lovers may not be specially attractive, but surely they are beautiful in their *abandon*, loving and being loved. Thanks to them the prosaic *Aigle* is an Arcadian hostelry, with green retreats and winding paths of dalliance, lawns, rocks and leafy trees.

> Was there a tree that did not know
> The love betwixt those two?

The glacier nearest to the hotel is much discoloured by the *débris* from the mountain. Tennyson's farewell words were: "That glacier is a filthy thing; it looks as if a thousand London seasons had passed over it." Such was our retrospect of Grindelwald.

1st July. To-day at Giessbach he said that if he had been one of the "Wise Men of Greece," and had been asked for a *dictum*, he would have given "Every man imputes himself," meaning that a man, unless he is very sane indeed, in judging of others, imputes motives, etc. which move himself. "No man can see further than his moral eyes will allow him."

He has been talking of Lord Bacon. He says that certain passages of his writings, their pregnant eloquence and vivid completeness, lifted him more than those of almost any writer. We happened to see a little fountain in the hotel, which danced a wisp; he stopped, looked at it attentively, and said: "It is a pretty toy, it would have pleased Bacon."

Lucerne, *2nd July*. To-day we hired a boat and two men, and had a row on the lake. As we returned, the wind rose, the men pulled well, but they tired, so Tennyson bent to an oar. He rowed very pluckily for half-an-hour, till Mr Eardly our travelling companion relieved him. Then came my turn. When we got back to the hotel, the people said that the wind had risen so much that they had been watching us with anxiety.

A few days afterwards, on the Wengern Alps, we came across a man who blew a loud blast through a cow's horn, which produced a varied and prodigiously prolonged echo. Tennyson said: "You'll have to pay half a franc for that noise. The man subsists on a ghost of a sound."

Hôtel d'Angleterre, Strasbourg, *3rd July*. Tennyson does not like his eggs too lightly cooked. To-day at breakfast there was a pretty waitress, and he sent his eggs to be more boiled, and then, in the damsel's native tongue, expostulated with her as to the softness of her eggs and the apparent hardness of her heart. It was very pleasant to hear his grave but gallant remonstrance and her merry laugh. He is delightful.

Rheims, *5th July*. We have just returned from visiting the Cathedral and the Church of St Remi (one of the most remarkable churches in Europe). As we passed through the immense wide-open door of the cathedral, which seemed to spread its arms to receive all who wished to enter, Tennyson said: "How grand it must have been, when the lower windows were all filled with stained glass, to have looked into the divine twilight, and gazed up at that huge window, glowing like jewels sprinkled in gloom! What a mystery is the Christian religion! It requires an act of Faith to believe and accept it."

We arrived in Paris on 7th July. On the 10th we breakfasted with Gustave Doré, the painter, at the Moulin Rouge. His enormous studio was in the Rue St Dominic. We were much pleased with the good Doré. Although Tennyson had not been entirely satisfied with the publication of the folio edition of the "Idylls," which Doré illustrated, the two met and parted with perfect cordiality.

One afternoon I was packing Tennyson's portmanteau,

packing for both of us, as he was suffering from gout. The weather was so hot that we had taken off our coats, he, the while, being seated on the edge of his bed, smoking his pipe.

As the packing was almost completed, and it was near the hour of departure, I cleverly hoisted him into his coat, and bade him be easy; however, he complained that the garment was tight, and that he would rather wear his other coat, his older and bigger coat. He would much prefer his bigger one. As the time was getting on, and as I did not covet the labour of unpacking and repacking, I insisted that the coat he already had on did as well as possible, infinitely better than the older one.

" Now, be aisy," says I, " or if you can't be aisy, be as aisy as you can."

This quenched my poet; he returned to his pipe. He was plaintive, but he submitted. When I had quite finished and looked round for my own coat, I found that I had not only packed up both of Tennyson's, but that I had squeezed him into mine, my comparatively little coat. At last when my blunder was set right and when all was comfortably arranged, the dear fellow volunteered something very kind about the trouble I took for him. I assured him it was no trouble, quite the contrary. He was silent for a while and then he said: " Locker, I think you have a physical pleasure in packing."

Later in London. This morning we were at the marriage of Miss Louisa Simeon to Mr Richard Ward. She was the daughter of our old friend, Sir John Simeon, one of the best beloved by Tennyson and me of all Tennyson's circle. The youngest of the bridesmaids was a five-years-old sister, and as she knelt before us in sweet unconscious reverence, she displayed the soles of her little white shoes. These, and her little face and her general adornment were altogether very engaging, and Tennyson whispered to me: " She and her shoes remind me of one of your poems."

I once met Tennyson at dinner at the Conservative Club, in company with Dick Doyle, Sir J. Emerson Tennent, Sir Arthur Buller (Charles Buller's brother) and others whom I have forgotten. Tennyson read " Maud " to us and was very gay and companionable

After dinner one or two of the younger spirits got round him, and pelted him with all sorts of questions, some highly

indiscreet, all of which he listened to most benignantly; at last
our host, Mr. Cholmondeley Pennell, cut in with : "Mr. Tennyson,
which do you consider the greatest poet, Browning or Blank?"
On this Tennyson withdrew his pipe from his lips, straightened
himself in his chair, and said emphatically : " Blank, as compared
with Browning, is as the dung beneath my feet." He afterwards
expressed regret that he had spoken so freely. You see, dear
reader, that in telling this story, I have not betrayed my friend.

In 1870, my distinguished friend, Lord Stratford de Redcliffe,
expressed a warm and very laudable desire to make Tennyson's
acquaintance. At that time the Laureate was confined with
gout to his room, on a fourth floor in Albert Mansions, and the
gartered statesman, often a martyr to the same malady, was
a good deal past eighty. However, Lord Stratford was not only
a hero, but he was also a hero-worshipper, and, like his great
kinsman, was no mean poet; so he gallantly and gaily breasted
the staircase. The introduction was happily accomplished, the
visit satisfactorily paid, and I thought that the bearing of these
two remarkable and very striking-looking men was worthy
of their high reputations, and that it was characteristic of
both.

I do not think anything specially to be remembered was said,
unless when Lord Stratford described being at Lords' Cricket Club,
I suppose the Dorset Square ground, and seeing a big Harrow
boy, hat in hand, limp back to the pavilion having just lost his
wicket, and evidently not over-pleased. This moody-looking
boy was Lord Byron.

Lord Stratford added that he afterwards met Lord Byron at
John Murray's, and then at Constantinople, and that on each
occasion Byron talked a great deal, and very brightly, but that a
mocking spirit ran through his conversation. However, he did
not appear to have said anything that had impressed Lord
Stratford, or lingered in his memory. " Byron had a fine head,
eyes and hair, but the expression of the lower part of his face
was not agreeable." Perhaps Lord Byron, on the sneering side
of his nature, was not the sort of man to greatly interest Lord
Stratford.

Tennyson says that as a boy he had a great thirst to be a
poet, and to be a *popular* poet. He would rove through the
fields composing hundreds of couplets, and shouting them to the
skies; but that now he is inclined to think popularity is a

bastard fame, which sometimes goes with the more real thing, but is independent of and somewhat antagonistic to it.   He appears to shrink from his own popularity.   He maintains that the artist should spare no pains, that he should do his very best for the sake of his art, and for *that* only.

Balzac's remark that " Dans tout l'homme de génie il y a un enfant" may find its illustration in Tennyson.   He is the only grown up human being that I know of, who habitually thinks aloud.   His humour is of the dryest, it is admirable.   Did anybody ever make one laugh more heartily than Alfred Tennyson ?   He tells a story excellently, and has a catching laugh.   There are people who laugh because they are shy or disconcerted, or for lack of ideas, or to bridge over some conversational gap or obstruction: only a few because they are happy or amused or perhaps triumphant.   Tennyson has an entirely natural and a very kindly laugh.

I and mine have a warm regard for Tennyson.   He has been very kind to Mrs Locker and me.   The more we see of him the more we appreciate his singular charm, which has never deserted him in this world, and which I trust will be secured to him in the next.   His friendship has been and still is one of the solaces of my life.

It is easy to criticize a great man, it is not so easy to estimate him, and certainly it is not for me to attempt it ; however, I may say that Tennyson, as a poet, has mental and moral gifts, most rare in the high quality of their separate excellence, and marvellous in the harmony of their combination. "The Muse may give thee, but the gods must guide," and this the gods have done.   So future generations will not suffer his happiest poems, and there are many such, to die.   These poems will remain the highest expression of the imaginative mind of his epoch, and he will continue to shine, a beautiful and serene star, in the poetical heavens.

On again reading this paper of mine, I am painfully conscious of its inadequacy.   Lady Tennyson's name is not even mentioned, but there is little need.   Is not there a Book where all noble actions are recorded ?   I spare her my praise.

My mother's journal. — Mr Fox, Aldworth, Arthur
Hallam, Miss Thackeray.

After the journey, Mr Locker gave us a drawing by Guercino and a print by Marc Antonio of Mary standing over the dead body of Christ.

A. wrote to Mr Locker:

ALDWORTH, *August 6th*, 1869.

My DEAR LOCKER,

I am rather shocked at receiving your magnificent M. Antonio and Guercino: I feel myself (as compared with you, who know so much more of these matters) unworthy to be the possessor, at least blame-worthy in accepting them. Nevertheless I do accept them, and value them not only as they are beautiful, but as memorials of your friendship.

We have got into our new house, which is very charming; nothing in it pleases me more than the bath, a perennial stream which falls thro' the house, and where I take three baths a day.

I hope presently, when we get things a little arranged, you will come and see us.

Yours ever, A. TENNYSON.

And to the Duke of Argyll:

ALDWORTH, *Aug. 17th*, 1869.

MY DEAR DUKE,

I apologise in the first place for troubling you with this letter rather than Gladstone, but I wrote to him lately in behalf of another petitioner, and am loth to intrude on him again so soon: moreover I thought that, being yourself a geologist, you were more likely to be interested in the writer of the letter. However that may be, Mr Fox is a very worthy man, and poor, and has

been for many years curate at Brixton near me in the
Isle of Wight, whose whole delight, always and excepting
that which he takes in the discharge of his clerical duties,
lies in exploring on our coast; and it would break his
heart I believe to be separated from the localities of his
favourite study. If the government would give him this
living, they would make him happy for life: for the worth
and value of his contributions to geology, Owen will
answer.

I will say no more, and what I have said comes I fear
too late: for I have been living here in my new house
near Haslemere, to which as yet there is no post, and all
my letters arrive irregularly, and so his was delayed in
reaching me: still, if the living be not already promised, I
should be grateful if you could help him to it.

I do not know where you are at present, but I direct
this to Inveraray.

With best remembrances to your Duchess,

Believe me always yours,

A. TENNYSON.

Sept. 13*th*. At night a fearful clap of thunder. We seemed
in the very heart of the storm. A. said he did not think that he
had "ever seen anything more sublime than the great plain of
Sussex beneath us, covered with moving mist, in the dim
twilight, and bellowing from end to end with thunder:

> With sullen thunders to and fro
> That to a dreary distance go."

Read the "Idylls" thro' in their proper sequence during
these months, also Tom Hughes' *Alfred the Great*, Pressensé's
Life of Christ, Martineau's *Endeavours after a Christian Life*,
and Lecky's *European Morals*.

Oct. 7*th*. We laid the first turf of our (Aldworth) lawn. All
the turf is brought from our Farringford Down.

He gave me his beginning of "Beaumains" ("Sir Gareth")

to read, written (as was said jokingly) to "describe a pattern youth for his boys."

He "would like the blank shields on his mantelpiece to be emblazoned with devices to represent the great modern poets, Dante, Chaucer, Shakespeare, Milton, Goethe, Wordsworth."

Nov. 1st. A. and I talked a long talk together, sitting over the fire in our room at night. We were very busy about the new volume of poems, "The Holy Grail."

Dr Martineau came. He struck us as having a subtle and wonderful mind : he is mournful and tender-looking, "a noble gentleman."

A. went to London. Tilly (Matilda Tennyson) in the evening told me how, on an autumn evening at Somersby, just before Arthur Hallam's death, she and her sister Mary saw a tall figure, clothed from head to foot in white, and they followed it down the lane, and saw it pass thro' the hedge where there was no gap : and how she was so awed that on reaching home she burst into tears. She then related how, being at Spilsby for her dancing lessons, she had brought home the letters, and one among them from Clevedon. This was addressed to A. She gave it to him, as he sat at dinner, and went to take off her bonnet, and she heard afterwards that he had suddenly left the table, and that poor Emily was then summoned to him to have the terrible news broken to her.

Then Tilly talked of Arthur Hallam's goodness to the younger children; how she and they "roared" when he went away with A. and Charlie to college ; and said that Arthur Hallam was so delightful, that they were all in love with him from the first, when they saw him on the lawn, where he and A. were playing with "Billy," the monkey. She added that he always begged that the children might be of any pleasure-party that was made : but that A. was kindest of all to the children, often taking them on his knee, and telling them ghost-stories and other stories of his own invention.

A. wrote to me that he thought of giving up "The Lover's Tale," and publishing "The Golden Supper" with a preface.

Dec. 11th. Farringford. A. read me some of Maurice's *Social Morals ;* "a noble book" it seemed to me, as A. called it. He wrote to Z. expressing the hope that Cabinet Ministers would think how to make England and her colonies one, body and soul, instead of casting the colonies off : and he continued —

" I cannot but feel that those who think otherwise must be blind to our real interest, and our high calling."

Throughout these years we saw a great deal of Mr and Mrs Cameron, who had bought a house near Freshwater Bay.   My father described him as "a philosopher with his beard dipt in moonlight."   Not only was he an excellent classical scholar, but while in the East, where he lived for many years, he had codified the laws of Ceylon.   Mrs Cameron was one of the most benevolent of human beings, always thinking of something for the good or pleasure of others.   Her photographs are well-known.   She herself took an absorbing interest in making them.

Writing to Mr Digby, she gives an account of the life at Freshwater [1].

After speaking of the party of young people assembled at Freshwater ; of Annie Thackeray as the queen of all hearts, of her cousins the Miss Ritchies, like Gainsboroughs to look at, one sister "singing perfectly, the other playing as perfectly," both as if inspired ; and after telling of the dances and the walks, " Alfred taking walks of several miles daily," and of the silent and deep enjoyment of Henry Taylor, "my peculiar friend," — Mrs Cameron adds : "Then we have feasts of intellect.   Sometimes we dine at Farringford, sometimes Farringford dines here."

One evening she describes, when Annie Thackeray, and the Miss Prinseps, Alfred Tennyson, and Henry Taylor, were dining at her house.   "We dined at 7 and only got up from dinner at 11.   All this while the most brilliant conversation.   The whole range of poetry comprised, every immortal poet brought to life, and living again in the glowing and wise breath of Alfred Tennyson, in the quotations from Henry Taylor's rich and faithful memory.   Each one recited favourite passages from Beaumont and Fletcher, favourite sonnets of Shakespeare's, all that was finest in my adored Wordsworth, and the god of poetic fire, Milton.   They were like two brilliant fencers crossing their rapiers, or flashing their foils, giving and evading clean thrusts [1]."

From 1869 to 1880 my brother, myself and the younger members of the Cameron family spent many of

[1] See Appendix, p. 523, for Freshwater Society.

our evenings during the Christmas and Easter holidays in Mrs Cameron's little theatre.   Here we acted plays by Sheridan, Gilbert, Robertson and Tom Taylor, and my father was seldom absent, for he loved the stage.   He was a careful critic and never missed a point.   As one of the actors said of him: " Criticism only came when sought, and seldom then ; but, if conceded at all, he had the faculty of putting in a few forcible phrases the warmth of his approval, or the *douche* of his disapproval, as I never heard them put."

Miss Emily Ritchie writes of her first visit at this time :

The first day (in 1869) I ever saw Alfred Tennyson he was walking on the downs at Freshwater.   Annie Thackeray was with him and she introduced me and made me walk on his other side.

He swooped down the hillside, his large black cloak flying in the wind, and his massive tread seeming to carry him at an astonishing pace.   After that, a large party of us led by Mrs Cameron spent the evening at Farringford ; the fact of being in so august a presence seems to have obliterated the actual memory of what he said ; but I remember how, in the course of the evening, a sudden transformation took place in all our appearances, which gave us assurance from an unexpected quarter.   One of the subjects which came up in the course of conversation was the fashion for young ladies of wearing their hair.   He said the most becoming fashion was to wear it flowing, without being put up at all, and wished that we would let ours hang down our backs.   He suggested our trying the effect at once.

We all therefore sat round the dessert table with our hair down, and for the rest of the evening he approved of us very much, and said he wished the Empress Eugénie would set the fashion.

What he especially disliked was seeing the whole ear, as " So few women have specially small, well-shaped ears to show."

Some time after this I spent three nights at Farringford, and

on one of them a dance took place at Mrs Cameron's, to which I
went, and my return from it was memorable.   It was two in
the morning, and I came back expecting to be let in by the
manservant, but it was he himself who opened the door, and
the invitation to come up to his den, where he was still smoking,
took me aback.   He led me up the winding stairs to his study
(a much smaller and less stately one than the present study),
and talked delightfully whilst he finished his pipe.   What
I chiefly remember was the way in which he told me "never
to get spoilt by the world."

His talk ranged over every possible subject, from the most
trivial thing of the passing moment, to which he somehow gave
raciness and importance, to the greatest heights of thought and
speculation.   The unexpected was one of the most striking
fascinations of his company, the utter child-like simplicity of
his great nature revealed itself in this.

His judgments of men were wonderfully kindly.   He had
a refreshing hatred of the commonplaces of intercourse, and a
mistrust of what he called the " humbug of society," which made
him dread ever attending anything in the shape of a party : but
to visitors in his own house he showed ideal hospitality, giving
his friends a feeling that they had come to a home indeed,
bestowing *himself* upon them in a way which the most genial
of the earth alone understand.

He used the fewest words I ever heard anyone use to express
his ideas, or to recount an experience, or to tell an anecdote
(always a large element in his talk), but each word was the
right one, and his use of the English language was unlike
anybody else's for force and dignity.

The strongest vein of common sense characterised his talk,
and he disliked exaggeration of all sorts.

Mrs Cameron's wildly romantic ideas and performances used
to call forth growls of amused dissatisfaction from him, and he
hated the adulatory attitude of some people.   Praise, which he
felt due, he accepted as a matter of course, being himself the
most censorious critic of his work.   At the same time he was
very sensitive to any critical opinion, so sensitive that I have
heard him say, all the praise he had ever received didn't out-
weigh for the moment a spiteful and unkindly criticism, even
though the criticism (he once added) was directed against the
straightness of his toe-nail.

Amongst the experiences of intercourse with him, nothing was more memorable than to hear him read his poetry. The roll of his great voice acted sometimes almost like an incantation, so that when it was a new poem he was reading, the power of realizing its actual nature was subordinated to the wonder at the sound of the tones. Sometimes, as in "The Passing of Arthur," it was a long chant, in which the expression lay chiefly in the value given to each syllable, sometimes a swell of sound like an organ's; often came tones of infinite pathos, delicate and tender, then others of mighty volume and passionate strength.

UNFINISHED POEM OF THIS PERIOD.

Reticence.*

Not to Silence would I build
A temple in her naked field;
Not to her would raise a shrine:
She no goddess is of mine;
But to one of finer sense,
Her half sister, Reticence.

Latest of her worshippers,
I would shrine her in my verse!
Not like Silence shall she stand,
Finger-lipt, but with right hand
Moving toward her lip, and there
Hovering, thoughtful, poised in air.
Her garment slips, the left hand holds
Her[1] up-gather'd garment folds,
And veils a breast more fair to me
Than aught of Anadyomené!

[1] The two *Her's* coming together vexed him and he threw the poem aside — unfinished — and forgot all about it.

* Copyright, 1897, by The Macmillan Company.

Near the shrine, but half in sun,
I would have a river run,
Such as never overflows
With flush of rain, or molten snows
Often shallow, pierced with light,
Often deep beyond the sight,
Here and there about the lawn
Wholly mute, but ever drawn
Under either grassy brink
In many a silver loop and link
Variously from its far spring,
With long tracts of murmuring,
Partly river, partly brook,
Which in one delicious nook,
Where the doubtful shadows play,
Lightly lisping, breaks away;
Thence, across the summit hurl'd,
Showers in a whisper o'er the world.

CHAPTER IV.

"THE HOLY GRAIL," 1869, AND MY MOTHER'S JOURNAL, 1870–1872.

Trinity College (Cambridge), his old College, had this year made my father an Honorary Fellow; and it was from Cambridge men in particular that he received commendations of his " Holy Grail." Among others Maurice wrote:

CAMBRIDGE, *Dec. 18th*, 1869.

MY DEAR TENNYSON,

I did not give myself credit for so much of Diomedean craft in changing brass armour for golden. But if I can persuade any who listen to me to seek for the " Holy Grail " and to increase the "Arthur " standard of character above any Greek one, my aim will be accomplished and I shall thankfully own how much more you have contributed to it than we lecturers and parsons can.

Pray remember me affectionately to Mrs Tennyson as well as to my godson and Lionel. I had hoped we might have seen you this winter in the Isle of Wight, but we have been urged to try Torquay and have taken a house there for two months.

Believe me very truly yours,

F. D. MAURICE.

About "The Holy Grail" my father said to me: "At twenty-four I meant to write an epic or a drama of King

Arthur; and I thought that I should take twenty years about the work. They will now say that I have been forty years about it. 'The Holy Grail' is one of the most imaginative of my poems. I have expressed there my strong feeling as to the Reality of the Unseen. The end, when the king speaks of his work and of his visions, is intended to be the summing up of all in the highest note by the highest of human men. These three lines in Arthur's speech are the (spiritually) central lines of the Idylls:

> In moments when he feels he cannot die,
> And knows himself no vision to himself, ⸺
> Nor the High God a vision.

The general English view of God is as of an immeasurable clergyman; and some mistake the devil for God."

He said again to us with deep feeling, in January 1869: "Yes, it is true that there are moments when the flesh is nothing to me, when I feel and know the flesh to be the vision, God and the Spiritual the only real and true. Depend upon it, the Spiritual *is* the real: it belongs to one more than the hand and the foot. You may tell me that my hand and my foot are only imaginary symbols of my existence, I could believe you; but you never, never can convince me that the *I* is not an eternal Reality, and that the Spiritual is not the true and real part of me." These words he spoke with such passionate earnestness that a solemn silence fell on us as he left the room [1].

The new volume contained besides " The Holy Grail," " Lucretius[2]," " The Coming of Arthur," " Pelleas

---

[1] I have taken the words of this paragraph from Mrs Bradley's diary written at the time : I remember the scene well.

[2] Munro, the great Lucretian, wrote praising "Lucretius," and saying the poem was perfect but for one word, "neat-herd."

and Ettarre," " The Passing of Arthur," " Northern
Farmer (New Style)," " The Golden Supper," "The
Victim," " Wages," " The Higher Pantheism," " Flower
in the crannied wall."

After the publication of this book his fame in America
grew extraordinarily, and every post brought him innumerable American letters.

One little incident pleased him much. A literary
society at Philadelphia called itself after him " The
Tennyson Society," and asked him for a motto. He
sent this answer:

Sept. 9th, 1869.

Dear Sir,

You have done me honour in associating my
name with your institution, and you have my hearty
good wishes for its success. Will the following Welsh
motto be of any service to you ? I have it in encaustic
tiles on the pavement of my entrance hall: " Y Gwir yn
erbyn y byd " (The truth against the world). A very
old British apophthegm, and I think a noble one, and
which may serve your purpose either in Welsh or
English. Your letter arrived when I was away from
England, or would have been earlier answered.

Believe me yours truly,

A. Tennyson.

When certain adverse critics discovered that throughout all the new " Idylls of the King " there was a great
moral significance, he was attacked with the cry of "Art
for Art's sake." After reading one of these attacks he
reeled off this epigram:

Art for Art's sake
(*instead of Art for Art — and — Man's sake*)[1].

Art for Art's sake! Hail, truest Lord of Hell!
Hail Genius, Master of the Moral Will!
" The filthiest of all paintings painted well
Is mightier than the purest painted ill!"
Yes, mightier than the purest painted well,
So prone are we toward the broad way to Hell.

These lines in a measure expressed his strong and
sorrowful conviction, that the English were beginning to
forget what was, in Voltaire's words, the glory of English
literature — " No nation has treated in poetry moral
ideas with more energy and depth than the English
nation."
Of all the " Idylls of the King " " The Holy Grail "
seems to me to express most my father's highest self.
Perhaps this is because I saw him, in the writing of this
poem more than in the writing of any other, with
that far away rapt look on his face, which he had whenever he worked at a story that touched him greatly, or
because I vividly recall the *inspired* way in which he
chanted to us the different parts of the poem as they
were composed [2].

[1] He quoted George Sand: " L'art pour art est un vain mot: l'art pour
le vrai, l'art pour le beau et le bon, voilà la religion que je cherche."
[2] An able review of the four first published " Idylls " (*Ed. Rev.* 1859),
written by Coventry Patmore, remarks (what is eminently true of " The Holy
Grail ") that " Since the definite formation of the English language no poetry
has been written with so small an admixture of Latin as the ' Idylls of the
King,' and what will sound still stranger in the ears of those who have
been in the habit of regarding the Latin element as essential to the dignity
of poetry, no language has surpassed in epic dignity the English of these
poems."

1870.

At the beginning of the new year the Bradleys again visited us.

My father was extraordinarily happy now that he felt that his great work of the Epic of Arthur was nearing its completion: and it impressed the Bradleys that, in spite of vexatious publishing matters, he was marvellously calm and genial.

. *January* 11*th.* Mrs Bradley wrote:

Both at dinner and afterwards at the " Round Table " (where we have dessert in the drawing-room) Mr Tennyson talked a great deal, unusually much at dinner, when he is oftenest rather silent. I asked him, " Did he know that 'gleam' was an old Lincolnshire word used formerly in the Fens for the cry of the curlew ? " alluding to the line in " Locksley Hall," "dreary gleams about the moorland flying over Locksley Hall." " I never heard it," he said, " I wish I had." He thought it curious and interesting, explained that the passage in question "meant nothing more than to express the flying gleams of light across a dreary moorland, when looking at it under peculiarly dreary circumstances. 'Curlews' only a feature in the scene; but an unfortunate misprint, merely the omission of a comma, had given rise to very various interpretations of the passage." A great many were quoted. He wished he had used the word "sweeping" instead of "flying," as it would have been more explicit. He read aloud "The Holy Grail."

He said: "The first poetry that moved me was my own at five years old. When I was eight, I remember making a line I thought grander than Campbell, or Byron, or Scott. I rolled it out, it was this : 'With slaughterous sons of thunder rolled the flood ' — great nonsense of course, but I thought it fine." He was very jovial, and talked on all imaginable topics.

Spoke a little of the stir being made just now about " Women's Rights." The account of some meeting on the subject in America amused him. He said that all the great men that had ever lived were made out as sort of beasts with a view to exalt women.

" You know," he added, " that I think women much better (morally) than we are."

My father sent this answer to a letter from James Spedding approving of " The Holy Grail ":

FARRINGFORD, *Jan.* 19*th*, 1870.

MY DEAR JAMES,

Send the box, please, not without your new volume hither. I shall be grateful for both. I am glad that you find anything to approve of in the " H. G." I have not yet finished the Arthurian legends, otherwise I might consider your Job[1] theme. Strange that I quite forgot our conversation thereupon. Where is Westbourne Terrace? If I had ever clearly made out I should assuredly have called. I have often when in town past by the old 60, the " vedovo sito," with a groan, thinking of you as no longer the comeatable, runupableto, smokeablewith J. S. of old, but as a family man, far in the west, sitting cigarless among many nieces, clean and forlorn, but I hope to see you somewhere in '70, for I have taken chambers in Victoria Street for three years, though they are not yet furnished.

Where is the difficulty of that line in the " Flower "? It is rather rough certainly, but, had you followed the clue of " little flower " in the preceding line, you would not have stumbled over this, which is accentual anapæst,

What you are, root and all:

rough — doubtless.

Believe me yours ever,

A. TENNYSON.

[1] Mr Spedding said he wanted a " Modern Job " by Tennyson.

Edward Fitzgerald also wrote about "The Holy Grail":

WOODBRIDGE, *Jan.* 1870.

MY DEAR OLD ALFRED,

I bought your vol. (the "Holy Grail") at Lowestoft; and, when I returned home here for Xmas, found a copy from your new publisher. As he sent it I suppose at your orders, I write about it what I might say to you were we together over a pipe, instead of so far asunder.

The whole myth of Arthur's Round Table Dynasty in Britain presents itself before me with a sort of cloudy, Stonehenge grandeur. I am not sure if the old knights' adventures do not tell upon me better, touched in some lyrical way (like your own "Lady of Shalott") than when elaborated into epic form. I never could care for Spenser, Tasso, or even Ariosto, whose epic has a ballad ring about it. But then I never could care much for the old prose romances either, except *Don Quixote.* So, as this was always the case with me, I suppose my brain is wanting in this bit of its dissected map.

Anyhow, Alfred, while I feel how pure, noble and holy your work is, and whole phrases, lines and sentences of it will abide with me, and, I am sure, with men after me, I read on till the "Lincolnshire Farmer" drew tears to my eyes. I was got back to the substantial rough-spun Nature I knew; and the old brute, invested by you with the solemn humour of Humanity, like Shakespeare's *Shallow,* became a more pathetic phenomenon than the knights who revisit the world in your other verse. There! I can't help it, and have made a clean breast; and you need only laugh at one more of "Old Fitz's crotchets," which I daresay you anticipated. To compare X— to my own "paltry Poet" is, I say, to compare an old Jew's Curiosity Shop with the Phidian Marbles. They talk of "metaphysical depth and subtlety," pray is there none in "The Palace of Art," "The Vision of Sin" (which last touches on the limit of disgust without ever falling in), "Locksley Hall" also, with some little passion, I think! only that all these being clear to the bottom, as well as beautiful, do not seem to cockney eyes so deep as muddy waters? I suppose you are at Farringford with your boys for the holidays. Let me wish you all a Happy New Year, and believe me your faithful old crotchety Retainer,

E. F. G.

P.S. I also think I shall one day send you my little piece of knightlihood (*Euphranor*), of which Cowell told me you liked parts, and from which (in consequence) I have cut out what seems to me the most disagreeable part, leaving much behind, together with what still seems to me pretty. I had not looked at it for 15 years till Cowell told me what you said; and that made me cut out, and insert some pages.

January 25*th*. The Ritchies and Annie Thackeray dined with us.

My father said to them: " I don't find it difficult to believe in the Infinity of Worlds." Then, after trying to make us all realize the rate at which the earth whirls through space, and that every two days the solar system has rushed one million miles towards a certain point in the constellation of Hercules, and that light takes millions of years to travel from some of the stars, the light of which has not yet reached us, and other astronomical sublimities — he observed, "From the starry spheres to think of the airs given themselves by county families in ball-rooms! One lady I remember early in the century in Lincolnshire, drawing herself up on hearing that the daughters of a neighbouring family were taking lessons in drawing and singing, and saying, ' My daughters don't learn drawing.' " He continued: " Miss Austen understood the smallness of life to perfection. She was a great artist, equal in her small sphere to Shakespeare. I think *Persuasion* and *Mansfield Park* are my favourites. There is a saying that if God made the country, and man the town, the devil made the little country town. There is nothing equal to the smallness of a small town."

After a magnificent recitation of " Lycidas " came the unexpected outburst, " I don't suppose one blessed

German can appreciate the glory of the verse as I can," and on hearing that one of the party had not read through *Paradise Lost* he called out, "Shameless daughter of your age." The indifference to religion of the age was touched on, and X— began to uphold Shelley's views for the regeneration of mankind.

A. T.   Shelley had not common-sense!

X—.   Well, but had Christ common-sense?

A. T.   Christ had more common-sense than you or I, Madam.

My mother's journal. — Death of Sir John Simeon,
Franco-German War.

March 1st.   Aldworth.   Hallam read the 4th *Æneid* with A.; they study Virgil together daily.   We were interested by an article of Froude's on *Government and the Governed.*

He received from a stranger, Mr John White of Cowes, a melancholy letter, and a present of a cartload of wood — old oak from one of the broken up men-of-war.   A. wrote to him.

FARRINGFORD, *March 8th,* 1870.

DEAR SIR,

Your present has rather amazed me, though not unpleasantly: so I accept it with thanks, and I will sit by the "blue light" gratefully, and hope for you that *your* light may be no longer "low," and if you ever come my way I shall be glad to see you.

Yours faithfully, A. TENNYSON.

May 23rd.   The terrible blow of Sir John Simeon's death at Friburg fell on us just as we were starting for Aldworth.

May 31st.   A. went to Swainston for the funeral.   He wrote

"In the Garden at Swainston[1]" (smoking one of Sir John's pipes in the Swainston garden). "All dreadfully sad and trying, and seeming all the sadder, for the sun shone and the roses bloomed profusely[2]."

A. very sad, his loss haunted him. Sir John was a brother to us.

A. wrote to Lady Simeon :

ALDWORTH, *June 27th*, 1870.

MY DEAR LADY SIMEON,

Of course nothing could be more grateful to me than some memorial of my much-loved and ever honoured friend, the only man on earth, I verily believe, to whom I could, and have more than once opened my whole heart; and he also has given me in many a conversation at Farringford in my little attic his utter confidence. I knew none like him for tenderness and generosity, not to mention his other noble qualities, and he was the very Prince of Courtesy; but I need not tell you this; anything, little book, or whatever you will choose, send me or bring when you come; and do pray come on the 4th July, and we will be all alone; and Louie can come, when she will, and you can spare her.

Believe me, always affectionately yours,

A. TENNYSON.

This June A. was asked to become President of the Newsvendors' Benevolent Institution. His letter to Mr Walter Jones ran as follows :

June, 1870.

SIR,

First let me thank the Committee and yourself for the honour you have desired to confer upon me,

---

[1] First published in the Cabinet Edition of the Collected Poems, 1874.
[2] Letter from my father.

which, however, I feel obliged to decline accepting; for I am neither a diner out, nor a speaker after dinner, nor could without violence to the truth be called a man of business. I should be but a *roi fainéant*, which I don't wish to be — the square man in the round hole — but, if you wish for the square man in the square hole, I am sure Lord Houghton would be proud to serve your cause as President.

At the same time, with the permission of your Committee, I should be happy to be one of your Vice-Presidents by the side of my friend Longfellow.

I have the honour to be, Sir,

Your obedient Servant, A. TENNYSON.

July 26th. Aldworth. A. was laid up with gout in town. Hallam and I went to town to fetch him, and that I might receive instructions from our kind friend Sir James Paget[1]. Lady Augusta Stanley took us in her carriage to the station. Lady Charlotte Locker with us. A. told us that war between France and Germany was declared.

At this time he constantly anticipated that England, if she continued as she was, unprepared, would be some day invaded and smashed; and said, " We rashly expose ourselves to danger, and in our press offend foreign powers, being the most beastly self-satisfied nation in the world."

Nov. 1st. What a craze the tendency now-a-days to invent gossiping stories! Emily[2] copied the passage in Miss Mitford's letters, which states that A. dug the garden of Miss Repton's

---

[1] Sir James had strictly charged my father not to touch his leg. One day he said : " The doctor says that I mustn't scratch my leg, but I can't help it, and last night I scratched it till I could have shrieked with glory."

[2] My father's sister.

father at Sevenoaks, whereas A. never saw him or his garden. Then there was an illustrated paper came, which stated that he was at Louth School until he went to Trinity, the fact being, he says, that he remained at Louth two or three years; and after ten he was taught at home by his father, until he went to Trinity.

Another story the paper gave of his having been taken into custody as a smuggler, when watching a stormy sea, — the only foundation for this being that one wild night on the Farringford Down the coast-guard said to him, "Who goes there? O you, Sir! a stormy night!" or some such words.

Mrs Bowen told us a nice story of a little boy in the village who had informed her that Mr Tennyson was " the gentleman who made *poets* for the Queen under the stars, — that policeman had often seen him at it."

Nov. 4th. Mr Arthur Sullivan, Mr Knowles, and Mr Strahan came. Mr Sullivan wished to publish the "Window Songs[1]." A. did not like publishing songs that were so trivial at such a grave crisis of affairs in Europe; but he had given his promise to Mr Sullivan about them, and " He that sweareth unto his neighbour and disappointeth him not " determined us. So they are to be published with the protest : " I am sorry that my four-year-old puppet should have to dance at all in the dark shadow of these days ; but the music is now completed, and I am bound by my promise."

Nov. 8th. Mr Peach, the dear old Cornish geologist, is here. A. read me Pepys' *Diary*. At night he repeated some of " The Last Tournament " which he had just written. We read about starlings in Morris ; I did not know (what A. had put into his Idyll from his own observation) that the starlings in June, after they have brought up their young ones, congregate in flocks in a reedy place for the sake of sociability.

Nov. 12th. Aunt Franklin (Lady Franklin) and Sophy Cracroft came to luncheon from Moor Park. Both charmed with our view. A. declined going in a ship with the astronomers to Cadiz as he had hoped to do, finding that a poem on the eclipse was expected from him, " a thing absurd and out of

[1] Printed first at the Canford Manor Press in 1867, when my father was staying with the Guests. Published by Strahan, with music by Arthur Sullivan, December, 1870.

the question." Likely enough that no one will go if this insolent despatch of Gortschakoff brings war, as it should do if not withdrawn. A. talked, as he had done of late, chiefly of the state of England and Europe. He cared so much for this that most other things just then seemed matters of indifference to him. He thought of writing to Lord Granville, to tell him how grateful he was for his spirited remonstrance: and he said, "How strange England cannot see her true policy lies in a close union with our colonies!" He added: "We ought to have all boys at school drilled, so that we may be more ready for defensive war than now."

1871.

My mother's journal. — Death of Spedding's brother, Despondency, Jenny Lind, "The Last Tournament," Tourgueneff, George Eliot, Gladstone, Wales, Huxley, Illness of the Prince of Wales.

On New Year's day A. received this touching letter from Mr Spedding:

WESTBOURNE TERRACE,
Dec. 21st, 1870.

MY DEAR TENNYSON,

I should have answered your very kind letter sooner, but I doubted which house to direct to, as you seemed to be on the point of moving. I suppose I shall be safe now in writing to Farringford.

My brother's death was altogether sudden and unexpected; for he had been remarkably well all the year and showed no symptoms of failing in any way, unless possibly a very slight appearance of the " bowed shoulder of a bland old age " reminded you that he had just completed his threescore years and ten, and how lightly they lay upon him. Till within two days of his death there had been no symptoms of illness observable by anybody; nor were the symptoms which appeared then such as to cause immediate alarm. His first attack of pain was on Saturday. It was not till Monday afternoon that another severe attack made them send for the doctor, who pronounced the seat of disorder to be in the heart but did not apprehend any present danger. He died in the middle of that night without a word or a struggle or a sign of distress. " God's finger touched him and he slept."

When death comes in the middle of life, I do not mean in middle age but with no symptoms of decay by way of warning, people think it an aggravation. To me the premonitory decay seems the worst part of the business, a business in which man and nature between them are too apt to make ugly work. To have lived till 70 in full health of body and mind, and then to depart without knowing it, is surely for a mortal man a lot not to be regretted or repudiated. And though for the survivors the shock is greater at the time, it brings far less suffering even to them, than the more ordinary fate of tedious and distressing sickness, with all its miserable anxieties, and things painful not only to witness but ever after to remember. In this case there is nothing to remember which is in any way distressing. While the life lasted it was pleasant to look upon : it departed in pure peace and rest : leaving no troubles behind, — only the sense of a good thing gone, and the want which is the measure of its value.

Such a blow could not have been better borne (according to my notions) than this has been by all the family : no shutting up with grief : no hanging of the past with black and making remembrance uncheerful : but such a state of mind as becomes those who look upon death as upon the entrance of a future life, who know that their sorrow is for themselves, not for him, and to whom the memory of the past remains a secure possession, sacred but not sad. The house when I left it was going on almost as it would have done if he had only been absent on a journey, leaving his son to take his place in the meantime.

Yours very truly, JAMES SPEDDING.

A. wrote to Mr Oscar Browning :

FARRINGFORD, *Sunday, Feb. 12th,* 1871.

MY DEAR MR BROWNING,

I ought before this to have thanked you for having sent me the apparition-story [1], and your friend

---

[1] The story of Professor Conington's wraith being seen in Oriel Lane at the time of his death

for having written it out for me.　Pardon the delay, and
accept my thanks now for him, and for yourself.　Could
he and would he get for me Miss Cobbe's?　I rejoice
that my few words about the teaching of history seem
to have borne fruit at Eton, and I am glad that Lionel
was present at your lecture: he has, I believe, a mind
really capable of great thoughts, but is so impressionable
that it is more important to him than to most boys to
have these continually put before him.　Will you tell
Mr Johnson[1] how exquisite I think his translation of
" Hesper," which I have just now seen in this Sunday's
Spectator?　My wife's kind remembrances, and

Believe me yours ever,

A. TENNYSON.

February.　A. received Mr Jowett's four volumes of Plato, a
most welcome gift for itself and for the donor.　I cut open the
Phædo for him.　He talked on the subjects nearest his heart,
the Resurrection and the Immortality of the Soul.　He read to
me some of the *Edinburgh Royal Society Transactions.*

Lord and Lady Elcho called: he and A. discussed Cardwell's
army reforms; something more radical seems to be needed.

Feb. 26th.　In Maiden's Croft.　He spoke despondingly of
the tone of literature, as is his wont now from time to time.　He
foreboded "the fiercest battle the world has yet known between
good and evil, faith and unfaith."

What does midnight to-night bring?　Peace or War for
France and Germany?　Surely peace.　The continuance of
such a war is too horrible to think of.

A. has been taking pains to help the Committee of the City
of London Fund for the relief of Paris.

He copied "Break, Break," for Lady F. Cavendish, as the
first MS of it had been burnt at Holker: and wrote to Mr Palgrave inclosing the copy.

---

[1] The author of *Ionica* had translated "In Memoriam," CXXI.

FARRINGFORD, *May* 4*th*, 1871.

Dear P.

Here it is! a weariness of the flesh writing out my own things, but I have done it. I only wish that the Gainsboroughs and Reynolds were as easily replaceable as this MS. Love from myself and wife to yours.

Ever yours, A. Tennyson.

P.S. This place has been very full. Jenny Lind coming to dine here to-day. We go to the mountains about the end of this month.

May 4*th*. Jenny Lind came to Farringford and sang "Auld Lang Syne" and "Auld Robin Gray" for A. at his especial request. Of these and " Bonnie Doon " (the words of the last ruined for the music he thought) he was very fond.

She sang Handel and some of the *Elijah*-magnificently. She is full of feeling and of fun, and is deeply religious.

May 21*st*. He read me his "Tristram[1]" ("Last Tournament"), the plan of which he had been for some weeks discussing with me. Very grand and terrible. We went into the kitchen garden to see the splendid crimson poppies with their black marks inside the blossom (favourite flowers with A.).

June 5*th*. Mr Edward Fitzgerald wrote:

Very imperfect as Laurence's portrait[2] (of A.) is, it is nevertheless the *best* painted portrait I have seen; and certainly the *only* one of old days. " Blubber-lipt " I remember once Alfred called it; so it is; but still the only one of old days, and still the best of all to my thinking. I like to go back to days before the beard, which makes rather a Dickens of A. T. *in the photographs*—to my mind. If you are at all of this mind, tell Laurence to send it back to you, swept and garnished with a suitable frame, and hang it up, where *you* at any rate may have it before your eyes, with all its imperfections on its head. When last I heard from Spedding, half a year ago, I think, he said that Alfred had never called for the drawing by Thackeray of the Lord of Burleigh[3]

---

[1] Just written.   [2] Now at Aldworth.
[3] Now in my father's study at Farringford.

which I sent him.   Tell him I don't think Browning would have
served me so, and I mean to prefer his poems for the future.

The following letter was written by A. to Mrs Elmhirst
(née Rawnsley) on the death of her son:

HASLEMERE, *June*, 1871.

MY DEAR SOPHY,

I ought to have written to you before to
express my sympathy with you on the loss of your son,
and I thought of writing at the moment when I first
heard of your great affliction, but somehow I myself have
always felt that letters of condolence, when the grief is
yet raw and painful, are like vain voices in the ears of
the deaf, not heard or only half heard. "The heart
knoweth its own bitterness," and a stranger intermeddleth
not therewith, though I am not a stranger indeed, but
your old friend from your childhood.   However, when
Drummond and Catherine were here the other day, he
said he thought you would be soothed by hearing from
me; so I write, though I doubt whether I can bring
you any solace, except indeed by stating my own belief
that the son, whom you so loved, is not really what we
call dead, but more actually living than when alive here.

You cannot catch the voice, or feel the hands, or kiss
the cheek, that is all; a separation for an hour, not an
eternal farewell.   If it were not so, that which made
us would seem too cruel a Power to be worshipped, and
could not be loved, but I trust that you believe all this,
and by this time have attained to some degree of tran-
quillity: and your husband also.

I hear that *he* was very amiable and full of promise,
and the manner of his death, and its taking place far
away from you, and its suddenness, must have so added
sorrow to sorrow, that I almost fear you will think I

write coldly, but I do not feel coldly. Kindest remembrances to Elmhirst, and also to the Hallidays, and

Believe me affectionately yours,

A. TENNYSON.

June 22nd. A. and Hallam went to town for the Royal Academy.

June. Aldworth. Tourgueneff the Russian novelist (whose *Lisa* and *Pères et Enfants* A. liked much) and Mr Ralston arrived. Tourgueneff (a tall, large, white-haired man with a strong face) was most interesting, and told us stories of Russian life with a great graphic power and vivacity.

He told us how, in the Cossack council, they used all to stand in a circle and talk or fight until they were unanimous, whether the question was great or small. It might be an election of "Peter" or "John," and they would fight till all said "Peter."

He spoke too of a wonderful instance of the "Origin of legends" as he called it, which A. recounted in these words afterwards.

"Before the actual enfranchisement of the serfs by the Czar, many became unruly. So the Czar resolved to go on a progress thro' his dominions. At each place the serfs were assembled, and he made a little speech, telling them that he was the Czar who had freed them, and that he expected them to be obedient to their old masters until nine years were passed (which he had fixed as the limit of their serfdom, and) that then they were to be entirely free.

When the Czar came to Tourgueneff's village, Tourgueneff was ill, and could not accompany his serfs, but the Starosta or head man of the village went.

Presently he, with about thirty serfs, rushed into the room where Tourgueneff was sitting, and they all began talking together, 'Oh we have seen such a wonderful thing.' Tourgueneff said, 'I cannot hear you, if you speak all at once : let the Starosta speak!' Accordingly the Starosta spoke : 'There came a chariot drawn by four horses, and inside the chariot was a beautiful man in glittering armour, but he was not the Czar. He passed by us and vanished into the wilderness. Then came another magnificent chariot with a still more beautiful man, in resplendent and bejewelled armour; and this was the White Czar of all the Russias! And he stood up in his chariot, and spread his arms abroad! Then he beat upon his breast, and he said, 'Do you know who I am?' Then we all fell to the earth with our heads in the dust, and we saw nothing, but he beat upon his breast again three times, and cried aloud, 'Obey, obey, obey,' and then the chariot began to move, and we watched him as far as eye could see, and the chariot whirled him away, and he vanished into the wilderness.'

And all the serfs of the village chimed in, whenever the Starosta paused, 'Yes, yes, it is all as he says.' When Tourgueneff was well enough, he went to the station, and asked what had really happened, and was informed that the Czar did not once get up in his carriage, that he was dressed in an ordinary frock-coat like an English gentleman, and that he made the same little quiet speech he had made at all the villages in the country. Tourgueneff said: 'No doubt all the serfs had their heads in the dust and dared not look at the Czar, and were too scared to hear what he said, and had imagined the whole scene.'"

Tourgueneff and A. had great games at German backgammon.

June 28th. Tourgueneff received a letter about the sale of his home in Baden, and to our regret had to go to-day.

July 14th. A. travelled down from London with G. H. Lewes, who took him to his home at Witley and introduced him to Mrs Lewes (George Eliot). A. thought her "like the picture of Savonarola." She told him that Professor Sylvester's laws for verse-making had been useful to her. A. replied that he could not understand this. He likes her *Adam Bede, Scenes of Clerical Life, Silas Marner* best of her novels. *Romola* he thinks somewhat out of her depth.

July 20th. We drove to Cowdray Park, and home by Fernhurst. A. specially admired the large Spanish chestnuts and the Templar's walk of yews at Cowdray.

July 22nd. A. and Hallam drove to meet Mr and Mrs Gladstone and their daughter Helen. A telegram came to say they would not arrive till a later train, so A. and Hallam called on Mr and Mrs Lewes. She is delightful in a *tête-à-tête*, and speaks in a soft soprano voice, which almost sounds like a fine falsetto, with her strong masculine face. An interesting evening with talk ranging everywhere. At the Gladstones' request A. read "The Holy Grail," which Mr Gladstone admired. We discussed the Goschen parish council plan and other social reforms.

July 23rd. Hallam and our guests attended a schoolroom service at Haslemere (for the church was being enlarged).

After luncheon A., Hallam, and the Gladstones walked to the end of Blackdown. Mr and Mrs Gladstone frisked about like boy and girl in the heather. "A very noble fellow," A. called him, "and perfectly unaffected."

At dinner the conversation most interesting, about politics and the stormy times ahead; and Lacordaire, and his liberal Catholicism. Mr Gladstone assured us that he was a "Conservative," and that he * * * feared "extreme measures from the Opposition." He is a man of versatile mind and great impulsiveness. One could not but feel humbled in the presence of those whose life was evidently one long self-sacrifice, and, one would hope, quickened to more of it in one's own life. Mrs Gladstone wears herself out by all her hospital work in addition to the work of a prime minister's wife. Her daughter helps her, and helps her brother also in his bad Lambeth parish.

A good many people were at the station on the 24th when they went away to London.

July 29th. Mrs Greville, Mrs Fanny Kemble, and Lord Houghton came to luncheon. Fanny Kemble read Shakespeare magnificently, with tears streaming down her cheeks. She told us that, when she was nearly drowned, she did not recall the scenes of her former life, but the "terrible thing was that all her life appeared a blank." As they drove away up the hill, we heard her command Lord Houghton in her tragic way, "Get down, my lord, from off the box, for you are no inconsiderable weight."

A. is rejoiced that the National Education Bill has been passed: he admires Mr Forster's courage. "No education, no franchise," is A.'s epigram.

August 7th. A. and Hallam set off to-day for North Wales; Llanberis and Snowdon by way of Uriconium, staying with the Archibald Peels [1] at Wrexham.

A letter, English hexameters, from the travellers. They had

---

1 Mr Archibald Peel was a most faithful friend from 1851 onwards.

arrived at Llanberis: a jovial party apparently in the room above theirs in the Hotel Victoria.

Dancing above was heard, heavy feet to the sound of a light air,
Light were the feet no doubt but floors were misrepresenting.

Next morning they started early.

Walked to the Vale Gwynant, Llyn Gwynant shone very distant
Touched by the morning sun, great mountains glorying o'er it,
Moel Hebog loom'd out, and Siabod tower'd up in æther:
Liked Beddgelert much, flat green with murmur of waters,
Bathed in a deep still pool not far from Pont Aberglaslyn —
(Ravens croak'd, and took white, human skin for a lambkin).
Then we returned. — What a day! Many more if fate will allow it.

Aug. 31*st.* The travellers have come back. A. drove to the Lewes'. He read to them, and last of all at G. H. Lewes' request "Guinevere," which made George Eliot weep.

Sept. 1*st.* A. takes long walks in the evenings. He is very cheerful, and is reading me a book about Russia. He is interested in the strange sects among the Russians, and the character of the Russian peasant and the strong feeling of unity in the nation. He has read and given me to read *Fraser's Magazine* with suggestive articles on colonial federation, and against the inclosure of commons, against which he has always protested. A general Colonial Council for the purposes of defence sounds to us sensible. He advocated inter-colonial conferences in England; and was of opinion that the foremost colonial ministers ought to be admitted to the Privy Council or to some other Imperial council, where they could have a voice in Imperial affairs.

Sept. 4*th.* We both read Browning's *Balaustion.* Heracles the free, the joyous, the strong, the self-sacrificer, a grand creation.

Sept. 8*th.* A. went to the George Howards at Naworth Castle. He liked the free, independent peasantry. He talks of an ancient stone trough, about which the members of an Archæological Society were discoursing, when a countryman stepped forward, still bitter with the old border spirit: " It is where we washed them Scots in before we hanged them."

Nov. 10*th.* Aldworth. A. sent his poem "England and America" to the *New York Ledger.*

Nov. 11*th.* Mr Huxley and Mr Knowles arrived here on a visit. Mr Huxley was charming. We had much talk. He was chivalrous, wide, and earnest, so that one could not but enjoy talking with him. There was a discussion on George Eliot's humility. Huxley and A. both thought her a humble woman, despite a dogmatic manner of assertion that had come upon her latterly in her writings. Mr Knowles and Mr Arnold White [1] have been kind in arranging A.'s publishing business. Mr Knowles's active nature, I think, sometimes spurs A. on to work when he is flagging [2].

Nov. 19*th.* The new poem, " Sir Gareth," which he has almost written down, is full of youth, vigour, and beauty.

Dec. 11*th.* Anxious telegrams about the Prince of Wales. Touching accounts reach us of the Princess; her speech failed her from anxiety, and when she was allowed to go into the Prince's room, she stood for hours looking at him through a hole in the screen.

This illness has quelled the chatter about the expense of royalty to England. A. says, " Our Government plus Royalty is the cheapest government of any great country in the world."

His new study was not quite finished, and he wandered about drying the wet places on the walls with a hot poker.

Christmas. I was very unwell, and he said, " I leave you to your two sons' nursing," but he did not, and watched over me as tenderly and carefully as ever.

He does his work in the morning regularly after his breakfast at 8 o'clock; then walks before luncheon with the boys or a friend, and one or two dogs.

He has inserted his " Last Tournament " in the December *Contemporary,* and wrote on Dec. 21st a letter thanking Mr Browning for his *Prince Hohenstiel-Schwangau.*

---

[1] Afterwards Sir Arnold White, the well-known lawyer.

[2] My father would at this time point his finger at Mr Knowles with a grim smile and say: " I was often urged to go on with the 'Idylls,' but I stuck: and then this beast said, ' Do it,' and I did it."

1872.

Letters, My mother's journal, Paris and the Chartreuse, "Gareth," "Epilogue to the Idylls."

Mr Emerson wrote about his daughter's visit to England:

Jan. 21st, 1872.

MY DEAR MR TENNYSON,

I cannot let my daughter pass through London without tasking your benevolence to give her the sight of your face. `Her husband Colonel Wm. H. Forbes (himself a good soldier in the Massachusetts Volunteers in the War of the Rebellion) and Edith set forth to-morrow for England, France and Italy, and I of course shall not think they see England unless they see you. I pray you to gratify them and me so far. You shall not write a line the less, and I shall add this grace to your genius. With kindest remembrance of my brief meeting with you,

Yours always, R. W. EMERSON.

The following letter was sent to Mr Gladstone about an application from Z— for a pension:

Feb. 5th, 1872.

MY DEAR GLADSTONE,

You see that I am requested by Browning, Houghton, and others, to forward the enclosed to you, and I do not suppose that you can go far wrong in pensioning poor Z—, who has done hard work in more ways than one, and is now on the threshold of old age. Heaven help you fair through the Session, like enough to be a rough one — but if you let those Yankees get anything like their way of you in the Alabama claims, I won't pay my "ship-money" any more than old Hampden.

Ever yours, A. TENNYSON.

Answer from the Right Honourable W. E. Gladstone.

11 CARLTON HOUSE TERRACE,
Feb. 9th, 1872.
MY DEAR TENNYSON,

   With respect to literary pensions I think it was the intention of parliament that they should be given to really distinguished literary men.   I need not name the great instances in which this practice has been pursued.   Gradually the standard seems to have declined; in part no doubt because the endowment supplied by public approbation is now, as a general rule, materially improved.   An article in the *Quarterly Review* recently exhibited (perhaps with exaggeration) the insignificance of many recent recipients.   Since assuming my present office I have found that it was necessary, in practice, to recognise loss of health, old age or calamity, as elements in the case for pensions of this class; but I have endeavoured to limit this admission to those cases only where some real service had been rendered, by works of intrinsic value, to the cause of letters.   I am afraid upon enquiry that this case may not be up to the mark according to this rule.   I am constantly refusing applications where personal character, undoubted need, and *respectable* authorship are combined.   The pension list would I fear become a source of mischief were it made available for this class. All this, because I am desirous you should understand that the application you have sent me is not treated lightly.   Minor aid, I may add, is sometimes given from another fund, by small grants not annual; and in these cases the standard of literary merit is not lifted quite so high.

Yours very sincerely,

W. E. GLADSTONE.

P.S.   Be assured we are all ears and eyes and thought too I hope in the American matter.

Lady Charlotte Locker died suddenly; and my father wrote to Mr Locker:

FARRINGFORD,
April 28th, 1872.

I scarcely dare to write. The shock must have been so terrible, just when things seemed better. I would we could know how you have borne it. Sure at least I am that, even in this first anguish of grief, you can think with thankfulness that the weary days of suffering are over for ever with your dearest one, and can trust that she is happy now with the God and Saviour she has loved and served. May He strengthen you to bear your immeasurable loss. Is there not even in its greatness, that which helps to make it bearable? Had she been less a creature of light and love, you could not have had the beautiful memory, or the sustaining help you now have.

Vain words all, I know: forgive them as all that one poor human sympathy can do at such an hour.

When you are able to come to us, and it will be good for you to come, you must come. We will do all the little we can for you you know, with all true love.

Ever your affectionate

ALFRED AND EMILY TENNYSON.

June 22nd. Farringford. Every night A. has read Shakespeare, or Pascal, or Montesquieu (*Décadence des Romains*).

On July 9th A. went to London about " Gareth," and wrote: " I have sent ' Gareth [1] ' to press this morning. The MS is so ill-written that I expect much confusion."

---

[1] On April 5th my father had written to Mr Knowles (then Editor of the *Contemporary Review*): " ' Gareth ' is not finished yet. I left him off once altogether, finding him more difficult to deal with than anything excepting perhaps 'Aylmer's Field.' If I were at liberty, which I think I am not, to print the names of the speakers ' Gareth ' ' Linette ' over the short snip-snap of their talk, and so avoid the perpetual 'said' and its varieties, the work would be much easier. I have made out the plan however, and

Aug. 7th. We went to Paris. A. said that the hollow eyes
of the ruined Tuileries looked out very ironically, with " Liberté,
Égalité, Fraternité " written above them. The maid at the Hôtel
St Romain gave us a pitiful account of her living through the
siege, half-starved, for four months in the cellars. A. and the
boys spent the day in the Louvre. He told the boys that in
1848 he saw two Englishmen come to look at the Venus of Milo.
They were discussing Peel and the corn laws. " This is the finest
statue in the whole world." " Yes, but about Peel now," and so
back they went to the corn laws, and the " finest statue in the
world " was left unheeded. He immensely admired the portraits by Velasquez with a far-away look in the eyes : and
Titian's Entombment.

He bought and read many volumes of Victor Hugo and
Alfred de Musset. He praised the *Chasseur Noir.* Alfred de
Musset's *On ne badine pas avec l'amour* and his other comedies
were favourites of A.'s [1].

Aug. 14th. To Dijon, thence to Mâcon and Vienne.

We drove along the valley of the Isère to Grenoble, and A.
said, " This is our best day." A magic, dreamy light on the
crags which stretched far away into the distance. Beneath
were vines, and fruit-trees, and full crops. From Grenoble we
drove to Sassenaye.

Aug. 21st. Grenoble. A. and Lionel went to the Chartreuse
Monastery, a splendid drive by the side of a torrent. A. told
me to read Victor Hugo's *Burgraves.* He wanted to know what
I thought of the "strange confusion of times." There seems to
me something fine in the ideas, though Uther Pendragon is out
of place.

At midnight mass A. and Lionel had a dim view of the two
chanting lines of white cowled monks each with his little lantern.
This nightly service had gone on for hundreds of years, and is
very solemn and affecting. A good dinner was served, no charge
was made, and A. and L. were waited on by a silent monk with
courtly bearing; "a great gentleman," A. said, "who looked as if

perhaps some day it will be completed; and it will be then to consider
whether or no it should go into the *Contemporary* or elsewhere." " Gareth "
was published by Strahan in the autumn (1872) along with " The Last
Tournament."

[1] My father was fond (about this time) of dipping into French history;
Thierry, Thiers, Lavallée, Montalembert, Michelet, Guizot, Lanfrey.

he had been a distinguished officer in the French army." Next day the Procureur showed them over the Monastery, which is bare and stern, and every now and then opened the doors of the cells. A. inquired if any of the monks kept skeletons or skulls to remind them of their mortality. The Procureur shook his head.

Aug. 29th. A. and Lionel climbed the Dent du Chat, more than 6000 feet high. They had a beautiful view of Mont Blanc, A. saying it "looked like a great cathedral with three naves." The guide approved of his powers of endurance, and called both father and son good mountaineers.

Sept. 2nd. Geneva. A. took me to the meeting of the rivers, "the clear stream with the muddy one." When the night deepened (as he and I had noticed at Cauteretz and elsewhere) the rushing of the Rhone sounded louder and louder.

Sept. 5th. Returned by Lausanne and Amiens to Aldworth. A. read *Le Lendemain de la Mort* on the way.

On our return we found the following letter from Walt Whitman:

WASHINGTON, *Sept. 2nd,* 1872.

DEAR MR TENNYSON,

After a long absence in the mountains and lakes of Vermont and Northern New York I am now back again at work and expect to remain here. Your letter of May 23rd, also the one with the picture [1], safely reached me. The picture is superb and I consider myself in luck possessing it. It brings you very near me. I have it now before me.

I send you by same mail with this in a little book my piece lately delivered for Dartmouth College Commencement up North. Did *Democratic Vistas* reach you?

We have had in this country a summer more fit for the infernal regions, but now the delicious Virginia September has set in balmy cool and one dilates and feels like work again.

With best respects and love,

WALT WHITMAN.

[1] The frontispiece of Vol. II.

Sept. 24th.   Aldworth.   A. sent off corrections of "Gareth" to the press.   His lines on the honeysuckle in "Gareth" were made on the lawn about the honeysuckle that climbs up the house at Aldworth.

> Good lord, how sweetly smells the honeysuckle
> In the hush'd night, as if the world were one
> . Of utter peace, and love, and gentleness.

He finished *Coriolanus* to us, which he reads dramatically and magnificently.

Oct. 7th.   Alan and Mary Ker (A.'s sister) and Walter Ker their son arrived.   A. chaffed Mary about her sonnet-writing.

He said to her: "This is the sort of sonnet you would write to Swedenborg," then, without drawing breath, he spouted a sonnet, and at the end observed, "There is a sonnet with the most intricate rhymes, and now I do not remember a word of it." Many of his shorter poems were made like this, in a flash.

Oct. 29th.   A. went to Clapham.

My father's letter-diary.

Oct. 31*st.*   The Hollies.   I believe we are going to the theatre to-night to see "Bijou" which is great as a "spectacle."   Gassiot, with whom I dined the day before yesterday, has a great voltaic battery and he showed us wonderful lights.   K. is going to 'interview' Strahan about Charles' sonnets.   Strahan has joined himself to King.

Nov. 1*st.*   I have not set eyes on the Canada paragraph, but Knowles, who has gone off to Brighton to-day, says he will get it for me.   I saw "Bijou" last night, and was ashamed of my countrymen flocking to such a wretched nonentity, miserable stagey-toned, unmeaning dialogue: only one thing made amends, a young damsel whose dancing was music and poetry.   By the

bye I read in the bill that one of the actresses was Miss
Tennyson. I think it is a fancy name assumed by her.
I have not yet got my sheets back from the printer.

Nov. 4th. I called on Carlyle yesterday but he was
out.

Nov. 6th. I haven't seen Palgrave yet or Woolner.
K. has asked Pollock to dinner to-morrow, and Mr King
the publisher, who once visited at Farringford, is coming.
I have not written to Browning yet or seen him, but
must one or other. I am trying to write a war song for
the knights in the first " Idyll."

November 8th. Lady Franklin has sent me that
Canadian bit of the *Times*[1]. Villainous.

November 10th. It seems to me all right for the
knights going forth to break the heathen[2]. It is early
times yet, and many years are to elapse before the more
settled time of " Gareth." I must say that to me the
song rings like a grand music. An article in the *Spectator*
on Twickenham where Hallam is mentioned.

November 11th. I think of coming home on
Wednesday, for I stop for the " Metaphysical" on
Tuesday.

November 13th. There are several reasons why I
cannot fulfil my promise of coming to-day,—one is

---

[1] In answer to this article he wrote:

> And that true North, whereof we lately heard
> A strain to shame us "keep you to yourselves;
> So loyal is too costly! friends — your love
> Is but a burthen; loose the bond, and go."
> Is this the tone of empire? here the faith
> That made us rulers? this, indeed, her voice
> And meaning, whom the roar of Hougoumont
> Left mightiest of all peoples under heaven? etc.
>
> Epilogue to the "Idylls of the King."

[2] Referring to the war-song "Clang battle-axe, and clash brand! Let the
King reign."

I must go to my rooms in Victoria Street[1] and put things in order, as I have to vacate at the end of the year, and there are others. Archbishop Manning thanked me warmly last night for "Gareth," and I sat by Father Dalgairns, whom I gratified by telling of my wife's approval of his essay on God.

A poem arrived from Dr W. C. Bennett which was acknowledged as follows:

Nov. 13th, 1872.

My dear Mr Bennett,

Thanks for your flattering poem. I could wish that I had something of what Master Swinburne calls " the Divine arrogance of genius," that I might take it into my system and rejoice abundantly; but as Marvell says:

> "At my back I always hear
> Time's winged chariot hurrying near;
> And yonder all before us lie
> Deserts of vast eternity,"

where most of us will be left and swallowed up. Nevertheless, true thanks.

Yours ever, A. Tennyson

My mother's journal.

Dec. 25th. A. thought of writing a poem about a shipwreck on the Yorkshire coast, which Lord Houghton had described to him. One mid-winter a stranded vessel was found near Redcar; women tied to the masts with men's coats thrown round their shoulders, and the sailors lying about the decks; all of them, men and women, frozen to death. The name of the ship was " The Happy Home."

---

[1] Rooms in Albert Mansions which my father took (1870–1872) in order to be, during his visits to London, near his friends, Dean Stanley and Lady Augusta Stanley, and Frederick and Lady Charlotte Locker.

I have copied out for press the " Epilogue to the Idylls " he has just written : " O loyal to the royal in thyself." A. burnt with indignation and shame at one eminent statesman saying to him, " Would to God Canada would go ! "

There was the usual Christmas letter from Edward Fitz-gerald :

WOODBRIDGE, *Dec.* 30*th*, 1872.

To make amends for the audacious remarks I made, I trans-scribe what poor Savile Morton wrote to me.

"When I look into Alfred's poems, I am astonished at the size of the words and the thoughts. No man clothes an idea in language at once so apt, and so full of strength, music and dignity. Were a poet to be judged by single lines, I am not sure he would not deserve the first place among them all. How many of the lines of 'Locksley Hall' are perfect as a Sicilian tetradrachm, which is esteem'd the most beautiful of all coins, so round, so chisell'd, and of the purest metal. Virgil's *Georgics* have also the same perfection. Like Alfred's his lines coil themselves up in the mind.

I am satisfied that Goethe wanted the burning impressions of Tennyson on the mind, which rap the poet into the lyrical heaven. He was rarely impassioned ; his nature was for most part a cold, classifying, methodical one, fitter for a philosopher than a poet."

There, Sir, is something for wife and son to read and *keep*, if they please. I lit upon it the other day in a MS vol. of quotations from Morton's letters, all so good that I have wanted to get someone to put them in some magazine, but, of course, no one will do as I ask.

Believe me hers and yours always,

E. F. G.

To my father's favourite Library Edition (1872), pub-lished by Strahan, were added during this year the two early sonnets " Alexander " and " The Bridesmaid," also " The Third of February, 1852," " Literary Squabbles," " On a Spiteful Letter," and the " Epilogue " to the

"Idylls of the King." He was asked to publish his vigorous answer to the attack made upon him by Lytton Bulwer (in 1847), but he would not comply with the request. " Let those wretched literary squabbles be forgotten." Spiteful attacks irritated him, for, as he would explain, " I hate spite: I am black-blooded like all the Tennysons. I remember all the malignant things said against me, but little of the praise." In his later years, when he was attacked, these moods of irritation were very rare, and he would quote his own lines:

> Surely, after all,
> The noblest answer unto such
> Is perfect stillness when they brawl.

CHAPTER V.

"THE IDYLLS OF THE KING," AND 'BALIN AND BALAN."

> For an ye heard a music, like enow
> They are building still, seeing the city is built
> To music, therefore never built at all,
> And therefore built for ever.

With the publication of "Gareth and Lynette" in 1872 my father thought that he had completed the cycle of the "Idylls"; but later he felt that some further introduction to "Merlin and Vivien" was necessary, and so wrote "Balin and Balan."

From his earliest years he had written out in prose various histories of Arthur. His prefatory MS note about the historical Arthur is: "He lived about 500 A.D. and defeated his enemies in a pitched battle in the Welsh kingdom of Strathclyde: and the earliest allusions to him are to be found in the Welsh bards of the seventh century. In the twelfth century Geoffrey of Monmouth collected the legends about him as an European conqueror in his *History of the Britons:* and translated them from Celtic into Latin[1]. *Morte d'Arthur* by Sir Thomas Malory was printed by Caxton in 1485." On Malory, and later, on Lady Charlotte Guest's translation of the *Mabinogion*, and on his own imagination, my father said

[1] Wace translated them into French and added the story of the Round Table.

that he chiefly founded his epic; he has made the old legends his own, restored the idealism, and infused into them a spirit of modern thought and an ethical significance, setting his characters in a rich and varied landscape; as indeed otherwise these archaic stories would not have appealed to the modern world at large.

In 1832 appeared the first of the Arthurian poems in the form of a lyric, " The Lady of Shalott" (another version of the story of Lancelot and Elaine), and this was followed in 1842 by the other lyrics, " Sir Launcelot and Queen Guinevere" (partly if not wholly written in 1830), and " Sir Galahad."

The 1842 volume also contained the " Morte d'Arthur," which now forms part of the " Passing of Arthur."

The earliest fragment of an epic that I can find among my father's MSS in my possession was probably written about 1833, and is a sketch in prose. I give it as it stands.

King Arthur.

On the latest limit of the West in the land of Lyonnesse, where, save the rocky Isles of Scilly, all is now wild sea, rose the sacred Mount of Camelot. It rose from the deeps with gardens and bowers and palaces, and at the top of the Mount was King Arthur's hall, and the holy Minster with the Cross of gold. Here dwelt the King in glory apart, while the Saxons whom he had overthrown in twelve battles ravaged the land, and ever came nearer and nearer.

The Mount was the most beautiful in the world, sometimes green and fresh in the beam of morning, sometimes all one splendour, folded in the golden mists of the West. But all underneath it was hollow, and the mountain trembled, when the seas rushed bellowing through the porphyry caves; and there ran a prophecy that the mountain and the city on some wild morning would topple into the abyss and be no more.

It was night. The King sat in his Hall. Beside him sat the sumptuous Guinevere and about him were all his lords and knights of the Table Round. There they feasted, and when the feast was over the Bards sang to the King's glory.

———

The following memorandum was presented by my father to Mr Knowles at Aldworth on October 1, 1869, who told him that it was between thirty and forty years old. It was probably written at the same time as the fragment which I have just quoted. However the allegorical drift here marked out was fundamentally changed in the later scheme of the "Idylls."

K. A.   Religious Faith.

King Arthur's three Guineveres.

The Lady of the Lake.

Two Guineveres. ye first prim. Christianity. 2^d Roman Catholicism. ye first is put away and dwells apart. 2^d Guinevere flies. Arthur takes to the first again but finds her changed by lapse of Time.

Modred, the sceptical understanding. He pulls Guinevere, Arthur's latest wife, from the throne.

Merlin Emrys, the enchanter. Science. Marries his daughter to Modred.

Excalibur, war.

The sea, the people.   ⎱ the S. are a sea-people
The Saxons, the people. ⎰ and it is theirs and a
                              type of them.

The Round Table, liberal institutions.

Battle of Camlan.

2^d Guinevere with the enchanted book and cup.

———

Before 1840 it is evident that my father wavered between casting the Arthurian legends into the form of an epic or into that of a musical masque; for in one of his 1833–1840 MS books there is the following first rough draft of a scenario, into which the Lancelot and Elaine scenes were afterwards introduced.

First Act.

Sir Mordred and his party. Mordred inveighs against the King and the Round Table. The knights, and the quest. Mordred scoffs at the Ladies of the Lake, doubts whether they are supernatural beings, etc. Mordred's cringing interview with Guinevere. Mordred and the Lady of the Lake. Arthur lands in Albyn.

Second Act.

Lancelot's embassy and Guinevere. The Lady of the Lake meets Arthur and endeavours to persuade him not to fight with Sir Mordred. Arthur will not be moved from his purpose. Lamentation of the Lady of the Lake. Elaine. Marriage of Arthur.

Third Act.

Oak tomb of Merlin. The song of Nimue. Sir Mordred comes to consult Merlin. Coming away meets Arthur. Their fierce dialogue. Arthur consults Sir L. and Sir Bedivere. Arthur weeps over Merlin and is reproved by Nimue, who inveighs against Merlin. Arthur asks Merlin the issue of the battle. Merlin will not enlighten him. Nimue requests Arthur to question Merlin again. Merlin tells him he shall bear rule again, but that the Ladies of the Lake can return no more. Guinevere throws away the diamonds into the river. The Court and the dead Elaine.

Fourth Act.

Discovery by Mordred and Nimue of Lancelot and Guinevere. Arthur and Guinevere's meeting and parting.

Fifth Act.

The battle. Chorus of the Ladies of the Lake. The throwing away of Excalibur and departure of Arthur.

After this my father began to study the epical King Arthur in earnest. He had travelled in Wales, and meditated a tour in Cornwall. He thought, read, talked about King Arthur. He made a poem on Lancelot's quest of the San Graal; "in as good verse," he said, "as I ever wrote — no, I did not write, I made it in my head, and it has altogether slipt out of memory[1]." What he called "the greatest of all poetical subjects" perpetually haunted him. But it was not till 1855 that he determined upon the final shape of the poem, and not until 1859 that he published the first instalment, "Enid[2]," "Vivien," "Elaine," "Guinevere." In spite of the public applause he did not rush headlong into the other "Idylls of the King," although he had carried a more or less perfected scheme of them in his head over thirty years. For one thing, he did not consider that the time was ripe. In addition to this, he did not find himself in the proper mood to write them, and he never could work except at what his heart impelled him to do. — Then, however, he devoted himself with all his energies and with infinite enthusiasm to that work alone.

[1] Letter from my father to the Duke of Argyll, 1859.

[2] He found out that the "E" in "Enid" was pronounced short (as if it were spelt 'Ennid'), and so altered the phrase in the proofs "wedded Enid" to "married Enid."

Had married Enid, Yniol's only child.

He also gave some other reasons for pausing in the production of the "Idylls." "One," he wrote, "is because I could hardly light upon a finer close than that ghost-like passing away of the King" (in "Guinevere"), although the "Morte d'Arthur" was the natural close. The second was that he was not sure he could keep up to the same high level throughout the remaining "Idylls." "I have thought about it," he writes in 1862, "and arranged all the intervening 'Idylls,' but I dare not set to work for fear of a failure and time lost." The third was, to give it in his own words, "I doubt whether such a subject as the San Graal could be handled in these days without incurring a charge of irreverence. It would be too much like playing with sacred things." "The Holy Grail" however later on seemed to come suddenly, as if by a breath of inspiration; and that volume was given to the world in 1869, containing (see previous chapter) "The Coming of Arthur," "The Holy Grail," "Pelleas and Ettarre," and "The Passing of Arthur."

In 1871 "The Last Tournament" was privately printed, and then published in the *Contemporary Review:* republished with "Gareth and Lynette" in 1872. These with "Balin and Balan" (published in 1885) make up the "twelve books," — the number mentioned in the Introduction to the "Morte d'Arthur."

In 1870 an article on the "Idylls" by Dean Alford, the old college friend of Arthur Hallam and of my father, came out in the *Contemporary*[1]: an able letter also by J. T. Knowles appeared in the *Spectator*[2]. These reviews my father considered the best. But in later years he often said, "They have taken my hobby, and ridden

---

[1] See *Contemporary Review*, May, 1873.

[2] Mr Knowles writes to me: "He encouraged me to write a short paper, in the form of a letter to the *Spectator*, on the inner meaning of the whole poem, which I did, simply upon the lines he himself indicated. He often said, however, that an allegory should never be pressed too far."

it too hard, and have explained some things too
allegorically, although there is an allegorical or perhaps
rather a parabolic drift in the poem." "Of course
Camelot for instance, a city of shadowy palaces, is everywhere symbolic of the gradual growth of human beliefs
and institutions, and of the spiritual development of man.
Yet there is no single fact or incident in the ' Idylls,'
however seemingly mystical, which cannot be explained
as without any mystery or allegory whatever." The
Bishop of Ripon (Boyd Carpenter) once asked him
whether they were right who interpreted the three
Queens, who accompanied King Arthur on his last
voyage, as Faith, Hope and Charity. He answered:
" They are right, and they are not right. They mean
that and they do not. They are three of the noblest of
women. They are also those three Graces, but they are
much more. I hate to be tied down to say, '*This*
means *that*,' because the thought within the image is
much more than any one interpretation."

As for the many meanings of the poem my father
would affirm, " Poetry is like shot-silk with many
glancing colours. Every reader must find his own
interpretation according to his ability, and according
to his sympathy with the poet." The general drift
of the " Idylls " is clear enough. " The whole," he said,
" is the dream of man coming into practical life and
ruined by one sin. Birth is a mystery and death is
a mystery, and in the midst lies the tableland of life,
and its struggles and performances. It is not the history
of one man or of one generation but of a whole cycle of
generations." Dean Alford writes,

One noble design warms and unites the whole. In Arthur's
coming — his foundation of the Round Table — his struggles
and disappointments, and departure — we see the conflict continually maintained between the spirit and the flesh; and in the

pragmatical issue, we recognize the bearing down in history and in individual man of pure and lofty Christian purpose by the lusts of the flesh, by the corruptions of superstition, by human passions and selfishness.

Yet in spite of the ebbs and flows in the tide of human affairs, in spite of the temporary bearing down of the pure and lofty purpose, the author has carefully shadowed forth the spiritual progress and advance of the world, and has enshrined man's highest hopes in this new-old legend, crowning with a poet's prophetic vision the vague and disjointed dreams of a bygone age.

About the characterization Alford says: "As the pages are turned over...and as name after name again catches the eye, one is newly struck by the abundant and *dramatic* variety of the men and women moving to and fro! All, as before said, are *alive* and recognisable at a glance, at the sound as it were of their voice." This seems to me true. Lancelot the "noblest brother and the truest man," Tristram the bold and careless hunter, Galahad the pure, unearthly knight, Bors the blunt and honest, Bedivere the warm-hearted, all have been to me from boyhood living personalities, natural human characters, each with some dominant trait; and the allegorical (if alone accepted) would be to me the death-warrant of many an old friend.

" The vision of Arthur as I have drawn him," my father said, " had come upon me when, little more than a boy, I first lighted upon Malory[1] "; and it dwelt with him to the end; and we may perhaps say that now the completed poem, regarded as a whole, gives his innermost being more fully, though not more truly, than " In Memoriam." He felt himself justified in having always pictured Arthur as the ideal man by such passages as this from Joseph of Exeter: " The old world knows not his peer, nor will

[1] My father's MS.

the future show us his equal: he alone towers over other
kings, better than the past ones and greater than those
that are to be." So this from Alberic,

" Hic jacet Arturus, flos regum, gloria regni,
Quem probitas morum commendat laude perenni."

And this from the *Brut ab Arthur*, " In short God has
not made since Adam was, the man more perfect than
Arthur."

My father felt strongly that only under the inspiration
of ideals, and with his "sword bathed in heaven," can
a man combat the cynical indifference, the intellectual
selfishness, the sloth of will, the utilitarian materialism
of a transition age. " Poetry is truer than fact[1] " he
would say. Guided by the voice within, the Ideal Soul
looks out into the Infinite for the highest Ideal; and
finds it nowhere realized so mightily as in the Word
who "wrought With human hands the creed of creeds."
But for Arthur, as for everyone who believes in the
Word however interpreted, arises the question, " How
can I in my little life, in my small measure, and in my
limited sphere reflect this highest Ideal?" From the
answer to this question come the strength of life, its
beauty, and above all its helpfulness to the world.

On the other hand, having this vision of Arthur,
my father thought that perhaps he had not made the
real humanity of the King sufficiently clear in his
epilogue; so he inserted in 1891, as his last correction,
" Ideal manhood closed in real man," before the lines:

Rather than that gray king, whose name, a ghost,
Streams like a cloud, man-shaped, from mountain peak,
And cleaves to cairn and cromlech still.

---

[1] In this phrase he expressed what Matthew Arnold has said somewhat
differently, that " Poetry is the reality, philosophy the illusion."

Gladstone says [1]:

We know not where to look in history or in letters for a nobler or more overpowering conception of man as he might be, than in the Arthur of this volume. Wherever he appears, it is as the great pillar of the moral order, and the resplendent top of human excellence. But even he only reaches to his climax in these two really wonderful speeches (at the end of "Guinevere"). They will not bear mutilation: they must be read, and pondered, to be known.

To sum up: if Epic unity is looked for in the "Idylls," we find it not in the wrath of an Achilles, nor in the wanderings of an Ulysses, but in the unending war of humanity in all ages, — the world-wide war of Sense and Soul, typified in individuals, with the subtle interaction of character upon character, the central dominant figure being the pure, generous, tender, brave, human-hearted Arthur, — so that the links (with here and there symbolic accessories) which bind the "Idylls" into an artistic whole, are perhaps somewhat intricate [2].

My father would explain that the great resolve (to ennoble and spiritualize mankind) is kept so long as all work in obedience to the highest and holiest law within them: in those days when all the court is one Utopia:

The King will follow Christ, and we the King,
In whom High God has breathed a secret thing.

Thus in "Gareth [3]" the "joy of life in steepness overcome, And victories of ascent," lives in the eternal

---

[1] *Gleanings of Past Years*, Vol. II. p. 166.

[2] Edmund Lushington called the "Idylls of the King" "Epylls of the King." According to him they were little Epics (not Idylls) woven into an Epical unity, but my father disliked the sound of the word "Epylls."

[3] The epitome which follows is a summary of the chief points on which my father would dwell.

youth of goodness. But in the later "Idylls" the allowed sin not only poisons the spring of life in the sinner, but spreads its poison through the whole community. In some natures, even among those who would "rather die than doubt," it breeds suspicion and want of trust in God and man. Some loyal souls are wrought to madness against the world. Others, and some among the highest intellects, become the slaves of the evil which is at first half-disdained. Tender natures sink under the blight, that which is of the highest in them working their death. And in some, as faith declines, religion turns from practical goodness and holiness to superstition :

This madness has come on us for our sin.

These seek relief in selfish spiritual excitement, not remembering that man's duty is to forget self in the service of others, and to let visions come and go, and that so only will they see "The Holy Thing." In the Idyll of "Pelleas and Ettarre" selfishness has turned to open crime; it is "the breaking of the storm"; nevertheless Pelleas still honours his sacred vow to the King and spares the wrong-doers. Whereas in "The Last Tournament" the wrong-doer "suffers his doom," and "is cloven thro' the brain." We have here the deadly proof of the kinship of all wilful sin in murder following adultery in closest relation of cause and consequence, — the prelude of the final act of the tragedy which culminates in the temporary triumph of evil, the confusion of moral order, closing in the great "Battle of the West."

Throughout the poem runs my father's belief in one strong argument of hope, the marvellously transmuting power of repentance in all men, however great their sin :

As children learn, be thou
Wiser for falling.

The lost one found was greeted as in Heaven.

> Have ye look'd
> At Edyrn? Have ye seen how nobly changed?
> This work of his is great and wonderful,
> His very face with change of heart is changed.

So of Guinevere's repentance and the King's forgiveness: so too of the repentance of Lancelot, whose innocent worship of beauty had turned into the "guilty love," and of whom we are told that he died a "holy man." But repentance could not avert the doom of the Round Table. The "last dim weird battle" my father would quote as some of his best work, and would allow that it was a "presentment of human death" as well as of the overthrow of the "old order":

> And ev'n on Arthur fell
> Confusion, since he saw not whom he fought.
> For friend and foe were shadows in the mist,
> And friend slew friend not knowing whom he slew;

> *   *   *   *   *

ending with the lines:

> And rolling far along the gloomy shores
> The voice of days of old and days to be.

And he liked to read the last passage in "The Passing of Arthur," that one when Arthur himself finds the comfort of the faith with which he comforted Bedivere in his passing "from the great deep to the great deep"— for the individual man may seem to fail in his purpose, but his work cannot die—

> The old order changeth, yielding place to new,
> And God fulfils himself in many ways;

and that other, when Bedivere hears from the dawn, the East, whence have sprung all the great religions, the triumph of welcome given to him who has proved himself "more than conqueror":

> As from beyond the limit of the world,
> Like the last echo born of a great cry,
> Sounds, as if some fair city were one voice
> Around a king returning from his wars[1].

My father made this further manuscript note on another phase of the unity of the poem. "The Coming of Arthur is on the night of the New Year; when he is wedded 'the world is white with May'; on a summer night the vision of the Holy Grail appears; and the 'Last Tournament' is in the 'yellowing autumntide.' Guinevere flees thro' the mists of autumn, and Arthur's death takes place at midnight in mid-winter. The form of the 'Coming of Arthur' and of the 'Passing' is purposely more archaic than that of the other 'Idylls.'"

Concerning the love of Nature, shown especially in the metaphors and similes, Gladstone has a remarkable passage:

"Nowhere could we more opportunely than at this point call attention to Mr Tennyson's extraordinary felicity and force in the use of metaphor and simile.

This gift appears to have grown with his years, alike in abundance, truth and grace. As the showers descend from heaven to return to it in vapour, so Mr Tennyson's loving observation of Nature and his Muse seem to have had a compact of reciprocity well kept on both

---

[1] "Elaine," "Guinevere," "The Holy Grail," and "The Passing of Arthur," were his favourite "Idylls" for reading aloud: he would show that throughout each of the twelve "Idylls" his blank verse varied according to his subject. If he differentiated his style from that of any other poet, he would remark on his use of English — in preference to words derived from French and Latin. He revived many fine old words which had fallen into disuse: and I heard him regret that he had never employed the word "yarely."

sides. * * * Sometimes applying the metaphors of Art to Nature, he more frequently draws the materials of his analogies from her unexhausted book, and however often he may call for some new and beautiful vehicle of illustration, she seems never to withhold an answer. With regard to this particular and very critical gift, it seems to us that he may challenge comparison with almost any poet, either of ancient or modern times [1]."

Most explanations and analyses, although eagerly asked for by some readers, appeared to my father somewhat to dwarf and limit the life and scope of the great Arthurian tragedy; and therefore I will add no more, except what Jowett wrote in 1893: "Tennyson has made the Arthur legend a great revelation of human experience, and of the thoughts of many hearts."

Some passages of the "Idylls" were first written in prose: and I find among his manuscripts prose-sketches for part of "The Holy Grail," "Pelleas and Ettarre," "Gareth and Lynette," and for "Balin and Balan." I give as a specimen the last-mentioned, which he dictated to Mr Knowles, almost without a pause.

The "Dolorous Stroke."

There came a rumour to the King of two knights who sat beside a fountain near Camelot, and had challenged every knight that passed, and overthrown them. These things were told the King, and early one morning the spirit of his youth returned upon him, and he armed himself, and rode out till he came to the fountain, and there sat two knights, Balin and Balan;

---

[1] Gladstone's *Gleanings*, Vol. II. p. 159. Jowett wrote: "Tennyson may be said to have *always* lived in the presence of Nature."

and the fountain bubbled out among hart's-tongue and
lady-fern, and on one side of the fountain sat Balan and
on the other side sat Balin, and on the right of Balan
was a poplar-tree, and on the left of Balin was an
alder-tree, and the horse of Balan was tied to the poplar-
tree, and the horse of Balin to the alder-tree. And
Arthur said, " Fair sirs, what do ye here ? " And they
said, " We sit here for the sake of glory, and we be
better knights than any of those in Arthur's hall, and
that have we proven, for we have overthrown every
knight that came forth against us." And Arthur said,
" I am of this hall ; see, therefore, whether me also ye
can overthrow." And Arthur lightly smote either of
them down, and returned, and no man knew it.

Then that same day he sent for Balan and Balin, and
when they were brought before him he asked them,
saying, " Answer ye me this question : who be ye ? "
And Balin said, " I am Balin the savage, and that name
was given to me, seeing that once in mine anger I
smote with my gauntlet an unarmed man in thy hall and
slew him, whereupon thou didst banish me for three
years from thy court as one unworthy of being of thy
table But I yearn for the light of thy presence, and the
three years are nigh fulfilled, and I have repented me
of the deed that was unknightly ; and so it seemed to
me that if I sat by yon fountain and challenged and
overthrew every knight that passed thou wouldst receive
me again into thy favour. And this is my brother
Balan, not yet a knight of thine."

Which when the King heard and saw that he had
indeed repented him, he received him again and made
his brother Balan knight. And the new knight demanded
the first quest. And there came one into Arthur's hall,
and Balan rode away with him.

And as Balin moved about the court he marvelled at
the knightliness and the manhood of Sir Lancelot, and

at the worship he ever gave the Queen, and the honour
in which the Queen held him. Then he thought within
himself, "Surely it is this Queen's grace and nobleness
which have made him such a name among men, wherefore I too will worship the Queen an I may. And I
will forget my former violences and will live anew, and I
will pray the King to grant me to bear some cognisance
of the Queen in the stead of mine own shield."

And Arthur said, "Ask thou my Queen what token
she will give thee, and wear thou that." And he was
bold, and asked for the Queen's crown to wear upon his
shield, and that he would amend himself, under the lustre
thereof, of his old violence. So she turned her to the
King and smiled and asked him, and the King said,
"Yea, so that thereby he may be holpen to amend
himself." And Balin said, "The sight thereof shall
evermore be bit and re. to all my savage heats." Then
Balin ever hovered about Lancelot and the Queen, so
that he might espy in what things stood truest knight-
hood and courtesy toward women. Anon he came to
wonder how so great a tenderness of love might be
between two such as were not lover and damosel, but
ever thrust away from him such thought as a shadow
from his own old life. Yet he grew somewhat gloomy of
heart and presently took his shield and arms and rode
privily away to seek adventure.

So, many days, he traversed the thick forests, till he
came upon the ancient castle of King Pelles, and there
they said to him, "Why wearest thou this crown royal
on thy shield?" and he answered them, "Because the
noblest and the chastest of all ladies hath granted me to
wear it." So at the high banquet in the hall sat one Sir
Garlon, who likewise said, "Why wearest thou a Queen's
crown royal?" Unto him Sir Balin made the same
answer. Whereat Sir Garlon grimly smiled and said,
"Art thou so simple, and hast yet come but now, as thou

sayest, from the court? Hast thou not eyes, or at the least ears, and dost not know the thing that standeth (shame that groweth) between Lancelot and the Queen?" To which Sir Balin fiercely answered, "Yea surely, because I have both eyes and ears and because I have diligently used them to learn how he, the greatest of all knights, doth gain his valour from the noblest of all ladies, I know that such a thing as this thou sayest is but a foul thing and a felon's talk." But none the less Sir Garlon's talk made him full heavy and gloomy of heart, so that he wandered to and fro among the churls, and there heard marvellous tales. For they told him that Sir Garlon rode invisible and had wounded unto death many strong and good knights, striking them through the back, and they warned him to beware of Sir Garlon.

Also they told him how that King Pelles was the true descendant of Joseph of Arimathea, and also how in hidden chambers of the castle lay wondrous treasures from the days of our Lord Christ—even the spear which ever bled since Longus smote our Lord withal, and many more such marvels, till Sir Balin doubted him whether he could believe aught that they told him of Sir Garlon or aught else. But on the morrow when Sir Garlon met him by the Castle walls and mocked him, saying, "Still then thou wearest that shameful token — that crown scandalous," then did Sir Balin's old nature break through its new crust, and he smote him on the helmet with his sword. But though he overthrew and left him lying, yet his sword was broken into diverse pieces, so that he cast the handle from him, and ran hastily to find some other weapon. For by now he saw men running upon him from the castle, and thought but to flee and to fight for his life. And as he fled he saw within a loophole window where a stack of spears lay piled, and burst the door and caught the tallest of them all, and, crying to his war-horse, leaped upon him and departed. And as he went he heard the voice of King Pelles to his knights: "Stay, stay him: he defileth holy things beyond his wit to know of." But being hot and fleet with madness he plunged far into the woods, and drew no rein until his horse was nigh to dying. Then did he spy his golden crown and bemoaned himself, saying, "Alas that I should so soon turn as a dog to his vomit! Alas! for now were I but wounded with the bleeding spear itself, and of a wound that should for ever bleed, I could be none too wounded for my deserts."

So there as he lay bitter of heart he turned the shield away from him, not bearing to look upon it, and hung it to a bough hard by, and there it glistened in the sun the while he turned the other way and raged, and felt that he would dwell a savage man for evermore within the woods.

But anon came through the woods a damsel riding on a palfrey, and but a single squire attending. And when she saw the shield she stayed her horse and called her squire to search for him who owned it, for she marvelled to see Queen Guinevere's crown thereon.

Then when she had found Sir Balin she demanded straightway that he should help her through the woods, for that she was journeying to King Mark of Cornwall, and her good knight had met some misadventure and had left her with none but this squire. "And I know thee for a worshipful man and one from Arthur's hall, for I see by this cognisance that thou art from the court." Then did Sir Balin redden and say, "Ask me not of it, for I have shamed it. Alas! that so great a Queen's name, which high Sir Lancelot hath lifted up, and been lifted up by, should through me and my villainy come to disgrace!" Thereon the damsel, looking keenly at him, laughed, and when he asked her why, laughed long and loud, and cried that little shame could he do to the Queen or Lancelot either which they had not themselves already done themselves.

And when he stood as Lot's wife stood, salt-petrified, and stared at her, she cried again, " Sir Knight, ye need not gaze thus at me as if I were a reder of fables and a teller of false tales. Now let me tell thee how I saw myself Sir Lancelot and the Queen within a bower at Camelot but twelve months since and heard her say, ' O sir, my lord Sir Lancelot, for thou indeed art my true lord, and none other save by the law.' "

But when he heard her thus, his evil spirit leapt upon him and tare him and drove him mad, and then he cried with a great yell, and dragged the shield from off the tree, and then and there he cast it to the ground, drave his mailed foot through the midst of it, and split the royal crown in twain, and cast the two halves far from him among the long weeds of the wood. Then at that cry came Balan riding through the forest, and when he saw the broken shield and crown lie on the earth he spurred his horse and said, " Sir Knight, keep well thyself, for here is one shall overthrow thee for the despite thou hast done the Queen!" At that Sir Balin, for he knew not that it was Sir Balan, seeing that his newly granted shield had yet no bearing, called to the squire to lend him his shield, and, catching up the spear he gat from Pelles' castle, ran his horse fiercely to meet Sir Balan. And so sore was their onset that either overthrew the other to the earth; but Balin's spear smote through Sir Balan's shield and made the first mark it had ever borne, and through the rent it pierced to Balan's side and thrust him through with deadly wounds, wherefrom the blood streamed and could not be stayed until he fainted with the loss of blood; and Balin's horse rolled on him as he fell, and wounded him so sorely that he swooned with agony.

But when they thus lay, the damsel and her squire

unlaced their helms and gave them air, and presently
when they came to themselves they gazed as men gone
newly wild upon each other, and with a mighty cry they
either swooned away again, and so lay swooning for
an hour. Then did the damsel wait and watch to see
how this might end, and withdrew herself behind the
leaves.

Anon Sir Balin opened first his eyes, and then with
groanings which he could not hide for pain he slowly
crawled to whither his brother lay. And then did he put
from off his brother's face his hair, and leaned and kissed
him, and left his face beblooded from his lips, for by
now his life began to flow away from his hidden inner
wounds.

Then presently thereafter Balan woke up also from
his swoon, and when he saw his brother so hang over
him he flung his arm about his neck and drew his face
again down to him and said lowly in his ear, "Alas, alas,
mine own dear brother, that I should thus have given
thee thy death! But wherefore hadst thou no shield, and
wherefore was it rent asunder and defiled? O brother!
for it grieveth me more than death to see this thing."
Then did Sir Balin tell him all that Sir Garlon and afterwards the damsel had told him of the Queen, and when
Sir Balan heard it he moaned greatly and cried out that
Garlon was a felon knight, well known about those
marches for his evil deeds and lies, and the damsel he
well believed, if she were going to King Mark, was as
bad as he. "Perchance Sir Garlon," said he, "was the
very knight she said had left her: and would I could find
her or her squire," he said, "for even dead man as I am
I fain would now abolish her, lest she work more evil
than this dolorous stroke she hath caused betwixt us
two."

When the damsel heard them thus speak, she feared
for her life lest the wounded knight might be recovered

and might find her, and stealthily she sped away to King
Mark and after to Arthur's court, and there she told how
she had overheard from Knights of Arthur's Table scandal
beyond all disproof about Sir Lancelot and the Queen.
And thus in truth the Dolorous Stroke was struck, which
first shook to its base the stately order of the Table
Round.

Then when the damsel left them came the Lady of
the Lake and found Sir Balin and Sir Balan at their last
breaths, and caused them to be solemnly buried, and
sang above them an high song.

CHAPTER VI.

MY MOTHER'S JOURNAL, AND LETTERS 1873-74.

The Revenge, Connaught, Dr Tennyson in Russia,
Macugnaga, London, Cambridge

On March 6th my father went to Windsor, in obedience to a command from the Queen; and he wrote to my mother: "The visit to Windsor went off very well, and we were first ushered into a long corridor in the Castle. There the Queen came, and was very kindly, asking after all at home, pitying Lady Simeon (for the loss of Sir John). We talked too of Romanism and Protestantism. Then I walked with the Dean and Lady Augusta to Frogmore, and pottered about till the Queen and Princess Beatrice arrived. The Queen took me into the building and explained everything."

On March 9th he met Mr Markham (now Sir Clements Markham), the secretary of the Hakluyt Society, who had undertaken to give him all information about Sir Richard Grenville; and he wrote to my mother: "Sir Richard Grenville in one ship, 'the Revenge,' fought fifty-three Spanish ships of the line for fifteen hours: a tremendous story, out-rivalling Agincourt."

The line, "At Florés in the Azorés Sir Richard Grenville lay," was on my father's desk for years, but he finished the ballad at last all at once in a day or two.

When he returned from London, he read the account of Sir Richard Grenville in Froude. A telegram arrived saying that the Dean was commanded by the Queen to ask whether, if some honour were offered to A., it would be acceptable. A. wrote that he did not himself care for any honour except as a symbol of the Queen's kindness. The old life had been too good to desire any change even in outward things.

March 17th. Professor Tyndall and Mr Huxley called. Mr Huxley seemed to be universal in his interest and to have keen enjoyment of life. He spoke of "In Memoriam [1]." Professor Tyndall and Dr (now Sir Joseph) Hooker came to tea. Lord Dufferin's letter to A., telling of the happy effect that his words about the "True North" in the Epilogue to the "Idylls" have had in Canada, pleased him. It is a blessing to think that they may have done good, and helped somewhat to a more perfect union of England with her Colonies. —

OTTAWA, *Feb. 25th*, 1873.

MY DEAR MR TENNYSON,

I cannot help writing a line to thank you on behalf of the generous and loyal people whose government I am now administering, for the spirited denunciation with which you have branded those who are seeking to dissolve the Empire, and to alienate and disgust the inhabitants of this most powerful and prosperous colony. Since arriving here I have had ample opportunity of becoming acquainted with the intimate convictions of the Canadians upon this subject, and with scarcely an individual exception, I find they cling with fanatical tenacity to their birthright as Englishmen, and to their hereditary association in the past and future glories of the mother country. Though for two or three generations his family may have been established in this country, and he himself has never crossed the Atlantic, a Canadian seldom fails to allude to England as "Home." They take the liveliest interest in her welfare, and entertain the strongest personal feeling of affection for their Sovereign.

Moreover it must be remembered that these sentiments are perfectly unselfish and disinterested. Not a penny of British money is spent in the country, and some imagine their purely material interests might be benefited by annexation to the States. On the other hand the assertion that their connection with Great Britain weakens their self-confidence or damps the ardour of Canadian Nationality is a pure invention. Amongst

---

[1] "He (Huxley) once spoke strongly of the insight into scientific method shown in Tennyson's 'In Memoriam.'" "Thomas Henry Huxley," by Wilfrid Ward, *Nineteenth Century*, August, 1896.

no people have I ever met more contentment with their general condition, a more legitimate pride in all those characteristics which constitute their nationality, or a firmer faith in the destinies in store for them. Your noble words have struck responsive fire from every heart; they have been published in every newspaper, and have been completely effectual to heal the wounds occasioned by the senseless language of the *Times*.

I hope you will forgive me for thus troubling you, but you have invariably shown me so much kindness and indulgence, that I cannot resist my inclination to let you know how deeply all in this " True North " feel indebted to you.

Yours sincerely, DUFFERIN.

To Lord Dufferin.

February, 1873.

MY DEAR LORD DUFFERIN,

Since you have so near an interest in " that true North," I thought it might not displease you to receive from myself my lines to the Queen. I send therefore the two volumes of the " Idylls " containing them, with the assurance of the great interest we take in your work there, and our best wishes that it may prosper, and you and yours also.

Believe me, yours ever,

A. TENNYSON.

From Lord Dufferin.

CANADA, *March 3rd*, 1873.

MY DEAR MR TENNYSON,

I cannot say how inexpressibly delighted I have been by the arrival of your two noble volumes, or how deeply I feel your kindness in having remembered me. I am all the more pleased, as by the previous mail I had already written to tell you of the happy effect produced in Canada by the glorious lines with which the " Idylls of the King " conclude. Canada may well be proud that her loyal aspirations should be thus imperishably recorded in the greatest poem of this generation.

Ever yours sincerely and gratefully, DUFFERIN.

March 25th. This day brought the kindest of letters from Mr Gladstone, offering a baronetcy from the Queen. "Nothing can be kinder," wrote A., "than your letter, and I shall always treasure it; but will you allow me to meditate your proposal for a day or two before returning a definite answer?" The following reply was subsequently sent:

March 30th.

My dear Gladstone,

      I do not like to trouble you about my own personal matters in the midst of your absorbing public work; but not only on account of my feeling for yourself, but also for the sake of that memory [1] which we share, I speak frankly to you when I say that I had rather we should remain plain Mr and Mrs, and that, if it were possible, the title should first be assumed by our son at any age it may be thought right to fix upon: but like enough this is against all precedent, and could not be managed: and on no account would I have suggested it, were there the least chance of the Queen's construing it into a slight of the proffered honour. I hope that I have too much of the old-world loyalty left in me not to wear my lady's favours against all comers, should you think that it would be more agreeable to Her Majesty that I should do so. * * *

Believe me yours ever, A. Tennyson.

Mr Gladstone answered that to give Hallam a baronetcy during his father's lifetime would be an innovation, but that the innovation *might be* attempted.

April 16th. A. again wrote to Mr Gladstone:

Accept my thanks for having made clear my wish and my motives to the Queen. Now that I have Her Majesty's sanction as well as your own, I am not likely to change my mind on the subject. Hallam, to whom we have spoken regarding it since my last, would not like

---

[1] Arthur Hallam was the friend of both.

to wear the honour during my lifetime. For the rest I leave myself in your hands, being quite sure that you will do what is best and when best. You have much good work, I trust, to accomplish before the time of your retirement from office.

With kindest regards from my wife and myself,

I am yours ever, A. TENNYSON.

May 8th.   Mr Browning's *Red Cotton Nightcap Country* came from himself.

Among the lines which my father liked were

" Palatial gloomy chambers for parade,
And passage lengths of lost significance,"

and he praised the simile about the man with his dead comrade in the lighthouse. He wrote to Mr Browning:

FARRINGFORD, FRESHWATER,
ISLE OF WIGHT, *May 8th*, 1873.

MY DEAR R. B.,

My wife has just cut the leaves. I have yet again to thank you, and feel rather ashamed that I have nothing of my own to send you back, but your Muse is prolific as Hecuba, and mine by the side of her, an old barren cow.

Yours ever, A. T.

June 10th.   The Bishop of Winchester (Wilberforce), Bishop of Albany and others. Six Americans tramped up the drive and rang at the door-bell, and asked to see A. He did not feel up to entertaining six strange Americans, so rushed up the tower followed by the two bishops — but eventually asked the Bishop of Winchester to go down and receive them, saying, " A live Bishop will be much more appreciated than a Poet Laureate." So down the Bishop went from the study, and made himself most agreeable, and they departed charmed. Before, he seemed to be only brilliant, but to-day, he seemed more like an old friend, full of strength, earnestness, and wide knowledge.

A. repeated this anecdote of his once being driven by "the King of Connaught."

"The waiter at the inn told me that there was a stream that leapt down Hungry Head clear for several hundred feet. I accordingly ordered out a car, and before I had gone far, the carman began to talk to me, and pulled out a great seal from his pocket and said, 'Do you know those arms, your honour?' I answered, 'No,' and he said, 'These are the MacCarthy More, and the Sullivan! great names, your honour!' I assented, and he continued, 'If I had my rights I should be king of Connaught.' I daresay that he would be. We drove on, and it began to rain in cataracts, and we got drenched, and went into an Irish shanty where there were a woman and her little son. The king dried my stockings and went to sleep on a bench. The woman drew me up a stool to the turf fire with the courtly air of a queen. While he was asleep, I heard the mother say to the boy 'Johnny' several times (she didn't speak a word of English). The king awoke, and, as we were going out, I said 'Johnny,' and the little boy with a protuberant paunch (protuberant I suppose from eating potatoes) ran forward, and I gave him a sixpence. The woman, with her black hair over her shoulders, and her eyes streaming with tears, passionately closed her hands over the boy's hand in which was the sixpence. When the king and I climbed into the car, I, in my stupid Saxon way, thinking it was the beggarly sixpence that had made the woman grateful, expressed my astonishment at such gratitude. He said, 'It was not the sixpence, your honour, it was the stranger's gift.' We drove on to the waterfall. It was, as I expected, a poor affair, and trickled down the side of the mountain, tho' in full flood after rain it might have leapt some hundred feet or so clear of the rock. When we returned to the inn, the waiter said to the king, who was a jolly good fellow, 'Have you been telling the gentleman of your great blood?' and he drew himself up, answering, 'The gentleman is a gentleman, every inch of him.'"

Then A. told the thrilling story of his father's stay in Russia: how, as a very young man, he was dining with our English Minister, Lord St Helens, at St Petersburg, when he said, across a Russian, to Lord St Helens, "It is perfectly well-known in England who murdered the Emperor Paul: it was

Count So and So." Whereat a dead silence fell on the company. After dinner Lord St Helens called Dr Tennyson aside and said, " Ride for your life from this city : the man across whom you were speaking to me was the Count So and So, whom you accused of murdering the Emperor Paul." Dr Tennyson took horse and rode for weeks and weeks through Russia, till he came to the Crimea where he fell ill. He became delirious, and remembered the wild country-people dancing round his bed with magical incantations. Once in every three months an English courier passed through this village where he lay ill, and as he passed through the village blew a horn. It all depended on Dr Tennyson's hearing this horn whether he could escape from Russia, for he had no money. In his delirium he would perpetually start up agonized lest he had missed it. At last the courier came, the horn was blown and he heard the sound, and applied to the courier to take him. The courier agreed, and Dr Tennyson journeyed with him. He was a drunken fellow and dropt all his despatches on the road. Dr Tennyson picked them up, but did not say that he had done so. The courier was in despair, and at last Dr Tennyson gave them to him, with a warning that he must not be drunken in future. At one frontier town the sentries had barred the gates, because it was late night. The courier, not to be daunted, shouted out " Le duc de York." An immediate unbarring ensued, and the sentinels all sprang to attention, and saluted him with deference. So, after less drunkenness on the part of the courier, and many adventures, they managed to reach England.

September. A. and Hallam went off to Pontresina, thence to the Italian lakes, Val Sesia, and Val d' Anzasca. Hallam writes :

Sept. 4th. Val d' Anzasca. All to-day Monte Rosa has been wrapped in cloud, except at 5 o'clock this morning when we had a beautiful view. Above fold on fold of mountain, covered with walnuts and vines, rose the pinnacles of Monte Rosa, flushed with the morning sun, and slowly becoming bright gold. He has begun a poem, 'The Voice and the Peak[1],' describing the torrent in this valley,

> Green-rushing from the rosy thrones of dawn.

[1] Included, with "England and America," in the Cabinet Edition, 1873–74.

The Val d' Anzasca is, he thinks, *the grandest valley that he has seen in the Alps*. He is in good spirits and quoting the *Cinque Maggio* of Manzoni.

Sept. 5*th.*   Ponte Grande.   Last night saw the mountains silvered with moonlight over black pines.   This morning walked back from Macugnaga, going to Domo d' Ossola.

Bauer-Sierre.   Returned through Domo d' Ossola over the Simplon.   The coming over was a great disappointment.   Thick mist the whole of the way except the first half-hour when we started from the Simplon Inn.   He was full of these lines on the Simplon by Wordsworth :

> ' The immeasurable height
> Of woods decaying, never to be decayed,
> The stationary blast of waterfalls,
> And in the narrow rent, at every turn,
> Winds thwarting winds bewildered and forlorn.'

During the evening we consoled ourselves by reading *Lélia* by George Sand : whose *Consuelo* and *Petite Fadette* were favourites of his.   Nothing was to be heard at night thro' the mist but the shrill ticking of a church clock, which sounded, he said, ' in the thick darkness like the cry of a dying man.'   He says he once lived near a stable clock which he never *heard* but which he *felt*, most ghostlywise, through the boards.

Sept. 10*th.*   Arrived at Neufchâtel : deep-coloured rainbow over the lake.   He has been telling me that ' the only cheerful thing he ever saw in going home by coach over the flats from Cambridge to Lincolnshire was the gray line of dawn over Whittlesea mere.'   Every foreigner seems to talk of nothing else but the Tichborne trial."

From Neufchâtel they returned straight home.

Seamore Place, London.

Early in November A. received the following letter from a stranger (who did not sign his name).   The letter and the packet of flowers sent with it greatly touched him.

CHATHAM, U. S. AMERICA,
25*th October*, 1873.

MY DEAR SIR,

These "nurslings" of our fall and summer skies which, thinking of you, I plucked, I send as messengers of the love and respect and affection, nay the gratitude, which I bear to one whom God has so greatly blessed with such good gifts, with so true an eye, so exquisite an ear for all sights and sounds of this our beautiful and mysterious world.

Could I express in words all that I owe to you, all those pleasures and delights of the past, which seem so interwoven with words and scenes and thoughts of your making, I might seem almost untruthful, or at least prone to exaggeration. Yet I can say in all truth that the purest and truest pleasures of my life have been derived from you.

The times have been very bitter to most of us, and we still suffer from the results of our disastrous conflict, and the terrible pressure, but we think that we are just beginning to see the dawn, or we hope so at any rate. Going to my daily work this fall through the pine lands, all purple and golden, and looking too over "the happy autumn fields" with their rich harvest, I seemed to feel happier than for many a year since that bitter time from which we date so many evils.

I thought of that delightful time still further back, old college times, those famous discussions in which you too seemed to take a part: while round us "All the thickets rang to many a flute of Arcady."

Many of those companions and friends sleep their last sleep in the far West, but some are left.

I thought to myself (but it may be a weak thought, born of sentiment or weakness) that these words from a far-off land, these humble flowers from the same, might please you. Certainly it is a thought of pleasure to me that your eye will rest on them, mayhap but for a moment, that your hand may touch them. That all things good may attend you and yours now and for all time, is my hearty prayer.

I am, with respect and gratitude,

Your very obliged

* * *

Oct. 28th. London. 4 Seamore Place. We took up our abode at Seamore Place in the house we shared with Lady Franklin, and A. likes it the best of any house we have had in London. He is reading *The Mystery of Matter* by Hinton who is an aurist by profession, and who on giving a prescription one day wrote (so absorbed was he in the mysteries of the universe), " To be rubbed round the world night and morning."

Nov. 8th. A. and the boys went with Annie Thackeray to Irving's *Richelieu*.

He did not care for *Richelieu*, but one thing he remembered, after the play was over, as good :

"Ye safe and formal men
Who write the deeds and with unfeverish hand
Weigh in nice scales the motives of the great."

He described to Irving his conception of the manner in which " Hamlet " ought to be acted.

Mrs Thackeray Ritchie wrote of a similar evening in 1874 after *Hamlet*:

The play was over, and we ourselves seemed a part of it still ; here were the players, and our own prince poet, in that familiar simple voice we all know, explaining the art, going straight to the point in his own downright fashion, criticising with delicate appreciation, by the irresistible force of truth and true instinct carrying all before him. " You are a good actor lost," one of them, the real actors, said to him, laughing as he spoke.

The parts of Irving's *Hamlet* which my father thought best were the dreamy and poetical sides, and when he showed the " method in his madness as well, as the madness in his method." To Irving he said, " *Hamlet* is a many-faceted gem, and you have given more facets than anyone I have seen."

He was daily at Mr Woolner's studio because of the new bust [1].

Nov. 15*th.* A. went to Cambridge.

He had lunches and dinners, and walks with Trinity fellows and undergraduates, and was as happy as a boy.

He was full of reminiscences too: remarking, for instance, how he had idealized Nevile's Court in "The Princess": and how the "six hundred maidens clad in purest white" was taken from the striking memory of the white-surpliced undergraduates in Trinity Chapel; and he described the effect of the Trinity organ upon him:

> While the great organ almost burst his pipes,
> Groaning for power, and rolling thro' the court
> A long melodious thunder to the sound
> Of solemn psalms, and silver litanies.

He said: " I see a ghost of a friend in every corner of the old place."

On his return Mr Furnivall called about the Shakespeare Society, which he wishes to found, and to make A. president. This honour he has declined, hating to push himself forward as a learned Shakespearian, but he has agreed to join the Society.

The boys walked with him to call on Mr Carlyle, who thought that we were to be ruined by a "government of party, headed by a gentleman Jew who sits at the top of chaos." However he preferred Disraeli to Gladstone. Mr Carlyle called upon me, and was very interesting and touching about old days, and was afraid of tiring me by over-talking.

Edward Fitzgerald wrote:

My dear Alfred,

I write my yearly letter to yourself this time, because I have a word to say about " Gareth " which your publisher sent me as "from the author." I don't think it is mere perversity

---

[1] In 1894 the people of Freshwater generously wished to buy this bust (which represented my father with his beard) and to place it in their church, but Mrs Woolner reserved it for some public gallery.

that makes me like it better than all its predecessors, save and
except (of course) the old "Morte." The subject, the young
knight who can endure and conquer, interests me more than all
the heroines of the 1st volume. I do not know if I admire
more *separate* passages in this "Idyll" than in the others; for I
have admired *many* in *all*. But I do admire several here very
much, as

> The journey to Camelot, pp. 13–14,
> All Gareth's vassalage, 31–34,
> Departure with Lynette, 42,
> Sitting at table with the Barons, 54,
> Phantom of past life, 71,

and many other passages and expressions "quæ nunc perscribere
longum est." I doubt that Mrs A. T. will have to let me know
how you all of you are. I suppose got back to your Island
by this time. Your eldest boy at Cambridge too! I won't
write any more in mercy to your eyes as well as mine. But I
am

> Yours and wife's always devotedly,

> E. F. G.

December. A. went with Hallam to see Lady Martin (Helen
Faucit) in *As You Like It.* Her 'Rosalind,' he felt, had great
distinction. He held that one of the most exquisite things for
simplicity and eloquence in Shakespeare is Rosalind's saying to
Orlando,

> "Sir, you have wrestled well
> And overthrown more than your enemies."

Dec. 19*th*. Mr Browning dined with us. He was very
affectionate and delightful. It was a great pleasure to hear
Mr Browning's words — that he had not had so happy a time
for a long while as since we have been in town.

We have been troubled again by publishing affairs. It is a
pity that these splitting up of partnerships drive A. from one
publisher to another. Let us hope however that he has found a
steadfast publisher in Mr King, with whom he may stay to the
end. That he is most liberal there can be no doubt.

A. wrote to Mr Gladstone about Mr Furnivall's Shakespeare
Society: "As to Furnivall I believe him to be a hard-working,

painstaking, conscientious man....I have refused the Presidency and even a Vice-Presidency of the Shakespeare Society. I am now merely a subscriber, though I have promised, if need be, to give them a donation. I think you cannot do better than subscribe..."

1874.

My mother's journal. — "Welcome to Alexandrovna," "Queen Mary," Pyrenees, Letters and Recollections.

"Old Brooks" (W. H. Brookfield), A.'s old and true friend, has passed away. A. wrote to Mrs Brookfield:

FARRINGFORD, FRESHWATER,
ISLE OF WIGHT, *Jan.* 18*th*, 1874.

MY DEAR JANE,

You will believe that I feel with you, and that I feel that the *dead* lives whatever the pseudo-savants say, and so

May God bless you and yours.

A. T.

After Mr Gladstone had announced the dissolution of Parliament at Greenwich, A. wrote to him:

Feb. 17*th*, 1874.

MY DEAR GLADSTONE,

We have, I need not say, been pained and disgusted at much that has occurred within the last few days; but action and reaction are the law of the world, for which one sometimes hates the world, tho' such a law is, I believe, in the main wholesome for the common weal. Care not, you have done great work, and if even now you rested, your name would be read in one of the fairest pages of English history. I say this, however on some points of policy we may have differed. * * *

Yours ever, A. TENNYSON.

And on March 6th to Lord Houghton, on the death of Lady Houghton:

MY DEAR HOUGHTON,

I was the other day present at a funeral here, and one of the chief mourners reached me her hand silently almost over the grave, and I as silently gave her mine. No words were possible; and this little note, that can really do nothing to help you in your sorrow, is just such a reaching of the hand to you, my old college comrade of more than forty years standing, to show you that I think of you. You have your children; she must live to you more or less in them, and to you and others in the memory and result of her good and charitable life: and I may say that I think I can see as far as one can see in this twilight, that the nobler nature does not pass from its individuality when it passes out of this one life. If you could believe as much, it would be a comfort to you, and perhaps you do. I did not intend to say even so much as this, and will say no more, only that

I am yours affectionately,

A. TENNYSON

March 11*th*. I persuaded A. to go to town to see to-morrow's procession (the Duke and Duchess of Edinburgh entering London after their marriage), he having never seen London in festival. We had had telegrams from Windsor saying that they all liked the "Welcome to Alexandrovna[1]." A. talked of making a play of "Lady Jane Grey."

[A. wrote: *March* 12*th*. Here it began to snow early in the morning and was snowing when we started at 10 o'clock for Regent Street, where K. had hired seats for the show; for-tunately the snow just ceased falling a little before the Queen passed. How she and the Princess did shake their heads incessantly right and left, as if they had necks of india-rubber,

---

[1] Printed in the *Times*, March 7th, 1874, and on separate sheets.

and that for miles. The people were very enthusiastic, but the lack of sunshine took away all the splendour from the house-decorations and the helmets. The Princess looked large and imperial, I thought. People say that the accent is on the antepenultimate, Alexándrovna. If so, it rather spoils my chorus.

March 17*th*. Sir Samuel and Lady Baker, Dr Quain, and Mr Leland (the American author of the *Breitmann Ballads*, very humorous) came to dinner. Lady Baker is plump and pretty, and does not look as if she had gone thro' all that in Africa among the savages. I have not called anywhere as yet, and I think I may come home at the end of the week. There is another party to-day here and I wish there was not, and another to-morrow at Knowles' and I wish there was not.

March 21*st*. Dined at Lady Franklin's and met Stanley, the Livingstone finder.]

March 28*th*. Review of the Ashantee troops by the Queen at Windsor. We are glad that the Government have taken strenuous steps to relieve the famine in Bengal. A. returned: another photograph of him by Mayall.

April 10*th*. Professor Tyndall, and the Claud Hamiltons, and Sir John Lubbock called. Lately we have been reading Holinshed and Froude's *Mary*, for A. has been thinking about a play of "Queen Mary," and has sketched two or three scenes. For a time he had thought of "William the Silent[1]," but he said that our own history was so great, and that he liked English subjects best, and knew most about them, and that consequently he should do "Queen Mary."

Mr K— wrote that he wanted A. to do a play of "The Armada," or rather to make a sort of panoramic view of Edward's, Mary's and Elizabeth's reigns, but that would be impracticable[2].

---

[1] He had been reading Motley's *Dutch Republic*.

[2] He wrote a few lines of a play on "Elizabeth," in which he had imagined a great Armada scene.

Popularity (an unpublished impromptu, made about this time).

Popular, Popular, Unpopular!
" You're no Poet"— the critics cried!
" Why?" said the Poet. " You're unpopular!"
Then they cried at the turn of the tide —
" You're no Poet!"   " Why?"—" You're popular!"
Pop-gun, Popular and Unpopular!

Tour in France.

In the summer of this year we went to Paris and St Germain. When in Paris, A. saw some plays at the Théâtre Français, and especially admired Got, the Coquelins, and Mdlle Reichemberg. [From Mdlle Reichemberg in *L'École des Femmes* he took the idea of his " Margery" in " Becket." He looked upon Molière's plays as great works of art, and said, " The *Bourgeois Gentilhomme* contained the germ of the French Revolution."] We afterwards stayed at Tours, where A. and Hallam left myself and Lionel, and proceeded to the Pyrenees.

The sight of the cleft peak of the Pic du Midi d'Ossau A. thought " grand " from the head of the valley, and made an outline sketch of it. " The Pyrenees," he said, " look much more Homeric than the Alps." Many of the mountains are wooded up to the summit.

On our return I had to answer many letters from unknown correspondents, asking advice from A. as to religious questions, and desiring criticism of poems, etc., and I became very ill[1], and could do but little, so my journal ends here. After a time Hallam came home from Cambridge to help A. in reading books for him, writing letters, and in his work generally.

[End of my mother's journal.]

[1] My mother was never strong, but after this she was almost entirely confined to her sofa. The Master of Trinity (Dr Butler) writes to me (Aug. 13th, 1896) : " Your mother's life has been one of exceptional beauty and power. How few will ever be able to estimate all she did, while lying for years on that sofa. It always seemed to me a kind of sanctuary, from which issued words of the ' Sursum corda ' order, words of patriotism, and . fearlessness, and faith."

Letters of this Period.

Among the letters of this year is the following rough copy of part of a letter from my father to someone unnamed:

May 7th, 1874.

SIR,

I have to thank you for your essay and. your photograph; the face is that of one born to grapple with difficulties, metaphysical or other; and the essay does not belie the face — a vigorous subtle résumé of metaphysic, ending yet once again in the strange history of the human race, with the placid Buddha, as verified by the xixth Century anæsthetics. But what need you my praise when you have secured the approval of him, who is by report our greatest or one of our greatest Hegelians, whereas I have but a gleam of Kant, and have hardly turned a page of Hegel, almost all that I know of him having come to me "obiter" and obscurely thro' the talk of others; and I have never delivered myself to dialectics.

With respect to anæsthetic treatment, I cannot say my slight experience of chloroform (the only anæsthetic I have ever tried) has tended to confirm what you advance.

I was in Scotland about the time when Dr Simpson brought chloroform into use, and I had a slight but very painful operation on the nail of the great toe to undergo, and the friend with whom I was staying urged me to try Simpson's prescription. When I came out of the trance, I took the surgeon for the waiter of Gliddon's cigar divan, a place which has disappeared from the face of the world whole decades ago, and where I had been once, or perhaps twice, many years before, and thro' all those

years, as far as I know, the recollection of my one or two
visits had never occurred to me.

Then, seeing my foot bare, I said to the surgeon,
"Where the deuce have you put my stocking and boot?
do you think I can walk thro' the streets barefoot?"
Immediately after this I laughed, and said, "Oh, I see."
I could not but conclude that, during the operation, the
mind had been passing thro' a little history and had
arrived easily and "gradatim" at this all-but-forgotten
Gliddon's cigar divan. To be sure, the friend who held
my hand and supplied the handkerchief, told me that first
of all I bolted out a long metaphysical term, which he
could not re-word to me.

A. TENNYSON.

To F. T. Palgrave (about the tour in France).

FARRINGFORD,
October 16th, 1874.

DEAR PALGRAVE,

We had not much of a tour. We stayed a
week in Paris and then went on to St Germain, which she
found too cold for her; then to Tours, where we stopt
some weeks at the Hôtel de l'Univers, but where it was
still very blustering and by no means warm. Some
Italians, who were at the inn with us, said the cold made
them shudder.

I and Hallam started for a few days to the Pyrenees,
leaving the wife and Lionel at Tours. I remembered
seeing, from the Esplanade at Pau, the cleft peak of the
Dent du Midi d'Ossau far away; and steamed away
south to make a nearer acquaintance with that, and found
him worth seeing; then to Cauteretz, where I had been
twice before, and to Gavarnie. So after a few days
returned to Tours, and then home, not much of a tour.

As for the "May Queen," King and Co. hire my copyright for five years: you must ask them.

I congratulate you upon the birth of your fourth daughter, and am

Yours ever,
A. TENNYSON.

We shall take no house in London this winter, and I cannot tell you when I shall be there.

The following was in answer to a letter about two fine lines (in E. F. G.'s "Omar Khayyám") which my father greatly admired; Fitzgerald had taken into his head that my father had said they had been "copied from some lines in 'The Gardener's Daughter[1].'" The lines were

"The stars are setting, and the caravan
Starts for the dawn of nothing! O make haste!"

DEAR MRS TENNYSON,

I had really meant to write again to Alfred this evening; to say that I repented of having bothered him about "Omar"! His (Alfred's) letter is come to-day however: and I am glad that he is not bothered at all and for the best of reasons: having no alternative to be bothered with.

I had meant to say besides, that what I asked him about "Omar" had reminded me of what I had often thought and meant to say about a very different thing indeed; namely two of that "paltry Poet's" own wretched effusions: the "Gardener's and Miller's Daughters": of which I have always thought he should reprint the *first drafts*. I do not say they were better than the accepted copies: I do not think they are: but there are I think some things better in them; some, at any rate, which should not be lost. There was something more of the "Wine and Walnut" vein of recollection in the first edition of

---

[1] The summer pilot of an empty heart
Unto the shores of nothing!

the Miller story, and I still retain in my copy the opening stanza
(partially altered by the paltry one himself) beginning —

> I met in all the close green ways,
> While walking with my *rod and line* [1] —

the paltry one having been frightened out of "line and rod" by
C. North. Then there was a touch of *Titian landscape* (I
guessed it, and was right) in the "Gardener," "Autumn touching
the fallows [2]," etc., which I thought and think threw the living
figures better into relief than the Daughters of the Year, who
now pass thro' the Garden. I repeat that I do not maintain
the poem is not altogether improved by the change, which
would be setting my wits against a very poor bird, but I should
publish, for posterity to see, the first draft of both these paltry
poems.

When I look at the *Athenæum* I see there are at least
four poets scarce inferior to Dante, Shakespeare, etc., Browning,
Morris, D. G. Rossetti, Miss Do. They will have their day.

But when I talk so, my bile is invariably on fire. *I! I!* crib
from the "Gardener," which the paltry poet charges me with!
Oh, Dem! But really, I should like to hear what this *Paltry-
Innuendo-maker* alludes to: if it be any gloss of mine on "Omar,"
very little doubt it came from some of those paltry poems; but if
it *should* be old Omar, not even the spite of a poet *inferior* to
Browning can accuse the old Persian of theft. I should like to
find that the *so-called* poet had jumped at one thought. So do
tell me what *runkles* in poor Alfred's mind, and I will relieve
him at once.

Ever your E. FITZGERALD.

On December 29th the Queen, through Mr Disraeli,
offered my father a baronetcy.

From the Right Hon. B. Disraeli.

BOURNEMOUTH, *Dec. 29th*, 1874.

DEAR MR TENNYSON,

A government should recognize intellect. It elevates
and sustains the spirit of a nation. But it is an office not easy

---

[1] See quotation in Vol. I. p. 117.
[2] See quotation in Vol. I. p. 198.

to fulfil, for if it falls into favouritism and the patronage of mediocrity, instead of raising the national sentiment, it might degrade and debase it. Her Majesty, by the advice of Her Ministers, has testified in the Arctic expedition, and will in other forms, her sympathy with science. But it is desirable that the claims of high letters should be equally acknowledged. This is not so easy a matter, because it is in the nature of things, that the test of merit cannot be so precise in literature as in science. Nevertheless there are some living names, however few, which I would fain believe will reach posterity, and yours is among the foremost. I should be glad, therefore, if agreeable to yourself, to submit your name to the Queen for the distinction of a baronetcy, so that, by an hereditary honour, there may always be a living memorial of the appreciation of your genius by your countrymen. Have the kindness to inform me of your feelings on this subject; I shall remain here to the 4th of January. After that it will be best to direct to me at 10 Downing Street, Whitehall.

I have the honour to remain, dear Mr Tennyson,

Faithfully yours, B. DISRAELI.

My father answered Mr Disraeli that Mr Gladstone had offered a baronetcy before, and that he would prefer to adhere to the decision to which he had then come: that he respectfully declined the honour himself but wished it might be conferred if possible after his death on his son. Mr Disraeli replied that such a course as reserving a baronetcy for a son was contrary to all precedent. My father then wrote as follows:

ALDWORTH, BLACKDOWN,
HASLEMERE.

DEAR MR DISRAELI,

It is quite certain that I never desired anything contrary to precedent; nor did Mr Gladstone pledge himself to anything contrary, as (for I have been looking over his letters) he expressly stated. I am therefore fully aware that his promise on the subject was to be interpreted according to precedent, with whatever reserves this may imply. Be the issue what it may, my son is happy in the knowledge of the Queen's gracious intention to his father, and of Mr Gladstone's kindness, and your own.

I have the honour to be yours faithfully,

A. TENNYSON.

At the end of this year my father received a letter from a bricklayer in America, the son of an old Somersby bricklayer, which delighted him, and which obtained a line or two of cordial thanks.

TRENTON, MISSOURI, 1874.

MR TENNYSON,

Sir, I don't know whether this will gain me a response; I know it ought. I have long wished I could get a line from you, since your poetry is in almost every house considered respectable, and your name a household word even out here in the far west. I will relate one anecdote in proof. A good little sewing girl had gained my esteem. I wished to make her a present, and she said, "If I had Tennyson's poems!"

I am H. H. Atkinson, son of Thomas Atkinson, bricklayer, Hagg, near Somersby, and am a bricklayer myself. You will scarcely remember my father building the Doctor's dining-room, you were very young then, about my age. My reminiscences of the Tennyson family run away back. My mother was a Tealby woman, and was in her young days dressmaker for the old Squire's lady, and my father thought so much of the Doctor who was always the Doctor par excellence. The public papers here describe you as a stout broad-shouldered man, and I remember the Doctor so well that if you resemble him I think I should know you. Ah me! it only seems like yesterday, when the Doctor came down to scold the old coachman for ordering my father to build the new carriage-house on too large a plan (coachee would say to the Doctor what no one else dare), said he, " By.G—d, sir, you have a twopenny coachman, I have a twopenny master." I can just now see the good Doctor smile, and walk away, and the coach-house was built. I can just now see the apple-trees that bore such fine yellow apples running up from the stables to the house, the broad lawn where some boys, whom I wot of, used to astonish me by coming out with those wondrous gauze helmets and long foils, and I was afraid mischief would be done. You were not very broad-shouldered then I remember. Do you remember the Siberian crab-tree down the garden, the old Scotch firs at the house-end where the rooks used to build, and those tiny bantams that made their home over the oven, and the handsome cock who was burned to death? I remember one Good Friday we were working for the Doctor. I see him coming, and hear him saying, " Atkinson, you must leave work and go to church," and I remember he preached from " As Moses lifted up the serpent," the first time I had ever heard it as a text and that is near fifty years ago. Ah sir! perhaps no man in America knows as well as I where you first heard the wrens twitter, the blackbirds, thrushes, the robins sing. Many a speckled trout and silver eel have I caught in the brook, running through the meadow below.

And now I am here about fifteen hundred miles west of New York, asking for an autograph all the way from the Isle of Wight.

If you can spare me a line, I would like to know how many children you have, also if Mr Fred is living, Mr Charles (Turner now), also Miss Emily whom everybody loved, also Mr Arthur.

I was burnt out in Chicago, and have lost a fine boy since then from consumption, my only boy. I live in a house and garden of my own here between two groves; we can grow fine peaches here, also all kinds of melons, etc. etc. without extra care. Have I tired you? Well, my heart grows soft and young again in looking over the long past, tho' I have sail'd the seas over, I've crossed the wide ocean.

If this goes into your waste basket, please excuse the scrawl and

> Believe me, sir, yours truly, H. H. ATKINSON.

At this time my father often felt oppressed by the compliments and curiosity of undiscerning critics, and would say: "I hate the blare and blaze of so-called fame. What business has the public to want to know all about Byron's wildnesses? He has given them fine work, and they ought to be satisfied. It is all for the sake of babble. As for the excuse, 'Tôt ou tard tout se sait,' nothing can be falser as far as this world is concerned. The surface of the *tout* may be, but the *tout* never is, correctly known. 'If one knew all, one would pardon all,' is much more likely to be the truth. The worth of a biography depends on whether it is done by one who wholly loves the man whose life he writes, yet loves him with a discriminating love. Few of these gossiping biographies are the man, more often the writer." He wrote out these lines then.

Fame. (*Unpublished.*)

Well, as to Fame, who strides the earth
   With that long horn she loves to blow,
I know a little of her worth,
   And I will tell you what I know —
This London once was middle sea,
   These hills were plains within the past,
They will be plains again, and we,
   Poor devils, babble "we shall last."

CHAPTER VII.

METAPHYSICAL SOCIETY.

Our true seamates regather round the mast —

*   *   *   *   *

For some, descending from the sacred peak
Of hoar high-templed Faith, have leagued again
Their lot with ours to rove the world about;
And some are wilder comrades, sworn to seek
If any golden harbour be for men
In seas of. Death and sunless gulfs of Doubt.

My faith is large in Time
And that which shapes it to some perfect end.

The Metaphysical Society was founded, in 1869, by my father, Mr Pritchard, and Mr Knowles, the idea being first mooted by Mr Knowles. The latter writes to me: " The Metaphysical Society owed its existence to your father, for it was entirely through his adhesion to the plan for it that this remarkable club was set on foot. At first it was intended that no distinct and avowed opponents of Christianity should be invited, though Anglicans of all shades, Roman Catholics, Unitarians, and Non-conformists should be eligible. But it was soon felt that if any real discussion of Christian evidences was to take place, the opposition ought to be fully and fairly represented. This extension of the plan commended itself especially to Dean Stanley, whom I consulted early about it, and it was when talking over it at the Deanery one day, with him and Lady Augusta, that she suggested the name of 'Metaphysical Society' as being better than 'Theological Society' in the altered circumstances of its composition." The object of the Society therefore was, that those who were ranged on the side of faith should meet those who were ranged on the side of unfaith, and freely interchange their views. Darwin's theory of evolution was prominent in men's minds, and my father for one thought that, although evolution in a modified form was partially true, some of Darwin's disciples had drawn unwarrantable inferences from the theory, and had arrogated to themselves too much. His friends and himself were grieved at the scorn that the theological and the agnostic parties showed toward each other, and considered that meeting on a friendly footing would do much toward the ventilation of new doctrines, and the clearing up of misunderstandings, as well as toward the cultivation of charity in controversy, and mutual esteem [1].

I give the earliest members of the Society in order of the names signed in the minute-book: Dean Stanley, Seeley, Roden Noel, James Martineau, W. B. Carpenter, Hinton, Huxley, Pritchard, Hutton, Ward, Bagehot, Froude, Tennyson, Tyndall, Alfred Barry, Lord Arthur Russell, Gladstone, Manning, Knowles, Lubbock, Alford, Alexander Grant, Bishop of St David's, Frederic Harrison, Father Dalgairns, G. Grove, Shadworth Hodgson, Henry Sidgwick, Edmund Lushington, Bishop of Gloucester and Bristol, Mark Pattison [2].

---

[1] Towards the end of his life he rejoiced that the churches were standing shoulder to shoulder in works of charity and education.

[2] The following were afterwards elected: (1870) The Duke of Argyll, Ruskin, Robert Lowe, Grant Duff. (1871) W. R. Greg, A. C. Fraser, Henry Acland, F. D. Maurice, The Archbishop of York, J. B. Mozley. (1872) The Dean of St Paul's, The Bishop of Peterborough, J. Croom Robertson. (1873) FitzJames Stephen, Sylvester, J. C. Bucknill. (1874) Dr Andrew Clark, W. K. Clifford, St George Mivart, Matthew Boulton. (1876) Lord Selborne, John Morley. (1877) Leslie Stephen. (1879) Frederick Pollock,

The subjects originally suggested for discussion were the comparison of the different theories respecting the ultimate grounds of belief in the objective and moral sciences, the logic of the sciences whether physical or social, the immortality of the soul and its personal identity, the personality of God, conscience — its true character, the material hypothesis.

At one of the preliminary meetings, my father said humorously that " Modern science ought at all events to have taught men to separate light from heat," and this was certainly adopted as the rule of the Society.

The first meeting after the formation of the Society took place at the Deanery, Westminster, June 2nd, 1869, under the presidency of Sir John Lubbock, when my father's poem " The Higher Pantheism " was read. With the poem he sent this note to the secretary. " I am not coming up for your meeting, i.e. I believe so, to-day, and your request that you may read the poem at that meeting abashes me. If you are to read it, it ought to be stated surely that I have but ceded to your strongly expressed desire. Hutton can have a copy of it if he choose; but an I had known that such as he wanted it, I would have looked at it again before I let it go." Mr Ward was elected President of the Society in 1870, and my father was always struck with his reckless candour, his liberality, and his " swift dimicatory " ways; and would observe, when Ward was depressed, " If I had Ward's blind faith, I should always be happy." The finest argumentative duels that he had heard, he said, and those which impressed him most, were between Huxley and Martineau. F. D. Maurice he thought was probably " the greatest mind of them all," although often his thoughts were too deep to be easily understood. Grant Duff writes to Mr Wilfrid

Gasquet, C. B. Upton, William Gull, Robert Clarke. (1880) A. J. Balfour, James Sully, A. Barratt.

Ward of one of these meetings, "I do not remember that the Laureate took any part in the discussion, but his mere presence added dignity to a dignified assemblage."

Father Haythornethwaite, W. G. Ward's chaplain, reminds me of one of Ward's stories about my father and Cardinal Manning, which I give in Father Haythornethwaite's words.

" 'Why did you show such deference to Manning?' reprovingly asked an agnostic friend of Tennyson, who had seen him and the Cardinal talking together at a 'Metaphysical' meeting, when Tennyson had apparently been as deferential as Johnson on his introduction to the Archbishop of York. 'Because Manning,' Tennyson had replied, 'is the distinguished head of a great Church.' He had a profound respect for sincere religion in every shape, and though it cannot be said that he pinned his faith to formulæ, all Christian Creeds had his sincere good-will and sympathy, and it was his constantly repeated wish that they 'should sink their differences and pull together for the bettering of mankind[1].' "

[1] Father Haythornethwaite's note on this is interesting, but has nothing to do with the Metaphysical Society. "Tennyson liked to tell the story of the French priest he had met abroad, with whom he had conversed in dog-Latin: 'If our Cardinals,' said the priest, 'were not so proud, and your Bishops not so obstinate, there might be some chance of the Union of the Churches.' Tennyson clearly saw the need of Churches and sympathised with all forms of religious belief,

'Thou knowest I hold that forms are needful' ('Akbar'),

and he looked forward, not always unhopefully, to the day when there would be one Shepherd and one Flock. He wished that the Church of England could embrace, as he felt that Christ would have it do, all the great Nonconformist sects that loved the name of Christ. He recognised to the full that an organized religion was the needful guardian of morality. He was indignant at the expulsion of the Religious Orders from France, calling Paul Bert roundly 'a beast,' and angrily asking, 'What is left for poor people if you take away their religion?' He was full of compunction at once having shown a poor man what he thought an inconsistency in the Gospel, lest he should have weakened his faith in the Bible. He would repeat chant-like in his rich voice the hymns of the Roman breviary: his delicate ear particularly revelling in the sonorous roll of the 'Ave Regina Cœlorum.' "

From the discussions of the Metaphysical Society he came out as strongly convinced as ever of the irrationality of pure materialism, while respecting the earnestness and lofty aims of many agnostics. He was glad to receive the impression that theologians of this age were more enlightened than their predecessors, and that there was an endeavour in the Churches to march side by side with science, and bring their teaching into living relation with the movement of contemporary thought.

As for pure metaphysics I have heard him say: " I do not think that we have advanced much beyond the old philosophers."

The last meeting of the Society was held at Dr Martineau's house on May 16th, 1880. Huxley asserted that it " died of too much love "; my father declared that it " perished because after ten years of strenuous effort no one had succeeded in even defining the term ' Metaphysics.' "

Subjoined is an account of my father's metaphysical views as understood by Dr Martineau.

35 GORDON SQUARE, LONDON, W. C.
1893.

MY DEAR LORD TENNYSON,

As the Metaphysical Society arose from your noble father's suggestion, and he was its first President, it is natural to seek in its history for some characteristic traces of his genius and influence; and they would have been found there in abundance, had he assumed the control over its proceedings which he was too willing to leave in other hands. But in such a society the deeper thinkers, especially if they be rare attendants, seldom come to the front; being outstripped by ready talkers who are always there, and who move upon an intellectual plane level to the eye of all. By reference to the secretary's Minute Book I find that out of 100 Meetings between April 21st, 1869, and your father's resignation December 9th, 1879, he was with us only eleven times; usually as a silent listener, exceptionally interposing some short question or pregnant hint. On June 2nd, 1869, being unable to join us, he sent his poem on " The

Higher Pantheism " to be read to us by Mr Knowles. Nothing that he ever wrote was more likely to lead to interesting discussion : but the evening was pre-engaged to a paper of Mr R. H. Hutton's on Herbert Spencer's theory of the Genesis of apparent Moral Intuitions ; so that the admiration of that memorable poem remained untouched by a word of criticism.

I seem to remember a special interest shown by your father in a paper contributed by the Rev. F. D. Maurice on the meaning of the words " Nature," " Natural," " Supernatural," November 21st, 1871, the only time that Maurice was ever present (he died April 1st, 1872). The Coleridgian acceptation of these words was not less congenial to the Poet than to the Divine, harmonising and consecrating for both the uniformity of the material and the freedom of the spiritual world. I have the impression that in this fellowship of thoughts with the truest *Vates* of his age, Mr Maurice found a powerful inward support.

The other subjects on which papers were read in your father's presence were the following :

July 14, 1869. *The commonsense philosophy of Causation:* Dr W. B. Carpenter.

June 15, 1870. *Is there any Axiom of Causation?* Myself. (Mr Tennyson in the chair.)

June 13. *The relativity of Knowledge:* Mr Fred. Harrison.

Dec. 13. *The emotion of Conviction:* Mr Walter Bagehot.

July 11, 1871. *What is Death?* Bishop of Gloucester and Bristol.

July 9, 1872. *The supposed necessity for seeking a solution of ultimate Metaphysical Problems:* Mr F. Harrison.

Nov. 12. *The five idols of the Theatre:* Mr Shadworth H. Hodgson.

Dec. 16, 1873. *Utilitarianism:* Professor Henry Sidgwick.

Feb. 12, 1878. *Double truth:* Rev. M. Pattison, Rector of Lincoln College, Oxford.

I cannot recall anything that fell from your father in the discussion of these topics. But in general his sympathies went with the advocate of the more conservative aspects of moral and metaphysical questions, as presented by such Roman Catholic members as Cardinal Manning, Dr W. G. Ward, Father Dalgairns ; and such independent writers as Dean Stanley, Prof. H. Sidgwick, Mr R. H. Hutton and the Duke of Argyll.

That in a certain sense our great Laureate's poetry has nevertheless had a dissolving[1] influence upon the over-definite dogmatic creeds within hearing or upon the modes of religious thought amid which it was born, can hardly be doubted. In laying bare, as it does, the history of his own spirit, its conflicts and aspirations, its alternate eclipse of doubt and glow of faith, it has reported more than a personal experience : he has told the story of an age which he has thus brought into Self-knowledge. And as he has never for himself surrendered the traditional form of a devout faith, till he has seized its permanent spirit, and invested it with a purer glory, so has he saved it for others by making it fairer than they had dreamt. Among thousands of readers previously irresponsive to anything Divine he has created, or immeasurably intensified, the susceptibility of religious reverence.

I was aware that my last book did not meet with your father's approval. I need not say what support I should have found in his sympathy. The message, however, which he sent me, that his objection had reference not to the book itself but to the act of *publishing* it, somewhat consoled me; by showing that we differed less about the *quest* of truth than about its *presentation ;* his tenderness towards others' beliefs leading him to favour an *esoteric* teaching distinct from the exoteric. So long as for certain subjects Latin remained the literary language of Europe it was easy to address a selected audience by writing *ad cleros* in Latin, *ad populum* in the *vernacular* tongue. But now that every book must be accessible to every reader, the choice lies between total suppression or free utterance of conviction. I cannot see that we are entrusted with any right of suppression when once profoundly convinced of a truth not yet within others' reach[2].

Yes, I know and glory in every line of "Akbar," except that I cannot, like Akbar, trust the "hand that rules" to "mould" or choose the "forms" of faith and worship that suit the needs of all the people.

Ever yours most truly, JAMES MARTINEAU.

[1] What I mean by "dissolving" is not *destroying* religious faith, but *releasing* it from imprisonment within tight propositions which *define the Infinite.*   J. M.

[2] Dr Martineau's last book seemed to my father to be "founded on doubts rather than on profound convictions."   T.

CHAPTER VIII.

HISTORICAL PLAYS.

"QUEEN MARY" (*published* 1875).

"Queen Mary," the first play of what my father called his "historical trilogy" ("Harold," "Becket" and "Queen Mary"), was published in 1875. "This trilogy of plays," he notes, "pourtrays the making of England." In "Harold" we have the great conflict between Danes, Saxons and Normans for supremacy, the awakening of the English people and clergy from the slumber into which they had for the most part fallen, and the forecast of the greatness of our composite race.

In "Becket" the struggle is between the Crown and the Church for predominance, a struggle which continued for many centuries.

In "Mary" are described the final downfall of Roman Catholicism in England, and the dawning of a new age: for after the era of priestly domination comes the era of the freedom of the individual.

"In 'The Foresters,'" my father wrote, "I have sketched the state of the people in another great transition period of the making of England, when the barons sided with the people and eventually won for them the Magna Charta."

To begin publishing plays for the stage after he

was sixty-five years of age, was thought to be a
hazardous experiment. He had, however, always taken
the liveliest interest in the theatre; and he bestowed
infinite trouble on his dramas, choosing these three great
periods of ' Harold,' ' Becket,' and ' Mary,' so as to complete the line of Shakespeare's English chronicle-plays,
which end with the commencement of the Reformation.
He was quite alive to the fact that for him to attempt this
dramatic work would be at first unpopular, since he was
then mainly regarded as an Idyllic, or as a lyric, poet.
But Spedding, a first-rate Shakespearian scholar, George
H. Lewes and George Eliot admired his plays, and
encouraged him to persevere in spite of all discourage-
ment. He felt that he had the power; and even at the
age of fourteen he had written plays which were "extraordinary for a boy," and full of vivid contrasts and
striking scenic effects. All his life he enjoyed discovering the causes of historical and social movements; and
had a strong desire to reverse unfair judgments, and
an eager delight in the analysis of human motive
and character. With the great dramas of ancient and
modern times he was acquainted; hating in consequence
the hideous realism and unreality of plays like "La
Tosca"; but he believed in the future of our modern
English stage when education should have made the
masses more literary. "Clever enough but wants
nature" was his criticism of much of the dramatic
work in the present day. He regarded the drama as
one of the most humanising of influences. He always
hoped that the State, or the municipalities, as well as
the public schools, would produce our great English
historical plays, so that they might form part of the
Englishman's ordinary educational curriculum. For himself he was aware that he wanted intimate knowledge
of the mechanical details necessary for the modern
stage; although in early and middle life he had been

a constant playgoer, and would keenly follow the action of a play, criticizing the characterization, incidents, scenic effects, situations, language and dramatic points. His dramas were written with the intention that actors should edit them for the stage[1], keeping them at the high poetic level; yet he did not always approve when they omitted those soliloquies and necessary episodes which reveal the character and, so to say, the mental action of a piece; nor did he speak favourably of some of the modern sensational *curtains*. He said that "The public are often left poised on the top of a wave, and the wave is not allowed to break"; that this might be modern theatrical art, but is entirely opposed to the canons of true literary dramatic art: and that the theatric and the dramatic were always being mistaken the one for the other[2].

He would observe that "Critics are so exacting now-a-days, that they not only expect a poet-playwright to be a first rate author but a first-rate manager, actor and audience all in one." He said they did not consider that the conditions of dramatic art are much more complex than they were, and that to be a first-rate historical playwright means much more work than formerly, seeing that "exact history" has taken the place of the chance chronicle, and that a dramatist is expected to be cognisant of all the newest phases of contemporary drama.

As his "Queen Mary," "Cup," "Becket," "Falcon" and "Foresters" were all more or less successful on the stage, partly no doubt owing to the admirable

---

[1] Mary Anderson writes to me: "In reading 'The Cup' and 'The Foresters' Lord Tennyson showed by his remarks that he had the instincts of the true dramatist; and he moreover asked me to tell him of any lines that might seem to me to overweight the dramatic action of these plays. He thoroughly appreciated the need of action, and was ready to sacrifice even his *most* beautiful lines for the sake of a real dramatic effect."

[2] The same complaint was made by Fanny Kemble.

stage-management, I cannot but feel sorry that he did not add to his plays another which he had in his mind, " Simon de Montfort," wherein he would have pourtrayed some of his favourite historical characters, de Montfort, and the greatest of the Plantagenets, Edward, and Roger Bacon. The England of the thirteenth century, its great architecture, its Common Law, its new-made constitution (the archetype of all modern free constitutions), its literature, its Universities for rich and poor, moved him only less than " the spacious times of great Elizabeth." Both " The Cup " and " Becket " hold the stage, but whether these or his other plays will continue to do so is of course a question which only time can answer.

During 1874 and 1875 my father worked hard and unceasingly at his " Queen Mary," " more of a chronicle-play " he called it. The first list of books which he read on the subject is written down in his note-book : " Collier's *Ecclesiastical History*, Fuller's *Church History*, Burnet's *Reformation*, Foxe's *Book of Martyrs*, Hayward's *Edward*, Cave's *P. X. Y.*, Hooker, Neale's *History of the Puritans*, Strype's *Ecclesiastical Memorials*, Strype's *Cranmer*, Strype's *Parker*, Philips' *Pole, Primitive Fathers No Papists*, Lingard's *History of England, Church Historians of England, Zürich Letters, and Original Letters and Correspondence of Archbishop Parker* (published by the Parker Society)," in addition to Froude, Holinshed and Camden.

With respect to character-painting my father considered " Queen Mary " the most successful of his plays, but with his keen sense of truth always regretted that he had not, through lack of knowledge, done justice, as he thought, to Sir Thomas White, Lord Mayor of London.

The following remarks by Hutton seemed to him to bring out his own conceptions of the characters:

Almost all the characters who play a real part in the drama, however slightly touched, are clearly defined; Philip, whose disgust for the Queen is powerfully painted, but who remains otherwise something of a cold, cruel and sensual shadow, being perhaps in some degree an exception. Courtenay, Earl of Devon, the vain and flighty Catholic Plantagenet, "this prince of fluff and feather," as Lord Howard in speaking to Elizabeth calls him; Reginald Pole, the fair-weather Papal Legate, who shrinks alike from being persecuted and from persecuting, but is easily driven into the latter policy under fear of the former; Bishop Gardiner with his fierce Romanising dogmatism and his English hatred of Italian interference in English concerns,

> His big baldness,
> That irritable forelock which he rubs,
> His buzzard beak, and deep incavern'd eyes.

Bonner and his moral brutality, Lord Paget with the half-confessed Protestantism of his statesman's intellect, and yet that craving for English influence abroad which makes him support the alliance with Spain; Lord Howard, with his aristocratic Catholicism, his complete contempt for the vulgarity and ignorance of the new schismatics, and yet his thoroughly rooted antipathy to the bigotry of the sacerdotal spirit; Sir Thomas Wyatt, with his tasteful literary cravings, and the keen audacious soldier beneath them; Sir Ralph Bagenhall, with his bold, meditative insubordination and his hopelessness of active resistance; Sir Thomas White (the Lord Mayor), with his political indecision, and his wonderful dexterity at swaying the London Guilds directly the feather's weight has turned the scale which he is pleased to call his mind, so as to decide him on his own course; Cranmer with his somewhat questionable faith and courage, questionable we mean as regards historical fact, not questionable at all in Mr Tennyson's picture, his humility, penitence and sweetness; and lastly, the imaginary servants and peasants, both men and women, who are made parties to the drama, — these are all drawn with a firm hand and painted with a delicate touch. But the great characters of the piece are, as of course they ought to be, Mary and her half-sister Elizabeth, whose star declines as the Catholic Queen's rises, and rises fair again as Mary's sets. Of course the portrait of Elizabeth is comparatively slight as compared with that of Mary, but though much less carefully filled in it is to the full as dramatic and life-like.

In few ages of the Christian era can the words " I came not to send peace but a sword " have been more sorrowfully verified than in the life of Mary Tudor. The wrong, done by her father to her mother and herself, was a sword that early pierced through Mary's own soul. She had, my father thought, been harshly judged by the popular verdict of tradition, therefore he had a desire to let her be seen as he pictured her in his imagination. Hence he was attracted toward the subject. He pitied the poor girl, who not only was cast down by her father from her high estate, but treated with shameless contumely by the familiar friends of her childhood. What wonder that a nature originally bright should thus have been clouded! He sympathised with her queenly courage, dramatically expressed by him, when, after her accession, triumphant over revolt, she flashes out with:

My foes are at my feet and Philip King.

He held that all allowance ought to be made for her, when, her high hopes for the Church and for the kingdom having been rekindled and quenched, the clouds of youth gathered again into a settled gloom. Throughout all history, he said, there was nothing more mournful than the final tragedy of this woman, who, with her deep longing for love, found herself hated by her people, abandoned by her husband: and harassed in the hour of death by the restlessness of despair [1].

---

[1] The well-known critic Mons. Augustin Filon writes in *Le Théâtre Contemporain* (1895): " Vienne une main pieuse qui dégage ces deux drames (" Queen Mary " and " Harold "), fasse circuler l'air et la lumière

The real difficulty of the drama, as my father was aware, is to give sufficient relief to its intense sadness, especially to the scenes in which Mary's devotion is repelled by Philip's coldness, consummated in that last scene, where she sits upon the ground, rocking herself to and fro, making her lament.

Nothing less than the holy calm of the meek and penitent Cranmer can be adequate artistic relief[1].

He pass'd out smiling, and he walk'd upright;
His eye was like a soldier's, whom the general
He looks to and he leans on as his God
Hath rated for some backwardness and bidd'n him
Charge one against a thousand, and the man
Hurls his soil'd life against the pikes and dies.

*   *   *   *

The following close of the last act, which my father wrote in 1876 for the acting edition[2], he never printed, but left as a note:

After Mary's speech, ending " Help me hence."
        [*She falls into the arms of Lady Clarence.*
Alice.   The hand of God hath help'd her hence.
Lady Clarence.   Not yet.
        [*To Elizabeth as she enters.*
Speak, speak, a word of yours may wake her.

autour de leurs lignes essentielles; vienne un grand acteur qui compresse et incarne Harold, une grande actrice qui se passionne pour le caractère de Marie, et, sans effort, Tennyson prendra sa place parmi les dramaturges."

[1] Cf. the remarkable review in the *Times*, June 19th, 1875.

[2] As produced at the Lyceum Theatre with Irving as Philip, and Miss Kate Bateman as Queen Mary. Miss Bateman played some of her part finely, and Irving's " Philip " my father always pronounced to be a consummate performance, ranking it for powerful conception of character with Salvini's " Othello."

On the Australian stage Miss Dargon won a triumph in " Queen Mary." It was very popular when produced at the Melbourne Theatre Royal, and had a long run; and when reproduced at the Bijou Theatre in the same city had a second long run.

Elizabeth (kneeling at her sister's knee). Mary!

Mary. Mary! who calls? 'tis long since any one
Has called me Mary, she,
There in the dark she sits and calls for me,
She that should wear her state before the world.
My father's own true wife. Aye, madam. Hark!
For she will call again.

    Elizabeth.   Mary, my sister!

    Mary.   That's not the voice!
Who is it steps between me and the light?

                [*Puts her arm round Elizabeth's neck.*
I held her in my arms a guileless babe,
And mourn'd her orphan doom along with mine.
The crown! she comes for that! take it and feel it!
It stings the touch! It is not gold but thorns!

                   [*Mary starts up.*
The crown of crowns! Play not with holy things!

             [*Clasps her hands and kneels.*
Keep you the faith!...yea, Mother, yea, I come!

                        [*Dies.*

Lady Clarence. She is dead.

Elizabeth (kneeling by the body). Poor sister! Peace
be with the dead.   [*Curtain.*

Letters about "Queen Mary."

From J. A. Froude.

5 ONSLOW GARDENS,
May 7th, 1875.

MY DEAR TENNYSON,

       I cannot trust myself to say how greatly I admire
the play. Beyond the immediate effect, you'll have hit a more
fatal blow than a thousand pamphleteers and controversialists;
besides this you have reclaimed one more section of English
History from the wilderness and given it a form in which it will

be fixed for ever. No one since Shakespeare has done that. When we were beginning to think that we were to have no more from you, you have given us the greatest of all your works. Once more I thank you for having written this book with all my heart. ·

Most truly yours, J. A. FROUDE.

From Robert Browning.

19 WARWICK CRESCENT, W.,
June 30th, 1875.

MY DEAR TENNYSON,

Thank you very much for "Queen Mary," the gift, and even more for "Queen Mary," the poem: it is astonishingly fine. Conception, execution, the whole and the parts, I see nowhere the shade of a fault, thank you once again! I am going to begin it afresh now. What a joy it is that such a poem should be, and be yours!

All affectionate regards to Mrs Tennyson from

Yours ever, ROBERT BROWNING.

Count Münster wrote about Prince Bismarck:

He now has real holidays at Varzin and has for a short time given up all public business, and told me that he has already read parts of "Queen Mary" with the greatest pleasure and admiration.

From the Right Hon. W. E. Gladstone.

11 CARLTON HOUSE TERRACE,
June 30, 1875.

MY DEAR TENNYSON,

It was most kind in you to send me the book; and I wish I had or could have anything to cap it with that would not seem like a mocking echo.

However I am going to reprint in a volume my recent tracts and I shall perhaps make bold to send them to you.

Perhaps we may appear in the "Index" together.

I cannot but be glad that, in turning to historic times, you have struck a stroke for the nation. For my own personal share, I have found my interest in your work on this occasion enhanced and cumulated by the novelty of form and by having to enjoy a careful historic study. It must have cost you great pains to qualify for such an assemblage of portraits : of whom five or six at least are of personages whose names never can be effaced from our annals, nor do I know that Mary, Philip (in England), Gardiner or Cranmer have ever yet been fully drawn. The two last are still in a considerable degree mysteries to me! Was Cranmer a great weak man? Do great and weak contradict and include one another? He was certainly weak, I think, in the everlasting fluctuation of his opinions; for surely fluctuation of opinion had much to do with the six recantations. Elizabeth on the other hand was to my mind one of the great theologians of the period (who were exceedingly few) as well as the greatest among women-rulers. I think you may not dislike the following sentence from Jeremy Collier on Cranmer at the stake : " He seemed to repel the force of flames, and to overlook the torture by strength of thought."

My judgment is worthless, but I heartily congratulate you on the Poem, on the Study, and on the grace and ease with which you move in new habiliments.

Ever sincerely yours, W. E. GLADSTONE.

From Edward Fitzgerald.

WOODBRIDGE, *July 9th*, 1875.

MY DEAR OLD ALFRED,

I had bought your Play a few days before your gift-copy reached me. I have not had sufficient time to digest either you see, though I have read through twice. I must leave it for the Papers and Magazines to judge in a few hours, what took you, I suppose, weeks and months in concocting. I could speak of parts, I think : but not yet of the whole : and you can very well afford (can't you ?) to wait till "The Great Twalmley" pronounces ? One thing, I don't quite understand why you have so much relinquished "*thee*" and "*thou*" with their relative verbs for "*you*," etc. I know that we have had more than enough of "Thee" and "Thou" in modern Plays and Poems; but it should surely rule in the common *talk* of Mary's time. I suppose however that you have some very good reason for so often supplying the old form by the new.

Still your old Fitzcrotchet, you see, still! And so will be to the end, I suppose. I am not over-well just now, and see very little of books; all day on the river, and talking to the ducks and barndoors.

But ever yours the same,

"OLD FITZ."

From Sir Henry Bedingfeld, Bart.

OXBURGH, STOKE FERRY,
20th August, 1875.

SIR,

As a great admirer of your genius, I eagerly read your drama "Queen Mary," but was so surprised and pained at the ignoble part which is allotted to Sir Henry Bedingfield, that I cannot refrain from addressing you on the subject. I feel justified in so doing, as I am the direct descendant of Sir Henry, and date from the house which was his home. The millions who will read "Mary Tudor," or witness the play on the stage, will carry away the impression that my ancestor was a vulgar yeoman in some way connected with the stables, whereas he was a man of ancient lineage, a trusted friend and servant of the Queen, who confided to him in time of danger the Lieutenancy of the Tower, and the custody of the Princess Elizabeth. This Princess so respected Sir Henry that, although she complained of his severity during her captivity, she visited him at Oxburgh after her accession to the Throne, and treated him with the greatest consideration. Numerous documents in my possession, including letters from the Sovereign, from the Privy Council, and from the most eminent men of the time, would prove, were such proof required, the high position held by Sir Henry. I trust therefore to your feeling of justice, that you will, if possible, either strike out Sir Henry's name from future editions, or allot to him a more dignified part on the stage, and one which will convey a more correct view of his character and position.

I am, Sir, your obedient servant,

HENRY BEDINGFELD.

Answer to Sir Henry Bedingfeld, Bart.

FARRINGFORD, *April 15th*, 1876.

SIR,

Your letter arrived when I was abroad, else would have been answered at once: and therefore I waited till the play should be announced for acting. I had made your ancestor an honest gentleman tho' a rough one, as I found him reported to be, whether that were true or no; and I regret that you should have been pain'd by my representation of him. Now, in deference to your wishes, his name is not once mention'd on the stage, and he is call'd in the play-bill merely "Governor of Woodstock." Moreover I have inserted a line in Elizabeth's part, "Out, girl, you wrong a noble gentleman[1]."

I have the honour to be, Sir,

Your obedient servant,

A. TENNYSON.

It may be as well to insert here a letter from Robert Browning, written in April 1876, describing the production of "Queen Mary" on the stage. My father said that in his opinion Philip and Richard III were Irving's best parts.

[1] Sir Henry expressed himself satisfied with the explanation and the added line.   T.

19 WARWICK CRESCENT, W.
April 19th, 1876.

MY DEAR TENNYSON,

I want to be among the earliest who assure you of the complete success of your "Queen Mary" last night[1]. I have more than once seen a more satisfactory performance of it, to be sure, in what Carlyle calls "the Private Theatre under my own hat," because there and then not a line nor a word was left out; nay, there were abundant "encores" of half the speeches: still whatever was left by the stage scissors suggested what a quantity of "cuttings" would furnish one with an after-feast.

Irving was very good indeed, and the others did their best, nor so badly.

The love as well as admiration for the author was conspicuous, indeed, I don't know whether you ought to have been present to enjoy it, or were not safer in absence from a smothering of flowers and deafening "tumult of acclaim," but Hallam was there to report, and Mrs Tennyson is with you to believe. All congratulations to you both from

Yours affectionately ever,

ROBERT BROWNING.

---

[1] One of the lines most applauded was :

"I am English Queen, not Roman Emperor";

which hit the temper of the London democracy, for the Queen had lately assumed the title of Empress of India.

"HAROLD."

(*Published* 1876.)

"Harold" my father called his "Tragedy of Doom," citing the scenes of the comet, Harold's shipwreck and capture, the oath, Edward's curse and death, the marriage and coronation of Harold and Aldwyth, and the great battle of Senlac.

Winds and waves, Harold's own acts, so alien to his nature, and even circumstances fight against him and yet he still holds to duty, nobleness and patriotism. The truthful Harold's false oath by the saints of Normandy gives the tragic unity to the action.

It becomes his avenging destiny. In his short career, it is what the inherited curse was to the house of Pelops. Harold can say in the true sense which Euripides meant, "My tongue has sworn, but my soul has not sworn." Nothing in the play seems to us finer than the contrast between Harold's own view of his predicament and the casuistry of the theologians who seek to re-assure him. He has a foreboding that he must suffer the immediate doom of the defiled; but beyond that doom he looks up to that Justice which shall give him the reward of the pure in spirit [1].

[1] From the review in the *Times*, Oct. 18th, 1876, by Professor Jebb. When my father was writing the notes to his poems, such as are often quoted throughout these chapters, he read this review, and thought that it contained most of what he had to say about "Harold" as a subject for drama. Harold's character he considered very ably drawn: "No historical character unites more completely than Harold all the elements of dramatic effect. His military genius, his civil virtues, his loyal and fearless championship of England against the dominion of strangers; his liberality, which has for its perpetual monument his secular foundation of Waltham; his frank and open bearing, in which prudent contemporaries blamed too slight a regard

In vain Harold defeats the Danes and his own treasonable brother Tostig who has brought them into England. The bloody victory does but weaken him in the struggle for supremacy with William.

In vain does he sacrifice his Edith and marry Aldwyth to secure, as he thinks, the aid of her brothers Edwin and Morcar. They stand aloof in his hour of need; and his own high courage itself does but expose him to the fatal arrow which seals his doom and that of England.

When we were at Battle Abbey in 1876, where my father wrote his prefatory sonnet to "Harold," we found a rising ground to the English right, and he pictured Edith and Stigand and the English canons of Waltham and the camp followers standing to watch the battle, and to catch a glimpse of their great Harold between the English standards which flapped high above the roof of flying arrows, and the deadly gleam of axes "that lightened with a single flash about the summit." And when we saw the streams of tourists flowing over the lawns, and not seeming much to care for this mighty Harold or for the momentous field of Senlac, he turned to me and said

"Another England now we come and go,
A nation's fall has grown a summer show."

But those tragic days of the "nation's fall" were the prelude of a new birth for England, as Edward foresaw in his death-vision, — one of those passages in which my father thought he had been successful :

Then a great Angel past along the highest
Crying "the doom of England," and at once

for self-interest; his generous courage, which panegyrists could not wholly vindicate from the charge of rashness; his tall stature, his comely countenance, that mighty physical strength to which the pictures of the Bayeux tapestry bear witness — all these things make Harold a man fit to stand as the central figure of a drama."

He stood beside me, in his grasp a sword
Of lightnings, wherewithal he cleft the tree
From off the bearing trunk, and hurl'd it from him
Three fields away, and then he dash'd and drench'd,
He dyed, he soak'd the trunk with human blood,
And brought the sunder'd tree again, and set it
Straight on the trunk, that thus baptized in blood
Grew ever high and higher, beyond my seeing,
And shot out sidelong boughs across the deep
That dropt themselves, and rooted in far isles
Beyond my seeing: and the great Angel rose
And past again along the highest crying
" The doom of England!"

To meet the conditions of the modern drama, before writing " Harold " my father had studied many recent plays. He had also refreshed his mind with the dramas of Æschylus and Sophocles, which always seemed to him "full of noble reality and moral beauty."

It has been asked· why in his historical trilogy he does not give free rein to his sense of humour; the answer is, he held that a certain formal humour was the only humour possible now-a-days in stage-tragedy, which in its rapid action does not allow scope for original humour; and that even this formal humour must be kept in strict subservience to the plot.

Letters about "Harold."

From Henry W. Longfellow.

CAMBRIDGE, *Dec.* 21*st*, 1876.

MY DEAR TENNYSON,

I have just been reading your "Harold" and am delighted with its freshness, strength and beauty. Like " Boadicea " it is a voice out of the Past, sonorous, strange, semi-barbaric. What old ancestor of yours is it thus speaking through you?

The Fifth Act is a masterly piece of dramatic writing. I know not where to look for anything better.

This being the shortest day of the year I make my letter correspond.

I wish you knew, I wish you could possibly know, the power of your poetry in this country. It would make your heart go forth towards the thirty or forty million of English on this side of the Atlantic.

With cordial congratulations on your great success, and kind remembrances,

Your friend and admirer,

HENRY W. LONGFELLOW.

From Robert Browning.

19 WARWICK CRESCENT, *Dec. 21st*, 1876.

MY DEAR TENNYSON,

True thanks again, this time for the best of Christmas presents, another great work, wise, good and beautiful. The scene where Harold is overborne to take the oath is perfect, for one instance. What a fine new ray of light you are entwining with your many coloured wreath!

I know the Conqueror's country pretty well: stood last year in his Castle of Bonneville, on the spot where tradition is that Harold took the oath; and I have passed through Dives, the place of William's embarcation, perhaps twenty times: and more than once visited the church there, built by him, where still are inscribed the names of the Norman knights who accompanied him in his expedition. You light this up again for me. All happiness befall you and yours this good season and ever.

Yours affectionately, R. BROWNING.

Answer to Robert Browning.

ALDWORTH, HASLEMERE.

After-dinner talk between husband and wife.

W. Why don't you write and thank Mr Browning for his letter?

H. Why should I? I sent him my book and he acknowledged it.

W. But such a great and generous acknowledgement.

H. That's true.

W. Then you should write: he has given you your crown of violets.

H. He is the greatest-brained poet in England. Violets fade, he has given me a crown of gold.

W. Well, I meant the Troubadour crown of golden violets; pray write: you know I would if I could; but I am lying here helpless and horizontal and can neither write nor read.

H. Then I'll go up and smoke my pipe and write to him.

W. You'll go up and concoct an imaginary letter over your pipe, which you'll never send.

H. Yes, I will. I'll report our talk.

He goes up and smokes, and spite of pipe writes and signs himself

A. TENNYSON.

From Aubrey de Vere.

December 28th, 1876.

MY DEAR ALFRED,

I do not like to defer longer sending you my most cordial thanks for sending me your "Harold." I have already read the whole of it twice, and many parts of it much oftener, and it is probably better that I should write with the general effect of the work still broad and plain on my mind, than after a minute analysis of details had to some extent clouded my estimate of it as a whole. You know how heartily I admired it when you read it aloud to me: and I can honestly assure you that that admiration has not been less on reading it to myself. On that first occasion it may have derived an advantage from your reading; but if so, the more careful attention one gives to what one reads with one's own eyes fully compensated for whatever was lost. The great characteristic of this drama is to me that of an heroic strength blended with heroic simplicity, and everything in it harmonious with that predominant characteristic. Nearly all the characters are simple and the plot is eminently so. Perhaps the simplest of all the characters is that of Harold himself, and for that reason there is quite an extraordinary paths in the malicious might of those circumstances which force his feet off the straight ways and into those perplexed paths for which they have no inclination. The extreme simplicity of the drama requires a corresponding amount of strength to make it effective, and a sort of Æschylean strength seems to me to belong to it everywhere, to its characters, its action, its passions, its style and diction, and to all its most remarkable passages. This strength increases to the end, and sums itself up in that grand battle-scene with its Latin "choruses" (as they might be called) which constitutes the chief part of the fifth Act. In Greece (and I suppose everywhere) Dramatic poetry came later than Narrative; and though more an expansion of the Choral Ode, yet in some of the earlier specimens retained something of an Epic character also; and I think that your Drama has something also of an Epic spirit combined with its dramatic form. It is a great thing to have had this wonderful crisis in our early English History added to our great dramatic gallery.

Ever affectionately yours,

AUBREY DE VERE.

From Dean Stanley.

DEANERY, WESTMINSTER,
December 25th, 1876.

MY DEAR TENNYSON,

I will gladly contrive if you wish to transmit your poem to the Queen. I know that Her Majesty is expecting it.

I ought ere this to have thanked you for my own copy. It cheered some mournful winter evenings for me, and it will, I trust, for the country at large, revive or rekindle the dying torch of Truth and the belief that there is something greater and nobler than capricious Norman Saints.

Yours sincerely, A. P. STANLEY.

From Edward Fitzgerald.

LOWESTOFT, *December 30th*, 1876.

MY DEAR OLD ALFRED,

"Harold" came, King Harold. But I still yearn after a Fairy Prince who came from other skies than these rainy ones, with his joyful eyes, "foxfooted step," and his mantle glittering on the rocks. Impute this to my old prejudice, childish taste, whatever you will, except my ceasing to be your loyal old Fitz.

I scarce know if it be worth writing to say this : you knew it all beforehand : still, I suppose it is proper to acknowledge such a present. At any rate it gives me an opportunity to wish you and yours all good for coming 1877, a wish that I think you would also guess without my writing. Here I have a book of old Spanish Romances familiar to Don Quixote and Sancho. I shall write you out a *rather* pretty one which I read yesterday, and remain

Yours as ever, E. F. G.

There is not much in it, if you take the trouble to construe ; but I like the lady with her old husband partner, managing to address the young Count, perhaps as she passes him in the dance, bit by bit as the figure brings her round again.

From G. H. Lewes.

THE HEIGHTS, WITLEY,
GODALMING, 18*th June*, 1877.

MY DEAR TENNYSON,

We have just read "Harold" (for the first time) and "Mary" (for the fourth) and greatly wished you had been here to read certain scenes, especially that masterly interview between Harold and William, or that most pathetic close of "Mary." It is needless for me to say how profound a pleasure both works have given us — they are great contributions ! and your wretched critics who would dissuade you from enriching literature with such dramas must be forgiven, "for they know not what they say." It is not however to carry the coals of applause to your Newcastle that I scribble these lines, but to enquire whether there is a hope of your being at Blackdown this summer and of our seeing you ?

Yours truly, G. H. LEWES.

"BECKET."

(*Printed* 1879; *published* 1884.)

In 1879 my father printed the first proofs of his
tragedy of "Becket," which he had begun in December
1876. But he considered that the time was not ripe
for its publication; and this therefore was deferred
until December 1884. We had visited Canterbury in
August 1877, and gone over each separate scene of
Becket's martyrdom. "Admirers of Becket," my father
notes, "will find that Becket's letters, and the writings
of Herbert of Bosham, Fitzstephen, and John of Salisbury throw great light on those days. Bishop Lightfoot found out about Rosamund for me."

The play is so accurate a representation of the
personages and of the time, that J. R. Green said that
all his researches into the annals of the twelfth century
had not given him "so vivid a conception of the
character of Henry II. and his court as was embodied
in Tennyson's 'Becket.'"

To my father it was interesting to learn the impression made upon Roman Catholics by this work. He
first asked the opinion of his neighbour at Freshwater,
W. G. Ward. He could not have asked a more candid, truth-speaking critic than this "most liberal of
all Ultramontanes," who was deeply versed not only
in the spirit and doctrine of his own Church, but also
in the modern French and English drama. My father

once said of Ward when speaking to a friend of Roman Catholic casuistry: "Well, one of the most truthful men I ever met was a strict Ultramontane: he was grotesquely truthful." They thoroughly understood each other, for Ward was "full of fun and faith." So it came to pass that my father often discussed religion and Roman Catholicism with him in their walks together. He once said to Ward, "You know you would try to get me put in prison if the Pope bid you." Ward replied, "The Pope would never tell me to do anything so foolish."

It may be imagined that we looked forward with some anxiety to the evening when Ward had promised to be at Farringford to hear "Becket." He came, as it afterwards appeared, to listen patiently, though convinced "that the whole play would be out of his line." At the end of the play he broke out into enthusiastic praise. "Dear me! I did not expect to enjoy it at all. It is splendid! How wonderfully you have brought out the phases of his character as Chancellor and Archbishop! Where did you get it all?"

Struggle for power under one guise or another has doubtless been among the most fruitful sources of theme for tragedy. During many centuries, as we know, "spiritual power," clothed in earthly panoply, seemed to most men to be the one embodiment of the Divine Power. What struck Ward in my father's play was the clear and impressive manner in which he had brought out Becket's feeling that in accepting the Archbishopric he had changed masters, that he was not simply advanced to a higher service of the same liege lord, but that he had changed his former lord paramount, whose fiery self-will made havock of his fine intellect, for one of higher degree; and had become a power distinct from and it might be antagonistic to the King. Thus Becket says, still loving his old friend:

The worldly bond between us is dissolved,
Not yet the love: can I be under him
As Chancellor? as Archbishop over him?

My father's view of Becket was as follows: Becket was
a really great and impulsive man, with a firm sense of duty,
and, when he renounced the world, looked upon himself
as the head of that Church which was the people's
"tower of strength, their bulwark against throne and
baronage." This idea so far wrought in his dominant
nature as to betray him into many rash acts; and later
he lost himself in the idea. His enthusiasm reached a
spiritual ecstasy which carries the historian along with it;
and his humanity and abiding tenderness for the poor,
the weak and the unprotected, heighten the impression
so much as to make the poet feel passionately the
wronged Rosamund's reverential devotion for him (most
touchingly rendered by Ellen Terry), when she kneels
praying over his body in Canterbury Cathedral[1].

As a stage tragedy (adapted by Irving) Irving has
told us that " Becket " is one of the three most successful
plays produced by him at the Lyceum. " ' Becket' is a
finer play than ' King John,' " he wrote to my father.
Palgrave has observed that " Becket " has two excellent
characteristics of the old Greek drama, that of bringing
the four protagonists prominently throughout before the
audience: and that of introducing the crisis of the
tragedy in a scene of first-rate comedy. Irving's arrangement has been criticised as too episodical; but the thread
of human interest remains strong enough for its purpose,
as from first to last it holds the audience in an attitude
of rapt attention. Assuredly Irving's interpretation of
the many-sided, many-mooded, statesman-soldier-saint
was as vivid and as subtle a piece of acting as has been
seen in our day.

[1] In the play Rosamund is the king's wife by a left-handed marriage.

13—2

He says truly that one of the chief keynotes of the
character is to be found in the following lines, which
he always gave with an indescribable tenderness, as if
looking back to and recalling the daydream of his youth.

Becket.   There was a little fair-hair'd Norman maid,
　　　　Lived in my mother's house: if Rosamund is
　　　　The world's rose, as her name imports her — she
　　　　Was the world's lily.

John of Salisbury.   Ay, and what of her?

Becket. She died of leprosy.

John of Salisbury.   I know not why
　　　　You call these old things back again, my lord.

Becket.   The drowning man, they say, remembers all
　　　　The chances of his life, just ere he dies.

In 1879 Irving refused the play: but in 1891 he
asked leave to produce it, holding that the taste of the
theatre-going public had changed in the interval, and
that it was now likely to be a success on the stage.

He writes to me (1893):

We have passed the fiftieth performance of " Becket," which
is in the heyday of its success. I think that I may, without
hereafter being credited with any inferior motive, give again
the opinion which I previously expressed to your loved and
honoured father. To me " Becket" is a very noble play, with
something of that lofty feeling and that far-reaching influence,
which belong to a " passion play." There are in it moments of
passion and pathos which are the aim and end of dramatic art,
and which, when they exist, atone to an audience for the endurance of long acts. Some of the scenes and passages,
especially in the last act, are full of sublime feeling, and are
with regard to both their dramatic effectiveness and their poetic
beauty as fine as anything in our language. I know that such a
play has an ennobling influence on both the audience who see
it and the actors who play in it [1].

[1] Professor Stanford's incidental music has not received the credit which
it deserves, for it is eminently artistic and imaginative. — His identification
of Becket with the Gregorian melody " Telluris ingens conditor" is
particularly impressive.

Some of the last lines which my father ever wrote are at the end of the Northampton scene, an anthem-speech written for Irving.

The voice of the Lord is in the voice of the people.
The voice of the Lord is on the warring flood,
And He will lead His people into peace!
The voice of the Lord will shake the wilderness,
The barren wilderness of unbelief!
The voice of the Lord will break the cedar-trees,
The Kings and Rulers that have closed their ears
Against the Voice, and at their hour of doom
The voice of the Lord will hush the hounds of Hell
In everlasting silence.

The story of Henry and Rosamund had long ago attracted him, and the germ of the play is to be found in a little song written before 1842.

Rosamund's Bower. (*Unpublished.*)

Rosamund loquitur.

What rustles hither in the dark?
    A step? a footfall? What is that I hear?
The night is black and still; the deer
    Bleat as with human voices in the park.
Is it the king? is it my love
    Coming along the secret ways?
The man that round me wove
    Inextricable brickwork maze in maze?

It is not he; far off from England's shore,
    He comes no more.
An idle hope was in my breast,
    My hope is false, my terror's true!
I shudder in my lonely nest,
    And think a cunning hand has found the clue —
God be gracious to my soul!

Letters about " Becket."

Dedication to the Lord Chancellor (Selborne).

MY DEAR SELBORNE,

To you, the honoured Chancellor of our
own day, I dedicate this dramatic memorial of your
great predecessor; — which, altho' not intended in its
present form to meet the exigencies of our modern
theatre, has nevertheless, for so you have assured me,
won your approbation.

Ever yours, TENNYSON.

From the Earl of Selborne.

30 PORTLAND PLACE.

I have been prostrated for several days by a feverish
cold, and when your present of " Becket " arrived here on
Monday was not in a fit state to write.

But I can no longer delay thanking you for it and for the
dedication. All of us, I suppose, who have so far come out
conquerors in the great internal struggles of life as to have been
enabled to play some part, in the hope that it may be for good,
in the world, must share in the natural feeling of the ancients,
who did not look upon death as Christians do, that there would
be something, not the mere memory of places, offices or titles,
and still less pompous memorials, to rescue our names from the
obscurity and virtual oblivion which history has in store for all
but a very few of those whose inner lives are as little known as
mine. This makes me accept your dedication as the greatest
real honour that has ever been done me : that you should be my
vates sacer and let those remote generations of the best spirits
among the English-speaking race, who will read your works,
know that there was something in me which had won your
friendship and esteem, is more than I could have hoped for.

Believe me ever affectionately yours,

SELBORNE.

From the Right Honourable J. Bryce.

As I have been abroad for some time it was only a little while ago that I obtained and read your "Becket." Will you, since you were so kind as to read me some of it last July, let me tell you how much enjoyment and light it has given me? Impressive as were the parts read, it impresses one incomparably more when studied as a whole. One cannot imagine a more vivid, a more perfectly faithful picture than it gives both of Henry and of Thomas. Truth in history is naturally truth in poetry; but you have made the characters of the two men shine out in a way which, while it never deviates from the impression history gives of them, goes beyond and perfects history. This is eminently conspicuous in the way their relations to one another are traced; and in the delineation of the influence on Thomas of the conception of the Church, blending with his own haughty spirit and sanctifying it to his own conscience. There is not, it seems to me, anything in modern poetry which helps us to realize, as your drama does, the sort of power the Church exerted on her ministers: and this is the central fact of the earlier middle ages. I wish you were writing a play on Hildebrand also. Venturing to say this to you from the point of view of a student of history, I scarcely presume to speak of the drama on its more purely literary side, how full of strength and beauty and delicacy it is, because you must have heard this often already from more competent critics

Believe me always sincerely yours,

J. BRYCE.

CHAPTER IX.

REMINISCENCES BY THE RIGHT HONOURABLE
W. E. H. LECKY.

From 1874 to 1880 I have but few notes, except about our visits to London. Mr Lecky, however, has kindly supplied me with the following recollections of this period:

You ask me to put down a few recollections of your father. It is with some difficulty that I do so, for many years have passed since I had the privilege of being much with him, and I knew too well his deep hatred of the common fashion of journalising in a great man's house, and writing down for future publication the careless utterances of free conversation, to be guilty of such an act. I must rely wholly on my memory, and I am afraid that to you, who knew him so much better than I did, these few notes can be of little use.

It was towards the close of the sixties that I had first the honour of knowing your father, and he invited me to accompany him to Farringford. We spent the night at Winchester, and next day went together over the cathedral, and visited the nonagenarian Dean Garnier, whose gracious courtesy in extreme old age, and whose solemn words of blessing as he said farewell to your father, still remain vividly in my memory. In many days at Farringford, on this and other later occasions, I came to know your father well, and long walks with him gave me much insight into his ways of thinking and feeling. His natural shyness seemed to me to have been afterwards considerably mitigated by periods of residence in London, but when I first knew him it was very apparent, and it was a good deal aggravated by his great short-sightedness. I well remember in one of our first walks his alarm at a flock of sheep which he took for tourists.   There always seemed to me to be a strange and somewhat pathetic contrast between his character and his position.   Nature evidently intended him for the life of the quietest and most secluded of country gentlemen, for a life spent among books and flowers and a few intimate friends, and very remote from the noise and controversies of the great world. Few men valued more highly domestic privacy.   But a great gift had made his name a household word among the English race.   True privacy, as he bitterly complained, became impossible to him, and troops of tourists, newspaper writers and interviewers were constantly occupied with his doings.

It was a surprise to me to find that he possessed a strong sense of humour, delighted in witty stories and told them admirably.   This was a side of his nature which never, I think, appeared in his writings before "The Northern Farmer," which was published early in the sixties.

I found too that he was not only a great poet, but also the best critic of verse I had ever known.   His ear for all the delicacies of rhythm has, I suppose, very seldom been equalled. He had an admirable verbal memory for the poetry of others as well as for his own, and he had the true instinct of genius in detecting among commonplace surroundings some happy phrase or some original metaphor.   His taste lay chiefly in sixteenth and seventeenth century poetry, in which he was widely read, and which he used to quote with admirable power.   I can still remember the almost terrible force he threw into the noble lines of Rochester on the "Vanity of Human Reason."

> "Reason, an *ignis fatuus* of the mind,
>   Which leaves the light of Nature, sense behind,
>   Pathless and dangerous wandering ways it takes,
>   Through Error's fenny bogs and thorny brakes;
>   While the misguided follower climbs with pain
>   Mountains of whimsies heaped in his own brain.
>   Till Old Age and Experience hand in hand
>   *Lead* him to Death and *make* him understand,
>   After a search so painful and so long,
>   That *all* his life he has been in the wrong."

In eighteenth century poetry he especially admired Burns, whom he placed, I think, on almost as high a level as Carlyle did, and his admiration was rather increased than diminished by the skill with which Burns, by a few strokes of genius, immortalised so many of the old songs of Scotland and incorporated great parts of them in his own poetry. "Burns did for the old songs of Scotland," he said, "almost what Shakespeare had done for the English drama that preceded him." Among nineteenth century poets I think he placed Keats on the highest pinnacle. He maintained (like Landor) that he had more of the real gift even than Shelley, and he thought it difficult to over-estimate the height to which he might have risen if he had lived. Byron he seemed to place on a lower level, and he considered his poetry too much akin to rhetoric. In discussing him I once quoted the exquisite passage in "The Giaour" beginning,

> "He who hath bent him o'er the dead
> Ere the first day of death is fled,"

comparing Greece to the dead man in the moment after death. Your father admitted its beauty, but said that to his taste the idea was too beaten out. "A Greek poet would have conveyed it by a single stroke. He would have said 'The face of the land is as the smile of the dead.'" He lamented that Campbell in "The Battle of the Baltic" had spoilt the intense reality and truthfulness of one of the noblest patriotic odes in the language by one false and jarring note:

> "And the mermaid's song condoles."

He admired much the plays of his old friend Henry Taylor, but complained that they were too uniformly stately, that he "never laid aside the cothurnus."

We naturally talked much about his own poetry. He said that he had great difficulty about a subject and a framework, a definite beginning and ending, but when these were found composition cost him very little trouble. "Guinevere," perhaps the most perfect of his "Idylls," was written in a fortnight. He had written out parts of the last "Idylls" in old English prose before turning them into verse. A letter once appeared in the *Spectator* written by Mr Knowles, who at that time was scarcely known in the literary world, representing King Arthur as conscience, and treating the "Idylls" as an allegory or picture of the different ways in which men looked on conscience, some reverencing it as a heaven-born king, others ascribing to it a purely earthly origin, while others simply obeyed it without forming any theory about its source. Your father gave me this letter, saying that it was the best account that had yet been given of his poem. I confess, however, that in spite of a beautiful image in " Guinevere " which seems to corroborate this view I have always thought that the allegory must have been in a great measure an afterthought. He had originally intended to write twelve " Idylls," one for each knight of the Round Table. He mentioned as an illustration of the uncertainty of critical judgments, that while the great majority of his critics complained that the " Idylls " had deteriorated after the first series, Fitzgerald, the author of the translation of " Omar Khayyám," whose opinion he valued very highly, steadily maintained that " The Holy Grail " was the best of them all.

In his conversation that minutely accurate observation of nature which is so conspicuous in his poetry, was very evident. He had a strong sense of the force and rhythm of words, and his knowledge of old English and of vivid provincial expressions was very great. " How infinitely superior," he said, " is the provincial word *flitter-mouse* to the orthodox *bat!* " With his love for old English he combined some taste for old forms of pronunciation. He once rebuked me for pronouncing "knowledge " in the way which is now usual, maintaining that the full sound of " know " should be given. I defended myself by quoting Swift's lines on the Irish Parliament:

" Not a bow-shot from the college,
Half the world from sense and knowledge,"

but he only said he hoped I would never pronounce the word in this way in reading his poetry.

He had no kind of sympathy with the theory which would divorce art from morals, and I have known no literary man who had a more uniformly high sense of duty in connection with his work. It was a sense of duty not only to the living and the unborn, but also, and in a very marked degree, to the dead. In speaking of the character of Becket, I remember his expressing the dread he always felt, lest he should do some injustice to the actions or motives of those who are in their graves. He hated with an intense hatred all literary quarrels, and rivalries, and jealousies, and his literary judgment seemed to me not only singularly sane and unexaggerated, but also singularly unbiassed by his personal likings. On the other hand, his many and close friendships had little or nothing to say to literary affinities. Carlyle, who never cared for his poetry, and indeed seemed always to think that he would have done better to have written in prose, was one of his oldest and most valued friends. Many persons spoke of your father as too much occupied with his own poetry. It did, no doubt, fill a very large place in his thoughts, and it is also true that he was accustomed to express his opinions about it with a curiously childlike simplicity and frankness. But at bottom, his nature seemed to me singularly modest. No poet ever corrected so many lines in deference to adverse criticism. His sensitiveness seemed to me curiously out of harmony with his large powerful frame, with his manly dark colouring, with his great massive hands and strong square-tipped fingers. It is probable, however, that it was closely connected with the gift that made him so delicate an interpreter of the finer shades of feeling, and also with the extreme tenderness of nature with which he shrank from all infliction of suffering. He once told me the well-known story of how some mischievous men made a bet that they would drive a strong young farmer of their acquaintance in alarm to his bed, and how they succeeded by coming to him one by one, inquiring with well simulated anxiety about his health, deploring his bad looks, asking him if he felt no strange sensation, and entreating him to take care of himself, and he owned that a few friends could in the same way persuade him that anything he wrote was worthless. The popularity of his poems sometimes seemed to bewilder him, and I have heard him gravely express his belief that it was largely due to his official position as Laureate.

As is always the case with great writers, resemblances to something he had written were often found in books which he had never read, and in languages which he did not know, and he complained with much reason that there were critics who imagined that the same idea could never occur independently to two men looking on the same aspects of Nature. "Tennyson suspected of plagiarism!" I once heard Browning say, when this subject was mentioned: "Why, you might as well suspect the Rothschilds of picking pockets." He had, however, the skill which most great writers possess, of drawing knowledge and thought from all about him. Among his friends was Mr G. F. Watts, and though your father, I think, had little real technical knowledge of art he fully *felt* the charm of that great imaginative painter. He once asked Mr Watts to describe his ideal of what a true portrait-painter should be, and he embalmed the substance of Mr Watts's reply in some of the noblest lines in the " Idylls [1]. "

> As when a painter, poring on a face,
> Divinely, thro' all hindrance, finds the man
> Behind it, and so paints him that his face,
> The shape and colour of a mind and life,
> · Lives for his children, ever at its best —

Freshwater society, in the days of which I am writing, had a singular charm. Among the permanent residents in the neighbourhood were Mr Watts, Mr Ward the well-known Catholic metaphysician and reviewer, and that true artist and most gifted woman Mrs Cameron. Miss Thackeray made many long visits. Sir John Simeon ("the prince of courtesy" of a very beautiful poem) sometimes came over from Swainston, and Farringford received many illustrious visitors from London, Oxford and Cambridge. Among the strangers who stayed there was Longfellow, for whom your father conceived a deep affection, and whom he described as one of the most enchanting of men. There was a delightful flavour in the house of the best intellectual society mingling with the tastes and habits of the most genuine country life. The country, however, always seemed to predominate, and some of us were made duly conscious of our town ignorance by the searching questions that were put to us about the flowers and trees which your father knew so well and loved so much. I remember myself once falling into some disgrace when having judiciously confessed my ignorance in many cases, I too confidently pronounced a flower to be a cowslip which was in truth an oxlip; and your father declared that he had persuaded one charming town-bred lady, to whom he was much attached, that a common daisy was a peculiar kind of rhododendron only found in the Isle of Wight. Apart from poetry there were several subjects on which he had read widely. He followed with keen and intelligent interest the great scientific discoveries of the day, and he delighted in

---

[1] My father had thought of writing for his last volume a poem to Watts on his great imaginative pictures, and on their common love of the golden spring crocus.

travels and natural history. His later works were largely historical, and he read for them very conscientiously.

Your father thought much about religious matters, and often dwelt with great force on his intuitive conviction of immortality, with its corollaries of Theism and Providence. These beliefs he held very strongly, but they were, I think, wholly detached in his mind from the dogmas of particular creeds. He had a decided leaning to some kinds of metaphysics, and the writings of James Hinton especially came home to him in a way which I could not share, or indeed understand. As all attentive readers of his poetry will have perceived, he was much occupied with, and disturbed by, the subversive theories that were abroad, but chiefly I think on account of their bearing on the great primal beliefs which I have mentioned, which he believed to be the main pillars on which the goodness, happiness and dignity of man must ultimately rest. Among his poems relating to these subjects the one which fascinated me the most was " Lucretius," in which he described with wonderful skill and subtlety the feelings of a convinced Materialist, who, having drunk the love-potion which his wife had given him, sees palpable visions of what seemed spirit-forms around him, and at last cuts the knot of his perplexity by suicide; and who when his wife confessed what she had done, died without a word of anger or reproach in his firm belief that all human actions are linked together in a chain of inexorable necessity. I do not think, however, that your father altogether approved of my preference, and when I quoted with admiration the lines:

Poor little life that toddles half an hour
Crown'd with a flower or two, and there an end —

he said that my liking for them only showed the morbidness of my nature.

My memory of your father goes back to many different scenes, to the garden and downs of Farringford, to the lovely terrace at Aldworth, to great uninteresting London crowds, in which I think he was much out of his element, to small dinners with Browning and a few other congenial spirits. I was once with him at the Lyceum at a representation of " The Cup," to which he had just added a new passage, and when between the acts Ellen Terry came into the box where we were sitting, I was much struck with the skill and judgment of his criticism of the acting. Perhaps, however, the most pleasing recollection of all is our journey together to Salisbury. I had been staying at Farringford, and was going thence to visit Stonehenge, which I had never seen, when about a quarter of an hour before the time of starting your father very unexpectedly declared that he would accompany me. You will remember the two lovely May-days (in 1880) we spent in visiting Stonehenge, and Salisbury cathedral, and Amesbury, the last home of Guinevere, and George Herbert's church, and the great Vandykes at Wilton. Carlyle and Emerson once made the same excursion, and Emerson has described it in his *English Traits*. We knew or visited no one, and the gardens of Wilton, where we long sat together, were a perfect dream of beauty. It is one of those recollections which abide with one for a life, and it never rose more vividly before me than when twelve years later I stood by your father's coffin in Westminster Abbey.

CHAPTER X.

ALDWORTH AND LONDON.

1874–1879.

Farringford he never forsook, though he added another home to it; and assuredly no poet has ever before called two such residences his own. Both of them were sweetened by the presence there, so graciously prolonged, of her to whom the lovers of Song owe so deep a debt of gratitude. The second home was as well chosen as the first. It lifted England's great poet to a height from which he could gaze on a large portion of that English land which he loved so well, see it basking in its most affluent summer beauty, and only bounded by "the inviolate sea." Year after year he trod its two stately terraces with men the most noted of their time, statesmen, warriors, men of letters, science and art, some of royal race, some famous in far lands, but none more welcome to him than the friends of his youth. Nearly all of those were taken from him by degrees; but many of them stand successively recorded in his verse. The days which I passed there yearly with him and his were the happiest days of each year. They will retain a happy place in my memory during whatever short period my life may last: and the sea-murmurs of Freshwater will blend with the sighing of the woods around Aldworth, for me, as for many more worthy, a music, if mournful, yet full of consolation.

MS Note, Aubrey de Vere.

In April 1874 the regular journal, giving the bare facts of our daily life, which my father had wished my mother to keep for his private use, comes to an end, so that I have no longer this on which to depend for the exact date as to days.

Owing to my mother's illness I did not return to Cambridge after the Christmas of 1875, but remained at home as my father's secretary, a capacity in which there was much to be done.

Yet he would willingly have set me free for a more

definite career; and at one time he consulted Mr. Gladstone as to my taking up a political life.   Gladstone
wrote in answer that my father must recollect that a
political life was "surrounded by an adamantine wall,"
that a man in politics was apt to "lose the finer moral
sense," and that the political outlook ahead was "full of
storms."

Our life did not undergo much change.   We
stayed at Farringford, as of late, till the end of June
or the beginning of July, and then went to Aldworth.
That fine air effectually cured my father's summer
hay-fever: and he could now thoroughly enjoy his walks
and drives in the beautiful country round Blackdown
and Haslemere.

Two places he particularly liked.   One was "Wegner's
Wells" on Hindhead, where he wrote his "Flower in the
crannied wall," and of which George Eliot said to him,
"What a good place for a murder in a novel!"   The
other was the "Silent Pool" near Albury, beneath the
Merrow downs that look over Guildford.   I have often
heard him describe this pool — "The splendour and
ripply play of light on the stream as it gushes from the
chalk over the greensand bottom, the mackerel colours
which flit about in the sunshine, and the network of the
current on the surface of the pool like crystal smoke."
"The water itself," he said, "was like what Keats says
of Neptune's cave, the 'palace floor breath-air.'"

The motto he proposed for a new sundial in his
garden was the old "Horas non numero nisi screnas."
As years went by he became calmer and more restful in
himself.   To plant new trees, and to watch the growth
of what were already planted, continued to be unfailing
sources of pleasure to him.   His hours of work were
somewhat changed, Sir Andrew Clark having insisted
on his walking before luncheon, and resting afterwards.

With his crook-handled stick, and accompanied by

my brother, or myself, or a friend, and by a dog, he
would tramp over hill and dale, not caring if the weather
were fair or foul, every now and then stopping in his
rapid walk to give point to an argument or to an anecdote. When alone with me, he would often chant a
poem that he was composing, and add fresh lines.
There was the same keen eye as of old for strange
birds and flowers, and, as of old, he would make a point
of looking up a strange bird or a new flower as soon
as he returned home from his walk. If a tourist were
seen coming towards him, he would flee: for many
would recognize from a distance his broad-brimmed
wideawake (the kind of hat that Carlyle, Sir Henry
Taylor, and others of his contemporaries wore) and his
short blue cape with velvet collar, and would deliberately
make for him in order to put some question. His hours
were quite regular: he breakfasted at 8, lunched at
2, dined at 7. At dessert, if alone, he would read to
himself, or if friends were in the house, he would sit
with them for an hour or so, and entertain them with
varied talk. He worked chiefly in the morning over his
pipe, or in the evening after his pint of port, also over
his pipe. Rare books or books with splendid bindings
he never cared for; yet he treasured his first edition
of Spenser's *Faery Queen*, and his second edition
of *Paradise Lost*. He would read over and over
again his favourite authors, and his delight was genuine when he came across a new author who "seemed
to have something in him." He was not unfrequently
abstracted in mood for days while he was composing,
which made him appear brusque to strangers, but alone
with his family he was never so happy as when engaged
on a great subject. His very directness and simplicity
moreover caused him sometimes to be misunderstood.
With strangers doubtless he was shy at first, owing
mostly to his short-sight, though none could be more

genial when he thawed. No one could have been more tolerant of or more gracious to dull people; and out of his imaginative large-heartedness he usually invested everyone with higher qualities than he or she possessed. As Jowett observed, "he would sit by a very commonplace person, telling stories with the most high-bred courtesy, endless stories not too high or too low for everyday conversation." With the country folk he loved to converse; especially seeking out the poor *old* men, from whom he always tried to ascertain their thoughts upon death and the future life.

His afternoons he generally spent on one of our smaller lawns, surrounded by birch and different sorts of pine and fir and cypress, after the fashion of separate green parlours. Here he would read the daily papers or some book to my mother lying out in her sofa-chair, or would receive friends from the neighbourhood, or would talk to guests staying in the house.

By degrees luncheon became later, partly because of the two hours' walk which had been ordered in the morning, and partly because of the trains which brought friends from London; and not seldom he went to town.

In March 1875 I find a note after he had seen Irving in *Hamlet*: "It is not a perfect Hamlet: the pathetic side of him well done, and the acting original. I liked it much better than Macready's. Irving came into the box, and we had a talk: he is a taking man."

In the summer my mother had sufficiently recovered to go with my father, my brother and myself to Pau, whence my father[1] and I made a tour in the Western Pyrenees. At Pau, meanwhile, Lionel became engaged to Eleanor Locker, whom as a child we had known well,

---

[1] On this journey he took Balzac's novels with him, especially delighting in *Le père Goriot* and *Eugénie Grandet*.

and who was like one of our own family. The engagement had not been in any way foreseen; but it was as welcome as so anxious an event can be to those whose life has been with and for their children. My father writes thus to the Duke of Argyll:

MY DEAR DUKE,

I had my garden gravelled when I made the terrace in front of the house at Aldworth. Many cartloads came over the hill. I should think it more probable that the flint found by you was dropt there, than that it had been left there since the denudation.

Tell the Duchess if she do not know it that Lionel, my youngest son, is engaged to Miss Eleanor Locker, who is half a Bruce and half a " London Lyric." The Queen has been very kind about it; we have known her from a child and approve of her heartily; but as he is only twenty-one they must wait till he get some employment, of which at present I see small prospect.

I trust the Duchess is bearing the winter well.

With our love to her, yours ever,

A. TENNYSON.

On our return to Farringford Mrs Procter came to visit us, and wrote after:

I cannot tell you what a happy time we had at Farringford. If I am not better for it, I ought to be; talking with A. T. seemed to lift me out of the earth-earthy. It was like what a retreat is to the religious.

In November[1] 1875 my father said: " I know it is the custom to prophesy change in France, but I am not so

[1] See Appendix, p. 526, for translations of Franklin epitaph sent to him by Gladstone this November.

sure that the Republic, which M. Rouher denounced, will not surprise many of them in its duration. They can have perpetual change of their men in power now."

December brought Edward Fitzgerald's usual Christmas letter.

My dear Alfred,

The time of year has come about when I have earned a right to hear a little about you all — Mrs Tennyson especially. But I suppose I must wait till one of your boys is at home ; which must soon be, for here is Christmas close by. Then a son must write me a bit of a letter. You know that I wish you all well and happy at Christmas and after. I have been told of Mrs Leslie Stephen's death, which must be a terrible thing for Annie Thackeray. Only about a fortnight ago she was telling me by letter what a sister she had.

As Spedding and Pollock (whom I asked about it) told me they had given their names to the Carlyle conspiracy, so did I, much wondering how Masson came to know of my existence. But I must say I thought the whole thing rather a cockney affair — *Address and Medal and White Satin Scroll*, which some dozen years ago, I think Carlyle would have been tempted to blow his nose upon, as the Sandwich Islanders did with their playbills at the Theatre. Only I never did see Carlyle use a handkerchief.... It is fine of him to be eighty ; I shall write him also my best 1875 letter. He seems to have passed the summer cheerfully and well in Kent. I see —— has another of his uncouth works out: I call him the great Prophet of the Gargoyle School : in France they have a man equally disagreeable to me — Victor Hugo. I think it partly is because the beautiful things have been done from the time of the Greeks to A. T., and so those who can't do them better prove their originality by descanting on the Ugly ; and they have their day. And I am your sincere and trusty old bedesman,

E. F. G.

In September 1876 my father and I visited Fitzgerald at Woodbridge. He was affectionate, genial, and humorous, declaring that the captain of his lugger was

one of the greatest of men. The views that Fitz expressed to me on literature were original and interesting,
but the old man never got off his own platform to look
at the work of modern authors. He had always wanted
men like Thackeray and my father to go along with his
crotchets, which were many. He had not been carried
away by their genius out of himself and out of his own
old Cambridge critical groove; and had not, like them,
grown with the times. After we had arrived home he
wrote:

WOODBRIDGE, *Sept. 26th*, 1876.

I am glad you were pleased with your short visit here.
Perhaps you will one day, one or both of you, come again : and,
if you will but give warning, and no nieces are in possession of
the house, it shall be ready for you, and some *tender* meat provided. Somehow I, when you were gone, felt somewhat abroad,
and a few hours after went to an old village by the sea, Dun-
wich, once a considerable town, now swept into the sea, with
the remains of a church on the cliff and the walls of an ancient
priory beside. I was wishing that I had made you come with
me, over a stretch of wild heath too, but there was no room in
the little Inn : and dare say *very tough meat!* *That* fatal reed
sticks in my side you see. But I am still yours, and all yours,
sincerely,

E. F. G.

In October we stayed with the Gladstones at Hawarden, my father accepting the invitation thus:

October 25th, 1876.

On Monday then, if all be well. As you are good
enough to say that you will manage anything rather
than lose my visit, will you manage that I may have my
pipe in my own room whenever I like?

The talk between Gladstone and my father was
on Dante, "Harold," Gladstone's late speech about

remitting the Income Tax, modern morality, the force of public opinion, the evils of materialism and the new Biblical criticism.

My father expressed the view that, "as the English language is much finer than the Italian for variety of sound, so Milton for sound is often finer than Dante." He quoted Milton, Virgil, Dante and Homer[1] to illustrate his meaning; then said:

"What, for example, can be more monotonous than the first lines of the ' Inferno' with their ' a-s'?

> 'Nel mezzo del cammin di nostra vita
> Mi ritrovai per una selva oscura,
> Chè la dirritta via era smarrita' —

and so on."

After the visit my father wrote from Farringford:

My dear Mrs Gladstone,

Here we are returned to our winter-quarters, which however we find at present colder than Aldworth. We retain golden memories of our visit to Hawarden, and your statesman, not like Diocletian among his cabbages but among his oaks, axe in hand. Has he anything to say about my drama ("Harold")?

Always yours, A. Tennyson.

Gladstone answered:

It seems to me you have worked the history up to the acme of its capability... I propose to quote, but without acknowledgement, in an article for the current *Contemporary Review* about the Hellenic part of the Eastern Question the two lines about the voice of the people...

The voice of any people is the sword
That guards them or the sword that beats them down.

[1] Cf. the fine effect of the monotonous ending of words in -ων at the beginning of the thirteenth book of the *Iliad*.

A letter of Jan. 13th, 1877, from the Hon. Sec. of the Burns' Memorial, asks my father to be present at the unveiling of the statue in Glasgow. The Secretary says: "So enthusiastic are the people of the West of Scotland that the 25th (the date of unveiling) is to be held as a general holiday, and a procession of thirty or forty thousand is to take part in the proceedings." My father answered that he could not go — "Though I have as much veneration for the poet as if I had been born a Scotchman."

Great pleasure was given to my father by the following letter from Lord Lytton; a graceful and cordial recognition of the intention shown in the dedication of " Harold " to obliterate the memory of the old literary passage-of-arms with his father [1].

CALCUTTA,
19th Jan., 1877.

DEAR MR TENNYSON,

I am told by the English newspapers, received to-day, that you have dedicated to me your new dramatic poem " Harold." I have not yet seen the poem; but there must be an exception to every rule, and assuming that in this instance at least the newspapers tell the truth, I cannot let a mail go by without asking you to believe how flattered I am by the honour you have done me, and how sensibly touched by your manner of doing it. Memories the tenderest and most cherished of my life are strangely mingled with the hope your generosity has sanctioned, that I may live hereafter on your pages, associated with the name of their great author, to whom in common with all our countrymen, I already owe so much, and with that of my dear father, to whom I owe life itself, and all great things in life,

---

[1] See Vol. I. p. 244.   The dedication ran :

MY DEAR LORD LYTTON,

After old-world records — such as the Bayeux tapestry and the Roman de Rou, — Edward Freeman's *History of the Norman Conquest*, and your father's Historical Romance treating of the same times, have been mainly helpful to me in writing this Drama. Your father dedicated his *Harold* to my father's brother; allow me to dedicate my " Harold " to yourself.

A. TENNYSON.

nor least of all my share in the valued tribute so generously
offered to his memory by England's greatest living Poet.   In his
name and for his sake, I thank you no less warmly than on my
own behalf.   It is a fact of which I was not aware until after his
death, that the plot of almost every one of my father's novels
was first worked out in the form of a play; and probably he
owed to the habitual employment of this method much of his
success as a romance writer in the dramatic development of character and situation.   In the mass of his unpublished manuscripts
I have found an unfinished dramatic sketch entitled " William
the Norman" or " William the Conqueror" (I forget which), containing the undoubted germ of the historical romance to which
reference is made in the dedication of your own poem.   This
manuscript is not with me in India; but, should I live to return
to England, I hope you will then accept from me a private copy
of it, as a literary curiosity which will henceforth derive its
chief interest from your own work.   Meanwhile pray accept
the sincere assurance of those grateful sentiments with which
I am,

Dear Mr Tennyson, your obliged

LYTTON.

In March 1877 my father wrote " Montenegro,"
which he always put first among his sonnets, writing
thus to Mr Gladstone: " Your talk interested me and my
son so much that we quite forgot one of my two objects
in calling on you, the first to gain your approval of that
sonnet of which you were the inspirer; the second to ask
if you could give us tickets of admission to the House
for the great debate to-morrow, if it come on to-morrow,
and about what time you may be expected to speak."

On March 28th my father and I dined with Lord
Houghton at Almond's Hotel to meet Schliemann.   In
the course of conversation Schliemann said: " Hissarlik,
the ancient Troy, is no bigger than the courtyard of
Burlington House."   " I can never believe that," my
father replied.   As we were leaving the room after
dinner, Schliemann, duly impressed with the splendour

of the entertainment, remarked to us of our host: "Our lord is a very glorious lord, is he not?"

In June Victor Hugo thanked my father in the following letter for the sonnet, addressed to the great French poet, after my brother had visited him in Paris:

4 *Juin*, 1877, PARIS.

MON ÉMINENT ET CHER CONFRÈRE,

Je lis avec émotion vos vers superbes, c'est un reflet de gloire que vous m'envoyez. Comment n'aimerais-je pas l'Angleterre qui produit des hommes tels que vous! l'Angleterre de Wilberforce! l'Angleterre de Milton et de Newton! l'Angleterre de Shakespeare! France et Angleterre sont pour moi un seul peuple comme Vérité et Liberté sont une seule lumière. Je crois à l'unité divine.

J'aime tous les peuples et tous les hommes et j'admire vos nobles vers.

Recevez mon cordial serrement de main.

VICTOR HUGO.

J'ai été heureux de connaître votre charmant fils — il m'a semblé, que serrer sa main, c'était presser la votre.

In July I find a note from Sir Alexander Grant to Mr. Palgrave describing a visit to Farringford:

After I saw you in London I had a delightful visit to Freshwater, at least I found it so in spite of the most inclement weather. As the *Saturday Review* wisely remarks, "Nature brings not back the mastodon," in the case of visiting houses where of old we had divine hours. But yet at Farringford mine heart burned within me. The bard would not smoke as much as I could have wished, *he is very regular and methodical*, and walks and sleeps by rule, which is uninteresting, but which, I hope, will cause him to live till ninety. I never knew him more hearty and kind.

In the evenings my father would now play at Dummy Whist, and on one occasion he so terrified a young lady by talking to Dummy as to a real person that she forthwith vanished to her own room. About this time a beautiful setter was given him. It suddenly struck him at midnight that the new dog might feel hungry and lonely, so he went downstairs and stole a chicken for the dog, " Dear old Don." Great was the discomfiture in the kitchen next morning as to what had become of the chicken.

In October he wrote to Mrs Brookfield on her son's marriage:

Oct. 11th, 1877.

MY DEAR J. O. B.,

　... Out of the distance I spread my hands over your son, and his future, if that — tho' I trust it may in some measure please you — can in any way avail him.

Your old friend who remembers you coming out on the balcony of the house at Southampton — I was walking with *him* [1] and he had just told me of his engagement.

A, TENNYSON.

At Christmas Longfellow sent him a friendly greeting:

CAMBRIDGE, *Nov.* 27th, 1877.

MY DEAR TENNYSON,

　Accept this brief Christmas greeting from me, with all good wishes for yourself and household.

Yours faithfully,

HENRY W. LONGFELLOW.

---

[1] In 1869 my father had written an elegiac sonnet to his old college-friend Brookfield for Lord Lyttelton's memoir.

Wapentake to Alfred Tennyson.

Poet! I come to touch thy lance with mine,
  Not as a knight who on the listed field
  Of tourney touched his adversary's shield
In token of defiance, but in sign
Of homage to the mastery, which is thine
  In English song; nor will I keep concealed,
  And voiceless as a rivulet frost-congealed,
My admiration for thy verse divine.
Not of the howling dervishes of song,
  Who craze the brain with their delirious dance,
  Art thou, O sweet historian of the heart!
Therefore to thee the laurel-leaves belong,
  To thee our love and our allegiance,
  For thy allegiance to the poet's art.

HENRY W. LONGFELLOW.

My father answered:

MY DEAR LONGFELLOW,

  You have sent me a Christmas greeting: more than that, a Christmas gift in the shape of a very perfect flower from your own spacious garden: wherefore I exult and stick it in my cap and defy my foes. I and wife and sons salute you and thank you and wish all happiness to you and yours here and hereafter.

With our kindest remembrances,

Yours ever, A. TENNYSON.

À propos of Longfellow's greeting Edward Fitzgerald wrote:

LITTLE GRANGE, WOODBRIDGE, *Dec.* 1877.

Will anyone tell me anything of old Frederick? Three months ago, I think, he wrote me word of a house he had bought near Jersey, a wonderful bargain, which I told him would be about the first wonderful bargain he ever made in his life, so

far as I could guess. Now a month or so ago I wrote to ask
him about himself and his bargain : and, though he is not so
liberal a letter-writer as the present, he generally satisfies me
with some answer within such a time. Does anyone at Farringford know about him ? And will tell me ? Be it noticed that
being on distant terms with the whole Laureate Family, I
address no one in particular : only am obliged to direct to that
paltry poet who is the unworthy head. And, in spite of my
wrongs, I do wish them all a happy Christmas and New Year,
and am theirs according as they shall behave to

They know Whom.

That was a nice sonnet of Longfellow's to "The Laurell'd
Head"; the "howling dervishes" will tire out in their dance
before long, I do think : never doubted but they would.

> O but then my Bil-ly listed,
>   Listed and cross'd the roaring main :
> For King George he fought brave-ly
>   In Po'tig'l, France, and Spain :
> Don't you see my Billy a-coming,
>   Coming in yonder cloud :
> Gridiron Angels ho-vering round him,
>   Don't you see him in yonder clouds ?

E. F. G.

On the 28th of February, 1878, Lionel and Eleanor
Locker were married in Westminster Abbey. Dean
Stanley was too ill to officiate; but he sent for the young
bride and bridegroom to his bedroom and gave them his
blessing.

Frederick Locker writes to me in June 1878 :

I have a letter from Arthur (Dean Stanley) asking me if
Herkomer may take a portrait of A. T. Herkomer himself
says he will go to you wherever you may happen to be, and
it will only occupy about three hours. I write in great haste,
and I know I bore you by writing, but I do not like to refuse
my brother, who, I fancy, likes Herkomer.

Herkomer's offer was accepted, and he came to
Farringford and had sittings from my father.

From 1875 to 1882 we every year took a house in London, in Wimpole Street, in Upper Belgrave Street, Eaton Place and Eaton Square, in order to be near my brother whose work was at the India Office; and as my father said, " To rub our country rust off." We always kept Christmas at Farringford, moving to London in February to stay till Easter. During these years my father made many new acquaintances. Among these I may name the Selbornes, with whom my parents became close friends; and who, fortunately for us, lived within driving distance of Aldworth.

On one occasion Ruskin lunched with us, adorned by his accustomed blue tie, kind and courteous as ever. He said that his inclination was to devote himself still to Art, but that he felt it a duty to give the remainder of his life to the education of the poorer classes. In his opinion " Everything bad is to be found in London and other large cities; and only in life and work in country fields is there health for body and for mind." My father and he deprecated in the strongest possible language the proposed Channel Tunnel.

Before Ruskin took his leave, my father said to him:

" Do you know that most romantic of lyrics?

> He turn'd his charger as he spake,
>   Upon the river shore,
> He gave his bridle-reins a shake,
>   Said Adieu for evermore,
>   My Love!
> And adieu for evermore."

" Do I not? " said Ruskin, " I am so glad you like it, Tennyson; I place it among the best things ever done by anyone."

Upon a day, memorable to me, my father took me to Pembroke Lodge. He had a high esteem for Lord and Lady Russell; " Plucky Lord John " he would call him. Lord Russell and my father had a strong bond in their common conviction that the English race was " destined to be the greatest among races." Both gloried in the " Imperii porrecta Majestas " of England and advocated an ever-closer union with our colonies [1]. My father believed that the federation so formed would be the strongest force for good and for freedom that the world has ever known. I have heard him say that he did not believe it hopeless that America should enter into a close alliance with such a league.

" The craven fear of being great " my father felt was among the besetting sins of certain English statesmen, and in reply to this Lord Russell would cry that there must be no niggardliness with regard to armaments, he being convinced that " If need were, we should be able to stand alone." My father particularly liked Lord Russell's high expectations from " the independence of nationalities." They both shook hands over the hope that now-a-days foreign ministers, whether Liberal or Conservative, had learnt to be alive to the need of continuity in our foreign policy.

On another not-to-be-forgotten day General Gordon came to us. He had lately arrived from Ireland, after having made there certain suggestions with regard to the land question. These were, I believe, the foundation of the "Ashbourne Act."

In answer to our invitation to luncheon he arrived suddenly, and asked to see me in the hall. Having

[1] A letter which I wrote to the Colonial Institute after his death summarises my father's views on this subject :

"One of the deepest desires of his life was to help the realisation of the ideal of an Empire by the most intimate union of every part of our British Empire. He believed that every different member so united would, with a heightening of individuality to each member, give such strength and greatness and stability to the whole as would make our Empire a faithful and fearless leader in all that is good throughout all the world."

learnt that we were alone, he glided spirit-like into the dining-room where we were already seated. Going straight up to my father, he said in a solemn voice: "Mr Tennyson, I want you to do something for our young soldiers. You alone are the man who can do it. We want training-homes for them all over England." As it happened, we were at that time much interested in a project of James Baillie Hamilton's — a camp where gentlemen's sons might be prepared for the army or the colonies. We told the General of this and he allowed us to introduce Mr Baillie Hamilton to him. It was finally agreed that if such a camp were founded the General would take the head, on condition that arrangements were made to admit also the sons of the poorest. The camp was never formed, the General was ordered to Mauritius, and the scheme of a training-home for the army fell through; until the Gordon Home was initiated by my father, and founded by the Prince of Wales, after Gordon's death and in his memory.

What struck my father about Gordon was, he said, "his look of utter benevolence and bonhommie." He was to have returned and given my father more detail as to his young soldiers' camp, but he wrote:

I fear I must deprive myself of a great pleasure, viz. a smoke with Mr Tennyson, for I am engaged, and on Sunday evening I generally stay at home. I hope when these east winds have ceased, and when you are back in town, I may come and see you unless I am already gone.

Believe me with kind regards yours sincerely,

C. E. GORDON [1].

[1] The following is an extract from a letter from Lady Cardwell:

74 EATON SQUARE, *April 9th*, 1878.

......It may interest you to know another instance of the solace you have given to those in distant lands severed from all those with whom they could hold converse.

You know all about Col. Gordon (Chinese Gordon) and the immense

For Matthew Arnold my father always had a warm
regard, not only because he admired his best work, but
also because he had known him at Coniston as a young
man just entering on life. They met frequently in
London. On one occasion, when he called, I remember
my father was amused at what he called " Mat's sublime
waggery," for " Mat " had said to me, probably to call
forth a retort, " Your father has been our most popular
poet for over forty years, and I am of opinion that he
fully deserves his reputation."

Later I met Matthew Arnold at Mr Goschen's, and
my father gave me this message for him : " Tell Mat not
to write any more of those prose things, like *Literature
and Dogma* but to give us something like his ' Thyrsis,'
' Scholar Gipsy,' or ' Forsaken Merman.' " " Mat " took
the message in the best possible spirit, and told it
gleefully about himself all over London.

Two or three times we met George Eliot in town,
and she expressed herself much pleased that the poet
who, she said, had " so much human blood in his poems
and plays," should have told her that her " flight of Hetty
in *Adam Bede* and Thackeray's gradual breaking down
of Colonel Newcome were the two most pathetic things
in modern prose fiction." He had the highest admiration for her insight into character, but did not think

pressure upon him and the heroic services he is rendering to the cause of
humanity in putting down the slave trade, as Governor of the Soudan, by a
wonderful sacrifice of himself. I often hear from him of his long solitary
rides of hundreds of miles in the desert and wilderness, and wished to find
the most acceptable companion I could send to him.

It must be in a very small compass. Happily I found the beautiful
edition of all your books in the small green case, and I sent it a few months
ago.

He is intensely delighted with it and mentions it in every letter. In his
last, lately received from Khartoum, he says: "I find the reading of
Tennyson is my great relief, and the volumes are so small and of such clear
print that they will always go with me. I have long wanted a small copy,
but never knew that he had published one," etc.

her quite so true to nature as Shakespeare and Miss Austen [1].

I read somewhere an account of a quarrel between her and my father, carried on in loud tones, with red faces and clenched fists, the subject being her want of belief in an after-life. I showed this to him, and he wrote down what actually happened. "I and she never had one moment of discussion, much less of quarrel. She called, and when she went away I pressed her hand kindly and sweetly, and said, ' I wish you well with your molecules.' She replied as gently, ' I get on very well with my molecules.' "

I have also the record of a later conversation between them which took place at Aldworth. They agreed as to " the namby-pambyism of the age, which hates a story to end in tragedy, as if the greatest moral lessons were not taught by tragedies." My father added, " What the public do not understand is that the great tragedy is all balance throughout." She then objected to the many English writers who set up French literature against our own, for " Is not ours," she said, " one of the greatest in the world ? "

She wanted my father to make a poem of this story, which she narrated as true, and as having occurred in one of the midland counties. A drunkard boasted that he would " fight any bull ever born." He went out into the starlight and walked up to a well-known ferocious bull, dealing him a blow on the forehead which felled both man and bull. By that shock the man became " undrunk " and never drank again, so great was the terror which seized on him while lying there: the bull " nozzling " him; those big eyes, head and horns between him and the sky. George Eliot thought that my father would make a fine analysis of what passed in the man's mind as he lay there under the starry heavens.

[1] For instance, the character of Adam Bede was " too much idealized."

In return for this my father told her a story of real life, about a sailor, devoted to music, who was always in requisition for sailors' dances, as he played superbly on the violin. But whenever he played his nerves were so excited that he took brandy to quiet them, and became in consequence invariably drunk after his music. One night when sailing up the Mississippi he brought out his violin under the broad moon, and then broke it over the side of the vessel; having resolved never to play violin more or get drunk again.

When the restoration of St Mark's was contemplated George Eliot wrote to my father (she had asked him to protest against it):

Please, dear friend, send the letter about St Mark's, Venice, without delay,—a dying struggle against the vandalism of the present age.

M. Lewes.

In November 1878 the lively, witty, kindly George Lewes died, and my father wrote as follows to George Eliot, who was all but broken-hearted:

Dear Friend,

Our affectionate sympathies are with you. That is all that can be said at present, and these "words" are nothing to you at present, but for his sake accept them.

A. Tennyson.

My father's first meeting with the Princess of Wales took place at Mrs Greville's in Chester Square. The Princess asked him to read the "Welcome to Alexandra." When he had read it, the fact of his reading his own complimentary poem to the Princess herself somehow struck them both as being so ludicrous, that he dropt the book on the floor and both went into fits of uncontrollable laughter.

It was at this time that Lady Simeon had a wish to bring Newman and my father together. She therefore forwarded a message from my father to the effect that he would like to meet Newman whenever they happened to be in London together. Newman wrote as follows:

April 17th, 1877.

DEAR MR TENNYSON,

I hope you will not think it a liberty in me thus to address you, but the kindness of your message to me by Lady Simeon encourages me to do so. While I acquiesce in the purport of it, I cannot help expressing the pleasure and the honour I should feel it to be allowed to make your acquaintance. Great differences of opinion and personal history lie between us, but it would be strange if I *alone* of Englishmen did not feel the *force* of those endowments of mind which have made your name so popular. I am with great respect,

Sincerely yours, J. H. NEWMAN.

Dr Dabbs has recorded the following conversation that he had with my father about " In Memoriam " and Newman :

D. Do you think there is any really insuperable obstacle or series of obstacles between science and religion ?

T. I have tried to say my say about it in " In Memoriam."

D. Certainly no lack of religion there.

T. I hope not.

D. And all proper reverence for scientific facts ?

T. So there should be — (long pause). I sometimes think it is the least misunderstood of all my work. I don't mean that the commentators have been more right, but that the general reading public has been less wrong than usual as to my intentions.

D. I often wish, sir, that commentaries might cease or the poet himself supply them.

T. That can never be. And (after another long pause) the poet might not do them well.

D. He could not, in many cases, do them worse.

T. I am not sure (half smiling). He might!

D. I see Newman was asked as to his meaning of two lines in "Lead, kindly Light" and frankly acknowledged he had forgotten "what he was driving at."

T. He never used such a phrase as "what he was driving at."

D. No, no, that is mine.

T. Is that paraphrase or commentary, eh?

D. Ah! (Then there was a good laugh at my expense.)

T. I daresay Newman may have forgotten. It would be hard indeed to remember the "atmosphere" of each thought. When young men ask me the interpretation of some of my *early* lines, I sometimes forget, and can only answer with Goethe, "You probably know better than I do, being young."

Among the compliments paid my father, that which he valued most was his old friend Browning's dedication of a selection of his own poems:

To Alfred Tennyson.

In poetry illustrious and consummate,
In friendship noble and sincere.

Browning frequently dined with us. The *tête-à-tête* conversations between him and my father on every imaginable topic, when no one but myself was with them, were the best talk I have ever heard, so full of repartee, quip, epigram, anecdote, depth and wisdom: but it is quite impossible to attempt to reproduce them, owing to their very brilliancy. These brother-poets were two of the most widely-read men of their time, absolutely without a touch of jealousy, and revelling as it were in each other's power.

On rare occasions my father would rally Browning playfully on his harshness of rhythm, the obscurity and length of his poems. The retort would be: " I cannot alter myself: the people must take me as they find me." My father would repeat his usual dictum about literary work: " An artist should get his workmanship as good as he can, and make his work as perfect as possible. A small vessel, built on fine lines, is likely to float further down the stream of time than a big raft." They would laugh heartily together at Browning's faculty for absurd and abstruse rhymes. I remember a dinner where Jebb, Miss Thackeray, and Browning were present. Browning said he thought that he could make a rhyme for every word in the English language. We gave him "rhinoceros." Without a pause he said :

> " O, if you should see a rhinoceros
>   And a tree be in sight,
>   Climb quick, for his might
> Is a match for the Gods, he can toss Eros."

At another time Browning produced for my father's amusement impromptu verses on Carlyle and his wife, " Terse Verse, being a contribution to Scottish Anthology," as he called it:

> " Hail ye hills and heaths of Ecclefechan!
>   Hail ye banks and braes of Craigenputtock!
>   T. Carlyle was born in Ecclefechan,
>   Jane his wife was born in Craigenputtock.
>   She, a pearl where eye detect no speck can,
>   He, ordained to close with and cross-buttock
>   Cant, the giant — these, O Ecclefechan,
>   These your glories be, O Craigenputtock!"

My father on the other hand confessed that he believed he knew the quantity of every word in the English language except perhaps "scissors." We asked him to make a Sapphic stanza in quantity, with the Greek cadence. He gave us this:

Sapphics [1].

Faded ev'ry violet, all the roses;
Gone the glorious promise; and the victim,
Broken in this anger of Aphrodite,
      Yields to the victor.

Browning had sent us his *Aristophanes' Apology:* "another jet from his full fountain," as my father said; and then he gave his *Inn Album* to my father, who wrote:

MY DEAR BROWNING,

      You are the most brotherly of poets, and your brother in the muses thanks you with the affection of a brother. *She* would thank you too on paper if she could put hand to pen.

                    A. T.

While in London we often walked to the Westminster Deanery, for about Lady Augusta and the Dean there was "a good atmosphere of high work." Dean Stanley's courage and truth, and his delicate perceptions of things beautiful and spiritual, and his broad and generous sympathies and interests, fascinated my father. He often quoted a remark of the Dean's: "So far from being effete, Christianity is as yet undeveloped." A story that Stanley told (not mentioned in his *Life*) was, that after a great function in the Abbey he was coming

---

[1] Printed in Professor Jebb's *Primer of Greek Literature*, 1877.

out with Disraeli. The Dean was saying that the
Athanasian Creed ought to be omitted from the Prayer
Book. Disraeli looked up at him and replied, "Mr Dean,
no dogmas, no deans."

When Cleopatra's Needle was brought to London,
Stanley asked my father to make some lines upon it;
to be engraven on the base. These were put together
by my father at once, and I made a note of them:

Cleopatra's Needle.

Here, I that stood in On beside the flow
Of sacred Nile, three thousand years ago!—
A Pharaoh, kingliest of his kingly race,
First shaped, and carved, and set me in my place.
A Caesar of a punier dynasty
Thence haled me toward the Mediterranean sea,
Whence your own citizens, for their own renown,
Thro' strange seas drew me to your monster town.
I have seen the four great empires disappear!
I was when London was not! I am here!

Renan called. My father thought him genial, acute
and epigrammatic, and approved much of one of his
epigrams, "La vérité est dans une nuance." Stories
were told of Brittany and the Bretons; and Renan
was delighted when my father narrated how the landlady of the inn at Lannion had recognized "Monsieur
Tennyson" as the poet of their King Arthur.

My father said that he had been disappointed with
Carnac, and that Stonehenge was far finer. Renan
discoursed on Carnac, and said that stones similar to
the Carnac stones had been discovered in Algiers; he
believed that they were all symbols of tribal covenants.
My father and he then discussed Villemarqué, and my
father said "Villemarqué est plus poète que savant"; to
which Renan assented. The talk turned to the ma-

terialism and realism of the present day, against which my father inveighed. Renan said, "Ah yes, it is better to illuminate history with genius as you and others have done, than with mere research." The retort was quick: " You are a prose-poet, Monsieur Renan, and perhaps in this instance too imaginative."

My father was fond of asking Joachim to play to him in his own house. One particular evening I remember, at 86, Eaton Square. My father had been expressing his wonder at Joachim's mastery of the violin, — for Joachim had been playing to us and our friends numberless Hungarian dances, — and by way of thanks for the splendid music I asked him to read one of his poems to Joachim. Accordingly after the guests had gone he took the great musician to smoke with him in his ' den ' at the top of the house. There they talked of Goethe, especially praising a poem of Goethe's old age, " Der West-östliche Divan," and then my father read " The Revenge." On reaching the line

And the sun went down, and the stars came out far
        over the summer sea,

he asked Joachim, " Could you do that on your violin ? " — the peace of nature after the thunder of the battle. There was no more reading however that night, for he suddenly turned round to me, saying, " I must not read any more, else I shall wake up the cook who is sleeping next door."

Whenever a chance offered itself, we called on the Carlyles. My father would say, " Mr and Mrs Carlyle on the whole enjoyed life together, else they would not have chaffed one another so heartily."

Carlyle made a point of not unfrequently paying his respects to my mother, who he knew could not go to see him; and the last time he called my nephew, " golden-haired Ally," was brought in to the great man. Carlyle put his hands on the little fellow's head and said solemnly, " Fair fall thee, little man, in this world, and the next." Upon which my father said to me: " Carlyle is the most reverent and most irreverent man I know."

I subjoin some talks which my father had with Carlyle, jotted down in my note-book.

A. T. People say you are writing your autobiography.

Carlyle. Do they? Do they want me to make away with myself that they talk like that?

A. T. Why don't you try your hand at a great novel? you have seen life enough.

Carlyle. No, no. I write a novel! I know nothing of human character.

After going with my father to the British Museum and looking at the Greek and Roman statues, Carlyle said, " Neither man nor god can get on without a decent jaw-bone, and not one of them has a decent jaw-bone."

Carlyle became in later years reconciled to my father's writing poetry. He admired " Harold," saying that it was "full of wild pathos," and founded on the Bayeux tapestry, which he called "a very blessed work indeed."

My father read him " The Revenge."

Carlyle. Eh! Alfred, you have got the grip of it.

A. T. There's a man for you. The Spaniards declared he would "carouse" three or four glasses of wine and take the glasses between his teeth and crush them to pieces and swallow them down.

Carlyle. (Half to himself.) I knew that Alfred would treat that episode in a masterful manner, and he'd not allude to Elizabeth's starving the poor sailors.

And then he spoke of " The May Queen." " Oh! but that's tender and true; my niece says it sometimes to me!"

Through " The First Quarrel " he gave little cries of sympathy.

Carlyle. Ah, but that's a dreary tragic tale.

A. T. That's a true tale. My doctor in the Isle of Wight told it me.

Carlyle, going on about the poem : Ech! poor fellow, he was just an honest plain man, and she was a curious production of the century, and I'm very sorry for that poor girl too.

One day Carlyle was full of Holman Hunt's " Shadow of the Cross."

Carlyle. I think, poor fellow, he painted that picture in a distraction.

A. T. The Christ I call Christ-like is Sebastian del Piombo's in the National Gallery [1].

Then they talked of Goldsmith and Goethe.

Carlyle. Goldie was just an Irish blackguard, with a fine brain and sun-like eyes, and a great fund of goosery.

A. T. And of tender-heartedness : I love Goldie.

He made Carlyle laugh by giving a humorous imitation of Dr Johnson and Goldsmith talking together.

Carlyle. Goldsmith was much read in Germany in Goethe's time.

A. T. You know we visited Goethe's house at Weimar. The " Salve " on the door-mat, and the legion of Goethe's old boots there looked to me terribly pathetic.

Then my father told how we had found a book " From T. Carlyle " on his table, which pleased the old man mightily.

They made merry over the statues of Goethe and Schiller in the market-place, " for all the world like drunken sailors quarrelling over a wreath."

Carlyle. Ay, ay. Art is at a low ebb ; and among the nations England, unless she takes great heed, will go down to the devil.

[1] My father also had a high admiration for Leonardo da Vinci's sketch of the head of Christ in the Brera at Milan.

A. T. Come! we are not so bad as in Charles II.'s reign.

Carlyle. O yes, there were more Andrew Marvells then. True, the Parliament was so coxcombed at having cut a king's head off that there was no doing anything with them. Those days indeed were very like the days now, no real strong ruler, all just a confusion of jackassery.

He called Gladstone " The man with the immeasurable power of vocables."

A. T. I love the man, but no Prime Minister ought to be an orator.

They touched on Macaulay.

A. T. Macaulay, Guizot, Hallam and I went over the Houses of Parliament and Westminster Hall together; Macaulay said to me on going away, " I am delighted to have met you, Mr Tennyson "; but I never saw him afterwards.

Carlyle. Eh (looking at him grimly), Alfred, Macaulay was afraid of you, you are such a black man (with a tremendous guffaw).

The last time we saw Carlyle he was in his dressing-gown, reading Masson's *Milton*.

A. T. Milton is a grand old fellow.

Carlyle. Yes, yes, and this man Masson is the first man who has properly sorted the Mosaic cosmogony, and I can now tell which way Satan went; but Masson has hung on his Milton peg *all* the politics, which Milton, poor fellow, had never much to do with except to print a pamphlet or two.

They then talked about death.

A. T. In my old age I should like to get away from all this tumult and turmoil of civilization and live on the top of a tropical mountain! I should at least like to see the splendours of the Brazilian forests before I die.

Carlyle. I would also like to quit it all.

A. T.   If I were a young man, I would head a colony out somewhere or other.

Carlyle.   O, ay, so would I, to India or somewhere: but the scraggiest bit of heath in Scotland is more to me than all the forests of Brazil.   I am just twinkling away, and I wish I had my Dimittis long ago.

Carlyle gave my father his tobacco box as a pledge of eternal brotherhood, and at the bottom of this I found a letter from Carlyle introducing Mrs Oliphant.

Mrs Oliphant, whom this note accompanies, is an old and esteemed friend in this house; distinguished in literature, *Life of Edward Irving*, etc., and what is best of all, a highly amiable, rational and worthy lady.

Yours ever truly, T. CARLYLE.

CHAPTER XI.

1879–80.

In the Spring of 1879 a great sorrow came upon
my parents. My father's favourite brother Charles (Tennyson) Turner died at Cheltenham on April 25th, and
on May 20th his wife, my mother's sister, followed him.
His sonnets, " Letty's Globe," " Time and Twilight,"
" On seeing a child blush on his first view of a corpse,"
" The Buoy Bell," " The Schoolboy's Dream," " On
shooting a swallow in early youth," had in my father's
judgment all the tenderness of the Greek epigram,
and he ranked sonnets such as " Time and Twilight,"
and " The Holy Emerald," among the noblest in the
language.

My uncle with his aquiline nose, dark eyes and
black hair was very like my father, and Thackeray
seeing him in middle life called him a " Velasquez
tout craché." As Vicar of Grasby he was known as the
bountiful and loving father of his flock, his wife being
in all things his devoted helpmate. We often spent
part of the summer with them in their Vicarage. At
their own expense they had built this and the church
and the schools. Both had great delight in a simple
country life, and my uncle had especial pleasure in

his garden, his dogs, and his horses. These last he would train to obey his voice rather than whip or rein. No one who reads his poems can fail to see the "alma beata et bella" breathing through them. My father's "At Midnight," June 30th, 1879, was written as a preface to the *Collected Sonnets*, published in 1880.

Mr Gladstone wrote a pleasant letter about the volume, and my father answered, with an allusion to the elegy by Catullus on his brother:

My dear Gladstone,

I am, as you will believe, very glad to have your appreciative estimate of my brother's son-nets. I wish indeed that you had known him: he was almost the most loveable human being I have ever met. I am glad too that you are touched by my little prefatory poem, so far as to honour it by a comparison with those lovely lines "Multas per terras et multa per æquora vectus," of which, as you truly say, neither I nor any other "can surpass the beauty": nor can any modern elegy, so long as men retain the least hope in the after-life of those whom they loved, equal in pathos the desolation of that everlasting farewell, "Atque in perpetuum frater ave atque vale." It would be pleasant to talk to you on these things instead of writing, but I fear that I cannot accept your kind invitation to Hawarden this year.

Ever, my dear Gladstone, yours,
A. Tennyson.

In May my father published in a revised form a poem written when he was seventeen, "The Lover's Tale." The publication was forced upon him, as it was being extensively pirated. He had already in 1875 suppressed an edition brought out by Mr Herne Shepherd, paying the costs of the decree of the Court of Chancery, since he heard that Mr Shepherd was very poor and that his aged mother depended on him for her livelihood.

In June Fitzgerald wrote:

LITTLE GRANGE, WOODBRIDGE,
June, 1879.

MY DEAR ALFRED,

I do not write to you now, because when I have done so lately, Mrs Tennyson has taken the trouble to answer me, which I do not wish her to have the trouble of doing.

Spedding tells me he has been on a visit to Farringford to arrange with you about an edition of your brother Charles' sonnets. Six months ago did I beg Spedding to make them more known to the world by some review, which he was the one man to do; and now he is going to do something of the kind, for a better, if sadder, reason than any request of mine. I believe that these sonnets, along with your own poems, are the *only* poetry of our times destined to survive: I could wish some of the sonnets omitted; but *that* I suppose even *you* must not do.

Then I have to thank you for your last, of some lines of which I have an echo in my head from some 50 years ago. Was not the original name *Cadrilla*[1], which I thought too remindful of Paine's first set (of quadrilles), which you used to talk about and in which I believe you greatly excelled?

Now, in my turn, I shall send you my Readings (not Recitations) in old Crabbe's *Tales of the Hall:* which you will just look into. Had I published, I should have used your authority, though not your name, for advising the world to read a little of the old chap, now buried, but "post tres dies" to rise again, if the critics and creators of two generations agone were not mistaken. So I should have quoted one of our time (A. T.) saying to me "Crabbe has a world of his own," which I suppose means originally the poems will live, as your brother's will, when others lie past howling. Well: had I thought proper to *name* you, I might have published: for then I should have succeeded in getting two or three hundred people perhaps to try a taste of my old boy before his regular turn comes; but no one would be tempted by my solitary recommendation; a

[1] Instead of "Camilla" in "The Lover's Tale."

critic or two might quash me and mine — so "enfin" I keep the book for my friends; some of whom may think that, as my old Montaigne says, "Tout abrégé d'un bon livre est sot abrégé." When you get the book you had better say nothing to me about it; which I do think is the best to be agreed on beforehand by friends in such cases, give or take.

Think of old Carlyle (who has been but weakly this winter) reading right through Shakespeare during the Spring months! So his niece writes me. I do not hear of his doing the same by his Goethe. I lately made another shot at *Faust* in B. Taylor's translation, but I am as deaf to the charmer as ever. I really do suppose it is my obtuseness, as so many great people believe in him.

Are you ever coming this way again? It was very good of you to think of me in your travel three years ago. Three years! A consideration; when one has left 70 behind one. I only wonder to find myself alive after this most mortal winter.

Farewell: do *not* let Mrs Tennyson write in reply. I take for granted from Spedding's letter that all is well with you all, and do you believe that I am always your ancient

E. F. G.

Mrs Greville also wrote about Carlyle:

MILFORD, *June*, 1879.

Let me hear your plans. I will not ask Carlyle till I can make sure of finding you all at Aldworth. I cannot tell you how enormously curious and interesting it is to listen to Carlyle. His hands shake with a sort of palsy so that his meat must be cut for him: he feels this with painful acuteness. This is the only sign of age. He can walk any distance. He surprised me by putting Browning next Alfred Tennyson. He has the tenderest contempt for the fellow-creatures he despises, and mixes up in his conversation the dead, the living, and characters in fiction with the greatest method. He said, "Alfred always from the beginning took a grip at the right side of every question." He cares for goodness more than genius, and the *truth* of "The Grandmother" *quite* upset him — he kept saying, "Poor old body, poor old body. And Alfred wrote that: well, I didn't know it."

SABINE GREVILLE.

Mr Fields the American publisher paid us a visit this spring at Farringford. In a lecture, delivered afterwards, Fields said that in passing through the park by moonlight with my father, the poet suddenly fell on his knees and said, " Violets, man, violets! smell them and you'll sleep the better."

His keen sense of smell may well have discovered the flowers in the night, but he writes to a poet who had indited a sonnet on the incident: " What Mr Fields has said about the violets is *doubtless* authentic, still (the fact) has altogether faded out of *my* memory, but I shall not easily forget your graceful sonnet for which I pray you to accept my best thanks."

On Sept. 29th he wrote to a sculptor who wished to make a bust of him: " I thank you for the photograph of Longfellow's bust, but having had my own executed by Woolner some years ago [1], I then made up my mind not to sit again to any sculptor however excellent in his art."

In December Mr and Mrs Kendal produced " The Falcon " at the St James' Theatre, and it had a run of sixty-seven nights. Fanny Kemble saw the piece, and her criticism was that it was an exquisite little poem in action, like one of Alfred de Musset's, such as *Les Caprices de Marianne*. " Mrs Kendal," my father said, "looked magnificent, and Kendal spoke his lines well."

In February 1880 my father sent two child-songs, " The City Child " and " Minnie and Winnie " (set to music by my mother), to *St Nicholas' Magazine*.

It was in the following month that the students of Glasgow University endeavoured to obtain my father's consent to his nomination for the Lord Rectorship of Glasgow. He had understood that the invitation had come from the whole body of students irrespective of

[1] He alluded to the bust by Woolner made in 1857, which he much preferred to Woolner's later bust.

political party, and accepted, on condition that this was the case. The manifesto of the Glasgow University Independent Club recognized his condition.

He found however that he had been put forward as a nominee of the Conservative party and at once withdrew.

To Matthew Fraser.

May 6th, 1880.

DEAR SIR,

I only consented to stand for your Lord Rectorship when informed by the letter of introduction which your agreeable deputation brought, that my nomination was "supported by a large majority, if not the totality, of the students of Glasgow." It now seems necessary that I should, by standing at your invitation, appear what I have steadfastly refused to be — a party candidate for the Conservative Club. The mere fact of a contest between the supporters of a nominee for a Liberal and of that for a Conservative Club leads, I suppose, inevitably to this conclusion in the minds of the public, and therefore I must beg to decline the honour of your candidature.

You are probably aware that some years ago the Glasgow Liberals asked me to be their candidate, and that I in like manner declined. Yet I would gladly accept a nomination, after what has occurred, if at any time a body of students, bearing no political name, should wish to nominate me, or if both Liberals and Conservatives should ever happen to agree in foregoing the excitement of a political contest, and in desiring a Lord Rector who would not appear for installation, and who would in fact be a mere *roi fainéant* with nothing but the literary merits you are good enough to appreciate.

I thank you for all the trouble you have taken,

16—2

and I am, with best wishes for the prosperity of your University,

Yours faithfully, A. TENNYSON.

I now received the following letter from Froude:

5 ONSLOW GARDENS, S.W.

June 7th, 1880.

MY DEAR MR TENNYSON,

I am sorry that I shall lose the pleasure of paying you a visit but I am far more sorry for the reason. Your father has two existences. Spiritually he lives in all our minds (in mine he has lived for nearly forty years) in forms imperishable as diamonds which time and change have no power over. The mortal case of him is of frailer material, and, as I believe he takes extremely little care of it himself, the charge falls on you, and the world will expect an account of it at your hands. Centuries will pass before we have another real full-grown poet. The seeds of time I suppose are sown and grow for a bit, and the reviews clap their hands. But they come to nothing. The moral atmosphere is too pestilential. The force which there is in the world is all destructive and disintegrating, and heaven knows when any organizing life will show itself again.

We must keep what we have got to the latest moment and be thankful for him.

Serus in cœlum redeat.

" Cœlum " can do without your father better than we can.

Faithfully yours, J. A. FROUDE.

After my uncle Charles' death my father was very unwell, suffering from a liver attack, and hearing perpetual ghostly voices.

Sir Andrew Clark ordered him either to America or to Venice. We applied for berths in the next liner to Canada but found that all the best had been taken, so we determined to go to Venice, and the journey did in effect restore his health and silence the ghosts.

June 13*th.* We were at Munich and saw the modern picture gallery, where my father liked Wilkie's "Reading of the last Will," and a shipwreck off the coast of Essex, lit up by a weird light "like one of Danby's pictures."

In the evening we went to the Countess d'Alberg's (Lord Acton's mother-in-law) and met Dr Döllinger. He had a fine earnest countenance and my father was delighted with him. He told my father that since his youth a great change had come over Germany. Now, Germany was full of materialistic unbelief, whereas England, he thought, had "much of the true, broad and liberal faith, a faith which developes and grows more real as the centuries advance."

Next day we visited the Pinakothek. My father admired a picture of a sunny young man, with his hands crossed, by Rembrandt, also a Virgin by Titian, who, he said, "looked out on the world with a sad commanding eye." Charles V. with his projecting jaw and large massive hands struck him "as a truthful portrait."

From Munich we journeyed into a Bavarian valley where

> The mountain breaks,
> And seems with its accumulated crags
> To overhang the world;

and thence to Tegernsee to Lord Acton's, the most hospitable of houses. From Tegernsee we went to Innsbrück. There Professor Bickel called upon us from the University, full of having discovered a metre in the Hebrew of the Psalms.

We left Innsbrück for Landro (the Dolomites). The reflection of Monte Cristallo in the green lake, and the drive to Cortina my father thought remarkable. Innumerable ragged peaks rose about one, as he said "like ghosts of Chimborazo." The mountain meadows

were gay with forget-me-nots, blue gentians and pink
daphnes, glorifying the upland slopes.

We asked a young maiden on the way whether she
was not happy in this beautiful land. She answered, " I
have been three summers in Cortina and my heart is
always laughing like the summer." My father admired
the great lonely mountain throne of Antelao with its
sloping canopy of ridged snow, which rises in a grand
sweep from the valley of Cortina. Next day we drove
through a tract of firs, past the Antelao to Pieve di
Cadore, the birthplace of Titian. The entrance of the
valley looked sublime, and we seemed to recognize many
backgrounds of Titian's pictures in the different valleys.
We passed one lake, the Lago Morte, which my father
said was like the lake from which " The Lady of the
Lake rose ": and pushed on to Venice, which we reached
in a great thunderstorm. The best picture in Venice,
he thought with Burne-Jones, is Venice itself as one
glides in a gondola along the Grand Canal: but, having
dreamt all his life of this city on the sea, he was disappointed with the side canals. The pictures themselves
in the churches were generally in such dim light that
he could scarcely see them, but Tintoretto's " Presentation of the Virgin" in the Church of the Madonna del
Orto he particularly praised.

The Tintorettos struck him as most original, dramatic, and sublime in their treatment of subjects which
had been often painted before. He stood long before a
beautiful Bellini in the Church of Il Redentore.

He was fascinated by St Mark's, by the Doge's
Palace and the Piazza, and by the blaze of colour in
water and sky. We climbed the Campanile : thence we
walked to the Library, where he could scarcely tear
himself away from the Grimani Breviary.

" In gondolas by day and night" he quoted " Julian
and Maddalo," and went out to see the sunsets, and

wished to wander by himself on the Lido, but liked most of all the burial-ground of the Jews, overgrown with poppies and thistles, a pathetic place. At the Armenian monastery the pomegranates were in flower, and a fat little Armenian monk brought him a book to sign, whereupon he wrote, to the monk's satisfaction:

> With all good wishes
> And all good dishes
>
> A. T.

In the Piazza San Marco we met the sculptor Story, and on my father talking of " the lin-lan-lone of evening bells," heard from him how wonderful the winter ringing in a wind of the ice-sheathed forests in North America is: like the tinkle of innumerable bells all round, from far and near.

From Venice we went to Verona, and my father was enchanted by the romance of the situation, nestled among vine-clad hills, with the Adige rushing round the walls, and by the beautiful Giusti garden, — famous for its cypresses throughout two centuries, — that looks out toward the western hills.

From Verona we returned home by the Lago di Garda and Milan.

Over Sirmio, the peninsula of Catullus, we roamed all day. My father liked this, I think, the best of anything we had seen on our tour: its olives, its old ruins, and its green-sward stretching down to the blue lake with the mountains beyond.

Here he made his " Frater Ave atque Vale."

> Row us out from Desenzano, to your Sirmione row!
> So they row'd, and there we landed — O venusta Sirmio!
> There to me thro' all the groves of olive in the summer glow,

There beneath the Roman ruin where the purple
    flowers grow,
Came that " Ave atque Vale " of the poet's hopeless
    woe,
Tenderest of Roman poets nineteen hundred years
    ago,
" Frater Ave atque Vale " as we wander'd to and
    fro
Gazing at the Lydian laughter of the Garda lake
    below,
Sweet Catullus' all-but-island, olive-silvery Sirmio!

Miss Ritchie was staying at Farringford when we
came back from our foreign travels.   To her he dwelt
with more pleasure on the row to Desenzano than on
almost anything else, and on the associations of Sirmione
with Catullus.   The long July twilight had at last died
away whilst he talked of all he had been seeing, and
lights were brought, and I fetched him a volume of
Catullus.

He made Miss Ritchie, who was no Latin scholar,
follow the words as he read through some of his favourite
poems.   His finger moved from word to word, and he
dwelt with intense satisfaction on the adequacy of the expression and of the sounds, on the mastery of the proper
handling of quantity, and on the perfection of the art.

CHAPTER XII.

BALLADS AND POEMS. MY FATHER'S NOTES. "THE CUP."

1880.

The volume of the ballads and poems, dedicated by my father to his grandson "Golden-hair'd Ally," was published in my father's 71st year in 1880, and contains some of his most vigorous and dramatic poems.

His manuscript notes on them are as follows:

"'The First Quarrel' was founded on an Isle of Wight story. Dr Dabbs was the doctor. The poor woman quarrelled with her husband. He started the night of the quarrel for Jersey; the boat, in which he was, struck a reef and went down."

"'Rizpah' is founded on an incident which I saw thus related in some penny magazine called *Old Brighton*, lent me by my friend and neighbour Mrs Brotherton[1]:

"A conspicuous tombstone (at Brighton), to be read

---

[1] "I told him the story one day at Farringford, knowing it would touch him, and he came up to see my husband and me next day, and asked me to tell it him again: on which I gave him the little penny magazine I found it in. It was an unpretentious account of 'Old Brighton.' Many months after he took me up to his library, after a walk, and read me what he called 'Bones.' That was before it was called 'Rizpah' and published."

MARY BROTHERTON.

249

by everyone passing through the churchyard, bears the
following truly extraordinary inscription:

PHŒBE HESSEL.

Who was born at Stepney, in the year 1713.
She served for many years as a Private Soldier in the
Fifth Regiment of Foot in different parts of Europe,
And in the year 1745 fought under the command of the
Duke of Cumberland, at the Battle of Fontenoy,
Where she received a Bayonet Wound in her Arm.
Her long life, which commenced in the Reign of
Queen Anne, extended to that of King George IV,
By whose munificence she received comfort and support
In her latter days. She died at Brighton,
Where she had long resided,
December 12th, 1821, aged 108.

"This epitaph gives the complete history of one of the
most notable characters of Brighton, concerning whom it
seems scarcely possible to say more than her tombstone
records.   For many years before her death, it should be
mentioned that George IV. allowed her half-a-guinea a
week.   When the king saw her, and talked with her, he
called her 'A jolly old fellow,' and offered her a guinea
a week, which, with a rare moderation she refused,
saying, 'Half that sum was enough to maintain her.'
She is well remembered in Brighton still, as she used to
sit in the sun against a house on the lower part of the
Marine Parade.   Her life was indeed an extraordinary
one.   After the death of her second husband, William
Hessel, by the assistance of some friends she purchased
a donkey, and travelled with fish and other commodities
to the villages about Brighton.

"It was in one of these journeys that she obtained
such information as led to the arrest and conviction of
Rooke and Howell for robbing the mail, a circumstance
which made a considerable sensation at the close of the
last century.   They were gibbeted on the spot where
the robbery was committed, and there is an affecting
story connected with the body of Rooke.   When the

elements had caused the clothes and flesh to decay, his aged mother, night after night, in all weathers, and the more tempestuous the weather the more frequent the visits, made a sacred pilgrimage to the lonely spot on the Downs, and it was noticed that on her return she always brought something away with her in her apron. Upon being watched it was discovered that the bones of the hanging man were the objects of her search, and as the wind and rain scattered them on the ground she conveyed them to her home. There she kept them, and, when the gibbet was stripped of its horrid burden, in the dead silence of the night she interred them in the hallowed enclosure of Old Shoreham Churchyard. What a sad story of a Brighton Rizpah!"

"'The Northern Cobbler,'" wrote my father, "is founded on a fact that I heard in early youth. A man set up a bottle of gin in his window when he gave up drinking, in order to defy the drink."

"The story of 'The Revenge,'" he wrote again, "is told finely by Sir Walter Raleigh and Froude, also by Bacon. Sir Richard Grenville commanded Sir Walter Raleigh's first colony which went out to Virginia." "'This story of 'The Revenge,'' says Froude, 'struck a deeper terror, though it was but the action of a single ship, into the hearts of the Spanish people, it dealt a more deadly blow upon their fame and moral strength than the Armada itself.'

"Sir Richard, after this desperate fight of his one ship against the Spanish fleet, 'commanded the master gunner' whom he knew to be a most resolute man, to split and sink the ship, that thereby nothing might remain of glory in victory to the Spaniards, seeing in so many hours they were not able to take her, having had fifteen hours' time, fifteen thousand men, and fifty-three sail of men of war to perform it withal.'"

When Sir Richard is dying, he cries out in the poem:

"I have fought for Queen and Faith like a valiant
    man and true;
I have only done my duty as a man is bound to do:
With a joyful spirit I Sir Richard Grenville die!"
And he fell upon their decks, and he died.

"His exact words were [1]: 'Here die I Richard Green-
field, with a joyful and quiet mind, for that I have ended
my life as a true soldier ought to do, that have fought for
his country, Queen, religion and honour. Whereby my
soul most joyful departeth out of this body, and shall
always leave behind it an everlasting fame of a valiant
and true soldier that has done his duty as he was bound
to do.' When he had finished these or such other like
words, he gave up the Ghost with a great and stout
courage, and no man could perceive any true sign of
heaviness in him."

The germ of the poem of "The Revenge" was, as
has been stated in the Journal, the one line

At Flores in the Azores Sir Richard Grenville lay.

"The Sisters" was partly founded on the story,
known to him, of a girl who consented to be bridesmaid to her sister, although she secretly loved the
bridegroom. The night after the wedding the poor
bridesmaid ran away from her home. They searched
for her, high and low, and at last she was discovered
knocking at the church door, in "the pitiless rush of
autumn rain," her wits gone:

"The great Tragedian, that had quench'd herself
In that assumption of the bridesmaid."

The simile taken from the lake at Llanberis was a
personal experience. He always said that he remem-

---

[1] This is Linschooten's account.

bered the lake as it looked in a flash of lightning, not as
he saw it afterwards in the daytime.

The scene of the picnic in the wood was also a
personal experience in the New Forest.

And these lines he would quote as his own belief:

> My God, I would not live
> Save that I think this gross hard-seeming world
> Is our misshaping vision of the Powers
> Behind the world, that make our griefs our gains.

Among his Lincolnshire poems " The Village Wife "
is the only one that is in any way a portrait.   The rest
of them are purely imaginative.

> Heäps an' heäps o' buoöks, I ha' see'd 'em, belong'd to
>   the Squire,
> But the lasses 'ed teärd out leaves i' the middle to kindle
>   the fire.

This really happened to some of the most valuable
books in the great library formed by Johnson's friend,
Bennet Langton.

My father's note on " The Children's Hospital " is:
" A true story told me by Mary Gladstone.   The
doctors and hospital are unknown to me.   The two
children are the only characters, in this little dramatic
poem, taken from life."

Miss Gladstone's letter ran thus:

There was a little girl in the hospital, and as the doctor
and nurse passed by her bed they stopped, for her eyes were
shut and they thought she was asleep. "We must try that
operation to-morrow," he said, "but I am afraid she will not get
through it."   I forget what the child said, until Annie the girl in
the next bed suddenly suggested, "I know what I should do, I
should ask Jesus to help me." "Yes, I will, but oh! Annie,
how will he know it's me, when there are such a lot of us in the
ward?" "I'll tell you," said Annie, "put your arms outside the

counterpane." The next morning the little girl's arms were outside the counterpane and her eyes were closed. She was dead.

About "The Defence of Lucknow" my father says: "The old flag, used during the defence of the Residency, was hoisted on the Lucknow flagstaff by General Wilson, and the soldiers who still survived from the siege were all mustered on parade in honour of this poem, when my son Lionel (who died on his journey from India) visited Lucknow. A tribute overwhelmingly touching."

"I took as subject of a poem," he goes on, "Sir John Oldcastle, Lord Cobham, because he is a fine historical figure. He was named by the people 'The good Lord Cobham,' a friend of Henry V. As follower of Wyclif, he was cited before a great council of the Church, which was presided over by Archbishop Arundel, and was condemned to be burnt alive for heresy."

"My poem of 'Columbus' was founded on the following passage in Washington Irving's *Life of Columbus*":

The caravels set sail early in October, bearing off Columbus, shackled like the vilest of culprits, amid the scoffs and shouts of a miscreant rabble, who took a brutal joy in heaping insults on his venerable head, and sent curses after him from the island he had so recently added to the civilized world. The worthy Villejo, as well as Andreas Martin, the master of the caravel, felt deeply grieved at his situation. They would have taken off his irons, but to this he would not consent. "No," said he proudly, "Their Majesties commanded me by letter to submit to whatever Bobadillo should order in their name; by their authority he has put upon me these chains; I will wear them until they shall order them to be taken off, and I will afterwards preserve them, as relics and memorials of the reward of my services." "He did so," adds his son Fernando in his history; "I saw them always hanging in his cabinet, and he requested that when he died they might be buried with him."

It was written after repeated entreaties from certain prominent Americans that he would commemorate the discovery of America in verse.

My father continues: "The oldest form of 'Maeldune' is in the *Book of the Dun Cow* (1160). I read the legend in Joyce's *Celtic Legends*, but most of the details are mine."

By this story he intended to represent in his own original way the Celtic genius, and he wrote the poem with a genuine love of the peculiar exuberance of the Irish imagination.

The blank-verse lyric of "The Battle of Brunanburh[1]" suggested to Edward Fitzgerald that the choruses of Greek plays ought to be rendered in this fashion. My father himself liked the rush of the alliterative verse, as giving something of the old English war song.

> The struggle of standards,
> The rush of the javelins,
> The crash of the charges,
> The wielding of weapons —
> The play that they play'd with
> The children of Edward.

The few lines addressed to Dante have a curious history. In 1865 Lord Houghton met a brother of my father's friend Canon Warburton, and said to him, "Tennyson is not going to the Dante Centenary, but he has given me some lines which I am to recite to the Florentines," and he then repeated the lines. The same evening Canon Warburton met his brother who observed, "Milnes has just been saying to me some lines which Tennyson has given him to recite at the Centenary, for he is not going himself." He then repeated the lines. Some fifteen years or so later, my father was talking to the Canon about the probably short-lived duration of all modern poetical fame. "Who," said he, "will

[1] See page 272.

read Alfred Tennyson one hundred years hence? And look at Dante after six hundred years!" "That," Warburton answered, "is a renewal of the garland-of-a-day superstition." "What do you mean?" "Your own words!" "What can you mean?" "Don't you remember those lines you gave to Milnes to recite for you at the Dante Centenary?" My father had quite forgotten the lines. Warburton then wrote out the lines as far as he could remember them, and shortly afterwards I sent a letter to the Canon, telling him that my father had recalled the correct version of the poem.

My father received many complimentary sonnets about this volume.

The following is the kind of brief acknowledgment which he sent.

Pray accept my best thanks for your energetic and too complimentary sonnet.

A. TENNYSON.

I thank you for your kind words. I rejoice to hear that you are happy in the possession of those good gifts of which you speak.

As to the rest, the poet can scarcely be judged with fairness in one age or another. He must abide the judgment of the ages.

A. TENNYSON.

Late in 1880 my father had completed "The Cup," begun after he had finished "The Falcon" in Nov. 1879[1]. This story from Plutarch first commended itself to him in a paragraph by Lecky in his *History of European Morals*[2]:

A powerful noble once solicited the hand of a Galatian lady named Camma, who, faithful to her husband, resisted all his

---

[1] Both plays were published (Macmillan) 1884.
[2] Lecky, Vol. II. p. 342 (ed. 1894).

entreaties. Resolved at any hazard to succeed, he caused her husband to be assassinated, and when she took refuge in the temple of Diana, and enrolled herself among the priestesses, he sent noble after noble to induce her to relent. After a time he ventured himself into her presence. She feigned a willingness to yield, but told him it was first necessary to make a libation to the goddess. She appeared as a priestess before the altar bearing in her hand a cup of wine, which she had poisoned. She drank half of it herself, handed the remainder to her guilty lover, and when he had drained the cup to the dregs, burst into a fierce thanksgiving that she had been permitted to avenge, and was soon to rejoin, her murdered husband. (Plutarch, *De Mulier. Virt.*)

Sir Charles Newton helped my father in the archæology of the period. He wrote:

March 6th, 1879.

I see no reason for doubting Plutarch's statement that Artemis was worshipped in Galatia, tho' it is not corroborated as yet by coins or inscriptions, and the particular Artemis so worshipped would most probably be closely allied in attributes to the Tauric Artemis, and would thus correspond with your conception of the Galatian Artemis (the goddess of Nature). The epithet πατρῷος in the *Amatorius* applied to the priesthood shows that the priesthood was hereditary. It may be inferred therefore that Camma was of noble birth. The story as told by Plutarch is most dramatic. If I find anything more you shall have it. In the meantime you may rely on my silence.

Mr Knowles writes, Dec. 4th, 1880:

Irving is in a great state of enthusiasm and excitement, and he is most anxious that you should read over the Play, not only to himself and Ellen Terry but to all the Company which is to enact it. This is a most admirable suggestion, and I hope extremely that you will see your way to say " yes " to it. He would like it to be on next Thursday week, the 25th inst., when Ellen Terry will be back in town and everything advanced enough to make such a reading of the greatest and most opportune value.

My father accepted the invitation, and happily but few alterations from the first manuscript copy were found necessary for the stage-edition. Three short speeches for Synorix were added, Act I. Sc. 3; and at the end of Act II. the quarrel between Sinnatus and Synorix was lengthened by two lines, and Camma was made to interrogate Sinnatus as to what Synorix had said, and three or four entrances were made less abrupt. Irving inserted most of the stage-directions, and devised the magnificent scenery[1], and the drama was produced by him with signal success at the Lyceum, and played to crowded houses. He wrote to my father, " I hope that the splendid success of your grand Tragedy will be followed by other triumphs equally great[2]."

Ellen Terry, who played the noble part of " Camma " magnificently, thanked him for his " great little play."

Browning was loud in praise of " The Cup[3] "; and my father wrote to him:

FARRINGFORD, FRESHWATER,
Feb. 8th, 1880.

MY DEAR BROWNING,

That you, whom Professor Morley calls a born dramatist, should approve of my little play, is good news to me and mine. I hope to see you soon. * * * *
We three greet you lovingly, and are all yours.

A. TENNYSON.

---

[1] I understand from Mr Knowles that he helped Irving to design the Temple scene.

[2] My father said, " Irving has not hit off my Synorix, who is a subtle blend of Roman refinement and intellectuality, and barbarian, self-satisfied sensuality."

[3] " The Cup " was produced January 3rd, 1881; and ran for over one hundred and thirty nights.

Of our Aldworth life in 1880 and of my father's talk about " Becket " and " The Cup " William Allingham gives a pleasant account in his private diary.

Haslemere. *Thursday, Aug. 5th,* 1880. Very fine. Helen and I started about 3.30 to walk to Tennyson's as invited. In the shady lane the carriage overtook us. Tennyson had kindly called for us. He was in the carriage, with his little grandson, Alfred, on his nurse's lap, and Mr Field, an American guest. Little Alfred, aged 3, had on the great Alfred's black sombrero, and the child's straw hat with a blue ribbon was stuck on the top of the poet's huge head, and so they drove gravely along. I followed on foot along the heath-fringed road on Blackdown, overlooking the vast expanses of light and shadow, golden cornfields, blue distances from Leith Hill to Chanctonbury Ring. Walked through the house, long hall open at each end, and found tea on the further lawn, smooth, shut in with shrubs. The view of the lower windows of the house is now shut up by the growth of twigs and leaves. On the lawn, Mrs Tennyson lying horizontal in an invalid chair with a hood to it, wrapt in furs, and looking sadly pale and worn. Mrs Hodgson (of Lythe Hill) and sister, visitors. Mr and Mrs Field of Philadelphia (from Egypt and Spain) two days' guests, Hallam, alert and friendly, Alfred Tennyson in sombrero, a gray suit, broad-shouldered, somewhat stooping, looking peaceful and contented. He has been at Venice, Cadore, etc. with Hallam.

I told him Dr Martineau, who is 75, had just climbed a mountain in Strathspey 4000 ft. high.

T. When I was 67 I climbed a mountain 7000 ft. high ; the guide said he never saw a man of my age *si léger.*

We spoke of the stage. " Irving won't answer letter." Perhaps the only way, I suggest, to have any peace.

T. I often think I ought to have gone on the same plan. (But in fact Mrs Tennyson has done nearly all the answering.) I gave Irving my " Thomas à Becket " : he said it was magnificent but it would cost him £3000 to mount it : he couldn't afford the risk. If well put on the stage it would act for a time, and it would bring me credit (he said), but it wouldn't pay. He said, " If you give me something short I'll do it." So I wrote him a play in two acts " The Cup." The success of a piece doesn't depend on its literary merit or even on its stage effect, but on its *hitting* somehow.   Miss Terry said, "We act mechanically after a long run, but on a first night nobody suspects how we have our hearts in our mouths."

Tennyson did not much approve Irving's "Shylock," "He made you pity Shylock too much."

T.   I told Miss Terry she ought, as advocate, to stand on the steps to gain advantage, instead of standing on the level, a little female thing, and looking up at him.   The worst of writing for the stage is, you must keep some actor always in your mind.

As we went to another part of the grounds he recalled the direction in *Sakontala*, "You will go straight on till you come to a Brahmin buried to his middle in a pit full of termite ants and then turn to the left."   He said the story of the Mayor of Galway, who for the sake of justice condemned his own son to death, and then hanged him, was fine, would make a tragedy.

CHAPTER XIII.

SPEDDING'S DEATH. "THE PROMISE OF MAY."
GLADSTONE.

1881–1883.

At the beginning of 1881 we were again in London.
My father sat to Millais for his portrait[1], now in
Mr Knowles' possession, and Mrs Andrew Hichens
generally drove him to his sittings. She says that she
remembers what numberless stories, suggested by any
passing sight in the streets, he would tell her.

An interesting discussion took place one evening
after dinner between Mr Gladstone, Froude, Tyndall
and my father on historical belief in the immortality of
the soul. My father and Gladstone spoke strongly on
the side of belief. The latter ended the discussion by
saying: "Let the scientific men stick to their science,
and leave philosophy and religion to poets, philosophers
and theologians."

My father's letters were at this period generally of the
shortest, as for instance this which he wrote to Sir Henry
Parkes, the Premier of New South Wales, in May 1881:

I always feel with the Empire, and I read with great
interest of these first steps in Federation.

Go on, and prosper in the good work, and with many
thanks for the Blue Book,

I am yours very truly,

A. TENNYSON.

[1] Millais said to me that this was the finest portrait he had ever painted.

And this which he sent to Roden Noel:

"I congratulate you on your new volume, and trust that it will fight the good fight against materialism successfully."

And this to an unknown correspondent:

"I thank you for your poem 'To the Dead Premier.'

The feeling of American brotherhood which it bespeaks cannot but be welcome to an Englishman.

Thank you also for your courteous words to myself."

In this year Spedding, one of my father's oldest and most intimate friends, died in St George's Hospital, having been run over by a cab in Hill Street. His loss was deeply mourned by my father.

Edward Fitzgerald wrote:

Laurence has written me some account of his visit to St George's: J. S. all patience, only somewhat wishful to be at home ; somewhat weary with lying without book or even watch for company. What a man! as in life so in death, "which," as Montaigne says, "proves what is at the bottom of the vessel." I had not seen him for more than 20 years, and should never have seen him again unless in the street, where cabs were crossing! He did not *want* to see me, he wanted nothing I think, but I was always thinking of him and should have done till my own life's end. I know I only wrote to him about twice, a year: he only cared to answer when one put some definite question to him, and I had usually as little to ask as to tell. I was thinking that, but for the cab, I might even now be asking him what I was to think of his cousin Froude's *Carlyle Reminiscences*. I see but one quotation in the book, which is "of the days that are no more," which clung to him when his sorrow came, as it will to many and many who will come after him.

I certainly hope that some pious and judicious hand will gather and choose from our dear Spedding's letters: no fear of indelicate personality with *him*, you know: and many things

which all the world would be the wiser and better for.   Archdeacon Allen sent me the other day a letter about Darwin's
Philosophy, so wise and so true, so far as I could judge, only,
though written off, unfit to go as it was into print, and do all
the world good.   Will not Master Alfred say something on this
score?   Why it would be a good work for Hallam, a pious
work.

It was fine too of Carlyle ordering to be laid among his own
homely kindred in the village of his birth without questions of
Westminster Abbey.   So think I, at least: and dear James
Spedding at Mirehouse, where your husband and I stayed, very
near upon 50 years ago, in 1835 it was, in the month of May,
when the daffodils were out in a field before the house and I see
them, though not in such force, owing to cold winds, before my
window now.   Does A. T. remember them?   And what J. S.
persisted in calling "gale" which grew by the lake?   No other
answer could be got in spite of demand for extra definition.
"If not *gale* I don't know what it is."

Matthew is in his grave, but now methinks I see him stand
as at that moment

In the days that are no more.

Tell Alfred that, since this happened, I have turn'd to him "for
Auld Lang Syne," and did not write to any of the Spedding
party, whom I scarce ever saw, because I thought they would
have enough of nearer and dearer friends to write to.   I should
still wish them to know, if they know of my existence, that I
had a report every day from Mowbray Donne, who lives near
them.

Here is a long letter, dear Mrs Tennyson, which you will
like well enough.   You give me no address with your letter.

Mr Norman Lockyer wrote as to a red rainbow my
father had seen at Aldworth opposite the sunset:

I have been much interested by Macmillan's account of the
red rainbow which you saw.   It is I think the first I have
heard of, and I hope you will send us a note to *Nature* on
the subject, as it gives a fresh interest to sunrise and sunset
phenomena.

In November his poem of " Despair " was published in the *Nineteenth Century*. Much bitter criticism followed, since the public did not recognize it. as a "dramatic monologue." Miss Gladstone (Mrs Harry Drew) had suggested the subject in a short paragraph which she sent my father, and which he somewhat altered, and put as the heading of his poet's protest against the denial of these two great truths of his faith which were to him the life of life.

"A man and his wife having lost faith in a God, and hope of a life to come, and being utterly miserable in this, resolve to end themselves by drowning."

1882.

When we were at 86 Eaton Square in February, the old version of " Hands all round," written in 1852, was recast by request of Sir Frederic Young into a patriotic song for the Empire. The reprint was published with my mother's setting (arranged by Professor Stanford), and sung all over Great Britain and the Colonies on the Queen's birthday.

Sir Alfred Lyall writes about the reception of the song in India :

I think I should write a line to tell you that your song of " Hands all round," part of which you repeated to me one day last spring when I had the pleasure of walking with you across Blackdown, was sung in chorus, and very well sung, on the Queen's birthday here. We had collected all the English folk for a ball, and the song was new to by far the greater part of them : it interested all very much.

India is just now, so far as one can see, quiet throughout its length and breadth ; and when the country is quiet it is apt to be dull, except to those for whom it finds incessant work. Of course the Mahommedans, of whom we have between thirty and forty millions, are watching very closely our proceedings

in Egypt, and are not easily disabused of the idea that we intend
to seize the country and to upset another Mahommedan dynasty.
But I hope we shall rapidly and successfully clear away the
complications that have been gathering there; it does not suit
us to be constantly fighting against Mahommedans; and, however plainly we may prove that our expeditions are just and
necessary, the Asiatic persists in believing us still to be a fierce,
unscrupulous, earth-conquering race.

Nainee Tal, where I now am, is a very picturesque little settle-
ment in the Himalayas; my house looks down on a fine mountain
lake; and beyond, the level plains stretch far away. I may take
this occasion of expressing the pleasure that my good fortune
in meeting you at home gave me. I fear it may be some years
before I see England again.

The Executive Committee of the " Good Templars "
were offended because " First drink a health " was the
opening line of the poem. I had to answer a letter of
remonstrance in these terms:

" My father begs to thank the Committee of the
Executive of the Grand Lodge of England Good
Templars for their resolution. No one honours more
highly the good work done by them than my father.
I must, however, ask you to remember that the common cup has in all ages been the sacred symbol of
unity, and that my father only used the word ' drink '
in reference to this symbol."

Further, I might have mentioned that my father
had supported a movement for the closing of public
houses on Sunday throughout the Isle of Wight.

On Aug. 9th my father and I started for Dovedale. From
Ashbourne we drove through wide-sweeping valleys to Ilam,
and stayed in the " Izaak Walton " at the entrance of Dovedale.

Ilam is a " land of streams," and round the hotel were the
greenest of meadows. We walked up by the Dove, through a
richly-wooded glen with gray pinnacles of limestone here and

there. The vivid green of the ash trees, the islands of meadow-sweet, willow-herb and harebell, and the rippling stream itself, enchanted my father. We lunched at the Doveholes, about which were circling innumerable martins. We then sauntered down the stream, and he smoked a lonely pipe near where the Dove rushes round beech-boles into the Manifold. He always kept up the habit of smoking a solitary pipe when he came to a place which he particularly liked. "I want my pipe alone for ten minutes," he would say.

Aug. 10*th.* Went by the Manifold, gliding under witch-elms, to Ilam Hall. This valley is Johnson's "Happy Valley." In the afternoon we strolled up Dovedale again. My father said, "The Dove is various in its dales, like a great genius. Does not this particular Dovedale remind you of 'lætantia loca aquarum'?" He quoted an unpublished line of his on a Norway torrent,

Storming and streaming through its wooded isles.

Aug. 11*th.* Drove over broad backs of downs, strewn with villages, to Hartington, walked to Hall Dale and beautiful Beresford Dale — fine piles of rock there with trees and rich green-sward. Mill Dale a contrast — sinuous, spacious and bare.

After another day we returned, and his verdict was that Dovedale was one of the most unique and delicious places in England.

"THE PROMISE OF MAY."

In October Mrs Bernard Beere resolved to act "The Promise of May" at The Globe, after having heard my father read it at Aldworth. She wrote thus:

October 7*th,* 1882.

Even at the risk of troubling you, I must write to thank you for letting us have the immense advantage of hearing you read your play. The comedy-touches alone, as you read them, ought to make the success of the piece. I am particularly fascinated by Dora's speech in the 3rd Act, when left alone after paying her people. I hope to be able to interpret it in a way that would please you.

Previously Mr and Mrs Kendal had read the play, and Mr Kendal had written as follows:

It is full of dramatic incident and character, but it appears to me, if I may be allowed to say so, that the dramatic incident and character are so *strong*, the whole requires to be very much more fully developed! When next we meet I can better explain myself.

In November "The Promise of May" was produced. I am bound to say that my father had written it, somewhat unwillingly, at the importunate entreaty of a friend who had urged him to try his hand on a modern village tragedy.

The unlucky piece ran for five weeks, but received very rough treatment on the first night, owing to the advertisements having announced that it was an attack on Socialism, and to the fact that it had been imperfectly edited for the stage. The public had mistaken the purpose of the author. The temper of the house was shown even before the performance began, for the pit doors were broken. One of the most popular playwrights of the day said, "If I had had that play for twenty minutes, I could have made it one of the successes of the season. The hero is unconventional; he is a thinker and is consequently not understood." This is probably a true criticism. The dialect scenes and the songs, and especially "The last load home," were very effective.

In the middle of one of the performances Lord Queensberry rose, and in the name of Free Thought protested against "Mr Tennyson's abominable caricature."

I subjoin the analysis of the hero's character by my brother, as it best gives my father's conception.

Edgar is not, as the critics will have it, a freethinker, drawn into crime by his Communistic theories; Edgar is not even an honest Radical, nor a sincere follower of Schopenhauer; he is nothing thorough and nothing sincere. He has no conscience until he is brought face to face with the consequences of his crime, and in the awakening of that conscience the poet has manifested his fullest and subtlest strength. At our first introduction to Edgar, we see him perplexed with the haunting of a pleasure that has sated him. "Let us eat and drink, for to-morrow we die" has been his motto; but we can detect that his appetite for all pleasure has begun to pall. He repeats wearily the formulæ of a philosophy which he has followed because it suits his mode of life. He plays with these formulæ, but they do not satisfy him. So long as he had on him the zest of libertinism he did not, in all probability, trouble himself with philosophy. But now his selfishness compels him to take a step of which he feels the wickedness and repugnancy. He must endeavour to justify himself to himself. The companionship of the girl he has betrayed no longer gives him pleasure; he hates her tears because they remind him of himself — his proper self. He abandons her with a pretence of satisfaction; but the philosophical formulæ he repeats no more satisfy him than they satisfy the poor girl whom he deserts. Her innocence has not, however, been wantonly sacrificed by the dramatist. She has sown the seed of repentance in her seducer, though the fruit is slow in ripening. Years after he returns, like the ghost of a murderer to the scene of his crime. He feels remorse. He is ashamed of it; he battles against it; he hurls the old formulæ at it; he acts the cynic more thoroughly than ever. But he is changed. He feels a desire to "make amends." Yet that desire is still only a form of selfishness. He has abandoned the "Utopian Idiocy" of Communism. Perhaps, as he says, with a self-mockery that makes the character so individual and remarkable, "because he has inherited estates." His position of gentleman is forced on his notice; he would qualify himself for it, selfishly and without doing excessive penance. To marry the surviving sister and rescue the old father from ruin would be a meritorious act. He sets himself to perform it. At first everything goes well for him; the old weapons of fascination, that had worked the younger sister's ruin, now conquer the heart of the elder. He is comfortable in his scheme of reparation, and lays that flattering "unction to his soul."

Suddenly, however, the girl whom he has betrayed, and whom he thought dead, returns; she hears him repeating to another the words of love she herself had heard from him and believed. "Edgar!" she cries, and staggers forth from her concealment, as she forgives him with her last breath.

Then, and not till then, the true soul of the man rushes to his lips; he recognizes his wickedness, he knows the blankness of his life. That is his punishment.

He feels then, and will always feel, aspirations after good which he can never or only imperfectly fulfil. The position of independence, on which he prided himself, is wrested from him, he is humiliated. The instrument of his selfish repentance turns on him with a forgiveness that annihilates him; the bluff and honest farmer whom he despises triumphs over him, not with the brute force of an avenging hand, but with the pre-eminence of superior morality. Edgar quits the scene, never again, we can believe, to renew his libertine existence, but to expiate with lifelong contrition the monstrous wickedness of the past.

In the midst of the storm among the Freethinkers my father answered one of the many correspondents who admired the play:

"I am grateful for your letter. I had received others to the same purport.

I had a feeling that I would at least strive (in my plays) to bring the true drama of character and life back again. I gave them one leaf out of the great book of truth and nature."

———

Through Lowell the Pennsylvanians asked for a poem on Penn, which my father felt himself at that time unable to write, although he had a great love for Penn:

10 Lowndes Square,
Nov. 7th, 1882.

My dear Tennyson,

I enclose the note of our Quaker friends and hope you will say yes to them if you can. Perhaps a few verses are harder to do than a good many.

At any rate, you can do them if anybody can, and a few will answer.

I think it pretty that they should recognize you as the laureate of the Tongue and not only of the Nation.

I send also a small tribute of baccy. I can't see that it does you any harm if I may judge by your latter harvest.

Very sincerely yours,

J. R. Lowell.

To the Pennsylvanians.

86 Eaton Square, S.W.

My Friends,

I would have written ere this to thank you for the honour you have done me, in asking me to write a few verses on the 200th anniversary of the founding of Pennsylvania, but I have had the gout in my right hand and writing was impossible, and just now it seems to me that a verse upon anything is beyond my power; but does that matter much while you have your noble old Longfellow among you and other poets, who might be more likely than myself to give you something which would not fall below the subject? I do not say that I will not make the attempt, but I cannot promise you anything, except that I will be with you in spirit on the 8th of November (1883), and rejoice with your rejoicing; for, since I have been ill, I have read the life of your noble countryman, and mine, William Penn, and find him no " comet of a season," but the fixt light of a dark and graceless age, shining on into the present, not only great but good, καλὸς κἀγαθός as the Athenians said of their best.

Believe me most faithfully yours,

A. TENNYSON.

Letters from Edward Fitzgerald to Hallam Tennyson.

Nov. 30th, 1882.

Thank you very much for your letter. I know that you have plenty to do in that way: but I will look to you for a few lines of reply to my half-yearly enquiries. I expect no more; and you will not have to write what little I ask for many years to come.

I used to require the same from Carlyle's niece when he grew unable to write, and, latterly, to dictate for himself. Now he is gone, I wrote about a fortnight ago for a word about herself: for she had always been very kind in answering me before. In her reply it "came into her head," she says, to tell me how she happened to see our Spedding about half-an-hour before you know what, walking briskly toward Piccadilly, looking cold, and wearing a cape such as her uncle used. When you speak of having lately returned from Newstead, and Sherwood (whither you had gone to gather local colour for "The Foresters"), I suppose you mean *before* the leaves had fallen from the trees; or were you content with the gnarled trunks? The gale of a month ago (which blew down four of my few trees) play'd the deuce even with the foliage of the oak which generally hangs on for months longer: but it may not have been in merry Sherwood as hereabout. And you did not go to old Lincolnshire? Aldis Wright, who went on Bursar business to Horncastle, went also to Somersby, not on business, and sent me a large photo of the Rectory, but it looked to me new and hard: not half so good in my eyes as the feeble lithograph which your father (I suppose) gave me years ago.

I think he must have been good-humouredly amused at Lord Selborne's adjudicating the palm between me and Mr Morshead (in our translations of *Agamemnon*). I did not know he had that great work to lend: till I remembered my poor Donne writing me something about it. I say "my poor Donne" because he is now in a very helpless state of mind and body; so

much so that he scarce seems conscious of any but his own
family's society (so Mrs Kemble writes me), otherwise I should
go up to see him.   Thompson, Trinity's Master, is also in a very
feeble state of *body*.   All this is rather for your father than for
you : and not very cheerful matter either for him or me.

But tell him (à propos of the Greek) that, when I saw his
version of your "Battle of Brunanburh," I said to myself, and
afterwards to others, "There's the way to render Æschylus'
Chorus at last!" unless indeed it might overpower *any* blank
verse dialogue.   When I said in my printed word of apology,
that such a work was for a *poet* to do, I was not thinking of Mr
Browning.   But the poet must follow his own will and genius.

Annie Thackeray's paper on Mrs Barbauld is very pretty, as
also her book on Sévigné, but of the latter she gives little more
than *one* side as probably best suited to the purpose of her book.
How can she say, however, that there is more of the laughable
than of the humorous in those letters ?

Well, you have had enough of mine at any rate.   I need not
say that I am right glad that your father is well, and your
mother fairly so.   You are I take for granted "all right" as the
fashion is now to say.   Of myself I need not complain, though
not quite, as Sévigné somewhere says, so well that "I cannot
think what God means to do with me."

I am yours sincerely,

The Laird of Littlegrange.

WOODBRIDGE, 1882.

MY DEAR HALLAM,

I believe I ought to be ashamed of reviving the little
thing (*Euphranor*) which accompanies this letter.   My excuse
must be that I have often been asked for a copy when I had no
more to give ; and a visit to Cambridge last summer, to the old
familiar places, if not faces, made me take it up once more and
turn it into what you now see.   I should certainly not send a
copy to you or yours but for what relates to your father in it.
He did not object so far as I know to what I said of him,
though not by name, in a former edition ; but there is more of
him in this, though still not by name, nor, as you see, intended
for publication.   All of this you can read to him if you please at
pp. 25 and 56.   I do not ask him to say that he approves of

what is said or meant to be said in his honour, and I only ask you to tell me if he disapproves of it going any further. I owed you a letter in return for the kind one you sent me, and *if I do not hear from you to the contrary*, I shall take silence, if not for consent, at least for publication. I really did and do wish my first, which is also my last, little work to record, for a few years at least, my love and admiration of that dear old fellow, my old friend.

Ah, if you all of you were living out of the reach of many guests, at Locksley Hall even, I might answer your kind invitations in person. I tell my dear old Frederick that, if ever I cross the seas again, it will be to visit him, but I am not the less grateful to you and yours for your thought of me, being ever yours and theirs.

E. F. G.

1883.

In April 1883 my father and I stayed with Dr Bradley at the Deanery, Westminster, where, when in London, in the later years of his life he oftenest liked to be.

On this occasion Archdeacon Farrar asked him to write an epitaph on Caxton for the painted window in St Margaret's, placed there by the printers of London to his memory. He willingly complied with the Archdeacon's request, and wrote the lines:

Thy prayer was " Light more Light while Time
    shall last,"
Thou sawest a glory growing on the night,
But not the shadows which that light would cast,
Till shadows vanish in the Light of Light.

With the exception of that on Sir John Franklin in Westminster Abbey, he thought this the best of his epitaphs.

One evening Mr Gladstone came to the Deanery to meet my father. Among other subjects they talked of Ireland. Mr Gladstone told us that he felt irritated, having been badgered to death by Irish obstruction.

Then he related this story. "Some Irish labourers from South Ireland had walked up to the North of Ireland, and crossed to the northern English counties to cut the 'Sassenach's wheat,' and a Yorkshire farmer had lent them a barn where they might sleep, and next season, when they came north, they carried on their shoulders by turns a keg of whiskey as a present to the farmer." Whereupon my father observed that he feared that the Irish people were seldom grateful to England: adding however that, when he was in Ireland during the great famine year, he had one day watched an English ship, laden with corn, sail into an Irish harbour, and a peasant had said to him, "There, your honour, there's England like a good sister doing what she can to save Ireland."

The Dean, I think, interposed: "I hear one of the Phœnix Park murderers has been let off to-day." Mr Gladstone became much excited and raising his voice very loud exclaimed, "What! is it possible?"

It turned out to be the driver of the car which had carried the murderers.

The Prime Minister had softened about Parnell. In Downing Street, a year or two before, he had denounced him to us as if he were the leader of a great revolution and the real cause of the implacability of Ireland; but Parnell's offer to resign his seat in the House of Commons, after the murders of Lord Frederick Cavendish and Mr Burke, had evidently impressed Mr Gladstone as most unselfish, and he now felt generously towards him. Throughout Lady Frederick Cavendish had behaved nobly. When she saw Gladstone just after the tragedy she spoke of her husband: "Uncle William," she said, "you did right to send him."

On another evening my father went to *Much Ado About Nothing* at the Lyceum.

He liked the acting of " Beatrice " best in the later scenes; but thought that Ellen Terry ought to have been more of 'the great lady' in her playing of the part. He spoke highly of the trouble which Irving had taken; but he still considered Irving's best Shakespearian study was Richard III., especially in his witty and sardonic moments.

The next morning we wandered about the Abbey for a long time. We climbed up to the chantry, and, while the organ and voices of the choristers were sounding through the cathedral, my father suddenly said: " It is beautiful, but what empty and awful mockery if there were no God!"

This year his old and valued friend Fitzgerald died, and my father wrote of him:

> Gone into darkness, that full light
>   Of friendship! past, in sleep, away
> By night, into the deeper night!
>   The deeper night? A clearer day
> Than our poor twilight dawn on earth —
>   If night, what barren toil to be!
> What life, so maim'd by night, were worth
>   Our living out? Not mine to me
> Remembering all the golden hours
>   Now silent, and so many dead,
> And him the last.

Fitz's last letter had been as humorous and full of warm friendship as ever.

From Edward Fitzgerald to Hallam Tennyson.

April 19th, 1883.

My dear Hallam,

It is now some six months since I heard of you all, from Annie Ritchie, I think. So be a good boy and write me just enough to tell me how it fares with mother, and father, all your party.

Of myself I will tell you that I got through what should have been winter well enough; yes, and even through the March that was winter; but, since sun and wind (east wind) combined, I have been somewhat croaky again.

By the way, do you understand by Lady Macbeth's raven the bird himself, or (as I had always supposed) the messenger who had but breath to deliver his message, as Aldis Wright interprets? and *may* old Hamlet's (does papa remember my "Gimlet Prince of Dunkirk"?) "eternal Blazon" mean not so much of the *Eternal* as of the *Infernal* world, as Wright thinks *possible* from the use of the word in other places by "Williams," "the divine Villiams," as in the case of Fags, an "eternal" villain. I fear I had never even thought of the word but as meaning "*long-winded*," which however I do not propose to the commentators.

This, among other things, Wright and I talked about when he was with me here at Easter, which reminds me of a *crow* (not a *raven*) I have to pick with your father. For Wright had heard from someone that he, the Laureate, had added to his wreath one of the very grandest lines in all blank verse,

"A Mister Wilkinson, a clergyman"—

of which I was the author while speaking of my brother-in-law, but which the paltry poet took up as it fell from my inspired lips and has adopted for his own.

You see that bronchitis, ever flourishing his dart over me, fails to make me graver, that is at least while referring to my dear old comrade, whom I should call "master," and with whom (in spite, perhaps *because*, of his being rather a "gloomy" soul sometimes, as Carlyle wrote to Emerson) I always did talk more nonsense than to anyone, I believe. Pray heaven I may not be trifling unseasonably with him now, that is, when he or his may not be in the proper mood for it. Write me word of this, dear Hallam, and believe me in sober earnest,

Yours and all yours as ever at 75,

E. FITZGERALD.

At this time the following letter was sent by my father to a working man who asked whether he should adopt poetry as a profession:

" I write in compliance with your request, tho' I fear that I can say little to comfort you.   Believe me, however, that I am grieved for your loneliness and your sorrow.

Let me hope that you, having, as I think, found the God of Love, will feel day by day less lonely among your fellow-men: for, loving God, you cannot but grow in love towards them, and so forget yourself in them, since love begets love.

As to your poem it is so much the habit of the age to try and express thought and feeling in verse, each one for himself, that there are not I suspect many listeners (for such work as yours), and therefore poetry is not generally profitable in a money point of view. By all means write, if you find solace in verse, but do not be in a hurry to publish.   Poetry should be the flower and fruit of a man's life, in whatever stage of it, to be a worthy offering to the world."

CHAPTER XIV.

VOYAGE ON THE "PEMBROKE CASTLE," SEPT. 1883.
TALK ON POETS AND POETRY.

The following is taken from my journal kept on the voyage:

My father and I met the Gladstones at Chester. Thence to Barrow we had a triumphal progress, crowds shouting "Gladstone" at every station. At Barrow we embarked on a tug for the "Pembroke Castle," and left our native land in a tumult of acclaim! Thousands of people lining the shore, and cheering for "Gladstone" and "Tennyson."

The first evening, Sept. 8th, we anchored off the Isle of Man. Gladstone and my father talked of the fact that in England poets and literary men were less known by face to the people than actors and orators. Gladstone advanced the theory that writers being supposed by the public to live in strict seclusion, the public deemed it useless to learn their faces by photographs, since the said public would never see them. Someone noted in the course of the conversation that the photographs of preachers were said by a photographer to sell better than those of any other literary men.

They then discussed the allocution of the Archbishop at the coronation of Edward III. which had been based on the old proverb *Vox populi, vox Dei*. The Tudors, according to Gladstone, soon stamped out this ancient English feeling.

The next morning the two at breakfast were deploring Arthur Hallam, and saying what a noble intellect he had, and, as a student, how great a loss he had been to Dante scholarship.

We steamed past the Ailsa Crag up the coast, and arrived at Islay in the evening.

During the day Sir Arthur Gordon (now Lord Stanmore) was closely questioned by my father as to what he thought Nirwana was. "I understand," said my father, "that the Buddhists hold their end to be a negation of the known, which equals, according to them, a positive apprehension of the unknown." Sir Arthur said that Nirwana was undoubtedly a quenching of all human passion, and that a Buddhist on being asked what Nirwana was, after pondering some time, answered, "I cannot explain, Nirwana is Nirwana." My father suggested as an illustration that "The soul is like a cork in a bucket of water rising through the different strata, until at last it reaches the top and is at rest."

From Oban we went to Loch Hourn. Gladstone and my father conversed on Homer, both admiring Worsley's translation of the *Odyssey*. My father wanted "a translation of the *Iliad* and *Odyssey* into Biblical prose." Gladstone said that he fully approved of young men taking up the translation of Homer. "It was like warriors storming the walls of a city; all the warriors were slain, but perhaps some day the city might be taken."

Sir William Harcourt met us at Ardnamurchan Point, and accompanied us to Tobermory. We were talking about tobacco, and my father said that his morning pipe after breakfast was the best in the day. Sir William interposed (laughing at his own burlesque), "The earliest pipe of half-awakened birds."

At Tobermory we took on board Sir Andrew and Lady Clark and Miss Clark. In the evening the Gladstones and Miss Laura Tennant ("the little witch" as my father nicknamed her, begged him to read "The Promise of May." Gladstone expressed his admiration of the play, and his opinion that the row on the first night of the play was "because it was above the comprehension of the vast mass of the people present."

From Tobermory we steamed past the grand headlands of Skye to Gairloch. We landed, and drove to Loch Maree — between ferny, heathery hills, covered with gray crags, very wild, — by the side of a rushing burn. The loch is about eighteen miles long, with rich pine-grown islands scattered here and there, and wooded hills, on either hand, sloping up to a grand fellow, Ben Slioch. Gladstone and my father thought the whole land-scape one of the most beautiful they had ever seen.

We returned on board, and rounded Cape Wrath. Sir Arthur Gordon's Fijian servant amused us this afternoon by striking fire with two bits of stick.

On arriving at Kirkwall at ten in the morning of Sept. 13th, the "Pembroke Castle" was boarded by a deputation of the Town Council and Magistrates, who wished Gladstone and my father to accept the freedom of the Burgh. Their petition being granted, we rowed ashore, walked up through a narrow winding street, gay at intervals with Orkney and Shetland wool-shops, to the Cathedral of St Magnus. Gladstone and my father admired the noble simplicity of the church and its massive stone pillars, but we all shuddered at the liberal whitewash and the high pews. From the Cathedral we went to the Bishop's palace, and the banqueting hall described in (*The Pirate*). We had a drive of ten miles to Maeshowe, a Pict burial-mound, and lunched there. We then returned to Kirkwall, and drove to the United Presbyterian Church. The freedom of the Burgh was conferred. There were throngs of people and children, all enthusiastic, very stalwart, and independent-mannered.

My father said to me: " I am never the least shy before great men. Each of them has a personality for which he or she is responsible : but before a crowd, which consists of many personalities, of which I know nothing, I am infinitely shy. The great orator cares nothing about all this. I think of the good man, and the bad man, and the mad man, that may be among them, and can say nothing. *He* takes them all as one man. *He* sways them as one man."

So Gladstone spoke for himself and for my father in acknowledgment of the honour done to them, and ended his speech as follows :

" Mr Tennyson's life and labours correspond in point of time as nearly as possible to my own, but Mr Tennyson's exertions have been on a higher plane of human action than my own. He has worked in a higher field, and his work will be more durable. We public men — who play a part which places us much in view of our countrymen — we are subject to the danger of being momentarily intoxicated by the kindness, the undue homage of kindness, we may receive. It is our business to speak, but the words which we speak have wings, and fly away and disappear. The work of Mr Tennyson is of a higher order.

I anticipate for him the immortality, for which England and
Scotland have supplied in the course of their long national life
many claims.   Your record to-day of the additions which have
been made to your municipal body may happen to be examined
in distant times, and some may ask, with regard to the Prime
Minister, 'Who was he, and what did he do? We know nothing
about him.'   But the Poet Laureate has written his own song,
on the hearts of his countrymen, that can never die.   Time is
powerless against him, and I believe this, that were the period
of the inquiry to be so long distant as between this day and the
time when Maeshowe was built, still in regard to the Poet
Laureate of to-day there would be no difficulty in stating who
he was, and what he had done to raise the intellects and hearts
of his fellow-creatures to a higher level, and by so doing acquire
a deathless fame.   It is an unmixed pleasure, on behalf of Mr
Tennyson and myself, to acknowledge the great kindness we
have received.   For any services rendered to the country, on
this and on many other occasions, in a thousand other places,
I have been received with a tribute far beyond anything I could
by any possibility deserve."

It seemed to me that, in the conversations between my father
and Gladstone, my father was logical and brilliant in his talk,
made his points clearly, and every word and phrase of his, as in
his poems and plays, bore directly on the subject under discussion; that Gladstone took longer to go from point to point,
and wrapt up his argument in analogies which he thoroughly
thrashed out before he returned to his thesis.   What struck me
most in Gladstone's expression of his thoughts was his eagerness,
and mastery of words, coupled with a self-control and a gentle
persuasiveness; and a certain persistence in dwelling on those
topics which he had himself started for discussion.   Yet, like my
father, he was always most anxious to learn from anyone whom
he thought better informed than himself on the matter in hand.
He made some remarkable statements, such as that " No man
since Æschylus could have written *The Bride of Lammermoor.*"

Both men were as jovial together as boys out for a holiday;
but they took good care to keep off the quagmire of politics.

A dense fog came upon us in the middle of the North Sea,
and our fog-horn blew all one morning.   The lane of moon-lit

sea behind us, as we rushed along at night, seemed to my father
" Like a glorious river rushing to the city of God."

After a calm voyage we reached Christiansand. The entrance to the fiord is very rocky. The Norwegians my father
thought " English-looking " ; and the town was clean. From
Christiansand we drove through wooded walls, like the Tros-
sachs, by the side of the river Torreschal to see a cataract.
Our ponies trotted along well, and we passed many one-seated
curricles.

Gladstone said, " The Norwegians are a happy, unambitious
people." They seemed, by what they said to us, to be fond
of the English. As we left the quay they cheered with a shrill
sharp cheer, like the old English war-cry at the battle of Senlac,
" Harou ! Harou ! "

When again on board, my father was interested by a story
which Captain —— told as having happened " when his ship
conveyed the Rifles to the Crimea." In the hold they found a
French girl hiding : " Je cherche mon amant," she said. They
took her as far as Constantinople, and then turned her out of
their ship, as they were bound by law to do. But there was
a collection made among the men to enable her to go on to the
Crimea, which she eventually reached, found her lover, and
married him.

We had a fine voyage from Christiansand to Copenhagen,
and my father was continually leaning over the bulwarks, and
watching the ' rainbow hang on the poising wave."

We passed between Denmark and Sweden, and saw the Castle
of Elsinore, but Elsinore is by no means a " wild and stormy
steep," but a very flat shore. As we drew into Copenhagen the
sailors on board the colliers cheered, and it was almost dark
when we got into harbour. In the evening we sallied forth to
the illuminated gardens of Tivoli, where the old moat with trees
on either side glittered in the light of thousands of coloured
lamps, festooned among the bushes and the summer-houses.
On Monday morning we visited the Thorwaldsen Museum.
The Apostles and the Hebe my father recognized and admired,
and he liked the statue of the dancing girl. The canal through
the town looked picturesque with its yellow-sailed boats and the
red-tiled roofs on its banks ; the fishermen with their blue
aprons standing in groups along the streets, or marketing. We
walked to the Rosenberg Palace, and Gladstone and my father

wcre presented with gorgeous bouquets of violets and red roses by Mrs Harris, the wife of the consul.

An invitation from the king came to us for dinner at the Castle of Fredensborg, far out into the country. Mr and Mrs and Miss Gladstone, Sir Arthur Gordon, Sir Donald Currie and I went. The palace is like an old-fashioned English country house, and we were charmed with the freedom and unconventionality of the large family party.

We sat down, about eighty, to dinner at a horse-shoe table. The King and Queen of Denmark, the Princess of Wales, the Czar and Czarina, the King and Queen of Greece, the Princess Mary of Hanover, the Duchess of Cumberland, and many other notabilities were present.

Next day, Sept. 18th, we visited the Scandinavian museum, and saw in their oak coffins, buried three thousand years ago, human bodies which had been dug up out of the peat-bogs in Jutland, wrapt in fur cloaks, with hair on the skulls. There were besides old horn trumpets, flint-sickles and spear-heads, and a third century kind of Boadicea chariot with scythes on the wheels.

In responsc to an invitation from the hospitable Sir Donald the Royalties came to luncheon on board, amid salvoes of artillery; three royal ensigns at the bows of the boats.

Danish Admirals, and different Ministers and Diplomatists and Consuls were present to meet the royal visitors.

Gladstone proposed the health of the King of Denmark, the point of his speech being that we English and Danes had sprung from common ancestors. The Czar proposed the health of our Queen; and the King of Denmark that of Mr and Mrs Gladstone. Then the Queen of Denmark rose and drank to my father. The Czarina said to him, " What a kind and sympathetic man Mr Gladstone is ! how he stood by little Montenegro ! " Everybody was most friendly and everything went without a hitch.

In the small smoking-room after luncheon my father, at the request of the Princcss of Wales, read " The Bugle Song " and " The Grandmother." The Czarina paid him some very pretty compliment, and he, being very short-sighted, and taking her for a Maid of Honour, patted her on the shoulder and said, " Thank you, my dear."

The Czar observed to my father, " I should like to be King of Denmark ! " and in his talk he seemed full of love for the Danes, who are a simple people.

There was a roar of cannon when the King and Queen left: and at four o'clock we steamed out of harbour, the sailors cheering from all the battle-ships of England, France, Russia and Denmark, and the Russian band on board the Russian man-of-war, playing "God save the Queen."

We arrived at the Nore about 7 p.m. next day, and the morning after landed at Gravesend. The last evening my father and Gladstone had a long talk about the clergyman-poets of England, and about poetry in general. Mr Gladstone noted, what I have before touched on, my father's promptitude in praising anything in which he saw merit, written by writers however obscure [1].

It may not be out of place if I give here some of my father's criticisms on poets, — "who," as he said, "enrich the blood of the world," — in addition to those already quoted. I put down a few random notes of his sayings at this time and at other times on the subject.

Chaucer was to him a kindred spirit, as a lover of nature and as a word-painter of character: and he enjoyed reading him aloud more than any poet except Shakespeare and Milton.

When he talked of the "grand style" of poetic diction he would emphasize his opinion that he considered that of Milton even finer than that of Virgil, "the lord of language." "Verse should be *beau comme la prose*."

[1] To one of these talks Mr. Gladstone has referred in the *New Review*, July, 1896: "The next of my sub-classes is that of persons who may be said to have deserved fame without obtaining it, or obtaining even for the moment either fame, or anything which resembled it. My readings in poetry led me to hold this belief so strongly that very long ago I resolved on testing it by a reference to Lord Tennyson, who at once gave it the stamp of his authority — an authority which I take to be quite conclusive, for he was one who would be at once a candid and a strict or even fastidious judge. He was strongly of opinion that a number of poems of real merit had been published during the period I am dealing with, of which the public had taken no notice whatever; which were in effect still-born. It would be invidious to mention names, though some are in my recollection : and in truth they would convey no information. But I may refer to the case of the late Lord de Tabley," etc.

"Browning," he said, "never greatly cares about the glory of words or beauty of form : he has told me that the world must take him as it finds him. As for his obscurity in his great imaginative analyses, I believe it is a mistake to explain poetry too much, people have really a pleasure in discovering their own interpretations. He has a mighty intellect, but sometimes I cannot read him. He seldom attempts the marriage of sense with sound, although he shows a spontaneous felicity in the adaptation of words to ideas and feelings. I wish I had written his two lines :

'The little more and how much it is,
　　The little less and what worlds away.'

He has plenty of music in him, but he cannot get it out."

He would cite "Rabbi Ben Ezra," "Death in the Desert," "Caliban upon Setebos," "The Englishman in Italy," and "A Grammarian's Funeral," as poems of fine thought, and "Mr Sludge, the Medium" as an example of exceeding ingenuity of mind. The last, however, he said to Browning, is "two-thirds too long."

Among modern sonnets he liked some of Rossetti's, Mrs Browning's "Sonnets from the Portuguese," and Charles Turner's. For Christina Rossetti, as a true artist, he expressed profound respect.

Of Shelley he said : " He is often too much in the clouds for me. I admire his ' Alastor,' ' Adonais,' ' Prometheus Unbound,' and ' Epipsychidion,' and some of his short lyrics are exquisite. As for ' The Lover's Tale,' that was written before I had ever seen a Shelley, though it is called Shelleyan [1]."

Of Swinburne : " He is a reed through which all things blow into music."

---

[1] For his admiration of Shelley's blank verse see p. 70.

He was not a great reader of William Morris; but he liked *The Life and Death of Jason.*

Keats he placed on a lofty pinnacle. " He would have been among the very greatest of us if he had lived. There is something of the innermost soul of poetry in almost everything he ever wrote." He gave the unfinished " Eve of St Mark," and the following lines from the " Ode to a Nightingale " in illustration :

> " Perhaps the self-same song that found a path
>   Through the sad heart of Ruth, when, sick for home,
>   She stood in tears amid the alien corn ;
>   The same that oft-times hath
>   Charm'd magic casements, opening on the foam
>   Of perilous seas, in faery lands forlorn."

" If the beginning of ' Hyperion,' as now published, were shorter," he said, " it would be a deal finer : that is, if from ' Not so much ' to 'feathered grass ' were omitted."

He felt what Cowper calls the " musical finesse " of Pope, and admired single lines and couplets very much ; but he found the " regular da da, da da " of his heroic metre monotonous.   He quoted

> " What dire offence from amorous causes springs."

" ' Amrus causiz springs,' horrible !   I would sooner die than write such a line !!   Archbishop Trench (not then archbishop) was the only critic who said of my first volume, ' What a singular absence of the 's '!'"

" Pope here and there has a real insight into Nature, for example about the spider, which

> ' Feels at each thread and lives along the line.'

His lancet touches are very fine.

> ' Now night descending, the proud scene was o'er,
>   But lived in Settle's numbers one day more.'

" What a difference," he would add, " between Pope's little poisonous barbs, and Dryden's strong invective! And how much more real poetic force there is in Dryden!

Look at Pope:

' He said, observant of the blue-eyed maid,
Then in the sheath return'd the shining blade ':

Then at Dryden:

' He said; with surly faith observed her word,
And in the sheath reluctant plunged the sword.'

The ' Elegy on the Unfortunate Lady ' is good, but I do not find much human feeling in him, except perhaps in ' Eloisa to Abelard.' "

He liked Crabbe much, and thought that there was great force in his homely tragic stories. " He has a world of his own. There is a ' tramp, tramp, tramp,' a merciless sledge-hammer thud about his lines which suits his subjects." And in speaking of him he would cite Byron's

" Nature's sternest painter yet the best."

In early boyhood he had been possessed by Byron's poetry, but he could not read it in later life, except perhaps " The Vision of Judgment," and parts of " Childe Harold," and of " Don Juan." He would say: " Byron is not an artist or a thinker, or a creator in the higher sense, but a strong personality: he is endlessly clever, and is now unduly depreciated [1]."

" One must distinguish," he would add, " Keats, Shelley, and Byron from the great sage poets of all, who are both great thinkers and great artists, like Æschylus, Shakespeare, Dante, and Goethe. Goethe

[1] See Vol. 1. p. 141.

lacked the divine intensity of Dante, but he was among the wisest of mankind as well as a great artist. He could not quite overcome the harshnesses of the German language. 'Kennst du das Land?' is a perfect poem, but 'Beschützer ziehn' is a hideous sound in the middle. Goethe was supposed to be cold. I can only say that when told of his son's death he seemed quite calm, but shortly afterwards from repressed emotion he broke a blood-vessel."

"Goethe thought it a sign of weakness to lose faith in Immortality, and said, 'I hope that I shall never be so weak-minded as to let my belief in a future life be torn from me.' 'Edel sei der Mensch' is one of the noblest of all poems."

He had a hearty admiration for Wordsworth, the purity and nobility of whose teaching he highly reverenced. "He seems to me," my father would say, "at his best on the whole the greatest English poet since Milton. He is often too diffuse and didactic for me: for instance, in 'Tintern Abbey' the repetition of 'that blessed mood, that serene and blessed mood' becomes ridiculous. The line

'Whose dwelling is the light of setting suns'

is almost the grandest in the English language, giving the sense of the abiding in the transient."

Of Gray he said, "Gray in his limited sphere is great, and has a wonderful ear." The following he held to be "among the most liquid lines in any language":

"Though he inherit
Nor the pride, nor ample pinion
That the Theban eagle bear,
Sailing with supreme dominion
Through the azure deep of air."

Also:

"And drowsy tinklings lull the distant folds."

He liked Collins' and Campbell's *Odes*. " I admire the ' Ode to Evening,' " he said, " but what a bad, hissing line is that in the poem on the death of Thomson,

' The year's best sweets shall duteous rise.' "

" Campbell's unquantitative line

' The sentinel stars set their watch in the sky

is as bad as the following line is good :

' The weary to sleep and the wounded to die.' "

Of Shakespeare's sonnets he would say, " Henry Hallam made a great mistake about them : they are noble. Look how beautiful such lines as these are :

' The summer flower is to the summer sweet,
    Though to itself it only live and die,'
and

' And peace proclaims olives of endless age.' "

Of Shakespeare's blank verse he said, " Almost any prose can be cut up into blank verse, but blank verse becomes the finest vehicle of thought in the language of 'Shakespeare and Milton. As far as I am aware, no one has noticed what great Æschylean lines there are in Shakespeare, particularly in *King John :* for instance,

' The burning crest
Of the old, feeble, and day-wearied sun,'

or again,

' The sepulchre
Hath oped his ponderous and marble jaws.' "

He would say, "There are three repartees in Shake-speare which always bring tears to my eyes from their simplicity.

One is in *King Lear* when Lear says to Cordelia, 'So young and so untender,' and Cordelia lovingly answers, 'So young, my lord, and true.' And in *The Winter's Tale*, when Florizel takes Perdita's hand to lead her to the dance, and says, 'So turtles pair that never mean to part,' and the little Perdita answers, giving her hand to Florizel, 'I'll swear for 'em.' And in *Cymbeline*, when Imogen in tender rebuke says to her husband,

'Why did you throw your wedded lady from you?
Think that you are upon a rock; and now
Throw me again!'

and Posthumus does not ask forgiveness, but answers, kissing her,

'Hang there like fruit, my soul,
Till the tree die.'"

After reading *Pericles*, Act v. aloud:
"That is glorious Shakespeare: most of the rest of the play is poor, and not by Shakespeare, but in that act the conception of Marina's character is exquisite."

Of *Henry VI*. he said, "I am certain that *Henry VI*. is in the main not Shakespeare's, though here and there he may have put in a touch, as he undoubtedly did in *The Two Noble Kinsmen*. There is a great deal of fine Shakespeare in that. Spedding insisted that Shakespeare, among the many plays that he edited for the stage, had corrected a play on Sir Thomas More in the British Museum. It is a poor play, but Spedding believed that the corrections were possibly in Shake-speare's actual handwriting."

" I have no doubt that much of *Henry VIII.* also is not Shakespeare. It is largely written by Fletcher, with passages unmistakeably by Shakespeare, notably the two first scenes in the first Act, which are sane and compact in thought, expression and simile. I could swear to Shakespeare in the *Field of the Cloth of Gold:*

> ' To-day the French
> All clinquant, all in gold like heathen gods,
> Shone down the English; and to-morrow they
> *Made Britain India; every man that stood*
> *Show'd like a mine.' "*

"*Hamlet* is the greatest creation in literature that I know of: though there may be elsewhere finer scenes and passages of poetry. Ugolino and Paolo and Francesca in Dante equal anything anywhere. It is said that Shakespeare was such a poor actor that he never got beyond his ghost in this play, but then the ghost is the most real ghost that ever was. The Queen did not think that Ophelia committed suicide, neither do I."

" Is there a more delightful love-poem than *Romeo and Juliet?* yet it is full of conceits.

"One of the most passionate things in Shakespeare is Romeo's speech :

> ' Amen, amen! but come what sorrow can,
> It cannot countervail the exchange of joy
> That one short minute gives me in her sight,' etc.

More passionate than anything in Shelley. No one has drawn the true passion of love like Shakespeare."

For inimitably natural talk between husband and wife he would quote the scene between Hotspur and Lady Percy (*King Henry IV.,* Pt. i.), and would exclaim : " How deliciously playful is that —

> ' In faith, I'll break thy little finger, Harry,
> An if thou wilt not tell me all things true '! "

" Macbeth is not, as is too often represented, a noisy swash-buckler; he is a full-furnished, ambitious man. In the scene with Duncan, the excess of courtesy adds a touch to the tragedy. It is like Clytemnestra's profusion to Agamemnon; who, by the way, always strikes me as uncommonly cold and haughty to his wife whom he had not seen for years."

"*King Lear* cannot possibly be acted, it is too titanic. At the beginning of the play Lear, in his old age, has grown half mad, choleric and despotic, and therefore cannot brook Cordelia's silence. This play shows a state of society where men's passions are savage and uncurbed. No play like this anywhere — not even the *Agamemnon* — is so terrifically human."

" Actors do not comprehend that Shakespeare's greatest villains, Iago among them, have always a touch of conscience. You see the conscience working — therein lies one of Shakespeare's pre-eminences. Iago ought to be acted as the 'honest Iago,' not the stage villain; he is the essentially jealous man, not Othello."

Parts of *The Two Noble Kinsmen* he considered were by Shakespeare. " For instance such lines as these bear his impress:

' That makes the stream seem flowers,'

and

' Who dost pluck
With hand armipotent from forth blue clouds
The mason'd turrets: that both mak'st and break'st
The stony girths of cities.' "

Of Marlowe too he was very fond, and would often quote Ford's *Broken Heart*.

On American poets: " I know several striking poems by American poets, but I think that Edgar Poe is (taking his poetry and prose together) the most original

American genius." When asked to write an epitaph of one line for Poe's monument in Westminster Church-yard, Baltimore, he answered: " How can so strange and so fine a genius, and so sad a life, be exprest and com-prest in one line?"

He said of writing poetry: "Simple poems with simple thoughts and in simple language are most difficult to write. I might say that in blank verse 'The easiest things are hardest to be done': and the converse is often true with me, 'The hardest things are easiest to be done.' I feared for years to touch the subject of the 'Holy Grail,' and when I began finished it in a fortnight."

CHAPTER XV.

1883–84.

After our voyage in the *Pembroke Castle* my father was in great spirits, and wrote to the Queen of Denmark:

As soon as I came home I gave orders to my publishers to bind the books which your Majesty and others of your family had desired me to send them.

They have taken nearly five weeks to do so. I sent them off yesterday to your Majesty, and I trust they will reach you in a day or two.

Allow me to say how much I, old man in my 75th year, was charmed by the kindliness and true-heartedness of your royal Danish children, and believe me, I can't say loyally, for your Majesty is not my Queen, yes, at any rate loyally in the old knightly way —

A. TENNYSON.

In the spring of 1882 my father had first met Mary Boyle who was a guest at "The Briary," Mr. G. F. Watts' house at Freshwater, then occupied by Lord and Lady Kenmare. Her gentle voice and manner, her sympathetic nature, her conversational powers, and playful wit, made her from time to time henceforward a welcome guest in our homes as she was in so many others.

To her he wrote:

" I have just returned from my cruise with Gladstone. There were many pleasant people on board, but I found myself often wishing that you and Audrey were among them.

I verily believe that the better heart of me beats stronger at 74 than ever it did at 18."

It was during one of Mary Boyle's first visits to Farringford with her niece Audrey that Phillips Brooks (afterwards Bishop) came to see us. The more my father saw of him in future years the more he reverenced his cheerful Christianity, his hard work in the cause of truth, and his common-sense criticism of men and public affairs. Nor less high was the regard returned by the Bishop.

Bishop Brooks' journal supplies a notice of this visit:

FARRINGFORD.

I came down here yesterday, a long three hours' run from London, through a very pretty country, passing Winchester cathedral and other attractive things upon the way. At last we crossed the Channel in a little cockleshell of a steamboat, and landed at Yarmouth, where Hallam Tennyson was waiting for me with the carriage. Then a pretty drive over the Downs, with two or three small villages upon the way, brought us, in about three miles, to this house. Here the great poet lives. He is finer than his pictures, a man of good six feet and over, but stooping as he walks, for he is seventy-four years old, and we shall stoop if we ever live to that age. A big dome of a head, bald on the forehead and the top, and very fine to look at. A deep bright eye, a grand eagle nose, a mouth which you cannot see, a black felt hat, and a loose tweed suit. These were what I noticed in the author of " In Memoriam."

The house is a delightful old rambling thing, whose geography one never learns, not elegant but very comfortable, covered with pictures inside and ivies outside, with superb ilexes and other trees about it, and lovely pieces of view over the Channel here and there.

He was just as good as he could be, and we all went to a place behind the house, where the trees leave a large circle, with beautiful grass, and tables and chairs scattered about. Here we sat down and talked. Tennyson was inclined to be misanthropic, talked about Socialism, Atheism, and another great catastrophe like the French Revolution coming on the world. He declared that if he were a Yankee he would be ashamed to keep the Alabama money, but he let himself be contradicted about his gloomy views, and by and by became more cheerful. We had tea out of doors, took a walk for various views, then, having come to know me pretty well, he wanted to know if I smoked, and we went up to the study, a big, bright, crowded room, where he writes his Idylls, and there we stayed till dinner-time.

Dinner was very lively. Mrs Tennyson is a dear old lady, a great invalid, as sweet and pathetic as a picture. Then there are staying here Mr Lushington, a great Greek scholar, a Miss B., who knows everybody and tells funny stories, and another Miss B., her pretty niece, with the loveliest smile. After dinner, Tennyson and I went up to the study again, and I had him to myself for two or three hours. We smoked, and he talked of metaphysics, and poetry, and religion, his own life, and Hallam, and all the poems. It was very delightful, for he was gentle, and reverent, and tender, and hopeful. Then we went down to the drawing-room where the rest were, and he read his poetry to us till the clock said twelve — "Locksley Hall," "Sir Galahad," pieces of "Maud" (which he specially likes to read), and some of his dialect poems. He said, by the way, in reading "Locksley Hall," that the verse beginning

Love took up, etc.

was the best simile he ever made; and that and a certain line in "The Gardener's Daughter" were the ones on which he most piqued himself [1]. Just after midnight we came to bed. They

---

[1] For effects of sound he instanced
    The mellow ouzel fluted in the elm,
from "The Gardener's Daughter," and
    By the long wash of Australasian seas,
from "The Brook." "I should like to hear," he added, "from afar the deep roar of the Pacific."

had the prettiest way at dinner of getting up before the fruit came and going into the drawing-room, where there was a fresh table spread by the window looking out on the lawn and Channel.

In November of this year Sir Edward Hamley and Mr Locker-Lampson visited us at Aldworth. Sir Edward Hamley and my father discussed the incidents of the charge of the Heavy Brigade, and my father's poem on the subject, published in *Macmillan's Magazine*, March, 1882.

During the afternoon we walked through the grounds and woods. Sir Edward stayed till evening, when he rose to take leave. My father asked him to stay the night: adding, " There are three ladies here who wish it," meaning my mother and two guests in the house. Sir Edward answered that there were three other ladies who opposed it. "Who are they?" said my father. "The Fates," Sir Edward replied. Whereupon my father rejoined, "The Fates may be on one side, but the Graces are on the other."

The lines, addressed to Sir Edward Hamley, as a prologue to " The Charge of the Heavy Brigade," describe the visit, and the autumnal view from Aldworth.

> Our birches yellowing, and from each
> The light leaf falling fast,
> While squirrels from our fiery beech
> Were bearing off the mast,
> You came, and look'd, and loved the view,
> Long known and loved by me,
> Green Sussex fading into blue
> With one gray glimpse of sea.

My father had many interesting conversations with Lord Wolseley, who is alluded to in this prologue, both in London and at Aldworth. I need hardly remark how much of a soldier at heart the poet was who had written "The Charge of the Light Brigade," "The Defence of Lucknow," and the "Ode on the death of the Duke of Wellington," or what true, admiring sympathy he felt always for the self-sacrificing lives to which those who command and serve in our army are often called. He would proudly remember he had been taken three times into battle. He said that one soldier wrote: "I escaped with my life and my Tennyson."

With reference to "The Charge of the Heavy Brigade," Kinglake forwarded a letter from Colonel A. Elliot[1], who had been there with Scarlett:

Of course I am proud to be mentioned again in connexion with that ride into the Russian column, and to be associated with the memory of my dear old chief. It is an honour in every sense. I read the ballad (or poem?) with a renewal of that blood-rising which I recognized on the day when we wheeled into line, and started to meet the big foe above us on that hillside, now twenty-eight years ago, for the sketch is very graphic, and fine, and worthy of the Laureate.

This autumn a Peerage was offered by the Queen to my father. The part of my journal relating to the offer may be inserted here:

"Mr Gladstone caught sight of me reading by the bulwarks of the *Pembroke Castle* one day, and beckoned me to walk with him. He said literature was one of the noblest callings he knew, that he honoured my father greatly, and that for the sake of literature he would like to offer him a distinction from the Queen, about which he had been corresponding with Lord Granville — a barony. 'Do you think that your father would accept it?' I replied that the offer was so startling that I did not know how he would take it, but I thought that he might

---

[1] He was one of the

Three that were next in their fiery course.

accept it for the sake of literature (remembering how various literary men had cried 'shame upon him' when he did not take the baronetcy offered three successive times). The only difficulty in Gladstone's mind was that my father might insist on wearing his wide-awake in the House of Lords. He begged me to lay the matter before my father. I answered that he had better let me take my time, as the offer would fluster him and mar his enjoyment of the voyage, since he never thought about or cared for titles. He said, 'Very well, let me know when I may speak to him.'

Next day (Wednesday) I let go by without breathing a word. I spoke to Mrs Gladstone and told her I was not anxious that he should accept the honour, but that I knew he would be touched by the feeling of delicacy shown by Mr Gladstone, and by the friendship that prompted what he had said.

On Thursday Sir Arthur Gordon asked me whether I had spoken to my father about the barony, as Gladstone was growing anxious to have the answer, and wished to write definitely to the Queen.

I then told my father of the plot against him as he was smoking, and left him to ruminate. When I returned, I found Mr Gladstone and my father deep in Homer, discussing the beauty of the similes. I said to Mr Gladstone, 'I have spoken.' 'I may speak then,' he said, and proceeded to urge the peerage.

He said that a baronetcy was not the same honour as in Sir Walter Scott's day, that he had always thought a baronetcy an inadequate honour for my father, and then he cited Grote as being offered a peerage, on purely literary grounds, which he had refused for good reasons. As for my father's politics, he assured him that he believed that his (Laureate) political poems were among the wisest of political utterances.

My father shook his head and said that he felt nervous about it, and did not want to alter his plain Mr., that the peerage might have been a good to him twenty years ago, when he could have spoken in the House of Lords.

I could not find out what my father's mind was, as he had many 'cons' and very few 'pros.' I then asked Sir Arthur Gordon to help me. He returned perplexed. So I appealed to Algernon West, as Mr Gladstone said that he wanted to communicate with the Queen. West came from my father after some time, saying that my father had consented to Gladstone's writing to Her Majesty, and that he was going to Gladstone, but I begged him not to do so : 'Don't say anything until my father expresses his views more clearly.' After dinner I discussed the question with my father, and he said, ' By Gladstone's advice I have consented to take the peerage, but for my own part I shall regret my simple name all my life.' "

I may here give two letters from my father to Mr Gladstone after he had accepted the Peerage.

ALDWORTH, 1883.

MY DEAR GLADSTONE,

I cannot but be touched by the friendliness of your desire that this mark of distinction should be conferred on myself, and I rejoice that you, who have shown such true devotion to literature, by pursuing it in the midst of what seems to most of us overwhelming and all-absorbing business, should be the first *thus* publicly to proclaim the position which literature ought to hold in the world's work.

Faithfully and affectionately yours,

A. TENNYSON.

P.S. I have totally forgotten what passage in Dante we were discussing on board the P. C. I have written my thanks to the Queen.

December, 1883.

MY DEAR GLADSTONE,

...Her Majesty must decide as to when I am to be Peered. The younger branch of my father's family, who succeeded to the fortune, took the name of Tennyson d'Eyncourt. Would that do? They say they are descended from the old branch of the d'Eyncourts who came in with William, and from the later creation of the

same name in tempore Charles II. If they, then I. It
is a small matter, I will let you know later on. Many
thanks for your congratulations on Hallam's engagement.
I trust that Mrs Gladstone, to whom my best and
kindest remembrances, is better.

Yours ever, A. TENNYSON.

P.S. I heard of an old lady the other day to whom
all the great men of her time had written. When
Froude's *Carlyle* came out, she rushed up to her room,
and to an old chest there wherein she kept their letters,
and flung them into the fire. " They were written to
me," she said, " not to the public!" and she set her
chimney on fire, and her children and grandchildren ran
in — " The chimney's on fire! "   " Never mind! " she said,
and went on burning. I should like to raise an altar to
that old lady, and burn incense upon it.

*From the Right Hon. W. E. Gladstone to
Hallam Tennyson.*

Dec. 27th, 1883.

I am very glad to learn that the title is fairly launched and
the apotheosis accomplished. I think that by it we certainly
succeed in decorating the House of Lords, and I think your
father will also be pleased with having given, as I believe, some
real pleasure to the Queen in the grant of this honour. Thank
him very much for having sent me Mr Seeley's book[1]. Although
I think a Professor gets upon rather slippery ground when he
undertakes to deal with politics more practical than historical
or scientific, yet it is certainly most desirable that English folk
should consider well their position, present and prospective, in
the world. It is fearful in moral responsibility, but magnificent

---

[1] *The Expansion of England.*

in strength, in security, in magnitude and in moral capabilities. Have you heard of the pamphlet of Mr Zincke who shows, by fair probable argument, that the English-speaking peoples of the world are likely in 1983 to be a thousand millions? At some time or other, but at the proper time and if it is allowable, I want to ask for a copy of the "Promise of May"; there is so much delightful dialogue that I wish not to be without record in my mind.

All best wishes of Xmas and New Year to you all.

My father wrote to another friend: "Why should I be selfish and not suffer an honour (as Gladstone says) to be done to literature in my name? For myself I felt, especially in the dark days that may be coming on, that a peerage might possibly be more of a disadvantage than an advantage to my sons: I cannot tell. I have been worried because, being of a nervous, sensitive nature, I wished as soon as possible to get over the disagreeable results, and the newspaper comments and abuse." Nevertheless he felt grateful to the Queen who desired that he should belong to what he regarded as "the greatest Upper Chamber[1] in the world," and have a voice among many men of mark and among the descendants of those who had made England what she is. He looked upon the House of Lords as foremost

---

[1] I suppose that this was repeated, for it was said that he approved of the English constitution for all countries. On the contrary I have heard him often say: "This English constitution would never do for every sort and condition of country. The fault of the Englishman is, that he thinks that he and his ways are always right everywhere." He was of opinion that the hereditary principle in the House of Lords might be further qualified by life-peerages (to be given more especially to the most remarkable representatives of Art, Science and Literature, and to the heads of the great professions and industries), although our Upper House, as now constituted, has shown that it possesses the political common-sense to compromise whenever democratic passions are likely to be excited. In 1885 Maine's *Popular Government* was published, and he would advise his friends to read this as an exposition of the views of moderate men in England.

in debating power, a stable, wise, and moderating influence in these changeful democratic days.

He said indeed, "Since we have no American referendum (with a two-thirds majority necessary before any constitutional change is undertaken), what safeguard is there against the destruction of the Constitution and the disruption of the whole Empire, except a chamber like the House of Lords?"

On March 11th, 1884, my father was staying at the Deanery, and took his seat.

The Duke of Argyll and Lord Kenmare introduced him, — the latter in place of his old college friend Lord Houghton, who was unable to be present. Lord Selborne as Chancellor received him.

He sat on the cross benches, for, as he told Mr Gladstone, he could not pledge himself to Party, which he considered was made "too much of a god in these days." He felt that he must be free to vote for that which seemed to him best for the Empire.

He voted for Extension of the Franchise in July, not that he deemed the time altogether ripe for such a measure, on the contrary. But the promises of statesmen and agitators had so deeply stirred the popular mind, that delay, he thought, was no longer safe.

"Perhaps," he said, "it is the first step on the road to the new social condition that is surely coming on the world. Evolution has often come through revolution. In England common-sense has carried the day without great upheavals, and I believe that English common-sense will save us still if our statesmen be not idiotic.

If there is a revolution it will be world-wide, the mightiest ever known.

May I not live to see it."

Among many messages of congratulation, a poor old blind servant of his mother's, Susan Epton, sent to congratulate him. He wrote: "I have received many letters of congratulation, some from great lords and ladies, but the affectionate remembrance of good old Susan Epton and her sister touched me more than all these. I am grieved that the former is stone blind. Will you, please, give her my kindest remembrance?"

On March 21st he wrote to an old blind Sheffield blacksmith:

I should have a heart harder than your anvil if I were not deeply interested by what you tell me. I thank you for your pretty verses. The spirit which inspires them should give the lesson of cheerful resignation and thankfulness and faith to all.

Being able to do this by writing such verses you will always have work of the noblest and best to do.

Accept from me my best wishes, and believe me

Truly yours, TENNYSON.

To Monsieur Francisque Michel, who had translated the "Idylls of the King" into French, he wrote:

I have such sheaves of letters, not only from here and there in Great Britain, but America, Australia, India, &c., that I am sometimes, as they say, "at my wit's end" how I am to answer them all; and my son generally answers them for me, for my eyes are failing, and I fear that I may be slowly growing blind; but I cannot resist responding to your kindly letter with my own hand.

I have not forgotten you, nor that pleasant day and night when you were with us, and enlivened us with hundreds of stories and anecdotes. You talked a whole volume. Very agreeable it was and very rememberable.

You will despise my ignorance. I am so little of an antiquarian that, though of course I have heard of John Gower, I don't think I have ever read more of him than a few lines in a chance quotation; and as for Chandos, I am ashamed to tell you that till I read your advertisement I knew not even his name; but I have no doubt that your forthcoming book supplies a want, and will be most interesting.

I thank you for your kind congratulations about the peerage; but being now in my 75th year, and having lost almost all my youthful contemporaries, I see myself, as it were, in an extra page of Holbein's " Dance of Death," and standing before the mouth of an open sepulchre while the Queen hands me a coronet, and the skeleton takes it away, and points me downward into the darkness.

Pardon me, if this sound too tragic.

"Freedom" in *Macmillan's Magazine* for December was his first political utterance as a peer. It carried on the feeling of his old political poems, the same feeling which Bacon had expressed, that " Men in their innovations should follow the example of time itself, which indeed innovateth greatly, but quietly, and by degrees scarce to be perceived."

A correspondence with Mr Gladstone on my father's vote for the Extension of the Franchise follows.

From the Right Hon. W. E. Gladstone to Lionel Tennyson.

10 DOWNING STREET, *July 3rd*, 1884.

MY DEAR LIONEL TENNYSON,

We should be sorry to make any unnecessary demand on your father, but the motion of Lord Salisbury on Monday raises issues of the utmost importance to the country and to the Order, and I make no doubt that we may count upon his being in his place on Tuesday for the Division.

Believe me sincerely yours,

W. E. GLADSTONE.

From Lionel Tennyson to his father.

Here is a letter from W. E. G. I have simply said that I will write and talk to you on the subject, but that in the meantime I know nothing of your plans. I do not know what you feel about the Franchise, but one thing is certain, that W. E. G. has not the smallest chance of a majority in the House of Lords. Lord Salisbury's motion is, I think, identical with Albert Grey's in the Lower House, viz. that Extension of Franchise should be coincident with redistribution. The Liberal argument in favour of their separation is that Extension of Franchise is a question of principle, and that the chances of carrying a bill on the subject should not be imperilled by the petty and personal interests which would be brought into play by a measure of redistribution. Principle first, detail afterwards. The other side says : As matters stand, the Liberals would derive an undue advantage from the Extension of Franchise; and that they will go to the country with these odds in their favour.

Mr Gladstone at the same time writes to my mother:

.........I was so sorry to miss you at Hallam's marriage [1], and so pleased to receive any message, but it almost provoked me to send you a couple of tracts of mine, published six or eight years ago. This however would be too vindictive. It is most true, as Mr Burke says, that the right to govern lies in wisdom and virtue. It is not less true that irresponsive power is a dangerous thing unless curbed by wisdom, which often finds this curbing difficult.

My father answered :

ALDWORTH, *July*, 1884.

I did not write more fully knowing how overwhelmed you are with business and anxiety, but you have found time to write to me notwithstanding, and I

[1] With Audrey Boyle in Westminster Abbey on June 25th, 1884.

must answer, and you must read my answer or not as you can and will. Here is something of my creed.

The nation is one and includes all ranks of people.

I take for granted that both Houses are equally anxious to do justice to all.

Certainly the House of Peers has the prior claim to confidence, being the older of the two, and it would be a base abdication, if it forewent its right and its duty to reconsider an all-important question.

The Extension of Franchise I hold to be matter of justice; the proper time for bringing forward the question, matter of opinion.

Whether this was the proper time or not — Extension I now hold to be an accomplished fact. But I think that at this time, and at all times, redistribution is necessarily an integral part of a true Franchise Bill.

For instance, whether the towns are to dominate and absorb the country votes, or the country votes to have their due weight, whether loyal North Ireland is to be overridden by disloyal South, seem to me all-important facts in the true representation of the country.

(A Franchise Bill, I take it, is intended to facilitate the choice of those supposed to be best fitted to understand the needs and the claims of the people, and to devise means for satisfying them.)

If you solemnly pledge yourselves that the Extension Bill shall not become law before redistribution has been satisfactorily settled, I am quite willing to vote with you, and in proof I come up to town notwithstanding gout. My wife is very grateful for your letter, but will not of course trouble you with a reply.

Ever yours, TENNYSON.

I am oppressed with gout, and therefore beg you will excuse my employing my daughter-in-law's hand.

My brother then writes:

Gladstone gives a positive pledge that redistribution follows at the earliest opportunity. You may rest assured the Liberal party is pledged to a Redistribution Bill, and further that now resolutions are to be adopted, putting the pledge into definite shape. I saw Gladstone this morning.

My father accordingly went up to London and voted for Lord Wemyss's motion:

"That this House being in possession of full knowledge of all that has passed with reference to the Franchise Bill, the principle of which has already been accepted by this House, is of opinion that it should be proceeded with and considered with a view to its being passed in the present session: and this House is further of opinion that an humble address should be presented to Her Majesty to summon Parliament to assemble in the month of October next for the purpose of considering the Redistribution Bill which Her Majesty's Ministers have undertaken to use their best endeavours to pass so soon as the Franchise Bill has received the royal assent."

On division this was rejected by 182 to 132: Lord Salisbury stating that he could not accept the mere promise of a Redistribution Bill, for though the Government might promise to bring in such a Bill, they did not and could not promise what that Bill would be. On November 13th the Franchise Bill was formally introduced into the House of Lords, and my father wished Mr Gladstone to make the main provisions of a Redistribution Bill the subject of friendly communication with the Conservative opposition, and to bring on the second reading of this Bill simultaneously with the Franchise Bill going into committee. On November 14th he forwarded the following lines to the Prime Minister:

Steersman, be not precipitate in thine act
    Of steering, for the river here, my friend,
    Parts in two channels, moving to one end—
This goes straight forward to the cataract:
    That streams about the bend;

But tho' the cataract seem the nearer way,
Whate'er the crowd on either bank may say,
Take thou the "bend," 'twill save thee many a day.

From the Right Hon. W. E. Gladstone.

10 DOWNING STREET,
Nov. 15th, 1884.

MY DEAR TENNYSON,

I think it a great honour to receive from you a suggestion in verse. For three months I have laboured to the best and utmost of my ability to avert a crisis and an era of organic change, which it seems to me that the Tory benches have been inviting; and I have been quite willing to tread any path, direct or circuitous, which could lead me to the attainment of this end. Indeed I have, as you advised, toiled in the circuitous method; but unfortunately with this issue, that, working round the labyrinth, I find myself at the end where I was at the beginning. However, in any and every way open to us we shall continue to work for peace. "The resources of civilisation are not yet exhausted," and I will not despair, provided our friends, and you among them, continue, as I feel sure it will be, to give us their firm and united support.

Believe me most sincerely yours,
W. E. GLADSTONE.

To the Right Hon. W. E. Gladstone.

ALDWORTH, HASLEMERE,
November 16th, 1884.

MY DEAR GLADSTONE,

It is very good in you to take my lines so kindly. I know nothing of parliamentary party tactics, but I have a strong conviction that the more simple the dealings of men with men as well as of man with man are — the better. Therefore, were I your mentor, I should earnestly advise you and urge upon you that you would do a noble and an English act, if you went straightway to the House and said — "When the Lords have passed the second reading of the Franchise Bill, we pledge ourselves to lay on the table our Redistribution Bill."

You can scarce expect the Opposition to give you their scheme of a Bill. It is your duty (or so it seems to me) to give *your* scheme.

As your friend, I should then feel it a triumph to vote for you; and I have little doubt that your Bill would be moderate.

Yours ever, TENNYSON.

Mr Gladstone's secretary answered:

November 17*th*, 1884.

Mr Gladstone desires me to express to you his thanks for your letter. He hopes that you may think the declaration which will be made by the Government this afternoon on the Franchise question reasonable and sufficient.

The declaration was in accordance with the hopes my father had expressed in his last letter: and on the 18th Lord Hartington stated that the Government would receive in trust a communication from the Opposition that they would go into consultation on the Redistribution Bill and would not ask for an assurance as to the passing of the Franchise Bill as a preliminary to such a consultation. The Franchise Bill was therefore read a second time without a division [1].

By my father's wish I then wrote to Mr Gladstone:

" My father desires me heartily to congratulate you on the declaration, and on the explanation that you gave in your letter to the leaders of the Opposition. We cannot but feel that all your *real* friends, and all true Englishmen, will rejoice at your magnanimous act."

" The Cup " and " The Falcon " and " Becket " were published this year; also new editions of the complete works in seven volumes, and in one volume, both carefully revised by my father.

[1] See Irving's *Annals of our Time.*

CHAPTER XVI.

LETTERS. THE GORDON HOME. "TIRESIAS," WITH
NOTES BY MY FATHER.

1885.

Roden Noel's article on the "Idylls" was the subject of much conversation in February, and my father wrote to him as follows:

"Your article in the *Contemporary* has been sent to me * * *. My eyes are very bad. One is entirely gone for all reading purposes, and the other — I hope it will not fail me utterly before I die; — but I have looked into your book, and find it full of true poetry [1] — not concentration enough, perhaps. You are wrong about the 'Idylls of the King,' but wrong in a gracious and noble way, for which I am obliged to you."

To E. V. B., the charming and gifted lady who had illustrated his "May Queen," and whose drawings of children he admired, he sent these lines for her *Ros Rosarum*.

The Rosebud.

The night with sudden odour reel'd,
The southern stars a music peal'd,

---

[1] Two of Roden Noel's lines which he quoted after reading were

"The life of life whene'er we cry
Fills our low springs with personality."

Warm beams across the meadow stole ;
For Love flew over grove and field,
Said, " Open, Rosebud, open, yield
    Thy fragrant soul."

Among many varying testimonies to his work, one
such as the following was sure to give him real pleasure.
This was an album of his own verses, copied out by some
young pupils of a large school at Brooklyn, with this
inscription :

" To Alfred Lord Tennyson from his young friends
in Public School No. 9, Brooklyn, New York, U.S.A."

On receiving the album he sent the following answers
to the mistress and the scholars :

To the Mistress.

Will you present my little note to your scholars
and give my best thanks to Miss Kate Stewart for her
explanatory letter, and accept them yourself for your
interesting account of American schools ?

To the Scholars.

March, 1885.

MY DEAR YOUNG FRIENDS,

Your Christmas greeting only reached me
the day before yesterday, and it was very welcome. I
thank you heartily for having taken so much trouble to
show me that what I have written gives you pleasure.
Such kindly memorials as yours make me hope that, tho'
the national bond between England and America was
broken, the natural one of blood and language may bind
us closer and closer from century to century.

Believe me your true old friend,

TENNYSON.

To the American poet Whittier, who had asked
him to write some lines on General Gordon's death at
Khartoum, he sent this reply:

"Your request has been forwarded to me, and I
herein send you an epitaph for Gordon in our Westminster Abbey, i.e. for his cenotaph:

Warrior of God, man's friend, not here below,
   But somewhere dead far in the waste Soudan,
Thou livest in all hearts, for all men know
   This earth hath borne no simpler, nobler man."

He was so fearful of seeming to obtrude himself
on the public, that, much as he had desired to help in
realizing the idea of a camp for the training of poor
boys as soldiers or emigrants, which he had discussed
with General Gordon, it was not until encouraged by
Miss Maude Stanley, ever energetic in all good work,
that he consented to write to the Duke of Cambridge
on the subject, and to allow me to send a letter to the
Times[1].

Earlier in the year my father had been not less
interested in the company for the purchase of land in
different parts of England, to be resold at moderate prices
to agricultural labourers.   Although he took no public
part in the work of forming the company, a task undertaken by Mr Auberon Herbert and Mr Albert Grey[2] and
myself, his strongly expressed opinion no doubt furthered
the cause.   He believed that the agricultural labourer must
be persuaded to remain in the rural districts, and he was
convinced that to give him a freehold interest in the land

[1] See page 224.   He always took the keenest interest in the 'Gordon
Boys' Home,' and as late as August 1891, at the request of Sir Dighton
Probyn and Sir George Higginson, wrote a letter to Sir Edwin Arnold in
the *Daily Telegraph*, "Have we forgotten Gordon?" appealing for further
subscriptions.

[2] Now Earl Grey.

he tilled was the best means of persuading him to do this, and also of insuring the stability of the Empire. A year or two later it was a gratification that a colony of agricultural labourers, some of them from the Isle of Wight, was taken out by Mr Arnold White to South Africa, and called "The Tennyson Colony."

In April the *Pall Mall Gazette* had some articles on the weakness of our navy, which roused my father to write for the *Times* his lines on "The Fleet." "These lines," Cardinal Manning said, "ought to be set to music and sung perpetually as a National song in every town of the Empire."

In August my father and I stayed at Gavelacre, a farm on an island in the Test, most kindly lent to us by Mr Stewart Hodgson. The Test here is a babbling stream, running by banks of loose-strife, meadow-sweet, and willow-herb.

My father wrote to Mr L. Vanderpool of New York, denying a malicious statement in some newspapers concerning Mr Bayard Taylor:

"An utter lie: according to the fashion of this cowardly and unchivalrous generation of bookmakers, which kicks the dead.

De mortuis nil nisi *malum*."

In the November *Macmillan* appeared one of the most remarkable of his later poems, "Vastness": and for the Royal Family he privately printed his lines on the marriage of Princess Beatrice, published in the *Times*, July 23rd.

The volume of *Tiresias, and other Poems* was published at the end of the year.

Letters to friends, 1885.

In December my father sent the following letter to Mr Bosworth Smith in defence of the Church:

Dec. 12th, 1885.

I thank you for your collected letters on the subject of Disestablishment. The letters, as they have reached me separately, I have read with the greatest interest. With you I believe that the Disestablishment and the Disendowment of the Church would prelude the downfall of much that is greatest and best in England. Abuses there are, no doubt, in the Church, as elsewhere, but these are not past remedy.

As to any vital changes in our Constitution, I could wish that some of our prominent politicians, who look to America as their ideal, might borrow from her an equivalent to that Conservatively restrictive provision under the Fifth Article of her Constitution[1]. I believe it would be a great safeguard to our own in these days of ignorant and reckless theorists.

I am yours truly, TENNYSON.

To a correspondent, who was writing the life of Rossetti and who asked for some original drawings by him, my father wrote:

I have neither drawing nor picture by Rossetti. I am sorry for it, for some of his work which I have seen elsewhere I admired very much. Nor have I any letter from him, nor do I remember his being present when I was reading the proofs of "Maud." Indeed I would willingly have known so fine a spirit

---

[1] No change can be made in the American Constitution unless it is ratified by conventions in three-fourths of the several states or by their Legislatures.

more intimately, but he kept himself so shut up that it
was all but impossible to come at him. What you call
"intimacy" never advanced much beyond acquaintance.

Yours truly, TENNYSON.

To Dr A. B. Grosart he wrote, thanking him for
his edition of Spenser:

FARRINGFORD, 1885.

I owe you golden thanks for your magnificent
edition of Spenser, of which I count myself very
unworthy, for I am very unlearned not only in Spenser,
but in most of our old poets, and I delight (not being
a Bibliophil) rather in the "consummate flower" of a
writer than in the whole of him, root and all, bad and
good together. But of Vaughan, with the exception of
"They are all gone into the world of light," I know
absolutely nothing. I accept him on your authority,
and willingly make one of your Committee. Again
thanking you,

I am yours truly, TENNYSON.

*Notes by my father on "Tiresias, and other
Poems," 1885.*

The Prologue describes Edward Fitzgerald, as we
had seen him at Woodbridge in 1876.

His vegetarianism had interested my father, and he
was charmed by the picture of the lonely philosopher, a
"man of humorous-melancholy mark," with his gray
floating locks, sitting among his doves, which perched
about him on head and shoulder and knee, and cooed
to him as he sat in the sunshine beneath his roses.

Fitzgerald wrote to Fanny Kemble of our visit, Sept.
21st, 1876: "Who should send in his card to me last
week, but the old poet himself — he and his elder son
Hallam passing through Woodbridge from a town in

Norfolk. 'Dear old Fitz,' ran the card in pencil, 'we are passing thro.' I had not seen him for twenty years — he looked much the same, except for his fallen locks; and what really surprised me was, that we fell at once into the old humour, as if we had only been parted twenty days instead of so many years. I suppose this is a sign of age — not altogether desirable. But so it was. He stayed two days, and we went over the same old grounds of debate, told some of the old stories, and all was well. I suppose I may never see him again."

The vegetarian dream, to which allusion is made in the poem, my father related to us in these words:

" I never saw any landscape that came up to the landscapes I have seen in my dreams. The mountains of Switzerland seem insignificant compared with the mountains I have imagined. One of the most wonderful experiences I ever had was this. I had gone without meat for six weeks, living only on vegetables; and at the end of the time, when I came to eat a mutton-chop, I shall never forget the sensation. I never felt such joy in my blood. When I went to sleep, I dreamt that I saw the vines of the South, with huge Eshcol branches, trailing over the glaciers of the North."

Edward Fitzgerald did not live to read the poem, dedicating the volume to him; but on its publication his widow wrote the following letter, which greatly touched my father.

I hope you will not think me intrusive, but I must especially thank you for the volume of poems just received. I had been eagerly looking for its appearance for some days, and that it should have come to me first from you touches me deeply.

I need not tell you that Lord Tennyson's tribute to the memory of his old friend has wakened in me many thoughts which, perhaps, you can better understand than I can tell, so few are now left who have the least idea of what he really was!

The very sight of this fresh volume, and even a hasty perusal of its passages, has brought back so many memories of "Days that seem to-day" (for I often live in them still), when that first volume, which took us all captive, and many a later one, used to be brought to our fireside, and read to my dear father [1] by that well-remembered voice......

It was good of you to know how much I should value your gift.

The passage which my father liked to quote from the poem of "Tiresias" as a sample of his blank verse was:

-But for me,
I would that I were gather'd to my rest,
And mingled with the famous kings of old,
On whom about their ocean-islets flash
The faces of the Gods — the wise man's word,
Here trampled by the populace underfoot,
There crown'd with worship — and these eyes will find
The men I knew, and watch the chariot whirl
About the goal again, and hunters race
The shadowy lion, and the warrior-kings,
In height and prowess more than human, strive
Again for glory, while the golden lyre
Is ever sounding in heroic ears
Heroic hymns, and every way the vales
Wind, clouded with the grateful incense-fume
Of those who mix all odour to the Gods
On one far height in one far-shining fire.

The poem of "The Wreck" was suggested by a catastrophé which happened to an Italian vessel, named the *Rosina*, bound from Catania for New York. "One day, at the end of October, she was nearly capsized by a sudden squall in the middle of the Atlantic. All hands were summoned instantly to take in sail, and all, together

---

[1] Bernard Barton, the "Quaker poet."

with the captain, were actively engaged, when an enormous wave swept the deck of every living person, leaving only one of the crew who happened to be below. For eight days he struggled against wind and sea, without taking an instant's repose, when the *Marianna*, a Portuguese brigantine, bore down upon her, as she was sinking, and rescued him."

The "Idyll of the King" in this volume, "Balin and Balan," was written soon after "Gareth and Lynette," but was not then published.

The simile beginning—

Thus as a hearth lit in a mountain home,

was suggested by what he often saw from his own study at Aldworth: the fire in the grate at night reflected in the window, and seemingly a fire raging in the woodland below.

Of "The Ancient Sage" he writes: "The whole poem is very personal. The passages about 'Faith' and the 'Passion of the Past' were more especially my own personal feelings. This 'Passion of the Past' I used to feel when a boy."

"The Flight," my father notes, "is a very early poem."

Of "Tomorrow" he writes that Aubrey de Vere had told him this story.: "The body of a young man was laid out on the grass by the door of a Chapel in the West of Ireland, and an old woman came, and recognized it as that of her young lover, who had been lost in a peat bog many years before: the peat having kept him fresh and fair as when she last saw him[1]."

The "Epilogue" of "The Charge of the Heavy Brigade" was founded on a conversation that my father

[1] He corrected his Irish from Carleton's admirable *Traits of the Irish Peasantry*.

had had with Miss Laura Tennant (the late Mrs Alfred Lyttelton) on board the *Pembroke Castle*. He was offended by the way in which those who did not know him repeatedly accused him of loving war. So he wrote:

> And who loves War for War's own sake,
> Is fool or crazed or worse.

"To Virgil" was written at the request of the Mantuans for the nineteenth centenary of Virgil's death. There was at first a curious misprint in the poem: "Thou that singest wheat and woodland, *tithe* and vineyard," instead of "tilth and vineyard"; recalling to my father's mind the misprints of earlier poems: in "The Palace of Art," "Europa's mantle *blue*" for "blew": in "The Talking Oak," "The *modest* Cupid of the day" for "modish Cupid": in "The Princess," "Follow'd up by a hundred *hairy* does" for "airy does": in "Guinevere," "To where beyond these *vices* there is peace" for "voices."

"'The Dead Prophet,'" he notes, "is about no particular prophet."

He wrote it because he felt strongly that the world likes to know about the roughnesses, eccentricities, and defects of a man of genius rather than what he really is.

The whole volume was affectionately dedicated

"'To my good friend Robert Browning, whose genius and geniality will best appreciate what may be best, and make allowance for what may be worst."

Sketch of the beginning of an unpublished poem,
" Ormuzd and Ahriman " (1885).

In the eternal day before the days were, the Almighty created Freewill in the two great spirits Ormuzd and Ahriman.

And these two came before the throne of the Almighty, and spoke to Him, saying, " Thou hast shown thyself of Almightiness to make us free ; now therefore to be free is to act, how should we be idle ? "

And the Lord said to them, " The elements are in your hands."

And they answered and said, " We will make the world."

And the Lord said, " One of you is dark, and one is bright, and ye will contend each against each, and your work will be evil. Ormuzd will put pleasure into that which he does, and Ahriman will put pain."

And Ormuzd said, " The pleasure will overbear the pain." And Ahriman said, " The pain will overbear the pleasure." And the Lord said to Ahriman, " Why wilt thou work against Ormuzd ? " And Ahriman said, " I know not, Thou hast made me." And the Lord said, " I know why I have made thee, but thou knowest not." And the two went forth from before the Lord, and made the world.

CHAPTER XVII.

DEATH OF LIONEL. "LOCKSLEY HALL SIXTY YEARS AFTER."

1886.

> Not there to bid my boy farewell,
> When That within the coffin fell,
> Fell and flash'd into the Red Sea,
> Beneath a hard Arabian moon
> And alien stars.

We had always been so united a family that my brother Lionel's death, in April 1886 as he was returning from India, was an overwhelming grief to us, "a grief as deep as life or thought." From earliest childhood his had always been an affectionate and beautiful nature. While at Eton and Trinity College, Cambridge, his imaginative qualities, his unselfishness, his open-heartedness, and humour were widely appreciated. After his engagement to Eleanor Locker he "passed well" into the India Office, which enabled him to marry (1879). It was a great pleasure to my brother that some of the higher official work was not seldom intrusted to his charge. None of his age there knew more about India, and I have not a few letters from his chiefs speaking in the warmest terms of his ability, and of the high place that, had he lived, he was destined to make for himself. With the natives of India in London he was popular, and his house (4 Sussex Place, Regent's Park) was always open to them.

His Blue Book on India is a model of clear style and condensation. As a relaxation from official work he wrote articles for magazines, and for the *Saturday Review*, and occasional poems, and took a great interest in music for the working classes. In 1885 at the invitation of Lord Dufferin he went with his wife on a tour to India, in order to see as much of the country as he could for himself. The part of his tour which he seemed to enjoy most was that in the old-world Rajputana. While shooting in Assam he caught jungle-fever. The poison was in his system when he attended the camp of exercise at Delhi, where during the military manœuvres he was exposed to very inclement weather. On his return to Calcutta he fell dangerously ill, and never recovered, but hung between life and death for three months and a half, bearing his sufferings with the utmost fortitude and with uncomplaining resignation. In the words of Lord Dufferin, " Nothing could exceed his courage, and his patience, and his goodness to us all." He started for home from Calcutta at the beginning of April. Then came the last days on the Red Sea. He spoke little and did not suffer much pain. He passed away peacefully at three in the afternoon of April 20th. The burial service was at nine that same evening, under a great silver moon. The ship stopped: and the coffin was lowered into a phosphorescent sea.

In June Dr Oliver Wendell Holmes and his daughter visited us at Farringford. My father told him that he admired his " Chambered Nautilus." When they parted, Wendell Holmes said to him, " We have points of contact, have we not ? " Which was true enough, especially in their humour. Holmes gives an account of this visit in his *Hundred Days in Europe*.

I saw the poet to the best advantage under his own trees and walking over his own domain. He took delight in pointing out to me the finest and the rarest of his trees, and there were many beauties among them. I recalled my morning's visit to Whittier at Oak Knoll, in Danvers, a little more than a year ago.

* * * * * *

In this garden of England, the Isle of Wight, where everything grows with such a lavish extravagance of greenness that it seems as if it must bankrupt the soil before autumn, I felt as if weary eyes and over-taxed brains might reach their happiest haven of rest.

* * * * * *

I am sorry that I did not ask Tennyson to read or repeat to me some lines of his own. Hardly anyone perfectly understands a poem but the poet himself. One naturally loves his own poem as no one else can. It fits the mental mould in which it was cast and it will not exactly fit any other. For this reason I had rather listen to a poet reading his own verses, than hear the best elocutionist that ever spouted recite them. He may not have a good voice or enunciation, but he puts his heart and his interpretative intelligence into every line, word and syllable. I should have liked to hear Tennyson read such lines as

"Laborious orient ivory, sphere in sphere."

My father was now in his seventy-seventh year. Wendell Holmes, Craik and his other guests were much struck "by his patience under his sorrow, and by his unselfish thoughtfulness for others."

Sometimes when he was with us alone he would say, "The thought of Lionel's death tears me to pieces, he was so full of promise and so young": and "to keep himself up" he worked harder than ever at his new "Locksley Hall." He was touched by one of the daily papers saying of his Ode "Welcome, welcome with one voice!" sung at the opening of the Colonial Exhibition, that "The twelve thousand people were deeply moved, remembering his sorrow."

The shepherd on our farm died this spring, an old fellow of ninety-two, with whom he had had many talks. On his tombstone was put, by my father's desire, "God's finger touch'd him and he slept." A little before his death he said: "I should like to see master again; he is a wonderful man for Nature and Life."

In the evenings my father would pace up and down Maiden's Croft, the meadow where "Enoch Arden" and "The Holy Grail" had come into being; he would admire the after-glow on the trees in St George's (the mediæval-looking field beyond), and would talk about the stars. The planet Venus was unusually bright, and he would say, "Can you imagine roaring London and raving Paris there in that point of peaceful light?" He would add, "While I said 'there,' the earth has whirled 20 miles."

For his "daily airings" he often drove instead of walking, and favourite drives of his were to Calbourne to see "the huddling brook," or by the old-world thatched cottages of Thorley and Wellow to Newtown creek, or through the fishing-hamlets along the southern coast of the island. "The greatest inventor, it seems to me, must have been the inventor of a wheel," he said to me in one of these drives, during which he would discuss many subjects with great animation. Once he stopped under a telegraph post "to listen to the wail of the wires, the souls of dead messages." One day he discussed Plato's saying that "Of all wild beasts boys are the most unmanageable." Another day the second part of *Faust* and his love for the phantasmal Helen were mentioned. "The poem is full of splendid imagery, but far inferior on the whole to the first part."

He anxiously impressed upon his political friends this summer the necessity that England should keep up a fleet equal to France and Russia combined. "The democracy," he said, "does not appreciate that our trade depends upon the strength of our fleet, and on our having docks and coaling-stations in the Mediterranean and elsewhere. England would not, as in old days, be able to depend upon her vast resources, since there could not be a continued struggle. There would be but a short preparation for a naval war now, and one naval defeat for us would mean that we should sink at once into a third-rate power. The fleet of England is her all in all."

In July we saw Lady Archibald Campbell and her company act scenes from "Becket" in the Canizzaro Wood, at Wimbledon, and my father thought them effective among the glades of oak and fern.

We then stayed with Mr and Mrs Knowles in St James's Park: and visited the Colonial Exhibition. Nothing pleased him more than Miss North's drawings and the Indians working at their trades: he much admired the inlaid alabaster from Agra; and the modelled landscape of old Australia also interested him greatly.

In the evening we went to a performance of *Faust* at the Lyceum: the representation he found too melodramatic for his taste.

Towards the end of the month we lunched with the Tyndalls at the Royal Institution on our way to Norfolk. At Cromer the Locker-Lampsons were our hosts, taking us excursions to Gunton, Felbrigg, and Hempsted, and one day we sailed on Wroxham Broad, a large inland lake, surrounded by woods and fringed with willow-herb and bulrushes. The variously coloured sails of the wherries made my father think the whole landscape like a picture of Holland. This part of Norfolk was pleasant to him, differing as it did from any other English scenery which he knew.

On August 7th we went to Cambridge. My father stayed at Trinity, in rooms belonging to Dr Glaisher, overlooking the lime avenue. On the first evening we dined with Jenkinson (the University Librarian), the second with Aldis Wright, the Vice-Master.

The conversation fell on Shakespeare and Miss Austen, and from this glanced at a letter (lately published) from Mrs Cameron to Sir Henry Taylor, reporting some sportive attack made by my father upon autograph hunters, which certain newspapers, in quoting, had taken seriously. On this letter my father commented: " It is very possible that I went on in a whirling way, saying I was afraid that every crime was attributable to autograph hunters. I can quite fancy myself saying this, but I could never have imagined that anyone could be so totally deficient in humour as to take it seriously."

On our return to Aldworth we had various guests. Among others Canon Ainger, the Euan-Smiths, Sir Andrew and Lady Clark, and Lord Napier of Magdala. Lord Napier, a truly great and simple man, talked freely with my father on many topics. On one occasion they discussed competitive examinations, which my father considered were overdone now-a-days. Lord Napier laughingly suggested that we might become so advanced that men would hire themselves out as in China to pass examinations for other men, " Crupper bachelors," as they are called there.

My father questioned him closely about the relief of Lucknow, and as to whether he might have put in his poem " And ever upon the topmost *tower* (instead of *roof*) our banner of England blew," as the sound was better. Lord Napier said that he might have done so, and added that from the poem he should have thought the author had been present at the siege; that he himself had gone up with Havelock and Outram, being in command of the rear guard, and had " got in at night." Then he told how he had mined under a house occupied by the rebels, which jutted out into the Residency ground, and found vaults underneath; and

how he had lurked in a dark corner, where the rebels
passed him so closely that the dust was actually wafted
on his face as they passed. There, nevertheless, he
placed three barrels of gunpowder, laid a train and
blew up house, rebels and all. " It was a terrible
time," said my father, "for England, but from this
mutiny our race grew in strength." The conversation
then reverted to China. My father observed that he
thought the Chinese, who lived on a very little, could
imitate everything, and had no fear of death, would,
not long hence, under good leadership be a great power
in the world. Lord Napier agreed with him, and said
that their contempt of death had on one occasion come
painfully home to himself. A whole family had drowned
themselves in a well, whether out of pique or fear
· he did not know, because he himself had refused to
accept a dog, which he had petted and they had offered
to him. " No incident," he added, " ever impressed me
with so much horror."

They then touched on vivisection, my father expressing his conviction that without anæsthetics no animal
should be cut open for the sake of science. " I have
been reading," he said, " of the horrible and brutal
experiments in Italy and France ; and my whole heart
goes out to a certain writer in the *Spectator*, who
declared he had yet to find out mankind was worth the
cruel torture of a single dumb animal." Lord Napier
replied he never carried a gun now or even walked with
shooters : " I have had enough of killing, and I can't
bear to see an animal killed."

At the end of the year, as my father was walking with
Ralston (the Russian scholar), in Freshwater, he came
across an old Wesleyan preacher dead in the road, who
had died on his way to the Wesleyan Chapel. My
father wrote to one of the near relatives : " I cannot but
look upon his death as a happy one ; sudden, painless,

while he was on his way to his chapel, to render thanks and praise to his Maker. Our Liturgy prays against sudden death; but I myself could pray for such a sudden death as Isaac Porter's."

In December " The Promise of May " and " Locksley Hall Sixty Years After" were published (dated 1887).

" Locksley Hall " was dedicated to my mother, partly because it seemed to my father that the two " Locksley Halls " were likely to be in the future two of the most historically interesting of his poems, as descriptive of the tone of the age at two distant periods of his life: partly perhaps because the following four lines were written immediately after the death of my brother, and described his chief characteristics:

Truth, for Truth is Truth, he worshipt, being true
    as he was brave;
Good, for Good is Good, he follow'd, yet he look'd
    beyond the grave!
Truth for Truth, and Good for Good! The Good,
    the True, the Pure, the Just!
Take the charm "For ever" from them and they
    crumble into dust.

My father said that the old man in the second " Locksley Hall " had a stronger faith in God and in human goodness than he had had in his youth; but he had also endeavoured to give the moods of despondency which are caused by the decreased energy of life.

His MS note on the poem is: " A dramatic poem, and Dramatis Personæ are imaginary. Since it is so much the fashion in these days to regard each poem and story as a story of the poet's life or part of it, may I not be allowed to remind my readers of the possibility, that some event which comes to the poet's knowledge, some hint flashed from another mind, some thought or feeling

arising in his own, or some mood coming — he knows not
whence or how — may strike a chord from which a poem
evolves its life, and that this to other eyes may bear small
relation to the thought, or fact, or feeling, to which the
poem owes its birth, whether the tenor be dramatic,
or given as a parable ? "

These four unpublished lines of the old " Locksley
Hall " were the nucleus of the " Locksley Hall Sixty
Years After " :

> In the hall there hangs a painting — Amy's arms
>   about my neck :
> Happy children in a sunbeam sitting on the ribs of
>   wreck.
> In my life there was a picture — she that clasp'd my
>   neck had flown ;
> I was left within the shadow, sitting on the wreck
>   alone.

The following letter from Lord Lytton to Miss Mary
Anderson was kept by my father, as containing valuable
remarks on the drift of the poem :

It is a great poem, worthy of the maturity of a great poet;
and, so far from suggesting to my mind any unpleasing sense of
incongruity with the first part of " Locksley Hall," it enormously
enhances the interest and spacious significance of that delightful work.   In this respect it is a most felicitous exception to the
generally unsatisfactory character of sequels, written in later life,
by the authors of early masterpieces.   Goethe's *Helena* has no
vital connection with his *Faust*.   But the old lover of " Locksley
Hall " is exactly what the young man must have become, without any changes of character by force of time and experience,
if he had grown with the growth of his age. — For that reason
alone, the poem in its entirety has a peculiar historical importance
as the impersonation of the emotional life of a whole generation.   Its psychological portraiture is perfect — its workmanship exquisite — and its force and freshness of poetic fervour
wonderful.   But I admire it not alone as a work of genius and

a work of art, I admire it, if possible, still more as a *work of courage* — that is to say, as a moral action.   An influential writer has many responsibilities to those his writings have influenced. But there is this curse in literary popularity.   It stimulates self-consciousness, and makes the popular author afraid of risking popularity, by wandering out of the groove in which it has been acquired.   Tennyson's earlier poems, which are household words, and more especially " Locksley Hall," have furnished misunderstood and misapplied texts to a whole tribe of traders in silly and pernicious rubbish of Neo-Radicalism.   In deprecating his high literary authority from such abuse of it, and repudiating the worship of false prophets, he discharged a literary duty sure to expose him, in the fulness of his fame, to a good deal of unjust and more or less spiteful criticism.   His publication of this poem was therefore a courageous act.

Letters to and from friends.

1886.

To Charles Esmarch, Malvern Links (about " Locksley Hall" and a German translation).

SIR,

I thank you for the gift of your translation, but I must object and strongly to the statement in your Preface that *I* am the hero in either poem.   I never had a cousin Amy, " Locksley Hall " is an entirely imaginative edifice.   My grandsons are little boys.   I am not even white-headed, I never had a gray hair in my head.   The whole thing is a dramatic impersonation, but I find in almost all modern criticism this absurd tendency to personalities.   Some of my thought may come out into the poem, but am I therefore the hero?   *There is not one touch of biography in it from beginning to end.*   Thanking you for your elegant volume,

I am yours very faithfully,

TENNYSON.

Of Mr Gladstone's Home Rule scheme for Ireland my father said at this date: "Gladstone and the Radicals know that it is infinitely easy to destroy the constitution of a state, but do not realize that it is infinitely hard to reconstruct it"; and he sent Mr Gladstone the following lines from Pindar:

῾Ρᾴδιον μὲν γὰρ πόλιν σεῖσαι καὶ ἀφαυροτέροις·
ἀλλ᾽ ἐπὶ χώρας αὖτις ἕσσαι δυσπαλὲς δὴ γίγνεται, ἐξαπίνας
εἰ μὴ θεὸς ἀγεμόνεσσι κυβερνατὴρ γένηται.

To Miss Chapman (author of an "Analysis of In Memoriam" lately published by Messrs Macmillan).

ALDWORTH, HASLEMERE,
Nov. 23rd, 1886.

MADAM,

I am grateful to you for your book which contains an analysis of "In Memoriam." I like this much better than Mr Gatty's, which perhaps you have seen, and which is too personal to please me. Yours is excellent in taste and judgment. I like too what you say about Comtism. I really could almost fancy that p. 95 was written by myself. I have been saying the same thing for years in all but the same words. I think that you have not touched upon one argument against *their* subjective immortality, viz. that, according to astronomical and geological probabilities, this great goddess Humanity in a certain number of ages will breathe her last gasp, and leave the earth without even a Comtist.

I should say, as Napoleon is reported to have said. When someone was urging upon him how much more glorious was the immortality of a great artist, a painter for instance, than that of a great soldier, he asked how long the best painted and best preserved picture would last. "About 800 years." "Bah! telle immortalité!"

Yours very faithfully, TENNYSON.

From the Honourable James C. Reed.

THE UNION LEAGUE CLUB,
NEW YORK CITY, *Nov. 27th*, 1886.

MY LORD,

For some years I had the honor to be the private secretary of Chester A. Arthur, lately the President of the United States. Shortly before the death of President Garfield, but subsequent to his wounding, some thoughtful Englishman had sent the Vice-President some unpublished lines of yours, which I remember Mr Arthur quoted to me as he and I rode from his private residence in New York to the train that was to take General Grant and himself to Elberon, where President Garfield had died the previous day.

As nearly as I can now recall, the lines ran thuswise:

Not he that breaks the dams; but he
That, through the channels of the State,
Convoys the people's wish, is great.
His name is —

Will you do me the honor to correct and to finish the quotation?

I should not trouble you in this if I knew where to find the verse quoted.

It has always seemed to me that it was the keynote of Mr Arthur's life as President of the United States, and I judge it fitting to inscribe upon his tomb.

Yours faithfully, J. C. REED.

My father answered him that the line for which he asked was printed in the "Shakespearian Show-Book," 1884:

His name is pure, his fame is free.

From Robert Browning.

19 WARWICK CRESCENT, *Dec.* 16*th*, 1886.

MY DEAR TENNYSON,

Once more, and just as ever, you make me grateful for a new poem, strong and fine indeed. I could wish it were a substantively new and independent piece; you cannot write such a wonder as the old "Locksley Hall" without startling us by any sort of change of its perfection, even the introducing into it of other and novel perfection. I am myself printing something which will go to you ere very long, and with it I shall send an old book from my father's library which has somehow strayed from the keeping of a kinsman of yours, I am ignorant in what degree. I had it in my mind to return it many years ago, and will not let the present opportunity go by. I have to thank Hallam heartily for his clever *Jack*. Somehow the modernised giant does not suit my memories, but that is Caldecott's affair. I know you will believe in my truest wishes of all happiness for you all; as long as I live I am ever

Affectionately yours, ROBERT BROWNING.

CHAPTER XVIII.

SOCIETY, POLITICS, CRUISE IN THE "STELLA."

1887–88.

In January Stanford's "Revenge" was sung in the Albert Hall, and my father thought the setting of his poem dramatic and fine.

He went to London and paid a visit to his old friend Mrs Procter. I asked him how it had passed, as it was the last time he saw her. He wrote that the talk ended thus:

"*I.* I am 78 and you are 87, and in all probability we shall not meet again.

Mrs Procter. Don't you young folk be impertinent to your elders. (Gallant old girl.)"

"The Jubilee Ode" was finished in February[1], and "Demeter" in May,

He would now quote long pieces from Andrew Marvell to us, "The Bermudas," "The Garden," and he told us that he had made Carlyle laugh for half-an-hour at the following line from "The character of Holland"—

"They, with mad labour, fish'd the land to shore."

"And," he continued, "about poetry or art Carlyle knew nothing. I would never have taken his word about either; but as an honest man, yes—on any subject in the world."

His memory was certainly still as wonderful as ever,

[1] Published in *Macmillan's Magazine*, April, 1887.

and, when his eyes were tired with incessant reading of all manner of books, on Travel, on Astronomy, on Natural Science, — not to mention novels by the dozen, — he reaped the gains of remembrance, and would say: " It is a great advantage to learn first-rate poetry and prose early by heart, because they recur to the memory when we lose later things. I have found them a great comfort and solace. We grow old and, from weariness or weakness, become incapable of retaining new things properly."

In August Professor Jebb was with us, and he watched an eclipse of the moon from the balcony of the sitting-room window with my father, who said that, according to analogy, at least one of the planets belonging to each sun should be inhabited, though perhaps with beings very different from ourselves: and that the spectroscope was destined to make much greater revelations even than it had already made, in charming

> Her secret from the latest moon.

Jebb's visit and favourable opinion of my father's later poems gratified him, and set him working with fresh vigour.

In this month we had many guests.

Miss Mary Anderson was acting in *The Winter's Tale* in London and came to visit us, and signed an agreement to produce " The Cup." My father wrote four new lines for her, to be sung before the priestesses in the Temple:

> Artemis, Artemis, hear us, O mother, hear us and
> bless us!
> Artemis, thou that art life to the wind, to the wave, to
> the glebe, to the fire,
> Hear thy people who praise thee! O help us from
> all that oppress us.
> Hear thy priestesses hymn thy glory! O yield them
> all their desire.

Some of his talk was at this time roughly noted down:

" Evil must come upon us headlong, if morality tries to get on without religion."

" When I see society vicious and the poor starving in great cities, I feel that it is a mighty wave of evil passing over the world, but that there will be yet some new and strange development, which I shall not live to see."

He quoted Bacon's " Opportuni magnis conatibus rerum transitus."   " You must not be surprised at any-thing that comes to pass in the next fifty years. All ages are ages of transition, but this is an awful moment of transition. It seems to me as if there were much less of the old reverence and chivalrous feeling in the world than there used to be. I am old and I may be wrong, for this generation has assuredly some spirit of chivalry. We see it in acts of heroism by land and sea, in fights against the slave trade, in our Arctic voyages, in philanthropy, etc. The truth is that the wave advances and recedes. I tried in my ' Idylls ' to teach men these things, and the need of the Ideal. But I feel sometimes as if my life had been a very useless life."

" Especially do I want people to recognize that the women of our western hemisphere represent the highest type of woman, greatly owing to the respect and honour paid to them by men, but that the moment the honour and respect are diminished, the high type of woman will vanish."

About reticence in art he said: " I agree with Wordsworth that Art is selection. Look at Zola for instance: he shows the evils of the world without the ideal. His Art becomes monstrous therefore, because he does not practise selection. In the noblest genius there is need of self-restraint."

" The higher moral imagination enslaved to sense

is like an eagle caught by the feet in a snare, baited with carrion, so that it cannot use its wings to soar."

Speaking of Ireland and England, he said: "The Celtic race does not easily amalgamate with other races, as those of Scandinavian origin do, as for instance Saxon and Norman, which have fused perfectly. The Teuton has no poetry in his nature like the Celt, and this makes the Celt much more dangerous in politics, for he yields more to his imagination than his common-sense. Yet his imagination does not allow of his realizing the sufferings of poor dumb beasts. The Irish are difficult for us to deal with. For one thing the English do not understand their innate love of fighting, words and blows. If on either side of an Irishman's road to Paradise shillelahs grew, which automatically hit him on the head, yet he would not be satisfied. Suppose that we allowed Ireland to separate from us: owing to its factions she would soon fall a prey to some foreign power. She has absolute freedom now, and a more than full share in the government of one of the mightiest empires in the world. Whatever she may say, she is not only feudal, but oriental, and loves those in authority over her to have the iron hand in the silken glove."

"I do not the least mind if England, when the people are less ignorant and more experienced in self-government, eventually *becomes a democracy*. But violent, selfish, unreasoning democracy, would bring expensive bureaucracy, and the iron rule of a Cromwell. Let the demagogues remember, ' Liberty forgetful of others is licence, and nothing better than treason.' The hero of the morning is too often the traitor of the afternoon. It was the mob who smashed the Duke of Wellington's windows on the anniversary of Waterloo. As Goethe says, ' The worst thing in the world is ignorance in motion.' The world would grow into the wickedest of worlds should all this babble and gabble ever succeed in impressing on the people that the obligation of contract is mere tyranny, and that law is nothing but coercion.

"At present we are freer, so most Americans tell me, than America. I have trust in the reason of the English people (who have an inborn respect for law), when they have time to reason; I believe in 'our crown'd republic's crowning common-sense.'"

He acknowledged that there is a greater feeling of the Unity of Society than there was in his young days. But he would say: "The whole of Society at present is too like a jelly; when it is touched, it shakes from base to summit. As yet the Unity is of weakness rather than of strength. The difference of individualities must always exist, and since we are members of one body, different gifts are needed to supply the wants of that body. Our aim therefore ought to be not to merge the individual in the community, but to strengthen the social life of the community [1], and foster the individuality."

Speaking of the ultra-Radicals' passion for change, he said: "Stagnation is more dangerous than Revolution. But *sudden* change means a house on sand. Action and Reaction is the miserable see saw of our child-world. If these extreme men had their way, the end of the century would be plunged in blood, a universal French Revolution. What we have to bear in mind is that, even in a Republic, there must be a guiding hand. Men of education, experience, weight, and wisdom, must continue to come forward. They who will not be ruled by the rudder will in the end be ruled by the rock.

> There be rocks old and new!
> There a haven full in view!

---

[1] He had a great belief in the Cooperative movements of the day, from the "Rochdale pioneers" onwards.

Art thou wise?   Art thou true?
Then, in change of wind and tide,
List no longer to the crew!
Captain, guide!"

*Cruise in the "Stella" to St David's, Clovelly, Tintagil,
and the Channel Isles during the Summer of 1887.*

We took Sir Allen Young's yacht, the *Stella*, for a short
cruise this summer.   The sea was calm as a mill-pond, and the
sunshine glorious.

Many of the crew had been more than once to the Arctic
regions, and interested my father by their yarns, and their love
for their wives and families impressed him much.

We anchored at Dartmouth, and the pretty harbour, winding
in among the hills, had quite an Italian look, when we sailed
out in the early morning.   We passed the Lizard, very wild,
and when we rounded the Land's End innumerable mackerel
boats with their brown sails made " pretty Cuyp pictures."   My
father often gazed into the depths of the sea, searching, as he
said, for some ruins of town or castle, parts of the ancient
Lyonnesse.   " Dark Tintagil " was sighted at some distance, then
we left the "thundering shores of Bude and Bos," and steamed
across to Lundy Island.   The green sea and the red sunset
made a rich contrast, and at night my father called our attention
to Venus, reflected twenty or thirty times in the ripples.   Wild
fowl screamed overhead.   From Lundy we sailed next morning
to Solva (the little river), a creek in St Bride's Bay.

Guided by a friendly sea-captain, we found a tax-cart, and
drove to St David's.   What a drive it was!   My father grew
melancholy, and declared that we should " soon see his spine
piercing the top of his head."

He liked the Cathedral of St David's, with its square tower,
and spacious nave, and sumptuously carved arches.   We saw
the ancient croziers of several bishops, and my father asked if
there was one belonging by tradition to the holy Dubric, who
wedded Arthur and Guinevere.   The ruined Bishop's Palace is
the finest building of its kind anywhere, and the banks of the
little stream, which runs by it, were beautiful with lady-fern
and yellow iris.

After dinner we listened to Welsh songs sung by the school-children, and as we left for the yacht the townspeople crowded round our carriage, to see my father, and shake him by the hand. "Very simple, cordial folk" he thought them.   After touching at Milford Haven, Tenby, and Saundersfoot, we arrived at Ilfracombe in the dark, and pilots came out to meet us, burning lights, to find out if we wanted a pilot.   "These mystic lights, and the buoy-bell perpetually ringing at the Land's End," my father said, "would have furnished good similes for Dante."

Next day we landed at Clovelly, and he thought it one of the most beautiful places he had seen.   It reminded him of Enoch Arden's village, although "Long lines of cliff breaking had left a chasm" was not true of Clovelly; he did not think of any particular village when writing the poem.   We climbed the steps to the top of the village, and walked to Clovelly Court, "the most paradisal country seat next to Wilton," he said.   The white May-trees were in full bloom, and over them, and the oaks, and the limes, one saw the broad belt of the sea: and he quoted —

Bowery hollows crown'd with summer sea.

Then we weighed anchor, sailed to Tintagil, and landed with extreme difficulty in the cove where king Arthur, as a babe, was borne in on a wave.   Two sailors helped my father up the cliff.   An old woman rushed out of her cottage, and said that she had seen him in that same spot fifty years ago, and began to recite passages from the "Idylls."

The ruined castle on the promontory is jagged and weird, and the height, where Iseult sat in the last tournament, had evidently in old days been "crowned with towers."   My father gazed at what he called "the secret postern" arch, through which the babe had been handed to Merlin.   He enjoyed the rushing of the sea under the great cave, and the splendour of the many-coloured sea-weeds, and carefully examined each bit of sorrel and thrift that grew among the ruins.   The old memories and visions of the "Idylls" came upon him, and he regarded the whole place with a kind of first-love feeling.

We drank to the health of the *Stella*, and to "Arthur's Return."

On our way home we stopped at Falmouth, Fowey, and Plymouth, and crossed the Channel to Guernsey and Jersey.

My uncle Frederick lived near St Heliers, and we visited him in his house, overlooking the town and harbour of St Heliers, Elizabeth Castle, and St Aubyn's Bay. The two old brothers talked much of bygone days; of the " red honey gooseberry," and the " golden apples " in Somersby garden, and of the tilts and tourneys they held in the fields; of the old farmers and " swains "; of their college friends; and of the waste shore at Mablethorpe : and then turned to later days, and to the feelings of old age. My father said of Frederick's poems that " they were organ-tones echoing among the mountains " : and quoted a fine sonnet of his :

Poetic Happiness.

There is a fountain, to whose flowery side
By diverse ways the children of the earth
Run day and night, athirst to measure forth
Its pure sweet waters, health and wealth and pride,
Power clad in arms, and wisdom argus-eyed;
But One apart from all is seen to stand,
And take up in the hollow of his hand
What to their golden vessels is denied,
Baffling their utmost reach. He, born and nursed
In the glad sound and freshness of the place,
Drinks momently its dews, and feels no thirst;
And sorrows for that troop as it returns
Thro' the waste wilderness with empty arms.

My uncle had grown more of a spiritualist than ever, believing in table-rapping; and in an unmusical girl being " made to play the most difficult music on the piano by invisible influence ": and in an old gentleman having been " conveyed through solid walls all in a moment, and found in the courtyard of a house a mile and a half distant, the gates of which were closed and locked." A lively discussion took place between him and my father about these so-called revelations. My father spoke after this fashion : " I grant you that spiritualism must not be judged by its quacks : but I am convinced that God and the ghosts of men would choose something other than mere table-legs through which to speak to the heart of man. You tell me it is my duty to give up everything in order to propagate spiritualism. I cannot see what grounds of proof (as yet) you have to go on.

There is really too much flummery mixed up with it, supposing, as I am inclined to believe, there is something in it."

Nevertheless the brothers parted on the best of terms, and Frederick told Alfred, as they parted, that "not for twenty years had he spent such a happy day."

Thence we went to Alderney, and explored the island; then to Cherbourg; and next morning anchored in Freshwater Bay.

The last entry for this year is that on Dec. 15th "Owd Roä" was finished for press. My father's note on the poem is: "I read in one of the daily papers of a child saved by a black retriever from a burning house. The details in this story are of course mine."

During this year "Vastness" was published in *Macmillan's Magazine* of March; and his MS note is, "What matters anything in this world without full faith in the Immortality of the Soul and of Love?"

Letters to and from friends, 1887.

A kindly recognition of his "Will Waterproof," in the shape of an old tankard from the Cock Tavern, pleased him. He answered:

FARRINGFORD, FRESHWATER, I. W.

I have this morning, Jan. 13th, received the old Cock Tavern tankard. Will you give my best thanks to Messrs Spiers and Pond for their present, and tell them that I shall keep it as an heirloom in my family, as a memorial not only of the old vanished Tavern but also of their kindness?

Yours faithfully, TENNYSON.

To Walt Whitman.

1887.

DEAR OLD MAN,

I, the elder old man, have received your article and the *Critic*, and send you in return my thanks and New Year's greeting on the wings of this East wind, which I trust is blowing softlier and warmlier on your good gray head than here, where it is rocking the elms and ilexes of my Isle of Wight garden.

Always yours, TENNYSON.

Extract from a letter from the Master of Balliol to my mother.

WEST MALVERN, *July 3rd,* 1887.

I hope you have good accounts of the travellers in the *Stella.* They have had a charming season for their voyage. Besides the gain to health many new thoughts will have been suggested by it. I always wish for Lord Tennyson, not that he should cease to write, because he has written so much and so well ; but that every year he should find something suited to his genius, and that all his friends should urge him not backwards but forwards. This seems to me the best for himself and for the world. His memory and his powers are so undiminished and his experience so increased, that I think he might even now surpass himself.

I should like some poems in which the truth of things or some side of the truth is clearly expressed, " a last vision of things."

Browning spent a few days with me at Commemoration. He is a very extraordinary man, very generous and truthful, and quite incapable of correcting his literary faults, which at first sprang from carelessness and an uncritical habit, and now are born and bred in him. He has no form, or has it only by accident when the subject is limited. His thought and feeling and knowledge are generally out of all proportion to his powers of expression. Since I have been ill I have been reading a good deal of his poems, and have come to like him, and in some measure to understand him. He spoke with great enthusiasm of the " Eastern Sage," and seemed to have caught the spirit. He is always generous and kind in what he says about Alfred.

To Walt Whitman.

November 15th, 1887.

DEAR WALT WHITMAN,

I thank you for your kind thought of me. I value the photograph much, and I wish that I could see not only this sun-picture, excellent as I am told it is, but also the living original. May he still live and flourish for many years to be. The coming year should give new life to every American who has breathed a breath of that soul which inspired the great founders of the American Constitution, whose work you are to celebrate. Truly, the mother country, pondering on this, may feel that how much soever the daughter owes to her, she, the mother, has, nevertheless, something to learn from the daughter. Especially I would note the care taken to guard a noble constitution from rash and unwise innovators.

I am always yours, TENNYSON.

1888.

At Easter Miss Mary Anderson was with us again and he read to her, whom he admired much, and held to be "the flower of girlhood," "The Leper's Bride," just finished.

In June we showed her parts of the New Forest, notably Mark Ash and the Queen's Bower, because she wished to perform "The Foresters," as well as "The Cup."

She reminds me that, when she had asked my father some years ago whether she should in *The Winter's Tale* play the parts of both "Hermione" and "Perdita," or whether this would be too much against stage tradition, he had urged her to undertake the double part, quoting as to "Perdita" the words, "The majesty of the creature in resemblance of the mother[1]." And then he burst forth: "Thank God, the time is past for

[1] *The Winter's Tale*, Act v. Sc. 2.

the Press to make or mar a poem, play, or artist. Few original things are well received at first. People must grow accustomed to what is out of the common, before adopting it. Your idea if carried out, as you feel it, will be well received generally, and before long." "You probably do not know," Miss Anderson adds, "what a great comfort and help your father was to his friends by his wisdom and decision[1]."

In August my father and I visited Chichester and Kingly Vale, where is a grove of yews which Mr Lear had sketched for " Oriana "; and we wandered far by the side of the Lavant, and among the beech-feathered coombs in the Downs. Leaning over a gate and looking over the woods he repeated his " Vastness," and " Far, far away," without hesitating for a moment.

One day he went off by himself to see an old labourer of ninety, and came back saying, " He tells me that he is waiting for death and is quite ready. What a sin it would be if anyone were to disturb that old man's faith!"

To Aldworth, in the early autumn, came for the last time our old friend Mr G. S. Venables, who with a highly cultivated intellect, a clear judgment, great strength of character, and a somewhat haughty bearing, had a deeply tender heart and was loved by children.

[1] Mrs de Navarro (Miss Anderson) writes in her *Memories*: " I had the happiness of joining him in the two hours' walk which, rain or shine, he took daily. His tender interest in every ' bud and flower and leaf' was charming. How many pretty legends he had about each ! The cliffs, the sky, the sea, and shrubs, the very lumps of chalk under foot, he had a word for them all. The things he read in Nature's book were full of the same kind of poetry as his own ; and the ' sunbeams of his cheerful spirit' flood all my memories of those delightful walks. Though nearer 80 than 70, his step was so rapid, he moved so briskly, that it was with difficulty I kept up with him. The last twenty minutes of the two hours generally ended in a kind of trot. Weather never interrupted his exercise. He scorned an umbrella. With his long dark mantle and thick boots, he defied all storms. When his large-brimmed hat became heavy with water, he would stop and give it a great shake, saying, ' How much better this is than to be huddled over the fire for fear of a little weather !' His great strength and general health were due, no doubt, to the time he spent so regularly in the open air."

CHAPTER XIX.

MY FATHER'S ILLNESS, 1888: AND CRUISE IN THE "SUNBEAM," 1889.

The following notes were written by desire of my father's doctors, who said that it was important to know not only the state of his physical health, but also something of what was occupying his mind.

Aldworth. On September 9th my father walked with Sir Alfred Lyall, and expressed great interest in Sir Alfred's conviction of the possibility of a religious revival in India. After the walk he complained that his knee hurt him. This was the commencement of his bad attack of rheumatic gout this winter, brought on chiefly by walking in the rain and storm, and getting drenched. As our friend Sir James Paget was away from London on his holiday, we telegraphed for Sir Prescott Hewitt, who came at once, and was most kind and wise in his treatment.

The doctors who attended my father were surprised at the simplicity of his bedroom. The room contained plain Chippendale, and oak chairs, an old oak table and wardrobe, a couch, and a brass bedstead with white dimity curtains, and a little table for his candles, since he read much at night. There were books lying about everywhere; and three or four good pictures hung on the walls — a forest pool, the interior of Chartres cathedral, the creek of Bosham (described in "Becket") whence Harold set sail for Normandy, Mrs Greville as his Queen Mary, and a Bartolozzi print of children dancing — the gift of Mrs G. F. Watts.

During the day he lay on his sofa near the south window of

his study, and told us that, looking out on the great landscape, he had wonderful thoughts about God and the Universe, and felt as if looking into the other world.   He liked my mother to be in the room with him even when he slept.   Strange dreams came to him of fir woods and cliffs and temples.   One night he thought that he was bound to visit all the ironclads in Her Majesty's fleet.   Another night he dreamt that he was Pope of the world, and that his shoulders were weighted down by all its sins and all its miseries.

He had two bad relapses.   The first day he came downstairs he talked with us about *Job*, which he thought one of the greatest of books.   He asked for St John, the 'little children, love one another' passage, and the Sermon on the Mount.

Among others he read or had read to him at this time the following books and essays: Leaf's edition of the *Iliad*; the *Iphigenia in Aulis*, expressing "wonder at its modernness"; Matthew Arnold on Tolstoi; Fiske's *Destiny of Man*; Gibbon's History, especially praising the *Fall of Constantinople*; Keats' poems; Wordsworth's "Recluse."   Of this last he said: "I like the passages which have been published before, such as that about the dance of the flock of birds, driven by a thoughtless impulse.   The poem is rambling, with fine lines, — for instance:

> 'The fierce confederate storm
> Of sorrows barricaded evermore
> Within the walls of cities.'"

He often looked at his Virgil, more than ever delighting in what he called "that splendid end of the second *Georgic*."

He was marvellously patient, and his humorous view of his own helpless condition helped him through some weary hours. At the crisis of his illness he made an epigram about himself, and on the pain killing the devil that was born in him eighty years back.   The doctors, fearing another relapse, ordered his removal in an invalid carriage to Farringford.   He remarked on his journey to the doctor in attendance, who was generalizing about humanity: "You see a great deal of mankind, but it is *mankind sick* — the devil a saint would be! do you therefore think you know mankind?"

Farringford.   To both Dr Dabbs and Dr Hollis he generally talked politics.   Some of his chance sayings are recorded below:

"I am afraid patriotism is very rare."

"The love of country, which makes a man defend his land-mark, that we all have, and the Anglo-Saxon more than most other races: but the patriotism that declines to link itself with the small fry of the passing hour for political advantage — that is rare, I say."

"The Duke of Wellington had both kinds of patriotism."

"Carlyle said of the Duke's speeches that they had effect because he kept hitting the nail on the head, repeating the same thing over and over again."

"It is the authors, more than the diplomats, who make nations love one another."

"To decry one original poet in order to magnify another is like despising an oak-tree because you prefer a beech, and almost as sensible."

"Every agitator should be made to prove his means of livelihood."

"True progress is gradation."

"Nihilism in Russia will never be laid at rest until an Emperor comes, bold enough to trust the people and chance the hatred of the nobles. He may be assassinated, but he will be the saviour of Russia. The Russians do not ask for much. Their men of thought, who are their men of action in domestic politics, ask for a graduated scale of liberty. Their moderation must have struck you."

"We ought not to show our Arsenals and Dockyards to the world, as we do. Want of confidence is hateful among members of a family, but want of confidence is necessary among nations."

"In a war we English do not listen to argument until we are victorious."

"In foreign affairs Palmerston saw further than he is ever credited with seeing."

"Education, as we call education, would have spoilt John Bright."

He said that there are many boys who would be far better equipped for their life's work if they learnt modern languages, or had a scientific training, instead of spending so many years on Greek and Latin: but that these ought to be made to study the old stories of heroism, and the masterpieces of ancient litera-ture in good translations, if they had not time to read them in the original. "Yet," he added, "the benefit of most translations from *poetry*, except they be by true poets, seems to me mainly to rest with the translators."

"Beware of breaking up the soil of any Faith, when you have no better seed to sow."

"The Queen has a wonderful knowledge of politics, quite wonderful: and her sagacity about them seems unerring. The Queen never mistakes her people."

At the crisis of his illness the following letters from Mr Jowett and Browning comforted him:

From the Master of Balliol to Hallam Tennyson.

I should have so liked to have spoken to your father once more but I must not intrude upon you at such a time.

Will you give again and again my love to him? He is one of two or three friends, for whom I have done so little, though I have received so much from them.

I hope that he will exert himself to recover if there is still time for such a word. A strong will has brought me back to life before now. But if the hour of hope is past, I commend him to God, and would have him consider that he is passing into the Invisible, of which all his life long he has been desirous to have a nearer view.

Ever yours most affectionately,
B. JOWETT.

From the Master of Balliol to Lady Tennyson.

Dec. 24th, 1888.

I am afraid that you must be in great anxiety but not without hope. May God strengthen and help you! I believe that the patient may at all times minister to himself if he is conscious, and that that strong frame and mind will not be easily overcome in its struggle. Give my love to him and tell him that I hope that he is at rest, knowing that we are all in the hands of God. I would have him think sometimes that no one has done more for mankind in our own time, having found expression for their noblest thoughts and having never written a line that he would wish to blot; and that this benefit, which he has conferred on the English language and people, will be an everlasting possession to them, as great as any poet has ever

given to any nation, and that those who have been his friends
will always think of him with love and admiration, and speak
to others of the honour of having known him. He who has
such record of life should have the comfort of it in the late years
of it: there may be some things which he blames, and some
which he laments, but as a whole he has led a true and noble
life, and he need not trouble himself about small matters. He
may be thankful for the great gift which he has received, and
that he can return an account of it. It seems to me that he
may naturally dwell on such thoughts at this time, although
also, like a Christian, feeling that he is an unprofitable servant,
and that he trusts only in the mercy of God.

Ever yours affectionately,

B. JOWETT.

1889.

From Robert Browning.

29 DE VERE GARDENS, W.

January, 1889.

MY DEAR TENNYSON,

I was at Venice when the first news of your illness
reached me, and I hardly know how I could resist so long the
impulse I at last gave way to, that of inquiring directly how
you are. Probably it came of needing only to know this more
exactly than was possible by the indirect means in my power,
for as to any object beyond it, I know that, being what you are,
there is no need to put in evidence the thorough love that I have
always had for yourself, no less than my absolute admiration
of your work. The circumstances of life never seemed to permit
me a neighbourhood, and intercourse, which would have been a
more valued honour and gratifying privilege than, with one
exception, ever befell me, still I could have taken observation of
the star beyond an actual reach which would have made me happy
indeed: all which, I repeat, you know and must have long
known; and it is only now that I trouble you with the telling,
because the last accounts I have heard of your condition are
favourable, and one's breath naturally ceases to be held when
the danger is, if God please, over: and mine relieves itself, and
you will forgive if it in any way importunes you: that it should

not do so is all I desire. I am sure my dear Hallam will let me know what he can, and give me what satisfaction he can : you shall merely tell him to tell me that you understand I mean well in saying thus much, little in comparison with what I might say. I shall ask also of his kindness that he adds a word concerning his mother, to whom belong my affection of old date, and my profoundest sympathy at the present time.

God bless you, my dear Tennyson.

ROBERT BROWNING.

Jan. 13*th.* Jowett told a story of Dan O'Connell, whom he had heard speaking on a steamboat. A man cried out, interrupting his speech : " I know you, Dan." Dan answered, " Now I will tell you a story. A friend of mine was walking down Merrion Street. A man came up to him and said, ' I know you.' My friend looked him in the face and replied, ' O yes, you're the man, aren't you, whom I defended on a charge of petty larceny.' " The man tried to interrupt again, but O'Connell after this always squashed him by saying, " O that's only petty larceny." Jowett and my father then talked of the Land League and of agrarian murders, and my father spoke of a murder that had happened in his childhood in Lincolnshire. A wild creature, Mad Bess, used to leap the dykes with a jumping pole, and was murdered by a labourer, who dug his way into her mud cottage, for the sake of 3*s.* 6*d.* that he had heard was hidden there.

Jan. 15*th.* My father asked Jowett whether his faith in God was more earnest than it had been. He answered, " Yes, certainly." He read my father the fine comparison between the philosopher and the lawyer in the *Theætetus.* My father said that he admired the skill of the *Timæus* dialogue, and often felt inclined to agree with Plato about the Demiurge, but that this would only put the difficulty one step further back.

Various prescriptions have reached him from strangers — one that burnt cork should be placed under his bed : another that a diet of snails should be tried, said by the country people here to be good for rheumatism.

Jan. 27*th and* 28*th.* We carried him down for the first time to the drawing-room. He was much struck with the beauty of the lights in the landscape and said, " This is certainly a very pretty place." Read Bret Harte's " Cressy."

Jan. 29*th.* Read *The Vision of Er.* He pitied Ardiæus and said, "That is eternal hell which I do not believe." I read to him some of Book II. of *The Republic*.

February. He had been making his poem "By an Evolutionist" between his attacks. Throughout the winter he fed the thrushes and other birds as usual out of his window. Towards the end of this month he sat in his kitchen-garden summer-house, listening attentively to the different notes of the thrush, and finishing his song of "The Throstle[1]": which had been begun in the same garden years ago.

> Summer is coming, is coming, my dear,
> And all the winters are hidden.

Talking of hopefulness he said, "Hope is the kiss of the future."

March. To my father's delight several crossbills were seen in our park. The fact was mentioned to the Duke of Argyll, who wrote in answer:

INVERARY, *March 4th*, 1889.

How your last letter did make me envious! 1000 crossbills! Not since 1837, when I was a boy, have I seen a flight of crossbills. In that year there was an enormous crop of cones on all the spruce firs. I was then living on the Clyde near *Roseneath*, where there was a famous wood of spruce, tall forest trees, 100 feet high. The tops were all loaded with cones. Unheard of before, a flight of crossbills appeared and fed on the cones. I used to cross a ferry often to shoot specimens, and it was not easy to kill them at such a height. The cocks were all *scarlet* with a few yellow feathers mixed with the scarlet. The hens were a dull brown with a little yellow. Never since that year have I seen the bird, except perhaps once at Balmoral: of that I was not sure. The habits are most curious. They cling head downwards like parrots to the cone, insert the bill between the scales, and then wrench them open by a side movement of the crossing pointed mandibles. A fresh spruce cone is a very tough affair. Yet the birds made mincemeat of them and the remains strewed the ground below the trees.

Yours affectionately, ARGYLL.

[1] Printed in *New Review*, October, 1891.

March 14*th.*　My father was astonished at the "living fingers of the cedar." "They look alive" he said.

He was pleased with the Press being called by someone "The whispering gallery of the world."

Father Haythornethwaite told him a story which amused him, and he retold it to me. Father Haythornethwaite had an interview with a job-gardener. The gardener said to him, 'That Shakespeare's a great poet, isn't he?' (Haythornethwaite) 'Yes.' (Gardener) 'And this Tennyson's a great poet, isn't he?' Haythornethwaite was kind enough to say 'Yes.' (Gardener) driving his spade into the clod, 'Then I don't think nothink o' neither of 'em.'"

March 21*st.*　He was able to see Lady Rosebery, who lunched with us, and he praised her husband's feeling for the empire. He spoke with enthusiasm about Challemel-Lacour's noble speech last December against the extreme danger of government by Opportunism.

April 17*th.*　He availed himself of the gleams of sunshine and sat in his summer-house in Maiden's Croft. As the spring came on, "the girlhood of the year" he called it, he grew much better, and was delighted with the primroses, cowslips, and the "ruddy-hearted blossom-flake" of the elm, and the turtle-doves "purring" in the garden.

When Sir Andrew Clark visited him for the last time in this illness, it was in spite of a summons from the Shah, to which Sir Andrew had replied that he could not obey His Majesty, as he had promised to visit his old friend the old poet. This struck the Shah so much that, far from being offended, he took a noble view, and, as a mark of signal honour to the great Hakim, gave him the order of "The Lion and the Sun."

Sir Andrew pronounced my father (although he had been as near death as a man could be without dying) perfectly recovered, quite healthy and sound, adding that he "could not see where the door would open for his exit from this life."

On May 21st Lord Brassey kindly lent us his famous yacht, the *Sunbeam*. Mr Andrew Hichens, my father and myself cruised in her down Channel to Dartmouth, Plymouth and Salcombe. During our cruise my father drew upon his wonderful memory for some of his endless stories:

Of his once telling a friend at a tavern-dinner about Dr Cumming having taken a house for twenty-one years, although

Dr Cumming had prophesied the end of the world in ten years, and of a waiter rushing forward, napkin on arm, and saying in a state of intense excitement: "Is that true, Sir? You have comforted me wonderfully, for I am a family man, and I did not see the use of my being waiter any longer at taverns, if the world was to end so soon."

Of an American clergyman, who wrote to assure him that he had once by an uncontrollable impulse recited "The Charge of the Light Brigade" in his pulpit instead of preaching a sermon, to the great scandal and indignation of his congregation. Some days later a man called on him and said, "Sir, I am one of the survivors of the Balaclava charge. I have led a wild, bad life, and haven't been near a church, till by accident and from curiosity I went into your church last Sunday. I heard you recite that great poem and it has changed my life: I shall never disgrace my cloth again." "So," said the clergyman, "though I may have lost my congregation, I have saved a soul by your poem."

Of a farmer, who saw a painting by Lady Margaret Majendie, of the Tennyson arms, the supporters being two leopards; and who said, "Why, I thought only one leper returned to give glory to the *Lord.*"

Of his father, urging him to try for the Cambridge Prize Poem although it was looked upon with the greatest contempt. Of the turning of an old poem on "Armageddon" into "Timbuctoo" by a little alteration of the beginning and the end, and of his utter astonishment when this poem won the medal.

Of Hallam (the historian) saying to him, "I have tried to read Carlyle's *French Revolution* but cannot get on, the style is so abominable." Of Carlyle groaning about Hallam's *Constitutional History*, "Eh! it's a miserable skeleton of a book."

Of X—, dining at an Irish inn (where a club was in the habit of holding convivial meetings), when a mouse ran out of the wainscot and played about his foot: upon which he went down on his knees to look at it. Meanwhile the waiter popped his head in at the door, and, seeing X— with eyes intent on the mouse, shouted: "It is a real mouse, your honour, it isn't *delirium tremens.*"

Of Aubrey de Vere giving his view of eternal punishment: "Of course it will be listening to Huxley and Tyndall disputing eternally on the non-existence of God."

Of Lowell asserting: "Wordsworth was no more an 'artist' than Isaiah"; whereupon my father answered: "I consider Isaiah a very great artist — everything he says is complete and perfect."

Letters to and from friends, 1889.

To the Rt. Hon. W. E. Gladstone.

FARRINGFORD,
June 17th, 1889.

My dear Gladstone,

I must write, tho' by another hand, something of my own warm thanks for all your kindly words. Better I certainly am as far as rheumatic gout goes, but it has left a good deal that is very trying to me, body and mind. However enough of this. The papers told much of your continued ovation in the West, and yesterday Mrs Elliot Yorke and her brother-in-law told more. We do not wonder at your feeling of exhaustion just now, but, when this is past, it will be a lasting pleasure to know that the people of England are not ungrateful for all you have done for them in days that are no more. I wish you could have looked in upon us here. The companionship of former years is, I need not say, a grateful memory to me. When you have resumed the old work, I hope you will find yourself renewed by the little voyage. Lord Brassey did all for me in his floating palace that princely munificence and friendly kindness could do, and with good result to my strength, tho' brought very low by a nine months' illness. Kindest remembrances from us all to Mrs Gladstone and yourself.

Believe me yours ever,

TENNYSON.

From Miss Elizabeth Fowler.

WINTERTON, LINCOLNSHIRE.

Two or three days ago I spent a short time with an aged cottager, Mrs "Bowskill," or "Bowskin," at Owston Ferry. She and her husband, palsied but "very bonny," live in an old wood-yard there, close by the Trent.

They and their "fore-elders" have been on the premises for 150 years.

This old lady always reads and asks about anything relating to "Master Alfred," who "used to come to visit at Dalby Hall [1]," near Langton, when she was in service there. "He used to *study* in an evening;—when I was sent with candles for him into another room. And he always was patikler, very, to say 'Thank you'; but you see, Miss, all that was before I knew that he *was tryin' for to be a poet.*"

The old man would not leave the cottage "on any account," and as he looked enquiringly, not hearing his wife's talk on the other side of the fire, she raised her voice and said, "I'm telling the ladies how that thou clings to the old yard." "Ay," he said laughingly.

The vicar's daughter had taken them some soup, and the old lady stood washing and drying the jug as she first began to talk.

I wonder if I may be forgiven for telling at this time of a clergyman's sister some years ago who read "Locksley Hall" to a poor woman at her own special request. This was in "The Marsh." The old lady sat knitting until the visitor came to the words,

Here about the beach I wander'd, nourishing a youth
    sublime,

when she laid down her hands, picturing the sand-hills, and ejaculated: "Nay, Miss, don't you believe a word o' that; for there's nothing to nourish *no*body here, be out it was a rabbit. An' its very rare you can get *that!*"

[1] His aunt Mrs Bourne's.

*Extract of letter from Aubrey de Vere
to Hallam Tennyson.*

1889.

I paid my annual visit to Cardinal Newman, sleeping one night at the Oratory. I found him considerably weaker than last year in his body but strong and clear in his mind. He is now 89. He looks forward to his end with a very bright and peaceful though humble Hope, equally unlike the coldness of the Sceptic or Stoic, and the presumption of the Puritan enthusiast. On no face, that of man, woman, or child, have I seen a smile like his, so rich in charity, sweetness and pathos, and yet often with a gleam of humour fleeting across it. It is a strong contrast to that strange look of *intensity* into which his features more often fix themselves. His great religious change has not prevented him from being also one of the most unchanged men I ever knew. He speaks with the most ardent affection of all his old friends, grieving deeply for Lord Blachford who is thought to be very unlikely to survive long. He looks to the progress of Democracy in this country and most others, with that profound distrust of its promises and pretensions with which he always regarded what is at heart but a system of political materialism. He spoke on several religious subjects too, among others on one which interests your father so much that I wished he had been present — e.g. Eternal Punishment, respecting which he remarked that though the " Pain of *Loss* " (that of the Vision and Fruition of God) never ceased, yet *Catholic* Theology allowed of a belief entertained by many Theologians, that the *"Pœna Sensus"* does not share that Eternity, but gradually diminishes and may wholly cease, as is implied by the expression "beaten by few *stripes*." This is wholly opposed to the Calvinistic Theology, especially when combined with the teaching that the " Fire " like the " Worm " is a *figure*, that Eternity includes no sense of *Succession*, and that the gates of Heaven are always open; so that the reason that the reprobate and impenitent does not enter is because he has no love for God and *does not desire* His presence.

On his birthday, August 6th, the tributes from Swinburne [1], Lewis Morris, Alfred Austin, Theodore Watts-Dunton, T. B. Aldrich, a writer in *Punch*, and others, greatly gratified him. In the afternoon of his birthday he planted a blue Colorado pine in Aldworth garden. The following are scraps of his talk :

"The newspaper attention which poets get now-a-days would be enough to prevent a young poet putting forward any poetry at all. Most of the things said of me in the papers are lies, lies, lies." Then he referred to a letter of extravagant flattery: "This fulsome adulation makes me miserable"; and after reading a beautiful letter from Edmund Lushington : "*That* is sincerely felt, and what a contrast! I don't know what I have done to make people feel like that towards me, except that I have always kept my faith in Immortality."

He talked of his past life — of "those old homes, which, though now far away in the morning twilight, are not forgotten": and of his future work, and set about beginning the second part of "Œnone." He was very cheerful and well. By his side in the study he kept a big box full of congratulatory letters and telegrams, into which he dived at intervals while he was smoking : and on his table was a splendid bouquet of eighty roses from Princess Frederica. He was especially touched by a letter from Browning.

To-morrow is your birthday, indeed a memorable one. Let me say I associate myself with the universal pride of our country in your glory, and in its hope that for many and

---

[1] My father wrote to thank Mr Swinburne, who answered thus :

MY DEAR LORD TENNYSON,

Your too kind note has just reached me here. I need not say how gratified I am by it, and how grateful for so generous a recognition of so brief and inadequate a tribute, or thank-offering. It adds yet another item to a debt which has been accumulating ever since I was twelve years old.

Believe me ever gratefully yours, A. C. SWINBURNE.

many a year we may have your very self among us : secure that your poetry will be a wonder and delight to all those appointed to come after; and for my own part let me further say, I have loved you dearly.   May God bless you and yours!   I have had disastrous experience, if I am to believe it, that words [1] may somehow mean the very thing most abhorrent to the habitual mood of the speaker : so may be explained and excused !   All I know is, at no moment from first to last of my acquaintance with your works, or friendship with yourself, have I had any other feeling expressed or kept silent than this, which an opportunity allows me to utter, that I am and ever shall be,

My dear Tennyson,

Admiringly and affectionately yours,

ROBERT BROWNING.

Birthday Letters to friends.

To Robert Browning.

ALDWORTH, *August*, 1889.

MY DEAR BROWNING,

I thank you with my whole heart and being for your noble and affectionate letter, and with my whole heart and being I return your friendship.   To be loved and appreciated by so great and powerful a nature as yours will be a solace to me, and lighten my dark hours during the short time of life that is left to me.

Ever yours, TENNYSON.

To Dr Van Dyke.

Aug. 19th, 1889.

I thank you for your kind and able articles [2], which you have sent me.   That on the two " Locksley Halls [3] " is also good.

---

[1] Edward Fitzgerald's words about Mrs Browning's poetry.

[2] In *Scribner's Magazine*, " Tennyson's First Flight," and in the *Century Magazine*, " The Bible in Tennyson."

[3] In *Scribner's Magazine*, " The Two Locksley Halls," by T. R. Lounsbury.

I should be very ungrateful if I were not grateful for the good wishes, and warm congratulations, which have reached me on my eightieth birthday. As a general rule, however, I think it wisest in a man to do his work in the world as quietly and as well as he can, without much heeding the praise or the dispraise.

The report (which you quote) that I dislike Americans is wholly without foundation, though it is true that I have protested against the manner in which some of the American publishers have pilfered my work.

Ever yours faithfully, TENNYSON.

In answer to a letter from a correspondent who asks my father to help start a Liberal Unionist Journal, he wrote:

SIR,

I am heart and soul a Unionist, but I confess that I think public opinion much more likely to be influenced by steady firm action than by much talking and writing.

At all events I live too apart from the world to feel justified in availing myself of the offer you are good enough to make me of being one of your hundred.

Believe me faithfully yours,
TENNYSON.

To the Hon. Sir Henry Parkes, K.C.M.G.

ALDWORTH, HASLEMERE,
September, 1889.

MY DEAR SIR HENRY,

I rejoice in your speech and your letter, and your remembrance of me. I have received innumerable congratulations on my eightieth birthday in the shape of telegrams, letters and poems, but none are more valued by me than your greeting from the Antipodes. I was obliged to advertise in the *Times* that I could not answer all my friends known and unknown, except thro' the medium of the newspaper, and indeed my doctor had told me that I was not to write letters for the present; for perhaps you may not be aware that I have had nine months of rheumatic gout, which he said would have made an end of most men at my age, but I answer you, however briefly, to show you that I have not forgotten your visits to me, and that I am

Always yours, TENNYSON.

CHAPTER XX.

"DEMETER AND OTHER POEMS."
NOTES BY MY FATHER.

1889–90.

Death of Browning, Long walks, Novels, Subjects for poems, Letters and Journals (1889–90).

" In the evening-tide there shall be light."

Demeter and other Poems appeared in Dec. 1889.

The general tone of criticism was gratifying, and to the effect that the poems were wonderful productions for a man of fourscore years, that they were especially remarkable for rhythm and strength, and close-packed diction, and that there was throughout a trustful peace and resignation in the evening of life, which touched the heart of the " great public."

In this year also had been published by Boussod Valadon and Co. the three poems " To Edward Lear," " The Daisy," and " The Palace of Art," illustrated by Edward Lear. The publisher accepted the book on condition that " one hundred copies were signed by Lord Tennyson "; and much as he disliked signing his name, he signed it in affectionate memory of his old friend.

Napier's *Homes and Haunts of Tennyson* (privately printed this year), and Alfred Church's *Laureate's Country*, published 1891, were the only two topographical books concerning him which he considered at all correct.

Very few MS notes have been left on *Demeter and other Poems*. The volume was dedicated to Lord Dufferin, as a tribute of affection and of gratitude; for words would fail me to tell the unremitting kindness shown by himself and Lady Dufferin to my brother Lionel, during his fatal illness.

The poem from which the book was named was written at my request, because I knew that he considered Demeter one of the most beautiful types of motherhood. He said, "I will write it, but when I write an antique like this I must put it into a frame — something modern about it. It is no use giving a mere *réchauffé* of old legends." He would give as an example of the "frame" the passage:

Yet I, Earth-Goddess, am but ill-content

*   *   *   *   *   *   *

And all the Shadow die into the Light.

"In a review," wrote my father, "of the Lincolnshire Poems it was remarked that I must have found these poems difficult to accomplish as being out of my way. I wrote to a friend that they were easy enough, for I knew the men, by which I meant the kind of men and their manner of speaking, not that my poems represented individuals whom I knew."

"A lady tells me that when she read 'The Northern Cobbler' at a village entertainment, the drunkard of the village, on her coming to the line,

An' I looök'd cock-eyed at my noäse an' I seeäd 'im a-gittin' o' fire,

left the room, saying, 'Women knoäws too much now-a-daäy.'"

About "The Ring" my father notes: "Mr Lowell told me this legend, or something like it, of a house near where he had once lived."

In answer to a letter respecting the legend Mr Lowell writes:

I shall only be too glad to be in any the remotest way the moving cause of a new poem by one to whom we are all so nobly indebted.

Henry James, by the way, to whom I told the legend many years ago, made it the subject of a short story. But this would be no objection, for the poet would make it his own by right of eminent domain.

The following lines my father would quote as giving his own belief that "the after-life is one of progress":

> The Voices of the day
> Are heard across the Voices of the dark.
> No sudden heaven, nor sudden hell, for man,
> But thro' the Will of One who knows and rules —
> And utter knowledge is but utter love —
> Æonian Evolution, swift or slow,
> Thro' all the Spheres — an ever opening height,
> An ever lessening earth.

"Happy" was suggested by a quotation in the *Isle of Wight County Press* from an archæological letter, written by the Reverend Bourchier James:

"At first there was a doubt whether wives should follow (into solitude) their husbands who were leprous, or remain in the world and marry again. The Church decided that the marriage tie was indissoluble. With a love stronger than this living death, lepers were followed into banishment from the haunts of men by their faithful wives."

Of "Merlin and the Gleam," written in August, 1889, he says: "In the story of 'Merlin and Nimue' I have read that Nimue means the Gleam, — which signifies in my poem the higher poetic imagination. Verse IV is the early imagination, Verse V alludes to the Pastorals."

Of "Romney's Remorse" he notes: "Edward Fitzgerald said in a letter, 'I read Hayley's *Life of Romney* the other day: Romney wanted but education and reading to make him a very fine painter; but his ideal was not high and fine. How touching is the close of his life! He married at nineteen, and because Sir Joshua and others had said that marriage 'spoilt an artist,' almost immediately left his wife in the North and never saw her till the end of his life; when old, nearly mad, and quite desolate, he went back to her and she received him and nursed him till he died. This quiet act of hers is worth all Romney's pictures, even as a matter of art, I am sure.'"

"Far — far — away," and "The Oak," are two poems in this volume which he liked.

> What sound was dearest in his native dells?
> The mellow lin-lan-lone of evening bells
> > Far — far — away.

Distant bells always charmed him with their "lin-lan-lone," and, when heard over the sea or a lake, he was never tired of listening to them.

"The Oak," he thought, might be called "clean cut like a Greek epigram. The allusion is to the gold of the young oak leaves in spring, and to the autumnal gold of the fading leaves."

"Crossing the Bar" was written in my father's eighty-first year, on a day in October when we came from Aldworth to Farringford. Before reaching Farringford he had the Moaning of the Bar in his mind, and after dinner he showed me this poem written out.

I said, " That is the crown of your life's work." He answered, " It came in a moment." He explained the " Pilot " as " That Divine and Unseen Who is always guiding us."

A few days before my father's death he said to me: " Mind you put ' Crossing the Bar ' at the end of all editions of my poems [1]. "

I give two of the many letters which he received relative to the volume:

HAWARDEN CASTLE,
Dec. 14th, 1889.

MY DEAR TENNYSON,

How kind of you to send me your new volume! I have lost no time in reading it, and I am, if not surprised, yet greatly pleased to find you still equal to new manifestations of power such as it contains.

Only I am not ready to part from the *Iliad* on any terms, not even on the condition of meeting its author. Your "lightning may shrivel[2], etc." is the grand expression of what I meanly spoke at Kirkwall as to your vocation and mine.

---

[1] My father considered Edmund Lushington's translation into Greek of "Crossing the Bar," one of the finest translations he had ever read :

Ἄλιος δέδυκε, λέλαμπεν ἀστὴρ
ἕσπερος, λαμπρά με καλεῖ τις ὀμφά·
μηδ' ἁλὸς βαρύστονος ἦχος εἴη
εὖτ' ἂν ἀπέλθω,
ῥεῦμα δ' οἷον ἦκα καθεῦδον ἕρποι
νόσφιν ἀφλοισμοῦ κελάδου τε πλῆθον,
ἃδ' ἀπόρροὰ βαθέων ἀπείρων
ὄκκ' ἀνακάμψῃ
οἴκαδ' αὖτις. Ἀμφιλύκα κνεφαῖον
νὺξ φέρει κώδωνα, τὰ δ' ἔνθεν ὄρφνα·
μηδὲ πενθήρης τις ὀδυρμὸς εἴη
ναυστολέοντος,
τῆλε μὲν χρόνου τε τόπου τ' ἄπουρον
τῆλε πλημμυρὸν πέλαγός μ ἀπάξει,
ἔλπομαι δ' εἰς ωπα πέραν κυβερνα-
τῆρος ἀθρήσειν.

[2] " Parnassus."

The death of Browning on the day of the appearance of your volume, and as we hear of one of his own, is a touching event. I was full of fear on seeing the word bronchitis. I hope you have no leanings that way. Requiescat in Pace. Wish for me, I pray you, a speedy deliverance, if God's will may so be, from the life of turmoil and contention which I have pursued for fifty-seven years and part of a fifty-eighth.

With our united love...

W. E. GLADSTONE.

Dec. 26th, 1889.

MY DEAR TENNYSON,

Accept my best thanks for your very kind present of "Demeter." I have not had a Christmas Box I valued so much for many a long year. I envy your vigour, and am ashamed of myself beside you for being turned out to grass. I kick up my heels now and then and have a gallop round the paddock, but it does not come to much. With best wishes to you, and, if Lady Tennyson has not forgotten me altogether, to her also,

Believe me yours very faithfully,

T. H. HUXLEY.

In December my father sent these lines to Bishop Westcott of Durham with reference to the strikes among the miners in the North of England, in return for a request for an autograph:

Well roars the storm to those who hear
A deeper voice across the storm.

The Bishop was hopeful as to the situation; but my father was sorely afraid of these continuous coal-strikes, that they might in the end have the effect of permanently increasing the price of coal for the poor labourer; of diminishing the numerous industries which depend on coal, and which support multitudes of hard-working men; and of eventually driving our gigantic coal-trade altogether out of England, and thus bringing wholesale ruin on the country [1].

1890.

Robert Browning's death, in December 1889, greatly distressed my father, who telegraphed to his son, "We deeply sympathize with you. The world has had a great loss and ourselves in particular." I was in London at the time and my mother wrote to me: "Browning has been so nobly free from envy, so loving and appreciative that one cannot but mourn his loss as a friend; and as a poet one feels that one has lost a deep mine of great thoughts, and pure feelings, and much else besides."

The death too of the Irish poet William Allingham took away from us yet another friend. My father often repeated Allingham's last words: "I see such things as you cannot dream of."

This winter my father amused himself by making water-colour sketches. Watts had urged him to do this and sent him the advice to "add a daub every day," saying he "would then soon have a picture." He was interested in every form of art and of craft, and at this time placed round the windows of a cottage at Farringford bricks moulded from a wreath of ivy leaves, which he had carved in apple-tree wood.

On April 21st my mother wrote to Mr Palgrave: "He has been entertaining large five o'clock tea-parties for the last three or four weeks, almost daily, and has often been even able to read to them. He has walked an hour and a half or two hours before luncheon, many days, between Mr Arthur Coleridge and Dr Stanford, all three telling merry stories; and at luncheon and at

---

[1] See p. 382.

dinner his spirits did not fail with others, though now he
is beginning to be weary of the many people."

His walks were still generally along his Downs from
Watcombe Bay by the Beacon towards the thymy
promontory that towers above the Needles [1]. The views
of sea and cliff, the gloom and glory over the waters on
either hand, were a perpetual delight to him. He often
wondered why the distant sunlight on the sea as seen
from the Beacon was so "amber": and would marvel
at the

> dead claps of thunder from within the cliffs,
> Heard thro' the living roar.

The birds that made their homes on the chalk ledges,
the peregrine falcons, the ravens with their "iron knell,"
the kestrels, the carrion-crows, the different kinds of
sea-bird, from the cormorants drying themselves on the
pinnacles of rock in heraldic attitudes to the sea-gull
sunning himself among the tufts of samphire and of thrift,
were ever a fresh interest. A special corner, that he
liked above all, was a platform of cliff over Scratchell's
Bay looking up to a dazzling white precipice, seen far
away by the ships at sea, and which he named Taliessin,
or the "splendid brow." At other times he would wander at low-tide among the green rock-pools on the shore,
and curiously examine the "branching sea-weed" and
the brilliant sea-anemones; or, when high-tide coincided
with sunset, would watch the great waves flinging their
"rosy veil of spray" behind them and "shouldering the
sun." Whenever I look at the sea at Freshwater, I
remember passages from his poems which he made as he
was walking or sailing there, such as

> The scream of a madden'd beach dragg'd down by
> the wave:

[1] The doctors had said, when my father was ill, that he would probably
never again have the use of his limbs or be able to move from the sofa. But
his great natural strength did not fail him.

and

                      a full tide
Rose with ground-swell, which, on the foremost rocks
Touching, up-jetted in spirts of wild sea-smoke
And scaled in sheets of wasteful foam, and fell
In vast sea-cataracts:

and

    For sure no gladlier does the stranded wreck
    See thro' the gray skirts of a lifting squall
    The boat that bears the hope of life approach
    To save the life despair'd of, than he saw
    Death dawning on him, and the close of all.

He read many novels after his evening's work, and among others he looked through *Henrietta Temple* again. He had told Disraeli that the "silly sooth" of love was given perfectly there. *Lothair* he did not admire, "altho' it was written to stir up the English gentry and nobility to be leaders of the people." To this end Disraeli had shown them as a handsome set of fellows who did nothing, but who had in them the stuff to be leaders of men if they would only exert themselves. It is interesting that Disraeli in later life expressed himself cordially about my father's poems, though earlier he had depreciated them in comparison with Byron's. My father in turn approved of "Disraeli's feeling for the true unity of our empire."

He would always talk of Thackeray's novels, *Esmond*, *Pendennis*, and *The Newcomes* as being "delicious: they are so mature. But now the days are so full of false sentiment that, as Thackeray said, one cannot draw a man as he should be." He would read and re-read them as well as Walter Scott's and Miss Austen's novels. His comments on Walter Scott and Miss Austen were:

" Scott is the most chivalrous literary figure of this century, and the author with the widest range since Shakespeare. I think *Old Mortality* is his greatest novel. The realism and life-likeness of Miss Austen's Dramatis Personæ come nearest to those of Shakespeare. Shakespeare however is a sun to which Jane Austen, tho' a bright and true little world, is but an asteroid."

Of *Clarissa Harlowe* he would say: " I like those great *still* books," and " I wish there were a great novel in hundreds of volumes that I might go on and on; I hate some of your modern novels with numberless characters thrust into the first chapter and nothing but modern society talk; and also those morbid, and introspective tales, with their oceans of sham philosophy. To read these last is like wading through glue."

In respect of contemporary novels he had a very catholic taste. Latterly he read Stevenson and George Meredith with great interest: also Walter Besant, Black, Hardy, Henry James, Marion Crawford, Anstey, Barrie, Blackmore, Conan Doyle, Miss Braddon, Miss Lawless, Ouida, Miss Broughton, Lady Margaret Majendie, Hall Caine, and Shorthouse. He liked Edna Lyall's *Autobiography of a Slander*, and the *Geier-Wally* by Wilhelmina von Hillern; and often gave his friends *Surly Tim* to read, for its " concentrated pathos." " Mrs Oliphant's prolific work," he would observe, " is amazing, and she is nearly always worth reading."

Various subjects for poems were suggested to him. The Master of Balliol urged him to write on the " Happiness of Old Age," or on the idea that " All religions are one," or on " The religions of all good men."

My father would have liked to make a poem of one of those great Egyptian legends, which describe how despair and death came upon him who was mad enough to try and probe the secret of the Universe; and he thought of weaving into a great stage drama the legend of " Tristram of Lyonnesse," as he had been obliged to cut it down to suit his treatment of the " Idylls of the King."

This narrative from the *Spectator*, given him by the Bishop of Ripon (Boyd Carpenter), he felt was a noble theme, and he laid it aside for future use:

In December last, the American ship "*Cleopatra*" was descried by Captain Hughes of the Liverpool steamer "*Lord Gough*," near the St George's Shoal, with her colours at half-mast and evidently sinking. The gale and the sea were so terrible that it seemed madness to help her; but volunteers came forward, and a boat was manned, when suddenly, the colours were hauled down. Captain Hughes however persevered, the desperate adventure succeeded, and the crew of the "*Cleopatra*" was saved.

The United States Government forwarded thanks and rewards to Captain Hughes and his men; but noble as their conduct was, Captain Pendleton of the "*Cleopatra*" had done a nobler thing. He was asked why his colours were hauled down, and replied, " Because we had no boats, and thought it wrong to imperil other lives in a hopeless attempt." The "*Cleopatra*" was then water-logged, and Captain Pendleton and his men faced the certainty of death by drowning rather than tempt others, strangers, into danger.

Honour to the name of the brave! That deed on the "*Cleopatra*" is equal to the conduct of the soldiers on the "*Birkenhead*," and should live like it in song.

Of the Bishop he had seen a good deal in late years and he talked freely with him as a sympathetic companion.

During one of the Bishop's last visits my father said to him: " Looked at from one point of view I can understand the Persian dualism; there is much which looks like the conflict of the powers of light and darkness." When the Bishop said that he thought this might be found in the word *education*, he said " Yes," and he repeated the lines:

The Lord let the house of a brute to the soul of a man,
  And the man said " Am I your debtor? "
And the Lord — " Not yet : but make it as clean as
  you can,
And then I will let you a better."

" It is hard," he said, "to believe in God ; but it is
harder not to believe.   I believe in God, not from what
I see in Nature, but from what I find in man."

Letters from friends, 1890.

From Oliver Wendell Holmes.

Feb. 2nd, 1890.

I had great pleasure in reading your last volume of poems,
and I thank you very heartily for sending me a copy.   All the
world honours and praises you, and I am a part of that world.
But besides that I am interested in you for one reason which
very few others can assign.   I had the honour of following
you into atmospheric existence at an interval of only twenty-
three days, having been born on the twenty-ninth of August
1809.   I am proud of my birth-year and humbled when I think
of who were and who are my coevals, Darwin the destroyer and
creator, Lord Houghton the pleasant and kindhearted lover
of men of letters, Gladstone whom I leave it to you to char-
acterise, but whose vast range of intellectual powers few will
question, Mendelssohn, whose music still rings in our ears, and
the Laureate whose "jewels five words long" — and many of
them a good deal longer — sparkle in our memories and will
shine till
        "Universal darkness buries all."

I said I feel proud to be even accidentally associated with such a
group.   But I said also that I feel humbled : perhaps I ought to
feel nothing about it, as the world at large is not very deeply
interested in the fact of my finding myself introduced into life in
such good company.   I might have spared you this letter, which
possibly your son or your secretary may read to you, but I could
not feel easy until I had thanked you for the welcome little

volume, and assured you that I have never forgotten the kindness with which you received my dear daughter, with me now only in memory, and myself.   With grateful remembrances and the hope that you may live many more years and sing many more songs,

I am, my dear Lord Tennyson,

Very truly yours,

OLIVER WENDELL HOLMES.

From the Duke of Argyll to Lady Tennyson.

Feb. 28th, 1890.

I have not been bothering you by letters and telegrams because I saw the daily report in the paper — with what anxiety I am sure I need not tell you.   I do trust soon to hear that he has weathered this new storm.   Will you tell him — it may amuse him — that his beautiful line in the last verses on "Spring,"

> Wavers on her thin stem the snowdrop cold
> That trembles not to kisses of the bee,

is true to nature *except* at Inverary?   We had, last Monday, an extraordinary hot sun, great calm, and a sudden awakening of the *hives*.   Out they came, and our snowdrop crop being still in full force the bees were all rushing to the snowdrops and for the first time in my life, sitting in the garden, I saw the bees all round my seat making the "thin stems" waver and tremble to their kisses!   But his observation is none the less true of the ordinary cycle of the season and of its flowers.

CHAPTER XXI.

OLD FRIENDS AND NEW POEMS.

My Journal.

1890–91.

A sudden attack of influenza had made my father ill again. Despite his growing weakness, his interest in the larger politics of the country never failed. Thus at his wish I read the new Tithes Bill to him, and he admired the courage of the graduated property tax in Victoria, saying that a modified tax of the same nature would soon have to be passed in England. He was much touched by an account of Mrs Moberley's (the wife of the late Bishop of Salisbury) being greatly comforted by "Crossing the Bar," when she was dying.

March 7th. He was pleased with Sir Henry Parkes' Dedication of his poems. He looked forward to Australian Federation as a prelude to Imperial Federation.

March 8th. He made me read Southwell's "Burning Babe" to him out of Palgrave's *Sacred Song*. Talked then of St Athanasius, who, as a boy, baptized his fellows in the sea; and remarked that the ceremony was at once treated by Bishop Alexander as valid. He added: "How much these old fellows believed in the divine nature of childhood!"

March 11th. Dined downstairs; told of his having addressed the boys at Louth School, in the person of his uncle Charles Tennyson, M.P. for Stamford, in a long and comic speech: and of his hating Louth School so much, that he would not go down the lane where it was, when in later life he was at Louth.

March 15th. My father quoted Goethe's "Kennst du das

Land?" and "Wer nie sein Brod" at dinner, admiring them greatly. He said he thought that seven of his own best songs (of the deeper kind) were "All along the Valley," "Courage, poor Heart of Stone," "Break, Break, Break," "The Bugle Song," "Ask me no more," "Tears, Idle Tears," and "Crossing the Bar."

March 16th. Talked about my brother Lionel, this being his birthday; and of the after-life being the cardinal part of Christ's teaching; and of *The Messiah*, *Pilgrim's Progress*, and *Paradise Lost*, as the three greatest religious works produced in England.

March 17th. He had all but recovered from his influenza, and sat in the sun in front of the study window, and read Jebb's *Homer:* quoted "Virtus repulsæ nescia sordidæ," and dwelt on the stateliness imparted by Horace to the Alcaic stanza.

March 20th. Said in the evening: " Love is the highest we feel, therefore we must believe that 'God is Love.' We cannot but believe that the creation is infinite, if God is infinite."

April. Miss Mary Anderson is to be married, so cannot act in " Robin Hood." My father said he was fond of Sherwood Forest, "the oaks with the bark of their trunks in waves like the flowing of the tides, each branch a grove," standing in the broad green glades. Then the talk touched on Rousseau.

My father went on to say he told Wordsworth that balloons would perhaps be fixed at the bottom of high mountains so as to take people to the top to see the views. Wordsworth grunted, thinking this a sacrilege.

In April Peter Bayne wrote:

A serious flaw has been allowed by you to remain in one of your masterpieces, in quality if not in size. When Lady Clare's nurse tells her that she is her own child, she, Lady Clare, uses in reply the words, " If I'm a beggar born." The criticism of my *heart* tells me that Lady Clare could never have said that.

I may mention also, though this is a matter of much less consequence, that the *one* word in " Sir Galahad " that seems to me to jar with the saintly and solemn atmosphere of the poem is the epithet " magic " applied to the boat that Galahad found.

My father answered:

April 29th, 1890.

MY DEAR SIR,

You make no allowance for the shock of the fall from being Lady Clare to finding herself the child of a nurse. She speaks besides not without a certain anger. " Peasant-born " would be tame and passionless. " Magic " includes " mystic."

Yours very truly, TENNYSON.

" Beggar-born." She is not calling her mother a beggar but thinking of Lord Ronald: " I that have nothing have kept him out of his own."

He also wrote to the daughter of the German poet Freiligrath:

FARRINGFORD,

May 1st, 1890.

MADAM,

I thank you for your translation of my " Snowdrop." It seems to me very good, tho' I do not profess to be a judge of German verse. I remember your father the poet with affection and regret.

Very truly yours,

TENNYSON.

May 28th. G. F. Watts left to-day, having done a fine portrait of my father (now in the Hall of Trinity). He was amused by Watts telling him that Carlyle had said that Watts had painted him like a mad labourer. At the request of Watts, my father read the " Ode on the Duke of Wellington."

He told Watts of my mother's dream after that ode was written. The Duke, she dreamt, called upon them, and as he rose from the sofa to shake hands with her, she feared to take the cold hand of death, and it was instead a warm, living hand which grasped hers. I read " The Golden Bough " and the " Story of a Balaclava Hero " to Watts and my father, while the portrait was in hand.

My father said that he used to act Dryden's plays with his brothers and sisters, and that the French governess assured him he would be a fine actor some day. He repeated to us the speech " O Laius Labdacus," etc.

June 13*th*. My parents kept their 40th wedding day. He gave my mother a pretty posy of roses, rosemary and syringa, and was very merry.

To the character of Edgar in " The Promise of May " he referred in an impromptu :

> A surface man of many theories,
> And yet not true to one : whose whims were meant
> For virtue's servants, but that heart of his
> Hard, and the slave of vice ; and he would weep
> For ills himself had practised on another,
> At some sad tale of wrong, and do the wrong
> He wept for, till the very wrong itself
> Had found him out.

He said that he never met Landor more than once or twice in his life, at the time when he himself was living with James Spedding, under the same roof as John Forster, 58 Lincoln's Inn Fields. Coming home about 10 o'clock one evening he saw Mr Fox, the member for Oldham, standing at the top of the doorsteps of the house. They shook hands, and he went into Forster's, where Landor had been dining. In the meantime Mr Fox had fallen down and broken his arm, and was brought into the dining-room, white from pain, and holding the injured arm with the hand of the other. Old Landor went on eloquently discoursing of Catullus and other Latin poets as if nothing particular had happened, " which seemed rather hard, but was perhaps better than utter silence."

Speaking of the original " Locksley Hall," he told us that two undergraduates were walking together some time after he himself had left Cambridge. One of the two mentioned " Tennyson." The other replied, " O do not mention that man's name. I hate him. I was the unhappy hero of ' Locksley Hall.' It is the story of my cousin's love and mine, known to all Cambridge when Mr Tennyson was there, and he put it into verse." Needless to say he had never heard either of the undergraduate or of his story. The poem was a simple invention as to place, incidents and people.

When the poem was first published Rogers observed to my
father, "That was something of my case. I was fond of a
girl, who was, as I thought, intellectual, and after all she
married a dog and horse man, and when she passed me after
her marriage she blushed, for she knew then what she had
done."

June 23rd. Aldworth. Walked on the Common. My father
is working at his Lincolnshire poem, "The Churchwarden":
and laughed heartily at the humorous passages as he made
them. He asserted that careful authors were good critics, only
apt to give too lenient criticisms if they felt a friendliness for
the man who asked for an opinion. "The ordinary critic," he
said, "is so hurried now-a-days that he not unfrequently mis-
quotes, or tears a passage from the context — misinterpreting
it, and then proceeds to base a contemptuous argument on his
own misquotation, or on his own misinterpretation [1]."

June 28th. He found some apple-blossoms and ripe straw-
berries and observed : "Miss Austen is not so wrong after all"
(in her garden-party in *Emma*). To-day Tyndall said to him,
"God and spirit I know, and matter I know ; and I believe in
both." And in answer to my father's profession of belief in
"individual immortality" Tyndall remarked, "We may all be
absorbed into the Godhead." My father said, "Suppose that
He is the real person, and we are only relatively personal." He
talked with Tyndall then about experiments as to the origin of
life — having frequently inspected Tyndall's hermetically sealed
bottles : and it interested him that Tyndall was convinced that
life could not originate without life. Tyndall on leaving us said
that he was glad to hear again my father's "full, deep, broad,
brotherly voice."

July 2nd. London. My father greatly admired Burne Jones'

---

[1] "Tennyson was very grand on contemptuousness. It was, he said, a
sure sign of intellectual littleness. Simply to despise nearly always meant
not to understand. Pride and contempt were specially characteristic of
barbarians. Real civilisation taught human beings to understand each
other better, and must therefore lessen contempt. It is a little or im-
mature or uneducated mind which readily despises. One who has lived
only in a *coterie* despises readily. One who has travelled and knows the
world in its length and breadth, respects far more views and standpoints
other than his own."
Wilfrid Ward's "Talks with Tennyson," *New Review*, July, 1886.

" Laus Veneris " ; and was interested by the " Briar Rose." He missed, however, the final picture, the going away :

> And o'er the hills and far away
> Beyond their utmost purple rim,
> Beyond the night, across the day,
> Thro' all the world she follow'd him.

In another Exhibition he liked Poynter's " Queen of Sheba," as a splendid piece of scenic painting ; but the picture by Poynter that he praised most was one of two naked boys sailing boats in a cavern. After a careful inspection of Leighton's two pictures in monochrome, " The Industrial Arts as applied to Peace and War," he said, " These are the greatest works by Leighton that I have seen."

Mr Knowles asked Mr and Mrs Gladstone, Lord Acton and others, to meet him at dinner. Gladstone and my father talked of Homer and Browning.

Aug. 6th. Aldworth. The Duchess of Albany came to luncheon with us in honour of my father's eighty-first birthday : and thanked him for what he had written about the Duke [1]. At her request he read " Guinevere " aloud.

. My father was much impressed by Martineau's book, *The Seat of Authority ;* but did not like parts of it. He had admired his *Types of Ethical Theory* and *The Study of Religion.*

Farrar told him the story of St Telemachus ; he was struck by the Christian regard for human life in contrast to the pagan recklessness in inflicting torture and death. In the reign of Trajan, after his victories over the Dacians, 10,000 men are said to have fought in the Colosseum. This subject he began to embody in a poem.

Another Roman story he kept in reserve for future use — that of Perpetua, the young Roman matron, with her child (born in prison) in her arms, who refused to give up her faith even at the entreaty of her father, and was eventually killed with her friend Felicitas in front of the howling Roman mob.

October. Mr Norman Lockyer visited us, and he was full of talk about Egypt, the orientation of the temples, and about meteorites. He said of my father : " His mind is saturated with astronomy."

[1] See page 437.

My father sent the following letter to Sir Henry Parkes about the strikes in Australia:

My dear Sir Henry,

Against my wont I must thank you for your most kind letter. I fear that it was written in pain and depression, for yours seems to have been a most serious accident, and coming as it did in the midst of such important work, you required a strong faith to believe that all was notwithstanding well. You will be sure that we have watched the telegrams respecting you with sincere interest, and have rejoiced that the last have been encouraging as to your health. You have indeed needed a renewal of health to face the new danger of your great strikes. You Australians appear to us to have met the monster bravely. Is there no hope of arbitration by mixed tribunals, governments having first distinctly shown a bold front against any attempt at illegal intimidation?

Many thanks for the promise of your book. We are, as you say, greatly interested in all that relates to the welfare of the Empire.

Yours ever sincerely, Tennyson.

He also wrote this stanza for an American lady, who had asked for an autograph:

Not such were those whom Freedom claims
    As patriot-martyrs of her creed:
    They were not slaves that names mislead,
Nor traitors that mislead by names!

At Christmas my father enjoyed the tree for the cottagers' children, saying to my wife about her baby: "Perhaps your babe will remember all these lights and this splendour in future days as if it were a memory of another life."

Talking about English schools he told an old Eton story:

"Provost Goodall and Keate were dining with William IV. The king said *sotto voce* to the doctor: 'When he,' pointing to

Goodall, 'dies, I will make you him.' Goodall overheard, and with a courtly bow retorted: 'I could not think of going anywhere before your Majesty.'"

1891.

With none of the publishers into whose hands circumstances had thrown my father, was the connection so uninterruptedly pleasant as with Messrs Macmillan, unless perhaps that with Mr Henry King. Alexander Macmillan's genuine enthusiasm for his authors was especially remarkable. The letter I give below refers to the purchase of the first proof-sheets of "In Memoriam" and "Maud" and the gift of them to himself.

To G. L. Craik of Messrs Macmillan's.

DEAR CRAIK,

I thank you and the Macmillans for your chivalrous gift. I value this more especially as showing your abhorrence of the sale of proof-sheets.

Yours gratefully, TENNYSON.

The following lines were inscribed by my father in a copy of his works to be presented by the Royal Guild of Nurses of England to Princess Louise Augusta of Schleswig-Holstein [1] on her marriage:

Take, Lady, what your loyal nurses give,
  Their full God-bless-you with this book of song,
And may the life, which, heart in heart, you live
  With him you love, be cloudless and be long!

During the winter he revised his poems for a new single volume edition. He walked regularly for an hour and a half on fine days, and on stormy days paced up

---

[1] Daughter of Princess Christian.

and down the music-room, or practised gymnastic exercises with his legs and arms. One day he was pacing up and down, somewhat disturbed by sundry ghostly noises, when he thought that he saw something fall. It turned out to be a large rough-legged buzzard which had flown in at the window, and caused all the commotion. When set at liberty, it flew to its mate, and they have since nested on our trees.

To Dr Gollancz he forwarded for his edition of *The Pearl*, an English poem of the fourteenth century, this prefatory quatrain:

> We lost you for how long a time,
> True Pearl of our poetic prime!
> We found you, and you gleam reset
> In Britain's lyric coronet.

In February he walked his three miles, uphill to the Beacon and back, with Princess Louise. He talked about Ireland and sculpture to H.R.H., and one of his sayings to her about his writing poems[1] in his old age was, " A crooked share, Madam, may make a straight furrow." The Princess described some tragic event to him and said it was "very *awful*" ; he turned round to her approvingly: " I am glad, ma'am, you use that word in the right way, and know the full meaning of it: not like the people of to-day who will say 'awfully jolly,'" etc.

At eighty-two my father preserved the high spirits of youth. He would defy his friends to get up twenty times quickly from a low chair without touching it with their hands, while he was performing this feat himself, and one afternoon he had a long waltz with M——— in the ball-room.

In April the President of Magdalen, Oxford, and Mrs Warren called upon us. My father spoke of Virgil to him, saying, " Milton had evidently studied Virgil's verse."

---

[1] He was working at his " Bandit's Death."

Warren mentioned the "lonely word" in the "Ode to Virgil":

"All the charm of all the Muses often flowering
    in a lonely word."

"Yes," my father said, and quoted "*cunctantem ramum*" in Book VI. as an instance. "In Dryden's time," he continued, "they did not understand or anyhow had forgotten how to write blank verse. Yet his paraphrase of Virgil is stronger than any of the translations. People accused Virgil of plagiarizing, but if a man made it his own there was no harm in that (look at the great poets, Shakespeare included)." He quoted Goethe's "Du bist ein Narr?" He himself had been "most absurdly accused of plagiarizing," e.g. "The moanings of the homeless sea," "moanings" from Horace, "homeless" from Shelley. "As if no one else had heard the sea moan except Horace." He quoted also out of "The Princess," "Like bottom agates in clear seas," etc., and said that he had been accused of taking it partly from Beaumont and Fletcher, and partly from Shakespeare, but that he had himself invented the simile (while bathing in Wales).

We talked about "The Cup." "Irving," my father said, "did not represent the character of Synorix rightly. Irving made him a villain, not an epicurean. Fanny Kemble's criticism was that he could not play an epicurean and so he played a villain." My father told us that he thought the *Agamemnon*, the *Prometheus* and the *Œdipus Coloneus* the finest of the Greek plays, adding, "Fitzgerald's version of the *Agamemnon* is most remarkable."

Mrs Richard Ward, who had joined us, wanted her little boy to hear my father read. My father answered, "I will only read you something old." He read the "Ode on the Duke of Wellington." He dwelt long on the final words, letting them ring so to speak, especially " *toll'd*, *Boom*." At the end he said, " It is a great roll of words, the music of words. For a hundred people who can sing a song, there are not ten who can read a poem. People do not understand the music of words." He then read the little Dedication to " Œnone," then the poem. He explained the story, pausing from time to time, asking a few questions, and saying he considered it even more strictly classical in form and language than the old " Œnone." Then he went to walk up and down the music-room, the weather being wet. He observed : " X— has said that Tennyson told him that ' Horace and Keats were his two masters.' X— must have misunderstood." He did not care for Horace at all until after he was thirty. He had said, " Horace and Keats are masters." After the *Poems by Two Brothers* he did not think he had taken anyone for master.

He was dominated by Byron till he was seventeen, when he put him away altogether[1].

Dulverton, "Akbar," "The Foresters."

My father spoke at this time warmly of the gallant spirit of Sir Edward Reed's lines on the Fleet in the *St James' Gazette ;* and said he liked much of Wallace's *Darwinism*, which he was reading. He talked of finishing the following little playful poem to Aubrey de Vere, and of alluding in a second verse to his youngest grandson, Alfred Aubrey ; but this second verse was never written :

Little Aubrey in the West! little Alfred in the East
Accepts the songs you gave, and he sends you his
    Salaam ;
And he prays that you may live. But as Earth her
    orbit runs,

[1] For most of the account of what my father said at this interview I am indebted to the President of Magdalen.

Little Homer, little Dante, little Shakespeare, can
    they last
                    In the vast
Of the rolling of the æons, of the changes of the suns?
Little poet, hear the little poet's epigram!

In June Colonel Crozier lent us his yacht, the
Assegai, and we went to Exmouth, and thence by rail
to Dulverton, "a land of bubbling streams" my father
called it.   Lord Carnarvon had told him years ago that
the streams here were the most delicious he knew.

We drove up the Haddon valley, and to Barlynch
Abbey on the Exe.   The ragged robin and wild garlic
were profuse.   We returned by Pixton Park.

The Exe is "arrowy" just before its confluence with
the Barle, running, as my father remarked, "too vehemently to break upon the jutting rocks."   We sat next
on the wooden bridge over the Exe, and he said to me:
"That is an old simile but a good one, 'Time is like a
river, ever past and ever future.'"

In the afternoon we drove through the Barle valley
to Hawkridge, then to the Tor steps, high up among
the hills, with an ancient bridge across the river, flat
stones laid on piers.   Some tawny cows were cooling
themselves in mid-stream: a green meadow on one side,
on the other a wooded slope.   "If it were only to see
this," he said, "the journey is worth while."

We climbed Haddon Down and then descended by
Higher Combe, a valley down which there was a most
luxuriant view, the Dartmoor range as background,
almost Italian in colouring.

The red of the rocks and the deep green of the grass
passing out of Exmouth harbour struck him.   We went
to Corfe Castle, and he called the ruins, "Gray relics of
an old world," and pointed out that the castle was as
"hollow as a skull," and liked hearing the "fierce east
scream thro' the eyelet-holes."

He began the Hymn to the Sun in a new metre for his "Akbar" at Dulverton, finishing it on the voyage home.

Even now, as in his youth, he loved the new metres which he invented, and took the keenest interest in fresh fields of thought, and in new subjects for poetry. In "Akbar" he thought that the language of theology had to be interchanged with that of philosophy, and that the highest good of Akbar's code of morals was, as far as he could make it out, quite within the Christian ideal. The philosophers of the East had a great fascination for my father, and he felt that the Western religion might learn from them much of spirituality. He was sure too that Western civilization had even in his time developed Eastern thought and morality; but what direction the development would ultimately take, it was impossible to predict.

The books which he took with him at this time were (1) the *Akbar-Náma* by Akbar's minister and friend Abul-Fazi, (2) *Ain-i-Akbarí*, a great survey of India (translated by Blockmann), (3) *Miscellaneous notices of Akbar in the orthodox Mohammedan histories*, (4) *The Asiatic Quarterly*, July 1890, *The Holy Mervi* or the Gospel according to Father Jerome Xavier, (5) Sir Henry Elliot's and Elphinstone's *Histories of India*, and *Asiatic Studies*, by Alfred Lyall. Some were lent him by the Master of Balliol, who first suggested an Indian subject, saying to me: "Your father appreciates the East."

In his poem of "Akbar" my father thought that the greatness of Christianity ought to be touched upon, and wrote accordingly:

I watch'd my son,
And those that follow'd, loosen, stone from stone,
All my fair work; and from the ruin arose
The shriek and curse of trampled millions, even

As in the time before.   But while I groan'd,
From out the sunset pour'd an alien race,
Who fitted stone to stone again, and Truth,
Peace, Love and Justice came and dwelt therein.

One June day an American suddenly appeared at
Aldworth, saying that he had worked his way over
the Atlantic in a cattle-ship in order to recite "Maud" to
the author.   Having pity on the man, my father allowed
him to do so, but suffered from the recitation.   We paid
the reciter's passage back to America, but never heard of
him again.

My father wrote in July to Gladstone about the death
of his eldest son:

MY DEAR FRIEND,
        Only one word from myself and my wife
to say how fully we sympathize with you.   More than
this one word at the present moment would be intrusive.

He spent his birthday, Aug. 6th, quietly, talking
over old days with Aubrey de Vere.

Many guests at Aldworth.   Lord and Lady Dufferin,
Lady Compton, the Leckys, Sir Daniel Wilson from
Toronto University, Mr and Mrs Rolfe and Mr McCabe
from America, the Bishop of Ripon, the Dean of Westminster, the Henry Sidgwicks, and Mr Lewis Morris
who paid us several visits during these last summers.

We often sat now on the heather at the top of
Blackdown to watch the sunset, and my father took
his friends there to talk with him.

Jowett could not come to us as he had hoped to do,
since he had fallen seriously ill; he wrote to me:

The doctors seem to think that I am seriously ill, and
although I think that I am very likely to recover, I should
like to send my most grateful love to your father and mother for

all their kindness to me.   At such a serious time some of my
old projects come back upon me.   One of these is, that your
father should write a few hymns in a high strain, to be a treasure
to the world and to the Church; and to come nearer to the
familiar thoughts of men than "In Memoriam," which is a very
great work of its kind, but not suited to be sung in Churches.   I
want him to think of millions of persons repeating his words
with the living voice, during many centuries.   Is this a crown to
be despised?   It is a thing which has never been accomplished
before in the Christian world, and therefore worth doing.   But I
do not press it upon you, well knowing that the Poet's mind
is not to be vexed, but inspired, whether in ancient or modern
times, by the Spirit of God.

Mr Daly and Miss Rehan came to arrange about
" Robin Hood."   Mr Daly said that such a thoroughly
English woodland play was sure to be popular in
America.   My father recommended him to look at
Whymper's pictures of Sherwood Forest, which he
straightway bought in order that they might be copied
for the scenes.   Sir Arthur Sullivan undertook to set
the songs.

My father said to Mr Daly: " I don't care for ' The
Foresters ' as I do for ' Becket ' and ' Harold.'   Irving
suggested the fairies in my ' Robin Hood,' else I should
not have dreamed of trenching on Shakespeare's ground
in that way.   Then Irving wrote to me that the play
was not ' sensational ' enough for an English public.   It
is a woodland play — a pastoral without shepherds.   The
great stage-drama is wholly unlike most of the drama of
modern times.   I do not like the idea of every scene
being obliged to end with a *bang*."   About " There is no
land like England," he added, " I wrote that song when
I was nineteen.   It has a beastly chorus against the
French, and I must alter that if you will have it."

Before Christmas he had written a new scene and
a new song for Miss Rehan — " Love flew in at the
window."

Letters to friends, 1891.

After the reports of the terrible persecution of the Russian Jews, the following letter was written by my father to the Secretary of the Russo-Jewish Committee·

Oct. 1st, 1891.

I have read what is reported of the Russian persecutions by your paper, and by the press generally; and if that be true, I can only say that Russia has disgraced her Church and her nationality. I once met the Czar. He seemed a kind and good-natured man. I can scarcely believe that he is fully aware of the barbarities perpetrated with his apparent sanction.

TENNYSON.

A letter was sent by my father to Henry E. Shepherd, Charleston, S. C., in reply to a request that he would explain the allusions in the first stanza of "In Memoriam," beginning

I held it truth, with him who sings,

as the question had led to a long and unsatisfactory controversy among Tennyson students.

ALDWORTH, *Nov. 3rd,* 1891.

I believe I alluded to Goethe[1]. Among his last words were these: "Von Aenderungen zu höheren Aenderungen," "from changes to higher changes."

Yours sincerely,

TENNYSON.

---

[1] Professor Sidgwick writes to me: "I remember sitting near your father at a dinner of the Metaphysical Society, when he talked very interestingly about poets and poetry. After some remarks on Goethe's dramatic work, noting its limitations, he said that he placed him foremost among the

One of the last letters which my father wrote this
year was to the young poet William Watson, whose
" Wordsworth's Grave " pleased him.

FARRINGFORD, *Dec. 20th*, 1891.

I thank you; for to me who receive every morning,
or all but every morning, in print or in MSS, verses,
verses, verses, the voice of a poet and a patriot must
all the more be grateful.

TENNYSON.

He praised too Mr Rudyard Kipling's " English
Flag," and Kipling's answer to his letter of com-
mendation gave him pleasure: " When the private
in the ranks is praised by the general, he cannot
presume to thank him, but he fights the better next
day."

moderns as a lyrical poet. One of his hearers demurred, mentioning great
lyrics by other writers. ' Yes,' your father answered, ' but Goethe is consummate in so *many different styles* ' : and then referred rapidly to four or
five examples — I remember that ' Kennst du das Land?' and ' Ueber allen
Gipfeln ' were two of them — dwelling on their great diversity of tone and
character. I did not like to interrupt him by an inquisitive remark: but I
said to myself ' Then it is undoubtedly Goethe who sings

To one clear harp in *divers tones.*' "

CHAPTER XXII.

THE LAST YEAR.

1892.

In January Dr Hubert Parry stayed with us at Farringford, for he wished to hear my father read " The Lotos-Eaters" which he was setting to music.

For the first time my father's voice, usually so strong, failed while reading this poem and the " Ode on the Duke of Wellington," which he was anxious that a great composer should set as he read it.

Someone said to my father: " No one has written finer things about music than you have done —

> Music that gentlier on the spirit lies
> Than tir'd eyelids upon tir'd eyes.
>
> The tides of music's golden sea
> Setting toward Eternity.
>
> The glory of the sum of things
> Will flash along the chords and go.
>
> Love took up the harp of life and smote on all
>   the chords with might,
> Smote the chord of self that trembling past in
>   music out of sight."

393

And these he too thought were among his most successful lines; the last simile especially.

Music seemed to him to be the language of spirits, and he would say: " I can feel the glory though I cannot follow the music. I know that I miss a great deal by not understanding it. It often seems to me that music must take up expression at the point where poetry leaves off, and expresses what cannot be expressed in words."

After hearing "Comfort ye" sung, by which he was greatly impressed (as he was generally by Handel), he said to Miss Ritchie, " It is difficult to believe that the man who wrote that was developed from the Ascidian," and after hearing Joachim play the "Trillo del Diavolo" (in 1878), " I can feel the magic and poetry of the *bowing*."

When his friends asked him now to write on every-day topics, he said, " I cannot; I must write what I am thinking about and I have not much time." The yearning of his whole heart was to

Follow the Gleam.

At the end of January he wrote his lines on the death of the Duke of Clarence.

The Princess of Wales had written (January, 1885) to my father on the coming of age of the Duke : that she had been in hopes that " the Poet Laureate would have been inspired " on that occasion, and that she might " have been gladdened by a few beautiful lines in honour of the event."

And my father had answered :

ALDWORTH.

MADAM,

I thank your Royal Highness for your kind letter, and congratulate the young Prince and trust that all Honour and Happiness may attend him thro' life.

To me the paths leading into the future seem somewhat gloomy and (as our Shakespeare says in his *Julius Cæsar*) "crave wary walking," but then I am an old man in my 76th year, and in spite of my apprehension, the age to come may have its own sunshine both for crown and people. That the Supreme Power may bless you and yours through both worlds is the wish of

Your affectionate servant,

TENNYSON.

As he had not sent a poem then, he was anxious, although unwell at the time, to speak some words of comfort for the poor mother, when the Duke died. He wrote his poem in two days but the strain told upon him severely. He said: Watts would make a fine picture of " The face of Death is toward the Sun of Life, His shadow darkens earth."

In March he recovered his voice and sang an octave to the piano as clearly as possible. He read " The Passing of Arthur" to Lord Houghton (now Lord Crewe) and his sister, Mrs Henniker, as well as ever, but he found the large Easter party too much for him.

On March 25th "The Foresters" was produced at New York by Daly. It gave him great pleasure to hear that American people were "appreciative of the fancy and of the beauty, and especially of the songs and of the wise sayings about life in which the woodland play abounds [1]." The houses were packed and the play had a long and most successful run.

[1] Jowett.

Before the production my father wrote to Augustin Daly:

I wish you all success with my "Robin Hood and Maid Marian." From what I know of Miss Ada Rehan I am sure that she will play her part to perfection, and I am certain that under your management, with the music by one so popular as Sir Arthur Sullivan, with the costumes fashioned after the old designs in the British Museum, with the woodland scenes taken from Mr Whymper's beautiful pictures of the Sherwood of to-day, my play will be produced to advantage both in America and in England. I am told that your company is good, and that Mr Jefferson once belonged to it. When he was in England, I saw him play *Rip Van Winkle*, and assuredly nothing could have been better.

With all cordial greetings to my American friends,

I remain faithfully yours,

TENNYSON.

And he received the following from Miss Ada Rehan:

Let me add my congratulations to the many on the success of "The Foresters." I cannot tell you how delighted I was when I felt and saw, from the first, the joy it was giving to our large audience. Its charm is felt by all. Let me thank you for myself for the honour of playing your "Maid Marian," which I have learned to love, for while I am playing the part I feel all its beauty and simplicity and sweetness, which make me feel for the time a happier and a better woman. I am indeed proud of its great success for your sake as well as my own.

P.S. The play is now one week old, and each audience has been larger than the last and all as sympathetic as the first.

And Professor Jebb wrote:

Being here on my way to the Johns Hopkins University
at Baltimore, where I have some Lectures to give, I naturally
went to see "The Foresters" at Augustin Daly's last night.
The Theatre, which is of moderate size, was densely packed,
and as I had not engaged my seat by cablegram from Liverpool, I bore no resemblance, in respect of spacious comfort,
to the ideal spectator, the masher or "dude," depicted on the
play-bill which I send you by this post. I was a highly compressed and squalid object in a back seat, amid a seething mass
of humanity, but I saw the play very well. It was very cordially
received and was well acted, I thought, especially by Ada Rehan
and Drew. The fairy scene in the third Act was perfectly
lovely, and the lyrics were everywhere beautifully given. The
mounting of the play was excellent throughout.

The criticism of "The Foresters" which pleased my
father most was in a letter addressed to Lady Martin
(Miss Helen Faucit) by the eminent Shakespearian
scholar, Mr Horace Furness of Philadelphia, when the
piece was being performed in New York:

After dinner we went to see "The Foresters." Men and
women — of a different time, to be sure, but none too good "for
human nature's daily food" — live their idyllic lives before you,
and you feel that all is good, very good. The atmosphere is so
real, and we fall into it so completely, that, Americans though
we be through and through, we can listen with hearty assent
to the chorus that "There is no land like England," and that
"There are no wives like English wives." Nay, come to think
of it, that song was encored. It was charming, charming from
beginning to end. And Miss Rehan acted to perfection. I had
to leave in the midnight train for home, and during two hours'
driving through the black night, I smoked and reflected on the
unalloyed charm of such a drama. And to see the popularity,
too! It had been running many weeks — six, I think — and the
theatre was full, not a seat unoccupied. I do revel, I confess, in
such a proof as this that there will always be a full response to
what is fine and good, and that the modern sensational French
drama is not our true exponent.

In answer to a poem sent by William Watson at this time my father wrote:

"I thank you once more for your fine lines, tho' they somewhat abash me, as overpraise.

If by 'wintry hair' you allude to a tree whose leaves are half gone, you are right, but if you mean 'white' you are wrong, for I never had a gray hair on my head."

In his morning and night solitudes my father was finishing "Akbar's Dream," in which was much of his own spirit of toleration.

He thought the "Hymn to the Sun" and "Spirit, nearing yon dark portal" the best of the smaller poems in his new volume.

"I should like," he said, "to write a long poem in the metre of 'Akbar's Hymn,' it is a magnificent metre."

After these were written he began "Kapiolani," and "Whirl and follow the Sun."

For forty-two years my father had had among his various strange letters an anonymous abusive letter, evidently from the same writer, on the appearance of every new volume. We generally contrive to burn them, so that he knew nothing of them. One such letter arrived this spring, and he saw it and was "sorry," he said, "for the man who had so much spite."

During these months my father talked about his early days, and his parents, and told Mr Douglas Freshfield, who frequently accompanied him on his morning walks, how his "grandfather and grandmother, when courting, were sitting on the steps of the Caistor House in the market-place. Part of the parapet fell on the step the moment after they had left it, or both would have been killed." " Where would you have been then, my dear?" his grandmother would say to him.

He spoke of his pleasure in Bishop Wilberforce's last visit to him, of his sudden death, and of the Bishop's story of the " table-turning" when he was staying with Judge Alderson at Farringford. A table moved towards the door where the Bishop was standing, he exorcised the supposed spirit, and then the table stood still, rapping out, " I can't abide a Bishop."

Half-way on his walks now he would sit down and rest, gazing up at the drifting clouds, or below over the blue waste of waters, or noting as of old with care the flight and song of the different birds, or looking at the flowers about him [1], or at the small insects in the grass, and wondering whether they felt no pain, only discomfort. " It is a comfort to think that it is only discomfort," he would say.

Hold thou, my friend, no lesser life in scorn,
All Nature is the womb whence Man is born [2].

I heard him quote more than once then:

" The wan moon is setting behind the white wave,
And time is setting for me, oh!"

In April my father had two or three talks with Mr. Herbert Warren, the President of Magdalen. The following is a sample taken down at the time partly by Warren, partly by myself.

---

[1] One day, looking at the flower of the spurge he said:

> Spurge with fairy crescent set,
> Like the flower of Mahomet.

[2] Lines he made on one of these walks.

He began about Catullus:

"Catullus says that a poet's lines may be impure provided his life is pure. I don't agree with him: his verses fly much further than he does. There is hardly any crime greater than for a man with genius to propagate vice by his written words. I have always admired him: 'Acme and Septimius' is lovely. Then he has very pretty metres. 'Collis O Heliconii' is in a beautiful metre. I wrote a great part of my 'Jubilee Ode' in it. People didn't understand. They don't understand these things. They don't understand English scansion. In the line 'Dream not of where some sunny rose may linger' they said the first syllable of 'sunny' was long, whereas it evidently is short. Doubling the *n* in English makes the vowel before short."

At his request Warren repeated some undergraduate lines about Jowett:

"What I know not is not knowledge:
I am the Master of this college."

"Very unfair," my father said, "Jowett never set up to be omniscient. It might possibly have suited Whewell. Jowett got his pronunciation of 'knowledge' from me (long o). 'Free-will, fore-knowledge absolute.' 'Fore-knŏlledge' would be horrible there."

The talk turned on religion and "God is Love," and he said that Jowett, who had liked the simple hymn for children in "The Promise of May," Act III. Sc. I, wanted him to write another hymn, and he quoted a prayer by Jowett, praying that "we might see ourselves as others see us." "I should not pray for that: others cannot see much of one's inner self."

Warren (*after a pause*). Is not the existence of evil (the "mystery of iniquity") the great difficulty?

A. T. Yes. I tried to bring that out in a poem that comes after the "Charge of the Heavy Brigade."

That charge was a wonderful affair. An officer who was there, after they came out said it was the finest excitement ever known, that drink, gambling, and horse-racing were nothing to it.

Warren. Will you write the hymn?

A. T. A good hymn is the most difficult thing in the world to write. In a good hymn you have to be commonplace and poetical. The moment you cease to be commonplace and put in any expression at all out of the common, it ceases to be a hymn. Of hymns I like Heber's [1] " Holy, Holy, Holy " better than most, it is in a fine metre too. What will people come to in a hundred years? do you think they will give up all religious forms and go and sit in silence in the Churches listening to the organs?

Warren. There is more religion now than there was twenty years ago.

A. T. I think there is more religion now among the parsons, though they are often very ignorant about modern criticism and about the great religions of the world, and they certainly cannot read aloud. Did you ever hear that story of Rawnsley's? The clerk told him not to read the service so fast: " For you mooöst gie me toime, Mr Rawnsley, you mooöst i'deed. You *mooöst* gie me toime, for I've a graäceless wife an' two godless soons to praäy for."

There's his other story too of the lady distributing a tract about invalids going for health's sake in the winter to sunny climates: (Mrs C.) I didn't like that book at all as your sister browt me. (Lady) Why what was it? (Mrs C.) Why it was 'Chaäsin' the soon'; and

---

[1] He would often quote this passage from the version of the Psalms by Sternhold and Hopkins:

> "And on the wings of all the winds
> Came flying all abroad."

I doän't think nothink to chaäsin' the soon! Chaäsin'
the soon i'deed! I think God A'Moighty 'ull soon let
folks know as cheevies him: he'll be taäkin' an' puttin'
it somewhere else I reckon. Chaäsin' the soon i'deed!
I doän't like sich waäys.

Lincolnshire is a fine broad dialect. Yorkshire is clipt.

I asked my way to Mr Robert —, of a Yorkshire
"swain." He answered, "Bob a Bob tapt-hill" (Robert
the son of Robert lives at the top of the hill).

(They walked to the house of "Ideal Ward." My
father quoted Shakespeare about Pompey the Great.)

Warren. If it is Shakespeare.

A. T. There is a great deal of Shakespeare that
Shakespeare never wrote, e.g. the speeches of Antonio
and Sebastian " Below you baggage," etc.

(They talked about Shelley and Byron, and my
father said that he would have sooner known Shelley
than Byron.)

A. T. I just escaped being in the battle of
Navarino. A relation of mine had secured a berth on
one of the men-of-war; then, as they say in the north,
he " rued " and offered it to my father. I was mad to
go, but my father would not let me. My cousin George
Tennyson went. He did not see much. The captain
had all the hatches closed and ordered him below, yet
in an electioneering speech at Stamford, when my uncle
beat the man who was afterwards the late Lord Exeter,
someone referred to his son George as "the hero
who had waved his chivalric sword at the battle of
Navarino."

(Then the talk turned on Walter Scott.)

A. T. I would have given anything to have seen
Walter Scott.

(They came upon the Roman kiln, like a beehive by
the side of the road to Alum Bay.)

A. T. It's odd that we know so little of the Roman

occupation of Britain. Tacitus has described the climate very well: "cœlum crebris imbribus ac nebulis fœdum: asperitas frigorum abest."

Warren asked if my father would write an installation Ode to Lord Hartington at Cambridge.

A. T. No, certainly not; writing to order is what I hate. They think a poet can write poems to order as a bootmaker makes boots. For the Queen I am obliged to do it, but she has been very kind and has only asked me once or twice. They call the "Ode on the Duke of Wellington" a Laureate Ode; nothing of the kind! it was written from genuine admiration of the man.

He told Warren the story about the Duke being piloted across Piccadilly and saying to his pilot, who was expatiating on the great honour done him, " Don't be a d—d fool." My father said humorously, " It is almost as great in its way as the battle of Waterloo. A Frenchman would have answered, ' Mais, oui, on m'appelle le grand.'"

April 10*th.* My father and Warren walked in the ball-room. My father quoted the line of Horace,

" Nec satis est pulchra esse poemata, dulcia sunto,"

and asked Warren to explain it.

Warren said he thought it meant " It is not enough for poems to be beautiful and correct in form, they must have a charm."

" Yes," my father said, " that's what I think." Then he quoted Milton, Virgil, Browning, and Molière, and said, " Molière is the greatest French poet, he is so sane."

The talk turned upon fame. My father said, " I hate spite more than I love fame."

O wretched race of slander-speaking men.

Οἴη περ φύλλων γενεὴ τοιήδε καὶ ἀνδρῶν.

Warren asked him about his blank verse, and my

father told him that it was very various, but variations in the metre were disliked by ordinary readers, such as

> Dust, and the points of lances bicker in it —

the short syllables expressing the movement of the light. He instanced Virgil's " Et vera incessu patuit dea," and wondered how many scholars saw the greatness in movement of such a line.   He quoted Pindar's Threnody " λάμπει δὲ —," and Euripides' chorus " ἀνὰ δὲ κέλαδος ἔμολε πόλιν."

Warren mentioned " The Foresters." My father repeated his songs " Down with John" and " Love flew in at the window[1]," which he had made shortly before Daly put " The Foresters " on the stage last month; then said: "'Robin and Richard!' Did you notice that I would not say '*Richard* and Robin?' It does not sound well. There's a mistake in the book about the wild goose and the wild swan. They are not seen in England now-a-days when the woods are in leaf. They might perhaps when England was wilder, but I do not know about that. I thought that I was wrong at the time, and since then I have consulted my bird-books, and have corrected it in a second edition."

My father quoted Pope and the description of a garden, "like his own," he said,

> " Grove nods to grove, each alley has his brother";

then Swift on the Irish Demon Club *à propos* of Home Rule in Ireland.

In June the Duke of Connaught called upon him. They discussed the state of India and talked on the splendour of the Himalayan Peaks at sunrise when they "hung like fiery lamps in the sky." My father was just then full of a letter from Woolner about a Japanese poet:

[1] The last song he ever wrote.

I heard a curious thing a time ago and I thought of telling you, but knowing your father must have numerous such stories told him, I did not. A gentleman I know lived a long time in Japan, and travelling in a remote part, he was received with great courtesy in a village he stayed at; and to show respect he was taken and introduced to the chief Japanese poet, who lived there. He was an old man over 80; and, on learning that my friend was an Englishman, he said that he had a great favour to ask of him, and went to a cabinet and fetched a book, and asked him to read those poems by the great Poet of England. They were pieces of " In Memoriam" he had copied out. My friend read them carefully and as well as he could. The old poet thanked him, and said, that, tho' he did not know the words, the music spoke to him, and he knew he felt as the poet felt when he wrote the poems, for the music talked in a tongue that could not be mistaken, and he knew the poems were very beautiful. This was immensely interesting to me, as it suggested that sound played so great a part of the meaning in all language. Consider the language of beasts. You do not know a syllable of their language, and yet how unmistakable is the meaning of every sound, of a cow lowing to go home, and the same cow lowing after her calf has been taken from her. I wish that I had written at the time for I forget the exact form of all the old poet said, but it was most gratifying to find the great man of Japan loving, tho' so imperfectly, the poetry of our great Poet— as he said, " We talk to each other across the World."

Colonel Crozier again lent us his yacht, and we made another pilgrimage to my uncle Frederick's in Jersey, taking Dartmouth, Guernsey, and Sark on our way. At Guernsey our pleasantest time was spent in the Bay " Moulin Huet," a craggy bay, with dark green satin water in pools among the rocks. My father quoted his own lines from " Enid" about the dress which Earl Doorm offered her,

> Where, like a shoaling sea, the lovely blue
> Play'd into green.

The next lines, he said, were made at Farringford: " After the Down had been wrapt in mist through one night, the next morning it looked as if covered with flashing jewels — all the colours of the rainbow."

> And thicker down the front
> With jewels than the sward with drops of dew,
> When all night long a cloud clings to the hill,
> And with the dawn ascending lets the day
> Strike where it clung; so thickly shone the gems.

Then the cuckoo began to sing, and he repeated from Wordsworth's "Reaper":

> "Breaking the silence of the seas
> Among the furthest Hebrides."

At St Peter's we visited the Museum, with its collections of butterflies and birds, and a library of 600,000 volumes.

On Sunday the Salvationists were singing somewhat loudly in the streets, and he said of them —

> For modes of faith let graceless zealots fight,
> His can't be wrong whose life is in the right.

The island of Sark he had long wished to see. The day was cloudless, and on landing we climbed up through the rock-tunnel.

From this tunnel we walked up a bowery lane, and secured a waggonette, but the jolting over the roads was terrific. We drove to Little Sark; and the narrow passage between Great and Little Sark, and the view from the rock bridge, the precipice with the "curve of white sand below on either hand," and the jagged rocks, like altars and spires, that rose out of the clear sea, struck him more than anything else.

At St Ewold's, Jersey, we found my uncle Frederick and his son Giulio at home. The two brothers again talked over the old times, and my uncle's poems, "The Isles of Greece," "Daphne and other poems," and my father especially praised "The Death of Alcæus."

The gasometer, which stands between St Ewold's and the fine view of St Heliers and the sea, rather troubled my father; his brother replied, "Oh, I have grown to think of it as the Temple of Vesta. You see the resemblance I hope." I found that my uncle's estimate of Arthur Hallam was as high as my father's. "At Eton," he said, "I think our impression was that Hallam, and not Gladstone, was the coming great man." We tried to persuade him to come on board the yacht and visit us in the Isle of Wight, but he said, "No, I shall never leave this place: it is the next best climate to Italy." When the brothers bade "good-bye," they thought that they would not in this life see each other again: "Good-night, true brother, here, good-morrow there!" We returned by Torquay to Farringford.

Before leaving for Aldworth we spent some delightful sunny days in the Farringford gardens. In the afternoons my father sat in his summer-house and talked to us and his friends.

This spring he had enjoyed seeing the unusually splendid blossom of apple and pear tree, of white lilacs, and of purple aubretia that bordered the walks.

At intervals he strolled to the bottom of the kitchen garden to look at the roses, or at the giant fig-tree ("like a breaking wave" as he said) bursting into leaf; or he marked the "branching grace" of the stately line of elms, between the boles of which, from his summer-house, he caught a glimpse of far meadows beyond. He said that he did not believe in Emerson's pretty lines —

"Only to children children sing,
Only to youth the Spring is Spring."

"For age does feel the joy of spring [1], though age can

---

[1] "What joyous things," he said, "are those larks in the spring sun! Do you know that pathetic story of the lark and of the man freed from the Bastille during the French Revolution? As he came from prison someone took pity on him and gave him a few sous. Passing down the street, he saw a lark in a cage: and the man, who had been in prison many years, could not bear the sight of the imprisoned bird. With his few poor sous he bought it and set it free. The lark shot up to heaven, singing a jubilant song of triumph — but the next moment had dropt dead at the man's feet, dead with excess of joy."

only crawl over the bridge while youth skips the brook." His talk was grave and gay together. In the middle of anecdotes he would stop short and say something of what he felt to be the sadness and mystery of life.

What impressed all his friends was his choice of language, the felicity of his turns of expression, his imagery, the terseness of his unadorned English, and his simple directness of manner, which none will ever be able to reproduce, however many notes they may have taken. His dignity and repose of manner, his low musical voice, and the power of his magnetic dark eye kept the attention riveted. His argument was clear and logical and never wandered from the point except by way of illustration, and his illustrations were the most various I have ever heard, and were taken from Nature and science, from high and low life, from the rich and from the poor, and his analysis of character was always subtle and powerful.

While he talked of the mysteries of the universe, his face, full of the strong lines of thought, was lighted up; and his words glowed as it were with inspiration.

When conversing with my brother and myself or our college friends, he was, I used to think, almost at his best, for he would quote us the fine passages from ancient or modern literature and show us why they are fine, or he would tell us about the great facts and discoveries in Astronomy [1], Geology, Botany, Chemistry, and the great problems in philosophy, helping us toward a higher conception of the laws which govern the world

---

[1] His knowledge of astronomy was most remarkable, and the accuracy of his talk about the stars surprised more than one of the great astronomers. Of late the spectrum analysis of light, and the photographs which reveal starlight in the interstellar spaces where stars were hitherto undreamt of, and the idea of the all-pervading luminiferous æther, particularly interested him.

and of "the law behind the law." He was so sympathetic
that the enthusiasm of youth seemed to kindle his own.
He spoke out of the fulness of his heart, and explained
more eloquently than ever where his own difficulties lay,
and what he, as an old man, thought was the true main-
spring of human life and action; and

> How much of act at human hands
> The sense of human will demands
> By which we dare to live or die.

The truth is that real genius, unless made shallow
by prejudice, is seldom frozen by age, and that, until
absolute physical decay sets in, the powers of the mind
may become stronger and stronger.

On one of these June mornings, Miss L—, who was
a stranger to us, but whose brother we had known for
some time, called upon us. My father took her over
the bridge to the summer-house looking on the Down.
After a little while he said: "Miss L—, my son says I
am to read to you," and added, "I will read whatever you
like." He read some of "Maud," "The Spinster's
Sweet-Arts," and some "Enoch Arden."

His voice, as Miss L— noticed, was melodious and
full of change, and quite unimpaired by age. There was
a peculiar freshness and passion in his reading of
"Maud," giving the impression that he had just written
the poem, and that the emotion which created it was
fresh in him. This had an extraordinary influence on
the listener, who felt that the reader had been *present* at
the scenes he described, and that he still felt their bliss or
agony.

He thoroughly enjoyed reading his "The Spinster's
Sweet-Arts," and when he was reading "Enoch Arden"
he told Miss L— to listen to the sound of the sea in the
line.

> The league-long roller thundering on the reef,

and to mark Miriam Lane's chatter in

He ceased; and Miriam Lane
Made such a voluble answer promising all.

We then went for a three miles' walk, my father
talking of the Passion Play at Ober-Ammergau, of
religion, of faith, and of immortality. While touching on
the life after death he spoke of Carlyle, and his dimness
of faith in the closing years of his life. He said that
when he was stopping at a coffee-house in London,
Carlyle had come to smoke a pipe with him in the
evening and the talk turned upon the immortality of the
soul; upon which Carlyle said: "Eh! old Jewish rags:
you must clear your mind of all that. Why should we
expect a hereafter? Your traveller comes to an inn,
and he takes his bed, it's only for one night, he leaves
next day, and another man takes his place and sleeps in
the bed that he has vacated." My father continued: "I
answered, 'Your traveller comes to his inn, and lies
down in his bed, and leaves the inn in the morning, and
goes on his way rejoicing, with the sure and certain hope
and belief that he is going somewhere, where he will
sleep the next night,' and then Edward Fitzgerald, who
was present, said, 'You have him there'": "which
proves," said my father, "how dangerous an illustration
is."

Miss L— writes:

We came home by the Farringford farm, and into the
garden. Before he went up the slope he seemed exhausted, and sat down to rest on a melon-frame, and
asked me to sit by him. It was the first sign I had
noticed of failing strength, and gave one a sudden pang.
He spoke rather sadly of his age, nearly 83, and of what
one must expect at that age. He seemed to love life,

and to have every reason to love it, surrounded by love, companionship, sympathy, and all that makes life sweet. There seemed so little reason why he should die, and it was impossible to associate any thought of death with him that day, except from his own words. As we walked up the garden he pointed out the splendour of the flowers to me. The garden was in all the beauty of the June mid-day brightness, and he spoke as if he were sorry to be leaving it to go away.

We sat some time in the summer-house, and then Mr H. joined us with the dogs. After a few minutes' talk I got up to go, and he asked me to stay to lunch. I did not do so, and he said playfully, " Naughty girl not to do as I tell you!" He walked with me back to the house and I thanked him for his reading. I said good-bye to him on the terrace.

I had never seen Lord Tennyson until this day. I think his greatest charm lay in his unworldliness and sincerity, in his tenderness and strong simplicity, and in a youthfulness which age could not destroy. That unworldliness and "apartness" had marked itself very impressively on his home. The home and garden, and surroundings at Farringford were like something not to be seen elsewhere One approached the house with a sort of awe. It seemed so remote and still, and as though the jar of the outside world had never entered it, a home at unity with itself.

On June 28th he wrote to an unknown correspondent, on the eve of the general election:

Sir,

       I love Mr Gladstone but hate his present Irish policy.

I am yours faithfully,

Tennyson.

He was gratified that the large Unionist meetings throughout Great Britain had adopted, as their motto, his line:

One life, one flag, one fleet, one Throne.

On June 29th the Rector of Freshwater, Dr Merriman, administered the Sacrament to us all in my father's study. The service was very solemn. Before he partook of the Communion he quoted his own words, put into Cranmer's mouth:

It is but a communion, not a mass:
No sacrifice but a life-giving feast;

impressing upon the Rector that he could not partake of it at all, unless it were administered in that sense.

June 30th. We left for Aldworth. My father at first took his regular walks of a mile out and a mile in, over Blackdown, but the walks dwindled down and he sat more and more in his summer-houses. One summer-house was used when the west wind was blowing; the other when the east wind was blowing, or when there was a gorgeous sunset. These command views quite different in character from his arbours at Farringford; from which, as I have said, we have glimpses of sea and meadows through bowers of elm-trees.

From the eastern summer-house at Aldworth you see under alders and birches, over a heather-glade, a stretch of cornland and woodland, with here and there a mellow grange nestled in some dell of the Sussex Weald, and far off the long line of Leith Hill and the Kentish Downs. The "sunset arbour" looks on Blackdown, bleak ridges "fledged with pine," or northward, beyond promontories of beech and holly, beyond the red roofs of Haslemere, up to the bold form of Hindhead. · Latterly his walks were confined to what he called "my demon-haunted hill"; with groves of oak close at hand — "grain storm-strengthened on a windy site "; — and larch and chestnut clothing the more distant slopes, haunts of woodpecker, jay, wood-pigeon and turtle-dove. The colours of the vegetation carpeting the moor behind Aldworth, as he saw them this last autumn, were very various, almost like a garden of flowers, ranging from the gray lichen, and the brown and the light green mosses, to the fading purple ling, the scarlet bramble bushes and whortle-berries, and the brilliant fields of golden fern. On the summit of Blackdown we used to watch many wild birds, owls of all sorts, night-jars, sparrow-hawks, hobby-hawks, pheasants, partridges, whose cries reminded him of a " rusty key turned in a lock [1]." Then if in the evening we wandered by the stone-diggers' cart-tracks, we often heard the "swish" of a flock of wild duck as they passed overhead, or the wail of a plover, winging its way to the chain of solitary pools. From either side of the Down gush clear fountains of water, some of them at this time half hidden by the "soft wool of the autumn willow-herb." These delighted him. Some flow down to join the Wey, others wend their course to the Arun, but the great want of our views, as he said, was the sight of " a full fed river winding through the landscape."

On July 12th we were staying with Mr Craik in Halkin Street, and visited the Royal Academy, where the heat and the crowd oppressed my father; then the Natural History Museum, where he insisted on walking through the geological part and seeing again his old friends the Ichthyosaurus, the Plesiosaurus, and the Giant Sloth. Professor Flower took us afterwards to the Bird's-nest room, and my father said, " I wish I could have seen this when I was a young man." In the evening my wife and I went to see Sarah Bernhardt's magnificent

---

[1] See "Lover's Tale."

rendering of *Phèdre.* My father would have liked to come with us but did not feel equal to it. He was anxious on our return to hear how she spoke " *Tu l'as nommé.*"

When we returned to Aldworth we saw many friends. We had no real summer weather and my father felt the cold.

On his eighty-third birthday he quoted some of Milton's blank verse with profoundest admiration:

> "That proud honour claim'd
> Azazel as his right, a cherub tall
> Who forthwith from the glittering staff unfurl'd
> The imperial ensign; which full high advanced,
> Shone like a meteor streaming to the wind,
> With gems and golden lustre rich emblazed,
> Seraphic arms and trophies; all the while
> Sonorous metal blowing martial sounds."

"What a grand line!" he said of the last. Then he quoted —

> "Whose wanton passions in the sacred porch
> Ezekiel saw, when by the vision led
> His eye survey'd the dark idolatries
> Of alienated Judah."

"This is very like Virgil in its movement," he continued. "If Virgil is to be translated it ought to be in this elaborate kind of blank verse."

He then repeated to Mr Frederic Harrison the following passage from De Quincey's *Opium Eater,* characterizing his prose as some of the finest in the English language — "not poetry," he observed, "but as fine as any verse":

"Yet I knew, even in my dream, that they had been in the grave for nearly two centuries. This pageant would suddenly dissolve; and, at a clapping of hands, would be heard the heart-quaking sound of *Consul Romanus;* and immediately come 'sweeping by,' in gorgeous paludaments, Paulus or Marius, girt round by a company of centurions, with the crimson tunic hoisted on a spear, and followed by the *alalagmos* of the Roman legions."

Mr R— asked my father: "Apart from the Bible, the Psalms, and the Book of Common Prayer, which, I know, you consider were written at the grandest period of English, in what six authors should you say you find the stateliest English prose?"

He answered: " Probably in Hooker, Bacon, Milton, Jeremy Taylor, De Quincey, Ruskin. Some of Sir Thomas Browne too is very stately; and some of the Acts of Elizabeth, Froude tells me, are written in the grandest language that he knows. Listen to this from Bacon: ' It is a heaven upon earth when a man's mind rests on Providence, moves in Charity, and turns upon the poles of Truth.'" Of the *Essays* he said: " There is more wisdom compressed into that small volume than into any other book of the same size that I know."

He liked the following birthday letter from Edward Wilkinson, a working-man:

87, ALBERT ROAD,
MIDDLESBOROUGH ON TEES,
YORKSHIRE, Aug. 5th, 1892.

MY LORD TENNYSON,

        All hail to your Lordship i send you a Real Yorkshire Greeting Comeing from an old Working man and i do from my heart congratulate you upon the Rare Event the Celebrating of your 83rd Birthday. God Bless you my very best are for your health and happiness and i wish your Lordship God's Speed with vigorous Health and Strength to Enjoy life with although at the ripe old age of eighty-three itz not too late yet to enjoy life and i see no Reason by God helping you that you should not live to Celebrate your 100 Birthday. believe me when i says my Poor congratulations and good wishes are as Sincear and true altho' Echoed from apoor Cottage as those Echoed from apalace trusting that You will Spend a happy time with all Your family that take part in the fastavel and ihope and trust that this Celebration will not be the last by avery great number and that this liberty from a poor old working man will give no offense.

May God smile upon you on this your 83rd Birthday.

Yours faithfully,

EDWARD WILKINSON.

The last letters written by my father, 1892.

To E. W. Whymper.

ALDWORTH, HASLEMERE,
SURREY, 1892.

DEAR SIR,

Accept my thanks for your most interesting volume.

I don't think that I have been higher than about 7000 feet, and so I look on your Chimborazos and Cotopaxis with all the greater veneration.

Yours very truly, TENNYSON.

To Sir Henry Parkes, K.C.M.G.

ALDWORTH, HASLEMERE,
SURREY, Aug. 13th, 1892.

MY DEAR SIR HENRY,

I have received your Australian opals which, as symbols of your kindly recollections of myself, are and will be to me more precious than ten times their weight in diamonds.

I have entered my 84th year. I have entirely lost, as far as reading is concerned, the use of my right eye, and I fear that the left is going in the same way, but I trust that my sight will last me till your *Fifty Years in the making of Australian History* is published.

Believe me yours ever,

TENNYSON.

To the Zemindar Bechari Lal.

HASLEMERE, *Aug. 27th,* 1892.

I thank my young brother of the East for all the good wishes he sends to his old brother of the West, and I rejoice that he has sung in their common tongue (English) the praises of that great and good sovereign, to whom all her subjects owe such deep reverence and love. Accept every best wish (not forgetting the wish that practice may, as you say, make your verse perfect) and thanks too for your little books.

Believe me truly yours,

TENNYSON.

In the beginning of September, though feeling very ill, my father looked over a book of poems at the earnest entreaty of a stranger, Mr Dalmon, and made one or two criticisms. He crossed out Mr Dalmon's despairing words about poetry — "*The end is failure*" — saying to him : "How can there be failure, if the divine speak through the human, be it through the voice of prince or peasant ? "

In the middle of the month his old friends Lord
Selborne and the late Master of Balliol visited him. One
of the principal topics of conversation was Max Müller's
speech at the Oriental Congress, the spirit of which my
father considered admirable. He did not feel himself
strong enough for religious discussions with Jowett, and
begged Jowett not to consult with him or argue with
him, as was his wont, on points of philosophy and religious doubt [1]. The Master of Balliol answered him in a
remarkable utterance. "Your poetry has *an element of
philosophy more to be considered than any regular philosophy in England.* It is almost too much impregnated
with philosophy, yet this to some minds will be its
greatest charm. I believe that your 'In Memoriam'
and your 'Crossing the Bar' will live for ever in men's
hearts [2]." And he spoke to me afterwards of my father's
"great and deep strength."

The qualities in Jowett which most attracted my
father were his childlikeness, his absolute simplicity of
life, his aversion from all that was unreal and affected,
his admiration of what seemed to him to be truthful and
naturally beautiful, and his power of imagination, which
my father thought essential in any philosopher. Another
bond between them was that both had it in their hearts
to help their brother men to the utmost of their power.
The poor student who needed help, the wealthy student
who needed guidance, could have no truer friend than
the Master of Balliol; and as for my father, I need
hardly say that wherever in the world help seemed to

[1] I remember my father saying of animated discussion, "You rarely find
dew after a windy night."

[2] Jowett has also left this utterance in a MS Note.

Mr Gladstone writes, October 25th, 1895: "I have a great conception
of your father as *philosopher*. The 'sage' of Chelsea (a genius too) was
small in comparison with him. Everyone admires your father: I look upon
him in his works and words with reverence."

be needed which he could give, he was sure to give it ungrudgingly and unostentatiously.

Later in the month Mr Dakyns, and Mr and Mrs Craik, Mr and Mrs Bram Stoker and Mr Walter Leaf came to see us. With Mr Craik he looked over all the proofs of his new volume, " Death of Œnone," " Akbar's Dream," etc. The last poem he finished was " Whirl and follow the Sun," and the last prose passage he inserted was the preface to " Kapiolani." This book he felt was his last will and testament to the world, and throughout there are echoes of the different notes that he had struck before, and a summing-up of the faith in which he had walked. With Mr Bram Stoker he talked of the arrangements for the production of " Becket," some misprints greatly amusing him.

He was sitting with an *Iliad* on his knee and the talk naturally turned on Homer. " You know," he said to Leaf, " I never liked that theory of yours about the many poets." Leaf spoke about his " splendid translation " of the simile at the end of *Il.* viii., three lines of which recur in *Il.* xvi., and asked him if he did not think they were far more appropriate in the latter book, and had the appearance of being borrowed in viii. " Yes," he said, " I have always felt that, I must say ": and he then enlarged for some time upon the greatness of Homer, quoting many lines from both the *Iliad* and *Odyssey*.

CHAPTER XXIII.

THE LAST CHAPTER.

Sunset and evening star,
  And one clear call for me!
And may there be no moaning of the bar,
  When I put out to sea,

But such a tide as moving seems asleep,
  Too full for sound and foam,
When that which drew from out the boundless deep
  Turns again home.

Twilight and evening bell,
  And after that the dark!
And may there be no sadness of farewell,
  When I embark;

For tho' from out our bourne of Time and Place
  The flood may bear me far,
I hope to see my Pilot face to face
  When I have crost the bar.

Some of my father's last talks have been recorded
and I quote them in brief. In his view of the Gospel of
Christ he found his Christianity undisturbed by jarring
of sects and of creeds; but he said, "I dread the losing
hold of forms. I have expressed this in my 'Akbar.'
There must be forms, yet I hate the need for so many
sects and separate services."

"The life after death, Lightfoot and I agreed, is
the cardinal point of Christianity. I believe that God

reveals Himself in every individual soul: and my idea of heaven is the perpetual ministry of one soul to another."

To some short notes on "In Memoriam" which he had written for future publication, one explaining Section XLIII. was added: "If the immediate life after death be only sleep, and the spirit between this life and the next should be folded like a flower in a night slumber, then the remembrance of the past might remain, as the smell and colour do in the sleeping flower; and in that case the memory of our love would last as true, and would live pure and whole within the spirit of my friend until after it was unfolded at the breaking of the morn, when the sleep was over."

Politics were to my father the good of the world, and passionately did he feel for all that concerned what he considered the welfare of the Empire. During these last months he talked with pride of the great work we had done in Egypt: and he took the greatest interest in the proposed schemes for Old Age Pensions for the poor. The mere working for party, as far as his own conviction went, was to him unintelligible, as well as the love of power and of rule for their own sakes. That all should work conscientiously and harmoniously together for the common weal, each with such differing power as had been given to each man, recognising the value of the difference, was his highest ideal of government.

While reading an article in the *Spectator* on blank verse, he observed: "I have been reading in the *Spectator* that Wordsworth and Keats are great masters of blank verse, who are also great in rhyme. Keats was not a master of blank verse. It might be true of Wordsworth at his best. Blank verse can be the finest mode of expression in our language."

He often quoted from Wordsworth now, and was

always greatly moved by "Yarrow Revisited," and particularly by the following stanza:

> "And if, as Yarrow, through the woods
>   And down the meadow ranging,
> Did meet us with unaltered face
>   Though we were changed and changing:
> If, *then*, some natural shadows spread
>   Our inward prospect over,
> The soul's deep valley was not slow
>   Its brightness to recover."

"I never could care," he said one day, "about French Alexandrines. They are so artificial. The French language lends itself much better to slighter things. Some of Béranger's Chansons are exquisite, for example his lyric to 'Le Temps,' with the chorus: 'O par pitié, lui dit ma belle, Vieillard, épargnez nos amours!' 'L'Agonie' by Sully Prudhomme I have just been reading, and think it beautiful, yet very sad; and there are things of Alfred de Musset like 'Tristesse' which seem to me perfect. I consider him a greater artist than Victor Hugo, but on smaller lines. Victor Hugo [1] is an unequal genius, sometimes sublime; he reminds one that there is only one step between the sublime and the ridiculous. 'Napoléon génait Dieu,' 'Napoleon irked God.' Was there ever such an expression?

"Among Hugo's poems I like some of the *Légende des Siècles*, and a lyric 'Gastibelza.' His finest play is *Le Roi s'amuse;* but *Mary Tudor* is a mere travesty."

"In his smaller poems such as those in *Wilhelm Meister*," he said, "Goethe shows himself to be one of

---

[1] In 1885 he came across Amiel's *Journal Intime*, and thought his criticisms on Hugo and literature in general good; but that the *Journal* throughout was too morbid for anything.

The modern French poets were read by him with genuine interest. The last French poems he read were by Coppée, and by Jean Aicard.

the great artists of the world.   He is also a great critic:
yet he always said the best he could about an author.
Good critics are rarer than good authors."

Talking of localisers, " I am told by a certain gentleman that this mill is the original mill in the ' Miller's
Daughter,' and that that oak was ' The Talking Oak,'
and that hall ' Locksley Hall.'   Never anything of the
sort.   Why do they give a poet no credit for imagination?
The power of poetical creation seems to be utterly
ignored now.   This modern realism is hateful, and
destroys all poetry.   No man with an imagination can
be tied down for his ideal.   " Turner was an imaginative
painter, and how absurd it would be to account for some
of his works.   There may be special suggestions."

Referring to the pictures at Blenheim, " I remember
the very strange simile which the gardener made to me
fifty years ago when he showed me over the place.   We
were talking of the stories told about the then Duke of
Marlborough's unpopularity.   He said, ' You see, Sir,
when a man goes down in his luck, everyone points at
him as if he were a church steeple.'

" The man himself was doubtless unaware that his
comparison answered the definition of humour, the
bringing together of violent contrasts."

Talking about his own life, " So much to do, so little
done."

" All the magazines and daily newspapers, which
pounce upon everything they can get hold of, demoralize
literature.   This age gives an author no time to mature
his works."

" Burlesque, the true enemy of humour, the thin bastard sister of poetical caricature, would, I verily believe,
from her utter want of human feeling, in a revolution
be the first to dabble her hands in blood."

" I have just had a letter from a man who wants my
opinion as to whether Shakespeare's plays were written

by Bacon. I feel inclined to write back : 'Sir, don't be a fool.' The way in which Bacon speaks of Love would be enough to prove that he was not Shakespeare. 'I know not how, but martial men are given to Love. I think it is but as they are given to wine, for perils commonly ask to be paid in pleasures.' How could a man with such an idea of Love write *Romeo and Juliet?*

Speaking of Walt Whitman, he said to me, " Walt neglects form altogether, but there is a fine spirit breathing through his writings. Some of them are quite unreadable from nakedness of expression."

Walt Whitman had sent my father a little book containing two addresses on *Giordano Bruno* by Daniel Brinton and Thomas Davidson. The death of Bruno was a subject which my father thought might be good for a poem [1]. Of Bruno he said, " His view of God is in some ways mine. Bruno was a poet, holding his mind ever open to new truths, and believing in an infinite universe as the necessary effect of the infinite divine Power ; he was burnt as a heretic. His age did not believe in him. I think that he was misunderstood, and I should like to show him in what I conceive to be his right colours : he was the author of much of our modern philosophy. He died the most desolate of deaths."

" Spinoza is another man who has been often misunderstood. He has been called an atheist, and yet he is so full of God that he sees Him everywhere, so much so that he leaves no room for man. He was said to be ' Gottbetrunken.' He thought joy was more real than sorrow."

" Matter is a greater mystery than mind. What such a thing as a spirit is apart from God and man I have never been able to conceive. Spirit seems to me to be the reality of the world."

" Vice," he said, " sometimes appears to me as the

---

[1] He also thought of the death of Savonarola.

shadow of Idleness." " I do not feel horror when I see sin and misery, but shame for the sake of God."

My father often now longed for the quiet Hereafter where all would be made clear.

On Sept. 3rd he complained of weakness and of pain in his jaw, which caused a difficulty in swallowing food.

On Wednesday the 29th we telegraphed for Sir Andrew Clark. That morning I drove with him to Haslemere[1]. He would point out his old accustomed haunts saying, " I shall never walk there again."

He read Job, and St Matthew, and Miss Swanwick's new book on *Poets as the Interpreters of the Age*. Sir Andrew arrived, and did not think so badly of him as I did. He and my father fell to discussing Gray's " Elegy."

On Thursday and Friday my father had a bad sore throat; on Friday my wife read him an article in the *Times* on the colonization of Uganda, for which he asked. He looked forward to the day when South Africa would be welded into one mighty state, linked in a strict federation with England.

On Saturday and Sunday he was very drowsy.

On Sunday afternoon he was much worse, and his breathing terribly uneven.

On Monday morning at 8 o'clock he sent me for his Shakespeare. I took him Steevens' edition, *Lear*, *Cymbeline*, and *Troilus and Cressida*, three plays which he loved dearly.

He read two or three lines, and told Dr Dabbs that he should never get well again. We asked him later whether he felt better; he answered, " The doctor says I am." At his request I read some Shakespeare to him; he was most patient, and in his courteous fashion always feared that he was troubling his nurses, and expressed

[1] The last drive he took.

much anxiety for my mother's health. In the morning
he told me that he was worse : he always counted the
striking of the clock correctly, and asked whether it was
night or morning. Dr Dabbs who had been in London
for the day had seen Irving. On his return my father
remarked : " What is he doing with my ' Becket ' ? It
will be successful on the stage with Irving as Becket."
He became excited towards night, saying that he must
look over the poems that had been sent him, and asking
me whether I had thanked an unknown author for a
certain book of poems. He said to me during the night,
" I make a slave of you."

On Tuesday he talked a great deal about a journey,
observing that he was not fit for his journey to Farringford to-day.

At noon he called out, " Where is my Shakespeare ?
I must have my Shakespeare." Then he said, " I want
the blinds up, I want to see the sky and the light." He
repeated " The sky and the light!" It was a glorious
morning, and the warm sunshine was flooding the weald
of Sussex and the line of South Downs, which were seen
from his window.

At 3 o'clock he was pleased with the telegram about
him from the Queen, but he muttered, " O, that Press
will get hold of me now!"

At five Dr Dabbs thought him better than he had
been for two days ; he asked Nurse Sanders how long he
had been ill, and she answered, " Four days." He told
Dr Dabbs that he " would take anything that he was
ordered." When the nurse put the thermometer under
his arm, she touched some nerve, and he said that a
" most beautiful vision of blue and other colours had
passed over his eyes."

At seven he asked me, " Have I not been walking
with Gladstone in the garden, and showing him my
trees ? " I answered, " No." He replied, " Are you sure ? "

On Wednesday he wanted to know whether his book had come, probably meaning the proofs of his new volume. I put them into his hand, and I kissed it, and he said, " Sir Andrew did that." He begged for his Shakespeare again. About 10.30 he called aloud, " Hallam," as I was leaving the room to fetch my mother. I questioned him as to whether he felt free from pain: he answered, " Quite, but I shall not get better."

At 2 o'clock he again asked for his Shakespeare and lay with his hand resting on it open, and tried to read it. Sir Andrew Clark had arrived from Christchurch: my father knew him, and said distinctly, " This is the worst attack I have had," and added, " I hope that you are not tired," for he had heard that Sir Andrew had started at seven o'clock.

All the afternoon he was much the same, occasionally saying a word or two to us, and hearing every sound, when he would open his eyes wide, look round the room, then close them again.

He had been talking to Dr Dabbs about death, and about " What a shadow this life is, and how men cling to what is after all but a small part of the great world's life." Then Dr Dabbs told him (for his interest was always keen " in the lot of lowly men ") of an incident that had lately happened. " A villager, ninety years old, was dying, and had so much pined to see his old bedridden wife once more that they had carried her to where he lay. He pressed his shrunken hand upon her hand, and in a husky voice said to her, ' Come soon,' and soon after passed away himself." My father murmured " True Faith "; and the tears were in his voice. Suddenly he gathered himself together and spoke one word about himself to the doctor, " Death?" Dr Dabbs bowed his head, and he said, " That's well."

His last food was taken at a quarter to four, and he tried to read, but could not. He exclaimed, " I have opened it." Whether this referred to the Shakespeare, opened by him at

> " Hang there like fruit, my soul,
>   Till the tree die[1],"

which he always called among the tenderest lines in Shakespeare: or whether one of his last poems, of which he was fond, was running through his head I cannot tell:

> Fear not thou the hidden purpose of that Power
>   which alone is great,
> Nor the myriad world, His shadow, nor the silent
>   Opener of the Gate.

He then spoke his last words, a farewell blessing, to my mother and myself.

For the next hours the full moon flooded the room and the great landscape outside with light; and we watched in solemn stillness. His patience and quiet strength had power upon those who were nearest and dearest to him; we felt thankful for the love and the utter peace of it all; and his own lines of comfort from " In Memoriam" were strongly borne in upon us. He was quite restful, holding my wife's hand, and, as he was passing away, I spoke over him his own prayer, " God accept him! Christ receive him!" because I knew that he would have wished it.

I give the medical bulletin published next day by Dr Dabbs:

The tendency to fatal syncope may be said to have really commenced about 10 a.m. on Wednesday, and on Thursday, October 6th, at 1.35 a.m., the great poet breathed his last. Nothing could have been more striking than the scene during the last few hours. On the bed a figure of breathing marble, flooded and bathed in the light of the full moon streaming through the oriel window ; his hand clasping the Shakespeare which he had

[1] *Cymbeline,* Act v. Sc. v.

asked for but recently, and which he had kept by him to the end; the moonlight, the majestic figure as he lay there, "drawing thicker breath," irresistibly brought to our minds his own "Passing of Arthur."

Some friends and the servants came to see him. He looked very grand and peaceful with the deep furrows of thought almost smoothed away, and the old clergyman of Lurgashall stood by the bed with his hands raised, and said, "Lord Tennyson, God has taken you, who made you a prince of men! Farewell!"

We placed *Cymbeline* with him, and a laurel wreath from Virgil's tomb, and wreaths of roses, the flower which he loved above all flowers, and some of his Alexandrian laurel, the poet's laurel. On the evening of the 11th the coffin was set upon our waggonette, made beautiful with stag's-horn moss and the scarlet Lobelia Cardinalis; and draped with the pall, woven by working men and women of the north, and embroidered by the cottagers of Keswick; and then we covered him with the wreaths and crosses of flowers sent from all parts of Great Britain. The coachman, who had been for more than thirty years my father's faithful servant, led the horse.

Ourselves, the villagers, and the school children followed over the moor through our lane towards a glorious sunset, and later through Haslemere under brilliant starlight.

The coffin was taken to Westminster Abbey[1], and, at

---

[1] The question of the burial in the Abbey or at Farringford was left to the decision of the Dean. My mother telegraphed to him: "Decide as you think best. If it is thought better, let him have the flag of England on his coffin, and rest in the churchyard of the dear place where his happiest days have been passed. Only, let the flag represent the feeling of the beloved Queen, and the nation, and the empire he loved so dearly." Owing to his detestation of the gloomy pomp of funerals, black plumes, black coaches, etc., the coffin was conveyed from Waterloo Station to the Abbey on a simple, covered van.

the request of the Prince of Wales, covered with a Union Jack — lent by Lord Methuen and the brigade of Guards quartered in London. He was laid that night in the chapel of St Faith.

On Wednesday the 12th the funeral procession was formed in the cloisters: the pall-bearers being the Duke of Argyll, Lord Dufferin, Lord Selborne, Lord Rosebery, Mr Jowett, Mr Lecky, Mr Froude, Lord Salisbury, Dr Butler (Trinity College, Cambridge), the United States Minister, Sir James Paget and Lord Kelvin. The Abbey was crowded from end to end by a vast multitude of mourners. The nave was lined by men of the Balaclava Light Brigade, by some of the London Rifle Volunteers, and by the boys of the Gordon Boys' Home, in token of their gratitude for what he had done for each and all of them. Two anthems were sung: both were settings of words by my father; one, "Crossing the Bar," by Dr Bridge; the other, "Silent Voices," a melody in F minor by my mother, and set by her at my father's express desire. Nothing could have been more simple and majestic than the funeral service[1]: and the tributes of sympathy which we received from many countries and from all creeds and classes were not only remarkable for their universality, but for their depth of feeling. What I said then I can only repeat: "God bless all for the love and reverence shown to the memory of him who above all things loved Love."

On God and Godlike men we build our trust.
Hush, the Dead March wails in the people's ears:
The dark crowd moves, and there are sobs and tears:
The black earth yawns: the mortal disappears;
Ashes to ashes, dust to dust;
He is gone who seem'd so great.—

[1] Many were seen reading "In Memoriam" while waiting before the service.

Gone; but nothing can bereave him
Of the force he made his own
Being here, and we believe him
Something far advanced in State,
And that he wears a truer crown
Than any wreath that man can weave him.
Speak no more of his renown,
Lay your earthly fancies down,
And in the vast cathedral leave him.
God accept him, Christ receive him.

Next to Robert Browning, and in front of the Chaucer monument, my father was laid: and for weeks after the funeral multitudes passed by the new-made grave in a never-ceasing procession. Against the pillar near the grave has been placed the well-known bust by Woolner[1].

[1] This replica by the sculptor himself, from the original at Trinity College, Cambridge (1857), was given me by Mr Charles Jenner of Portobello, Midlothian. Another replica is in existence and is the property of Mrs Charles Buxton. It may be remembered that Woolner executed the earliest medallion in 1850, the second a profile in 1856, the third a three-quarters head in 1867. We have always thought that the finest work of art and the best likeness was the bust done in 1857. The only other bust (from life) of my father was made by Woolner in 1873.

The portraits by G. F. Watts, R.A. are:

	Painted in
A profile, gone to Melbourne.	1856
A three-quarters, owned by Lady Henry Somerset.	1858–9
Another, owned by Sir William Bowman.	1859
A full face, in the National Portrait Gallery.	1865
A three-quarters, presented to Trinity College, Cambridge, by G. F. Watts.	1891

A replica of this last was painted by Mr Watts for the bequest which he has made to the nation. The portraits by other artists have already been named.

[It has taken me four years to complete this Memoir of my father. Throughout, my mother's assistance has been invaluable. She passed away peacefully at Aldworth, August 10th, 1896 (having entered her eighty-fourth year, the age at which my father died), and we laid her to rest in the quiet churchyard at Freshwater. A few days before her death she expressed her satisfaction that she had lived long enough to help me to correct the proofs for the press.

On the tablet, erected in the church to the memory of my father and mother, is the following inscription:

IN LOVING MEMORY

OF

ALFRED LORD TENNYSON

WHOSE HAPPIEST DAYS WERE PASSED AT FARRINGFORD

IN THIS PARISH

BORN AUG 6th 1809
DIED OCT 6th 1892
BURIED IN WESTMINSTER ABBEY OCT 12th 1892

SPEAK, LIVING VOICE ! WITH THEE DEATH IS NOT DEATH ;
THY LIFE OUTLIVES THE LIFE OF DUST AND BREATH.

ALSO IN LOVING · MEMORY
OF HIS WIFE

EMILY LADY TENNYSON

BORN JULY 9th 1813
DIED AUGUST 10th 1896

" DEAR, NEAR AND TRUE, NO TRUER TIME HIMSELF
CAN PROVE YOU, THO' HE MAKE YOU EVERMORE
DEARER AND NEARER."]

THE QUEEN.

These letters, which I have the Queen's gracious permission to publish, will, I am sure, be read with heartfelt interest: giving as they do fresh proof of Her Majesty's deep sympathy with her subjects, and of my father's earnest and chivalrous devotion to her.

From the Queen.

WINDSOR CASTLE,
Feb. 26*th*, 1873.

Though Lady Augusta Stanley has already conveyed the expression of the Queen's warmest thanks for and high admiration of the beautiful Epilogue[1] he has so kindly inscribed to herself, she wishes to repeat again herself to Mr Tennyson these feelings on the occasion of the arrival of the copy of the very fine new edition of the " Idylls of the King."

Pray accept the renewed thanks of the Queen for the noble heart-stirring words addressed to her, and which were a complete surprise. It would give the Queen much pleasure could she, some day, when he is within reach of Windsor, show him the Mausoleum

---

[1] Epilogue to the " Idylls of the King."

she has raised over the earthly remains of her dear
Husband, whom he knew how to appreciate, and so
beautifully described, as she feels sure he would admire
it and think it worthy of him who wore

" The white flower of a blameless life."

She also hopes that Mr Tennyson will not find Osborne
too far for a drive from Freshwater.

From my father (after a visit to Osborne).

August, 1883.

DEAR AND HONOURED LADY,

MY QUEEN,

Your Majesty's letter made me glad that
even in so small a matter I may have been of some
service to you. I will not say that "I am loyal," or
that "Your Majesty is gracious," for these are old
hackneyed terms used or abused by every courtier,
but I will say that during our conversation I felt the
touch of that true friendship which binds human beings
together, whether they be kings or cobblers.

Madam, when I left your presence, those lines of
our Shakespeare in his *Henry V.* came across my
memory,

" O hard condition twin-born with greatness,

*   *   *   *   *

What infinite heart's-ease must kings neglect
Which private men enjoy."

So it is, but I trust that in spite of the loneliness
of the throne and your Majesty's many losses, and
this latest[1] of your faithful servant, the return of your
beloved daughter may be of some solace to you. I

[1] Death of John Brown.

remember dear Princess Alice bringing her to me in the drawing-room at Osborne — a fair-haired child whom it was a pleasure to look upon.

My wife is very grateful for your Majesty's most kind remembrance, and

I am always your affectionate servant,

A. TENNYSON.

From my father.

(After our voyage to Copenhagen.)

ALDWORTH, HASLEMERE,
Sept. 22nd, 1883.

MADAM,

Our cruise was so unpremeditated as to direction that my wife could not forward your Majesty's letter to me, but could only place it in my hand just after my arrival at home yesterday evening.

I need not say that I have great pleasure in learning that the quotations suggested by me have been approved by your Majesty[1]. I feared that they were too elliptical.

The sight of the Princess of Wales in the midst of her own family, all of whom seem so royally simple and kindly, was, I think, the pleasantest thing that occurred in our whole voyage, delightful as it was; for the longer I live the more I value kindness and simplicity among the sons and daughters of men.

Believe me, dear Madam, your Majesty's

loyal and affectionate servant,

A. TENNYSON.

[1] Lines on a tablet in memory of John Brown, the Queen's Highland attendant.

My father's letter to the Queen, accepting the Peerage.

Sept. 1883.

MADAM,

I have learned from Mr Gladstone your Majesty's gracious intention toward myself, and I ask to be allowed to express to your Majesty herself my grateful acknowledgments.

You, Madam, who are so full of sympathy for your subjects, will, I am sure, understand me when I say that the knowledge of your Majesty's approval of what I have been enabled to do, is, as far as I myself am concerned, all that I desire.

This public mark of your Majesty's esteem, which recognizes in my person the power of literature in this age of the world, cannot, however, fail to be gratifying to my nearest and dearest.

Believe me, dear Madam,

Your Majesty's loyal

and affectionate servant,

A. TENNYSON.

From the Queen.

BALMORAL CASTLE,
Oct. 9th, 1883.

DEAR MR TENNYSON,

I thank you sincerely for your two last kind letters.

It affords me much pleasure to confer on my Poet Laureate, who is so universally admired and respected, a mark of my recognition of the great services he has rendered to literature, which has so great an influence on the world at large.

How I wish you could suggest means of crushing those horrible publications whose object is to promulgate scandal and calumny which they invent themselves!

Hoping to see you in the course of the next few months,

Believe me always yours most sincerely,

V. R. I.

The following lines on the Duke of Albany (who died in March 1884) were sent by my father to the Queen.

PRINCE LEOPOLD.

An Epitaph.

Early-wise, and pure, and true,
Prince, whose Father lived in you,
If you could speak, would you not say:
" I seem, but am not, far away;
Wherefore should your eyes be dim?
I am here again with him.
O Mother-Queen, and weeping Wife,
The Death from which you mourn is Life."

From the Queen.

(After the death of the Duke of Albany.)

WINDSOR CASTLE,
March 31st, 1884.

DEAR LORD TENNYSON,

I truly value your very kind words. My sorrows are many and great!

Almost all I needed most to lean on — and who helped and comforted — are taken from me! But tho' *all happiness* is at an end for me in *this* world, I am ready to fight on, praying that I may be supported in bearing my heavy cross — and in trying to be of use and help to this poor, dear young widow of my darling child [1], whose life, which was so bright and happy for barely two years, has been utterly crushed! But she bears it admirably, with the most gentle patience and courageous unmurmuring resignation.

All these terrible sorrows show us however, truly and really, that here is not our abiding home.

Still it is very hard to see such a young life, so full of talent, so gifted, and so useful, cut off so soon, and to feel that all the care and anxiety, which under Providence enabled him to attain full manhood, was unavailing at last.

I am well, and while I live shall devote myself to the good of my dear Country, which has on all occasions of sorrow or joy, but especially the former, shown such sympathy with me!

Ever yours truly,

V. R. I.

From the Princess Louise (Marchioness of Lorne).

WINDSOR CASTLE,
April 12th, 1884.

DEAR LORD TENNYSON,

The Queen desires me to send you the enclosed letter (dated March 31st), and to say that she is distressed to find that through some oversight of one of her gentlemen, owing to the great press of business, the letter was misdirected; and thus the delay.

The Queen was much touched by your beautiful lines, and had hoped you would have received her letter some days ago.

[1] The Duke of Albany.

The Queen is well, but the blow is a heavy one, and only by degrees will she realise what she has lost in that beloved son, who has been taken from her.

I do not like to tell you of my own sorrow. I have lost the truest and dearest friend (besides the best of brothers) I ever had, the joy and object of a lifetime.

Believe me yours sincerely,

LOUISE.

From the Queen.

OSBORNE.

DEAR LORD TENNYSON,

Though a very humble and unpretending author I send you my new book, which perhaps you may like to glance at. Its only merit is its simplicity and truth.

What a warm winter we have had!

Hoping that you are well, and wishing to be kindly remembered to Lady Tennyson,

Ever yours truly,

V. R. I.

From my father.

FARRINGFORD.

MADAM,

This beautiful morning has brought me the pleasant surprise of your Majesty's most gracious letter and gift [1].

I need scarcely assure you, Madam, of my gratitude at receiving the volume from your Majesty's own hands.

If I may venture to say so, I am certain beforehand of finding the lofty and tender sentiments and the hearty

[1] Second series of *Journal of our Life in the Highlands.*

enjoyment of nature, expressed in pure F████, w██ Ou cannot fail to make a book interesting, apart from the special interest which must of necessity belong to this particular volume.

My wife is most grateful for your Majesty's gracious remembrance.

Allow me, Madam, to subscribe myself

Your Majesty's devoted and affectionate servant,

TENNYSON.

From my father.

FARRINGFORD,
July, 1885.

MADAM,

I am honoured by your Majesty's most gracious letter, and, if I am fortunate enough to write what your Majesty would have me write[1], and as your Majesty would have it written, I shall have true pleasure in having written.

The account of the young Prince[2] is very interesting, and your Majesty may well believe that in him another will be added to your "army of Heroes."

England, whose heart has rarely, if ever, beaten more warmly for her soldiers, nor with better cause than now, will rejoice that the Princess, whom she has loved as the devoted daughter, has every prospect of being the happy wife of a soldier Prince, and of bringing a new solace to the life which year by year becomes more precious to the whole Empire.

Your Majesty's affectionate servant,

TENNYSON.

---

[1] Dedication of "The Defence of Lucknow."
[2] Prince Henry of Battenberg.

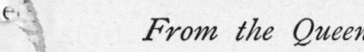

From the Queen.

WINDSOR CASTLE,
July 8th, 1885.

DEAR LORD TENNYSON,

I am so grateful and touched by your kind letter.

It would give me the greatest of pleasures if you would come over for the wedding in our village church [1], but I *fear* you will not do that! But pray come and see me when all is quiet again.

You will understand that Prince Henry, though an excellent soldier, has never been in the field as he was too young, the last German war being fifteen years ago, and he is only twenty-six.

You may also like to know that she will be followed by her ten nieces as bridesmaids, viz. my eldest son's three girls, Louise, Victoria, and Maud of Wales, dear Alice's two motherless girls, Irene and Alice of Hesse, Princess Christian's two, Victoria and Louise of Holstein, and my son Alfred's three, Marie, Victoria, and Alexandra Marie of Edinburgh.

I am yours very truly,

V. R. I.

[The Queen in a postscript speaks of " the death of that noble hero Gordon."]

From my father.

July 9th, 1885.

Your Majesty is most gracious, but I think that blind [short-sighted] as I am, and, I fear, growing blinder, I am best away from the wedding, and I would

[1] Whippingham.

pray to be excused, except that your Majesty had kindly anticipated my excuse for absence from the ceremony which cannot fail to be beautiful and touching.

Should the poem, which I send [1], be approved of by your Majesty and the Princess, shall I have some copies printed?

Very often in the sorrowful period through which we have passed, we have thought of what the Queen must have suffered.

It cheers one that the present Prime Minister [2] speaks only of the interests of the Empire, leaving at all events in abeyance the fatal cry of party. Change must needs come in all human things, but I wish that statesmen would oftener remember the saying of Bacon: — " Mere innovations should imitate the work of time, which innovateth slowly but surely" (or some such words). We might then have such stability in our policy as is possible to our poor human nature.

I fully sympathize with your Majesty's feelings for our great simple soldier-hero Gordon, and I rejoice that the Mansion House Committee have adopted, as the National Memorial, the scheme proposed by myself and my son, which had its origin in a conversation with Gordon.

Believe me your Majesty's

Loyal and affectionate servant,

TENNYSON.

[1] On the marriage of Prince Henry of Battenberg and Princess Beatrice.
[2] Lord Salisbury.

From my father.

July 20th, 1885.

MADAM,

I have sent your Majesty one hundred copies of the poem, printed. I am glad your Princess approves it, for I, who enter my 77th year on the 6th August, might well give in to the fear that the power of poetry was faded or fading in me. To the Royal bride the old poet sends his blessing; and for her he, and his, wish " Queen's weather " on the 23rd.

Your Majesty's loyal and devoted servant,

TENNYSON.

Mr Gladstone differs in *many* of his political views from myself.

From the Queen.

OSBORNE,
Aug. 7th, 1885.

DEAR LORD TENNYSON,

I was not unmindful of yesterday's anniversary, and would wish to offer my warm good wishes on the return of your natal day.

It was also my son Alfred's and my son-in-law Lorne's birthday, and there was always a gathering at Osborne Cottage of my children, grandchildren and relations, and, as I gazed on the happy young couple, and on my two sons Alfred and Arthur and their bonnie bairns, I could not but feel sad in thinking that their hour of trial might come, and earnestly prayed God would spare my sweet Beatrice and the husband she so truly loves and confides in, for long, long to each other.

Till sixty-one no real inroad of any kind had been made in our circle, and how heavy has God's hand been since then on me!

Mother, husband, children, truest friends, all have been taken from me, and yet I must "still endure," and I shall try to do so. Your beautiful lines have been greatly admired.

I wish you could have *seen* the wedding, for everyone says it was the prettiest they ever saw. The simple, pretty, little village church, all decorated with flowers, the sweet young bride, the handsome young husband, the ten bridesmaids, six of them quite children with flowing fair hair, the brilliant sunshine and the blue sea, all made up pictures not to be forgotten.

Believe me always yours affectionately,

V. R. I.

From my father.

ALDWORTH,
Aug. 9th, 1885.

MADAM,

Tho' feasts and flowers seem to me only properly to belong to the birthdays of the young, and tho' I myself always pass my own over in silence, yet believe me most thoroughly grateful for your Majesty's gracious and kindly congratulations.

As to the sufferings of this momentary life, we can but trust that in some after-state, when we see clearer, we shall thank the Supreme Power for having made us, thro' these, higher and greater beings.

Still it surely cannot be unlawful to pray that our children, and our children's children, may pass thro' smoother waters to the other shore.

The wedding must have been beautiful, the Peace of Heaven seemed on the day.

    *   *   *   *   *   *

Your Majesty's affectionate subject,

TENNYSON.

From the Queen.

OSBORNE,
April 16th, 1886.

DEAR LORD TENNYSON,

I cannot refrain from writing to express my deep concern and true sympathy with you and Lady Tennyson, who I know must be spared as much anxiety as possible at the present moment when you are in such trouble about your dear son [1].

I am indeed grieved beyond measure for you and your dear wife, and for poor little Eleanor, whom I have known from her earliest childhood.

God grant that you may yet get better news!

Beatrice shares my feelings, having known Eleanor so well.

I cannot in this letter allude to politics, but I know what your feelings must be.

Believe me always yours truly,

V. R. I.

From my father.

FARRINGFORD, FRESHWATER,
April, 1886.

MADAM,

I beg to offer your Majesty the assurance of my own and my wife's heartfelt gratitude for your Majesty's most welcome letter of sympathy with us.

---

[1] The illness of my brother in India.

Our latest telegram was from Colombo, "no improvement"; but in this pause, as it were between Life and Death, since your Majesty touches upon the disastrous policy of the day, I may say, that I wish I may be in my own grave beyond sight and hearing, when an English army fires upon the Loyalists of Ulster.

Believe me always your Majesty's

Loyal and affectionate subject,

TENNYSON.

From the Queen.

(After the death of Lionel.)

OSBORNE,
April 25th, 1886.

DEAR LORD TENNYSON,

I wish I could express in words how *deeply* and truly I feel for you in this hour of heavy affliction! You, who have written such words of comfort for others, will I am sure feel the comfort of them again *in* yourself. But it is *terrible* to lose one's grown up children when one is no longer young oneself, and to see, as I have done, and you will do now, the sore stricken young widow of one's beloved son!

I will not weary you or intrude on your grief by words of consolation, which in fact *can* offer none. But I say from the depth of a heart, which has suffered cruelly, and lost almost all it cared for and loved best, I *feel* for you; I know what you and your dear wife are suffering, and I pray God to support you.

Pray let your son Hallam write me a few words by the messenger, who takes this over, and say how you and Lady Tennyson are.

My dear Beatrice grieves deeply for her former playmate, poor dear Eleanor, and is very anxious to hear how she is.

Ever yours affectionately,

V. R. I.

I am very grateful for your kind letter.

From the Queen to Hallam Tennyson.

OSBORNE, *April 26th*, 1886.

The Queen is very thankful to Mr Tennyson for his kind sad letter, and for the enclosure from Lord Dufferin.

It is terribly sad.

She trusts his dear mother will be mercifully supported, and that fresh news will soon be received from poor Eleanor, and that the first meeting will not be too trying for her and for Lord and Lady Tennyson.

The Queen feels deeply for Mr Tennyson, to whom the loss of his only brother must be a heavy blow, and lasting sorrow.

From my father.

March 12th, 1887 (*the Jubilee Year*).

MADAM,

I am grateful for your Majesty's most kind letter... I do indeed feel how the sense of loneliness may oppress your Majesty in the midst of these loud rejoicings. "Ihr Beifall selbst macht meinem Herzen bang," as Goethe says in his preface to *Faust*. The multitude are loud, but *They* are silent. Yet, if the dead, as I have often felt, tho' silent, be more living than the living; — and linger about the planet in which their earth-life was passed — then *they*, while we are lamenting that they are not at our side, may still be with us; and the husband, the daughter, and the son, lost by your Majesty, may rejoice when the people shout the name of their Queen.

TENNYSON.

From the Queen.

WINDSOR CASTLE,
May 14th, 1887.

DEAR LORD TENNYSON,

I am anxious to tell you that your beautiful Ode[1] was performed at Buckingham Palace on the 11th with a full Orchestra.   It was conducted by Mr Stanford himself.   We greatly admired the music, which was very descriptive and well adapted to the words, and it was extremely well executed.   I wish you could have heard it.

We have just returned from opening the People's Palace.   There was an enormous crowd everywhere, and much enthusiasm and loyalty.

I must thank you for your last kind letter, and hope that you are well, as also Lady Tennyson and your family.

Believe me always yours affectionately,

V. R. I.

[1] " Jubilee Ode."

From my father to Princess Beatrice
(Princess Henry of Battenberg).

FARRINGFORD, FRESHWATER,
Feb. 15*th*, 1888.

MADAM,

I did not know, till after your Royal High-ness had left us yesterday, when I opened the parcel, that the memorial of the Jubilee Year was the photo-graph of the Queen. If I did not express my loyal thanks to your Royal Highness sufficiently by word of mouth for the kind and gracious gift, allow me to write them here.

Yesterday's visit will always be a pleasant memory to me, and I trust your Royal Highness has already forgiven me for introducing you to such low company, as my old " Spinster and her Cats [1]."

With our dutiful remembrances,

I am

Your Royal Highness' faithful servant,

TENNYSON.

From the Queen.

OSBORNE,
Aug. 9*th*, 1889.

DEAR LORD TENNYSON,

Though three days late, I hope I may still offer my best wishes for your eightieth birthday, and my hope that many more anniversaries may follow.

My time has been so much taken up by my grandson, the Emperor of Germany's visit, that I have hardly been

---

[1] Read to Prince and Princess Henry of Battenberg when they visited us at Farringford in February, 1888.

able to write, but my thoughts were with you on a day which is dear to me from being the birthdays of my second son, and son-in-law Lord Lorne.

My grandson the Emperor of Germany's visit went off very well, and much cordiality between the two countries was shown on both sides.

Trusting that you are now quite recovered from your long illness,

> Believe me always yours affectionately,
>
> V. R. I.

Pray remember me to Lady Tennyson.

From my father.

> ALDWORTH, HASLEMERE,
> *Aug.* 1889.

MADAM,

Your Majesty has given yet another proof of that universal kindness (which has rejoiced so many hearts), by remembering your old Poet's birthday, and making time to tell him so in the midst of almost overwhelming work.

That the Emperor's visit has passed off so well must be a source of thankfulness, not only to your Majesty but to the two nations, nations too closely allied by the subtle sympathy of kindred not to be either true brothers or deadly foes.

As brothers what might they not do for the world?

May those so near and dear to your Majesty as son and son-in-law find every 6th of August happier and happier to themselves, in the consciousness of good achieved.

I have had nine months of a most painful and

depressing illness. My doctors say that such an attack of rheumatic gout at my age very frequently is fatal. I am much better now, but possibly I shall never be quite the same man again, though always the same, I trust, in my devotion to the Queen, and my loyalty to her Throne of England.

TENNYSON.

My wife is most grateful for your Majesty's most gracious remembrance.

From the Queen.

OSBORNE, *Feb.* 9*th*, 1891.

DEAR LORD TENNYSON,

I venture to send you two photographs of the Tableaux Vivants of "Elaine," which your son will have told you of, and which I hope you will like.

Of course the want of colour prevents the effect being as fine as it was, but I think they are very good.

Our stage is very small, so that it cramps large groups. Our new room will be finished next year, when I hope we may be able to represent larger Tableaux, or at least to bring in more people without crowding.

Hoping that you and Lady Tennyson are well,

Believe me ever yours affectionately,

VICTORIA R. I.

From my father.

Feb. 9*th*, 1891.

MADAM,

I am very grateful for your Majesty's kind letter, and for the photographs of the Tableaux. That of Elaine in the boat seems beautiful, and Arthur's court with the splendid colouring of old armour must have been very effective.

May I be allowed to add how much my son and his wife felt the kindness of their reception at Osborne, and how much they enjoyed the Plays?

I am rejoiced to hear from them that your Majesty is looking so well.

With the loyal devotion of my wife and myself,

I am always your Majesty's

Ever affectionate servant,

TENNYSON.

The following inscription was sent by my father for the Prayer-book presented to the Queen by her children on the fiftieth anniversary of her wedding:

Remembering him who waits thee far away,
And with thee, Mother, taught us first to pray.
Accept on this your golden bridal day
The Book of Prayer.

From the Queen.

OSBORNE, *Feb. 10th,* 1891.

DEAR LORD TENNYSON,

How kind it is of you to have written those beautiful lines, and to have sent the telegram for this ever dear day, which I will never allow to be considered a sad day. The reflected light of the sun which has set still remains! It is full of pathos, but also full of joyful gratitude, and he, who has left me nearly 30 years ago, surely blesses me still!

Your son, whose acquaintance I was much pleased to make, was desirous of getting the photographs of our Tableaux, which he saw, and I send a set to-day for your acceptance, hoping you may be interested by them.

I hope that you are well, and that I may some day see you again.

Asking you to remember me kindly to Lady Tennyson and your son, believe me always

Yours affectionately, VICTORIA R. I.

From my father.

FARRINGFORD, *Feb. 10th*, 1891.

MADAM,

I am glad that your Majesty did not consider my lines out of harmony with the sacred day. No words could more entirely express the feelings which of right belong to it than your Majesty's. The photographs of the Tableaux are most interesting. They will, I need not say, ever be highly prized, both for the giver's sake, and as a memorial of the pleasant days my son spent at Osborne, when his Queen was so gracious and kind to him. My wife and son send their most loyal duty.

I am ever your Majesty's

Grateful and affectionate servant,

TENNYSON.

From my father.

(*After the death of the Duke of Clarence.*)

FARRINGFORD, *Jan.* 1892.

MADAM,

I venture to write, but I do not know how to express the profound sympathy of myself and my family with the great sorrow, which has befallen your Majesty and your children.

I know that your Majesty has a perfect trust in the Love and Wisdom which order the circumstances of our life, and in this alone is there comfort.

I am always your Majesty's affectionate servant,

TENNYSON.

From the Marquis of Lorne.

OSBORNE, *Jan.* 28*th,* 1892.

MY DEAR LORD TENNYSON,

The Queen was very much touched and very much pleased with what you wrote and sent to her[1].

She is specially anxious that you should not think that the delay, that has arisen in her acknowledgment, has been owing to any want of feeling; but it has come through want of time, for since her loss she has been overwhelmed with work. As soon as the touching lines came, she spoke with tears in her eyes of their beauty, and I know that she felt much your goodness in sending them, and that they were really a comfort to her.

Believe me, dear Lord Tennyson,

Yours very truly, LORNE.

From the Queen.

OSBORNE, *Jan.* 28*th,* 1892.

The Queen is very deeply touched by the beautiful lines Lord Tennyson has so kindly written (and sent) on this terrible tragedy, which is a real misfortune.

She thanks him warmly for writing and sending them. They are most affecting. But was there ever a more terrible contrast?

[1] The lines on the death of the Duke of Clarence.

A wedding with bright hopes turned into a funeral in the very chapel where the former was to have taken place.

The Queen hopes that Lord Tennyson is well in the midst of so much illness everywhere.

She keeps well, but she is deeply grieved by the loss of her dearly loved grandson.

From the Queen to Hallam Tennyson.

BALMORAL CASTLE, *Oct. 6th,* 1892.

The Queen thanks Mr Tennyson again for his very touching telegram, describing the passing away of his beloved father, whose latter years he soothed and sustained with so much devotion. That great spirit now knows what he so often reflected on and pondered over.

The Queen deeply laments and mourns her noble Poet Laureate, who will be so universally regretted, but he has left undying works behind him which we shall ever treasure.

He was so very kind and full of sympathy to the Queen, who alas! never saw him again after his last visit to Osborne.

Most deeply does the Queen feel for Lady Tennyson, whose delicate health will, the Queen hopes, not suffer from this great shock. The blank will be so terrible.

The Queen prays earnestly that they may all be sustained in this hour of grief and bereavement.

What was the cause of this fatal termination of his very short illness?

From the Queen to Hallam Tennyson.

BALMORAL CASTLE, *Oct.* 19*th*, 1892.

I am much touched by your two kind letters, and the copy of the beautiful lines [1], which I conclude were the last he ever wrote.

Everything must have been most touching and beautiful, and worthy of what the great poet was; the "passing away" with Shakespeare in his hand, the *very* simple and affecting departure from his own beloved home, and the last sad ceremony when the mortal part of this great man was laid in its final resting-place.

I am thankful that your dear mother is as well as could be expected, but the blank, which for some time must only increase, will be terrible.

May I ask who Miss Maud Tennyson [2] is, who has been mentioned several times?

I am anxious to have a bust of your dear father at Windsor, and would like to know which is the best to have copied.

I found this short account of your father's visit to me at Osborne in 1883, which I had hastily written down in my Journal, and have had it copied out, thinking it might perhaps interest you. Alas! I never saw him again. He was several times ill, and the weather prevented his moving, so that I had not the pleasure and comfort of again conversing with him once more.

Hoping to see you when I return south,

Believe me always yours truly,

V. R. I.

[1] "The Silent Voices."
[2] Daughter of my uncle Horatio Tennyson.

Extract from the Queen's private Journal.

OSBORNE, *Tuesday, Aug. 7th,* 1883.

After luncheon saw the great Poet Tennyson in dearest Albert's room for nearly an hour; and most interesting it was. He is grown very old, his eyesight much impaired. But he was very kind. Asked him to sit down. He talked of the many friends he had lost, and what it would be if he did not feel and know that there was another world, where there would be no partings; and then he spoke with horror of the unbelievers and philosophers who would make you believe there was no other world, no Immortality, who tried to explain all away in a miserable manner. We agreed that were such a thing possible, God, Who is Love, would be far more cruel than any human being. He quoted some well-known lines from Goethe whom he so much admires. Spoke of the poor Lily of Hanover[1] so kindly, asked after my Godchildren. He spoke of Ireland, and the wickedness of ill-using poor animals: " I am afraid I think the world is darkened; I dare say it will brighten again."

I told him what a comfort " In Memoriam " had again been to me, which pleased him; but he said I could not believe the number of shameful letters of abuse he had received about it. Incredible! When I took leave of him, I thanked him for his kindness, and said I needed it, for I had gone thro' much, and he said, " You are so alone on that terrible height; it is terrible. I've only a year or two to live, but I shall be happy to do anything for you I can. Send for me whenever you like."

I thanked him warmly.

[1] Princess Frederica of Hanover.

TENNYSON, BY THE LATE EARL OF SELBORNE.

BLACKMOOR, PETERSFIELD,
July 18*th*, 1893.

Lord Tennyson realized to me, more than anyone else whom I have known, the "heroic" idea. Even in person, he was such a man as I could conceive Thiodolf the Icelander, the hero of that romance of De la Motte Fouqué which Sir Walter Scott most admired, to have been, when no longer young. The consciousness, which he could not but have, of his great vocation, and of the work which he had done, was tempered by a vein of modesty, almost childlike. His domestic affections were very strong; and he had a happy home, in which the influence of others told upon him, hardly less (I think) than his own did on them. Wordsworth's wish, that his "days" should be "bound each to each in natural piety," seemed to be perfectly fulfilled in him. It was easy to see that he never forgot the influences which surrounded him in childhood, and never lost the habit of observing and sympathizing with Nature, which colours much of his poetry. There was nothing in him conventional or commonplace, nothing artificial or affected. If he spoke of or recited his own poetry, as he often did among friends, it was from pure kindness, because he knew that they wished for it. But his interests were not in his own vocation only; he thought much on religious, scientific and political questions, and expressed freely in conversation the opinions which he had formed on them. I did not see everything in exactly the same light that he did; but everything which he said had the stamp of reality, and it was wholesome and refreshing to listen to him. He looked at questions of truth and falsehood, of right and wrong, with a vision undisturbed by false sentiment, and free from the distortions of party spirit and personal sympathies or antipathies. He was noble, simple, manly, reverent as well as strong, with a frankness which might at times seem rough, but which was never inconsistent with the finest courtesy and the gentlest heart. I do not think I could better describe the impression which he made upon me by any multiplication of words. He was great in himself, as well as in his work; the foremost man, in my eyes, of all his generation; and entitled to be ranked with the greatest of the generations before him.

SELBORNE.

PERSONAL RECOLLECTIONS, BY THE LATE MASTER OF BALLIOL [1].

BALLIOL COLLEGE.

It is nearly forty years since I first made the acquaintance of Lord Tennyson. He was at that time living in the neighbourhood of Twickenham, and had recently married, and I was staying with Temple [2] at Kneller Hall, which in those days, was the scene of many a happy gathering of Dr Temple's old friends. He and I were invited to go and dine with the poet. There were no ladies present, but several of his Cambridge contemporaries; among them I remember particularly James Spedding and Tom Taylor. Our host was very cheerful and hospitable, and though I cannot remember what was said, I have a recollection that the dinner was what young men would call very jolly.

Tennyson was already a great man. Since the publication of the two volumes of poems more than ten years previously, he had shot up like a rocket, and, after the death of Wordsworth, there was no living poet who could be compared with him. In making his acquaintance we had the same kind of awe which Boswell describes himself to have experienced when he first met Johnson. Soon after the occasion of this dinner he removed to the Isle of Wight, where he kindly invited me to visit him. Those visits grew more and more frequent, until they were

---

[1] This short memoir was Jowett's last literary effort. Up to within a fortnight of his death he was working at it, and expressed the greatest anxiety to live long enough to make a faithful portrait of his friend.

[2] The present Archbishop of Canterbury.

repeated two or three times in each year, with scarcely an interruption, as long as he lived. I was in the habit of going both to Freshwater and to Aldworth: they were among the greatest pleasures of my life[1].

Having had the privilege of knowing Lord Tennyson intimately for so many years, it may be naturally supposed that I have something to communicate about him which is not known to the world in general. My own impression is, that anything which I or others may have to say of his daily life must, necessarily, be fragmentary and disappointing. A great man's character rarely, if ever, appears in the jests which he makes with his friends at table, or in the good stories which he narrates, although it is true also, as Dr Johnson says, that every man "may be judged of by his laughter." But his truest self must be estimated in his greatest efforts. The best and deepest nature of the poet will be found in the works of his genius, such as "In Memoriam," or, to take an instance of another kind in "The Northern Farmer," as our best conception of Shakespeare may be gathered, not from contemporary gossip about him, but from the *Sonnets*, from *Hamlet*, and the *Tempest*, and the life and death of Falstaff.

Those who read Tennyson attentively and consecutively know much more about him than can ever be learnt from passing observation. They will read him, as they read Shakespeare, with an ever-increasing wonder at the depth of his thought, and the fertility of his fancy.

If I were to describe his outward appearance, I should say that he was certainly unlike anyone else whom I ever saw. A glance at some of Watts' portraits of him will give, better than any description which can be expressed in words, a conception of his noble mien and look. He was a magnificent man, who stood before you in his native refinement and strength. The unconventionality of his manners was in keeping with the originality of his figure. He would sometimes say nothing, or a word or two only, to the stranger who approached him, out of shyness. He would sometimes come into the drawing-

---

[1] Since he became the possessor of Farringford, he found his quiet home and living with his wife and children the happiest place and life. Yet he was also extremely hospitable, often inviting not only his friends but the friends of his friends, and giving them a hearty welcome. For underneath a sensitive exterior he was thoroughly genial if he was understood. B. J.

room reading a book.   At other times, especially to ladies, he was singularly gracious and benevolent.   He would talk about the accidents of his own life with an extraordinary freedom, as at the moment they appeared to present themselves to his mind, the days of his boyhood that were passed at Somersby, and the old school of manners which he came across in his own neighbourhood: the days of the "apostles" at Cambridge: the years which he spent in London; the evenings enjoyed at the Cock Tavern, and elsewhere, when he saw another side of life, not without a kindly and humorous [1] sense of the ridiculous in his fellow-creatures.   His repertory of stories was perfectly inexhaustible; they were often about slight matters that would scarcely bear repetition, but were told with such lifelike reality, that they convulsed his hearers with laughter.   Like most story-tellers, he often repeated his favourites; but, like children, his audience liked hearing them again and again, and he enjoyed telling them.   It might be said of him that he told more stories than anyone, but was by no means the regular story-teller.   In the commonest conversation he showed himself a man of genius. His tales were full of dramatic life, owing to the great love and interest which he had for human things everywhere [2], far beyond the wonders either of Nature or of Art.   The latter was connected with the poetical side of him, the former with the human realization of life.

Most of Tennyson's friends remember a small room high up at the top of the house [Farringford], formerly very bare except for books, afterwards made more comfortable, to which, when dinner was over, he retired, and, sometimes after half-an-hour's solitude, invited his friends to join him [3].

We either smoked with him, or, if we did not smoke, we had the privilege of hearing him talk, and of talking with him. This was his temple, or it might be termed his den, where his poems and a few favourite books were kept.   It was a sign of more intimate friendship to be allowed to visit him there.   At

---

[1] His humour was constant; and he never or hardly ever made puns or witticisms, but always lived in an attitude of humour.   B. J.

[2] He was not a man of the world in the ordinary sense, but a man who had the greatest insight into the world, and often in a word or sentence flashed a light.   B. J.

[3] However many easy chairs there might be in a room, he always chose the hardest with the most upright back.

such times, if he was not deterred by shyness, he said just what came into his head. But, in general he was very free and frank; he had nothing to conceal, and he felt so keenly, that if he had, he could not have concealed it. He used to utter strong thoughts in strong language, about recent discoveries in Science, about the politics of the day, about the deeper mysteries of human life. On a few topics he would discourse again and again with undiminished energy. There was, perhaps, no political matter in which he took so deep an interest as the defence of his country. He would often, in fancy, draw pictures, half-ludicrous, of the consequences of an invasion to himself, as an inhabitant of the Isle of Wight. In projects for the extension of suffrage he took no part; it was another kind of ideal, much more distant, on which his eye was fixed. Hence he combined a singular affection for the great statesman who has become the wonder of the English world, with a recoil from his policy. "I love Gladstone," he said, "but I hate his Home-rule policy." This was the sum of many political conversations; but he never studied to put together or to systematize his views. "Locksley Hall," although spoken in the character of a disappointed lover, contains the sum of his politics when he was a young man, and though he wrote an epilogue to the poem sixty years later, the point of view from which he regarded the world in this poem was never really altered, but only underwent the natural change of old age. The daily and weekly movements of politics, which, like the weather, are always changing, made little or no impression upon him; the weight of the unknown seemed to fall upon him more heavily.

In Natural Science he took a deep interest. In the first years of his childhood his great-grandfather had taught him some of the wonders of the starry heavens, in a manner which remained with him throughout life. Some paragraph in a newspaper or magazine about a comet, or fixed star, would often catch his eye; these he would invest with a light and life which he himself gave to them. He was greatly pleased at being informed that Mr Procter had said of him that there were no mistakes about the stars in his poems, and a similar compliment was paid to him by an eminent botanist about flowers. He probably never went out on a starlight night without "thoughts too deep for tears" arising within him. He had the keenest and most delicate sense of the beauties of Nature. From his own windows he beheld, daily, one of the most perfect sea-views in England, — the line of coast stretching from the Downs at Freshwater along the whole south-east coast of the Isle of Wight. He rejoiced in the sun and sky and sea, and would often walk down to the sands at Freshwater, about half-a-mile distant from his house, to pay his respects to some unusual excitement of the ocean. He was a student, like Ruskin, of the ways of the clouds, as well as of the paths of the sea. They seemed to enter into his soul and to whisper new thoughts to him. Having been brought up in the country, and having lived there during the greater part of his life, he learned many things about plants and flowers which his capacious memory ever after-wards retained. It was not so much that his mind was always wandering from one scene to another, as that it seized upon things that he saw or imagined with an extraordinary power and intensity. He would have liked to have known more of astronomy and botany. It was one of his unfulfilled wishes, which he was continually repeating, to have seen the Tropics, but it is doubtful whether this greater variety and curiousness of knowledge would have made him a better poet.

He was very much of a scholar, but was not at all a pedant. Once he said to me, "I hate learning," by which I understood him to mean that he hated the minutiæ of criticism compiled by the Dryasdusts. They seemed to him to have no life in them, and to arrive at no result. More than thirty years ago I re-member his making what appeared at the time a very striking remark, namely, that "the true origin of modern Biblical Criticism was to be ascribed not to Strauss, but to Niebuhr, who lived a generation earlier." He was what might be called a good scholar, in the University or Public School sense of the term; his father before him had been a scholar, and he inherited as well as acquired a good, accurate knowledge of Latin and Greek. Yet I seem to remember that he had his favourite Classics, such as Homer, and Pindar, and Theocritus. The books which were chiefly read at Eton more than half a century ago were best known to him, and not those which, since the days of Porson and Hermann, have chiefly occupied the attention of the youths of England. He was also a lover of Greek fragments. But I am not sure whether, in later life, he ever sat down to read consecutively the greatest works of Æschylus and Sophocles, although he used occasionally to dip into them. French, German, and Italian he picked up by himself, not attaining any great proficiency in them, but sufficient to enable him to read them with ease. He had a profound respect for Goethe. It is worthy of remark, because it was a remark made by himself, that the description of Ulysses in the poem bearing that name is derived not from Homer, but from Dante.

Several of his poems are the result of deep study. Like Milton, he had early been impressed by the Legend of King Arthur, and had intended to weave it into a new form. This was, perhaps, the earliest of his poetical dreams, but it was not one of them which was destined to be carried out. The great work which he had designed was in no respect like the so-called "Idylls" which have become so familiar to the public. His purpose was to have in some way or other represented in it the great religions of the world: but although it was definitely planned, this poem never saw the light. He offered to show me the rough sketch of it, but on enquiring some years afterwards about it, I found that it had already been destroyed. This change of purpose may be attributed to two reasons. First, because the time when he was meditating this poem was the time at which the greatest calamity befell him. One can hardly conceive the overwhelming impression made on a mind like Tennyson's by the loss of a friend who was more than all the world to him [A. H. Hallam]. Secondly, at this time, there also came upon him another great blow, the coldness and even malignity which attended his first efforts, when he had a very few admirers, and a host of enemies.

It is a proof of Tennyson's genius that he should have thus early grasped the great historical aspect of religion.

It may further be doubted whether the work could have been executed, or would have been understood, sixty years ago, at a time when men's minds were so little acquainted with Oriental speculations, and were so hide-bound in the controversies of Protestantism and Romanism.

To return to the "Den." Tennyson was constantly speaking of the thoughts which occupied his own mind, in which the following characteristics might be traced : — A strong desire to vindicate the ways of God to man, and, perhaps, to demonstrate a pertinacity on the part of man in demanding of God his rights. He was not a sceptic in the least degree, though deeply impressed by the wonder and mystery of the world which surrounded him, especially its physical character. He was one of those who, though not an upholder of miracle-mongers, thought that the wonders of Heaven and Earth were never far absent from us. He had many stories to tell about Mesmerism, which had some effect upon his mind, though he can hardly be said to have seriously considered the subject. There is no trace of such stories anywhere in his writings. He was very impressible, and very willing to believe what he was told by anybody whom he *knew*. Yet it would be equally true to say that he was quite unaffected by the opinions of others. He had the susceptibility of a child, or of a woman; he had also (it was a strange combination) the strength of a giant, or of a God.

There was no one to whom he was so absolutely devoted, no poet of whom he had a more intimate knowledge, than Shakespeare. He said to me, and probably to many others, that there was one intellectual process in the world of which he could not even entertain an apprehension — that was, the Plays of Shakespeare. He thought that he could instinctively distinguish between the genuine and the spurious in them, e.g. between those parts of *King Henry VIII.* which are generally admitted to be spurious, and those that are genuine. The same thought was partly working in his mind on another occasion, when he spoke of two things, which he conceived to be beyond the intelligence of man, and it was certainly not repeated by him from any irreverence; the one, the intellectual genius of Shakespeare — the other the religious genius of Jesus Christ.

It was in the spirit of an old saint or mystic, and not of a modern rationalist, that Tennyson habitually thought and felt about the nature of Christ. Never did the slightest shadow of ridicule or profaneness mix itself up with the applications which he made of Scripture, although he was quite aware that there were many points on which he differed widely from the so-called Evangelical, or High-Church world, and he always strove to keep religion free from the taint of ridicule.

There were some other peculiarities about him, which have furnished endless material for gossip, and which have never yet been properly explained. Persons have often asked how such a king among men could have been so sensitive to the opinions of the public. It seems to them unmanly that he who was one of the greatest men of the century should have been unable to stand up against the prejudices of the vulgar. It was easier to understand when looked at a little more closely. It was not really a desire of praise, or fear of blame which actuated him — he was above such feelings as these: but he was grieved at the injustice and meanness of mankind which was always seeking to depreciate the fair fame of another, which, the greater or nobler a man is, is always the more eager to decry him. He doubtless experienced a great deal of pain from the attacks of his enemies. I never remember his receiving the least pleasure from the commendations of his friends. The truth seemed to be that, as his fame became established in the world, he hardly thought much of what was said of him[1]. The feeling of pleasure, which was not wanting in him, was due to an appreciation of himself in his own breast. He felt that he saw more truly than others how far he had succeeded and how far he had failed in the attainment of his purpose; all else was really as nothing to him. He once asked me which I thought the most touching lines in any of his works. I ventured to reply, the lines in "Maud," beginning:

O that 'twere possible
After long grief and pain
To find the arms of my true love
Round me once again!

He gave some sign of assent to the answer, adding, by the way, that they were not originally meant for that place. I have no doubt that innumerable verses of his, which gave so much pleasure to the rest of the world, have also given the truest and most natural pleasure to himself.

If it were possible, with propriety, I should like to say something about the wife who survives him, though I am aware that such a subject is beyond the proper limits of the biography. I can only speak of her as one of the most beautiful, the purest, the most innocent, the most disinterested persons whom I have ever known. He once told me, as indeed he told some things to everybody, which others keep to themselves, how she said to him, "When I pray I see the face of God smiling upon me." Such is the spirit of this remarkable life. As there is no chance of her giving me leave to repeat these words, and as I was not forbidden to do so by him, I venture to snatch them from the numberless sacred words which passed between them. It is no

[1] He never allowed himself to be puffed in the newspapers if he could possibly prevent it. B. J.

wonder that people speak of her with bated breath, as a person whom no one would ever think of criticising, whom everyone would recognize, in goodness and saintliness, as the most unlike anyone whom they have ever met. Though not claiming to possess intellectual powers, which she assuredly has, she was probably her husband's best critic, and certainly the one whose authority he would most willingly have recognized. Yet, with all her saintliness, she is not at all puritanical in her views, either in regard to him, or to anyone else. She has considerable sense of humour, and is remarkably considerate about her guests. The greatest influence of his life would have to be passed over in silence if I were to omit her name. These few lines I have ventured to insert without the permission of you, Hallam, lest by some inadvertence matters so important should pass out of remembrance.

She thinks a good deal about the conditions of society. She says that she is glad to have protracted life by a few years because she has come to see how small, comparatively, are the differences of good people, and how great the agreements. During the last thirty years and more, she has preserved not only life, but almost youth, on her sofa. She said to me, "About a future life we know hardly anything, but that little is enough." She is a lover of the good old times, and especially of the poor, though I must admit that she seems to me to wish to combine the happy condition of all classes, more than Political Economy can truly allow. And though she knows that "The old order changeth, yielding place to new," and that the liberties of England were not carried without many struggles, she thinks that the life of Christ and of St John may have a place in the world such as she has known in her youth. Yet she never for a moment desires that the world, or that mankind, should take a step backward in their course. By a happy inconsistency she thinks only of the good, and seems. to have forgotten all the evils of the past. To her, whatever is best in the past is the only type of good in the future which has been allowed to survive. A lady, well known in the world, who was a friend of Emily and Alfred Tennyson, Mrs Cameron, and through them, of myself, used to say to me, that, though unknown, "she was as great as he was."

Should this remark of Mrs Cameron's ever fall into Lady Tennyson's hands, she will only wonder that anyone should

seriously have thought that her husband shared his greatness
with her, yet one who knew them both intimately is conscious
that the poet himself was aware that these words were truly
spoken.

Jowett had not quite finished this paper, and a few days
before his death wrote to me as follows:

I had several more things to say about your father, but
I think I had better stop here, because I have a distinct recollection of these being his utterances, but of other things I cannot
be so sure, nor of the sense in which he meant them. I have
been myself caught rather more suddenly than I expected. I
cannot express the depth of gratitude which I owe to your
father and mother. Would that I could have done more justice
to their memories.

Yours affectionately, B. JOWETT.

1893.

LETTER FROM J. A. FROUDE.

1894.

I owe to your father the first serious reflexions upon life
and the nature of it which have followed me for more than
fifty years. The same voice speaks to me now as I come near
my own end, from beyond the bar. Of the early poems "Love
and Death" had the deepest effect upon me. The same thought
is in the last lines of the last poems which we shall ever have
from him.

Your father in my estimate stands and will stand far away
by the side of Shakespeare above all other English Poets, with
this relative superiority even to Shakespeare, that he speaks the
thoughts and speaks *to* the perplexities and misgivings of
his own age.

He was born at the fit time before the world had grown
inflated with the vanity of Progress, and there was still an
atmosphere in which such a soul could grow. There will be
no such others for many a long age.

Yours gratefully, J. A. FROUDE.

A GLIMPSE OF FARRINGFORD, 1858;
AND "THE ANCIENT SAGE," 1885[1].

MY DEAR HALLAM,

Rude and repeated assaults upon my health during the last two years have left me but little strength for the task you would impose upon me. Last summer was spent among the Alps, in the hope that the mere presence of scenes of former vigour and delight would do something towards restoring the forces I had lost. For eleven weeks we clung to our lofty solitude. Southwards and westwards the mountains rose in glory, while to the east and north stretched the noble glacier which for five-and-thirty years on and off had been my playground. I was never able to approach it. On the 3rd of October we set out for home. I could not ride downwards, while transport by chair was abhorrent to me; I therefore descended on foot, with a strong arm near me ready to help in case of need. My guide was a pious Catholic. Prompted by some local circumstance, he halted at a certain point and said: "*Herr Professor, Sie wollen es nicht übel nehmen?*" (You will not take it amiss?) He then described to me some wonderful cures that had been wrought at a neighbouring shrine, and most earnestly recommended the celebration of a solemn mass at that shrine for my recovery "It can do no harm," he urged; to which I cordially agreed. "But," I added, "the cures are always performed on believers, and I unfortunately am not a believer." This was admitted to be a difficulty, so we jogged amicably downwards.

From Brieg, with a loving companion beside me, I crept down the valley of the Rhone — halting two nights at Sierre, two at Vernayaz, and two at Lausanne. Here the news of your father's death reached us — Louisa first, me afterwards; for I was low at the time and she delayed the communication of intelligence which she knew must sink me lower still. On Monday the 10th, Miss Marryat, daughter of the celebrated novelist, secured for me a copy of the *Times*, wherein I read the brief and touching account by Dr Dabbs of the passing away of Tennyson.

Your father's interest in science was profound, but not, I believe, unmingled with fear of its "materialistic" tendencies. This, however,

[1] A Fragment, by John Tyndall, written in the autumn of 1892.

is to me a point of secondary importance. His influence on the life of a scientific man touches me more closely. You were not born when that influence in my case began. Fifty years ago, in the sixth chapter of Carlyle's *Past and Present* I found the line :

"There dwells the great Achilles whom we knew" ;

to which was attached a footnote referring the line to Tennyson. At the time here referred to, Thomas Carlyle was the inspirer and strengthener of the noblest minds known to me. This footnote assured me that Tennyson was a poet whose acquaintance must be made without delay. Not very long afterwards, two young men might have been seen eagerly engaged upon a volume, in the corner of a modest hotel in St Martin's Court, Covent Garden. The one read, the other listened. The one, after a life of usefulness and honour, was snatched from us last year by influenza, and now lies in Highgate Cemetery, the other remains to record the fact. The book in which my friend Hirst and I were then absorbed was entitled " Poems by Alfred Tennyson."

I do not know whether scientific men generally have found the warming up of the imagination as beneficial to them as it has been to me. Be that as it may, writings apparently far apart from science have often spurred me on in the pursuit of science. In 1849 I had gone to the University of Marburg in Hesse-Cassel ; and the antithesis of my intellectual disciplines at that time is revealed by a brief remark in my journal on October 19th, 1850 : "I must now turn from Tennyson, to whom I had appealed for inspiration, to Lefebre de Fourcy," a dry mathematician. I may anticipate matters here by quoting an entry of later date. I had declined a position in London which I might well have been proud to occupy, and in reference to this subject, I write : "Many of my friends will deem me unpractical for refusing such an offer. Bence Jones, indeed, has already discovered from my letters that I am ' poetical.' Be it so. If poetry make me a dreamer, so much the worse for me. If it make me a worker, so much the better."

Under the date of Sunday, 20th October, 1850, I find the following entry : "Up at 6 A.M. and began the day by reading Tennyson. I am acquainted with no spirit so strong, pure, and beautiful. Every line sparkles with empyreal fire, so that it is difficult to make a selection. I will, however, notice ' The Two Voices,' simply because Tom [Hirst] has not placed upon it his prize mark. In this poem the tempter to despair is furnished with his best weapons, and foiled though armed *cap-à-pie*." Your father's dear friend and mine, the late excellent James Spedding, first drew my attention to the definition of poetry as "a fine excess," and certainly the effect of your father's inspired language upon the two young men above referred to could not be better expressed. It was wine to our intellects, and many a night between ten and eleven, during the winter of 1850–51, after the scientific labours of the day were over, we quaffed together of this noble vintage.

In 1853, after a health-excursion to the Blocksberg, with *Faust* in my pocket and the scenes of the Walpurgis-nacht around me, I joined the Royal Institution. In his sweet wisdom, Faraday, perhaps on the whole the tenderest and most beautiful spirit that I have known, looked after my welfare. One of his earliest monitions to me was: "Tyndall, take care of your health." It occasionally broke down under stress of work, and I took strong measures to restore it. Cumberland, Westmorland and Wales were respectively laid under contribution. But the sanative influence brought to bear upon me was of a dual nature, and I am not sure whether in those excursions your father's verses had not as much to do as the mountain air with the restitution of my vigour. It was my habit as I walked to refresh myself by reciting passages aloud, sometimes from one poem, sometimes from another, most frequently perhaps from "Œnone." On one occasion I remember straining up Styehead Pass in Cumberland, with a horse-cloth thrown over me as a defence against the torrential rain, while the lines on *Will* at the end of "Maud," beginning:

O well for him whose Will is strong!

rang out cheerily among the crags.

But the place most frequently visited, because it was nearest to me, was the Isle of Wight. For many years my favourite expedition was a foot journey round the southern coast to the Needles; returning along the central spine of the island to Carisbrooke and Newport; thence to Cowes, and back by way of Southampton to London. Early in the month of April 1858, accompanied by the eldest son of Dr Bence Jones, I was upon the island. I took the usual coast line to Freshwater Gate, and put up at Plumbley's Hotel. Letters had been addressed to me to the post-office, Freshwater, and these, I know not why, had been forwarded to Farringford. The letters were afterwards sent to the hotel, accompanied by a note from Mrs Tennyson, inviting me to dinner. Her inherent courtesy expressed itself in the words: "Will you pardon Mr. Tennyson that he is not himself the bearer of this?" I had often wished to meet the poet, but had never made a move towards securing this pleasure. "It is wonderful," I remark in my journal, "how things gravitate in this world. Here is a great pleasure and a great privilege come to me without my seeking." On

Tuesday, 5th April, I first called on Mrs Tennyson. After a time the poet himself appeared — a fine, strong, frank-looking man, with large forehead and dark beard. The sound of his voice was straightforward and brotherly. It seemed the vehicle of perfect candour of thought. He always spoke without fear or concealment, as if animated by a grand and formidable innocence. The visit here referred to was a "morning call." We were engaged to dine, and were informed that we should meet Mr Jowett at dinner. After talking for half an hour, about Frederick Maurice, about the adjacent Down, the daffodils upon the lawn and the resemblance of their colour to the hues of sunset, I came away. At the hour appointed we went to Farringford, and found Mr Jowett already there. This was my first meeting with the learned and hospitable Master of Balliol. He was ruddy and of a fair countenance, and yet his hair was gray. Two fine little boys — probably in Tennyson's estimation his best poems — joined us at dinner. They came trustfully and lovingly forward and kissed me. They had inherited, or had been taught, their father's straightforwardness. We spoke of the Tyrol, which Mrs Tennyson would like to visit; of North Wales, of Switzerland and my climb up Mont Blanc. I also referred to my ascent of Styehead Pass with the poem on *Will* upon my tongue. But, wishing to be true to the science of the subject, I added that we must fall back in the long run on muscular force. This was a lowering of motive power from the moral to the physical; and, deeming probably that I had laid too much stress on the material side of the question, Mrs Tennyson turned towards me with that ethereal expression which Watts has seized so faithfully in his splendid portrait, and remarked quietly, "You can at all events walk till you die." Taken in conjunction with her obviously frail physique, I thought the remark an impressive example of spiritual force and resolution.

After talking for some time about the influence and limits of the will, Tennyson turned to me and said, "I am glad that you are not one of those who disdain to quote 'Maud.'" We discussed the poem for some time, and he laid some stress upon the manner in which it ought to be read. We passed on to speak of the moon, of the change in its apparent size as it approached the horizon, then to the colours of the clouds, the hue of the firmament, and my work among the mountains of Switzerland. Later on we joined Mrs Tennyson, for a moment, and then I accompanied the poet to his sanctum upstairs. There was a table on which lay a large scientific volume, a sofa, some chairs, and a rack over the chimney-piece in which were stuck fifteen or twenty pipes. The draws of the table were crammed with tobacco of various kinds. He warned me not to smoke if I was not accustomed to it. I was, however, sufficiently educated to bear a pull. He filled a pipe for me, lit it himself, and transferred it to my lips. We puffed sociably side by side and continued to speak about "Maud." Surely the critics ought to be careful of the power which they wield. "Maud" had been savagely reviewed by the London press; but no journal would venture to speak of it now save in terms of admiration. Tennyson affirmed that the oftener he read the poem the more he was convinced of its merits. It was, he considered, one of the best things he had ever done. The criticisms of the press irritated him. At Farringford, he pointed out, he was withdrawn from the world, and on taking up a paper and finding himself misconstrued and abused he suffered keen annoyance. "A flea will annoy me. Just feel my skin," he added, baring his wrist; "a flea-bite will spread a square inch over its surface. The term thin-skinned is perfectly expressive. I *am* thin-skinned, and I take no pains to hide it. I know it would be considered more dignified if I encased myself in a crust like Goethe; but that is not my nature. People imagine that I have described myself in 'Maud,' that it is the flower of my own life, and they ask, 'Is this all he has to give us?' Nothing could be more absurd. It is the vice of the age that a man cannot say anything without its being supposed to be personal." The writer of an article in the *Westminster Review* had affirmed that all kindness had deserted the poet. Among other things he was denounced for his supposed attack upon John Bright. Tennyson declared that he had no thought of John Bright when he spoke of the "broad-brimm'd hawker of holy things." He had no knowledge at the time that John Bright was a Quaker. The result of the reviewing, however, was that while 10,000 copies of the first edition of "Maud" had been sold, only 390 of the second edition had been disposed of.

We were joined by Mr. Jowett. Some time previously Buckle had lectured at the Royal Institution, and we spoke of his lecture and of scientific methods generally. While conceding its due place to "deduction," and admitting the power of imagination as an instrument of scientific discovery, both Jowett and Tennyson thought Buckle's lecture an empty performance. The "Master" having bidden us "Goodnight," we continued our conversation. It presently became intensely interesting. With great earnestness Tennyson described to me a state of consciousness into which he could throw himself by thinking intently of his own name. It was impossible to give anything that could be called a description of the state, for language seemed incompetent to touch it. It was an apparent isolation of the spirit from the body. Wishing doubtless to impress upon me the reality of the phenomenon, he exclaimed, "By God Almighty, there is no delusion in the matter! It is no nebulous ecstasy, but a state of transcendent wonder, associated with absolute clearness of mind." Other persons with powerful imaginations have had, I believe, similar experiences. Walking out with a friend one evening, the poet Wordsworth approached a gate, and laying hold of its bars, turned to his companion and said, " My dear sir, to assure myself of the existence of my own body, I am sometimes obliged to grasp an object like this and shake it." It was at the Bel Alp, and I believe by the late Professor Bonamy Price, that this incident was communicated to me. The condition here referred to appears to be similar to that " union with God" which was described by Plotinus and Porphyry. From this subject we passed on to the present condition of religion in this country. Tennyson looked with confidence to the development of Christianity, but the religion of our sects was not Christianity. The *Record* and the *Univers* though apparently hostile, were quite alike. He held undoubtingly the doctrine of a personal immortality, and was by no means content to accept our present existence as a mere preparation for the life of more perfect beings. He had once asked John Sterling whether he would be content with such an arrangement, and Sterling had replied that he would. " I would *not*," added Tennyson emphatically; " I should consider that a liberty had been taken with me if I were made simply a means of ushering in something higher than myself." Thus we conversed,  with perfect frankness and cordiality — he with his foot against the bar of the grate, and I with my shoulder against a shelf at my right. Descending from our attic and having bid Mrs Tennyson " Goodnight," I was led through a series of rooms hung with pictures to a back-door which enabled me to take the shortest route to my hotel. Our parting was exceedingly cordial. He wished me to come again — to tea, to dinner, at all events to come. In fact we separated as if we had known each other for years.

The weather was stormy during this visit to the island, and the sea at times was very wild. By day and night I occasionally sat near the shore observing the advance of the waves and listening to their thunder. The pebbles and shingles on the beach are mainly of flint, and emit a sharp sound on collision with each other. As the billows break and roll up the beach, they carry the shingle along with them, and on their retreat they drag it downwards. Here the collisions of the flint pebbles are innumerable. They blend together in a continuous sound which could not be better described than by the line in " Maud " :

　Now to the scream of a madden'd beach dragg'd down by the
　　wave [1].

[1] Actually written about the beach at Freshwater.

I thought the line when I first read it intensely pictorial. It was denounced as extravagant. In this respect, however, as in others, the reviewers, or their wiser successors, have attained to a sounder judgment.

On the 7th I was again with the poet in his little room at the top of the house. The noble Atlas of Keith Johnston lay upon his table. In regard to metaphors drawn from science, your father, like Carlyle, made sure of their truth. To secure accuracy, he spared no pains. I found in his room charts of isothermals and isobars intended to ensure the exactitude of certain allusions of his to physical science. In illustration of this, the late Lord Houghton, while still Mr Monckton Milnes, once told me that, having composed an exquisite poem upon a flower, Tennyson discarded it because of some botanical flaw. In comparing him with Carlyle, I notice that the latter drew his imagery, for the most part, from what we call inorganic nature. Physics and chemistry were well advanced when Carlyle wrote, but modern researches in biology had scarcely begun. These latter fell into your father's hands, and he has made noble use of them from "In Memoriam" onwards. I asked him on this occasion for some explanation of a passage in "The Vision of Sin":

God made Himself an awful rose of dawn.

He replied that the power of explaining such concentrated expressions of the imagination was very different from that of writing them. "What I say," he added, "will be considered nonsense by some, but you will not so consider it." We talked of Campbell and Wordsworth. He admired the bold swing of "The Battle of the Baltic," though it had some very faulty lines. He took me up rather quickly when I referred to the verse beginning:

"But the might of England flushed
To anticipate the scene";

remarking that it was the most faulty line in the piece. I did not however intend to detach the line from its context. I meant to refer to the whole passage.

"'Hearts of oak!' our captains cried; when each gun
From its adamantine lips
Spread a death-shade round the ships,
Like the hurricane eclipse
Of the sun."

These lines Tennyson considered very fine.

It may be worth while to mention here how I first made the acquaintance of "Maud." Rachel had come to the Haymarket Theatre for a few representations, and I, anxious to see and hear the great actress, engaged a stall. I had picked up "Maud" at a bookseller's in Piccadilly as I went to the theatre. I had never seen your father then, but his previous work justified my anticipations of delight. I had read several pages before the play began. I read between the acts, lowering the book to catch sufficient light from the stage. Once I went out, and walked to and fro between St James's Square and the theatre, still reading. Before I reached my lodgings I had finished the poem. I thought it true, strong and beautiful; and soon afterwards, meeting Mr Monckton Milnes in Glasgow, I expressed to him my opinion. He emphatically agreed with me. "It is beautiful," he exclaimed, "and the reviewers are blundering." Lord Houghton, I may say, was a loyal soul, and he was to the backbone an Englishman, proud of the historic greatness of his country. His mode of life was one that I should not desire to imitate, but his friendship was steadfast; and to none perhaps more steadfast than to your father and Carlyle.

In the year 1885, that is to say twenty-eight years after the time here referred to, were published *Tiresias, and other Poems*, by Alfred Lord Tennyson. For a copy of this remarkable volume I am indebted to its author. It contains a poem called "The Ancient Sage[1]." The Sage, who existed "a thousand summers ere the time of Christ," is described as having quitted his ancient city, followed by one who loved and honoured him, but who nevertheless was not his disciple. The younger man was "richly garb'd, but worn from wasteful living." He bore in his hand a scroll of verse. At the mouth of a cavern from which "an affluent fountain pour'd," the old man halted, turned and spoke:

> What hast thou there? Some deathsong for the Ghouls
> To make their banquet relish? let me read.

The allusions to "wasteful living" and "some deathsong for the Ghouls" indicate clearly the light in which Tennyson viewed the younger man. His moral and religious fibre are gone, and in particular he has lost all belief in a life after death. He is, briefly, what we should call a materialist, and the object of the nineteenth-century poet is to combat, through the mouth of the Sage, the errors of this view.

[1] "The Ancient Sage" is not the philosophy of the Chinese philosopher Laot-ze, but it was written after reading his life and maxims. A. T.'s MS note.

I would here remark, once for all, that the passages read from the young man's scroll, so far from being the language of a libertine — so far from being a "deathsong for the Ghouls" — are of a quality which no libertine or associate of Ghouls could possibly have produced. Supreme beauty and delicacy of language are not consistent with foul companionship, and never, even in Tennyson's own pages, has language assumed a form more surpassingly beautiful, more instinct with celestial melody, than in these passages quoted by the Ancient Sage.

> How far thro' all the bloom and brake
> That nightingale is heard!
> What power but the bird's could make
> This music in the bird?
> How summer-bright are yonder skies,
> And earth as fair in hue!
> And yet what sign of aught that lies
> Behind the green and blue?

This is exquisite. But to my mind the gem of the "Scroll" is to be found further on. The younger man had loved, and he had lost his love. My judgment may seem extravagant, but I do not think the English language has ever before been wrought into music equal to that of the lover's threnody.

> The years that when my Youth began
> Had set the lily and rose
> By all my ways where'er they ran,
> Have ended mortal foes,
> My rose of love for ever gone,
> My lily of truth and trust —
> They made her lily and rose in one,
> And changed her into dust.
>
> O rosetree planted in my grief,
> And growing, on her tomb,
> Her dust is greening in your leaf,
> Her blood is in your bloom.
> O slender lily waving there,
> And laughing back the light,
> In vain you tell me "Earth is fair"
> When all is dark as night.

My special purpose in introducing this poem, however, was to call your attention to a passage further on which greatly interested me.

The poem is, throughout, a discussion between a believer in immortality and one who is unable to believe. The method pursued
is this. The Sage reads a portion of the scroll, which he has taken
from the hands of his follower, and then brings his own arguments
to bear upon that portion, with a view to neutralising the scepticism
of the younger man. Let me here remark that I had read the whole
series of poems published under the title " Tiresias," full of admiration
for their freshness and vigour. Seven years after I had first read them
your father died, and you, his son, asked me to contribute a chapter
to the book which you contemplate publishing. I knew that I had
some small store of references to my interview with your father carefully written in ancient journals. On the receipt of your request, I
looked up the account of my first visit to Farringford, and there,
to my profound astonishment, I found described that experience of
your father's which, in the mouth of the Ancient Sage, was made the
ground of an important argument against materialism and in favour
of personal immortality eight-and-twenty years afterwards. In no other
poem during all these years is, to my knowledge, this experience once
alluded to. I had completely forgotten it, but here it was recorded
in black and white. If you turn to your father's account of the wonderful state of consciousness superinduced by thinking of his own name,
and compare it with the argument of the Ancient Sage, you will see
that they refer to one and the same phenomenon.

And more, my son ! for more than once when I
Sat all alone, revolving in myself
The word that is the symbol of myself,
The mortal limit of the Self was loosed,
And past into the Nameless, as a cloud
Melts into Heaven. I touch'd my limbs, the limbs
Were strange, not mine — and yet no shade of doubt,
But utter clearness, and thro' loss of Self
The gain of such large life as match'd with ours
Were Sun to spark — unshadowable in words,
Themselves but shadows of a shadow-world.

*   *   *   *   *   *

[Left unfinished and uncorrected Dec. 1893.]

IMPRESSIONS, BY T. WATTS-DUNTON.

1883–1892.

All are agreed that D. G. Rossetti's was a peculiarly winning personality, but no one has been in the least able to say why. Nothing is easier, however, than to find the charm of Tennyson. It lay in a great veracity of soul: it lay in a simple single-mindedness, so child-like that, unless you had known him to have been the undoubted author of poems as marvellous for exquisite art as for inspiration, you could not have supposed but that all subtleties — even those of poetic art — must be foreign to a nature so simple.

Working in a language like ours — a language which has to be moulded into harmony by a myriad subtleties of art — how can this great, inspired, simple nature be the delicate-fingered artist of "The Princess," "The Palace of Art," "The Day-Dream," and "The Dream of Fair Women"?

Tennyson knew of but one justification for the thing he said, viz., that it was the thing he thought. Behind his uncompromising directness was apparent a noble and a splendid courtesy of the grand old type. As he stood at the porch at Aldworth meeting a guest or bidding him good-bye — as he stood there, tall far beyond the height of average men, his skin showing dark and tanned by the sun and wind — as he stood there no one could mistake him for anything but a great forthright English gentleman. Always a man of an extraordinary beauty of presence, he showed up to the last the beauty of old age to a degree rarely seen. He was the most hospitable of men. It was very rare indeed for him to part with a guest without urging him to return, and generally with the words, "Come whenever you like."

Tennyson's knowledge of nature — nature in every aspect — was simply astonishing. His passion for "star-gazing" has often been commented upon by readers of his poetry. Since Dante no poet in any land has so loved the stars. He had an equal delight in watching the lightning; and I remember being at Aldworth once during a thunder-storm when I was alarmed at the temerity with which he persisted, in spite of all remonstrances, in gazing at the blinding lightning. For moonlight effects he had a passion equally strong, and it is especially pathetic to those who know this to remember that he passed away in the light he so much loved — in a room where there was no artificial light — nothing to quicken the darkness but the light of the full moon, which somehow seems to shine more brightly at Aldworth than anywhere else in England.

In a country having a composite language such as ours it may be affirmed with special emphasis that there are two kinds of poetry: one appealing to the uncultivated masses, the other appealing to the few who are sensitive to the felicitous expression of deep thought and to the true beauties of poetic art.

Of all poets Shakespeare is the most popular, and yet in his use of what Dante calls the " sieve for noble words " his skill transcends that of even Milton, Coleridge, Shelley, and Keats. His felicities of thought and of diction in the great passages seem little short of miraculous and there are so many that it is easy to understand why he is so often spoken of as being a kind of inspired improvisatore. That he was *not* an improvisatore, however, anyone can see who will take the trouble to compare the first edition of *Romeo and Juliet* with the received text, the first sketch of *The Merry Wives of Windsor* with the play as we now have it, and the *Hamlet* of 1603 with the *Hamlet* of 1604, and with the still further varied version of the play given by Heminge and Condell in the Folio of 1623. Next to Shakespeare in this great power of combining the forces of the two great classes of English poets, appealing both to the commonplace public and to the artistic sense of the few, stands, perhaps, Chaucer; but since Shakespeare's time no one has met with anything like Tennyson's success in effecting a reconciliation between popular and artistic sympathy with poetry in England.

LETTER FROM FREDERIC W. H. MYERS.

You have asked me, knowing well what pleasure the request would give me, to send you a few words, not of formal criticism, but of expression of intimate feeling as to your father's work ; — your father, a greater man than whom I have never looked and shall never look upon. You tell me to approach the subject, " not from the side of Plotinus, but from the side of Virgil." I understand what you mean. On your father's prophetic message, as I must deem it, I have already said my say ; and the other point at which my sympathy was deepest was in our common veneration for Virgil.

Such veneration is no chance preference or literary idiosyncrasy. Rather it implies the instructed, the comprehending acceptance of a certain ideal of the poetic art. It would be absurd, indeed, to draw up poets in two opposite camps ; especially absurd in treating of a poet whom those who best appreciated Romanticism held as romantic, while those who best appreciated Classicism felt him as classic to the core. Yet the words thus used express a real distinction ; and it is well to draw out their meaning and to realise how we regard their leading exemplars. In each art, then, we tend to call the type *romantic* when the artist strives above all things to make his work fresh, vivid, interesting ; infusing into it individual emotion, interweaving with it the attractiveness of other forms of art ; filling it, as one may say, with the pulse and breath of life. The aim of him whom we call the classical artist is at first sight a narrower one. For his absorbing and primary desire is to carry to its utmost height that innate and inexplicable charm in the relations of sound or line or rhythm or colour which makes the essential principle of his art. When he fails, he degenerates into a *virtuoso*. When he succeeds, he enters in some sort into the hidden heritage of emotion which maintains the life of Art itself ; and although his public may sometimes be small, he gives to *cognoscenti* a joy at least as penetrating and vital as any which the romanticist can bestow. Each type, I say, has its dangers, but there is need of both ; not only of Wagner, but of Beethoven ; not only of Shakespeare, but of Virgil.

Yet into such estimations there enters a practical question, which in judging of poetry is too often ignored. In order to appreciate the severer type of any art, long training is required. In music or painting no one questions the need of special and technical preparation, not only before a man can create, but before he can fully understand. In poetry, on the other hand, there seems to most men to be nothing to learn. The mere mechanism of verse, the scheme of English prosody, comes by nature, or may be mastered in an hour. This done, the boy thinks that he may read as he likes, and make his study of poetry a holiday thing. But it is not so; there is that to learn which takes years in the learning. For myself, I am no fanatical advocate of a classical education,—a form of training which must needs lose its old unique position now that there is so much else to know. But for one small class of students such an education still seems to me essential; for those, namely, who desire to judge the highest poetry aright. Must it not needs be so? In all else we may be wiser than the ancients, but Evolution has not again produced a language or a race like the Greek. The *Exemplaria Græca* should still, as in the days of Horace, be the study of night and morn; and with the Greek, too, we must rank that small group of poets on whose lips the language of Rome also was worthy of the mistress of the world.

Yet with modern studies, in this crowded age, the modern man of letters is often content. And classical education itself has felt the influence of science, and tends to make history and philology, rather than poetry, its leading aims. But surely not philology nor history, but such a vital sense of the spirit of classical poetry as your father possessed, *that* is the true treasure of antiquity and the flower of the Past. For indeed the highest use of language, the highest use, one may say, of history itself, has been to bestow upon mankind a few thousand lines of poetry for which all other study of bygone ages is but practice and preparation, and which should become by endless broodings no mere acquisition from without, but the inmost structure and prepotent energy of the onward-striving soul.

> Praise Him who gave no gifts from oversea,
> But gave thyself to thee.

And this the long line of poets themselves have been the first to feel. They have recognised the true tradition, and lived again the ancient song.

> Quam pæne furvæ regna Proserpinæ
> Et judicantem vidimus Æacum
> Sedesque discretas piorum, et
> Æoliis fidibus querentem—

Those complaints, indeed, might seem ill to befit the ears of the pious, in their discrete abodes. Yet nothing draws us closer to Horace than this; his instinct in the face of death itself, that from Sappho's lips "things worthy of a sacred silence" must sound across the underworld.

What Horace here has done for Sappho, that Dante in his noblest passages, your father in his most perfect poem, have done for the *altissimo poeta*. The one has expressed the veneration of the modern, as the other of the mediæval world. And surely that ode "To Virgil," read with due lightening of certain trochaic accents in the latter half of each line, touches the high-water mark of English song. Apart from the specific allusions, almost every phrase recalls and rivals some intimate magic, some incommunicable fire: "Landscape-lover, lord of language"; *Tum sciat aerias Alpes et Norica si quis;* "All the charm of all the Muses"; *Aonas in montis ut duxerit una sororum.*

But most Virgilian of all are the two central lines:

> Light among the vanish'd ages; star that gildest yet this phantom
> shore;
> Golden branch amid the shadows, kings and realms that pass to
> rise no more.

Ay, this it is which lives for us out of the confused and perishing Past! The gross world's illusion and the backward twilight are lit by that sacred ray.

And how noble a comparison is that of the elect poet himself to his one golden bough in Avernus' forest, which gleamed amid the sea of green!

> Talis erat species auri frondentis opaca
> Ilice; sic leni crepitabat bractea vento.

We are here among things that shall endure. It may be that our English primacy in poetry, now some four centuries old, is drawing to its close. It may be that the art must pass ere long to younger races, with fresher idioms and a new outlook on this ancient world. But whatever else shall pass from us, Tennyson shall remain. *His* rhythm also shall "sound for ever of imperial" England; shall be the voice and symbol of this age of mighty workings, this world-ingathering race.

> We sail'd wherever ship could sail;
> We founded many a mighty state;
> Pray God our greatness may not fail
> Thro' craven fears of being great!

How august, how limitless a thing is his own spirit's upward flight! In "The Voyage" he has given us the impulse of glorious youth; and in "Vastness" the old man's outlook, as of "one who feels the immeasurable world"; and in "Crossing the Bar" he has borne the soul onward, on "such a tide as moving seems asleep," into the infinity which men call death.

What honour for him, what progress still, in that unknown which we shall some day know !

Dicite, felices animæ, tuque optume vates; —

round him, as round Musæus of old, the souls shall press and cling ; of him too shall we ask the heart-stirring question, and receive the wise reply ; "things worthy of a sacred silence" he too shall utter among the dead.

PERSONAL RECOLLECTIONS BY F. T. PALGRAVE (INCLUDING SOME CRITICISMS BY TENNYSON).

1849–1892.

Despite the long privilege of Lord Tennyson's society with which I have been favoured, few and poor, I fear, will these recollections be found. My knowledge of him began with the youthful reverence due to one who, exception made of Wordsworth, then almost in his eightieth year and equally revered by both, was already accepted as the first poet wherever the "Yes" *si suona :* and this feeling towards the poet presently became that deeper, higher, and sweeter reverence for the man, which could only widen with the years. It was indeed on the very first day I visited him (April 2nd, 1849) that I see he gave me (first also of how many gifts !) the lines "You might have won...," just printed in a newspaper. Hence, impressed from the very beginning by the heart-felt praise which Tennyson here gave to "unrecording friends," I held myself absolutely barred by the fealty of friendship, from the attempt to make any memorial of his words. Deeply and often indeed did I long for such record, thinking with pain, after hours often carried past midnight in long dialogue, how much that one would not willingly let die, what golden streams had flowed by to waste and Lethe. But "The poet's work is his life, and no one has a right to ask for more," he would always say : reaching once even the barbarity, as I could not help calling it, that if Horace had left an autobiography, and the single MS were in his hands, he would throw it into the fire. And, consistently, he would never read such Lives.

Sometimes the thought also came, as the sense gradually grew, that against his recorded desire, he too must abide the natural fate, the penalty, in his eyes, of a "Life and Letters," — might not then some note be silently made, to be used when his, too, must be reckoned among the "Silent Voices"? Yet that, again, seemed a default in true and absolute loyalty ; and, over-scrupulous as this "self-denying ordinance " may appear to some judges worthy of respect, I can scarcely regret that I observed it.

On March 31st, 1849, through the kindness of Henry Hallam, youngest son to the great historian, and worthy himself to be Arthur's brother in beauty of character and pure nobleness of life, I was asked to meet Tennyson at the house of Hallam's cousin by marriage, W. H. Brookfield, in Portman Street. Tennyson's affectionate friendship has been one of the mainstays of my life ; and this was the unconscious beginning of it.

At that time the two green volumes of 1842, with " The Princess " in its first form (1847), had been to me, as to thousands more, Gateways into a new Paradise. Hence, a pride in the thought of looking upon this great enchanter ; a vague expectation ; a planless pleasure. But I was here in the circle of his own friends, Thackeray amongst others ; and except recognition of the features and abundant hair (familiar through the little print from S. Laurence's fine monochromatic portrait), and of a few words upon our common friendship with the Hallam family, I have preserved no memory of Tennyson during this evening. But at the close, discovering that our routes homeward began in the same direction, his to a house in the Camden Town Road, mine to Hampstead, we set forth together. As I always found it afterwards, his conversation (about " The Princess " inter alia) was on that evening frank, full, varied, yet never trivial : ending finally (if I may be excused for repeating words which vanity, maybe, fixed in my memory) with, " I like what I see of you : you do not seem to have the distant air (or, airs of superiority) which Oxford men show," and parting with an invitation to visit him in his lodgings. I had then just left that University, and tried to repudiate the charge ; a certain foundation for which, however, I have since recognized[1]. " He was very open and friendly," I wrote that evening : he had " the look of one who had suffered greatly : strength and sensitiveness blended."

Two days after, with a mixed sense of fear and delight (almost as if about to make a proposal), I accordingly climbed to the upper floor of the lodgings, one of a few houses fronting the Hampstead Road, just south of Mornington Crescent, and found Tennyson in a somewhat dingy room, sitting close over the fire, with many short black pipes in front, and a stout jar of tobacco by his side. Reverting to the Hallams,

---

[1] Bishop Charles Wordsworth when at Christ Church, some eighteen years earlier, similarly criticizes the common " donnishness " of Oxford society, compared with the tone of Cambridge. Tennyson made a line on the Oxford " masher's " general reception of a stranger :

With one Oxonian stare from heel to head.

although I had to confess ignorance of the elder son, beyond what was conveyed in the very rare privately printed memoir by his high-souled father, Tennyson offered to read me certain poems he had written about Arthur, which his friends "seemed to approve." He then brought forth a bundle of beautifully copied verse : the name "In Memoriam" I do not think he used ; and read several pieces. One was No. CIII, "On that last night...," which friends had specially admired : others from the early series describing the ship sailing " from the Italian shore " (No. IX) : and that, I think, where parents or sweetheart await a son's or a lover's return.

Poetry so rich and concentrated as this, and heard now for the first time from the lips of one who loved and mourned so deeply, I could but partly grasp, and knew not how to praise aright. But Tennyson's sweet-natured kindness, when he could give pleasure, down to the very last day and hour, I have never found exhaustible : and, taking up one of those note-books (upon which, as they lay about his room, many friends must have looked as mines of hidden treasure), he went on to read certain songs which he thought he might do well to place between the sections of "The Princess." Thus, "Sweet and low," "The splendour falls," "Ask me no more " (on which he mentioned having observed the cloud shaping itself as described above the mountain top), passed before me ; giving the sense of some great and splendid procession slowly unrolling itself, and that to the sound of its own music. In some cases also (whether in all, I have forgotten) he had provided second songs ; one of which, painting the assault of warriors on a town, if I rightly remember, struck me as singularly brilliant. But when I afterwards enquired, the precious note-book had been mislaid : and lay *perdu* during his lifetime.

Tennyson's ready friendliness led him to be my companion half-way to Hampstead ; and I left him with the sense that the Gateway before named had been personally opened to me, and a dim perception that the man was even greater than the work : a perception, as the years went by, to be revealed how clearly ! and, I trust, to be recognized throughout these memorials, like the deep rich bass note of the violoncello, supporting the melodies above it.

Yet, whether from lack of courage or of chance, the next meeting was not (I believe) till the late autumn of 1850, when Tennyson, married in the June preceding, had fixed himself in Twickenham, within two miles of which town my own employment had then carried me. Here, in an old-fashioned Queen-Anne-like house, one of those built for the Court, called Chapel-House from its situation, with tall narrow windows and fittings of carved oak, I saw Tennyson standing by a lofty fireplace, his bride, long sought and lately won, near him resting on a sofa.   A somewhat gruff-sounding " So you have found me out " were the first words.   No doubt I looked duly guilty.   But she, who was to be to me a friend no less loved and honoured — the

> Perfect woman, perfect wife,
> Tender spiritual face,

of the Duke of Argyll's deeply-felt " Elegy " (and she will not blame me for this quotation) — at once said, " You need not take Ally literally : he is glad to see you ; but we came here to escape from the too frequent interruptions of London."   He laughed and agreed.   *Causa finita est*, I might have thought when leaving ; for henceforth, through the three following years, either in Montpelier Row, or at top of a tower which had been allotted to me as a smoking-den study in the grounds of the house where I was living, we met often.   I remember long talks, and gay laughter, and things comic and serious discussed ; the impression, the charm, and the gain for life ; but the " effacing finger " has spared little beyond.   It was only those earliest meetings which engraved themselves ineffaceably upon the mind ; and with few more such detailed scenes shall I burden the reader.

In several of his summer journeys, whilst his own sons were children, Tennyson asked me to be his companion : — equally a privilege and a pleasure.   Travelling together is said to bring out the whole man, in his natural gifts, his manners, his good sense and temper, or otherwise. My sketch of the poet (so far as it goes) will easily make good these points.   Time after time I proved that no comrade could be more steadily charming, more deeply interesting, more considerate, not only to myself, but to all fellow-creatures in all stations of life he mixed with.   If any of the inevitable rubs of the road met us, they were presently evaporated by his cheery honest laughter : his force of observation, fine yet always discriminating, brought enjoyment and sunlight into every scene.   Like all eminently true men, Tennyson was a far simpler problem than some have fancied.   He would never spoil the pleasant *laissez aller* of a journey by strict planning for the future.   " We will talk of it after to-morrow's after-breakfast pipe," he would say.   It was also his way that when we had entered on some scene of special beauty or grandeur, after enjoying it together, he should always withdraw wholly from sight, and study the view as it were in a little artificial solitude. Unless he worshipped thus " in the Temple's inner shrine " the spirit of the scene could not fully reveal itself.

It is not, however, to be hence inferred that this dear and honoured companion had anything which could be rightly called a recluse or exclusive temper.   No one, in fact, could be less willing to be left to solitary wandering ; to hermit-like seclusion. But on this point I shall touch again.

With some of Tennyson's family, and early friends, Spedding, Venables, C. Spring Rice, and his own greatly loved and gifted brother Charles, a poet equally exquisite and unappreciated, A. de Vere, and others, now mostly passed away, then or afterwards I became gradually acquainted. In September, 1852, a great gathering of them was held at Hallam's christening. Thither came the baby's illustrious Godfather, in vigorous old age, nobly resigned, though overshadowed by the loss of his son Henry in 1850 ; there I first saw Robert Browning (his wife detained by sickness) ; and there also Mrs T. Carlyle, whose brilliant anecdotes and flashing incisive wit nearly sent some of us ignobly from the table to the floor. "Had her husband been here," said our host, " she would have sat in silence " : — adding, " he has more of the woman in him."

Sometime in 1852 Tennyson read over to me his " Ode on the Duke of Wellington," discussing various points of detail. I think this was the sole occasion upon which, moved by the greatness of the man and of the memories which that colossal career called forth, the national sorrow and the loss of heroic example, he showed a certain anxiety about his own work. Yet he need not have feared. Heroism, at least since the days of Pindar or of Virgil, surely has never been sung of more heroically.

One other remembrance must belong to this period. He was speaking of a new edition of the *Poems*, then in hand, and of its contents, and agreed at once with the suggestion which I ventured, that certain of the pieces now headed " Juvenilia " had best be omitted : " Let us look them out " : and between us, some six or eight were thus *obelized.* " It is, however, useless, I fear : the publisher (Moxon) will be sure to say that the edition would not sell, and *that* I cannot afford."

Some twelve or thirteen years later, when the further privilege of friendship with Browning had become mine, he also mentioned, with honest pleasure, that a fresh collected edition of his Poems was to appear. Remembering Tennyson's reception of my proposal, and thinking that it applied no less to Browning (as indeed to what poet, at least in modern days, would it not apply?) — to him in turn I suggested exclusion of his " earlier and less mature work." " Leave out anything !" cried he, in his animated way : " Certainly not: *quod scripsi, scripsi.*" By those who may read between the lines, these little anecdotes will be felt to go deep into the inner nature of the men, nor less, perhaps, into the quality of the legacies in their art which the two poets have respectively left us.

The low riverain position of Twickenham did not prove invigorating to the Tennysons, and he used laughingly to complain how malodorously thick and odious was the air from the many cabbage market-gardens all around. Hence by the close of 1853 the family removed to Farringford. They had nearly fixed themselves at S. Mary's, Trinity Hill, a house some three miles south of Axminster, which commanded a fine and uncommon view over tree and valley to the sea and lofty coast visible from Lyme. The ground of rejection was the want of sufficiently comfortable provision for the household: a point on which Master and Mistress were always sensitively considerate, with the natural result of faithful service, and an atmosphere of home comfort to the guest, as if the whole family joined in the welcome. I may illustrate this by a few words from a lady who (1881) had sent a body of working boys for a day's holiday to Aldworth: "When I told my maid how good your servants had been, she said '*that is just like them; they are the kindest people I know.*'"

At Farringford the ever-ready and genial hospitality of Tennyson and his honoured wife welcomed me at every Christmas-tide, I think, from 1854 to 1863. And either there or on his visits to London I enjoyed many other meetings. These, in after years (1875–1882), were often in London houses taken for a few weeks: and I may here note the free genial hospitality, the "honest talk and wholesome wine," with which friends (of all dates), or strangers desirous to become such, were received. The tales, in truth, which have painted Tennyson as a recluse, whether in London or in the country, could only amuse those acquainted with the ways of the family[1]. It was, indeed, more than most poets that Tennyson (as justly has been remarked about Horace[2]) felt the two impulses described by M. Arnold, one driving the poet "to the world without," and "one to solitude": although the happier circumstances of Tennyson's life allowed him less of Rome and more of Tibur and the Sabine farm than fell to the lot of the great Italian.

When it happened that Tennyson was our guest, he always begged

[1] If the poet, however, when at Farringford or Aldworth habitually reserved many hours to himself and solitary thought, he might have quoted the precedent of Michael Angelo. "Really zealous artists," as reported by a contemporary, he once said to Vittoria Colonna, "are bound to abstain from the idle trivialities and current compliments of society; not because they are haughty and intolerant by nature, but because their art imperiously claims the whole of their energies. The world is right in condemning a man who out of pure affectation or eccentricity shuts himself up alone....Those, however, who act in this way naturally, because their profession obliges them to lead a recluse life,...ought in common justice to be tolerated.... Do you not know that there are sciences which demand the whole of a man?" (J. A. Symonds: *Life of M. A. Buonarrotti.*)

[2] W. T. Sellar: *Horace* (1892).

that he might not go forth alone into the "great city"; his shortness of sight and the crowded streets and crossings, with which he had now grown unfamiliarized, rendering him grateful for the sympathetic and admiring companionship which he always found. On these walks I, indeed, was then rarely able to be present. But very charming, I heard (and indeed as a guest in every way), did he make himself: nor had photography and fame then rendered him subject to that *digito monstrari prætereuntium* which he hated. Once too he was nursed in our house (1863) in an attack of that troublesome enemy, eczema: during which Mr T. Carlyle came to see him.

To that house also (February 12th, 1864) Browning brought his will, in two autograph copies which he believed identical, to be signed in presence of Tennyson and myself as witnesses. Browning had taken Mr Procter's advice upon the document: so he laughingly said something to the effect that "It would be a wonder if it were legally accurate, advised by one poet, written out by another, and witnessed by a third." And accordingly, after that much-prized friend had been taken from England and us at Palazzo Rezzonico (December 12th, 1889), it proved that the two wills differed in some point (which, however, lapse of time and change of circumstances had now rendered simply *technical*): and it yet was legally desirable that I should try to point out which document had first received Tennyson's and my signature. But we, on that long past irrevocable day, had been gay together in no formal, Court of Chancery humour: and it was impossible for me to clear up the dilemma.

For a record (and the only one of the kind preserved) of the guests at the dinner (which, followed, or preceded, *quis dicat?*) I am indebted to the kindness of one among them, Canon T. Richmond. Most have been already named among Tennyson's friends: Mr Gladstone also was one: and I may here conveniently give a slight note of a dialogue which at the time struck me forcibly, although it fell earlier (May 3rd, 1862), when he and Tennyson were guests with myself of the large-hearted and gracious lady who was then Mistress of Cliveden. There, Tennyson and I had been walking under groves by

Sheets of hyacinth[1]
That seem'd the heavens upbreaking thro' the earth,

— words which he recalled to me as exemplified at that moment — and were joined by Mr Gladstone. The talk presently fell upon Oxford and Cambridge; the old contention, which had bred most men of first-class eminence. The familiar names on each side were quoted; and the representative of Cambridge could not repress his immense astonishment

[1] Made in the hyacinth wood at Farringford.

when the Member for Oxford as decidedly claimed not less than equal honours for his University. This claim (in which the earlier and truly greater Bacon was, I think, ignored) rested mainly upon Bishop Butler, as a giant unrivalled in religious argument, and upon the eminence of Oxford in the sphere of Dogma, in its technical sense. I thought Tennyson was hardly less surprised at the reasons given for Oxonian eminence than at the eminence itself asserted. For dogma, it may be conjectured, was commonly an alien thing from the tone of that gifted College circle by which the poet's current of thought, in some directions, had been deeply influenced. So the rival champions were fain to leave the great problem unsolved.

Returning to the evening above-named, another guest then present was my brother William Gifford, returning now to England for a short visit, after his strangely adventurous journey through Central Arabia. Even Tennyson was not a more devout and loving student of the highest poetry than he: and the " Locksley Hall " of 1842 was among his greatest loves. He[1] now, meeting Tennyson for the first time, ventured to remark on the truth of that poem to Arabian sentiment and manner. The conjecture proved correct: and Tennyson (as I noted at the time in the volume) told us that " Locksley Hall " had, in fact, been " suggested by reading Sir William Jones' prose translation of the old Arabian *Moallakat*" : — a famous collection from the work of pre-Mahommedan poets.

Upon our journeys, or at Farringford, in a low-roofed upper room, sacred to books and papers and a man's doctrine of tidiness, where we sat commonly till late (as afterwards at Aldworth), or traversing the long Down far as the Needles' Lighthouse, the lavish stores of a mind which to its own gifts added minute study of the master-works in poetry, classical, mediæval and modern, day by day were unfolded. Here, one felt, was a man who, like Wordsworth, had lived, not indeed exclusively, but essentially, *inter apices*, among the highest summits, the purest air, the region nearest Heaven. With Lucretius and Horace, *Iuvat integros accedere fontis* might have been his motto. Tennyson's conversation was hence of a peculiar quality and interest which I can rather recall in its general tone and tints than describe. Among many men gifted in talk, whom I have had the fortune to know, he, I felt, time after time, ranked highest. It would be, of course, an inaccurate impression if what has just been noted were taken to mean that the talk ran commonly upon the great aspects of life or literature or landscape. In fact, I have known no one who had so large a store of anecdote, serious and comic, but (with him) always illustrative of

[1] He said that Tennyson had the clearness of pronunciation — every syllable given — of an Arab.

human character in every phase, and always, also, given with lucid terseness clothed in perfect English speech. So sedulous, indeed, was Tennyson on this last point, that he would ever and anon good-humouredly correct certain Norfolk pronunciations which clung to me from youth; laughingly saying that he thought himself, as it were, officially a guardian of the Queen's English.

Everyone will have seen men, distinguished in some line of work, whose conversation (to take the old figure) either "smelt too strongly of the lamp," or lay quite apart from their art or craft. What, through all these years, struck me about Tennyson, was that whilst he never deviated into poetical language as such, whether in rhetoric or highly coloured phrase, yet throughout the substance of his talk the same mode of thought, the same imaginative grasp of nature, the same fineness and gentleness in his view of character, the same forbearance and toleration, the *aurea mediocritas* despised by fools and fanatics, which are stamped on his poetry, were constantly perceptible : whilst in the easy and as it were unsought choiceness, the conscientious and truth-loving precision of his words, the same personal identity revealed itself. What a strange charm lay here ; how deeply illuminating the whole character, as in prolonged intercourse it gradually revealed itself! Artist and man, Tennyson was invariably true to himself, or rather, in Wordsworth's phrase, he "moved altogether"; his nature and his poetry being harmonious aspects of the same soul ; as botanists tell us that flower and fruit are but transformations of root and stem and leafage. We read how, in mediæval days, conduits were made to flow with claret. But this was on great occasions only. Tennyson's fountain always ran wine.

Once more : In Mme. Récamier's *salon*, I have read, at the time when conversation was yet a fine art in Paris, guests famous for *esprit* would sit in the twilight round the stove, whilst each in turn let fly some sparkling anecdote or bon-mot, which rose and shone and died out into silence, till the next of the elect pyrotechnists was ready. Good things of this kind, as I have said, were plentiful in Tennyson's repertory. But what, to pass from the materials to the method of his conversation, eminently marked it was the continuity of the electric current. He spoke, and was silent, and spoke again : but the circuit was unbroken; there was no effort in taking up the thread, no sense of disjunction. Often I thought, had he never written a line of the poems so dear to us, his conversation alone would have made him the most interesting companion known to me [1]. From this great and gracious student of humanity, what less, indeed, could be expected? And if, as a converser, I were to compare him with Socrates, as figuréd for us in

[1] Fitzgerald once said : " I wish I had been A. T.'s Boswell."

the dialogues of his great disciple, I think that I should have the assent of that eminently valued friend of Tennyson's, whose long labour of love has conferred English citizenship upon Plato[1].

If we are lingering over these vanished hours, my excuse is, that in Tennyson conversation and recital expressed and indeed were the man, and cannot be omitted from any sketch which, even by imperfect hints, endeavours to perpetuate his likeness. One special charm of his society was the unvaried courteous good-nature, the simple pleasure in pleasing, which led him readily to comply with any wish expressed that he should read or repeat poetry. This was naturally most often his own : although if the choice were left free, he preferred the verse of others, notably, Shakespeare and Milton. Thus none of his friends, and few even among occasional visitors, failed to hear him read. What poetical recitation, as distinguished alike from mere reading and from dramatic utterance, should be, no definite theory seems to exist ; no authoritative code. Tastes at any rate here differ widely ; and casual hearers have found Tennyson's method too little varied or emphatic, his voice and delivery monotonous. Yet those who knew the speaker could easily see causes which explained and justified his method. Tennyson's grand range and " timbre " of voice ; his power of modulation ; his great *sostenuto* power ; the *portamento* so justly dear to Italian vocalists, might be the truer word ; the ample resonant utterance : all was simply no deliberate art of recital but the direct outward representative, the effluence at once of his own deepest sentiment as to what Poetry should be, and of the intention, the aspiration, of his own poems. Such had they sung themselves to him, as he thought them out, often keeping them, even when of considerable length, in memory before a syllable was placed on paper ; and in strict accordance with that inner music was the audible rendering of it. Whether this conformed to common practice or not, he " could no otherwise."

I spent some days at Farringford in September, 1854, when " Maud " was in course of completion. Alexander Grant, my much-loved college comrade, and endeared to Tennyson by his sympathetic enthusiasm and charm of nature, was, if I remember right, also there : and the entrancement, the intoxication (I hope I may be allowed the word), with which we listened for the first time, from the author's lips, and almost in the first flush of creation, to those passionate lyrics of indignation and love and sorrow is before me even now when writing. Nor could anyone, I think, who heard them so recited wonder at the preference which, it is well known, Tennyson at times expressed for this poem ; among his lyrical work, at least ; for " In Memoriam " and the " Idylls " were not, I think, in question. " Maud," in truth, the

[1] *Sic*, July, 1893. *Iam, Requiescat in pace.*

"Wellington Ode," "Guinevere," "Enoch Arden," the "Rizpah," the "Revenge," and, in a somewhat different way, "The Northern Farmer" with its brilliant companions, — I am sure many who heard them so spoken will agree, these can never be heard again, no, nor read, to similar advantage. Something of their music, some part of their very essence, has passed with the Maker.

Various tales, more or less of "The Spiteful Letter" character, ascribing to Tennyson now vanity, now rudeness, have circulated. Hence there may be some who will have read with a little surprise, perhaps a suspicion of partial over-praise, what has been said above on his courteous good-nature and habit of ready compliance. The censures alluded to, if conversance with Tennyson during many years and many moods may be trusted, had, however, but little foundation; would never have stood the test of familiarity. From childhood itself he had been haunted by a singularly sensitive shyness, a ghost which no resolution can wholly lay. Thus, for a moment, after which smiles and natural courtesy awoke, I have known him silenced, almost frozen, before the eager unintentional eyes of a girl of fifteen. And under the stress of this nervous impulse compelled to contradict his inner self (especially when under the terror of leonization, may Johnson and Murray excuse the word!), he was, doubtless, betrayed at times into an abrupt phrase, a cold unsympathetic exterior; a moment's "defect of the rose." Then, as in dreaming the nightmare will suddenly leave us, and we find it day, that involuntary spell would vanish, and a singular frank graciousness of conversation follow, only the more charming by contrast with the chill preceding. No one could pass more rapidly from reserve to confidingness : no one throw himself into confidence more fully from the whole heart; almost (I sometimes thought) pathetic in his entire trustfulness.

Tennyson, to turn now to him as poet, although at times, when wearied by gossip or ill-natured attack, he would energetically ban Fame, and pretend (as I called it) to wish he had been a farmer on four hundred a year in a Lincolnshire valley, was intensely interested in his work : he thought, doubtless, that into it he had put his very best : he wrote always, it was impossible not to feel, with such entire conscientiousness, that when lighting upon one of the felicitous descriptive epithets in which he excelled, his pleasure was not less great simply in feeling himself true to nature, than in his success as an artist. He had, it may be hence inferred, an encouraging satisfaction in his work, which the severest censor must admit to be not only justifiable, but in itself a well-deserved incentive to progress. Of personal vanity as a poet I never saw the very smallest trace. Doubtless, he was not insensible to the long chorus of praise which followed the comparative neglect of earlier years. But words which were sometimes referred to vanity, long experience convinced me were really due to that surprised sensitiveness I have already noticed. When reading and talking over any poem he had lately written, the point of merit, unless now and then by way of comparison with other of his analogous pieces, was never raised. One exception indeed to this silence on his own work there was which a hearer could hardly forget. We were sitting (1857 or so) late at night in the Farringford attic-room already mentioned : and Tennyson read over to me the little Theocritean Idyll " Hylas " ; eminent for beauty in a treasure-house where all are beautiful. He dwelt particularly on the tender loveliness of the lines which describe how the fair youth, carried to the depths of a fountain by the enamoured Nymphs, faintly answered the call of his companion Herakles :

τρὶς μὲν Ὕλαν ἄυσεν...
τρὶς δ' ἄρ' ὁ παῖς ὑπάκουσεν, ἀραιὰ δ' ἵκετο φωνὰ
ἐξ ὕδατος · παρεὼν δὲ μάλα σχεδὸν εἴδετο πόρρω ·

— thrice he called on Hylas, and thrice too the boy heard, and faint came the voice from the water, and near as he was, he seemed afar off. Tennyson, if I remember rightly, ended with that involuntary half-sigh of delight which breaks forth when a sympathetic spirit closes, or turns from, some masterpiece of perfect art, in words or colours. " I should be content to die," said the author of " Locksley Hall " and " Maud " and " In Memoriam," " if I had written anything equal to this." The scene need not be spoiled by any comments.

But another incident must be added, belonging to a much later date, when Tennyson's imperial position in Poetry was fully established. And if in relating this I expose myself to censure, I will receive it à cœur légère.

In the company of Locker-Lampson he read to me a poem, just then prepared for publication, which I shall not name. This appeared to me at the moment — probably one of the hasty incorrect judgments which a single hearing is too apt to engender — considerably below his habitual proper level ; and, with abruptness inexcusable, even had I been Rhadamanthus himself in cathedrâ, I owned that I could not find one good line in it. Little or no weight as this opinion was entitled to, a shade, a little shade, a hint, of vexation passed over the poet's face. But Locker kindly intervening said, " You should not feel vexed : he is probably the only one of your friends now left who would venture to speak out openly on such a matter." Tennyson smiled, and added (I think) a few modest words in defence of the perfunctorily ill-used poem. Nor did the occurrence (to give it too mild a name) ever make the smallest breach in his constant readiness to read to the critic his after-work : which indeed included some of his noblest, his most unique, efforts. How few, how very few, of the " irascible race " would show such forbearance !

Let us now try to enter a little into the studio of the artist, the inner secrets of his art. More than once he said that his poems sprang often from a " nucleus " ; some one word, may be, or brief melodious phrase which had floated through the brain, as it were unbidden. And perhaps at once whilst walking they were presently wrought into a little song. But if he did not write it down on the spot, the lyric fled from him irrecoverably. So, doubtless, did motives, one or two bars long, spontaneously come to Mozart or Beethoven, bringing with them a kind of inward assurance that, if seized and worked out, some " treasure for ever " of an air lay concealed behind them. The instances Tennyson mentioned have escaped me [1]: but in some of the shorter lyrics one can detect or imagine them.

I asked once, whether the praises of Arthur Hallam which " In Memoriam " sets forth did not outrun the actual facts : whether affection and poetry together had not led him to overcolour : whether now, looking back (cir. 1853), he believed that his friend would really have been

> A potent voice of Parliament,
> A pillar steadfast in the storm.

Tennyson's earnest look is still before me as he gave the assurance that he truly and fully believed that, in no form or way, had he exaggerated Arthur's wonderful promise. And perhaps I may be allowed here so far to diverge as to mention that more than one school or college contemporary of Hallam's, intimately known to me, have exactly confirmed Tennyson's judgment.

His own rule for writing participles in ed was to retain the vowel when it formed part of the verb ; to put the apostrophe in all other cases, unless the e was sounded metri gratia, when it should be accented. Verse, of course, is here thought of.

Did he ever use a rhyming dictionary? He had tried it in earlier days, but found it of little use : "There was no natural congruity between the rhymes thus alphabetically grouped together."

In regard to published criticism, more than once he remarked that it was his misfortune, and one which he felt unable to remedy, — to be little moved by praise, but long to remember points of censure.

A word may be here added on the illustrated editions of Tennyson's

---

[1] Several instances have been given in these volumes.

poetry. Whilst I believe he gratefully recognized the pains taken and skill shown by Maclise in "The Princess," by A. Hughes in "Enoch Arden," and the many eminent artists who were united to decorate the *Poems*, he would often say that in one sense these renderings did not satisfy him. "I can see every scene in my poems in the mind's eye: had I been trained to draw, I could set them all down according to my own idea of each." In this matter he must have envied the power which gives an exceptional value to many among his friend Thackeray's novels.

To take another point. Much discussion has been spent, or wasted, upon so-named "spontaneous" and "learned" poetry, and the great difference supposed to lie between these two classes. The distinction is, however, clearly one of more and less, not of essentially opposed kinds. The stream of art is always continuous; by the work of his predecessors every poet and painter is inevitably conditioned. *Vixere fortes ante Agamemnona;* and before Homer also.

It is among those poets with whom traceable references to their ancestors in art are frequent, allusions which, echo-like, multiply and sweeten their own strains; far-off hints, that render the spell over the soul more magical; that Tennyson, all know, is to be classed. Yet in whatever concerns the essence of his art, the substance of his verse, the form of his music, no poet (if I may venture the criticism) has truly been more constant to himself: *Qualis ab incepto:* — in the strict sense, more original. Tennyson's colouring indeed, the tone of his poems, has gradually passed from Titian to Rembrandt; the design, as a rule, has grown at once more precise and larger in style. Some flowers, but mostly from the gardens of old and of many lands, he has transplanted. in matter of form and substance he seems but little affected; and least by his own immediate contemporaries.

It is a favourite process of our day to trace the genesis of a poet as necessitated by the general circumstances of his period and country: as if he were evolved by natural law. An amusing instance of this very dubious argument, as applied to Tennyson, may be given.

Many years ago I met the accomplished French critic M. Taine. He asked whether Mr Tennyson in his youth had not been given to luxurious living, and surrounded with things of costly beauty. I told how I had then lately visited him in the Camden Town Road second-floor lodgings: that he had gone on his way from College days with little of the world's goods, and that the picture of his style of life now drawn by the critic was imaginary. Whence had he learned it? "From the 'Recollections of the Arabian Nights,' and a few other early poems," M. Taine replied. I was glad of this meeting, as it happily enabled me to offer him a correction, perhaps of some little value, for the book upon English literature which I understood he was preparing. Evidently his "siege was already made," at least in MS, for the lively critic listened with a disappointed air. However, when his elegant but somewhat flimsy and one-sided review of Tennyson soon after appeared, this conjecture about the poet's personal Sybaritism as the "milieu" of the early verses was barely perceptible.

Not a little ingenious labour has also wasted itself in the attempt to trace supposed previous authorities for this or that passage in Tennyson's poetry. Thus, to give another instance of these inferential fallacies; the influence of Shelley, supposed powerful and obvious in "The Lover's Tale" of 1827, I believe has been insisted on. Yet Tennyson recently assured me, when speaking of his early days, that the great lyrist was then, to his own belief, unknown to him. It was, in fact, after his College residence had begun (Feb. 1828) that Shelley became the study of the gifted Trinity circle.

Another and more vexatious error has now and then arisen from assignment to the poet's own opinion of the criticisms on life placed in the mouths of certain imaginary speakers. This misunderstanding may have been partly caused by the fact that he has carried the mono-dramatic form to a point of power and richness hitherto unreached, and employed it also on modern themes; more, however, from neglect by some readers to remember that in Monodrama it is essentially the mind of the character presented which lies before us, no less than in Drama proper. In each case the poet of course provides the sentiments and the words, but, even when these may happen in a general sense to accord with his own, they are only seen by us as modified in deference to the character: with the truth of which, not of his utterances, the poet is alone concerned. Shakespeare doubtless felt with, or perhaps through, Portia or Imogen: but this, because they represent womanhood in her simple loving graciousness. But the critic would almost exceed the wildness of Teutonic conjecture who should charge the dramatist with the misanthropy of Timon and Lear, or hold him personally identified with the mind of Juliet's nurse or of Emilia. Nor does anyone fancy that Tennyson's view of the mediæval Church is embodied either in Queen Eleanor or Queen Mary. But enough upon a point so obvious, that notice of it is only justified by the somewhat perverse allegations that Tennyson himself simply spoke his own thought through the madman-hero of "Maud," or the Hospital Nurse of "Emmie [1]." And, to close this subject, deeply as the spirit and the

---

[1] This singular blindness may be exemplified by the following extract from a professedly scientific journal (1881). Every word in the "Children's Hospital," it should be remembered, comes from the mouth of the Hospital Nurse, and, as in all

changes of his age, the great tidal waves of human thought, have moved Tennyson, throughout my intercourse, whilst he was ever ready to do justice to his contemporaries, yet never did I trace any symptom that he was affected by the latter in modes of thought or choice and treatment of his matter.

Returning now from these more general questions to actual life, let me put together such stray sayings as have survived in memory : poor gleanings, I fear, from that golden harvest of forty years.

Often, I believe, as life advanced, he would renew earlier familiarity with the great poets of all time ; living habitually with the high society of Parnassus. Thus a portable copy of Homer which some friend had given him he had in his hands on our Cornish journey (1860), and kept sitting down to read as we wandered over a wild rock-island in the Scillies. We took Homer, however, so much for granted, that I do not recall many discussions in honour of *Iliad* and *Odyssey*. It would have seemed like praising " Monte Rosa." — On Pindar he once said, " He is a kind of Australian poet ; has long tracts of gravel, with immensely large nuggets imbedded." This was in reference to the obscurity and inequality in the Odes : a hasty judgment, perhaps, on that colossal genius, if his work be closely studied as a whole.

One evening, in that upper room which could not be entered without a rising of the heart, a sense of exaltation, as of one admitted to the central shrine of Delphi, he read out off-hand Pindar's great picture of the life of Heaven in the second Olympian into pure modern prose, splendidly lucid and musical. This feat, incomparably more difficult and effective than when the pseudo-poetic facile disguise of some archaic form of language is resorted to, so struck me, that I begged him to think of preparing a version of these all but unique relics of the Greek Heroic Ode for English readers. But he smiled and said that " in his mind the benefit of translation rested with the translator [1]." These were memorable words ; but I fancy that ancient poets were at the moment before him. A decision even more trenchant by Shelley on the practical impossibility of translating poetry will be remembered by some readers.

dramatic writing, is necessarily and rightly modified to express sentiments natural to such a speaker.

The paper begins by quoting a statement that " Another of the London hospitals is in danger of entering upon a career of rampant *nursedom*"; then adding : " It is somewhat significant that in the poem in which the Laureate has recently libelled the medical profession he contrasts an angelic nurse with the coarse unfeeling doctor."

The charge of libelling a profession which Lord Tennyson, like every rational man, notoriously held always in honour, is of course nothing but an unconscious witness to the dramatic force of his poem.

[1] See p. 350.

"Why do you not write an Idyll upon the story of Ruth?" I once asked. The deep tone of conviction with which he answered still seems with me : "Do you think I could make it more poetical?"

Another time, late over the midwinter fire, reading the terrible lines in which Lucretius preaches his creed of human annihilation (Book III. especially ll. 912—977, ed. Munro) : and perhaps those (Book v. 1194—1217) on the uselessness of prayer, and the sublime but oppressive fear inevitable to the thoughtful mind in the awful vision of the star-lighted heavens : — so carried away and overwhelmed were the readers by the poignant force of the great poet, that, next morning, when dawn and daylight had brought their blessed natural healing to morbid thoughts, it was laughingly agreed that Lucretius had left us last night all but converts to his heart-crushing atheism.

More than once did Tennyson impress upon me that Milton, our " mighty-mouth'd inventor of harmonies," must have framed his metre upon that " ocean-roll of rhythm" which underlies the hexameters of Virgil : quoting as a perfect example the four lines, " Continuo ventis surgentibus..." (*Geor.* I. 356), in which the rising of a storm is painted. And similarly was he deeply moved by the Roman dignity which Horace has imparted to the Sapphic in the *Non enim gazæ*... (Book II. 16) : although in general Tennyson did not admire the Horatian treatment of that metre, which he would audaciously define, alluding to the " Adonic" fourth line, as " like a pig with its tail tightly curled." And he highly valued the solemn pathos of that great but heart-saddening Elegy on Cornelia by Propertius, *Desine, Paulle*...

Not less fragmentary are the stray relics surviving from discourse on later poetry. I had put the scheme of my *Golden Treasury* before him during a walk near the Land's End in the late summer of 1860, and he encouraged me to proceed, barring only any poems by himself from insertion in an anthology whose title claimed excellence for its contents. And at the Christmas-tide following, the gathered materials, already submitted to the judgment of two friends of taste (one, the very able sculptor, T. Woolner, lately taken from us), were laid before Tennyson for final judgment. This judgment, in some very few cases then not followed, has been now (1801) carried out by omission of Constable's " Diaphenia," xv. ; Sewell's " Damon," CLXIII., and Shelley's *Life of Life*... : about which Tennyson remarked that it was one of those flights in which the poet " seemed to go up, and burst." Between Shakespeare's Sonnets he hardly liked to decide, all were so powerful. With most by far of the pieces submitted he was already acquainted : but I seem to remember more or less special praise of Lodge's " Rosaline," of " My Love in her attire..." : and the " Emigrant's Song," by Marvell. For some poems by that writer then with difficulty accessible, he had a special admiration : delighting to read, with a voice hardly yet to me silent, and dwelling more than once, on the magnificent hyperbole, the powerful union of pathos and humour in the lines "To his coy Mistress," where Marvell that says

> Had we but world enough, and time,
> This coyness, lady, were no crime...
>   ....I would
> Love you ten years before the Flood,
> And you should, if you please, refuse
> Till the conversion of the Jews....
>
> But at my back I always hear
> Time's wingéd chariot hurrying near;
> And yonder all before us lie
> Deserts of vast Eternity....

Youth, therefore, Marvell proceeds, is the time for love;

> Let us roll all our strength, and all
> Our sweetness up into one ball,
> And tear our pleasures with rough strife
> Through the iron gates of life :

on this line remarking that he could fancy *grates* would have intensified Marvell's image.

After reading Cowper's "Poplar Field": "People nowadays, I believe, hold this style and metre light; I wish there were any who could put words together with such exquisite flow and evenness." Presently we reached the same poet's stanzas to Mary Unwin. He read them, yet could barely read them, so deeply was he touched by their tender, their almost agonizing pathos. And once when I asked him for the "Lines on my Mother's Portrait," his voice faltered as he said he would, if I wished it ; but he knew he should break down.

Petrarch, now stupidly undervalued, furnished a not dissimilar instance, in the ethereally-beautiful lines on the death of Laura ("Trionfo della Morte," Cap. 1) :

> Non come fiamma che per forza è spenta,
>   Ma che per se medesma si consume,
> Se n' andò in pace l' anima contenta ;
>   A guisa d' un soave e chiaro lume,
> Cui nutrimento a poco a poco manca,
>   Tenendo al fin il suo usato costume.

I remember still the tenderness with which he dwelt on the words, the sigh of delight — almost perhaps, the tears — that came naturally to the sensitive soul, as he ended. "It is the pathos of *beauty*," Chateaubriand finely remarks, "which is the most perfectly pathetic."

And Petrarch's own contemporary English admirer, again, supplied Tennyson with another favourite passage; that in the "Knight's Tale," where Arcite, dying, commends his soul as a legacy to his love, Emilie :

> Alas the wo! alas the peinës strong...
>
> *   *   *   *
>
> What is this world? what axen men to have?
> Now with his love, now in his coldë grave,
> Alone withouten any compagnie.

It is with a doubly pathetic echo that the tone, amorously lingering, which this dear friend always rendered Chaucer's last line, now returns to me.

These are small details, and somewhat egoistic : yet I hope for pardon. We shall hear that voice no more.

Here may be also noticed an incident of Tennyson's meeting with A. H. Clough, on a journey to the Pyrenees (1861). Clough's health was then fast failing; and Tennyson, speaking of him afterwards with the strong personal interest which he always exercised, as it were by some resistless spell, over those who knew him, said that Clough as he lay on the grass in some lovely valley near Cauteretz, had read aloud passages from his last and unfinished poem, the series of tales named "Mari Magno." These narratives of modern life have much delicately touched feeling, some passionate moments. "When he read them his voice faltered at times : like every poet, *he was moved by his own pathos.*"

Resuming Tennyson's *Golden Treasury* comments, which naturally fixed themselves in memory, another little poem greatly moved him : perhaps he was not very familiar with it : Scott's "Maid of Neidpath." This also he read, adding after the last stanza, "Almost more pathetic than a man has the right to be." We may perhaps say as much of "The Children's Hospital."

Tennyson was much struck by the plain force of Byron's "Elegy on Thyrza," and Moore's "Light of other Days"; saying of the last, "*O si sic omnia!*" In Wolfe's noble "Burial of Sir John Moore" he wished the last line but two could be changed; at the close of Hood's "Bridge of Sighs" "Her evil *behaviour*" was a slight defect in that masterpiece. And the infelicitous "mermaid's song *condoles*" of the "Battle of the Baltic" tempted him to a "How easily could a little blot like this be cured! If we had but Tom Campbell in the room to point it out to him" : adding, however, a tale how Rogers had done the same office for another poem; and how Campbell had bounced out of the room, with a "Hang it ! I should like to see the man who would dare to correct me ! "

Here let me add, that the selections from his own Lyrical poetry (1885), with the formation of which I was honoured by him, were submitted for his approval, and that those from "In Memoriam" (peculiarly difficult to frame, from the reasons which I have noted above in regard to Shakespeare's Sonnets) follow a list which he gave me.

Memory supplies little else upon the poets. Shakespeare and Milton, as before observed, he read aloud by preference : always coming to *Paradise Lost* with manifest pleasure and reverent admiration : like Keats, devoted to

> Miltonian storms, and more, Miltonian tenderness :

nor did voice and manner ever serve him better. I may name the passage describing the Gate of Heaven (*Par. Lost*, III. 501—509), specially singled out for delicate beauty : and the great vision of Eden (Book IV. 205—311), which he read aloud at Ardtornish in Morvern (August, 1853), and often afterwards ; dwelling always on the peculiar grace of lines 246—263. These are small points, and (with much else here written down) he would have laughed at me in his genial way for recording them. Yet some, I think, will look out the passages named, and read them with new interest.

One of Sir P. Sidney's songs to *Stella* he specially admired :

> Only Joy, now here you are,
> Fit to hear and ease my care...

with its pretty refrain —

> Take me to thee, and thee to me :
> "No, no, no, no, my Dear, let be ! "

From Donne he would quote the "Valediction, forbidding Mourning," the last four stanzas :

> Our two souls...

where the poet compares himself to the moving leg, his love to the central, of the compass when describing a circle : praising its wonderful ingenuity. And similarly he would often quote the lines from the "Dunciad" upon the evening of Lord Mayor's Day :

> Now Night descending, the proud scene was o'er,
> But lived in Settle's numbers *one day more.*

For their delicate music, again, he loved eight lines by his old friend S. Rogers, describing a girl imprisoned in some castle :

> Caged in old woods...

Keats, more than once, he said, "promised securely more than any English poet since Milton."

Edgar Poe's "Raven," with all its skill, was too artificial for genuine poetry. That writer's ingenious narrative, in one of his prose essays, how the whole poem had been generated first from the vowel *O*, then from the word *more*, and so forth even to the details, he would not accept : it was another piece of artificiality[1].

Tennyson often spoke of Goethe, in regard to his poetry. Much might be inferior : but as a lyrist certain pieces put him in the first rank. Amongst these favourites, which he gladly would read, were the "Nachgefühl" : "Der Abschied," admired for its exquisite tenderness : he had *les larmes dans la voix* when he reached the second stanza,

Traurig wird in dieser Stunde... :

and perhaps even more did he prize the beautiful song "An den Mond," where I find he has in my copy tremulously pencil-marked the last two stanzas ; familiar, doubtless, himself with the mysterious thoughts which at night-time "wander through the labyrinth of the bosom."

These poems are from Goethe's early *Lieder;* and in the same class of beauty is the much later "Elegie," of which Tennyson quoted two stanzas of "what I call Shakespearian beauty" ; those beginning

Du hast gut reden...

and ending

Da bleibt kein Rath als gränzenlose Thränen.

Highly rated also, for solemn thought and deep calm insight into human life, were the well-known "Gränzen der Menschheit" and "Das Göttliche." On *Faust* I remember no remark[2].

Another poem, valued for its stately beauty and tender feeling for a friend, was that upon the sight of Schiller's skull; which he read out in the Inn at York (1853) ; on the same occasion, as it chanced, repeating that graceful piece of colour, the

Go not, happy day...

which found a place in "Maud"; at once pleased and amused by his "red man" and "red babe," as effective points of crimson in that rosy landscape. Of Heine, he did not find the songs remained with him in memory, like Goethe's.

A few scraps remain. It was with a sort of reverence that he would name certain poets of supreme dignity. Thus with Wordsworth. Yet critical truth compelled him, when the point was raised, to confess the inequality of Wordsworth's work, the heaviness of style seen somewhat

---

[1] He ranked Poe's tales very high as works of genius; see p. 292.

[2] The Prologue and songs in *Faust* he often quoted with lavish praise. T.

too often in poems, the subjects of which more or less defied successful treatment.   In these, he would say, "Wordsworth seemed to him *thick-ankled.*" "Crabbe has given us the most varied and numerous portraits of character after Shakespeare." — In G. Meredith's first little volume he was delighted by the " Love in a Valley " (as printed in 1851 : the text in later issues has been greatly changed): in Rossetti's, the passion and imaginative power of the sonnet " Nuptial Sleep " impressed him deeply.   And the writer will here ask pardon, if he does not deny himself the pleasure of noting that a little lyric of his own,

Ask what you will, my own and only Love,

was warmly praised by Tennyson.   But enough, if not too much, of these side-gleams and snatches : although my hope is that in years to come, when Tennyson's great place in poetry shall be more fully and freely acknowledged than it has yet been, the slight notes here offered of the books and passages which he loved will have a peculiar interest of their own.   One would surely give much for details of this nature upon Shakespeare or Milton.

Sir W. Scott's short tale, *My Aunt Margaret's Mirror*[1] (how little known !), he once spoke of as the finest of all ghost or magical stories. The novel by Michael Scott, *Tom Cringle's Log*, Tennyson greatly admired for its marvellous vividness of description : instancing the narrative of the approach to Santiago de Cuba in chapter XII. *Euphranor*, that little dialogue, lively and discursive, by his gifted friend Edward Fitzgerald, which, here and there, in style comes so near Plato, he also highly esteemed; admiring especially (and no wonder !) the brilliant closing picture of a boat-race, with its glimpse of Whewell, " the high crest and blowing forelock of Phidippus's mare, and he himself shouting encouragement to his crew, conspicuous over all."

Tennyson about the same time, I think, commended to me warmly Fitzgerald's famous *Omar* paraphrase, in which old Oriental thought is so marvellously refracted through the atmosphere of modern English style.   This poem, at the date to which my literary notes mostly refer, was very scantily accessible to general readers in that limited first edition which contains the original preface in prose, one hardly knows whether more exquisite for its subtlety or its simplicity, and a text, not, perhaps, always altered in later issues to advantage.   To the *Omar*, and its highly-valued author, Tennyson afterwards did public honour in the " Prologue and Epilogue to ' Tiresias ' " : two lyrics which, short as they are, truly rank among masterpieces of rendering, in pure poetry, the humorous and the pathetic sides of common life : balanced evenly between realistic and ideal treatment : truly, a rare triumph.

[1] *The Tapestried Chamber* also he greatly admired

Gentleness, discriminating yet ever tolerant criticism, resolute — indeed, indignant — rejection of all " literary gossip," to sum up the general impression left, marked Tennyson's attitude towards contemporary writers.   I remember once attempting a silly joke about " balderdash " in reference to a recently published poem by S. Dobell. " That was a very easy and weak way of trying to dispose of a book," he at once said (nor was this the only time in which he performed analogous acts of a true friend's kindness): and then went on to point out the real merits of *Balder;* although, as he also noted about Mrs B. Browning's " Aurora Leigh," the fault was that both works, striking as they were in many phrases, might rather be defined as " organizable lymph " than as compacted and vertebrate poems.   And so, when I once casually remarked, Poland being mentioned, that all interest about that country was now dead, he replied with deep earnest feeling how passionately he in youth, and still, felt for the cruel fate of Poland ; and that such insensibility was morally wrong.

Kindness of heart, a deep and constant sense of human limitations, wide knowledge, natural refinement and penetration, the union of these essential elements in that much disputed quality, good taste, brought with it that rare and delightful result, the power of doing equal justice to the small as the great things of art.   Hence of all critics known to me Tennyson most surely and fairly would point out for praise the successful touches in minor poetry.   Much as he loved Horace, he rose above the epigrammatic narrowness of his brilliant *Non di, non homines...* : deeply conscious how difficult all fine art is, uniting always charity with justice, and prompt to be " kindly to his kind."

Let me in conclusion put together a few scattered memories (aided here by a brief journal) of the later visits when I was allowed to enjoy the society of this friend, faithful and true for more than forty years.

During many, perhaps most, of the summers since my first journey to Aldworth in the autumn of 1869, when the family was hardly yet settled in their new home, it was thither (not as of old, to Farringford) that its convenient vicinity to London led me.

Thus, on October 27th, 1886, he read aloud to me that piece of almost too terrible beauty, the " Locksley Hall Sixty Years After," in which he has concentrated a wealth of thought and observance of life, a passion, whether of tenderness or of " world-sorrow," such as had been reached neither in the youthful " Locksley," nor in the later " Maud." When, truly, has our Virgil-Lucretius thrown his whole soul into song more completely than in these (if of any human work one may speak so) imperishable lines, dark as they are with the sadness by which the poet ransoms, as it were, his prophetic insight into Humanity?   As he

read them, in the spacious dimly-lighted room, with that "large utterance" before noticed, it was a scene such as only Rembrandt, in his
mood of deepest intensity, could have adequately rendered.

The phrase "Virgil-Lucretius" I have used above, thinking of the
second "Locksley Hall" and perhaps a few other lesser lyrics of
Tennyson's later years, when the sense of the enormous significance of
Life and of Death, of Here and Hereafter, Shadow and Substance,
always vividly realized together by him, had naturally grown more vivid.
Yet the gay boyish humour, the sunny sweetness, the delight in life,
these never failed. For those solemn words, *as sorrowful, yet alway
rejoicing*, might be truly applied to the innermost being of this poet,
whether in regard to his life, or his poetry. The man, rather than the
writer, has been the subject of my story : but perhaps a few words of
general survey may be permitted. It is, however, for "the days that
remain" to bear witness to his real place in the great hierarchy,
amongst whom Dante boldly yet justly ranked himself. But if we look
at Tennyson's work in a two-fold aspect : — *Here*, on the exquisite art in
which, throughout, his verse is clothed, the lucid beauty of the form,
the melody almost audible as music, the mysterious skill by which the
words used constantly strike as the *inevitable* words (and hence, unfor-
gettable), the subtle allusive touches, by which a secondary image is
suggested to enrich the leading thought, as the harmonic "partials"
give richness to the note struck upon the string : *There*, when we think
of the vast fertility in subject and treatment, united with happy selection
of motive, the wide range of character, the dramatic force of impersonation, the pathos in every variety, the mastery over the comic and
the tragic alike, above all, perhaps, those phrases of luminous insight
which spring direct from imaginative observation of Humanity, true for
all time, coming from the heart to the heart — his work will probably
be found to lie somewhere between that of Virgil and Shakespeare :
having its portion, if I may venture on the phrase, in the inspiration of
both.

In Nov. 1888 I visited Aldworth shortly after death had suddenly
carried off my dearly-loved adventurous brother Gifford (September 30)
at Montevideo. He first met Tennyson in 1864, when the curious
remark about the Arabian influence operative upon "Locksley Hall,"
already recorded, was made : and again in 1868. They saw each other
no more until, in the late summer of 1887, Mr A. Macmillan kindly
brought Gifford to Aldworth for an afternoon from his house at Liphook
not far distant. Tennyson now read to me the beautiful lines named
"Ulysses" after the title of my brother's last narrative of travel : a commemoration the honour of which he did not live to enjoy. "I think
he was the cleverest man I ever met," when speaking of that visit,

Tennyson twice said, and his remark has been repeated to me by other witnesses. And I may perhaps be allowed to refer to my dear brother's narrative of his journey through Central Arabia, to the "Ulysses" and other volumes, as the justification of that eulogy, *laudes viri laudatissimi*.

In 1889 I found Tennyson in the gradual process of recovery from the terrible illness of the preceding year, when (as Sir A. Clark said to me at the time) "he had been as near death as a man could be without dying." Doubtless, from the care of that great physician, who has now followed him to the grave, Tennyson had received all the aid which human skill could give. And (at all but eighty) so great were his physical powers that he led me down one of his favourite walks to the Sussex weald some 400 feet below the house, and then climbed the hill, with steps that allowed no hesitation to his companions, and resting only here and there; as indeed the heat of July and the charm of a landscape so singularly beautiful rendered natural. That most true friend, one of the very few who, I think, really replaced for Tennyson the old fraternal circle of Trinity, the Duke of Argyll, was our companion. He was the sole other visitor at the time : and he will, I hope, not grudge my saying that never did I listen to better talk than that between those two as we sate at tea on the garden terrace. Even that noble view, sixty miles of landscape fading into the blue downs of Kent, the "immense plain" which Tennyson confessed "sometimes weighed upon his spirits," would have been unheeded by a lover of Nature, seeing it for the first time, in presence of discourse so equal, so sincere, so satisfying; never trifling, yet never didactic; poised equally, as it seemed to me, between seriousness and humour :

> Partem aliquam, venti, divom referatis ad auris !

one might have excusably said. From the indestructibility of Force some indeed have argued that the air-waves of sound somewhere in the Unknown preserve every human word ever spoken. But from my memory, alas ! that discourse has been swept into the void.

Upon this occasion it was that I noted Tennyson's first open concession to age and "the years as they retreated." Hitherto, after dinner and dessert, and a short time to himself, his guests had been invited to the poet's own room, whether first the attic at Farringford, or the high hall provided next at Aldworth, *novo Sublime ritu...atrium*, or that added in "the Island" home : in one or other of which, with an interlude, perhaps, below stairs, we might sit, and smoke, talk or be silent, hearing often the latest poem, through hours which no one cared to number. But in 1889 the interval of solitude was prolonged to 10 P.M. or later; the session, however, when it came, was hardly abridged.

At Aldworth in July, 1890, a friendliness welcomed me even more delicate and tender than I had met since the days of Twickenham. The greatest of all losses had fallen on me : I could not have come, but for the thought not only of the years during which the affection rendered me by Tennyson and his devoted wife had never slackened, but of the years, also, now gathering over them.   In contrast to such thoughts, I found the house brightened by the presence of the baby Lionel, and the grandfather himself seemingly restored to earlier health.   On the terrace he asked if I should care to hear a classical legend which he had lately completed upon the lines of an early attempt.   I thought it would have been read from the MS.   But he began at once where we sat, in the left-hand recess, and repeated without pause or lapse of memory the whole of that beautiful " Œnone " which, latest to appear of all his Hellenic Idylls, is perhaps the one most instinct with the peculiar grace of Grecian simplicity [1].

Illness in 1891 deferred a visit till October, when, after the lapse of near thirty years (traversing the street which meanwhile had grown up from Yarmouth onwards, "roofs of slated hideousness"), I was once more beneath the shelter of Farringford and among its trees, that ilex-*silva...iugerum paucorum*, so loved by its owner, which had meanwhile grown up to bowery overshadowing massiveness.   Much lessened were now the hours of converse : for the first time during three-and-forty years the evening session was in general exchanged for rest.   But the bright welcome, the readiness to please, the charm, even the ever-youthfulness which made it difficult to think of him and old age together, all were there.

But we are nearing the end.   In May, 1892, bodily decline had now too distinctly set in.   The extent of this was unknown to me ; nor, though lessened physical strength was perceptible, with Tennyson's unconquerable vigour of mind, and recent seeming rescue from the very grasp of death, did I admit any final fear.   To those who love, such old age in fact appears as if already immortal.

Daily, from the little bower beyond the bridge, at the foot of his great Down, now no longer, as of old, constantly, except in mid-winter, climbed and traversed, to the Needles' lighthouse, did I accompany him in a narrower two-mile circuit of his fields and farms and cottages. One picturesque little group, which Tennyson had built, and marked with tablets bearing the conjoined initials of his wife and himself, we found receiving graceful record at the hand of Mr Birket Foster [2].

[1] My father often said that this second "Œnone" had more of the pure Greek simplicity than the first "Œnone."   T.

[2] Mrs Allingham's pictures of the Farringford cottages are well-known to those who attend her exhibitions, and were much liked by Tennyson.

Tennyson was suffering from cough, by which, always physically sensitive in a high degree, he was much depressed.. But the old self would ever and anon break forth, as he pointed out to me some choice bit of that peculiar miniature beauty which marks the yet-unspoiled portions of the Island, or where in past days he had enjoyed the society of that singularly attractive and valued friend, Mr W. G. Ward. Ward's fervent Catholicism is well known; with Monteith, Simeon, and Aubrey de Vere, also friends so highly and so justly prized, he was devoted to the Roman Church. But it was eminently characteristic of Tennyson that this difference in belief seemed always only to strengthen the union between them.

Let me once more, as at the beginning of these notes, ask pardon, if, with too little of worth to tell, and too much, perhaps, of egotism, I linger over my story. At the close of this visit my hosts asked, " Would not I bring my daughters for a sight of Aldworth when Summer came?" Thus it was that, the customary migration from Farringford being somewhat delayed, July 19th, 1892, proved to be the last earthly meeting-time and sight of him whose friendship had been to me from youth onwards among the greatest blessings of life, — the most instructive, the most elevating.

" *Praise*," said Wordsworth, " *is a dangerous thing*": and, except inferentially or as it were inevitably, my desire has been to exclude it from these *Memorabilia;* if, indeed, I am not, rather, liable to censure for an unrepented unheroic over-familiarity. Now, however, whilst traversing the steep road from Haslemere to Blackdown, between ancient seemly cottages such as England only shows, and then, shadowy hedgerow trees, to the open downs, it seemed strange to my dear companions and me to remember that this visit was not only to the one who in all English-speaking lands could be truly named of all Englishmen at once both the most widely known and the most uniformly admired, but who also was, at any rate throughout every region. of European civilization, absolutely the greatest of living poets. But the simple kindliness of greeting which the girls met from Tennyson with his wife and son and son's wife soon put aside the sense of approaching Royalty. And we had the added happiness of a day when, free from special pain or weakness, we found ourselves with Tennyson in his almost boy-like humour of openness and enjoyment, and seeking only how to make the pleasure of the visit more pleasant to youthful guests. Laughingly he pointed out how, though unable then to boast of the luxuriance of locks conspicuous in that excellent *chiar' oscuro* portrait by Laurence (now at Aldworth), through which he was first made familiar to everyone, yet there was not a single white hair on his head. Overruling a little remonstrance from Hallam upon his cough, he took the sheets of the then-unpublished " Churchwarden," and read it through with due justice to the Lincolnshire dialect, clearly as ever, and like all true humourists, slyly enjoying his own fun. For as unless he weeps himself, who would make us weep, so it is with laughter.

Then followed a curious episode. Rain was falling, and only a short walk through the beautiful garden and hillside below Aldworth possible. So a phonograph which Mr Edison, a few years back, had presented to Tennyson was brought forth and set in motion. Into this machine, at the time when given, he had spoken the Bugle-song from "The Princess," —a lyric which, through its cadences from loud to low, from voice to echo, was specially adapted to display the powers of the instrument [1]. After a concert and some other show-pieces, followed this song. Tennyson said he could not now recite it with the fullness of voice which was his when he gave it to the keeping of the phonograph : yet, at my request, ever-kind, he repeated the first stanza ; and indeed there was little to be missed in his intonation. We found then, what the preceding musical reproductions had led me to expect, that it was a rough sketch of the real voice which we had heard, but all the finer tones, the higher delicate notes omitted. Tennyson remarked that the necessity of a decided *diminuendo* in the last line of his song had rendered the final words (which were inaudible) too faint for the wave of sound to record. When, however, the (second) " Northern Farmer" followed, that poem, spoken to the phonograph with less musically dramatic effect, was rendered more perfectly.

In this case the sound was carried to the ears of each person singly by elastic tubes. Hence all that was experienced by the rest of the party was an utterance at the mouth (so to speak) of the machine, of shrill tones almost too thin for hearing. Tennyson called it " the squeak of a dying mouse ". and then, with a certain shade of sadness in the voice, " I often think *that* represents fame after a man's death ; the *other*, contemporary glory." This was one of the very few occasions on which I have heard him touch on that subject, not perhaps, always treated by poets with such reticence.

This allusion to fame suggested to him two small stories which may be already known, although new to his hearers. Farringford, several years since, was the scene of both. Some traveller passing the gate in a carriage hired at Freshwater asked "Whose house was this?" "Nobody's in particular," the driver replied. "But whose is it?" "Mr Tennyson's." "Do you call him nobody? He is a great man!"

---

[1] Tennyson's baby grandson laughed uproariously as his father shouted down the tube; Tennyson thereupon laughed into the phonograph after the words — "Blow, bugle,.blow"; and this laugh has a most weird effect on the reproduction.

" He a great man ! why, he only keeps one man, and he don't sleep in the house."

Again : "A lady had been staying with us, and brought her maid. As the visit came to an end, she began a gossip with one of our housemaids (a temporary one) upon the family. 'What do you think of Mrs Tennyson?' 'O, she is an angel!' 'And what of your master?' 'Why (with an inexpressibly scornful air), he is only a public writer.'"

Trivial tales, are they not? Yet they may serve to show how the lightsome spirit of youth, the "royal heart of innocence" survived, even though he was already far on in mortal sickness. And thus, even as he himself wished it of what soon, too soon, was to come, there was no sadness about our parting that evening : only the long-known cordial grasp, the little *tenerezza* in the voice. I said to myself, "This we need not think of as Farewell." Six days later, the Duke of Argyll paid his last visit, and judged the situation more truly and more mournfully.

One word, as we quit this memorable family group, may be ventured upon that beauty of united life which for more than forty years I ever found the atmosphere of the house : the chivalrous tone of that "school for husbands," as I often named it to myself : the high spiritual nature and aim, "yes, higher than I am," he once said when twilight favoured such confidence, of her to whom the most deeply-felt of all his lines were addressed :

Dear, near, and true

to him from youth to age, the counsellor to whom he never looked in vain for aid and comfort ; but who now (May, 1893), in the words of Arthur Hallam's father, "submits to the righteous Will of Heaven which has ordained her to be his survivor."

Imperfect, sad, yet with a certain sweetness, my task is now ended. It is for others, for those nearer and dearer, for friends of more skill and insight, to frame some portrait in words of this man, emphatically not less good than great in the full range of his character. My attempt throughout has been only to offer truly, and "nothing extenuated," such lesser incidental traits as may, taken together, present a partial resemblance for the reader's own judgment. But the sketch will be a failure if it does not give those who care to read it the one impression which, above all others, these three-and-forty years of unwavering friendship have left with me as the dominant note of Alfred Tennyson, — Loveableness.

PERSONAL CHARACTERISTICS OF TENNYSON, BY THE DUKE OF ARGYLL.

My dear Hallam,

Were it not that even details, which would be trivial when they concern ordinary men, may well be of lasting interest when they concern one of the immortals I should reluctantly attempt to add anything to the many personal characteristics which you have so well indicated in your memorial pages. But having enjoyed your father's friendship for forty years I may be allowed on your invitation to say a few words about him.

The first words I heard him utter remain indelibly impressed upon my memory. On being introduced to him at an evening party in the house of Lord John Russell, I said, perhaps with some emotion, " I am so glad to know you." Not in the tone or voice of a mere conventional reply, but in the accents of sincere humility he answered, "You won't find much in me — after all." The effect which these words produced upon me at the moment was deepened every time I saw him. Your father was a man of the noblest humility I have ever known. It was not that he was unconscious of his own powers. It was not that he was indifferent to the appreciation of them by others. But it was that he was far more continually conscious of the limitations upon them in face of those problems of the universe with which, in thought, he was habitually dealing. In his inner spirit he seemed to me to be always feeling his own later words :

> " But what am I?
> An infant crying in the night :
> An infant crying for the light :
> And with no language but a cry."

In close connection with this frame of mind was the profound reverence of his character. In speculation he was often bold — in a sense he was sometimes even daring. But he was always reverent, — hating all levity or flippancy in thought or language about divine things. He was full of a kind of awful wonder, — of a silent worship. His direct theological utterances were few. But he said enough to show that he clung to the divine truths of the " creed of creeds." Although perfectly tolerant as regarded the doubts and difficulties of his time, he was impatient of any rough or contemptuous treatment of the great Christian verities, and sometimes indignantly rebuked it. Both his reverence and his humility were revolted by disdain. On one of the last occasions on which I ever walked with him in his garden at Aldworth, it had been a wet day and all the grass and shrubs were dripping with rain. We were walking in single file to avoid brushing the drop-laden boughs, when after something had been said in our conversation which brought up this subject, he suddenly stopped, turned round, confronted me, and said " I hate scorn " with an emphasis which showed how deep-seated in his nature that hatred was. We must all remember how finely this sentiment is expressed in the description of Modred in " Guinevere."

The absolute truthfulness of your father was a striking feature in his character. We are too apt to think of this as common, and so it is, up to a conventional standard which is determined by the public opinion of society from time to time. But in its highest manifestations, as they were seen in him, I always think that truthfulness is one of the rarest of human attributes. The degrees are innumerable in which truth is more or less compromised in the usages of society, in the pursuit of politics, and of business, as well as in controversy of all kinds. Your father's nature was in all things so simple and sincere that it made him sometimes abrupt and apparently rough in manner.

I recollect an amusing instance of this which occurred many years ago. At that time it was rather usual in a certain literary circle to give breakfasts in London at which very often there were most agreeable parties gathered together from all directions of the compass. Macaulay, Bishop Wilberforce, Lord Mahon, and Monckton Milnes were among the hosts whose breakfasts were most agreeable. I and my wife did our best occasionally to follow their example. On one occasion we had invited an excellent selection of friends to whom we were ambitious enough to hope that we might add the illustrious poet. He was then often with us, reading the proof-sheets of the " Idylls," and on one of these occasions the Duchess, who was an intense admirer, ventured to approach the subject, saying, " We have got so and so, and so and so, and so and so to breakfast with us next Wednesday morning at ten a.m. Do you think, Mr Tennyson, that you could be persuaded to join our party ? " Your father's reply left no room for further negotiations. It was simple and effective. " I should hate it, Duchess."

The inexhaustible fountains of tenderness opened in his poetry, and which " In Memoriam " more especially revealed, could hardly have been suspected from his manner. In his deeper feelings he was intensely reserved. I was therefore all the more gratified and surprised by an indication of personal friendship which was granted to me very near the close of his life. I was to return to London next morning from a visit to Aldworth. Your mother had been at dinner and had bidden us good night as usual. When, about an hour later, your father took me up to his smoking-room, as was also usual with him, we were surprised to find your mother lying on the sofa there. Your father expressed his astonishment and said, " My dear, you ought to have gone to bed long ago." Her kind reply was, " Oh, I wished to say good-bye to the Duke again as he leaves us to-morrow morning." At that moment you entered the room and at once carried your mother off. Your father, somewhat moved as I thought, occupied himself with putting fresh coals on the fire. Then, turning to me, he said in a deep and solemn voice, without mentioning your mother's name, " It is a tender, spiritual face, — is it not?" A better description, so full of truth and of poetry, could not be given of your mother's beautiful countenance, which I had so long known and had so often admired. These are the words I have interwoven into the last verse of the Elegy[1] written on your father's death, and which your mother was so good as to accept with some kind expressions of appreciation which have been a great pleasure to me.

Although I was a younger man than your father by a good many years, I am old enough to remember the first shining of his light above the horizon, and I have seen its steady culmination in a perfect day.

Very few men of the generation whose tastes have been formed on the older poets, and who had, for the most part, resisted even the popularity of Wordsworth, could easily appreciate your father's earlier poetry. It involved not only new rhythms, but also entirely new moods and tendencies of thought. Among those who stood absolutely aloof was Lord Macaulay. I had the happiness of being the medium of introduction through which he was at last subdued. When your father entrusted me with the proof-sheets of " Guinevere " I took them to Macaulay who was my next door neighbour for some years before his death. I left the poem with him, telling him I would return next day to hear his opinion I found him absolutely subdued, and I was much amused and interested in the few vain attempts he made even to qualify his admiration. He was, by natural disposition, highly critical. Himself a master in English prose composition, and the writer of some very beautiful bits of poetry, he could not easily surrender at discretion before an author whom he had hitherto regarded as at best the writer of some pretty lyrics. It was therefore with delight, but also with some surprise, that I heard him accost me at once, in a deeply impressed voice, with exclamations of unfeigned and reverent admiration. " Oh, it is very beautiful — very beautiful indeed," he repeated several times. Then, more moved than he was quite willing to confess, he tried to recover himself by making some critical reservations. " There is of course — " he would begin by saying, — or, " It is to be noticed however —," or some such phrase — repeated several times, but always broken off by a simple

[1] *Burdens of Belief, and other Poems* (J. Murray).

renewal of " Oh, it is very beautiful — very beautiful indeed — most touching." I confess I left him with a sense of your father's complete triumph over a very competent judge, — premonitory (as I felt assured) of his conquest over the living world and over the generations that are to come.

It was somewhere about the same time that I heard, and took a subordinate part in, a very interesting discussion in my own house on the question how far it is possible for any generation whatever to predict, with even tolerable security, how far any poet, however popular in his own time, would maintain at all a corresponding place in the estimate of future ages. The interlocutors in the discussion were old Lord Aberdeen, Mr Gladstone, Sir George Cornwall Lewis, and Lord Clarendon. The result seemed to be a general agreement that such a foreseeing is impossible. I venture to doubt the impossibility although fully admitting the many untraceable elements of deception. In your father's case I rest my assured confidence in his immortality on two strong foundations : — first, the mass, variety and elevation of thought in his poetry ; and, secondly, the extraordinary perfection of form by which it is distinguished. It seems to me that for example " In Memoriam" can never die until our existing world has passed away. Sorrow is always at home here. And sorrow has never had such a voice to express all its moods whether terrible or tender. Again, your father's blank verse is as peculiar as it is magnificent. Not even the stately march of Elizabethan English in its golden time, can overpass it in sweetness or in strength. In its description of Nature in all her aspects, it is quite incomparable, — as for example, in " The Gardener's Daughter," or in the description of the thunderstorm in " Vivien."

But I must not run on into an essay on so large a subject as his poetry. I am speaking now only of what I conceive to be a few of the elements in it which may well give us an assurance of its immortality. To have been numbered amongst his personal friends I esteem as one of the greatest honors of my life.

Yours affectionately,

ARGYLL.

EPILOGUE.

(*Unpublished.*)

Speak to me from the stormy sky!
  The wind is loud in holt and hill,
  It is not kind to be so still:
Speak to me, dearest, lest I die.

Speak to me, let me hear or see!
  Alas, my life is frail and weak:
  Seest thou my faults and wilt not speak?
They are not want of love for thee.

APPENDIX.

(P. 34.) *My father's talk on Milton's "Paradise Lost" to me when a boy at Marlborough.*

Bk. I. 60. "Our English language alters quickly. This great line would be almost commonplace now :

The dismal situation waste and wild."

Bk. I. 211. "I hope most of us have a higher idea in these modern times of the Almighty than this :

                       The will
And high permission of all-ruling Heaven
Left him at large to his own dark designs,
That with reiterated crimes he might
Heap on himself damnation."

Bk. I. 725. "I always like this, it is mystical :

                  From the arched roof
Pendent by subtle magic, many a row
Of starry lamps and blazing cressets."

Bk. II. 129. "Note the great pauses in Satan's speech."

"I think that Milton's vague hell is much more awful than Dante's hell marked off into divisions."

518

Bk. II. 634. "What simile was ever so vast as this?

> Then soars
> *Up to the fiery concave towering high.*
> As when far off at sea a fleet descried
> Hangs in the clouds, by equinoctial winds
> Close sailing from Bengala, or the isles
> Of Ternate and Tidore, whence merchants bring
> Their spicy drugs; they, on the trading flood,
> Through the wide Ethiopian to the Cape,
> Ply stemming nightly toward the pole : so seem'd
> Far off the flying fiend.

Then the next passage, the picture of sin that seems to be alluring at first, hideous afterwards, is fine."

Bk. II. 879. "A good instance of onomatopœia :

> On a sudden open fly
> With impetuous recoil and jarring sound
> The infernal doors, and on their hinges grate
> Harsh thunder, that the lowest bottom shook
> Of Erebus."

Bk. IV. 127. When Uriel saw Satan—

"This shows a fine dramatic feeling in Milton,—

> Disfigured, more than could befall
> Spirit of happy sort ; his gestures fierce
> He mark'd, and mad demeanour, then alone,
> As he supposed, all unobserved, unseen."

"A few lines below—'Sylvan scene' and the gentle gales 'fanning their odoriferous wings' are undoubtedly commonplace now, but Milton introduced the style."

"I hate the lines about 'the spouse of Tobit's son.' They are objectionable. I do not object to the thief simile as some do."

"*Blooming* ambrosial fruit." "'Blooming' is bold." In the description of the garden he quoted "flowers worthy of Paradise" down to "without thorn the rose."

Bk. IV. 242. "'Where the unpiercèd shade' is the right reading not 'th' unpierc'd shade,' in those beautiful lines about the flowers which

> Nature boon
> Pour'd forth profuse on hill, and dale, and plain,
> Both where the morning sun first warmly smote
> The open field, and where the unpiercèd shade
> Imbrown'd the noontide bowers."

Bk. IV. 248. "What liquid lines these too —

> Groves whose rich trees wept odorous gums and balm,

or   And sweet reluctant amorous delay,

or Bk. IV. 354,   And in the ascending scale
> Of Heaven, the stars that usher evening rose."

"This last line is lovely because it is full of vowels, which are all different. It is even a more beautiful line than those where the repetition of the same vowels or of the same consonants sometimes are so melodious."

Bk. IV. 810. "That is a wonderful simile —

> Him thus intent Ithuriel with his spear
> Touch'd lightly, for no falsehood can endure
> Touch of celestial temper, but returns
> Of force to its own likeness; up he starts
> Discover'd and surpris'd. As when a spark
> Lights on a heap of nitrous powder, laid
> Fit for the tun, some magazine to store
> Against a rumour'd war, the smutty grain,
> With sudden blaze diffused, inflames the air;
> So started up in his own shape the fiend."

Bk. V. 277. "A seraph winged" to "colours dipt in Heaven" he would quote with admiration.

Bk. V. 336–396. And my father would humorously quote of the French cooks abroad —

> "Taste after taste upheld with kindliest change —
>   *   *   *   *   *   *
> No fear lest dinner cool,"

Adding, "That is a terrible bathos after the beautiful imagery, but shows Milton's simplicity."

Bk. v. 525. My father said : " Certainly Milton's physics and metaphysics are not strong — though I fully agree with

> To persevere
> He left it in thy power ; ordain'd thy will,
> By nature free, not over-ruled by fate
> Inextricable, or strict necessity.
> Our voluntary service he requires,
> Not our necessitated ; such with him
> Finds no acceptance, nor can find ; for how
> Can hearts, not free, be tried whether they serve
> Willing or no, who will but what they must
> By destiny, and can no other choose? "

My father liked the gathering of the host " by imperial summons called," and the " mystical dance " which the mystical dance of the " starry sphere of planets resembles nearest." The angels' feast he called " delicious," and said " Old Milton the puritan must have been a bit of a sensualist in his nature."

Bk. v. 745. Of the coming of Satan with his host

> Innumerable as the stars of night,
> Or stars of morning, dewdrops, which the sun
> Impearls on every leaf and every flower —

and Satan mounting his royal seat, my father said, " What an imagination the old man had ! Milton beats everyone in the material sublime."

Bk. v. 791. " Milton could not help adding his political comment

> If not equal all, yet free,
> Equally free ; for orders and degrees
> Jar not with liberty, but well consist." .

Bk. v. 896. My father quoted the famous lines about Abdiel as very fine —

> Among the faithless, faithful only he ;
> Among innumerable false, unmoved,
> Unshaken, unseduced, unterrified,
> .... From amidst them forth he passed
> Long way through hostile scorn.

Bk. vi. 372. " Milton's proper names are often chosen for their full sounds,

> Ariel and Arioch and the violence
> Of Ramiel."

Bk. VI. 771. "The following is what made Wordsworth admire Milton's imagination —

(*The Messiah*)

He onward came ; *far off his coming shone.*
.... Under his burning wheels
The steadfast empyrean shook throughout
All but the throne itself of God.

What a grand pause in the blank verse after ' God ' ! "
And "This is a rushing line that describes the lightning course of his wrath —

Eternal wrath
Burnt after them to the bottomless pit."

Bk. VII. 23–26. "A beautiful beginning —

Standing on earth, not rapt above the pole,
More safe I sing with mortal voice, unchanged
To hoarse or mute, though fall'n on evil days,
On evil days though fall'n, and evil tongues."

Bk. VII. 216. "This is a magnificent line,

Silence, ye troubled waves, *and thou, deep, peace !*

How much finer than ' and, billows, peace,' the proper scansion, this break is, and the alliteration how subtle, ' and thou, dee*p*, *p*eace ' ! "
" Full of notable lines, e.g. 298 :

Wave rolling after wave, where way they found —
If steep, with torrent rapture ; if through plain,
Soft-ebbing.........
Then herbs of every leaf, that sudden flower'd,
Opening their various colours, and made gay
Her bosom, smelling sweet........."

Bk. VII. 431.   The air
Floats, as they pass, fann'd with unnumber'd plumes ;
From branch to branch the smaller birds with song
Solaced the woods.

Then my father would quote the pictures of the nightingale, the swan and the peacock as beautiful.

"How much finer than Thomson's lines are those on the peacock! They are as fine as can be —

> The crested cock, whose clarion sounds
> The silent hours, and the other whose gay train
> Adorns him, coloured with the florid hue
> Of rainbows and starry eyes."

Bk. VIII. The first three lines of this book are "beautifully expressed —

> The angel ended, and in Adam's ear
> So charming left his voice, that he awhile
> Thought him still speaking, still stood fix'd to hear."

Bk. IX. 568. "Satan begins well too —

> Empress of this fair world, resplendent Eve."

"This seems to be rather poor however —

> The blasted stars looked wan, etc."

Bk. XI. 491. "I hate inversions, but this line (after the many mighty lines about the many ways that lead to death's 'grim cave') is strong in its inversion —

> And over them triumphant Death his dart
> Shook."

Bk. XI. 553. And my father often quoted

> "Nor love thy life, nor hate; but what thou livest
> Live well."

(P. 84.) *Miss Weld wrote to a friend the following account of Freshwater society, published in "Lord Tennyson," by H. J. Jennings:*

"I must ask you to transport yourself back ten summers, and to picture to your mind's eye the figure of Tennyson emerging from the little green postern leading to the Down Lane. Bearing to the left, he lingers awhile at the first gate, to admire the beautiful view which, with its sea of Mediterranean blue and its foreground of pines, he compares to the Riviera; but not again does he slacken the rapid pace, habitual to him, till he has turned towards Freshwater Bay, and reached a house embosomed in ivy and garlanded to the very roof with roses in full bloom. He looks up to the window from which smiling faces are

nodding to him, but ere his foot can cross the threshold the genial
hostess of Dimbola has come out into her garden to meet and greet her
honoured guest; and by the way in which they plunge forthwith into
earnest converse, you can see what a true communion of spirit exists
between them on most subjects, though, to her great regret, she cannot
get Tennyson's full sympathy for the pursuit she at present finds so
engrossing, and he cannot see why, because she has devoted herself to
photography, he should be called upon to victimize himself by becoming
her sitter so often.   In vain does the lady of the camera lay before the
poet the muster-roll of his illustrious fellow-victims who have already sat
to her [1], and urge how successful his friends thought her last study of
him, and that the state of the atmosphere is even more favourable to
photography to-day than it was when that study was taken.   Mrs Julia
Margaret Cameron will not win her cause this time, her persuasions
being suddenly cut short by the entrance of two gentlemen and a lady.
The elder of the former at once arrests your attention by his patriarchal
mien, as he stands erect, leaning on his staff, his ample white beard and
snowy locks flowing down over a blue caftan, suggestive of the Eastern
land so long his home.   For this is Mr C. H. Cameron, the husband of
our hostess and a member of the Indian Council, who was for many
years resident in Calcutta, where he and his wife were most highly
esteemed by Lord Hardinge (after whom they have called one of their
sons, who is now in the Ceylon Civil Service).   Mr Cameron is a
first-rate classic, and he and the Laureate engage in an animated
discussion about the respective merits of certain great Greek and Latin
writers, and the peculiarities of their several styles, whilst Mrs Cameron
turns to inquire of the younger gentleman how it fares with the poor of
Freshwater.   None can better answer her question, for he to whom it
is addressed is Horatio Tennyson, seventh brother of the poet, now
resident at the Terrace, close to Mrs Cameron, who is devoting his
life to ministering amongst those 'who are any ways afflicted or distressed in mind, body, or estate,' winning the wanderers back into the
fold by showing them he still counts them his brethren in Christ.

After the bodily presence of Mrs Cameron was taken from us, her
spirit seemed to linger on in the person of a sister, who had come to
Freshwater in order to be near her.   This was Mrs Prinsep, the wife
of Mr Thoby Prinsep, the well-known East India Director.   To their

---

[1] A muster-roll not then complete, but afterwards embracing, among many other
names, those of Browning, Carlyle, Darwin, Herschel, Herr Joachim, Jowett, Lecky,
Sir Henry Taylor, Aubrey de Vere, Watts, the Emperor Frederick of Germany, etc.
When the last-named was sitting to her, she was so taken up with the desire of
getting a satisfactory likeness, that, to make him open his eyes wider, she shouted
out to him, "Big eyes! big eyes!" quite oblivious, at the moment, of his rank.

house, 'The Briary,' the Laureate (together with his eldest son, who, after leaving college, became his father's inseparable companion) was an almost daily visitor, and many were the hours spent by him in congenial conversation, on politics, literature, or science, with the master-mind that had long had so potent a share in the government of India, and whose ready grasp of almost every imaginable subject was only less wonderful than his marvellous memory. His keen interest in contemporary politics was unimpaired by the fact that his loss of eyesight compelled him to depend on others for his knowledge of passing events. Tennyson took delight in reading aloud to him the interesting letters which every mail brought him from his artist-son, Mr Val Prinsep, whilst the latter was engaged on his large painting of the 'Proclamation of the Queen as Empress of India' (which letters have since been published, almost without alteration, under the title of 'Imperial India').

With the Prinseps lived, for part of the year, the artist from whom their son Val had first learnt to handle the brush — Mr Watts, the Royal Academician ; and many a pleasant talk about art have the poet and the painter had together in the large studio at the Briary, on whose walls the colossal study of the 'Drayman and his Horses' used to hang. Many more of his pictures adorned the living-rooms, which were artistically furnished with costly objects from the East — so arranged that comfort was never sacrificed to appearance, but everything was made to minister to that hospitality of which the host and the hostess were the very soul. Amongst those who were the most frequently to be met here were Mrs Hughes and her children and grandchildren. Mrs Nassau Senior, so well known for her philanthropic labours, long shared her mother's Freshwater home ; but after her death, this noble hearted mother undertook the long voyage to Tennessee, in order to take her granddaughter out to her father, who was in charge of the colony of Rugby, founded by his brother, Mr Tom Hughes. Greatly to the regret of Tennyson and of all her Freshwater friends, she has never returned to the Isle of Wight, but continues to reside in the colony, respected and beloved by all as their common mother.

Tennyson has an intense dislike to dining out ; his habit being to retire soon after dinner to his study, and there to spend the evening in solitude with his books, unless he is tempted by the bright starlight to climb up to the flat roof of his house, to carry on his favourite pursuit of astronomy. I well remember one particular night on which there was a total eclipse of the moon, when he was so much struck by the number of constellations rendered visible to the naked eye through the veiling of the moon's light, that he insisted on his youngest son (Lionel) 'being got out of bed to look at the sight.'"

(P. 212.)   *The Franklin Epitaph in Greek and Latin.*

My father wrote to my brother and myself, enclosing a letter from
Mr Gladstone :

Nov. 19th, 1875.

My dear Boys,

Gladstone and others have been amusing themselves translating into Greek and Latin my " Epitaph on Franklin." He wants to
make a little book of it in various languages like that of the *Lady of the
Tree,* which you may remember Montagu Butler gave me. Lord
Lyttelton's is, I think, the best translation (of those he has sent) :

οἴχεται· ἐν Βορέου νιφοέσσαις ὀστέα κεῖται
ἀκταῖς· ναυτιλίαν Σὺ δὲ ναυτίλλει μέγ᾽ ἀμείνω,
Ἥρωος ψυχή, πόλον ἄμβροτον εἰσοιχνοῦσαν.

Would Macaulay, Butcher or any among you like to try your hand
on it ?

A. T.

I have added the original lest you should have forgotten it.

Not here ! the white North has thy bones ; and thou,
    Heroic sailor-soul,
Art passing on thine happier voyage now
    Toward no earthly pole.

*From the Right Hon. W. E. Gladstone (about translations of
my father's epitaph on Sir John Franklin).*

Hawarden Castle, Chester,
Nov. 16th, 1875.

My dear Tennyson,

Can you by chance, and will you by kindness, give me the
name and whereabout of a gentleman who is now preparing a work on
Sir John Franklin ? I have unhappily mislaid his letter.

The letter touched you and you may have been made aware of its
purpose. It invited me to translate, and to invite others to translate,
your fine epitaph, which is also in the old Greek sense epigram. I was
frightened, but thought I would ask of others what I dared not try. So

I accumulated a little store, which I send[1]. They may shock, or may amuse you. *Generally* they are by men of good or more than good name in scholarship. I have however (after all my coy fears) tried my hand. It is right that I should say that the two last, notwithstanding their remarkable verbal coincidences, are distinct in authorship and date. Do not look at the list of names till you have performed the part of the Queen of Beauty, or of Rhadamanthus. Query, is it murder or only manslaughter?

With all kindest regards and remembrances,

Ever sincerely yours,

W. E. Gladstone.

Do you and Mrs T. never come so near the "White North" as this? The place is worth a look.

No. 1.

Non hic, Nauta, jaces fortissime. Contegit ossa
  Semper Hyperboreo candida terra gelu.
Inde anima vehitur, cursu lætata secundo,
  Ardua, terrestrem non aditura polum.

Mr Rickards, Q.C.

No. 2.

οἴχεται· ἐν Βορέου νιφοέσσαις ὀστέα κεῖται
ἀκταῖς· ναυτιλίαν Σὺ δὲ ναυτίλλει μέγ᾽ ἀμείνω,
Ἥρωος ψυχή, πόλον ἄμβροτον εἰσοιχνῦσαν.

Lord Lyttelton.

No. 3.

Siste pedem: procul hinc albescunt ossa, sed Ille
Navita fortis agit cursum trans sidera, longi
Quò tandem detur metam tetigisse laboris.

Bishop of Rochester.

[1] The following were two of the best translations, the first by Edmund Lushington, the second by Canon David Melvill:

χαῖρ᾽ ἀγαθὴ ψυχή· κρυεραῖς σέθεν ὀστέα βήσσαις
κεῖται ἐν ἀρκτῴαις, οὐδέ σε πατρὶς ἔχει,
ἤδη δ᾽ ἐξανύεις σὺ μακάρτερα τέρμαθ᾽ ὁδοῖο,
οὐ χθονὸς ἀλλ᾽ ἄστρων ἐς πόλον ἀννέφελον.

σῶμα μὲν Ἀρκτῴαι νιφάδες λάχον· οὐρανίην δὲ
ἡμίθεος ψυχὴ στέλλεται εὐπλοΐην.

No. 4.

Non hic, sed Arcto membra sub albidâ;
Nauta ipse, et Heros lucida sidera
Polumque cælestem requirit,
Navigio potiore vectus.

W. E. G. (*Nov.* 12).

No. 5.

Non hic, sed niveâ requiescunt ossa sub Arcto;
Tuque, anima Herois pia Nautæ,
Trajicis, usque Polum cui non terrestris origo,
Navigio felicius, æquor.

LORD SELBORNE.

No. 6.

Non hic, sed niveâ jacent
Arcti relliquiæ plagâ.
Auris Ipse faventibus
Heros Navitaque impiger
Usque ad cæruleum bono
Pergit navigio Polum.

W. E. G. (*Nov.* 16).

My father writes to Gladstone :

I liked the Greek version best; but then it is easier to translate into Greek than Latin, Greek being so much more flexible. No. 1 " terrestrem non aditura polum " hardly gives " toward no earthly pole," and in No. 5 " cui non terrestris origo " seems bald and feeble. No. 4 " lucida sidera " is *de trop*. Altogether after the Greek I like No. 6. He seems to be continuing his voyage from the end of the earth's axis, the earthly pole to the heavenly one, only " auris Ipse faventibus " should be with more favourable winds, happier; and I doubt about " cæruleum." Might not our pole be called " cerulean "? " Cælestem " (as in No. 4) would seem to be the word wanted. My neighbour, Mr Prinsep, of the Indian Council, 83 years old, and as full of enthusiasm as a boy, but so blind he cannot write or read, spouted out to me yesterday morning a Persian translation of my epitaph.

Summer tours that my father made with me, 1874 *to* 1892.

1874. Stratford on Avon.

1875. Pau and the Pyrenees.

1876. Battle Abbey, Fitzgerald's at Woodbridge, and Hawarden.

1877. Canterbury, with a view to "Becket" (Canon Robertson showed us everything connected with Becket, and we went carefully over the scene of the murder).

1878. Ireland, Westport (Lord Sligo's), Galway, Mount Trenchard (Lord Monteagle's), and the Shannon, Killarney, Dublin and Wicklow.

1879. Salisbury, Stonehenge and Amesbury.

1880. Dolomites, Venice, Verona and Lago di Garda.

1881. Sherwood, with a view to "Robin Hood" and "The Foresters."

1882. Dovedale.

1883. Voyage in the *Pembroke Castle* to the Orkneys, Norway, and Copenhagen.

1884. Rowfant (the Locker-Lampsons').

1885. Gavelacre. Mr Stewart Hodgson's farm on the Test.

1886. Cromer and Cambridge.

1887. In the *Stella* to St David's, Clovelly, Tintagil and Channel Isles.

1888. Chichester and Kingly Vale.

1889. In the *Sunbeam* to Cornwall and Devon.

1890. Holmbury and Monkshatch near Guildford.

1891. In the *Assegai* to Exmouth and Dulverton.

1892. In the *Assegai* to Guernsey, Sark, and Jersey.

GERMAN TRANSLATIONS.

My father's works have been translated into various languages in many parts of the world. The German translations are the most numerous. A list is appended, sent me by Baron von Tauchnitz:

Title	Translator	Date of publication	Publisher
Gedichte	W. Hertzberg	1853, 1868	Gebrüder Katz in Dessau
In Memoriam		1854	Vieweg und Sohn in Braunschweig
Ausgewählte Gedichte	H. Fischer	1853	Th. Enslin in Berlin
Aylmer's Feld	H. A. Feldmann	1870	H. Gruning, Hamburg
„ „	F. W. Weber	1869	F. Naumann, Leipzig
Ausgewählte Dichtungen	H. A. Feldmann	1870	H. Gruning, Hamburg
Enoch Arden	R. Schellwien	1867	H. C. Huch, Quedlinburg
„ „	R. Waldmüller	1869, 1875, 1880, 1883	H. Gruning, Hamburg
„ „	F. W. Weber	1869, 1878	F. Naumann, Leipzig
Enoch Arden, Godiva	H. A. Feldmann	1870, 1872, 1880	H. Gruning, Hamburg
Freundes Klage	R. Waldmüller, Duboc	1870, 1871, 1879	„ „
Königs-Idyllen	W. Schotz	1867	Georg Reimer, Berlin
Ausgewählte Dichtungen	A. Strodtmann	1868	Bibliographisches Institut, Leipzig
„ „	M. Rugard	1872	Newmann Hartmann, Ebbing
Königs-Idyllen	H. A. Feldmann	1872	H. Gruning, Hamburg
Zum Gedächtniss	A. von Bohlen	1874	Gebrüder Bornträger, Berlin
Enoch Arden	C. Hessel	1873	Th. Reclam jun., Leipzig
„ „ illusttrit	A. Strodtmann	1876, 1881, 1891	G. Grote, Berlin
Harold	Graf Wickenburg	1880	H. Gruning, Hamburg

530

Title	Translator	Date of publication	Publisher
Enoch Arden	C. Eichholz	1881	T. F. Richter, Hamburg
„ „ illustrirt	R. Waldmüller, Duboc	1887	Verlags Anstalt, Hamburg
„ „ Volks-Ausgabe	„ „	1885, 1891, 1892, 1893	H. Gruning, Hamburg
Königs-Idyllen	C. Weiser	1884	Th. Reclam jun., Leipzig
Enoch Arden	H. Griebenow	1889	Otto Hendel, Halle
Bilder und Gestalten, illustrirt	Paget und Dickses	1890	Th. Strofer, München
Ausgewählte Dichtungen	A. Strodtmann	1887	Bibliographisches Institut, Leipzig
Locksley Hall	R. B Esmarch	1888	F. A. Perthes, Gotha
„ „	F. Freiligrath	1888	H. Gruning, Hamburg
„ „	T. Feis	1888	„ „
Maud. Ein Gedicht	F. W Weber	1891	F. Schoningh, Paderborn
Enoch Arden und Andere Dichtungen	A. Strodtmann	1892	W. Fiedler, Leipzig
Aylmer's Feld „ „ „	M. Mendheim	1893	„ „
	H. Grebenow	1893	H. Gesenius, Halle
Balladen und Lyrische Gedichte	von Harbon	1894	O. Brandner, Charlottenburg
Aylmer's Feld	E. V. Zenker	1893	Otto Hendel, Halle

F. Freiligrath translated some of the shorter poems.

INDEX.

533

INDEX TO FIRST LINES OF POEMS HITHERTO UNPUBLISHED, AND FRAGMENTS OF POEMS OCCURRING IN THE MEMOIR.

[1] Dr George Tennyson.
[3] A. H. Hallam.

[1] E. Fitzgerald.
[3] Frederick Tennyson.
[2] R. Browning.
[4] A. H. Hallam.